ENVIRONMENTAL CRIMES DESKBOOK
2ND EDITION

Judson W. Starr

Amy J. McMaster

John F. Cooney

Joseph G. (Jerry) Block

David G. Dickman

ENVIRONMENTAL LAW INSTITUTE

Washington, D.C.

Published 1996. Second edition published June 2014.

ISBN 978-1-58576-166-1

About the Authors

Lead Authors

Judson W. Starr has been a partner in the Washington, D.C., offices of Venable LLP since 1988. From 1982 to 1988, he was the first Director and then Chief of the Environmental Crimes Section, U.S. Department of Justice, Environment and Natural Resources Division. He has served as co-chair of various subcommittees on environmental crimes in the American Bar Association, and as a member of the Environmental Crimes Advisory Group, U.S. Sentencing Commission. For the past 17 years, he served as co-chair of the ALI-CLE (formally ALI-ABA) Criminal Enforcement of Environmental Crimes Conference. A frequent panelist and author on environmental enforcement issues, he was named by the *National Law Journal* and *Chambers* as one of the nation's leading white-collar-crime experts. He has been recognized in *Best Lawyers in America 2003–2013* and was named the *DC Environmental Lawyer of the Year for 2011.* He is a member of the Board of Directors for Medstar Georgetown University Hospital, the co-chair of the Georgetown Law School's Corporate Counsel Institute's Advisory Board and a board member for Somerset Prep DC Charter School. He is a graduate of Washington and Jefferson College and Georgetown University Law Center.

Amy J. McMaster is a partner in the Environmental practice group in Venable LLP's Washington, D.C., office. She has specialized in environmental criminal defense for over 10 years. Ms. McMaster is presently handling a criminal case related to wetlands impacted during a land development project, and recently worked on matters for a leading manufacturer of farm equipment and a major oil refinery. She also has extensive experience in civil enforcement, and focuses on providing clients with a holistic solution to their NEPA, NHPA and CWA issues. Ms. McMaster has authored several articles on wetlands and endangered species issues. She graduated with distinction from the University of Victoria and the College of William & Mary School of Law, where she was a member of Order of the Coif and an editor of the *William & Mary Law Review.*

John F. Cooney is a partner in the Washington, D.C., office of Venable LLP. He counsels clients on a broad range of regulatory issues involving federal agencies and has an active litigation practice in federal district courts, courts of appeals, and the Supreme Court. Mr. Cooney has had extensive experience in civil and criminal matters involving environmental problems, including obtaining an injunction in federal district court against the federal government's imposition of a moratorium on further deepwater drilling after the *Deepwater Horizon* explosion. Mr. Cooney previously served as Deputy General Counsel of the Office of Management & Budget, where he represented the Office of Information and Regulatory Affairs in its review of rules submitted for White House policy review, and served as an Assistant to the Solicitor General. Mr. Cooney graduated magna cum laude from Brown University and from the University of Chicago Law School, where he was a member of Order of the Coif and an editor of the *University of Chicago Law Review.*

Joseph G. (Jerry) Block is the former Chief of the Environmental Crimes Section of the U.S. Department of Justice from 1988-1991. He is a frequent author and commentator on environmental criminal issues and is a recently retired partner from Venable LLP's Environmental Group, which boasts one of the nation's preeminent environmental criminal defense practices. He received his law degree from Harvard Law School and did his undergraduate work at the University of Michigan.

David G. Dickman has been with Venable LLP since 1998 and represents clients on issues involving environmental, safety, security, and hazardous materials transportation laws and regulations, focusing primarily on the marine industry. He advises clients on international, criminal, civil, and administrative aspects of maritime and transportation legal issues. He served 24 years as an active duty officer in the United States Coast Guard. In addition to his Coast Guard legal experience, he has practical maritime law enforcement, pollution response, and port security experience, having served as a marine inspector, marine casualty investigating officer, oil and hazardous chemical pollution response officer, and port security planner during his service with the Coast Guard. He has a broad-based practice, working for legislative solutions on the Hill, on regulatory and enforcement matters involving executive agencies, and on criminal and civil litigation cases on behalf of a diverse group of clients. He has published numerous articles and been a panelist on the criminal enforcement of maritime environmental laws. He was recognized in the 2013 edition of *Chambers USA* (Band 3), Transportation: Shipping: Regulatory (outside New York), Nationwide. He is a graduate of the United States Coast Guard Academy and St. Louis University School of Law.

Contributing Authors

David L. Feinberg is an associate in Venable LLP's Washington, D.C., office. He focuses his practice on litigation, including the litigation of environmental civil and criminal claims. He has been involved with some of the most high-profile civil environmental matters in recent history, including *In re Polar Bear Endangered Species Act Listing and 4(d) Rule Litigation* (D.D.C.), *In re Oil Spill by the Oil Rig "Deepwater Horizon"* (E.D. La.), and *Waterkeeper Alliance, Inc. v. Alan & Kristin Hudson Farm and Perdue Farms Incorporated* (D. Md.). His experience also includes defending corporations and individuals who are under investigation for possible environmental crimes. He also conducts internal investigations concerning potential environmental violations. He is a graduate of Bowdoin College, Emory University's Candler School of Theology, and the University of Virginia School of Law.

Margaret K. Kuhn is an associate in the environmental practice group in Venable LLP's Washington, D.C., office. She has experience in a variety of environmental enforcement matters and counsels clients on proper compliance with environmental laws. She is a graduate of the University of Texas and Duke University School of Law.

Acknowledgements

The authors gratefully acknowledge the contributions of former Venable LLP attorneys Brian L. Flack, Lowell M. Rothschild, Thomas J. Kelly Jr., and Justin W. Curtis in the writing of this deskbook. Special thanks are also due to Kristen Rhodes and Colette McCrone, who tracked case developments and policy papers. In addition, the tireless administrative support of Danielle Pace, Janice Toepper, Barbara Taylor, Maria Uy, LaShawn Watson, and Julie Watkins in the preparation of this deskbook, while also supporting the authors' practices, is greatly appreciated.

Table of Contents

Index of Acronyms xiii
Foreword xv

Part One: The Basics

Chapter 1 — History of the Federal Environmental Crimes Program 1
- *I. Origins of the Criminal Enforcement Program* 1
- *II. The Political Crisis* 2
- *III. The Mature Criminal Enforcement Program* 3
  - A. Current Enforcement Priorities 4
  - B. Significant Victories of the Environmental Crimes Program 5
  - C. Policy Issues Currently Facing the Environmental Criminal Program 7

Chapter 2 — Operation—Infrastructure and Practice 9
- *I. Bricks and Mortar* 9
  - A. EPA 9
  - B. DOJ, ECS, and U.S. Attorneys' Offices 10
- *II. Policies and Paper* 11
  - A. EPA's Decision to Initiate a Criminal Investigation 11
  - B. DOJ's Decision to Bring Criminal Cases 12
  - C. Environmental Audits and Voluntary Disclosure Programs 13
  - D. To Disclose or Not to Disclose?—That Is the Question 17
  - E. American Bar Association—Standards on Prosecutorial Investigation 18
  - F. The Dual and Successive Prosecution Policy (Petite Policy) 18
  - G. Parallel Proceedings 19
  - H. Deferred Prosecution Agreements and Non-Prosecution Agreements 25

Chapter 3 — Case Initiation and Response 27
- *I. Case Initiation* 27
  - A. Voluntary Disclosure 27
- *II. The Warrant Requirement and Its Exceptions* 31
  - A. Pervasively Regulated Industries 31
  - B. Open Fields Doctrine 31
  - C. Imminent Environmental Harm 32
  - D. Other Exigent Circumstances 32
  - E. Consent to Search 32
- *III. Responding to a Surprise Search* 32
  - A. Administrative Inspections and Criminal Warrants 33
  - B. Protecting Rights and Protecting Evidence During a Surprise Search 33
  - C. Preventing Add-On Allegations 35

Part Two: Legal Theory and Strategy

Chapter 4 — General Principles of Criminal Liability 37
I. *Mens Rea* 37
A. Statutory "Intent" 38
B. Knowledge That the Conduct Will Violate a Law or Regulation 39
C. Knowledge That the Activity Requires a Permit 39
D. Knowledge of the Underlying Facts 40
E. Knowledge That the Conduct Will Violate a Permit Term or Condition 42
F. The "Public Welfare" Doctrine 43
G. Criminal Negligence 44
H. Negligent Endangerment 46
I. Demonstrating Proof of Knowledge 46
II. *The Responsible Corporate Officer Doctrine* 48
A. Origins of the Responsible Corporate Officer Doctrine 49
B. The Polar Decisions Extending the Responsible Corporate Officer Doctrine to Environmental Cases 50
C. Application of the Responsible Corporate Officer Doctrine in Recent Environmental Cases 52
D. Concluding Thoughts on the Responsible Corporate Officer Doctrine 53
III. *Defense Strategies in Environmental Criminal Cases* 53
Chapter 5 — Grand Juries, Subpoenas, Document Production Issues in the Digital Age, Internal Investigation, and More 57
I. *Grand Jury* 57
A. The Basics 57
B. The Grand Jury Subpoena 58
II. *Conducting an Internal (Shadow) Investigation* 59
A. Staffing the Investigation and Choosing the Right Counsel 59
B. Employee Rights Vis-à-Vis the Government 59
C. Employee Rights Vis-à-Vis the Company 60
D. More on Interviewing Witnesses 61
E. Collecting Documents 61
F. Preventing Add-On Allegations 62
G. Issues of Privilege and Waiver 62
H. Keeping the Investigation Privileged 63
III. *Responding to a Subpoena for Documents* 66
A. Basics of Document Subpoenas 66
B. Protect Your Rights When Responding to a Subpoena for Documents 66
C. Designate a Custodian of Record 66
D. Set Up a Fail-Safe "Litigation Hold" or "Document Hold" System 67
E. Establish a System for Identifying Privileged Documents 67
F. Track Evidence When Responding to a Subpoena for Documents 67
G. Prevent Add-On Allegations 68
IV. *Electronic Discovery* 68
V. *Other Issues That Commonly Arise During a Government Investigation* 70

A. Sampling and Testing 70
B. Taking Corrective Action 70
C. Disciplining Employees 71
D. Voluntary Disclosure 71
E. Identifying Whether Individual Employees Need Separate Counsel 72
F. Deciding Whether to Join Forces With Employees' Counsel in a Joint Defense Agreement 72
G. Protecting the Company From Parallel Proceedings 73
H Considering Collateral Consequences 73
I. Considering a Deferred Prosecution/Non-Prosecution Agreement 74
J. Disclosing the Results of the Internal Investigation 74
K. Global Agreements 75
L. The Role of Alleged Victims 76

VI. Going to Trial 77

Chapter 6 — Pre-Trial 79

I. Discovery 79
A. The Jencks Act 79
B. Federal Rules of Criminal Procedure 81
C. The Freedom of Information Act 84
D. *Brady* Material 85
E. *Giglio* Material 86
F. DOJ Guidance 86

II. Motion Practice 88
A. Bill of Particulars 89
B. Motion in Limine 89
C. Motion to Suppress 90

Chapter 7 — Trial 91

I. Evidence 91
A. Rules of Evidence 92
B. Rules of Criminal Procedure 92
C. Expert Witnesses 93

II. Confrontation Clause 96
A. *Crawford v. Washington* 96
B. *Melendez-Diaz v. Massachusetts* 97

III. Jury Instructions 98
IV. Jury Deliberations 99
V. Verdict 99

Chapter 8 — Sentencing 101

I. Consequences of an Environmental Criminal Conviction 101
A. Remedial Obligations and Negotiated Pleas 101
B. Federal Sentencing Guidelines 102
C. Criminal Sentencing for Individuals 103
D. Criminal Sentencing for Organizations 105
E. The Failed Attempt to Adopt Comprehensive Organizational Guidelines for Environmental Crimes 106

F. The Sentencing Guidelines Are Discretionary, Not Mandatory 109
G. Criminal Fines, the Alternative Fines Act and the *Southern Union* Case 109
H. Statistics Concerning Criminal Environmental Sentences 111
I. Factors to Be Considered in Imposing a Sentence 111
J. The Crime Victims' Rights Act 112
II. Collateral Consequences of Environmental Crimes Convictions 114
A. Mandatory "Listing" of a Facility Under the CWA and the CAA 114
B. Suspension and Debarment of a Company From Future Government Contracts 116
C. Federal Tax Consequences 118
D. SEC Disclosure Obligations 119
E. State "Bad Actor" Provisions 121

Part Three: Statutes and Cases

Chapter 9 — Specific Environmental Statutes 123
I. The Clean Water Act 123
A. Overview 123
B. Prohibitions 124
C. Penalties 125
D. Permits and Permit Requirements 126
E. Jurisdictional Considerations 126
F. Proposals to Expand Restitution and Increase Sanctions Under the CWA 131
G. Criminal Enforcement of the CWA 132
II. Ocean and Vessel Pollution 136
A. Jurisdiction to Enforce Environmental Laws—Defining the Interests 137
B. Lines in the Water—Geographic Jurisdiction 138
C. International Environmental Law Applicable to Vessels 140
D. Federal Environmental Statutes Addressing Ocean and Vessel Pollution 140
E. Issues Unique to Vessel and Ocean Pollution Prosecutions 144
F. Vessel and Ocean Pollution Prosecutions 149
G. The Current State of the Law in Prosecutions 153
III. The Clean Air Act 155
A. Legislative History 155
B. The CAA Regulatory Regime 155
C. Permitting 157
D. Enforcement Under the CAA 157
E. Cases Involving the CAA 159
IV. Resource Conservation and Recovery Act 163
A. Hazardous Waste 163
B. Entities Regulated by RCRA 164
C. Criminal Liability Under RCRA 165
D. Knowledge Requirement 166
E. Knowing Endangerment 167

F. Persons Liable Under RCRA 167
G. Passive Migration 168
H. Federal Enforcement of State Programs 169
V. The Comprehensive Environmental Response, Compensation, and Liability Act 169
A. Introduction 169
B. Criminal Liability 170
C. Title III of the Emergency Planning and Community Right-To-Know Act 176
VI. Toxic Substances Control Act 177
A. Introduction 177
B. Chemical Testing 177
C. Pre-Manufacture Notification and Significant New Use Rules 178
D. Substantive Control Rules 179
E. Imminent Hazard Authority 179
F. Reporting and Recordkeeping Requirements 179
G. Export and Import Notifications 180
H. Regulation of PCBs 180
I. Special Titles 181
J. Criminal Liability Under TSCA 181
K. Statutory Prohibitions 181
L. Elements of Criminal Liability 181
M. TSCA Criminal Enforcement 182
VII. Federal Insecticide, Fungicide, and Rodenticide Act 182
A. Definition of "Pesticide" 182
B. Registration Requirement 183
C. Trade Secrets and Data Compensation 184
D. Experimental Use Permits 184
E. EPA Inspections and Recordkeeping Requirements 184
F. Safe-Handling Disposal Restrictions 185
G. Import and Export Requirements 185
H. FIFRA Criminal Sanctions 186
I. Federal and State Enforcement Issues 187
J. Federal Enforcement Policy 188
VIII. Migratory Bird Treaty Act 188
IX. The Lacey Act 191
A. Overview 191
B. Criminal Application of the Lacey Act 193
C. Recent Examples of Criminal Enforcement Under the Lacey Act 193
X. The Endangered Species Act 196
A. Overview 196
B. Criminal Application of the ESA 197
C. Recent Examples of Criminal Enforcement Under the ESA 197
XI. The Convention on International Trade of Endangered Species of Wild Fauna and Flora 199

A. Overview 199
B. Recent Examples of Criminal Enforcement of CITES 200
XII. Safe Drinking Water Act 201
A. Safe Drinking Water Act Enforcement 202
B. Safe Drinking Water Act Criminal Provisions 202
XIII. Fracking—New Issues, Old Statutes 203
XIV. Transportation Statutes 206
A. Hazardous Materials Transportation Act 207
B. Pipeline Safety Act 207
XV. Common Title 18 Offenses in Environmental Crimes Cases 208
A. False or Misleading Statements 209
B. Obstruction of Justice/Destruction of Evidence 212
C. Conspiracy 215

Appendices

1. Memorandum From Earl E. Devaney, Director, Office of Criminal Enforcement, to All EPA Employees Working in or in Support of the Criminal Enforcement Program, The Exercise of Investigative Discretion (Jan. 12, 1994) 217
2. U.S. DOJ, Factors in Decisions on Criminal Prosecutions for Environmental Violations in the Context of Significant Voluntary Compliance or Disclosure Efforts by the Violator (July 1, 1991) 223
3. EPA Audit Policy (Website) 231
4. U.S. Attys. Manual-Prosecution of Organizations 237
5. U.S. EPA, Incentives for Self-Policing: Discovery, Disclosure, Correction, and Prevention of Violations, 65 Fed. Reg. 19618 (Apr. 11, 2000) 263
6. U.S. EPA, Small Business Compliance Policy, 65 Fed. Reg. 19630 (Apr. 11, 2000) 277
7. ENRD Parallel Proceedings Policy 285
8. EPA Criminal Enforcement and Compliance Results 297
9. U.S. Coast Guard Maritime Law Enforcement Manual, App. V, Environmental Crimes: Voluntary Disclosure Policy 301
10. Clipper Trojan Indictment 313
11. Mylonakis Jury Instructions 343
12. *United States v. W.R. Grace et al.* Superseding Indictment (Mont. 2005) 363
13. Gibson Guitar NPA 385
14. Search Warrant 411
15. McWane (N.D. Ala.) Court Jury Instructions (4.5.05) 419
16. Sample Employee Rights Form (Contracts) 453
17. Sample Document Hold Notice 457
18. Miranda Reading to Companies (*Upjohn* Warning) 461
19. Developing an Effective Environmental and Monitoring Compliance Program 465

Online appendices referenced in this book can be found at
www.eli.org/environmental-crimes-second-edition

Index of Acronyms

Act to Prevent Pollution From Ships (APPS)
Administrative Procedure Act (APA)
Antiterrorism and Effective Death Penalty Act (AEDPA)
Assistant United States Attorney (AUSA)
Atomic Energy Act (AEA)
Best Achievable Control Technology (BACT)
Clean Air Act (CAA)
Clean Water Act (CWA)
Comprehensive Environmental Response, Compensation, and Liability Act (CERCLA)
Conditionally Exempt Small Quantity Generator (CESQG)
Convention on International Trade of Endangered Species (CITES)
Deferred Prosecution Agreement (DPA)
Department of Environmental Conservation (DEC)
Department of Environmental Quality (DEQ)
Department of the Interior (DOI)
Department of Justice (DOJ)
Department of Justice Environmental Crimes Section (DOJ ECS)
Department of Natural Resources (DNR)
Department of Transportation (DOT)
Discharge Monitoring Report (DMR)
Emergency Planning and Community Right-To-Know Act (EPCRA)
Endangered Species Act (ESA)
Environment and Natural Resources Division (ENRD)
Environmental Protection Agency (EPA)
EPA Criminal Investigation Division (EPA CID)
EPA Suspension and Debarment Official (EPA SDO)
EPA Office of Criminal Enforcement, Forensics, and Training (OCEFT)
EPA Office of Enforcement and Compliance Assurance (OECA)
Excluded Parties List System (EPLS)
Exclusive Economic Zone (EEZ)
Extremely Hazardous Substances (EHS)
Federal Acquisition Regulation (FAR)
Federal Aviation Administration (FAA)
Federal Bureau of Investigation (FBI)
Federal Crime Victims' Rights Act (CVRA)
Federal Food, Drug, and Cosmetic Act (FFDCA)
Federal Insecticide, Fungicide, and Rodenticide Act (FIFRA)
Fish and Wildlife Service (FWS)
Food and Drug Administration (FDA)
Food, Drug, and Cosmetic Act (FDCA)
Freedom of Information Act (FOIA)
Hazardous Air Pollutant (HAP)
Hazardous and Solid Waste Amendment (HSWA)
Hazardous Materials Transportation Act (HMTA)
Hazardous Materials Transportation Uniform Safety Act (HMTUSA)
Information Technology (IT)
International Convention for the Prevention of Pollution From Ships (MARPOL)
Large Quantity Generator (LQG)

Lowest Achievable Emission Rate (LAER)
Mandatory Victims Restitution Act (MVRA)
Maximum Achievable Control Technology (MACT)
Migratory Bird Treaty Act (MBTA)
Mobile Offshore Drilling Unit (MODU)
National Ambient Air Quality Standards (NAAQS)
National Emission Standards for Hazardous Air Pollutants (NESHAPs)
National Enforcement Initiative (NEI)
National Enforcement Investigations Center (NEIC)
National Enforcement Program Managers Guidance (NPMG)
National Environmental Policy Act (NEPA)
National Marine Fisheries Service (NMFS)
National Oceanic and Atmospheric Administration (NOAA)
National Pollutant Discharge Elimination System (NPDES)
New Source Performance Standards (NSPS)
Non-Prosecution Agreement (NPA)
Occupational Safety and Health Administration (OSHA)
Office of Enforcement and Compliance Assurance (OECA)
Oil Pollution Act (OPA)
Oil Record Book (ORB)
Oily Water Separating Equipment (OWS Equipment)
Pipeline and Hazardous Materials Safety Administration (PHMSA)
Pipeline Safety Act (PSA)
Pollution Prosecution Act (PPA)
Polychlorinated Biphenyls (PCBs)
Prevention of Significant Deterioration (PSD)
Publicly Owned Treatment Works (POTW)
Resource Conservation and Recovery Act (RCRA)
Responsible Corporate Officer (RCO)
Safe Drinking Water Act (SDWA)
Securities and Exchange Commission (SEC)
Significant New Use Rule (SNUR)
Small Quantity Generator (SQG)
Solid Waste Agency of Northern Cook County (SWANCC)
Solid Waste Disposal Act (SWDA)
Standard Industrial Classification (SIC)
State Implementation Plan (SIP)
Superfund Amendments and Reauthorization Act (SARA)
Supplemental Environmental Project (SEP)
Toxic Substances Control Act (TSCA)
Treatment, Storage, and Disposal Facility (TSDF)
Underground Injection Control (UIC)
Underground Storage Tank (UST)
United Nations Convention on the Law of the Sea (UNCLOS)
Vessel General Permit (VGP)
Victim and Witness Protection Act (VWPA)

Foreword

The federal Environmental Criminal Enforcement Program is a highly successful cooperative effort between federal prosecutors in the Environmental Crimes Section of the U.S. Department of Justice (DOJ) in Washington, D.C., line prosecutors in the 94 U.S. Attorneys' offices, and criminal investigators at the U.S. Environmental Protection Agency (EPA) and other federal agencies including the United States Coast Guard, the Customs Service, and the U.S. Department of the Interior's Fish and Wildlife Service. Over the last two decades, these groups have established a solid foundation for the criminal enforcement effort by establishing clear policies for instituting criminal prosecutions, devising sensible enforcement priorities, and achieving a series of court victories that have created an effective deterrent threat. The program has enjoyed broad public support and achieved exceptional results.

Criminal environmental law relies on two areas of the law that are both complex and vital: history-driven criminal law and science-based environmental law. The innovations of criminal environmental law can, therefore, move beyond the basics familiar to many criminal practitioners. Traditional concepts of knowledge and intent and employer responsibility have evolved rapidly and expansively, much to the chagrin of any corporate manager who runs afoul of the law. Above all, the sheer size and complexity of the task of bridging the two fields challenges the novice and demands expert assistance.

Enter the *Environmental Crimes Deskbook* 2nd Edition. This Second Edition greatly expands upon the first edition, both in breadth of issues and depth of analysis, offering the insight and expertise of Judson W. Starr, Amy J. McMaster, John F. Cooney, David G. Dickman, David L. Feinberg, and Margaret K. Kuhn—attorneys in the Washington, D.C., firm of Venable LLP—and recently retired Venable partner, Joseph G. (Jerry) Block, who have over a century of combined experience representing corporations and individuals in criminal environmental cases. These attorneys are recognized leaders in this area with a background in both government and private practice. I have had the pleasure of working with, learning from, or associating with many of them.

In plain English, the authors lay out the basic concepts of criminal environmental law and how they fit into the larger context of environmental regulation. As specialists in criminal environmental law, the authors relate how the emerging criminal and environmental law comes together. And, they illuminate complex matters by placing policy decisions in the context of the historical development of the field—developments that they helped shape.

Divided into three main subparts, the first discusses the history of the federal environmental crimes program, the various policies and factors considered by DOJ, EPA, and U.S. Attorneys' Offices in deciding whether to bring a criminal environmental case, and the primary means by which a case is initiated including, voluntary disclosure, routine compliance information, audits, inspections, information requests, anonymous tips, whistleblowers, and administrative and criminal warrants. The second is devoted to legal theory and strategy, including a detailed discussion of the knowledge element as it is particularly applied in environmental criminal law, a detailed "how-to" guide for responding to an environmental criminal investigation, and suggestions and issue-spotting in the pretrial, trial, and sentencing stages of the case. The third subpart provides a detailed analysis of the primary environmental statutes, identifying key issues and considerations for each, as well as a brief discussion of landmark cases.

In addition to the analysis, the *Environmental Crimes Deskbook* includes agency guidance on such issues as general enforcement policy, specific EPA and DOJ investigative and prosecutorial procedures, parallel proceedings, and environmental self-audits. It also includes sample forms and pleadings, such as search warrants, indictments, deferred prosecution agreements, plea agreements, and jury instructions.

As with all ELI Deskbooks, the *Environmental Crimes Deskbook* should be your ready reference. It is practice-oriented with expert advice that can assist you daily. All of us who practice environmental law consider this to be the premier reference source.

John C Cruden
President
Environmental Law Institute

Part One: The Basics

Chapter 1: History of the Federal Environmental Crimes Program

The federal Environmental Criminal Enforcement Program is a highly successful cooperative effort between federal prosecutors in the Environmental Crimes Section (ECS) of the U.S. Department of Justice (DOJ) in Washington, D.C., line prosecutors in the 93 U.S. Attorneys' offices, and criminal investigators at the U.S. Environmental Protection Agency (EPA) and other federal agencies including the U.S. Coast Guard. Over the last two decades, these groups have established a solid foundation for the criminal enforcement effort by establishing clear policies for instituting criminal prosecutions, devising sensible enforcement priorities, and achieving a series of court victories that have created an effective deterrent threat. The program has enjoyed broad public support and largely avoided political controversy, with the exception of one rough passage in the mid-1990s.

I. Origins of the Criminal Enforcement Program

The first generation of environmental statues adopted in the 1970s provided for criminal enforcement of their provisions, generally through provisions that punished violations as misdemeanors. Initially, DOJ made little use of these authorities. EPA's Office of Criminal Enforcement referred many cases to DOJ's Division of Lands and Natural Resources (since renamed the Environmental and Natural Resources Division) for criminal prosecution, but the Division declined nearly 60% of the referrals due to poor investigative work.[1] The first tentative steps toward a freestanding criminal enforcement program occurred in fall 1982. In October, EPA hired its first cohort of experienced criminal investigators. In November, DOJ created a small contingent of prosecutors in the Environment Crimes Unit within its existing Civil Environmental Enforcement Section.

The Criminal Enforcement Program achieved its current institutional structure by 1987, when the U.S. Attorney General created an independent ECS within the then Lands Division, with a mission to prosecute individuals and corporations that had violated laws designed to protect the environment. The creation of ECS, under the leadership of Judson Starr, reflected a policy decision to maintain a degree of centralization in the administration of the program. By placing formal responsibility for approval of significant criminal prosecutions in the ECS, and ultimately the assistant attorney general in Washington, D.C., DOJ sought to ensure that: cases would be selected in a manner that minimized risk to crucial EPA regulatory interpretations; similar cases would be treated alike, even though they arose in different parts of the country; and potentially precedent-setting cases would be carefully presented and would have the attention of DOJ's high-level management. Given the difficulty in defining whether environmental violators should be prosecuted criminally, civilly, or administratively, this centralized policy control advanced the goal of consistency in charging decisions.

The environmental crimes initiative benefitted from this improved institutional structure, but initially suffered from limited resources and inadequate statutory authority. Many U.S. attorneys displayed little

1. *EPA's Law Enforcement Authority, 1983: Hearings Before the Subcomm. on Oversight and Investigations of the House Comm. on Energy and Commerce*, 98th Cong. 92 (1983) (testimony of Assistant Attorney General Habicht).

interest in the initiative. Local prosecutors had limited familiarity with environmental law, and some U.S. attorney's offices faced resource constraints that made it difficult to justify bringing misdemeanor cases. Nevertheless, centralized case selection and meticulous preparation by environmental experts helped ensure success in the initial generation of decisions that established the crucial precedents that remain the foundation of the program, notably decisions determining the mental state necessary to support an environmental criminal conviction.[2] Throughout the late 1980s, the executive branch worked with the U.S. Congress to clarify the scope of the criminal enforcement provisions, upgrade the crimes from misdemeanors to felonies, and provide for greater fines and longer terms of imprisonment.[3]

By 1992, the ECS had grown to 28 attorneys. Its work was complemented by the Federal Bureau of Investigation (FBI), which had 100 special agents working on environmental criminal cases. Between 1982 and 1992, EPA's enforcement staff grew from 6 to 62 criminal investigators.[4]

During this period, the vast majority of environmental prosecutions involved violations of the Resource Conservation and Recovery Act (RCRA) or the Clean Water Act (CWA). DOJ's enforcement policy concentrated on persons operating outside the regulatory or permit system, such as midnight dumpers, and persons operating inside the system who sought to avoid detection of regulatory violations by submitting false or incomplete information.[5] In October 1991, the Environmental Crimes Program enjoyed its largest nationally recognized success when former ECS Chief Joseph Block and other Justice Department officials, successfully concluded negotiations on a guilty plea with Exxon in the aftermath of the 1989 Exxon *Valdez* oil spill. Exxon and a subsidiary pleaded guilty to CWA and Migratory Bird Treaty Act (MBTA) offenses and agreed to a combined criminal and civil settlement of $1.125 billion, of which $250 million was for criminal fines and restitution.

II. The Political Crisis

The success of the Environmental Crimes Program was, to a substantial degree, a function of DOJ's original policy decision to centralize responsibility in the ECS. As the program proved its value, this policy generated friction both between DOJ and EPA and between Washington and the U.S. attorneys. EPA believed that DOJ was not sufficiently aggressive in bringing criminal cases, and the U.S. attorneys objected to the requirement of clearing cases through the ECS. Both sides argued strenuously for a more evenly distributed system in which they would have greater discretion and responsibility. This pressure intensified as environmental violations became more attractive targets for local prosecution, due both to the enhancement of the crimes to felonies and the issuance by the U.S. Sentencing Commission in 1987 of sentencing guidelines for individual offenders that virtually assured incarceration for persons convicted of environmental felonies.[6]

The Environmental Crimes Program encountered a political crisis in 1992, when the chairman of the U.S. House of Representatives' Energy and Commerce Committee accused the Bush Administration of deliberately refusing to prosecute environmental crimes.[7] Subsequent statistics demonstrated that this charge was unfounded, but the Environmental Crimes Program nonetheless suffered a substantial loss of credibility.[8]

To end the dispute and permit the Environmental Crimes Program to move forward, in August 1994, U.S. Attorney General Janet Reno delegated a substantial degree of additional authority to the U.S. attor-

---

2. *See, e.g.*, United States v. Weitzenhoff, 1 F.3d 1523 (9th Cir. 1993), *reh'g denied, opinion amended*, 35 F.3d 1275, 24 ELR 21504 (1994), *cert. denied sub nom.* Mariani v. United States, 513 U.S. 1128 (1995); United States v. Hopkins, 53 F.3d 533 (2d Cir. 1995).
3. Major benchmarks included the Hazardous and Solid Waste Amendments (HSWA) of 1984, which upgraded the RCRA criminal violations to felonies, Pub. L. No. 98-616, 98 Stat. 3221 (codified as amended at 42 U.S.C. §§6901-6992); the Superfund Amendments and Reauthorization Act of 1986 (SARA), Pub. L. No. 99-499, §109, 100 Stat. 1613, 1632-33 (codified as amended at 42 U.S.C. §9603(b)(d)); the Water Quality Act of 1987, Pub. L. No. 100-4, §312, 101 Stat. 7, 42-44 (codified at 33 U.S.C. §1319(c)); and the Clean Air Act Amendments of 1990, Pub. L. No. 101-549, §701, 104 Stat. 2399, 2672 (codified as amended at 42 U.S.C. §7413(c)).
4. Joseph G. Block, *Environmental Criminal Enforcement in the 1990s*, 3 Vill. Envtl. L.J. 33, 34-35 (1992).
5. Interview with Judson Starr, *Corporation Crime Reporter* 5, 7 (May 4, 1987). *See* F. Henry Habicht II, *The Federal Perspective on Environmental Criminal Enforcement: How to Remain on the Civil Side*, 17 ELR 10478, 10481 (Dec. 1987).
6. *See* U.S. Sentencing Commission, Guidelines Manual (Nov. 1994) [hereinafter Sentencing Guidelines].
7. *See* Staff of House Comm. on Energy and Commerce, 103rd Cong., Damaging Disarray: Organizational Breakdown and Reform in the Justice Department's Environmental Crimes Program (Comm. Print 103-T 1994).
8. The U.S. General Accountability Office, Environmental Enforcement: EPA Needs to Improve the Accuracy and Transparency of Measures Used to Report on Program Effectiveness 14 (Sept. 18, 2008) (GAO 08-1111R).

neys.[9] The 1994 policy, which essentially remains in effect today, divided prosecutions into "national interest cases" and lower priority cases.[10] The ECS and U.S. attorneys jointly handle "national interest" matters, including cases that present novel issues of law, simultaneous investigations in multiple federal judicial districts, cases with foreign policy implications, and urgent or sensitive issues, including those of major interest to Congress or the president.[11] In other cases, local prosecutors must notify Washington of an intended prosecution, but the ECS does not have formal veto authority over indictments or pleas.[12]

III. The Mature Criminal Enforcement Program

With its political problems resolved, the Environmental Crimes Program entered a stable period of development and expansion in the mid-1990s that continues to the present day. The ECS has grown to more than 40 lawyers, has trained hundreds of local federal prosecutors, and the majority of criminal cases are now handled either jointly with ECS or by prosecutors in the U.S. attorney's office. In the competition for funding, the Environmental Crimes Program fared reasonably well by comparison with other DOJ enforcement offices, whose resources were restricted after the 9/11 attacks to increase funding for the National Security Division. The involvement of FBI agents in investigating potential environmental criminal cases diminished, however, due to the FBI's concentration on national security matters.

In fiscal year (FY) 2008, the last period for which statistics for solely criminal enforcements were published, the Environmental Crimes Program brought criminal charges against 176 persons and entities. Defendants were sentenced to $64 million in fines and restitution, $12 million in court-ordered environmental projects, and 57 years of imprisonment.[13] In FY 2011, combined EPA civil and criminal environmental enforcement actions resulted in $168 million in penalties, and 89.5 years of imprisonment.[14] In FY 2012, combined EPA civil and criminal environmental enforcement actions resulted in $252 million in penalties.[15] During calendar year 2012, criminal violations of federal environmental and wildlife protection laws resulted in 342 defendants being sentenced to a combined total of over 86 years in prison and $26 million in fines.[16] According to DOJ, "[f]rom October 1, 1998 through June 30, 2013, ECS concluded criminal cases against more than 1,005 individuals and 373 corporate defendants, leading to 729 years of incarceration and $743 million in criminal fines and restitution (852 years with incarceration, halfway house and home detention)."[17]

---

9. Office of the Attorney General, Bluesheet Revision to the U.S. Attorney's Manual on Environmental Crimes (Aug. 23, 1994) (reproduced in Appendix __ of this deskbook).
10. *Id.* at 3 (amending DOJ manual §5-11.105).
11. *Id.*
12. *Id.* (amending DOJ manual §5-11.104).
13. U.S. EPA, Office of Enforcement and Compliance Assurance, FY 2008 Accomplishments Report 7 (Dec. 2008), *available at* www.epa.gov/compliance/resources/reports/accomplishments/oeca/fy08accomplishment.pdf (last visited May 28, 2013).
14. U.S. EPA, Office of Enforcement and Compliance Assurance, *Compliance and Enforcement Annual Results 2011 Fiscal Year*, www.epa.gov/compliance/resources/reports/endofyear/eoy2011/index.html (last visited May 28, 2013).
15. U.S. EPA, Office of Enforcement and Compliance, *Compliance and Enforcement Annual Results 2012 Fiscal Year*, http://www2.epa.gov/enforcement/enforcement-annual-results-fiscal-year-2012 (last visited Jan. 16, 2014). EPA also touts the following accomplishments in FY 2012:
    - 6.6 billion pounds of pollution and hazardous waste reduced, eliminated, properly disposed of or treated.
    - $44 million in additional investments for supplemental environmental projects that benefit communities.
    - Improving compliance with drinking water regulations by 60%: sustained and focused enforcement attention on serious violators of clean drinking water standards has resulted in dramatic improvements in compliance.
    - Progress cleaning up raw sewage and stormwater: 67% of large municipalities with combined sewer overflows are now on track to address their local water issues, many using innovations like green infrastructure to help reduce stormwater flows.
    - Bringing criminal prosecutions where criminal activity threatens public health: EPA is taking criminal enforcement action against companies or individuals who fail to use required pollution control equipment, knowingly violate pollution rules, resulting in death or serious harm, or falsify pollution information. See a case example in Louisiana, http://yosemite.epa.gov/opa/admpress.nsf/0/224A2AF1EC8927C7852579670063837A.
    - Advancing environmental justice: EPA incorporated fence line monitoring into settlements, ensuring that local residents have access to critical information about pollution that may be affecting their community. See an oil refinery case example, http://yosemite.epa.gov/opa/admpress.nsf/d0cf6618525a9efb85257359003fb69d/7edc0a75afdd90eb85257a07006719cd!opendocument.
    - Increasing transparency: EPA's enforcement and compliance online history tools, including the map of enforcement cases in 2012, state dashboards, and CWA pollutant loadings tool, provide the public with critical access to environmental information. See www.epa-echo.gov/echo/dmr_loadings_tool.php?template=echo, for more information.

    Id.
16. *Id.*
17. DOJ, Environmental Crimes Section, http://www.justice.gov/enrd/ENRD_ecs.html (last visited Oct. 8, 2013).

In the last two decades, relatively few environmental criminal cases against corporations have gone to trial. The combination of the non-demanding "general knowledge" standard of liability and the principle of *respondeat superior* means that an enterprise has relatively few defenses once the government proves the occurrence of an illegal discharge. The critical aspect of an environmental case is the prosecutor's decision whether a criminal resolution is warranted, based on such factors as the harm that occurred to the public interest and the adequacy of civil remedies. More, but still relatively few, individuals have assumed the risk of going to trial, because the *U.S. Sentencing Guidelines*, which once were thought to be mandatory, are now discretionary pursuant to an intervening U.S. Supreme Court decision.

A. *Current Enforcement Priorities*

Most federal environmental criminal charges involve violations of the CWA or illegal disposal of hazardous waste. DOJ's priorities, however, have shifted significantly over time.

In the mid-1990s, the ECS targeted the smuggling of ozone-depleting chlorofluorocarbons and pursued an initiative to prosecute fraud in environmental testing laboratories to assure the integrity of data reported to environmental regulatory agencies.

Since the late 1990s, the ECS has focused on prosecuting illegal discharges of oil from ships and the falsification of the Oil Record Books (ORB), which vessels are required to maintain and produce to the U.S. Coast Guard on request and in which each discharge of oil must be recorded. In recent years, more than one-quarter of all environmental criminal prosecutions have involved vessel pollution, and more than $250 million in fines have been collected from vessel owners. Intense litigation has occurred over the threshold legal issue whether, under the International Convention for the Prevention of Pollution from Ships (MARPOL) and its implementing statute, the Act to Prevent Pollution in Ships (APPS), the United States can prosecute on a false records theory oil discharges that occurred in international waters beyond U.S. jurisdiction.[18] In 2008, DOJ achieved a significant victory when the U.S. Court of Appeals for the Fifth Circuit upheld the jurisdictional theory on which the Vessel Pollution Initiative largely rests.[19]

The Occupational Safety and Health Act (OSH Act) does not contain a provision that punishes as a felony acts by corporations or managers that threaten worker safety. To fill this statutory gap, the ECS instituted a Worker Endangerment Initiative that targets corporations and individuals for prosecution under the environmental laws, on the theory that companies which violate environmental laws are highly likely to ignore worker safety laws as well.

Every three years, with input from states and the public, EPA sets national enforcement initiatives to focus its civil and criminal enforcement resources and expertise on serious pollution problems affecting communities. The 2011-2013 initiatives are[20]: (1) Reducing Air Pollution From the Largest Sources; (2) Cutting Hazardous Air Pollutants; (3) Keeping Raw Sewage and Contaminated Stormwater Out of Our Nation's Waters[21]; (4) Preventing Animal Waste From Contaminating Surface and Ground Water; (5) Assuring Energy Extraction Activities Comply With Environmental Laws; and (6) Reducing Pollution From Mineral Processing Operations. The public comment period on EPA's national priorities for FY 2014-2017 closed on February 27, 2013.[22]

In addition to supporting the six priorities for FY 2011-2013, EPA's Office of Enforcement and Compliance Assurance (OECA) notes that OECA and the regions will focus their enforcement efforts on several primary programs, including: (1) the Emergency Planning and Community Right-To-Know Act

18. *See* United States v. Royal Caribbean Cruises, Ltd., 11 F. Supp. 2d 1358 (S.D. Fla. 1998).
19. United States v. Jho, 534 F.3d 398 (5th Cir. 2008).
20. U.S. EPA, *National Enforcement Initiatives*, www.epa.gov/compliance/data/planning/initiatives/index.html (last visited May 28, 2013).
21. On Oct. 10, 2012, in one of the first stormwater pollution criminal case brought in the United States, a Washington State developer was sentenced to six months in prison, one year of supervised release, and a $300,000 fine by U.S. district court Judge Ronald B. Leighton in Tacoma, Washington, for a felony violation of the CWA (knowingly violating a national pollution discharge elimination permit). *See* U.S.A.O. (W.D. Wa.) Press Release, *Prominent Pierce County Developer Sentenced To Prison For Criminal Violations Of Clean Water Act* (Oct. 10, 2012), *available at* http://www.justice.gov/usao/waw/press/2012/October/stowe.html (last visited Jan. 28, 2014).
22. *See* www.regulations.gov/#!docketDetail;D=EPA-HQ-OECA-2012-0956 (last visited May 28, 2013).

(EPCRA); (2) the Resource Conservation and Recovery Act (RCRA); (3) the Toxic Substances Control Act (TSCA); and (4) the Clean Air Act (CAA).[23]

B. *Significant Victories of the Environmental Crimes Program*

Over the last decade, the Environmental Crimes Program has obtained a number of significant victories that have created a credible deterrent threat for potential violators of the environmental laws. In addition to the Exxon guilty plea in 1991, the most important cases include:

1. Royal Caribbean Cruise Lines

In 1999, Royal Caribbean Cruise Lines (RCCL) pleaded guilty in six federal district courts to a total of 21 felony counts based on alleged discharges of waste oil and hazardous chemicals by its vessels. RCCL paid a fine of $18 million, divided among the six jurisdictions.[24]

2. McWane

Between 2003 and 2005, the ECS brought five indictments in four district courts against the iron pipe fitting company McWane, Inc., for environmental and worker safety violations. The company pleaded guilty in four cases and was fined a total of $11 million. In the U.S. District Court for the District of New Jersey, after a jury trial lasting seven months, the company and four managers were convicted of conspiracy, environmental violations, false statements, and obstruction of Occupational Safety and Health Administration (OSHA) investigations. The company was fined an additional $8 million.[25] Finally, the company was convicted in the U.S. District Court for the Northern District of Alabama on 20 charges of conspiracy, false statements, and environmental violations. On appeal, after the Supreme Court narrowed the definition of "navigable waters" covered by the CWA,[26] the U.S. Court of Appeals for the Eleventh Circuit reversed the environmental convictions and remanded for a new trial.[27] The trial judge to whom the case was remanded wrote an opinion explaining why he was redirecting the case to another judge.[28] He questioned whether Justice Anthony Kennedy's ruling in *Rapanos v. United States*[29] was controlling, whether the "narrowest" reading test was applicable, and whether the double jeopardy clause barred another trial against the corporation. Rather than face a re-trial, the defendants defendants reached a plea agreement with the government. To date, the *McWane* convictions are the greatest achievement of the ECS' Worker Protection Initiative.

3. Overseas Shipholding Group (OSG)

In March 2007, OSG pleaded guilty in the U.S. District Court for the District of Massachusetts, in a proceeding that consolidated pleas in four other districts, to 23 felony counts involving conspiracy, obstruction of justice, false statements, and failure to maintain accurate ORBs. The company was fined $20.1 million and made community service payments of another $6.9 million. OSG also separately pleaded guilty in the U.S. District for the Eastern District of Texas, was sentenced to pay a fine of $7.7 million and to make community service payments of $2.3 million.

---

23. EPA, Office of Enforcement and Compli¬ance Assurance (OECA), National Enforcement Program Managers Guidance (NPMG) for FY 2013. This guidance applies to the OECA, all EPA regional enforcement programs, and state and federally recognized Indian tribes implementing EPA-approved inspection and enforcement programs. It is included as Appendix __.
24. ECS' practice of bringing essentially identical vessel pollution charges in multiple jurisdictions has been criticized as contrary to the provisions of the Principles of Federal Prosecution concerning charging decisions. John F. Cooney, *Multi-Jurisdictional and Successive Prosecution of Environmental Crimes: The Case for a Consistent Approach*, 96 J. Crim. L. & Criminology 435 (Winter 2006).
25. United States v. Atl. States Cast Iron Pipe Co., 627 F. Supp. 2d 180 (D.N.J. 2009), *aff'd*, United States v. Maury, 695 F.3d 227 (3d Cir. 2012), *cert. denied*, Atl. States Co. v. United States, 133 S. Ct. 1600 (U.S. Mar. 18, 2013).
26. *See* Rapanos v. United States, 547 U.S. 715, 36 ELR 20116 (2006).
27. United States v. Robison, 505 F.3d 1208 (11th Cir. 2007), *cert. denied*, 555 U.S. 1045 (2008).
28. United States v. Robison, 521 F. Supp. 2d 1247 (N.D. Ala. 2007).
29. 547 U.S. 715, 36 ELR 20116 (2006).

The trial judge in the Eastern District of Texas, however, dismissed criminal charges against a vessel officer for certain of the charges to which OSG had pleaded guilty, namely failing to maintain an ORB that accurately recorded discharges of oil in international waters. The court held that the government lacked jurisdiction to prosecute crimes based on acts that occurred outside U.S. jurisdiction. The Fifth Circuit reversed and remanded for trial, holding that the crimes charged in the indictment were for the failure to maintain an accurate ORB, not for the original act of making the false entry, and that this offense had occurred within U.S. navigable waters.[30] This decision validated the jurisdictional theory on which the ECS's Vessel Pollution Initiative rests.

4. BP Plc

In October 2007, BP and several subsidiaries pleaded guilty in the U.S. District Court for the Southern District of Texas to a one count felony violation of the CAA and a $50 million criminal fine related to a catastrophic explosion at a refinery in which 15 workers were killed. A BP subsidiary pleaded guilty in the U.S. District Court for the District of Alaska to a violation of the CWA relating to leaks of crude oil from its pipeline onto the tundra, and a fine of $12 million, with $4 million in criminal restitution to the state of Alaska and $4 million in other criminal recoveries. BP also entered into a deferred prosecution agreement in the U.S. District Court for the Northern District of Illinois related to propane market manipulation charges in Texas, for which it agreed to pay a total of $373 million in fines and restitution. These pleas were an important step forward for the ECS's Worker Protection Initiative.

5. BP Exploration and Production, Inc.

In January 2013, a federal judge in the U.S. District Court for the Eastern District of Louisiana approved a plea agreement entered into by BP for violations arising from the release of oil from the Macondo well in the Gulf of Mexico in 2010. The Macondo well was operated by BP, and had been drilled by the Mobile Offshore Drilling Unit (MODU) *Deepwater Horizon*, owned and operated by a subsidiary of Transocean Deepwater, Inc., a subcontractor of BP. The well failed. It eventually released between 4.5 and 5.5 million barrels of oil into the Gulf of Mexico. This was the worst oil discharge in U.S. history. In addition, gas discharged from the well enveloped the *Deepwater Horizon* and caused an explosion, which led to the sinking of the MODU and the loss of 11 crewmembers. BP pled guilty to 14 criminal counts, which included 11 counts under the maritime manslaughter statute, one count of obstruction of Congress, one misdemeanor count of violating the CWA provisions prohibiting the negligent discharge of oil, and one count under the MBTA. BP was sentenced to pay $4 billion in criminal fines and recoveries as provided in the plea agreement. In addition, Transocean agreed to plead to a single count of violating the CWA provisions prohibiting the negligent discharge of oil, and to pay $400 million in criminal fines and recoveries.[31]

30. United States v. Jho, 534 F.3d 398 (5th Cir. 2008).

31. The BP oil spill case also resulted in criminal indictments of several individual BP employees. In the first indictment, a former BP engineer was arrested and indicted on charges of obstruction of justice. The engineer had been involved in efforts to stem the discharge of oil from the well, and was involved in modeling flow rates of oil from the well—a significant point of controversy long after the well was capped. According to the indictment, the engineer shared estimates from the model within BP that were greater than the amounts estimated by the U.S. governement and shared with the public. Early on, BP and its employees, including the engineer were issued a legal hold order by the government mandating that all evidence regarding the incident be retained. The indictment alleges that the engineer, after receiving the evidence hold order, deleted hundreds of text messages from his phone regarding the estimated rate of discharge of oil from the well. *See* U.S. DOJ, Press Release, Former BP Engineer Arrested for Obstruction of Justice in Connection With the *Deepwater Horizon* Criminal Investigation (Apr. 24, 2012), *available at* http://www.justice.gov/opa/pr/2012/April/12-ag-524.html (last visited May 28, 2013).

Subsequently, a BP vice president was indicted for obstruction of Congress and making false statements to federal agents. Again these charges relate to statements made regarding the flow rate of oil being discharged from the well. According to the indictment, the BP vice president responded to a formal request for information regarding the amount of oil flowing from the well from a House subcommittee with oversight authority. The BP vice president allegedly falsely informed subcommittee staff members during a briefing that the flow rate was in accordance with initial federal agency estimates without disclosing information of which he was aware from a variety of other sources, including internal BP estimates, that the rate was significantly greater. Subsequently, it is alleged, he responded to a letter request from the subcommittee chairman accusing BP of understating the amount and flow rate of oil being discharged by again providing false and misleading information to support his original estimate. Finally, he is alleged to have made false statements to federal law enforcement agents investigating the obstruction of Congress charge. *See Indictment*, http://www.justice.gov/iso/opa/resources/2782012111514365832844 9.pdf (last visited June 4, 2013).

In addition, two BP well site leaders, who were on board the drilling rig *Deepwater Horizon* at the time of the explosion and fire, were indicted on 11 counts of involuntary manslaughter under 18 U.S.C. §1112, 11 counts of seaman's manslaughter under 18 U.S.C. §1115,

6. W.R. Grace & Co.

The greatest disappointment for the Environmental Crimes Program occurred in May 2009, when a jury in the U.S. District Court for the District of Montana acquitted W.R. Grace and three former executives on charges of multiple environmental violations involving the contamination of a town with asbestos emitted by a vermiculite mine.[32] DOJ invested substantial resources in this multi-week trial, but its position was undermined by its failure to disclose its relationship with a key witness.

C. *Policy Issues Currently Facing the Environmental Criminal Program*

The Environmental Crimes Program faces several policy problems that have significantly complicated determination of the appropriate cases to prosecute and the charges to file.

1. Restriction of the Scope of the CWA

The Supreme Court's 2006 decision in *Rapanos* has limited the scope of the CWA by narrowing the definition of the critical term "waters of the United States" as applied to wetlands. While explicitly rejecting the broad interpretation of "waters" that EPA had long applied, the Court did not provide an alternative standard. A four-Justice plurality and Justice Kennedy, separately concurring in the judgment, articulated different standards for defining "waters of the United States." Their inability to reach agreement has made it difficult to determine where "waters" end and a "wetland" subject to federal regulation might begin. This confusion in the definition of a fundamental statutory term has greatly complicated the role of courts called upon to determine the scope of federal jurisdiction. It thereby has created an obstacle to successful criminal prosecution of subsequent cases that involve discharges into wetlands. Congress has considered, but not adopted, statutory amendments that would restore the prior reach of federal prosecutorial jurisdiction. Accordingly, prosecutors contemplating bringing criminal charges under the CWA must address the threshold question whether any indictment will be subject to a motion to dismiss on the grounds that the waters into which a discharge was made do not fall within the scope of the statute.

2. Prosecutors' Demands for Privilege Waivers

Both EPA and the ECS have wrestled with how to create appropriate incentives to persuade corporations that have detected environmental violations to report their actions promptly to the government and cooperate with the ensuing investigation.[33] In particular, the Environmental Crimes Program has played an important role in a long-standing dispute between DOJ and the defense bar concerning whether, in order to receive credit for cooperation in the prosecutor's charging decision, a prosecutor may demand that the corporate target of an environmental investigation must disclose privileged material discovered by its attorneys in an internal corporate investigation.

In 1999, then-U.S. Deputy Attorney General Eric Holder announced revisions to the general principles governing prosecutions of corporations. These modifications suggested that in determining a company's willingness to cooperate with the government, line prosecutors could consider whether the entity

---

and one count of negligent discharge of oil in violation of the CWA. According to the indictment, the two well site leaders were responsible for supervising and determining the success of tests necessary to ensure the well was secure before it was temporarily abandoned. It is alleged that the well site leaders were negligent by ignoring glaring indications from the tests that the well was not in fact secure, and that they failed to investigate these indications further. According to the indictment, this negligence ultimately led to the loss of well control which caused the explosion and fire that resulted in the loss of life of 11 men aboard the *Deepwater Horizon*, and the discharge of oil from the well. *See Indictment*, http://www.justice.gov/iso/opa/resources/2520121115143638743323.pdf (last visited June 4, 2013). The trial court subsequently dismissed the seaman's manslaughter counts against the defendants because they were not involved with the marine operational and navigational functions on the vessel and therefore were not subject to the provisions of 18 U.S.C. §1115. U.S. v. Kaluza, Crim. Act. No. 12-265, 2013 U.S. Dist. LEXIS 173134 (E.D. La,, Dec. 10, 2013).

32. *See* United States v. W.R. Grace & Co., 504 F.3d 745, 37 ELR 20244 (9th Cir. 2007), *cert. denied* W.R. Grace & Co. v. United States, No. 05-1363, 2008 U.S. LEXIS 5196 (U.S. June 23, 2008).

33. *See* U.S. EPA, Incentives for Self-Policing: Discovery, Disclosure, Correction, and Prevention of Violations, 65 Fed. Reg. 19618 (Apr. 11, 2000).

was willing to waive the attorney-client and work product privileges.[34] In practice, this policy on cooperation evolved from encouraging self-disclosure to punishing a company's failure to disclose and relinquish protected rights. Over the last decade, prosecutors frequently made demands for such waivers in environmental criminal investigations. Arguments about the propriety and necessity of these demands became common as companies complained vigorously about the chilling effect of waiver demands on privileged communications.

In 2006, then-U.S. Deputy Attorney General Paul McNulty issued revisions to the principles of prosecution of corporations to address concerns expressed by Congress, the American Bar Association, and defense lawyers.[35] The McNulty memorandum divided the results of internal corporate investigations into two categories: (1) factual information; and (2) non-factual work product, such as the corporate attorneys' mental impressions and assessments of the credibility of witnesses. It provided that with proper approvals, line prosecutors were authorized to request disclosure of factual information and to consider the company's response in their charging decision. Prosecutors could not, however, request production of non-factual work product except in rare circumstances, with specific authorization from the attorney general or his deputy, and the company's response was not supposed to influence the charging decision. This revision neither stemmed criticism from the defense bar nor changed the culture of prosecutors' demanding waivers of the attorney-client privilege in return for avoiding a harsher charging decision.

Finally, in August 2008, DOJ responded to concerns about potential abuses by revising the *U.S. Attorneys' Manual* to provide that prosecutors may not request non-factual attorney-client communications and attorney work product with the exception of cases in which the crime-fraud exception or the advice of counsel defense are present.[36] For the moment, complaints about prosecutorial intrusions into privileged material have subsided, but it remains to be seen whether the 2008 modifications ultimately will produce a stable equilibrium.

34. Memorandum from Deputy Attorney General Eric Holder, to Heads of Department Components, U.S. Attorneys, *Principles of Federal Prosecution of Business Organizations* (June 1999).

35. Memorandum from Deputy Attorney General Paul McNulty, to Heads of Department Components, U.S. Attorneys, *Principles of Federal Prosecution of Business Organizations* (Dec. 12, 2006).

36. Memorandum from Deputy Attorney General Mark Filip, to Heads of Department Components, U.S. Attorneys, *Principles of Federal Prosecution of Business Organizations* (Aug. 28, 2008).

Chapter 2: Operation—Infrastructure and Practice

The Environmental Crimes Program has two parts. First is the "bricks and mortar" of the program, the organizational arrangements, personnel, and resources dedicated to the prosecution of federal environmental crimes. Second is the "policies and paper"—the statements of governance and aspirations that help guide the program, such as the policies that govern the exercise of the U.S. Department of Justice's (DOJ's) prosecutorial discretion. Among the most important policies are The Principles of Federal Prosecution of Business Organizations (the Principles)[1], which governs DOJ's decisions whether to charge a corporation; the Petite Policy, which governs its prosecution of crimes for which a state has already prosecuted; and policies governing so-called parallel proceedings when federal agencies initiate both civil and criminal investigations and/or enforcement actions. The Environmental Crimes Program's most controversial policies are those governing the disclosure of, and potential leniency toward, environmental noncompliance disclosed under DOJ's, the U.S. Environmental Protection Agency's (EPA's), or the U.S. Coast Guard's voluntary disclosure programs.

I. Bricks and Mortar

Since the mid-1990s, the Environmental Crimes Program has enjoyed a period of sustained development and expansion. The bricks and mortar of the program, including the EPA Criminal Investigation Division (EPA CID), the Environmental Crimes Section (ECS), and U.S. attorneys' offices, reflect this maturation and growth. In 2012, per Assistant Attorney General Ignacia Moreno, collaboration and close coordination between the Environment and Natural Resources Division (ENRD) and the U.S. attorneys' offices was more prevalent than ever: "[W]e are working together on joint prosecutions; launching initiatives and joint task forces; sharing referrals; exchanging information and advice regarding novel cases and issues; and providing training to Assistant United States Attorneys (AUSAs) and other federal, state, and local law enforcement personnel."[2]

A. EPA

The EPA CID is a cadre of special agents dedicated to investigating environmental crimes. The EPA CID is a division of EPA's Office of Criminal Enforcement, Forensics, and Training, headquartered in Washington, D.C, and its reach extends across the country. EPA maintains 10 regional investigation offices located in Atlanta, Boston, Chicago, Dallas, Denver, Kansas City, New York, Philadelphia, San Francisco, and Seattle. In addition, over the years, EPA has established 32 resident agent offices across the United States.[3]

1. *See* U.S. Attorneys' Manual §9-28.000, 9-28.200B (Principles of Federal Prosecution of Business Organizations) [hereinafter U.S. Attorneys' Manual], *available at* http://www.justice.gov/usao/eousa/foia_reading_room/usam/ (last visited Jan. 28, 2014).
2. U.S. Attorneys' Bulletin, Introduction to the Environmental Crimes Issue of the USA Bulletin 1 (July 2012), *available at* http:://www.justice.gov/usao/eousa/foia_reading_room/usab6004.pdf (last visited May 30, 2013).
3. U.S. EPA, *Criminal Enforcement Program Area and Resident Offices*, http://www.epa.gov/enforcement/criminal/contact (last visited May 28, 2013). In the mid-1990s, there were only 15 resident agent offices. *See* Donald A. Carr et al., Environmental Criminal Liability 8 (1995).

As of late 2010, EPA CID had succeeded in reaching 200 full-time investigators trained in traditional law enforcement techniques.[4] As often happens, the U.S. Congress adopted but did not fund its aspirations. The Pollution Prosecution Act of 1990 authorized a staff of 200 special agents by 1995.[5]

In recent years, EPA CID has increased efforts to train and support state and local investigators and police. EPA's Federal Law Enforcement Training Center in Georgia has trained hundreds of state law enforcement officers.

EPA CID conducts its work by using many customary investigative law enforcement techniques. It pursues tips, such as those provided by citizens, citizen watchdog groups, and state environmental protection agencies, and pursues cases referred internally by other components of EPA.

EPA CID investigates tips or referrals for potential criminal culpability. For technical assistance in conducting an investigation, it calls on EPA's National Enforcement Investigations Center (NEIC) in Denver—the only environmental forensic center for conducting complex criminal enforcement investigations.[6] With assistance from NEIC, EPA CID investigates suspected environmental crimes and refers meritorious cases to DOJ for prosecution, pursuant to established criteria for determining whether a case merits referral.

B. *DOJ, ECS, and U.S. Attorneys' Offices*

As noted in Chapter 1, responsibility for prosecuting environmental crimes is divided between the ECS of DOJ's ENRD and the U.S. attorneys in the various judicial districts.

ECS lawyers are dedicated exclusively to the prosecution of environmental offenses and related crimes. Historically, ECS has handled complex cases, multidistrict cases, and cases for which a U.S. attorney requested assistance from "Main Justice" in Washington, D.C.[7] ECS also has primary responsibility for the prosecution of cases referred directly from EPA CID.[8] ECS handles approximately 25% to 30% of all criminal cases, and ECS has tended to handle the larger, more complex environmental criminal cases, as well as those that involve national criminal enforcement policy priorities.[9] ECS cases account for approximately two-thirds of the total fines and restitution obtained in federal environmental criminal cases.[10] As of early 2013, there were 45 attorneys in the ECS, the most in its history.[11]

The 93 U.S. attorneys' offices handle the vast majority of environmental prosecutions. Many of these offices have a dedicated assistant U.S. attorney in charge of environmental criminal enforcement efforts. In general, U.S. attorneys handle all federal environmental criminal cases in their own districts, except for cases involving "novel issues of law," "simultaneous investigations into multiple districts," "international or foreign policy" issues, or those "of an urgent or sensitive nature."[12] The *U.S. Attorneys' Manual* states that those cases are more likely to be handled jointly between ECS and the local U.S. attorneys' office.[13]

When ECS and local U.S. attorneys act as joint co-counsel, the exact allocation of responsibilities varies case-by-case. The factors determining which office takes the laboring oar include the technical expertise of the assigned prosecutors; respective workloads; political considerations, including the local significance of a matter; and the case's importance in terms of overall national priorities.[14] In these cases, either ECS

4. Giles Says EPA Pursuing High-Impact Cases, Adding Criminal Investigators to Staff, Daily Env.t'l Rep. (BNA) No. 184, at A-7(Sept. 24, 2010).
5. Pollution Prosecution Act of 1990, Pub. L. No. 101-693, §201, 104 Stat. 2954, 2962-63.
6. U.S. EPA, *National Enforcement Investigations CenterCenter*, http://www.epa.gov/enforcement/criminal/neic.html (last visited May 28, 2013).
7. Carr, *supra* note 3, at 9.
8. *Id.*
9. John F. Cooney, *Multi-Jurisdictional and Successive Prosecution of Environmental Crimes: The Case for a Consistent Approach*, 96 J. Crim. L. & Criminology 435, 438 (2006) (citing David M. Uhlmann, Chief, ECS, U.S. DOJ, Speech to the District of Columbia Bar Association (Dec. 6, 2005)) and Interview by Corporate Crime Reporter with David M. Uhlmann, Chief, ECS, U.S. DOJ (Feb. 23, 2004), *reprinted in* 6 ABA Sec. Env't Energy & Resources 12, 13 (2005), *available at* www.abanet.org/environ/committees/environcrimes/newsletter/may05/ (last visited May 28, 2013).
10. *Id.*
11. U.S. EPA, *Criminal Enforcement Overview*, http://www.epa.gov/enforcement/criminal/basics.html (last visited May 28, 2013).
12. U.S. Attorneys' Manual, *supra* note 1, §5-11.104 (Responsibility for Case Development and Prosecution).
13. *Id.*
14. Cooney, *supra* note 9, at 439.

attorneys or local assistant U.S. attorneys may conduct the investigation, present the evidence to the grand jury, and take the lead at trial.[15]

For those cases that are not handled jointly, it is important to note that just because one part of DOJ has declined to prosecute is no guarantee that another will follow suit. The *U.S. Attorneys' Manual* specifically states that with respect to environmental criminal prosecutions, nothing limits "ECS' authority to prosecute a case declined by a United States Attorney's Office after consultation with that office, nor shall these provisions limit the authority of a United States Attorney's Office to prosecute a case that ECS has declined for reasons that ECS advises do not involve policy considerations."[16]

II. Policies and Paper

A. *EPA's Decision to Initiate a Criminal Investigation*

Every three years, EPA sets enforcement initiatives that guide the agency's allocation of criminal and civil enforcement resources.[17] These initiatives are determined based on input from the public, EPA programs divisions, EPA regions, state and tribal governments, environmental advocacy groups, and environmental justice groups. EPA determines the extent and severity of the problem and develops a goal statement for each initiative priority. DOJ also sets national priorities for prosecutions,[18] which evolve over time based on the perceived threats to the public welfare.

Once a violation has been discovered, the first step in the enforcement process is EPA's decision whether to initiate a criminal investigation. EPA's Devaney Memorandum[19] sets forth the criteria EPA uses to determine whether misconduct should be investigated criminally. Based on statutory intent, it concludes that criminal investigations should be targeted toward the most serious and egregious violations. In deciding whether it will investigate misconduct as a criminal matter, the two primary considerations for EPA are whether there is "significant environmental harm" and "culpable conduct."

"Significant environmental harm" includes both present harm and the threat of future harm to human health or the environment. The following factors are used to determine whether there is significant environmental harm:

- whether there is demonstrable actual harm that has "an identifiable and significant harmful impact on human health or the environment";
- whether there is the threat of harm to human health or the environment;
- whether there is a failure to report an actual discharge, release, or emission; and
- whether the action is part of a trend.[20]

EPA does not consider failure to report an emission or discharge, standing alone, as reason for initiating a criminal investigation. Nevertheless, this factor combined with an actual or threat of harm to human health or the environment may rise to the level of a target for a criminal investigation. When an action is part of a trend, rather than just an isolated violation, it generally is deemed to have a significant impact on human health or the environment.

"Culpable conduct" is not necessarily a determination of criminal intent. The following factors suggest that a criminal investigation is necessary:

- a history of repeated violations;
- deliberate misconduct resulting in a violation;

---

15. *Id.*
16. U.S. Attorney's Manual, *supra* note 1, §5-11.110 (Declinations).
17. *See* U.S. EPA, *National Enforcement Initiatives*, www.epa.gov/compliance/data/planning/initiatives/index.html (last visited May 28, 2013).
18. U.S. DOJ, *Priority Areas*, http://www.justice.gov/usao/briefing_room/index.html (last visited May 28, 2013).
19. Earl E. Devaney, Memorandum to All EPA Employees Working in or in Support of the Criminal Enforcement Program Re: The Exercise of Investigative Discretion (Jan. 12, 1994), included as Appendix 1.
20. *Id.* at 4.

- concealment of misconduct or falsification of required records;
- tampering with monitoring or control equipment; and
- business operation of pollution-related activities without a permit, license, manifest, or other required documentation.[21]

Other, non-public documents also guide EPA's enforcement decisions. For instance, Peter Murtha notes that during his time in charge of the EPA's Office of Criminal Enforcement, Forensics, and Training (OCEFT), he shifted "strategic direction toward pursuing 'high impact' cases—those with the greatest potential for maximizing deterrence and offering the greatest possibility for protecting human health and the environment—and away from 'stat-building' cases."[22]

After considering these factors, EPA will decide which enforcement tools are appropriate. Less serious violations may be addressed by administrative orders, while the most serious environmental cases are addressed through criminal investigation.

B. *DOJ's Decision to Bring Criminal Cases*

The Principles govern whether a federal prosecutor will criminally charge a company for alleged wrongdoing.[23] The Principles also contain guidance for prosecutors as to whether civil or administrative penalties would be preferable to criminal charges. Prosecutors are directed to consider all relevant factors to determine whether non-criminal alternatives would be adequate, including:

- the sanctions available under the non-criminal alternatives;
- the likelihood that an effective sanction would be imposed; and
- the impact of a non-criminal disposition on federal law enforcement priorities.

Because the Principles guide charging decisions, company counsel must structure an internal investigation with an eye toward the factors they set forth. Any effort to persuade a prosecutor that corporate charges are unwarranted must focus on the Principles.

Federal prosecutors, when exercising their discretion regarding whether to bring criminal charges against a company, consider at a minimum the following questions:

- What is the seriousness of the offense, including the actual or potential harm to human beings or to the environment?
- Was the wrongdoing at the company pervasive? Was management complicit in, or did it somehow condone, the wrongdoing?
- Is the company a repeat offender or has it received warnings (verbal or written) from regulatory authorities? What is the company's history of similar conduct, including prior criminal, civil, and regulatory enforcement actions against it?
- Did the company timely and voluntarily disclose the wrongdoing?
- Has the company been willing to cooperate in the investigation?
- Did the company have in place a compliance program at the time of the wrongdoing? Was that compliance program adequate?
- What remedial actions has the company taken since discovering or being informed of the wrongdoing?

---

21. *Id.* at 4-5.
22. *Available at* http://www.linkedin.com/pub/peter-murtha/7/231/983 (last visited May 28, 2013).
23. *See* U.S. Attorneys' Manual, *supra* note 1, §9-28.000 (Principles of Federal Prosecution of Business Organizations).

- What collateral consequences would attend a prosecution of the company? For example, would innocent shareholders or pension holders be harmed in a disproportionate manner following a prosecution? What would be the impact on the public if the company were to be prosecuted?
- Would prosecution of a responsible individual, or individuals for the wrongdoing better serve the public interest than prosecution of the company?
- Would civil or administrative enforcement be adequate to address the wrongdoing?[24]

C. Environmental Audits and Voluntary Disclosure Programs

The government encourages companies to engage in self-monitoring and auditing (oftentimes through an effective environmental compliance program)[25] on the ground that this approach serves the public interest by helping companies detect and address environmental problems before they become damaging. It also assists the government when companies identify and self-report problems, as such self-reporting frees up governmental resources that can be focused on facilities that do not audit and voluntarily disclose violations.[26]

Despite these recognized benefits, there can be risks to companies uncovering violations through self-auditing programs, including that the government will discover and use the information against it in criminal and civil enforcement actions.[27] To promote self-auditing, the EPA, DOJ, and the Coast Guard have established voluntary disclosure policies that reward companies which report violations found as a result of self-auditing program—typically by mitigating civil penalties or, in some instances, foregoing criminal enforcement. These voluntary disclosure programs, however, do not guarantee that a self-disclosing company will escape civil or criminal liability for the violations reported (or for additional violations the government may discover during the course of its ensuing investigation). Thus, companies often must choose between implementing a self-auditing program that encourages prevention of pollution and protection of the environment, or foregoing such a program because auditing reports may set up a paper trail to liability that can be followed by government investigators and prosecutors.

1. State Audit Privileges

Some courts have found that a self-audit or self-evaluation privilege exists under certain circumstances in the context of environmental audits.[28] Certain states have also recognized or created a self-evaluative privilege by legislation, which prevents the government from mandating forced disclosure of information discovered through an audit.[29] It is therefore important for counsel to consider whether a state's audit privilege may protect the disclosure of information in any civil or criminal investigation.

---

24. *Id.* §9-28.300. The policy regarding whether to bring criminal charges against an individual is also spelled out in the U.S. Attorneys' Manual. The Manual states that the attorney for the government should commence or recommend Federal prosecution of an individual where the person's conduct constitutes a Federal offense and the admissible evidence will probably be sufficient to obtain and sustain a conviction, unless, in the attorney's judgment, prosecution should be declined because no substantial interest would be served by prosecution, the person is subject to effective prosecution in another jurisdiction, or there exists an adequate non-criminal alternative to prosecution. Id. §9.27.220.
25. How to develop an effective compliance program is discussed in Appendix 19.
26. An empirical study concluded that the Resource Conservation and Recovery Act (RCRA) facilities that had self-reported violations to EPA had reduced the probability of an inspection in the following year by 80%. Sarah L. Stafford, Should You Turn Yourself In? The Consequences of Environmental Self-Policing 24 (College of William & Mary, Dep't of Economics, Working Paper No. 27, 2006).
27. This perception may drive firms to perceive self-reporting of violations as putting them at a competitive disadvantage. *See* Matthew Potoski & Aseem Prakash, *The Regulation Dilemma: Cooperation and Conflict in Environmental Governance*, 64 Pub. Admin. Rev. 152, 154 (2004) ("[F]irms may fear that opportunistic regulators may interpret voluntarily disclosed violations as admissions of guilt that are worthy of substantial punishment, leaving those firms at a competitive disadvantage . . . relative to their more evasive competitors.") [hereinafter Potoski & Prakash].
28. Reichold Chems., Inc. v. Textron, Inc., 157 F.R.D. 522, 25 ELR 20307 (N.D. Fla. 1994); James Cox, *The Case Against a Judicially Created, Common-Law Self-Audit or Self-Evaluation Privilege Applicable to Environmental Cases*, 15 Fordham Envtl. L.J. 1, 2-3 (2004).
29. As of March 2013, there were 26 states that had established state audit privilege and/or immunity laws. *See* EPA Region 5 Enforcement and Compliance Division, U.S. EPA, *State Audit Privilege and Immunity Laws & Self-Disclosure Laws and Policies, available at* http://www.epa.gov/region5/ enforcement/audit/stateaudit.html (last visited May 28, 2013).

   In addition, Wisconsin adopted a Green Tier program, Wis. Stat. §§299.80-.85, which provides incentives to business entities that take voluntarily measures to improve their environmental performance. The program is based upon a collaborative system of contracts and charters between businesses and the Wisconsin Department of Natural Resources (DNR). The program is divided into two parts. Generally speaking, Tier One participants are entitled to deferred civil enforcement as well as statutorily capped or stipulated fines for violations. Through contract,

The scope and criteria of the audit privilege varies from state to state. In general, however, it provides a qualified privilege that applies only when the audit was not required by law, the audit was not fraudulent, the company responded properly to any noncompliance it discovered as a result of the audit, and the company cooperates fully with enforcement personnel.[30] In civil proceedings, the privilege is usually absolute. In criminal proceedings, audit material is typically available to a prosecutor who can demonstrate a compelling need for the information, in a manner similar to that necessary to obtain access to attorney work product materials.[31] The privilege protects most materials related to the audit, not just the final report. In most instances, this includes all analyses of the primary report and any documentation implementing the findings of the report. In some states, such as Virginia[32] and Alaska,[33] the privilege is absolute and even extends beyond documents to protect testimony concerning environmental audits.

2. EPA's Voluntary Disclosure Program

In 1986, EPA established an initial policy on environmental compliance auditing.[34] It provides that the Agency will not routinely request a company's environmental audit reports for use in subsequent enforcement actions but still preserves EPA's ability to obtain and use a company's audit reports against it, including in a subsequent criminal investigation.[35] The policy states that in determining enforcement actions, EPA will consider good-faith efforts by companies to identify and correct violations.[36] Nevertheless, the guidance requires that in order to qualify, companies must cooperate fully with the government and have voluntarily disclosed their audit findings.[37]

Subsequent to the issuance of EPA's policy, several states implemented the state audit privileges discussed above. The Agency opposed the implementation of these state privileges for several reasons.[38] In 1995, in part to address the proliferation of state audit privilege laws, EPA revised its audit and voluntary disclosure policy to provide greater encouragement to companies to self-report. The new policy required self-reporting companies to comply with nine conditions to obtain the full benefits of self-reporting.[39]

DNR promises to not seek penalties for those businesses that self-disclose violations and take corrective action. Tier Two participants generally contract for a limited form of immunity from any civil action for self-disclosed violations. *Id.*

30. *See, e.g.*, Colo. Rev. Stat. §13.25-126.5; Or. Rev. Stat. §468.963.
31. *See, e.g.*, Or. Rev. Stat. §468.963.
32. Va. Code Ann. §10.1-1198.
33. Alaska Stat. §§09.25.450-490.
34. U.S. EPA, Environmental Auditing Policy Statement, 51 Fed. Reg. 25004 (July 9, 1986).
35. "EPA's authority to request an audit report, or relevant portions thereof, will be exercised on a case-by-case basis where the Agency determines it is needed to accomplish a statutory mission, or where the Government deems it to be material to a criminal investigation." *Id.* at 25007.
36. *Id.*
37. *Id.*
38. U.S. EPA, Incentives for Self-Policing: Discovery, Disclosure, Correction, and Prevention of Violations, 60 Fed. Reg. 66706, 66710 (Dec. 22, 1995) [hereinafter EPA 1995 Incentives for Self-Policing]. EPA stated that it was opposed to the state privilege laws because (1) creation of a privilege invited secrecy instead of the openness necessary to build public trust in the industry's ability to self-police, (2) surveys and hearings had failed to produce any evidence that a privilege was needed, (3) a privilege invited defendants to claim as audit material almost any evidence the government needed to establish a violation or determine responsibility, (4) audit privilege bred litigation over the scope of material subject to the privilege, (5) the EPA policy eliminated the need for any privilege by providing incentives for self-auditing and voluntary disclosure, and (6) the audit privilege was opposed by members of the law enforcement community.

    But see Potoski & Prakash, *supra* note 27, at 158 ("It follows, then, that firms are more likely to improve their environmental performance through voluntary programs when regulators establish policies on audit immunity, or at least provide credible institutional signals . . . that they are serious about fostering a trust-based regulatory environment.").
39. The conditions were: (1) the company discovered the violation through an environmental audit or an objective, documented, systematic procedure or practice reflecting its due diligence in preventing, detecting, and correcting violations; (2) the violation was identified voluntarily and not through a legally mandated monitoring or sampling requirement prescribed by statute, regulation, permit, judicial or administrative order or consent agreement; (3) the company fully disclosed the violation in writing to EPA within 10 days after it was discovered; (4) the discovery or disclosure was independent of government or third party plaintiff actions, such as commencement of a federal, state or local agency inspection or investigation or notice of a citizen suit; (5) the violation was corrected within 60 days of discovery, or as expeditiously as practicable, and correction is certified in writing; (6) the company agreed in writing to take steps to prevent recurrence of the violation, which may include improvements to its environmental auditing or due diligence efforts; (7) the specific violation had not occurred previously within the past three years at the same facility or was not part of violations by the facility's parent company; (8) the violation had not resulted in serious actual harm, or presented an imminent and substantial endangerment to human life or the environment; and (9) the company cooperated as required by EPA and, at a minimum, provided all requested documents, access to employees and assistance in investigating the violation. 60 Fed. Reg. at 66712. Regarding what EPA would look at to determine the adequacy of the due diligence or a systemic practice or procedure sufficient to qualify under the program, the agency referred to the Criminal Sentencing Guideline criteria. *Id.* at 66708. *See also* text accompanying note 25 *supra.*

    In 1996, EPA established a separate voluntary disclosure policy for small businesses. U.S. EPA, Interim Policy on Compliance Incentives for Small Businesses, 61 Fed. Reg. 27984 (June 3, 1996). A "small business" was defined as an entity that employs 100 or fewer individuals

In return for compliance with its voluntary disclosure policy, EPA stated that it would reduce civil penalties and limit criminal referrals related to the violation. With regard to civil penalties, EPA stated that it would eliminate the gravity component of the penalty for a violation if the company met all nine conditions.[40] EPA further stated that it would mitigate up to 75% of the unadjusted gravity component of the penalty in cases in which all of the conditions were met with the exception that the violation was not discovered through an environmental audit or systematic procedure.[41] With regard to criminal penalties, EPA stated it would not recommend that criminal charges be brought if all nine conditions were met and the violation did not demonstrate or involve: (1) a prevalent corporate management philosophy or practice that concealed or condoned the violations; or (2) conscious involvement in or willful blindness to the violation by high-level corporate officials or managers.[42] Finally, EPA stated that it would not request or use an environmental audit report to initiate a civil or criminal investigation of the company.[43]

In 1997, EPA established a policy to implement its self-policing and voluntary disclosure policy specifically in relation to possible criminal violations.[44] To maintain consistency in the application of the policy, EPA established a Voluntary Disclosure Board to receive, monitor, and consider all requests for treatment under the policy, and to make recommendations to the deciding official in all cases for which the disclosure indicated potential criminal violations.[45]

In April 2000, EPA liberalized its voluntary disclosure policy somewhat, but the basic components of the program remained essentially as first promulgated in 1995.[46] Of note, under the revised policy, a company may qualify for the "no recommendation for criminal prosecution" incentive even though the violation was not found as the result of an audit or other systemic procedure or practice, and provided it acted in good faith.[47] The incentive is not available, however, in instances in which corporate officials are consciously involved in or willfully blind to violations, or conceal or condone noncompliance.[48] In addition, EPA lengthened the period of time that companies have to disclose a violation after discovery from 10 to 21 days.[49]

---

across all facilities and operations. Under the policy, EPA stated that it would eliminate or mitigate penalty demands if (1) violations were discovered based either on receiving on-site assistance from the government or by conducting an environmental audit, (2) it was the business's first violation of the requirement, (3) the violation was corrected within 180 days, and (4) the violation did not cause actual serious harm, or present an imminent and substantial danger, to public health or the environment. Nevertheless, the policy only applied to civil penalties. *Id.* at 27985-86.

40. EPA 1995 Incentives for Self-Policing, *supra* note 38, at 66711.
41. *Id.*
42. *Id.*
43. *Id.*
44. Memorandum from Earl E. Devaney, Director, Office of Criminal Enforcement, Forensics and Training, to All EPA Employees Working in or in Support of the Criminal Enforcement Program, *Subject: Implementation of the Environmental Protection Agency's Self-Policing Policy for Disclosures Involving Potential Criminal Violations* (Oct. 1, 1997), *available at* http://www.epa.gov/ebtpages/fsgsearch/daily/pdfandwpf20120802_622.html (last visited May 28, 2013).
45. *Id.* at 2.
46. U.S. EPA, Incentives for Self-Policing: Discovery, Disclosure, Correction, and Prevention of Violations, 65 Fed. Reg. 19618 (Apr. 11, 2000) [hereinafter EPA 2000 Incentives for Self-Policing].

    On the same day, EPA also published revisions to its voluntary disclosure policy for small businesses. U.S. EPA, Small Business Compliance Policy, 65 Fed. Reg. 19630 (Apr. 11, 2000). The policy was narrowed to remain available only for reduction of civil penalties. It was revised to allow penalty relief if violations were discovered by any voluntary means, in addition to discovery as a result of government sponsored on-site compliance assistance activities or environmental audits as permitted under the original policy. *Id.* at 19631. In addition, as with the revised self-policing policy, the time period for reporting of violations was extended to 21 days. *Id.*

    In 2008, EPA published a notice establishing an approach to apply its audit policy to new owners of a facility. U.S. EPA, Interim Approach to Applying the Audit Policy to New Owners, 73 Fed. Reg. 44991 (Aug. 1, 2008). Under the policy, a "new owner" is defined as an entity that meets the following criteria: prior to the transaction, it was not responsible for environmental compliance at the facility that is the subject of the disclosure; the violation originated with the prior owner; and prior to the transaction in which the facility was acquired, neither the buyer nor the seller had the largest ownership share of the other entity, and they did not have a common corporate parent. *Id.* at 44995. The purpose of the policy is "to encourage owners of newly acquired facilities to undertake a comprehensive examination of and improvements to a facility's environmental compliance management systems." *Id.* at 44993. This policy focuses on the mitigation of civil penalties for new facility owners, and provides additional flexibility to new owners in relation to the conditions that are in the EPA 2000 Incentives for Self-Policing. It does not address the issue of criminal liability directly. Under the policy, a new owner may audit the newly acquired facility, either before or within nine months of the closing date, and benefit from the audit disclosure policy either by entering into an audit agreement with the EPA and disclosing any violations found during the audit; or in the absence of an audit agreement, disclosing violations within 21 days of discovery or 45 days of closing, whichever is later.
47. EPA 2000 Incentives for Self-Policing, *supra* note 46, at 19620, 19625.
48. *Id.* at 19620.
49. *Id.* at 19621-22, 19626.

In 2012, EPA's Office of Enforcement and Compliance Assurance (OECA) noted that, in light of its self-proclaimed "lean budget," EPA will be reducing investment in certain areas, including the Voluntary Disclosure Program:[50]

> Since implementation of the Audit Policy began in 1995, EPA's enforcement program has increased its understanding of environmental compliance auditing, and believes that internal reviews of compliance have become more widely adopted by the regulated community, as part of good management. In addition, EPA has found that most violations disclosed under the Policy are not in the highest priority enforcement areas for protecting human health and the environment. EPA believes it can reduce investment in the program to a limited national presence without undermining the incentives for regulated entities to do internal compliance reviews to find and correct violations. As we reduce investment in this program, EPA is considering several options, including a modified Audit Policy program that is self-implementing.[51]

3. DOJ's Voluntary Disclosure Program

In 1991, DOJ issued a policy regarding voluntary disclosure of environmental violations.[52] The policy encourages self-auditing, self-policing and voluntary disclosure of environmental violations by stating that these activities will be viewed as mitigating factors in the exercise of the agency prosecutorial discretion. Unlike the EPA's Voluntary Disclosure Program, the DOJ program does not address civil penalty mitigation.

The principal mitigating factors DOJ will consider are:

- whether the disclosing entity "made voluntary, timely and complete disclosure" and whether the disclosure "substantially aided the government's investigatory process";
- whether the disclosing entity gave full and prompt cooperation and made all relevant information available, "including the complete results of any internal or external investigation and the names of all potential witnesses"; and
- "the existence and size of any regularized, intensive, and comprehensive environmental compliance program," including an environmental compliance audit, which demonstrates a strong institutional commitment to environmental compliance.[53]

Other relevant factors include the pervasiveness of the noncompliance, effective internal disciplinary programs for environmental violations, and the promptness and completeness of actions taken to address the violation and remedy the environmental harm.[54]

4. U.S. Coast Guard Voluntary Disclosure Policy

On November 14, 2007, the Coast Guard issued an Environmental Crimes Voluntary Disclosure Policy.[55] In many ways, its policy mirrors EPA's program. A regulated entity disclosing environmental violations is assured that the Coast Guard "will not recommend" that criminal charges be brought against it, provided that the entity meets nine conditions, which are essentially the same as those under EPA's policy. Unlike EPA's policy, however, the Coast Guard policy does *not* include any relief from gravity-based civil penalties for violations of

---

50. OECA, U.S. EPA, National Program Manager Guidance FY 2013 (2012), *available at* http://nepis.epa.gov/Exe/ZyPDFcgi?Dockey=P100F6FG.PDF (last visited June 20, 2013). "This guidance applies to the Office of Enforcement and Compliance Assurance (OECA), all Environmental Protection Agency (EPA) regional enforcement programs, and states and federally recognized Indian Tribes (tribes) implementing EPA-approved inspection and enforcement programs." *Id.* at 1.
51. *Id.* at 15.
52. U.S. DOJ, Factors in Decisions on Criminal Prosecutions for Environmental Violations in the Context of Significant Voluntary Compliance or Disclosure Efforts by the Violator (July 1, 1991), *available at* http://www.justice.gov/enrd/3058.htm (last visited May 28, 2013).
53. *Id.* §II. A-C.
54. *Id.* §II. D.
55. U.S. Coast Guard, *Maritime Law Enforcement Manual, App. V, Environmental Crimes: Voluntary Disclosure Policy, available at* http://www.uscg.mil/foia/docs/CH-4%20Appendix%20V.pdf [hereinafter Coast Guard Voluntary Disclosure Policy] (last visited May 28, 2013).

federal environmental law.[56] Further, unlike EPA's policy, in order to benefit from the policy, the Coast Guard requires that the violations be discovered "through either an environmental audit, or a compliance management system that reflects due diligence in preventing, detecting, and correcting violations."

D. *To Disclose or Not to Disclose?—That Is the Question*

Companies must understand that each of the aforementioned disclosure policies is just that—a policy, not a law or a binding regulation. As such, they do not create any rights enforceable by companies who voluntarily disclose violations. Moreover, a determination by EPA or the Coast Guard not to recommend criminal prosecution does not bind DOJ prosecutors, U.S. attorneys or other federal agencies such as the Federal Bureau of Investigations (FBI), state prosecutors or state investigators, any of which may elect to exercise its independent law enforcement authority. In addition, to the extent that officers, managers, or employees are potentially culpable, any recommendation by EPA or the Coast Guard against criminal prosecution of the corporation will not apply to the criminal acts of individuals.

Even if a company wishes to take advantage of a disclosure program, EPA or the Coast Guard may not agree that the entity has met the rigid eligibility conditions. This is particularly true for the Coast Guard policy, which requires that the reported violations must have been discovered "through either an environmental audit, or a compliance management system that reflects due diligence in preventing, detecting, and correcting violations." Many violations are not discovered through compliance systems.

Participation in a voluntary disclosure program may require that the company waive legal privileges with regard to its audit documents or internal investigation.[57] Under the Coast Guard policy, the required level of "cooperation" may include a waiver of any attorney-client and work product privilege related to any investigation conducted into the reported violation, including statements made to internal investigators by managers or other employees.[58]

As a result of these limitations on the agency voluntary disclosure programs, few companies have concluded that the benefits of voluntary disclosure outweigh the risks. From 2000 through the end of 2007, the EPA Voluntary Disclosure Board received a total of 46 submissions, or an average of less than 6 per year.[59] In April 2014, the Coast Guard, for the first time, formally announced that a company, OSG, had made a voluntary disclosure, that it had been accepted, and that no criminal referral would be made.[60]

---

56. The Coast Guard did not discuss why its policy does not extend to civil penalties. Agency hearing officers who assess civil penalties for environmental violations are, however, directed to take into account the "circumstances, gravity, culpability, history of similar violations, and demonstrated good faith," in determining an appropriate penalty under Coast Guard's Civil Penalty Procedures. U.S. Coast Guard, Civil Penalty Procedures and Administration, Commandant Instruction (COMDTINST) 16200.3A at 4 (Oct. 16, 1992). Representatives of regulated entities dealing with hearing officers on civil penalties related to environmental violations that have been voluntarily disclosed under the policy should ensure that hearing officers are made aware of the voluntary disclosure as part of mitigation efforts. The voluntary disclosure is part of the circumstances of the violation; the audit or other compliance system process under which the violation was originally discovered could mitigate the gravity and culpability factors required to be considered; and the voluntary disclosure certainly would appear to demonstrate good faith on the part of the regulated entity.
57. The EPA policy and the Coast Guard policy both state that for criminal violations, cooperation requires a disclosing company to provide "access to all information relevant to the violations disclosed, including that portion of the environmental audit report or documentation from the compliance management system that revealed the violation; and access to the individuals who conducted the audit or review." *See supra* notes 46 and 55.
58. For a more detailed discussion of the issues associated with cooperating with the government in the context of a voluntary disclosure scenario, see Judson Starr et al., *"Waiving" Goodbye to the Internal Investigation*, 3 Benedict's Mar. Bull. 265 (2005).
59. Gregory F. Linsin, *Environmental Self-Audit and Voluntary Disclosure to What End?*, ALI-ABA Course of Study Materials—Criminal Enforcement of Environmental Laws 301, 303 (May 14, 2009). Even on the civil side, the vast majority of disclosures under the EPA policy since the program began involved violations of reporting requirements, which EPA itself acknowledges "may not produce significant reductions in pollutant emissions once the violations are corrected." U.S. EPA, Enhancing Environmental Outcomes From Audit Policy Disclosures Through Tailored Incentives for New Owners; Notice, 72 Fed. Reg. 27116, 27117 (May 14, 2007). *See also* Alexander S.P. Pfaff et al., Big Field, Small Potatoes: An Empirical Assessment of EPA's Self-Audit Policy 14 (Columbia Univ., Dep't of Economics, Discussion Paper No. 0102-55, 2002) (stating that as of the date of the study, over 70% of EPA audit policy violations were for reporting violations, while another 13% involved toxic release inventory and another 6% were for failure to notify. Thus, approximately 90% of the violations disclosed under EPA's audit policy concerned only reporting or submitting violations and not release or emission violations).
60. Michaela Noble, Chief, U.S. Coast Guard Envt'l Law Div., Presentation at the Maritime Law Ass'n of the United States, Joint Meeting of Committees on Regulation of Vessel Operations, Safety, Security & Navigation; Marine Ecology and Maritime Criminal Law; and Government Counsel (Apr. 29, 2014. Unlike EPA, the Coast Guard does not refer voluntary disclosures to a Review Board at the Headquarters level. The agency has in the past noted that most of its disclosures are handled at the local port official level, and, therefore, no real data existed as to how often, or if, the policy was being utilized by the regulated community.

Although disclosure to DOJ or a U.S. attorney's office may seem more attractive than to the EPA or the Coast Guard, given the relative liberality of the conditions that must be satisfied, there are still potential pitfalls that must be considered prior to disclosure. The DOJ policy is not legally binding. The lack of specific standards for qualification, combined with a lack of central oversight, means that individual prosecutors have significant discretion in making determinations under the policy. Further, DOJ preserved its discretion to use audit documents when necessary to prove its case, regardless of whether the disclosure was voluntary and complete. Finally, the disclosing company must give full cooperation and make all relevant material available to the prosecutors. Lastly, any agreement to not prosecute an offending company does not mean that individuals will not be prosecuted.

E. American Bar Association—Standards on Prosecutorial Investigation

Prosecutorial investigation standards are the subject of American Bar Association (ABA) Criminal Justice Standards approved by the ABA House of Delegates in February 2008.[61] They provide detailed guidance for government lawyers engaged in criminal investigative conduct. The standards provide guidance on the key decisions that must be made by the prosecutor both before and during the investigative phase of a potential criminal matter. These include guidance on:

- working with police and other law enforcement agents;
- victims, potential witnesses, and targets during the investigative process;
- contacts with the public during the investigative process;
- initiating or continuing a criminal investigation;
- selecting investigative techniques;
- the use of undercover agents, undercover operations, confidential informants, cooperation agreements, and cooperating persons;
- arrest, subpoenas, search warrants, the grand jury, technologically assisted surveillance, consensual and non-consensual interception and recording;
- parallel proceedings;
- terminating investigations, post-investigation analysis, and guidance and training;
- special prosecutors, independent counsel, and special prosecution units;
- use of information, money, or resources by nongovernmental sources; and
- prosecutor's role in addressing suspected misconduct by law enforcement personnel, judges, defense counsel, witnesses, informants, or jurors.[62]

The standards do not tell a prosecutor what to do, but rather identify the relevant factors, *i.e.,* risks and benefits, which must be considered prior to making key decisions regarding the initiation, continuation, and termination of a criminal investigation or pursing a particular strategy.

F. The Dual and Successive Prosecution Policy (Petite Policy)

The Petite Policy[63] sets forth guidance to federal prosecutors for determining whether to bring a federal prosecution based on the same acts that formed the basis for a prior state or federal action. The Petite Policy

61. ABA, Criminal Justice Standards (2008), *available at* http://www.americanbar.org/publications/criminal_justice_section_archive/crimjust_standards_pinvestigate.html (last visited May 28, 2013).
62. Steven P Solow & Anne Carpenter, *The State of Environmental Crime Enforcement: A Survey of Developments,* 39 Envt. Rep. (BNA) 472, 476 (Mar. 7, 2008).
63. U.S. Attorneys' Manual, *supra* note 1, §9-2.031 (citing Rinaldi v. United States, 434 U.S. 22, 27 (1977); Petite v. United States, 361 U.S. 529 (1960)).

states that in general, a prior state prosecution will not act as a bar to a subsequent federal prosecution, but that particular statutes may set forth certain offenses where a state conviction or acquittal will bar federal action based on the same act or acts. The Petite Policy is designed to promote efficient use of government resources and to protect persons from being prosecuted multiple times for the same act or acts. The Petite Policy does not apply to pre-charge investigations.

The assistant attorney general for the criminal division must approve a successive prosecution.[64] The Petite Policy states that federal prosecution should not be initiated unless three prerequisites are satisfied: (1) there is a substantial federal interest at stake; (2) the prior state or federal prosecution left the federal interest "demonstratively unvindicated"; and (3) the prosecutor believes the conduct is a federal offense and there is sufficient admissible evidence to obtain a conviction.[65] To determine whether there is a substantial federal interest at stake and whether the conduct constitutes a federal offense, prosecutors rely on the Principles of Prosecution of Business Organizations and evaluate whether the offense is a national or prosecutorial priority. The Petite Policy sets forth a rebuttable presumption that prior prosecutions have vindicated the federal interest. The factors that may be considered in overcoming the presumption include: corruption, jury nullification, unavailability of significant evidence, failure of the prior prosecution to prove an element of the contemplated federal offense, or prior exclusion of charges.[66]

The Petite Policy does not apply to cases where a prior prosecution involved only a small part of the contemplated federal charges.[67] For example, a prior prosecution on a single federal criminal charge will not preclude a federal conspiracy or Racketeer Influenced and Corrupt Organizations (RICO) charge.[68]

The Petite Policy is only an internal DOJ guidance document. It does not create any substantive or procedural rights enforceable by any party.[69] Federal courts of appeals have unanimously held that a defendant cannot invoke the Petite Policy as a bar to prosecution.[70]

G. *Parallel Proceedings*

"Parallel proceedings" are simultaneous criminal and civil proceedings against the same defendant that arise out of a single set of facts. Parallel proceeding questions arise frequently in the environmental area, due to the company's ongoing compliance obligations and the easy cross-over from civil to criminal enforcement resulting from the de minimis intent requirement.[71] DOJ's current policy encourages the use of parallel proceedings to "maximize the government's ability to share information among criminal, civil, and agency administrative teams to the fullest extent appropriate to the case and permissible by law."[72] Prior to this policy, DOJ and EPA long have had policies in place that restrict the circumstances in which parallel proceedings may be instituted and how they may be conducted, in order to avoid potential constitutional and ethical concerns.[73]

Parallel proceedings are a double-edged sword, which create procedural and substantive problems for both the government and the entity under investigation. The problems arise when one agency—typically EPA or a state environmental enforcement agency—wishes to file a civil injunctive action to enjoin ongo-

---

64. *Id.* §9-2.031(E).
65. *Id.* §9-2.031(A).
66. *Id.* §9-2.031(B).
67. *Id.*
68. *Id.*
69. *Id.* §9-2.031(F).
70. *See, e.g.*, United States v. Snell, 592 F.2d 1083 (9th Cir. 1979), *cert. denied*, 442 U.S. 944 (1979); United States v. Howard, 590 F.2d 564 (4th Cir. 1979), *cert. denied*, 440 U.S. 976 (1979); United States v. Frederick, 583 F.2d 273 (6th Cir. 1978); United States v. Thompson, 579 F.2d 1184 (10th Cir. 1978) (en banc); United States v. Wallace, 578 F.2d 735 (5th Cir. 1978); United States v. Nelligan, 573 F.2d 251 (5th Cir. 1978); United States v. Hutul, 416 F.2d 607 (7th Cir. 1969).
71. *See supra* II.A. (charging decisions).
72. *See* Memorandum from U.S. Attorney General Eric Holder, to All U.S. Attorneys, *Coordination of Parallel Criminal, Civil, Regulatory, and Administrative Proceedings* 3 (Jan. 30, 2012), *available at* http://www.justice.gov/usao/eousa/foia_reading_room/usam/title1/doj00027.htm (last visited May 28, 2013).
73. *See* U.S. DOJ, Land and Natural Resources Div., Directive No. 5-87, Guidelines for Civil and Criminal Parallel Proceedings (Oct. 13, 1987) (reproduced in Appendix A to ELI, Environmental Crimes Deskbook (1st ed. 1996) at 193) [hereinafter 1987 DOJ Parallel Proceeding Policy]; U.S. EPA, Memorandum, Parallel Proceedings Policy, Granta Y. Nakayama, Asst. Administrator, Office of Enforcement and Compliance Assurance (Sept. 24, 2007) [hereinafter EPA Parallel Proceedings Policy], *available at* http://www2.epa.gov/sites/production/files/documents/parallel-proceedings-policy-09-24-07.pdf (last visited Jan. 28, 2014).

ing environmental violations and accelerate the remediation process, while another agency simultaneously conducts a criminal investigation to determine if the infractions should be prosecuted. Civil discovery is far broader and less restrictive than discovery in criminal investigations, and there is substantial basis for concern that the government could use civil discovery as a means of avoiding many of the protections afforded in criminal cases.

The differences between the criminal and civil investigatory mechanisms create substantial tactical questions for counsel and raise concerns about due process for potential defendants. When parallel proceedings are instituted, however, the target and its defense counsel face difficult issues in coordinating their activities to address the conflicting demands of the two enforcement regimes.

I. Difficulties Created by Parallel Proceedings

From the company's perspective, problems from overlapping investigations are obvious from the outset, while others take more time to surface. The company must plan and act from the earliest stages of an investigation to be prepared to negotiate and litigate on multiple fronts. Internally, responding to the demands of several agencies can be onerous. The company must make adequate resources and corporate staff available to satisfy these demands. Both criminal and civil environmental counsel should be involved from the beginning of the investigation. Information released or statements made in one context, either voluntarily or due to regulatory reporting obligations, may have adverse effects in the other area. Likewise, strategies that are appropriate in the criminal context may hurt efforts on the civil side, and vice versa. For example, both the *U.S. Attorneys' Manual*[74] and the *U.S. Sentencing Guidelines*[75] provide an incentive for organizations to disclose environmental violations in order to benefit from leniency on the criminal side. Such disclosures, however, constitute confessions that could be used against the defendant in any civil suit the regulator may choose to bring.

RCRA provides an instructive example of how a company's response to a grand jury investigation may be affected by its compliance obligations. A facility's continued operations may be jeopardized if the regulator decides to suspend or revoke its permit. Thus, even before a determination has been made regarding the legality of its past environmental practices, the company may be pressured or legally required by civil enforcement authorities to remediate a situation, change its disposal method, or obtain a new or revised permit. The repercussions of these actions could be significant in both the civil and criminal contexts. The defense in the criminal case may well be that the waste generated at a facility was not properly characterized as a hazardous waste. If it is hazardous, however, a manifest is required, an EPA identification number must be obtained to fill out the manifest properly, and the waste must be shipped to a permitted hazardous waste facility for disposal. Once a dispute arises about the proper characterization of the waste, the conservative approach is for the company to satisfy the civil regulator and manifest the waste as hazardous. But on the criminal side, the changes necessary to resolve all doubts about continuing civil compliance may be interpreted as an admission that the prior conduct was illegal, and may be used against the company before the grand jury, as well as at trial. On the other hand, voluntary remediation has many benefits. It may demonstrate a positive corporate environmental stance, and thus be an important factor in demonstrating why no criminal charges should be filed. It also may lessen the chances of an injunctive action being instituted. How to strike the proper balance between these risks is a difficult question in every case, both as a matter of business judgment and of legal strategy.

To complicate the inherent problems in handling parallel proceedings, EPA or state authorities overseeing the ongoing compliance and remediation efforts may not be directly involved in the criminal prosecution. Moreover, corporate officials responsible for managing the cleanup may not be those working with criminal counsel. This division of authority, both internally and externally, must be managed carefully to

74. *See* U.S. Attorneys' Manual, *supra* note 1, §9-28.700(A) ("In determining whether to charge a corporation and how to resolve corporate criminal cases, the corporation's timely and voluntary disclosure of wrongdoing and its cooperation with the government's investigation may be relevant factors.").

75. *See* U.S. Sentencing Guidelines Manual §8C2.5(g) (2013) (providing for a reduction in the defendant organization's guideline fine multiplier if it self-reported the violation in a timely manner), *available at* http://www.ussc.gov/Guidelines/2013_Guidelines/Manual_PDF/Chapter_8.pdf (last visited Jan 28, 2014)..

avoid statements being made or actions being taken that could compromise the company's efforts to assert its legal rights in the criminal proceeding. For example, employees in the civil cleanup effort may be willing to answer leading questions or respond to hypothetical questions in a manner that could produce devastating admissions on the criminal side.

Accordingly, companies involved in parallel prosecutions need to coordinate their responses carefully. It is particularly important that counsel involved in the criminal matter review any reports or certifications before they are submitted to civil regulators. In such circumstances, counsel must make certain that a response is truthful but does not inadvertently create further problems, given the difference in perspective between the two enforcement mechanisms.

Another important difference between criminal and civil proceedings involves application of the Fifth Amendment privilege against self-incrimination. The U.S. Supreme Court has held that the fact that an individual has invoked the privilege and declined to answer questions may not be used against him in a criminal case.[76] No prosecutor, judge, or jury may draw an inference that a person is guilty from the fact that a person has invoked the privilege. Nevertheless, a litigant in a civil case is not accorded the same level of protection. While the individual retains the absolute right to decline to answer questions, the fact finder in a civil case may draw an adverse inference from the person's silence.[77]

The difference between the two enforcement systems thus places the subject of parallel investigations on the horns of a dilemma. The Fifth Amendment privilege against self-incrimination may be waived if not invoked in the civil case.[78] If an individual makes statements in a civil or administrative proceeding, they could be used as evidence against his or her employer in the criminal case. But if the individual invokes the constitutional right to decline to answer questions, that silence could be the basis of a negative inference in the civil proceeding, and thus be a significant factor in the government's determination whether to impose a civil penalty and remediation obligations.

2. From the Government's Perspective

At first glance, parallel proceedings would appear to have several attractive features for the government. They promote environmental compliance through civil injunctions and large monetary penalties; accelerate the start of remediation and mandating the terms of the cleanup; and may achieve deterrence through imposition of criminal sanctions. Thus, whenever the environmental problem sparking a criminal investigation is ongoing, the government will almost always start from the assumption that it should also bring a civil case. Indeed, a criminal prosecutor might encourage the filing of an injunctive action to demonstrate that the environmental harm is substantial.

On the other hand, there are several significant reasons why the government may decide, from a tactical viewpoint as well as from concern with fairness to the potential defendants, not to institute a parallel proceeding:

- two cases may, in the case of a minor violation, be an inefficient use of scarce enforcement resources;
- the defense may use civil discovery to gain information about the criminal investigation;
- the need to create a wall between civil and criminal proceedings, and the documentation of the civil discovery process necessary to avoid problems under Rule 6(e) of the Federal Rules of Criminal Procedure, may inappropriately delay and complicate the proceedings;
- additional delay may be encountered if the defendant files a motion seeking dismissal on the ground of bad faith use of compulsory processes;
- prior imposition of large civil penalties may lead to dismissal of an indictment on the basis that the civil fines were criminal in nature; and

76. *E.g.*, Carter v. Kentucky, 450 U.S. 288, 302-03 (1981); Griffin v. California, 380 U.S. 609, 615 (1965).
77. *See* Baxter v. Palmigiano, 425 U.S. 308, 316-20 (1976) (adverse inference is not an impermissible consequence of the exercise of privilege against self-incrimination in a civil case).
78. United States v. Kordel, 397 U.S. 1, 9-10 (1970).

- the prosecutor will have to guard against potential constitutional violations, which are always a possibility in parallel proceeding situations.[79]

Most of the problems stem from the fundamental differences in the fact-gathering mechanisms of criminal investigation and civil discovery. Criminal investigations are conducted by grand juries, and the law imposes substantial secrecy obligations upon these investigations, in order to preserve the integrity of the process and provide confidentiality to witnesses. These restrictions place substantial limitations on the ability of government investigators involved in the grand jury process to disclose information they obtain to other federal officials. These constraints also generally prevent counsel for potential defendants from determining directly what information the government is presenting to the grand jury, and thus shield the government's theory of the case from disclosure. Civil enforcement actions, however, are conducted under the ordinary rules of discovery. Those rules provide for early, mutual release of information and do not place significant limits on the extent to which federal officials may share material obtained through discovery with other law enforcement agencies.

The adverse effect that the principle of grand jury secrecy can have on parallel environmental proceedings was demonstrated in *United States v. Gold*,[80] where criminal charges of falsification of registration material for a pesticide were dismissed because of prosecutorial misconduct. A single government attorney acted as an EPA staff attorney, a special attorney for DOJ, and a grand jury witness. The court found that the attorney's presence in the grand jury room compromised its secrecy, due to the conflict of interest arising from his various roles. This defeat taught EPA and DOJ an important lesson about criminal procedure and maintaining separation of roles for their personnel.

3. Procedures Governing Institution of Parallel Proceedings

In recognition of the difficult tactical and legal questions presented by a decision to institute parallel proceedings, DOJ and EPA have long maintained policies on when such proceedings may be authorized and the processes that must be followed. The policies are largely intended to prevent errors from occurring that might inadvertently lead to limitation or dismissal of criminal charges. Thus, the DOJ guidelines are of particular importance for entities under investigation.

a. DOJ Parallel Proceedings Policy

Historically, DOJ would not institute parallel proceedings for environmental violations unless there were compelling reasons why both civil and criminal sanctions were appropriate.[81] The agency took the position that an environmental criminal proceeding generally should be brought and resolved before a civil action.[82] DOJ favored this ordering because criminal charges entail greater punishments and have greater deterrent effects. It wanted to avoid circumstances where a sentencing court might impose a more lenient sentence to avoid compounding a large prior civil penalty. The Speedy Trial Act,[83] is also a concern as a criminal trial must be commenced expeditiously, while civil proceedings may (and often do) lag. Finally, a criminal conviction may have collateral estoppel effects in a subsequent civil case against the defendant.

For these reasons, DOJ policy had in the past prescribed that civil cases ordinarily should not proceed at the same time as a criminal investigations.[84] In 2012, recognizing that courts had held there is nothing improper about the government undertaking simultaneous criminal and civil investigations provided that the government use those proceedings and associated investigative tools for their proper purposes and in

79. *See, e.g.*, United States v. Posada Carriles, 541 F. 3d 344, 353-61 (5th Cir. 2008) (outlining principles for when government's deceptive or outrageous conduct in parallel proceedings will amount to a constitutional violation); United States v. Kordel, 397 U.S. 1, 11-12 (1970) (Fifth Amendment right of self-incrimination not violated where the U.S. Food and Drug Administration (FDA) insisted that the defendant answer interrogatories while a grand jury investigation was underway); United States v. LaSalle National Bank, 437 U.S. 298 (1978) (parallel civil and criminal investigations in tax area are valid).
80. 470 F. Supp. 1336, 9 ELR 20713 (N.D. Ill. 1979).
81. *See* EPA Parallel Proceedings Policy, *supra* note 73, §III; *see also* U.S. Attorneys' Manual, *supra* note 1, §5-11.112.
82. EPA Parallel Proceedings Policy, *supra* note 73, §IV.D.
83. 18 U.S.C. §3161.
84. 1987 DOJ Parallel Proceedings Policy, *supra* note 73, §I.

appropriate ways,[85] Attorney General Holder updated the parallel proceedings policy to state "that criminal prosecutors and civil trial counsel should timely communicate, coordinate, and cooperate with one another and agency attorneys to the fullest extent appropriate to the case and permissible by law, whenever an alleged offense or violation of federal law gives rise to the potential for criminal, civil, regulatory, and/or agency administrative parallel (simultaneous or successive) proceedings."[86] Rather than limiting or prioritizing the types of investigations and enforcement actions that could or should proceed in cases involving potential parallel proceedings, the policy states that:

> Where parallel proceedings are conducted effectively, the government is able to make more efficient use of its investigative and attorney resources. If the government does not consider and properly manage potential parallel matters, it may not be able to realize all of the remedies available to the United States. For these reasons, it is important that criminal, civil, and agency attorneys coordinate in a timely fashion, discuss common issues that may impact each matter, and proceed in a manner that allows information to be shared to the fullest extent appropriate to the case and permissible by law.[87]

The policy states that "[a] case referral from any source, including an agency referral, a self-disclosure, or a qui tam action, to any component of the Department or to a United States Attorney's Office, is a referral for all purposes," and that "[f]rom the moment of case intake, attorneys should consider and communicate regarding potential civil, administrative, regulatory, and criminal remedies, and explore those remedies with the investigative agents and other government personnel."[88] In resolving a case, the policy states that DOJ attorneys consider the potential impact of resolution of one aspect of a case on other proceedings, including that "a prosecutor, when considering a plea agreement, should also consider the impact the charge used as a basis for the guilty plea (e.g., health care fraud as opposed to obstruction) and the facts set forth in support of the plea agreement could have on a subsequent civil case (collateral estoppel, res judicata) and/or administrative exclusion or debarment."[89] Targets and their counsel must also, in this area, consider these same potential impacts, and how these impacts may, in turn, provide opportunities to argue for resolution.

If the government chooses to pursue parallel proceedings, it must conform to Rule 6(e) of the Federal Rules of Criminal Procedure.[90] This Rule prohibits, with few exceptions, the disclosure of matters occurring before a grand jury. Although civil use of grand jury materials is not per se illegal, the Supreme Court has interpreted Rule 6(e) to prohibit federal prosecutors from disclosing grand jury matters to other DOJ attorneys for use in a civil suit, unless the prosecutor can demonstrate a "particularized need" for the materials on the civil side.[91] For these reasons, prosecutors are encouraged to seek evidence through channels other than grand jury subpoenas, such as searches, interviews, and administrative inspector general subpoenas issued through EPA.[92]

b. EPA's Policy

EPA's policy on parallel prosecutions provides that "[a]lthough the great majority of EPA's enforcement actions are brought as either civil or criminal matters, there are instances in which both enforcement responses are appropriate."[93] EPA recognizes two situations in which parallel proceedings are proper: (1) where the civil

85. *See, e.g.,* United States v. Stringer, 521 F.3d 1189 (9th Cir. 2006) (holding that failure to disclose ongoing criminal investigation at time of SEC deposition testimony was not cause to suppress SEC testimony in criminal trial when SEC's civil investigation was not conducted in bad faith solely to collect evidence for criminal trial, SEC did not affirmatively mislead or deceive subject of parallel civil and criminal investigation into believing investigation was solely civil in nature, and SEC apprised defendant of Fifth Amendment rights and disclosed SEC often makes files available to U.S. Attorney's offices and prosecutors).
86. U.S. DOJ, Memorandum from The Attorney General to U.S. Attorneys et al., Coordination of Parallel Criminal, Civil, Regulatory, and Administrative Proceedings (Jan. 30, 2012), *available at* http://www.justice.gov/usao/eousa/foia_reading_room/usam/title1/doj00027.htm (last visited Jan. 28, 2014) [hereinafter 2012 DOJ Parallel Proceedings Policy].
87. *Id.*
88. *Id.*
89. *Id.*
90. Fed. R. Crim. P. 6(e).
91. *See* United States v. John Doe, 481 U.S. 102 (1987); United States v. Sells Eng'g, Inc., 463 U.S. 418, 433-35 (1983).
92. 2012 DOJ Parallel Proceedings Policy, *supra* note 86.
93. EPA Parallel Proceedings Policy, *supra* note 73, at 1. EPA practice is to include the following warning in information requests: "[A]ll information sought maybe used in an administrative, civil judicial or criminal action." *Id.* at 7.

proceeding is an "administrative compliance or cleanup order . . . required for protection of human health or the environment," but no civil penalty is contemplated; and (2) where the actor's "conduct is sufficiently egregious that both civil and criminal responses are appropriate."[94] Each region is directed to develop its own procedures for determining which matters may go forward as parallel proceedings and, if so, the order in which the matters should proceed. Managers within both the Office of Regional Counsel and the Criminal Investigative Division of the Region must agree on parallel proceedings decisions; any disagreements must be resolved by the relevant EPA Office Directors or the Principal Deputy Assistant Administrator for the OECA.[95] Once the decision has been made to pursue a parallel proceeding, EPA's civil and criminal enforcement programs must jointly draft a Parallel Proceedings Memorandum which sets forth the timing and scope of the two proceedings.[96] EPA's policy also directs its civil and criminal enforcement personnel to consult with their colleagues at DOJ regarding all parallel proceedings matters.[97]

According to EPA, "[p]arallel proceedings under environmental laws do not give rise to double jeopardy concerns."[98] Citing the Supreme Court's decision in *Hudson v. United States*,[99] EPA's policy notes that civil penalties would have to be "so punitive in form and effect" as to be considered criminal penalties to create double jeopardy concerns. This is a marked departure from the previous EPA policy, which advised that civil penalty claims should be stayed (not assessed or collected) against a person who is a target of a criminal investigation until the criminal matter is resolved.[100]

4. Protection Against Abuse of Parallel Proceedings

If the government institutes parallel proceedings, in most instances, the potential defendants will be powerless to overturn that decision or stop the civil action altogether. The Fifth Amendment does provide some grounds, however, for mitigating the potential adverse effects.

a. Stays

The preferred defense strategy is to seek a stay or postponement of the civil action, pending resolution of the parallel criminal matter.[101] The argument can be made that even during the investigatory stage of the criminal proceedings, a stay is required to avoid presenting individuals with the Hobson's choice of either waiving the Fifth Amendment privilege by answering civil discovery, and thereby prejudicing the defense of the criminal action; or, invoking the Fifth Amendment and thereby prejudicing the defense to the civil action.[102] Thus, an alternative approach is for the target to seek a stay of civil discovery until the government decides whether to indict.[103] The target's probability of success is not high. If the government, however, seeks a stay, the courts are likely to grant it, especially if necessary to prevent the statute of limitations from expiring on civil charges pending resolution of the criminal matter.[104]

---

94. *Id.* at 3.
95. *Id.*
96. *Id.* at 5.
97. *Id.* at 2-3.
98. *Id.* at 7-8.
99. 522 U.S. 93 (1997).
100. *See* U.S. EPA, Memorandum, Parallel Proceedings Policy, Steven A. Herman, Asst. Administrator, Office of Enforcement (June 24, 1994) at 4 (reproduced in Appendix A to ELI, Environmental Crimes Deskbook (1st Ed. 1996) at 199.
101. The intermediate strategy of permitting the civil matter to go forward but imposing a protective order on its fruits, to prevent their use in the criminal case, was recognized at one point, *see* Martindell v. ITT Corp., 594 F.2d 291 (2d Cir. 1979), but later was disapproved, *see* In re Grand Jury Proceedings, 995 F.2d 1013 (11th Cir. 1993).
102. *E.g.*, Securities & Exchange Comm'n v. Dresser Indus., 628 F.2d 1368 (D.C. Cir. 1980) (en banc) (the Securities and Exchange Commission's use of civil investigative warrants was lawful, even though the agency previously had referred allegations about the company to Justice for criminal investigation).
103. *In re Grand Jury Proceedings*, 995 F.2d at 1013 n.11 (noting that the "civil trial court may stay discovery until the grand jury investigation is completed").
104. *See* United States v. Hugo Key & Son., Inc., 672 F. Supp. 656, 18 ELR 20272 (D.R.I. 1987) (granting government's motion to stay proceedings in a civil Clean Air Act case pending resolution of a parallel criminal investigation, to prevent harm to paramount government interest, including protecting the identity of informants against disclosure in civil discovery). Summary judgement was granted in favor of the government in *United States v. Hugo Key & Son, Inc.*, 731 F. Supp. 1135, 1136 (D.R.I. 1989).

Decisions in other regulatory areas demonstrate that courts are hesitant to restrict the government's ability to enforce the law, based only on an anticipatory claim that a subsequent action by the government might conceivably harm the defendant's rights.[105] A company seeking a stay must demonstrate a clear hardship or inequity arising out of the need to go forward on both fronts. In reaching its decision, the court will balance the harm to the moving party in the absence of the stay against the harm to the public interest that may result from granting the stay.[106] A private party seeking a stay must show that a criminal investigation is active or that indictment is likely, and must demonstrate clearly how continuation of the civil or administrative discovery would compel her to invoke the Fifth Amendment privilege. Any evidence of actual government misconduct in the two matters that has occurred can be an effective factor in persuading the court to stay the civil matter.

b. Double Jeopardy Constraints

The branch of the Double Jeopardy Clause that prohibits multiple punishments may provide limited protection against subsequent assessment of civil sanctions imposed for the purpose of punishment, after final judgment has been entered in a prior criminal case. The Supreme Court has ruled that the Double Jeopardy Clause does not preclude the government from imposing both civil and criminal sanctions based on the same behavior as long as the civil sanctions are not criminal in nature.[107] The burden is placed on a defendant to demonstrate by the "clearest proof" that the civil sanctions are, in fact, criminal in nature.[108] Whether a civil penalty can be deemed criminal is primarily a matter of statutory construction. The civil penalty scheme must be proven to be "so punitive either in purpose or effect . . . as to transfor[m] what was clearly intended as a civil remedy into a criminal penalty."[109]

The prohibition against double punishment does not apply to suits by private entities or to penalties imposed sequentially by both a state and the federal government. Under the Dual Sovereignty Doctrine, the Double Jeopardy Clause does not apply to suits brought by separate sovereigns. Therefore, the protections against multiple punishment do not apply in this situation; the potential defendants' best recourse may be under the Petite Policy.[110] In addition, a sizable settlement in an administrative action does not bar subsequent criminal penalties as duplicative punishment, where the consent agreement imposing the civil penalties explicitly recognizes the possibility of subsequent criminal proceedings.

H. Deferred Prosecution Agreements and Non-Prosecution Agreements

Deferred prosecution agreements (DPAs) and non-prosecution agreements (NPAs) are a species of federal pretrial diversion.[111] Under a DPA, the prosecutor charges a corporation in a criminal investigation, but agrees to defer prosecution for a given period of time.[112] If the corporation complies with the terms of the DPA, the prosecutor will dismiss the charges at the end of the agreement. Under a NPA, the prosecutor agrees not to file a charging document provided that the potential defendant adheres to the terms of the agreement. In the post-Arthur Anderson world, where the indictment and conviction of a company can be ruinous, the prospect of a DPA or an NPA might simply be viewed as the next best thing to a declina-

105. *See, e.g.*, *Dresser Indus.*, 628 F.2d at 1368.
106. *See* Golden Quality Ice Cream Co. v. Deerfield Specialty Papers, Inc., 87 F.R.D. 53, 56 (E.D. Pa. 1980) (resolution of stay issue requires balancing "the interests of the public in the pending civil and criminal litigation" against other factors, including the defendant's Fifth Amendment rights).
107. *See* United States v. Hudson, 522 U.S. 93, 105 (1977).
108. *Id.*
109. *Id.* at 99 (internal citations omitted).
110. *See* Heath v. Alabama, 474 U.S. 82 (1985).
111. *See* U.S. Attorneys' Manual, *supra* note 1, §9-22.010 (Pretrial Diversion—Criminal Resource Manual).
112. *See, e.g.*, Gibson Guitar NPA (July 27, 2012), included as Appendix 13 (resolving allegations that Gibson Guitar, for tariff purposes, improperly classified imported ebony and rosewood used in its guitars in violation of the Lacey Act (16 U.S.C. §3371), which combats trafficking in "illegal" wildlife, fish, and plants).

tion of prosecution.[113] But these types of agreements, which have become increasingly prevalent, cannot be entered into lightly.[114]

Counsel considering whether a DPA or NPA is in their client's best interest must be forewarned that prosecutors wield great discretion in this realm. Such agreement might place onerous demands on the company, and, while staying and avoiding criminal prosecution, might nevertheless invite other substantial consequences, such as suspension and/or debarment from serving as a government contractor.[115]

Where DOJ ECS is involved, DPAs and NPAs have historically been relatively few and far between, however.[116] DOJ ECS is typically reluctant to enter into these types of agreements, particularly when compared to other DOJ components, but occasionally does so based on case specifics.[117]

113. For a discussion and summary of major DPAs entered into in the past 10 years, as well as links to the actual DPAs, see Gibson & Dunn, 2012 Year-End Update on Corporate Deferred Prosecution Agreements (DPAs) and Non-Prosecution Agreements (NPAs) (Jan. 3, 2013), *available at* http://www.gibsondunn.com/publications/pages/2012YearEndUpdate-CorporateDeferredProsecution-NonProsecutionAgreements.aspx#_ednref38 (last visited May 28, 2013).

114. DPAs and NPAs have been applied in a wide variety of criminal cases, such as money laundering, public corruption, and violations of the Foreign Corrupt Practices Act. They are especially common in fraud cases, such as bank fraud, securities fraud, tax fraud, and healthcare fraud. For application of DPAs and NPAs in the environmental criminal context, see Joseph G. Block & David L. Feinberg, *Look Before You Leap: DPAs, NPAs, and the Environmental Criminal Case*, in The 22nd Annual National Institute on White Collar Crime V-1 (ABA 2008).

115. DPAs and NPAs, as well as considerations before entering into them, are discussed further in Chapter 5, Subpart J, *infra*.

116. *See* Douglas Gillison, *Criminal Divisions McInerney Defends Deferred Prosecution Agreements*, http://www.mainjustice.com/justanticorruption/2013/05/03/criminal-divisions-mcinerney-defends-deferred-prosecution-agreements/ (last visited May 28, 2013). *See generally* Joseph G. Block & David L. Feinberg, *Look Before You Leap: DPAs, NPAs, and the Environmental Criminal Case, in* The 22nd Annual National Institute on White Collar Crime V-1 (ABA 2008).

117. *See supra* note 112.

Chapter 3:
Case Initiation and Response

I. Case Initiation

A criminal case can begin in any number of ways, including through information discovered in voluntary disclosures, information submitted pursuant to routine environmental compliance documents, audits, administrative inspections and warrants, information requests, criminal search warrants, anonymous tips, or citizen and whistleblower complaints.

A. *Voluntary Disclosure*

To promote self-auditing, the U.S. Environmental Protection Agency (EPA), the U.S. Department of Justice (DOJ), and the U.S. Coast Guard have established voluntary disclosure policies to reward companies that report violations found as a result of self-auditing programs, typically by mitigating civil penalties, or in some instances, foregoing criminal enforcement.[1] These voluntary disclosure programs are discussed at length in Chapter 2, Section A.

1. Routine Compliance Information

Many environmental statues require the routine submission of compliance information, such as discharge monitoring reports pursuant to the Clean Water Act (CWA), national pollutant discharge elimination system (NPDES) permits or emissions monitoring reports pursuant to Title V of the Clean Air Act (CAA). Where such reports show evidence of "pencil-whipping" (for example, by the same information being submitted month after month, where some variation would normally be expected), total emissions that are "just below" a threshold trigger for stricter compliance, or other falsification of information (such as by a company keeping two sets of books—one with the "real" numbers and one for reporting to EPA),[2] such reports, which must be signed under penalty of perjury, routinely provide the impetus for a criminal investigation.

2. Audits

An environmental audit is a "systematic, documented, periodic and objective review by regulated entities of facility operations and practices related to meeting environmental requirements."[3] These audits may benefit companies in a number of ways. They help to:

---

1. *See, e.g.*, U.S. EPA, Incentives for Self-Policing: Discovery, Disclosure, Correction, and Prevention of Violations, 65 Fed. Reg. 19618 (Apr. 11, 2000); U.S. DOJ, *Factors in Decisions on Criminal Prosecutions for Environmental Violations in the Context of Significant Voluntary Compliance or Disclosure Efforts by the Violator* (July 1, 1991), *available at* http://www.justice.gov/enrd/3058.htm (last visited May 28, 2013); U.S. Coast Guard, *Maritime Law Enforcement Manual, App. V, Environmental Crimes: Voluntary Disclosure Policy*, *available at* http://www.uscg.mil/foia/docs/CH-4%20Appendix%20V.pdf (last visited May 30, 2013).
2. *See, e.g.*, United States v. Sinskey, 119 F.3d 712 (9th Cir. 1997) (affirming defendants convictions for falsifying monthly NPDES reports submitted to EPA).
3. U.S. EPA, Statement of Policy Incentives for Self-Policing: Discovery, Disclosure, Correction, and Prevention of Violations, 65 Fed. Reg. 19618, 19625 (Apr. 11, 2000).

- provide the ability to assess compliance status;
- address and minimize potential violations;
- provide potential costs savings;
- direct organization and management of environmental resources;
- minimize potential environmental liabilities;
- enhance public image with the local community and regulatory agencies; and
- improve the ability to anticipate future environmental requirements and potential hazards.[4]

Audits have some potential disadvantages for companies as well. They may require a substantial allocation of resources. Plant operations may need to be temporarily suspended in order to conduct the audit. The results of the audit may provide ammunition to enforcement agencies and private sector litigants. If a violation or liability discovered in an audit is not addressed, there may be enhanced penalties in future enforcement actions.[5]

3. Inspections

EPA conducts inspections pursuant to authority granted in the majority of environmental statutes it implements.[6] The inspections seek to determine whether a regulated facility is in compliance with statutory and regulatory requirements. Prior to the inspection, EPA will gather information regarding the compliance requirements. During the inspection, EPA may interview facility or site representatives, review reports and records, take photographs, collect samples, and make general observations. Inspections typically are limited to one medium, e.g., air or water, but facility-wide reviews may occur. Instead of inspections, EPA monitors compliance with the CAA through full or partial compliance evaluations.[7] The full compliance evaluation looks at all regulated pollutants at each unit and the facility's ability to maintain compliance. A partial compliance evaluation looks at a subset of pollutants or units.[8]

Inspections pursuant to federal statutory authority are considered "searches" for Fourth Amendment purposes. In *Marshall v. Barlow's Inc.*,[9] the U.S. Supreme Court placed limits on the federal government's authority to conduct administrative inspections. It held that a warrantless, non-consensual search conducted pursuant to §8(a) of the Occupational Safety and Health Act (OSH Act) violated the Fourth Amendment.[10] The Court concluded, however, that the inspection would have been valid if the administrative agency had obtained an administrative warrant prior to the search.[11] The Court further stated that an administrative agency would have to show probable cause before a neutral magistrate to obtain the warrant, but that the burden is less stringent than that required for a criminal warrant.[12] The Court concluded that the probable cause requirement is satisfied if the agency can show evidence of a violation or that the inspection was part of a neutral enforcement scheme.[13]

In the aftermath of *Barlow's*, the validity of EPA warrantless inspections has been upheld against court challenges. In *Mayes v. U.S. Environmental Protection Agency*,[14] the court rejected a defendant's motion to suppress evidence gathered by the agency during a Resource Conservation and Recovery Act (RCRA)-based administrative inspection of a registered underground storage tank (UST). During the inspection, EPA personnel found additional unregistered USTs that showed evidence of leaks or were improperly

4. *See* U.S. EPA, *Advantages and Disadvantages of Environmental Auditing*, http://www.epa.gov/nscep/index.html.
5. *Id.*
6. *See, e.g.*, 42 U.S.C. §6927(a) (RCRA), 33 U.S.C. §1318(a) (CWA), 42 U.S.C. §9604(e) (CERCLA).
7. *Id.* §7414(a).
8. U.S. EPA, *Inspections and Evaluations*, http://www.epa.gov/compliance/monitoring/inspections/ (last visited May 28, 2013).
9. 436 U.S. 307 (1978).
10. *Id.* at 325.
11. *Id.* at 323.
12. *Id.*
13. *Id.* at 320-21.
14. No. 3:05-CV-478 (E.D. Tenn. 2008).

closed. The defendant argued that the administrative inspection was unconstitutional because it was warrantless and conducted without consent. Citing an earlier U.S. Court of Appeals for the Seventh Circuit case, the court rejected this argument, finding that "RCRA 'vests broad authority in EPA to inspect and sample any facility at which the agency has probable cause to believe that violations of the statute are occurring.'"[15]

In *Palmieri v. Lynch*, the U.S. Court of Appeals for the Second Circuit upheld an administrative inspection under the "special needs" exemption to the prohibition against warrantless searches.[16] A waterfront home owner submitted a permit application to the New York Department of Environmental Conservation (DEC) to extend his dock and add a boat lift.[17] Before issuing the permit, a DEC representative requested an on-site inspection, which the property owner denied.[18] Notwithstanding the denial, the DEC representative arrived at the property and knocked on the door. When there was no answer, she opened a gate with a large "No Trespassing" sign and walked into the back of the property. The property owner chased the DEC representative off his property, threatening arrest, and later filed a civil rights lawsuit against the DEC inspector under 42 U.S.C. §1983 alleging a violation of his Fourth Amendment rights, conspiracy to violate those rights, and common-law trespass.[19] The district court granted the DEC representative's motion for summary judgment, and the Second Circuit affirmed. The court of appeals concluded that the property owner's privacy interest was compromised because the area was visually open to the public by way of the shoreline; the government intrusion, a technical trespass lasting less than three minutes, was minimal; and the government's interest in protecting tidal wetlands was significant.[20] The court noted, however, that other courts applying the special needs exception in other cases should proceed with caution, given that it allows for governmental intrusion into private areas.[21]

In *Riverdale Mills Corp. v. Pimpare*,[22] the U.S. Court of Appeals for the First Circuit upheld a warrantless search against a Fourth Amendment challenge in a case involving collection of a wastewater stream from a manufacturing facility. After an anonymous tipster alerted EPA that the system was not being run properly, the agency sent two representatives to investigate without a search warrant.[23] The investigators requested consent from the facility owner, who agreed so long as an employee accompanied the investigators.[24] The EPA representatives took one sample from a manhole on the adjacent street with facility representatives present. Later that day, they returned and took two additional samples from the manhole without the facility representatives present.[25] The company sued the EPA representatives for violations of the Fourth Amendment, and they defended on the grounds of qualified immunity. The district court rejected this defense, but the First Circuit reversed. The court of appeals concluded that the search did not violate the Fourth Amendment because the company did not have a reasonable expectation of privacy in the wastewater located in a manhole under a private street adjacent to the facility. The court relied heavily on the fact that the wastewater in the manhole "flowed irretrievably" into a public sewer located only 300 feet away.[26]

4. Information Requests

If an inspection or a review of records submitted by a facility warrants follow-up, EPA may send an enforceable, written request for information to a regulated, or potentially regulated, facility or entity. The authority for these information requests is found in multiple federal environmental statutes, including the Com-

15. *Id.* (citing National-Standard Co. v. Adamkus, 881 F.2d 352, 361 (7th Cir. 1989)).
16. 392 F.3d 73 (2d Cir. 2004), *cert. denied*, Palmieri v. Lynch, 546 U.S. 937 (2005).
17. *Id.* at 76.
18. *Id.*
19. *Id.* at 77.
20. *Id.* at 82-86.
21. *Id.* at 80.
22. 392 F.3d 55, 35 ELR 20004 (1st Cir. 2004).
23. *Id.* at 57.
24. *Id.* at 58.
25. *Id.* at 58-59.
26. *Id.* at 65.

prehensive Environmental Response, Compensation, and Liability Act (CERCLA).[27] These requests seek information on facility records, operations, reports or documents that will inform EPA as to whether there is a pattern of non-compliance or widespread criminal or civil violations are occurring. EPA also may submit an information request based on a referral from another agency.

5. Anonymous Tips and Citizen or Community Complaints

On occasion, individuals want to report a suspected environmental violation in their community, but do not want to be involved or identified in the subsequent investigation. EPA provides a website where any person can provide an anonymous tip.[28] This website also allows a person or community organization to provide contact information so that they can participate in any follow-up enforcement activities if they wish. Anyone providing a tip regarding a potential violation of an environmental law must indicate that he is aware the agency has the authority to impose criminal or civil penalties for false reports and that the information provided is true and accurate to the best of his or her knowledge.

6. Whistleblower Tips

Information provided by individuals who work inside a facility or company also can form the basis for a criminal investigation. Corporate employees are often the only individuals with firsthand knowledge of illegal discharges or dumping. The fear, however, of repercussions, e.g., harassment or firing, may prevent employees from providing this information to enforcement agencies. For this reason, whistleblower protection provisions are included in several major environmental statutes.[29] If a whistleblower is subject to retaliation, he or she may file a complaint with the U.S. Department of Labor, and the Occupational Safety and Health Administration (OSHA) will investigate the complaint. The environmental statutes provide for reinstatement, back pay, damages for loss of reputation and emotional distress, and recovery of attorney's fees if an employee has been subject to adverse action for identifying environmental violations for enforcement authorities. It should be noted that the Toxic Substances Control Act (TSCA) also allows for recovery of punitive damages.[30]

7. Administrative Warrants

If a property owner or facility manager refuses consent to an administrative inspection, EPA may seek an administrative search warrant pursuant to federal environmental statues. Further, information gathered during a routine inspection may provide the impetus for EPA to request an administrative warrant. In support of these applications, inspectors provide information regarding the premises to be searched, which items may be seized, and what laws may apply or have been violated.[31] According to EPA guidance, after a denial of access or on the basis of information gathered during an inspection, agency employees must contact the EPA Regional Counsel to discuss whether a warrant is required.[32] If EPA concludes that a warrant is necessary, it must contact DOJ, which must draft an application for a warrant, an affidavit in support of the warrant, and of course, the draft warrant itself.[33] The application must state the name of the statutory

27. *See, e.g.*, CERCLA §104(e), 42 U.S.C. §9604(e), which provides that if EPA has reason to believe that there may be a release or a threat of release of pollution, the agency may require a person who may have information to furnish information or documents relating to the matter. The demand for information may include the identity, nature, and quantity of materials treated, generated, or stored at the facility.
28. U.S. EPA, *Report an Environmental Violation*, http://www.epa.gov/tips/ (last visited May 28, 2013).
29. *See* 42 U.S.C. §7622 (CAA), 42 U.S.C. §9610 (CERCLA), 33 U.S.C. §1367 (CWA), 42 U.S.C. §300j-9 (SDWA), 42 U.S.C. §6971 (RCRA), 15 U.S.C. §2622 (TSCA).
30. 15 U.S.C. §2622(b)(2)(B)(iii). In the vessel and ocean pollution area, the Act to Prevent Pollution from Ships, which implements the International Convention for the Prevention of Pollution from Ships, provides that a whistleblower may collect up to half of any civil penalties or criminal fines to persons providing information leading to the assessment of penalties or convictions under the statute. 33 U.S.C. §1908(a)(b). For a more detailed discussion of whistleblower awards in vessel cases, *see* Part 3, Chapter 9, Section II.E.2 *infra*.
31. U.S. EPA, Federal Insecticide, Fungicide, and Rodenticide Act (FIFRA) Inspection Manual 15-3 (Feb. 2002).
32. *Id.;* Memorandum from Thomas L. Adams Jr., to Regional Administrators and Counsel, *Entry and Continued Access Under CERCLA* (June 5, 1987).
33. FIFRA Inspection Manual, *supra* note 31.

authority requesting the warrant and clearly identify the site to be inspected.[34] It also must set forth the basis for probable cause or the neutral enforcement scheme that is the basis for the warrant.[35]

Once the warrant is signed by a magistrate of the appropriate district court, the search can proceed.[36] If it is likely that the warrant will be resisted or met with a threat of violence, the inspector will be accompanied by a U.S. Marshal or local law enforcement official.[37] The search must be confined to the limits of the warrant; however, the inspector can use the "plain view" doctrine to seize any evidence of wrongdoing if that evidence is in a place where it can be seen by any person in a lawful position to do so.[38]

II. The Warrant Requirement and Its Exceptions

If no other pathway is available, an environmental enforcement agency must obtain a search warrant before entering a private facility and searching or seizing its contents. A search warrant is required prior to entry, search, or seizure on private property, unless: (1) there is sufficient cause for such actions,[39] and (2) the situation fits one of several exceptions allowing government officials to forego a warrant.

A. *Pervasively Regulated Industries*

Warrantless searches are permitted in a handful of "pervasively regulated industries."[40] Although environmental regulations are intensive, they do not "pervasively regulate" a specific industry, except perhaps in the case of industries that deal solely in regulated environmental products, i.e., waste transportation and disposal.[41] Therefore, this exception generally does not apply to federal investigations of businesses whose primary products or services are not limited to environmental matters. At least one state (New Jersey) appears to follow an exception to this rule.[42] Coast Guard searches of vessels may be another exception.[43]

B. *Open Fields Doctrine*

The "open fields" doctrine may permit a warrantless search of an industrial facility when violations can be observed from the air, from an adjacent property, or even from the defendant's own property.[44] Nevertheless, entering private property to take soil or groundwater samples usually requires a warrant containing a detailed sampling plan, unless the contamination is in "plain view" upon authorized entry.[45]

---

34. *Id.*
35. *Id.* at 15-3, 15-4.
36. *Id.* at 15-4.
37. *Id.*
38. *Id.*
39. To justify a criminal search, the government must demonstrate that the search is likely to reveal evidence of a crime, i.e., "probable cause." *See, e.g.*, Wong Sun v. United States, 371 U.S. 471, 479 (1963). To justify an administrative search, the government must demonstrate only that according to a neutral inspection scheme, the premises to be searched is covered by the applicable regulations. *See, e.g.*, Camara v. Municipal Court, 387 U.S. 523, 536-38 (1967).
40. *See, e.g.*, Colonnade Catering Corp. v. United States, 397 U.S. 72, 75 (1970) (liquor industry); United States v. Biswell, 406 U.S. 311, 315-16 (1972) (firearms industry); Donovan v. Dewey, 452 U.S. 594, 602-03 (1980) (mining industry).
41. *See, e.g.*, United States v. V-1 Oil Co., 63 F.3d 909, 911-12, 26 ELR 20058 (9th Cir. 1995), *cert. denied,* V-1 Oil Co. v. United States, 517 U.S. 1208 (1996) (warrantless search of liquefied propane gas dealer permitted in the context of an industry "pervasively regulated" under the Hazardous Materials Transportation Act).
42. *See, e.g.*, In the Matter of State DEP Certification, 177 N.J. Super. 304, 315-16, 426 A.2d 534, 540 (App. Div. 1981) (New Jersey's regulation of water pollution constitutes pervasive regulation and, therefore, allows for an exception to the Fourth Amendment warrant requirement).
43. *See, e.g.*, United States v. Royal Caribbean Cruises, Ltd., 24 F. Supp. 2d 155 (D.P.R. 1997). Addressing the defendant's claim that the Coast Guard had violated Fourth Amendment protections against search and seizure, the court held that the searches conducted by the Coast Guard, in this case, did not trigger the warrant requirement of the Fourth Amendment because they were objectively reasonable and minimally intrusive. For a detailed discussion of vessel searches, *see* Chapter 9, Section II.E.3 *infra*.
44. *See, e.g.*, Oliver v. United States, 466 U.S. 170, 182-83 (1984) (search of secluded marijuana field surrounded by a fence with a locked gate and a "No Trespassing" sign did not require a warrant); Dow Chemical Co. v. United States, 476 U.S. 227, 239, 16 ELR 20679 (1986) (aerial surveillance of plant permissible because the company had no reasonable expectation of privacy in open areas of its facility, even though it surrounded the complex with security barriers). In December 2012, a Texas grand jury returned an 18-count indictment against Columbia Packing Company for allegedly dumping blood into a creek that flows to the Trinity River. Amateur video surveillance (taken by a toy helicopter) alerted authorities, who investigated further. A court will likely find the video "search" falls within the open fields exception to normal warrant requirements.
45. United States v. Carasis, 863 F.2d 615, 617 (8th Cir. 1988) (taking a byproduct from a garbage pile in an otherwise natural, wooded area did not violate a legitimate expectation of privacy); *contra* Reeves Brothers, Inc. v. EPA, 956 F. Supp. 665, 670-71, 27 ELR 2111 (W.D. Va. 1995) (sampling to determine whether compounds were buried in a field violated an expectation of privacy).

C. *Imminent Environmental Harm*

Government officials may, under appropriate circumstances, enter private property without a search warrant to prevent potential environmental harm.[46] The threatened damage, however, must be substantial and truly imminent. The vast majority of potential environmental violations do not fit into this category.

D. *Other Exigent Circumstances*

Government officials may, where exigent circumstances exist, enter private property without a warrant. "Exigent circumstances," other than imminent environmental harm, exist only in rare instances, such as a threat to the availability of evidence.[47] While mobility of evidence may present an "exigent circumstance" in some cases, it does not qualify for an exception to the warrant requirement in most cases.[48]

E. *Consent to Search*

A person with appropriate authority may consent to government entry, search, or seizure of a facility without a warrant.[49] The grant of such consent may be appropriate in the case of most routine inspections by local regulatory authorities. In the case, however, of surprise inspections or searches, it is not usually advisable for a corporation to grant consent because there is no meaningful opportunity to weigh all potentially negative factors, such as the loss of rights, disclosure of violations, disruption of operations, and damage to facilities. If a company decides to grant such consent, it should carefully circumscribe in writing the scope of the search to which it agrees and make certain that the government stays within the defined scope.[50]

III. Responding to a Surprise Search

A company or facility typically first learns that a government investigation is underway in one of three ways: (1) a surprise government search; (2) an unannounced interview of an employee; or (3) a request/subpoena for documents. It behooves a company to know how best to react if the government knocks on its door.[51] The government has a distinct advantage if a company is not prepared. This section discusses issues that arise during a surprise government search. Chapter 5 discusses requests to interview employees and receipt of a grand jury subpoena for witnesses or documents. As a surprise search of a facility often leads to the company's receipt of a grand jury subpoena, many of the "follow-on" issues discussed in Chapter 5—including conducting an internal investigation, protecting rights and evidence, electronic discovery, issues of privilege and waiver, disciplining employees, taking corrective action, selection of counsel, whether to enter into a joint defense agreement, protecting the company from parallel proceedings, and collateral consequences—may also be relevant to a company that has found itself the subject of a surprise government search.

---

46. United States v. Warner, 843 F.2d 401, 404 (9th Cir. 1988) (holding warrantless entry invalid because officers knew suspect was not at home and that volatile chemicals had been stored there without incident for weeks).

47. In the maritime context, searches (even criminal ones) rarely require warrants because ships are mobile and evidence may be readily transported outside U.S. jurisdiction. *See, e.g.*, United States v. Varlack Ventures, Inc., 149 F.3d 212, 217, 28 ELR 21419 (3d Cir. 1998); United States v. Boynes, 149 F.3d 208, 212, 28 ELR 21410 (3d Cir. 1998). For a detailed discussion of warrantless searches in vessel pollution cases, *see* Chapter 9, Section Section II.E.3. and accompanying footnotes.

48. *See, e.g.*, Commonwealth v. Krisco Corp., 653 N.E.2d 579, 585 (Mass. 1995) (where surveillance revealed a pattern of illegal waste disposal, failure to obtain warrant between dumping of waste and removal of materials dumped on a particular day was not excused by exigent circumstances); Ohio v. Denune, 612 N.E.2d 768, 775 (Ohio Ct. App. 1992) (inspector who observed drums being loaded onto trailer, and who followed the trailer to the salvage yard and inspected it there, violated the trailer owner's expectation of privacy by failure to obtain a warrant first).

49. Most agencies seeking consent to perform administrative searches will request consent in writing in advance of arriving at a facility. *See, e.g.*, Memorandum from Assistant Administrator for Enforcement, to Regional Administrators, *Re: Conduct of Inspections After the* Barlow's *Decision* (Apr. 11, 1979); EPA, Memorandum from Frank Blake (EPA General Counsel), to J. Winston Porter (Assistant OSWER Director), *Re: Refusal of Entry and EPA's RCRA §3000(h) Authority* (Apr. 16, 1986).

50. The scope of any consensual search is limited to the terms of its authorization. *See, e.g.*, Walter v. United States, 447 U.S. 649, 656-57 (1980). For example, a company's invitation to the government to inspect and copy records does not authorize the seizure of the documents. *See* United States v. Leary, 846 F.2d 592, 599 (10th Cir. 1988).

51. In this section, we often use the direct voice, referring to our readers directly as "you," or "your company," to communicate the immediacy of being called into the position to defend against a government investigation.

A. Administrative Inspections and Criminal Warrants

Because virtually all searches have potential criminal implications,[52] a company should treat any inspection or search, including an administrative inspection, as a potential criminal search requiring a warrant (with the possible exception of some routine regulatory inspections). A criminal search must be treated with the utmost seriousness and urgency, as it is a strong signal that the government may be considering a criminal indictment. According to recent statistics cited by EPA's Director of the Office of Criminal Enforcement, 67% of all cases beginning with search warrants result in criminal charges being filed. Ninety-five percent of all defendants who are charged are convicted.[53] Regardless of whether a search is predominantly administrative or criminal in nature, a warrant is usually required, except under certain circumstances discussed in Section II of this chapter. Should the government attempt a warrantless entry, search, or seizure, the company may want to voice its objection for the record—to begin laying the groundwork for a legal challenge to any evidence that the government seizes.

B. Protecting Rights and Protecting Evidence During a Surprise Search

When government agents swarm a facility to execute a search warrant, panic and confusion may reign. This is undesirable for many reasons, including that this is the first impression that the company and its employees will make on government representatives. A good first impression can go a long way toward gaining the government's trust and minimizing the scope and intensity of the inspection, search, or investigation. The following list will help a company put its best foot forward when one of its facilities is subjected to a search.

1. Be Prepared

Take the time to train employees so that they are prepared for the prospect of government investigations. Holding training sessions and mock inspections will prepare employees on how to deal with the arrival of a government search team and how to supervise (escort) government agents during a search. These sessions can also educate employees on what their rights are if government representatives ask questions during the search.

2. Be Professional

Too much informality on the part of company representatives may suggest that the company does not take the government or its environmental obligations seriously. By the same token, challenging the government at every turn may only increase the tenacity of the investigators. The company must take a professional approach and avoid these extremes.

3. Contact Company Counsel

Ask to delay the search until counsel arrives. If the government does not grant a delay (and it need not), you should make certain that counsel receives a copy of the warrant as soon as possible.

4. Obtain, Copy, and Review the Warrant

Ask to see the warrant and photocopy it so that (1) designated escorts can carry a copy with them as they supervise the search efforts, and (2) the company has accurate information from which to prepare any later challenges to the warrant or search, if necessary. Ask for the affidavit in support of the warrant, which will

52. Evidence for use in a criminal investigation may be gathered under the auspices of an administrative search—so long as: (1) the "primary purpose" is administrative (and not investigative); and (2) the criminal aspect of the search does not exceed the scope of the administrative warrant. Michigan v. Clifford, 464 U.S. 287, 294-95 (1984). Further, any evidence obtained during an administrative search may be shared with state or federal prosecutors and later used as "probable cause" for a subsequent criminal search or as evidence in a criminal action.

53. Fred L. Burnside, Director, U.S. EPA Director of the Office of Criminal Enforcement, Forensics, and Training, Remarks at the ALI-ABA Criminal Enforcement of Environmental Laws Conference (May 14, 2009).

show the basis for granting the warrant. It is more likely than not, however, that the company will have to obtain the affidavit from the issuing authority at a later date, as it often is sealed.

- *Marshal Resources.* Try to get organized in the moments before the search begins. In particular: (1) designate employees who will escort government agents around the facility and observe their activities; (2) decide whether additional escorts are necessary, if the government will be searching more than one area; (3) gather necessary equipment in order to record the government's search, e.g., a notebook, a camera, and/or a digital video camera; and (4) if the government intends to take samples, designate persons knowledgeable about sampling to observe the procedures the government follows and request split samples.
- *Instruct employees not to interfere with agents, and remind them that they are not required to answer agents' substantive questions.* If employees do answer substantive questions, those answers can be binding on the company.
- *Accompany the government agents during the search.* Company representatives have the right to accompany government investigators during any inspection or search, as long as they do not interfere with the agents. It is important that company representatives carefully record everything that is said and done.
- *Choose the escort route carefully.* The government will scrutinize the facility while it is en route to specific areas identified in the warrant. The "plain view" exception to the warrant requirement may apply to anything they see en route. Avoid escorting investigators through areas with extensive operations, large numbers of employees, or environmental compliance activities. In other words, the most direct route may not always be the best route.

5. Exercise Specific Rights During the Search

Company representatives may exercise any of the following rights as appropriate:

- *Ask Agents to Identify Themselves.* It is perfectly acceptable, and advisable, for counsel or the lead escort to ask for the names and credentials of each member of the government team. This will facilitate the company's tracking of any evidence that the government seizes.
- *Ask About the Search.* Gather information about the logistics of the planned search, such as the length of the search, the number of search groups that the government will use, and specific items to be sought.
- *Answer Only Procedural Questions.* During the search, the government may ask questions about where certain items can be found (which generally should be answered). The government may also ask more substantive questions. (The company may decline to answer them.) At no time should the company volunteer information. Take time to prepare the company's answer and make sure the answer is specifically related to the original question.
- *Object to Scope.* If investigators stray from the terms of the warrant, the accompanying escort should immediately object and communicate with company counsel or the lead escort on how to proceed. The lead escort may then contact the authority who issued the warrant to clarify the warrant's scope and object to the investigation team's interpretation of it, if necessary. At a minimum, record how the government agents proceed after the objection.
- *Identify Privileged Information.* Company representatives should make every effort to identify any confidential materials and object to their seizure by government agents. If the agents insist on seizing the documents, encourage the agents to segregate the privileged materials from other seized items.
- *Obtain Samples.* If the warrant allows sampling, it should set out a specific sampling plan to be followed. Record detailed observations on the government's sampling, i.e., who, what, where, when, and

how the samples were taken, request "split samples,"[54] and/or obtain similar samples using approved sampling methods for a source of comparison to the government's sample results.

- *Obtain an Inventory of Items Seized.* The company is entitled to an inventory of all items taken by the investigators.
- *Ask to Meet with Investigators at the End of the Search.* Before the government's investigation team leaves, ask for a final opportunity to sit down and (1) go over the inventory of items seized, (2) obtain copies of documents that the government has seized, and (3) ensure that the company has split samples and find out what types of tests the government intends to conduct on the samples.

C. Preventing Add-On Allegations

While company representatives need to remain confident and decisive during a surprise inspection or search, they should not needlessly create problems by being overly aggressive. The last thing that the company wants is "added on" criminal allegations of obstruction of justice, witness tampering, making false statements or concealing evidence.[55]

By way of example, in *United States v. Tuma et al.*,[56] the defendant was convicted by a jury in the U.S. District Court for the Western District of Louisiana of three counts of CWA felony violations related to the discharge of wastewater into the Red River and into the publically owned treatment works in Shreveport. He was also found guilty of obstruction of justice and conspiracy in relation to his obstruction of an EPA inspection by inventing an equipment malfunction in order to prevent the EPA agent from collecting effluent samples.

To avoid these sorts of charges, train all persons who will serve as "designated escorts" to follow these basic ground rules:

- If the government presents a search warrant, you may not deny the government entry to your facility to prevent them from executing the warrant.
- If the government requests your company's consent to enter the premises, you may withhold consent and require a search warrant. Nevertheless, while the government is in the process of obtaining a warrant, you may not use this time to conceal problems that are clearly the focus of the government's inquiry.
- If government agents attempt to speak with employees, you may advise employees that they are not required to answer substantive questions posed by the agents (or that they may have an attorney present when doing so). Nevertheless, you may not instruct employees to refuse to answer government questions. *See* the discussion in Chapter 5, Section 2.A, on rights of employees when government representatives seek to interview them.
- If government investigators arrive at your facility unannounced, you may send company representatives around the facility to dismiss non-essential employees, apprise them of the situation, and/or remind them of their rights. Nevertheless, you must neither instruct nor encourage employees to conceal targeted problems, destroy documents, or coordinate their "stories."

---

54. A "split sample" is a sample that the government takes and then "splits," or divides evenly, with the company at the time the government takes the sample. This allows both parties to run their own independent analyses of the samples. Under RCRA (42 U.S.C. §6927(a)) and CERCLA (42 U.S.C. §9604(e)(4)(B)), the government is required to provide the company with split samples. The government's failure to provide split samples, however, is not a defense to criminal action. *See* United States v. Protex Indus., Inc., 874 F.2d 740, 745-46, 19 ELR 21061 (10th Cir. 1989).
55. Company lawyers should take heed as well. In 2010, at least two attorneys were indicted for their involvement in environmental matters on behalf of their clients. In connection with the sale of a former paper mill in upstate New York, attorney John M. Hogan Jr. was indicted on seven counts, including wire fraud. The former associate general counsel of GlaxoSmithKline LLC was indicted on charges of obstruction and making false statements to the U.S. Food and Drug Administration (after the company had received a letter of inquiry—not a formal statutory information request or subpoena).
56. No. 5:11-cr-00031-TS (W.D. La. Mar. 22, 2012).

Part Two: Legal Theory and Strategy

Chapter 4: General Principles of Criminal Liability

I. Mens Rea

Historically, mens rea (latin for "guilty mind") has been a necessary element in establishing criminal liability. "Mens rea is the rule of, rather than the exception to, the principles of Anglo-American criminal jurisprudence."[1] Thus, although one might be civilly liable in tort for an "innocent" act that injured others, criminal liability generally may not be established without showing some culpability or intent. Exceptions to the mens rea requirement have been rare, because of the significant consequences of criminal liability and issues of due process and equity. Exceptions typically involve areas where the general public interest is concerned and "dangerous" or "deleterious" substances are involved. Such "public welfare offenses" have included the sale of narcotics and contaminated food.[2]

During the 20th century, however, the explosion of regulatory law in the United States contributed to a gradual erosion of the mens rea requirement in criminal jurisprudence and an expansion of the concept of public welfare offenses and the public welfare doctrine. This trend has been particularly evident in the evolution of criminal prosecutions for violations of environmental laws. Federal courts have expressly labeled the Clean Air Act (CAA), the Clean Water Act (CWA), and the Resource Conservation and Recovery Act (RCRA) as public welfare offenses.[3] Thus, although the statutes criminalize "knowing" violations of the law, the courts have not required any showing of criminal intent to obtain a conviction. This lower standard of proof means that the distinction between civil and criminal cases has become blurred to the point that virtually every environmental violation is theoretically subject to criminal prosecution regardless of the subjective mind of the accused, even if that mind is "objectively" reasonable. This results in potential criminal liability for even the most environmentally responsible companies which, in turn, raises important questions about whether a lower standard of proof is appropriate or effective.

Since *United States v. International Minerals & Chem. Corp.*,[4] federal courts have applied the public welfare doctrine in environmental crimes cases, i.e., requiring only a showing of general intent, rather than specific intent, for conviction. Consequently, many courts have held that the government may obtain a conviction upon showing that the defendant was aware of his conduct, not that he was aware the conduct was unlawful. Environmental case law has imposed a new species of strict liability criminalizing conduct that may not have been negligent, much less knowing.[5] The government will almost always be able to meet this lower mens rea standard for facilities that have obtained environmental permits for their operations as they are "aware" of their regulated activities.

1. United States v. U.S. Gypsum Co., 438 U.S. 422, 436 (1978), *appeal after remand, cert. denied*, 444 U.S. 884 (1979).
2. *See, e.g.*, United States v. Dotterweich, 320 U.S. 277 (1943) (misbranded drugs), *rehearing denied*, United States v. Dotterweich, 320 U.S. 815 (1943).
3. Respectively, United States v. Alghazouli, 517 F.3d 1179 (9th Cir. 2008), *cert. denied*, 555 U.S. 904 (2008); United States v. Weitzenhoff, 35 F.3d 1275, 1283-84 (9th Cir. 1993), *cert. denied sub nom;* and United States v. Laughlin, 10 F.3d 961, 24 ELR 20221 (2d Cir. 1993).
4. 402 U.S. 558 (1971).
5. As Justice Clarence Thomas pointed out in *Staples v. United States*, use of the term "strict liability" is technically a misnomer. 511 U.S. 600, 607 n.3 (1994). Although courts have eliminated the requirement of mens rea, they do require that the defendant knows that he is dealing with a "dangerous or deleterious substance." *Id.*

Three environmental statutes—CWA, CAA, and RCRA—establish criminal liability for "negligent" as well as "knowing" violations.[6] Under the mens rea standards in these statutes, the government need not prove knowledge of all the operative facts, or premeditation, or intent to violate the law. Courts have interpreted the term "knowingly" to require only general awareness that the defendant was dealing with a substance likely to be regulated. This has raised significant constitutional questions of due process regarding notice and whether it is equitable to convict individuals who are unaware their conduct is criminal.

The risk of criminal liability for environmental violations is exacerbated by the complexity and technical nature of environmental statutes and regulations and the fact that some statutes, such as the CAA and the CWA, criminalize virtually all obligations under the statute. Under the CAA, for example, it is a felony to violate any permit provision or regulation, including detailed reporting requirements. Conflicting or vague permit and regulatory provisions mean that mistakes and errors in reporting are not uncommon. Further, state and federal regulations can contain aspirational language regarding how a permit program must be implemented, but the permits themselves may not incorporate these provisions.

A. *Statutory "Intent"*

During the 1980s, the U.S. Congress amended several environmental laws to include felony provisions, and Congress also amended certain statutes' mens rea requirements. For example, in 1987, Congress amended the CWA to change the mens rea requirement for misdemeanors from "willfully or negligently" to "negligently" and made "knowingly" the mens rea for felony offenses. The CAA Amendments of 1990 also added felony offenses for "knowing" violations and introduced "negligently" as the mens rea for misdemeanors. In *United States v. Frezzo Bros.*,[7] the U.S. Court of Appeals for the Third Circuit considered the original mens rea element of the CWA and affirmed the district court's holding that proof of specific intent was not required in order to sustain a CWA conviction for "willfully or negligently" dumping pollutants into navigable waters without a permit.[8]

Most federal environmental laws[9] prohibit "knowing" violations of their provisions, without further defining that term. The legislative history of environmental statutes rarely contains guidance as to what conduct the term "knowingly" covers.[10] Consequently, courts have had to define the term on a case-by-case basis. What is meant by the term "knowingly" has thus become the most frequently litigated issue in

6. *See* discussion *infra* Sections D & E.
7. 703 F.2d 62, 13 ELR 20584 (3d Cir. 1983).
8. United States v. Baytank (Houston), Inc., 934 F.2d 599, 618-19 (5th Cir. 1991), reached the same conclusion, finding that the use of the word "negligently" eliminated the need for specific intent.
9. There are two pure strict liability statutes that have been, and continue to be, used by DOJ prosecutors in environmental cases: the Refuse Act and the Migratory Bird Treaty Act (MBTA). *See* 33 U.S.C. §411; 16 U.S.C. §703 *et seq.* Under strict liability, a person can be convicted without any proof of intent or mens rea—proof that the person merely did the act prohibited is all that is required for a conviction. *See, e.g.*, United States v. American Cyanimid Co.,, 480 F.2d 1132, 1134 (2d Cir. 1973) (interpreting the Refuse Act broadly such that the court upheld convictions without requiring proof that the refuse (in this instance, overflow from a storage tank) had reached navigable waters). The Refuse Act, originally enacted in 1899, and provides that it is unlawful to "throw, discharge, or deposit, or cause, suffer, or procure to be thrown, discharged, or deposited, . . . any refuse matter of any kind or description . . . into any navigable water of the United States." 33 U.S.C. §407. The Refuse Act was the basis for the prosecution of the Exxon Valdez oil spill. *See* United States v. Exxon Corp., 2 Oil Spill Litig. New (Litig. Reporting Serv.) 1048 (D. Alaska Feb. 27, 1990). This was prior to the revision of the CWA in 1990, which until that time did not include criminal sanctions for discharges of oil or hazardous substances into navigable waters. Despite the fact that the CWA now does provide for criminal sanctions for knowing and negligent discharges of oil, prosecutors have on occasion utilized the strict liability of the Refuse Act to address discharges into navigable waters, primarily in vessel pollution cases, and prosecution of such discharges under the Refuse Act remains an option. *See, e.g.*, United States v. IMC Shipping Co. Pte. Ltd., No. 3:07-CR-00096 (D. Alaska, Aug. 22, 2007) in which the owner of the Motor Vessel Seledang Ayu, which ran aground and broke up on Unalaska Island in the Bering Sea in 2004, pleaded guilty to two Refuse Act violations and one violation of the MBTA for spilling approximately 340,000 gallons of bunker fuel, as well as several thousand tons of soy beans, into the Bering Sea in the Alaska Maritime National Wildlife Refuge in the Aleutian Islands, resulting in the deaths of several thousand migratory birds. The company was sentenced to pay a $10 million criminal penalty. The MBTA was originally enacted in 1918 to implement a treaty between the United States and several other countries. In general, the MBTA proscribes the hunting, capture, possession, and sale of more than eight hundred species of birds. 16 U.S.C. §703. Again, criminal liability under the MBTA does not require proof that the defendant had specific intent or guilty knowledge, or was negligent, but only proof that the proscribed action has occurred. For a detailed discussion of criminal enforcement under the MBTA, *see* Chapter 9, Section VIII *infra*. Prosecutions under the MBTA are more frequent than under the Refuse Act, and occur most frequently in oil discharge cases. *See, e.g., IMC Shipping Co., supra* note 159; *BP Exploration & Prod., supra* note 69.
10. *See* United States v. Weitzenhoff, 35 F.3d 1275, 1283-84, 1295-96, 24 ELR 21504 (9th Cir. 1993), *cert. denied sub nom.* Mariani v. United States, 513 U.S. 1128 (1995). The exception is the Ocean Dumping Act, 33 U.S.C. §1411(a), where the U.S. Senate Report provides that the term "refers to a conscious act or conscious omission . . . which amounts to a violation of law, regulation or permit." S. Rep. No. 451, 92d Cong. (1971), *reprinted in* 1972 U.S.C.C.A.N. 4234, 4249. On this basis, courts have held that the Ocean Dumping Act requires mere

environmental criminal prosecutions. In assessing the required level of "knowledge," courts have focused on such factors as whether the defendant must: (1) know that the conduct will violate a law or regulation; (2) know that the activity requires a permit; (3) have knowledge of the underlying material facts; and/or (4) know that the conduct will violate the terms or conditions of a permit.[11]

Notably, to sustain an environmental criminal conviction, courts have increasingly required, with few exceptions, proof only that the defendant was aware of his own conduct.

B. Knowledge That the Conduct Will Violate a Law or Regulation

In *United States v. Buckley*,[12] the U.S. Court of Appeals for the Sixth Circuit held that to sustain a conviction for failure to notify authorities of an asbestos release under the Comprehensive Environmental Response, Compensation, and Liability Act (CERCLA), the government need only prove that the defendant knew of the release of more than one pound of asbestos, the trigger level for liability defined only by regulation. The government did not need to prove that the defendant knew of the notification requirement or knew that asbestos was one of the substances regulated.[13] The court also held that for a conviction under the CAA, the government need prove only the defendant's knowledge of the asbestos emissions themselves, and not that the defendant knew the emissions were illegal or that they presented hazards to human health or the environment.[14]

C. Knowledge That the Activity Requires a Permit

In *United States v. Hayes International Corp.*,[15] the U.S. Court of Appeals for the Eleventh Circuit upheld convictions of defendants for illegally transporting hazardous waste in violation of RCRA §3008(1). The court rejected a proposed affirmative defense that the defendants misunderstood RCRA's implementing regulations, and held that the knowledge element did not require proof that the defendants knew that the wastes involved were regulated as hazardous.[16] The court held that the government need not show the defendants knew a permit was required. But, in a somewhat paradoxical holding, it also found that the defendants must have knowledge that the facility to which the waste was transported lacked a permit.[17] It stated that "[r]emoving the knowing requirement from this element would criminalize innocent conduct; for example, if the defendant reasonably believed that the site had a permit, but in fact had been misled by the people at the site."[18] Thus, a transporter could be held criminally liable if it knew a facility did not have a permit, even though it did not know a permit was required.

The U.S. Court of Appeals for the Fourth Circuit reached a similar conclusion in *United States v. Wilson*,[19] finding that a CWA conviction for illegal filling of wetlands need not be predicated on the defendant's knowledge that he needed a permit, but the defendant must be shown to have known that he did not have a permit.[20] In addition, both the *Hayes International* and *Wilson* courts observed that willful ignorance

---

consciousness of the action, and not proof that the defendant had knowledge of the relevant statutory provision. *See* United States v. Reilly, 827 F. Supp. 1076, 1078, 24 ELR 20097 (D. Del. 1993), *aff'd*, 33 F.3d 1396 (3d Cir. 1994).

11. *See* discussion in Chapter 4, Section I.C, *infra*.
12. 934 F.2d 864, 21 ELR 21113 (6th Cir. 1991).
13. *Id.* at 89.
14. *Id.* at 88-89.
15. 786 F.2d 1499, 16 ELR 20717 (11th Cir. 1986).
16. *Id.* at 1503.
17. The court stated in a footnote that "[i]t may seem anomalous to hold that the government need not show that the defendant had actual knowledge that the law requires a permit, but that it must show knowledge of the permit status of the disposal site at issue." 786 F.2d at 1504 n.6. (As Justice Byron R. White stated in *Liparota v. United States*, a seller need not know a license is required to sell a security as long as the seller knows he does not have a permit. Liparota v. United States, 471 U.S. 419, 436 (1985) (White, J., dissenting)). Here, if the transporter does not know a permit is required, but knows the facility does not have one, or knows he has not inquired, then sufficient knowledge is shown." 786 F.2d at 1504.
18. *Id.*
19. 133 F.3d 251, 28 ELR 20299 (4th Cir. 1997).
20. *Id.* at 264.

or conscious avoidance will not bar a finding of knowledge and ultimately found that the government had proved sufficient knowledge by circumstantial evidence.[21]

In *United States v. Speach*,[22] the U.S. Court of Appeals for the Ninth Circuit reversed a conviction under RCRA for knowingly transporting hazardous waste to an unpermitted facility on the ground that the government had failed to prove that the defendant knew or willfully failed to determine that the facility to which the hazardous waste was transported lacked a RCRA disposal permit. However, the court noted that a defendant would be in "the best possible position" to determine if his own facility had a permit, such that it would be reasonable to impose on such a defendant the risk of ascertaining the permit status of his own facility.[23]

The outlier is found in *United States v. Johnson & Towers, Inc.*, where the Third Circuit held that in order to sustain an indictment under RCRA for illegal disposal of hazardous waste without a permit, the government must allege and prove that the defendant had knowledge of each element of the offense, including that the defendant knew he required a permit.[24] Under this decision, the indictment must assert that the defendant knew that it was required to obtain a permit and that the defendant knew that it did not possess a permit.[25] The court did allow that knowledge "may be inferred by the jury as to those individuals who hold the requisite responsible positions with the corporate defendant." With respect to the defendant's knowledge of the law, however, the court held that "the government need only prove knowledge of the actions taken and not of the statute forbidding them."[26]

D. *Knowledge of the Underlying Facts*

In *United States v. Pruett*,[27] defendants owned and operated 28 wastewater treatment facilities in Louisiana. Though national pollutant discharge elimination system (NPDES) permits for the effluent discharges at these wastewater treatment facilities were obtained, the defendant failed to collect samples from these facilities, regularly submit test results, or keep records of discharges. Though the defendants conceded that the government presented sufficient evidence proving that violations of the CWA occurred, the defendant argued that the government did not present sufficient evidence to prove intent. The government relied on *United States. v. Aggarwal*,[28] which says that "[t]he intent necessary to support a conviction can be demonstrated by direct or circumstantial evidence that allows an inference of unlawful intent, and not every hypothesis of innocence need be excluded." The court found sufficient evidence to prove the defendant had knowingly violated the CWA. With regard to the effluent and records violations, the government further relied on *United States v. Greuling*,[29] to argue the defendant's knowledge of the industry and his experience in the field was sufficient to satisfy intent requirements. The defendant had worked in the industry since 1986 and was very familiar with permitting and record-keeping requirements.

In *United States v. Evertson*,[30] the defendant was convicted by a jury of one count of violating the Hazardous Materials Transportation Uniform Safety Act (HMTUSA), and of two counts of violating RCRA because he knowingly stored materials that he knew to be hazardous waste in violation of the statutes. On appeal, defendant challenged the conviction, the jury instructions, and his sentence. The appellate court affirmed the RCRA conviction, holding there was sufficient evidence because defendant's storage process was untested and failed within a year, he admitted to his sister and the Federal Bureau of Investigation (FBI) that the process was unsuccessful, and he left the materials in storage for over two years with incorrect contact information after leaving Idaho. The court further held that because a RCRA offense does not

21. Several other courts have made similar findings. *See, e.g.*, United States v. Hopkins, 53 F.3d 533, 537 (2d Cir. 1995), *cert. denied*, 516 U.S. 1072 (1996) ("One may not willfully or intentionally remain ignorant of a fact, material or important to his conduct to escape the consequences of criminal law.").
22. 968 F.2d 795, 22 ELR 21498 (9th Cir. 1992).
23. *Id.* at 797.
24. 741 F.2d 662, 669, 14 ELR 20634 (3d Cir. 1984), *cert. denied*, 469 U.S. 1208 (1985).
25. *Id.*
26. *Id.* at 670.
27. No. 11-30572, 2012 U.S. App. LEXIS 9769 (5th Cir. 2012).
28. 17 F.3d 737, 740 (5th Cir. 1994). *rehearding denied*, 1994 U.S. App. LEXIS 8709 (5th Cir. 1994).
29. No. 95-50705, 1996 WL 460109 (5th Cir. 1996).
30. 320 F. App'x 509 (9th Cir. 2009).

require intent to dispose of materials, criminal liability can be triggered simply by improper storage. The court found the jury instructions on the "willfulness" requirement of the HMTUSA were proper because the HMTUSA does not require actual knowledge of the specific regulations violated, but only requires knowledge that the conduct was unlawful.

In *United States v. Alghazouli*,[31] the Ninth Circuit affirmed a conviction under the CAA, for the illegal importation of an ozone-depleting air conditioning refrigerant for automobiles. In the process, the court expressly stated that the CAA is a "public welfare statute."[32] The district court had instructed the jury that to establish a "knowing" violation of the statute, the government need only prove that the defendant had knowledge of the facts that constitute the offense, not that the defendant knew his acts were unlawful."[33] The court of appeals agreed, relying on precedent from the U.S. Court of Appeals for the Second, Fifth, and Sixth Circuits as well as from the U.S. Supreme Court in *United States v. International Minerals & Chemical Corp.*[34]

In *United States v. Hansen*,[35] the court rejected the argument that the government must prove that the defendant knew that a release was in excess of the reportable quantity. The defendant directed plant employees to pump wastes into tanks that had once been used to store oil, although he knew that the wastewater mixed with oil could not be run through the plant's wastewater treatment system. The defendant requested that the trial judge instruct the jury that to obtain a conviction under CERCLA for failing to notify the EPA as soon as he had knowledge of a release of a hazardous substance in a reportable quantity, the government must prove that he "knew that the released hazardous materials exceeded the applicable reportable quantity." The court rejected this suggestion and instructed the jury instead that it need only find that a reportable quantity of the waste was released to impose guilt. On appeal, the Eleventh Circuit held that the government was required to prove only that a person in charge "knew of the release and knew that the release contained hazardous waste, and failed to report it."[36]

In *United States v. Weintraub*,[37] the Second Circuit considered the mens rea required by the CAA. Although it acknowledged that the statute "may plausibly be read to require either knowledge that the conduct in question violated the law or knowledge of the facts and circumstances that amount to a violation, without specific knowledge of the law," it ultimately held that "the phrase 'knowingly violates' requires knowledge of facts and attendant circumstances that comprise of violation . . . not specific knowledge that one's conduct is illegal."[38]

In *United States v. Bronx Reptiles, Inc.*,[39] the government prosecuted an importer and wholesale distributor of animals under the Lacey Act[40] after discovering that a shipment of reptiles sent to the importer had been improperly packaged, resulting in the deaths of many animals. The defendant challenged its conviction by arguing that the government must prove not only that it knowingly imported the animals, but also knew about the inhumane and unhealthy conditions.[41] The Second Circuit agreed, finding that it was "reasonably clear" that the word knowingly in the statute refers to all three clauses in the statute, i.e., that one "knowingly" (1) caused an animal to be transported; (2) to the United States; and (3) in inhumane conditions. The court rejected the government's arguments that illegal importation of wild animals constituted

---

31. 517 F.3d 1179 (9th Cir. 2008), *cert. denied*, 555 U.S. 904 (2008).
32. *Id.* at 1193. The public welfare defense is discussed *infra* in this chapter in subsection F.
33. *Id.* at 1192.
34. 402 U.S. 558 (1971).
35. 262 F.3d 1217 (11th Cir. 2001), *cert. denied*, 535 U.S. 1111 (2002).
36. *Id.* at 1254.
37. 273 F.3d 139 (2d Cir. 2001).
38. *Id.* at 146-47. *But see* United States v. Cooper, 482 F.3d 658, 664-68 (4th Cir. 2007) (holding in a CWA case that while the government did have to prove that the defendant knowingly discharged sewage into a creek, it did not have to prove that the defendant knew that the creek was a "water of the United States" as this was a "classic jurisdictional element" and "the *mens rea* requirements typically do not extend to the jurisdictional elements of a crime.")
39. 217 F.3d 82 (2d Cir. 2000).
40. The statute states in part that "it shall be unlawful for any person, including any importer, knowingly to cause or permit any wild animal or bird to be transported to the United States, or any Territory or district thereof, under inhumane or unhealthful conditions or in violation of such requirements." 18 U.S.C. §42(c).
41. 217 F.3d 82, 83 (2d Cir. 2000).

a public welfare offense. It also stated that with respect to proving inhumane conditions, circumstantial evidence could demonstrate criminal knowledge.[42]

In *United States v. Ahmad*,[43] the defendant emptied an underground storage tank by discharging gasoline into a municipal storm sewer and a local creek, in alleged violation of the CWA. In defense, the defendant argued that he thought he was discharging water, not gasoline, and thus could not be convicted of "knowingly" discharging a pollutant. He later challenged his conviction based on a jury instruction that did not make it clear that the jury must find that he knew the substance he was discharging was gasoline. The Fifth Circuit overturned Ahmad's conviction, holding that "[w]ith the exception of purely jurisdictional elements, the mens rea of knowledge applies to each element of the crimes."[44] "To hold otherwise would require an explanation as to why some elements should be treated differently from others, which neither the parties nor the case law seems able to provide."[45] The court also held that although the CWA appeared to implicate public welfare, it did not fit into the narrow exception for public welfare offenses.

In *United States v. Wilson*,[46] the Fourth Circuit reversed a defendant's conviction for filling wetlands in violation of the CWA because the trial court failed to require proof of mens rea for each element of the offense. The court found that by changing the mens rea requirement of the CWA from "willful" to "knowing," Congress had "intended to effect a change in meaning" that lessened the standard to exclude a requirement that a defendant understand the illegality of his acts.[47] The court, however, held that while knowledge of illegality was not required, the defendant must have knowledge of each element of the offense.[48] In so holding, the Fourth Circuit acknowledged the strict liability imposed by a true public welfare statute and declined to find that the CWA was such a law. The court did observe that "a statute which in some applications is a public welfare statue may in other applications be held to require different mens rea."[49]

E. Knowledge That the Conduct Will Violate a Permit Term or Condition

In *United States v. Dean*,[50] the Sixth Circuit followed other circuits in affirming a plant manager's conviction under RCRA §3008(d)(2)(A) for illegal storage and disposal of hazardous waste. It held that the word "knowingly" in that provision applies only to treatment, storage, and disposal of the hazardous waste, and did not require that the defendant know of the permit requirements for these activities.[51]

In *United States v. Goldsmith*,[52] the Eleventh Circuit affirmed RCRA convictions for transporting hazardous waste to an unpermitted facility and storing waste without a permit. The court held that the government did not need to prove that the defendant knew the waste was regulated. The court observed that

42. *Id.* at 89.
43. 101 F.3d 386, 27 ELR 20557 (5th Cir. 1996), *rehearing, en banc, denied*, 108 F.3d 335 (5th Cir. Tex. 1997).
44. *Id.* at 391.
45. *Id.* at 390.
46. 133 F.3d 251, 28 ELR 20999 (4th Cir. 1997).
47. *Id.* at 262.
48. In holding that the government must show that the defendant knew "the facts that make his conduct illegal" and that such knowledge be proven for each element of the offense, the court of appeals appeals relied on the Supreme Court decisions in Staples v. United States, 511 U.S. 600 (1994) and and United States v. X-citement Video, Inc., 513 U.S. 64 (1994). *Id.* at 262. In 2009, the Supreme Court, in addressing the question of what proof of knowledge the government must present to obtain a conviction, stated the general principle that "[a]s a matter of ordinary English grammar, it seems natural to read the statute's word 'knowingly' as applying to all the subsequently listed elements of the crime." Flores-Figueroa v. United States, 556 U.S. 646, 650 (2009). *See also* United States v. Metalite Corp., No. 99-008, 2000 WL 1234389 (S.D. Ind. July 28, 2000) (holding in a CWA criminal prosecution that wherever a mistake of fact defense attaches, the "knowing" requirement should apply).
49. 133 F.3d at 264.
50. 969 F.2d 187, 22 ELR 21296 (6th Cir. 1992).
51. In holding that the term, "knowing" can be construed as not applying to paragraph (A), the *Dean* court essentially construed it as a strict liability law. *See also* United States v. Hoflin, 880 F.2d 1033, 19 ELR 21140 (9th Cir. 1989), *cert. denied*, 493 U.S. 1083 (1990) (holding that interpretation of RCRA's knowledge requirement as a general intent provision was consistent with the express language of the statute and that the government was not required to prove that the defendant knew the wastes were regulated). *But see* United States v. Johnson & Towers, Inc., 741 F.2d 662, 14 ELR 20634 (3d Cir. 1984) (the court found that under §3008(d)(2)(A), which criminalizes storage, treatment, or disposal of hazardous waste without a permit, the government must prove knowledge for *all elements* of the crime, including knowledge of RCRA's requirements).
52. 978 F.2d 643, 23 ELR 20281 (11th Cir. 1992).

knowledge the waste had the potential to be harmful to humans or the environment was "sufficient to inform the jury that it must find that a defendant knew the substance he disposed of was hazardous."[53]

In *United States v. Weitzenhoff*,[54] the managers of a sewage treatment plant were convicted of multiple felonies under the CWA for knowingly discharging partially processed sewage into the ocean, in violation of the plant's permit limits on total suspended solids and biochemical oxygen demand. The defense argued that the phrase "knowingly violates" in CWA §309(c)(2),[55] differentiated this offense from other CWA criminal charges. The defendants claimed that government was required to prove that they knew that the release violated permit limits. The district court denied the defendants' request for a jury instruction that would have required the government to prove that the defendants knew that their acts were unlawful and also refused to submit to the jury the defendants' proposed affirmative defense that they mistakenly believed that the permit authorized their behavior in order to avoid a catastrophic plant failure.[56] The Ninth Circuit affirmed the convictions, finding that the district court had properly interpreted the phrase "knowingly violates" as requiring proof only that the defendants were aware that they were discharging pollutants, and not proof of actual knowledge that their acts violated the permit.[57] The court concluded that the CWA felony provision was also properly characterized as a public welfare offense.

In *United States v. Hopkins*,[58] the Second Circuit acknowledged that "[a]s a matter of abstract logic, it would seem that a statute making it unlawful to 'knowingly violate[ ]' a given statutory or permit provision would require proof that the defendant both violated and knew that he violated that provision," but affirmed a conviction under CWA §309(c)(2)(A) for violating the restrictions of a permit with respect to zinc discharges, and under 18 U.S.C. §371 for conspiracy to violate §309(c)(2)(A).[59] The court rejected the argument that the defendant must have known he was violating the permit, finding that the purpose and legislative history of §309(c)(2)(A) "indicate that Congress meant that that section would be violated if the defendants' acts were proscribed, even if the defendant was not aware of the proscription."[60]

Under *Hopkins* and *Weitzenhoff*, facilities with CWA permits are essentially subject to strict liability because the "enhanced awareness" of regulation implicit in receiving a permit virtually eliminates any possible (lack of) knowledge defenses.

F. *The "Public Welfare" Doctrine*

Under the public welfare doctrine, some courts have reduced the required knowledge element to a minimum. The public welfare doctrine applies when an activity or substance is so inherently dangerous that the defendant's knowledge of the likelihood of regulation is presumed. The doctrine originated with substances such as narcotics and ammunitions,[61] and was first extended to the environmental arena in *International Minerals*,[62] which involved a prosecution for a "knowing" violation of an agency rule that required shippers to disclose the presence of hazardous chemicals on container labels.[63] The U.S. Supreme Court upheld the validity of the criminal information filed in the case that failed to allege that the defendant had actual

53. *Id.* at 646 (citing United States v. Dee, 912 F.2d 741, 745, 21 ELR 20051 (1990), for the proposition that "the knowledge element of § 6928(d) does extend to knowledge of the general hazardous character of the wastes," thus preserving some mens rea). *See also* United States v. Laughlin, 10 F.3d 961, 24 ELR 20221 (2d Cir. 1993) (holding that the government need only prove that the defendant had a general awareness that he was performing the acts proscribed by the law, not that the defendant had actual knowledge of the lack of permit or that the specific waste involved was regulated); United States v. Wagner, 29 F.3d 264, 24 ELR 21353 (7th Cir. 1994) (noting that to require knowledge of the permit requirement for a violation of §3008(d)(2)(A) would render the use of the word "knowledge" in paragraphs (2)(B) and (2)(C) surplusage).

54. 1 F.3d 1523, 23 ELR 21322 (9th Cir. 1993), *reh'g denied, opinion amended*, 35 F.3d 1275, 24 ELR 21504 (1994), *cert. denied sub nom.* Mariani v. United States, 513 U.S. 1128 (1995).

55. Under §309(c)(2), it is a felony to "knowingly violate . . . any permit condition or limitation implementing any of [certain enumerated] sections in a permit issued under [§402]." 33 U.S.C. §1319(c)(2).

56. *Id.* 35 F.3d. at 1286. The evidence likely would have permitted the government to obtain a conviction under either standard, because it showed that the defendants released the illegal material at night and instructed their employees to keep quiet. *Id.* at 1289.

57. *Id.* at 1283-84.

58. 53 F.3d 533, 537, 25 ELR 21178 (2d Cir. 1995), *cert. denied*, Hopkins v. United States, 516 U.S. 1072 (1995).

59. *Id.* at 537.

60. *Id.* at 540.

61. *E.g.*, United States v. Freed, 401 U.S. 601 (1971), *rehearing denied*, United States v. Freed, 403 U.S. 912 (1971) (possession of unregistered grenade); United States v. Balint, 258 U.S. 250 (1922) (possession of narcotics).

62. 402 U.S. at 558.

63. The defendant was prosecuted under 18 U.S.C. §834(f), which made anyone who "knowingly violates" an Interstate Commerce Commission regulation subject to criminal liability. *Id.* at 558.

knowledge of the rule it allegedly violated. The Court stated that when "dangerous or deleterious devices or products or obnoxious waste materials are involved, the probability of regulation is so great that anyone who is aware that he is in possession of them . . . must be presumed to be aware of the regulation."[64]

The Court recognized two possible defenses under the public welfare offense doctrine. First, a factual defense is available if a "person think[s] in good faith that he [i]s shipping distilled water when in fact he [i] s shipping some dangerous acid . . . ."[65] Second, the Court recognized that products that are not obviously dangerous may also be regulated and that "substantial due process questions" might be raised if the statute did not require that mens rea be present as to each element of the offense.[66]

The public welfare offense doctrine is thus limited only by the Due Process Clause's requirement that a statute give notice that an act has been made criminal.[67] To date, this concern has been more theoretical than real as no environmental conviction has ever been overturned on this basis.

G. *Criminal Negligence*

The criminal negligence offense is a relatively new tool in environmental enforcement. Since its enactment over 20 years ago, the negligence provision of the CWA has been used most often as a means for obtaining convictions by pleading down felony charges. It also has been used when it was difficult to prove knowledge and to apply criminal liability to corporate officers and others in positions of authority who were not directly involved in a violation. The CAA differs from the CWA in that it does not create a penalty for negligent violation of the Act, but only for negligent endangerment when the offense places another person in imminent danger of death or serious bodily injury.[68] While the CWA negligence provision has been widely used, the CAA provision has not.

For instance, in January 2013, a federal judge in the U.S. District Court for the Eastern District of Louisiana approved a plea agreement entered into by BP for violations arising from the release of oil from the Macondo well in the Gulf of Mexico in 2010.[69] The Macondo well was operated by BP, and had been drilled by the Mobile Offshore Drilling Unit (MODU) Deepwater Horizon, owned and operated by a subsidiary of Transocean Deepwater, Inc., a subcontractor of BP. The well failed, eventually releasing between 4.5 and 5.5 million barrels of oil into the Gulf of Mexico. In addition, gas discharged from the well enveloped the *Deepwater Horizon* and caused an explosion, which led to the sinking of the MODU and the loss of eleven crewmembers. BP pled guilty to 14 criminal counts, which included 11 counts under the maritime manslaughter statute, one count of obstruction of Congress, one misdemeanor count of violating the CWA provisions prohibiting the negligent discharge of oil, and one count under the Migratory Bird Treaty Act. BP was sentenced to pay $4 billion in criminal fines and recoveries as provided in the plea agreement. In addition, Transocean agreed to plead to a single count of violating the CWA provisions prohibiting the negligent discharge of oil, and to pay $400 million in criminal fines and recoveries.[70]

---

64. *Id.* at 565.
65. *Id.* at 563-64.
66. *Id.* at 564.
67. *Id.* at 563; *see also* Kolender v. Lawson, 461 U.S. 352, 357 (1983); Jordon v. DeGeorge, 341 U.S. 223, 230 (1951), *rehearing denied*, Jordan v. De George, 341 U.S. 956 (1951).
68. 42 U.S.C. §7413(c)(4). It should be noted that low-level employees are expressly exempt from this provision. 42 U.S.C. §7413(h). United States v. BP Exploration & Prod., Inc., Case No.: 2:12-cr-00292-SSV-DEK (E.D. La., Jan. 29, 2013) (Reasons for Accepting Plea Agreement), *available at* http://www.justice.gov/criminal/vns/docs/2013/01/2013-01-30-bp-exploration-reasons-for-accepting-plea-agreement.pdf (last visited Jan. 31, 2014).
69. United States v. BP Exploration & Prod., Inc., Case No.: 2:12-cr-00292-SSV-DEK (E.D. La., Jan. 29, 2013) (Reasons for Accepting Plea Agreement), *available at* http://www.justice.gov/criminal/vns/docs/2013/01/2013-01-30-bp-exploration-reasons-for-accepting-plea-agreement.pdf (last visited Jan. 31, 2014).
70. The BP oil spill case also resulted in criminal indictments of several individual BP employees. In the first indictment, a former BP engineer was arrested and indicted on charges of obstruction of justice. The engineer had been involved in efforts to stem the discharge of oil from the well, and was involved in modeling flow rates of oil from the well, a significant point of controversy long after the well was capped. According to the indictment, the engineer shared estimates from the model within BP that were greater than the amounts estimated by the United States and shared with the public. Early on, BP and its employees, including the engineer were issued a legal hold order by the government mandating that all evidence regarding the incident be retained. The indictment alleges that the engineer, after receiving the evidence hold order, deleted hundreds of text messages from his phone regarding the estimated rate of discharge of oil from the well. *See* DOJ, Press Release, http://www.justice.gov/opa/pr/2012/April/12-ag-524.html (last visited May 28, 2013).

    Subsequently, a BP vice president was indicted for obstruction of Congress and making false statements to federal agents. Again these charges relate to statements made regarding the flow rate of oil being discharged from the well. According to the indictment, the BP vice presi-

In *United States v. Hanousek,*[71] the Ninth Circuit held that a person who acts with "ordinary" negligence in violating the CWA discharge prohibition may be subject to criminal penalties. The defendant was the supervisor of a construction project on a railroad that ran adjacent to an oil pipeline. Contrary to customary practice, precautions were not taken to protect the pipeline. When heavy equipment struck the pipeline, oil was discharged into a nearby river. Hanousek was convicted of negligent discharge in violation of the CWA. On appeal, he argued that a criminal conviction based on a showing of ordinary negligence, as opposed to criminal negligence, violated his due process rights.

The Ninth Circuit found that the term "negligence" is not defined in the CWA and applied traditional principles of statutory interpretation and the presumption that "the legislative purpose is expressed by the ordinary meaning of the words used."[72] The court rejected Hanousek's claims that the trial court should have instructed the jury that it could convict only if it found Hanousek was "criminally negligent." It held that the ordinary meaning of "negligently" is a failure to use such care as a reasonable prudent and careful person would use under similar circumstances. The court also relied on the fact that Congress had included other provisions in the CWA that provided for increased penalties for violations resulting from "gross negligence."[73]

The court stated unequivocally that "[t]he criminal provisions of the CWA constitute public welfare legislation."[74] Citing *United States v. Balint,*[75] among other cases, the Ninth Circuit observed that it was well established that public welfare statutes can subject a person to criminal liability for ordinary negligence without violating due process. Hanousek tried to distinguish *Weitzenhoff* on the ground that the defendants there were CWA permittees, while he was not a permit holder and thus not in a position to know what the CWA required.[76] The court held, however, that Hanousek should have been aware of the probability of strict regulations, relying on the fact that Hanousek admitted that he was aware of the pipeline and was aware that a break in the pipeline would pose a danger.[77]

The Supreme Court denied certiorari, but in a strong dissent from the denial, Justices O'Connor and Thomas expressed their concern that the public welfare doctrine was being construed too broadly, potentially imposing criminally liability on "ordinary industrial and commercial activity."[78]

In *United States v. Ortiz,*[79] the U.S. Court of Appeals for the Tenth Circuit applied an ordinary negligence standard and reversed a district court decision that set aside a jury conviction of a defendant who discharged wastewater via a toilet that ultimately connected with jurisdictional waters of the United States. In entering a judgment of acquittal, the district court found that the defendant could not be held liable unless he knew that using the toilet would result in a discharge.[80] On appeals, the government argued that the district court had conflated the mens rea standards for a negligent and a knowing violation. The defendant

dent responded to a formal request for information regarding the amount of oil flowing from the well from a U.S. House of Representatives' subcommittee with oversight authority. The BP vice president allegedly falsely informed subcommittee staff members during a briefing that the flow rate was in accordance with initial Federal agency estimates without disclosing information of which he was aware from a variety of other sources, including internal BP estimates that the rate was significantly greater. Subsequently, it is alleged, he responded to a letter request from the subcommittee chairman accusing BP of understating the amount and flow rate of oil being discharged by again providing false and misleading information to support his original estimate. Finally, he is alleged to have made false statements to federal law enforcement agents investigating the obstruction of Congress charge. *See* Indictment, http://www.justice.gov/iso/opa/resources/278201211115143658328449.pdf (last visited May 30, 2013).

In addition, two BP well site leaders who were on board the drilling rig *Deepwater Horizon* at the time of the explosion and fire, were indicted on 11 counts of involuntary manslaughter under 18 USC §1112, 11 counts of seaman's manslaughter under 18 USC §1115, and 1 count of negligent discharge of oil in violation of the CWA. According to the indictment, the two well site leaders were responsible for supervising and determining the success of tests necessary to ensure the well was secure before it was temporarily abandoned. It is alleged that the well site leaders were negligent by ignoring glaring indications from the tests that the well was not in fact secure, and that they failed to investigate these indications further. According to the indictment, this negligence ultimately led to the loss of well control which caused the explosion and fire that resulted in the loss of life of 11 men aboard the *Deepwater Horizon*, and the discharge of oil from the well. *See* Indictment, http://www.justice.gov/iso/opa/resources/25201211115143638743323.pdf (last visited May 30, 2013).

71. 176 F.3d 1116, 29 ELR 21049 (9th Cir. 1999).
72. *Id.* at 1120 (citing Russello v. United States, 464 U.S. 16 at 21 (1983)).
73. *Id.* at 1121.
74. *Id.* at 1121 (citing *Weitzenhoff*, 35 F.3d at 1286).
75. 258 U.S. 250, 252 (1922).
76. *Hanousek*, 176 F.3d at 1122.
77. *Id.*
78. United States v. Hanousek, 528 U.S. 1102, 1103 (2000).
79. 427 F.3d 1278 (10th Cir. 2005).
80. *Id.* at 1282.

did not dispute that an ordinary negligence standard applied, but argued that he could not be negligent because he did have knowledge of the risk that the toilet discharged to waters of the United States.

In considering the appropriate standard of negligence, the Tenth Circuit relied on the plain language of the statute. Observing that another section of the CWA contained civil penalty provisions for acts of "gross negligence,"[81] the court held that if Congress had intended a "heightened negligence standard, it could have done so explicitly" as it had in the civil provision.[82] The court disagreed with the defendant's contention that he could be held negligent only if he was aware of a known risk, relying on standard definitions of negligence as "a lack of ordinary care." It found that a reasonable jury could have found the defendant guilty of a negligent violation.

H. Negligent Endangerment

In *United States v. Little*,[83] the Tenth Circuit upheld a conviction for negligent endangerment against a municipal employee who directed a work crew that renovated a train depot, including the removal of insulation. The prosecution presented evidence that the defendant was aware of the possibility that asbestos was present but failed to take measures to protect the health of the work crew. The court did not consider what type of negligence was necessary for a conviction. Rather, it focused on whether there was sufficient evidence to determine that the work crew was exposed to imminent danger of death or serious bodily injury.[84]

I. Demonstrating Proof of Knowledge

Prosecutors rely on several approaches to prove a corporation's knowledge. Under the doctrine of respondeat superior, a corporation may be held criminally liable for the actions of its employees if the allegedly illegal acts were done on behalf of the company and were within the scope of the employees' authority.[85] Criminal liability may be imputed even if the company has an explicit policy against the activity.[86] Although actions by rogue employees occur on both sides of the equation,[87] mention of a rogue employee is often greeted by great skepticism on behalf of government investigators and prosecutors. After a corporation was found guilty of violating the Act to Prevent Pollution from Ships (APPS) for failure to maintain an accurate oil record book (ORB) by failing to disclose exceptional discharges of oil-contaminated waste made by an employee through a bypass hose,[88] the corporation appealed on the basis, among others, that conviction of the company required the government to prove more than that the employee was acting within the scope of his employment, and that the government was required to prove that the company also lacked effective policies and procedures to prevent and discover criminal actions by its employees.[89] The Second Circuit disagreed, holding instead that even without management condoning the activities, action by an employee within the scope of his employment is sufficient to hold the company vicariously criminally liable.[90]

---

81. 42 U.S.C. §1321(b)(7)(D).
82. 427 F.3d 1278, 1284, (10th Cir. 2005) (citing *Hanousek,* 176 F.3d at 1121 (1999)).
83. 308 Fed. App'x 256 (10th Cir. 2009).
84. *Id.* at 259.
85. *E.g.*, United States v. Marathon Dev. Corp., 867 F.2d 96, 19 ELR 20683 (1st Cir. 1989) (corporation found criminally liable for actions of a vice president who caused wetlands to be filled without a permit).
86. United States v. Hilton Hotels Corp., 467 F.2d 1000, 1004-07 (9th Cir. 1972), *cert. denied,* 409 U.S. 1125 (1973) (corporation liable for action of its agents even if they violated company policy in committing the act that constituted the crime).
87. On Sept. 30, 2011, U.S. district court Judge Rebecca Doherty found that former EPA CID Special Agent Keith Phillips had, "for his own purposes, set out with intent and reckless and callous disregard for anyone's rights ... and reckless disregard for the processes and power which had been bestowed upon him, to effectively destroy another man's life . . .." *See* Vidrine v. United States, No. 6:07-cv-01204, at 141 (W.D. La., *judgment entered* Sept. 30, 2011). Although his motive was never fully elicited, it appears Phillips headed an investigation that spanned three years and resulted in the indictment of Hubert Vidrine Jr. and Canal Refining Company of Church Point, Louisiana, for purposes of maintaining a sexual affair with an FBI agent who was also assigned to the case, despite Phillips' knowledge that there was insufficient evidence to indict Vidrine.
88. United States v. Ionia Management S.A., 498 F. Supp. 2d 477 (D. Conn. 2007), *decision reached on appeal,* United States v. Ionia Management S.A., 555 F.3d 303 (2d Cir. 2009).
89. United States v. Ionia Management S.A., 555 F.3d 303 (2d Cir. 2009).
90. *Id.*

Thus, a company's establishment of an environmental policy, even with diligent internal enforcement efforts, may not suffice to take the acts of the employee outside the scope of his or her employment.[91] This presents a frustrating reality for many corporations who spend millions of dollars on compliance training and other initiatives, and ultimately undermines a company's incentive for doing so. It also is contrary to the model jury instructions for Corporate Criminal responsibility in the Federal Jury Practice and Instructions.[92]

Under the doctrine of collective knowledge, the aggregate knowledge of all employees may also be imputed to the corporation. A company may be found to have knowingly engaged in conduct constituting a crime based on proof that one employee knew facts relating to one element of the offense and other employees had knowledge relating to other essential elements, even though no one person had knowledge of all necessary facts.[93] Interestingly, the Massachusetts Supreme Judicial Court recently refused to find a corporation liable under the collective knowledge doctrine where there was not a single employee who could be found liable for the offense.[94] The legitimacy of the U.S. Court of Appeals for the First Circuit's often-cited, but rarely followed reasoning in *Bank of New England*, which supports imposition of corporate liability based upon the collective knowledge doctrine, may therefore be questionable.

For individual defendants, prosecutors also have several avenues through which they may prove sufficient knowledge for conviction of environmental offenses, including: (1) direct evidence; (2) willful blindness/conscious avoidance; (3) circumstantial evidence; and (4) the responsible corporate officer doctrine.

1. Direct Evidence

Typically, the most effective means of proving criminal knowledge is through direct evidence that the individual personally was involved in the commission of the offense or personally aided and abetted the violation. A corporate officer who instructs his or her subordinates to perform acts that violate environmental laws is liable for such violations, even if the officer does not directly participate in the prohibited conduct.[95] For example, in *Hoflin*, the defendant was convicted of violating RCRA based on proof that he instructed his employees to bury drums containing hazardous wastes after receiving warnings that such disposal would violate certain permits.[96] Similarly, in *United States v. Carr*,[97] the defendant was convicted under CERCLA for failing to report a release of a hazardous substance based on evidence that he instructed workers to dump a truckload of paint cans into a pond, and then told the workers to dump earth into the pond.

2. Willful Blindness/Conscious Avoidance

The prosecution may obtain a conviction by proving that the defendant intentionally avoided learning, or was willfully blind to, the truth. For example, in *Hayes International*, the court held that a corporate

---

91. United States v. Beusch, 596 F.2d 871, 877-78 (9th Cir. 1979) (corporation may be liable for acts of employees done contrary to express instructions and policies, but existence of such policies may be considered in determining whether employee in fact acted to benefit the corporation).

92. The relevant Jury Instruction states, "A corporate defendant—like an individual defendant—however, may not avoid responsibility for its actions by meaningless or purely self-serving pronouncements. Similarly a corporate defendant— like an individual defendant—may not be held responsible for acts which it tries to prevent." 1A Fed. Jury Prac. & Instr. §18:05 (6th ed.) (2012). These proposed instructions are followed by a Note:

> There is nothing in the law that requires that a corporation be held criminally responsible for the action of a rogue employee that, in good faith, the corporation attempted to prevent. Unless a corporation is relieved of criminal liability for acts committed against genuine corporate policy and directives, there is absolutely no compelling reason for a corporation to either direct its agents to conform to the criminal law or to police such policies or, for that matter, to police its employees. To avoid criminal responsibility, however, the corporation must be acting in good faith when it prohibits the conduct and must make a diligent effort to police the directive.

93. *E.g.*, United States v. Bank of New England, N.A., 821 F.2d 844, 856 (1st Cir.), *cert. denied*, 484 U.S. 943 (1987) (collective knowledge instruction for corporation; the aggregate knowledge obtained by corporate employees constitutes the corporation's knowledge).

94. *See* Commonwealth v. Life Care Ctrs. of Am. Inc., 926 N.E.2d 206, 210-11 (Mass. 2010).

95. *E.g.*, United States v. Johnson & Towers, Inc., 741 F.2d 662, 666-67, 14 ELR 20634 (3d Cir. 1984), *cert. denied*, 469 U.S. 1208 (1985).

96. United States v. Hoflin, 880 F.2d 1033, 19 ELR 21140 (9th Cir. 1989), *cert. denied*, 493 U.S. 1083 (1990).

97. 880 F.2d 1550, 19 ELR 21137 (2d Cir. 1989).

employee's willful failure to determine the permit status of a facility to which hazardous waste had been shipped satisfied the requirement of knowledge of permit status under RCRA.[98]

The defendant also may be convicted based on a showing that he consciously avoided learning the truth after receiving substantial warning signs and therefore had the equivalent of knowledge. "A conscious avoidance charge is appropriate (a) when the element of knowledge is in dispute, and (b) the evidence would permit a rational juror to conclude beyond a reasonable doubt 'that the defendant was aware of a high probability of the fact in dispute and consciously avoided confirming that fact.'"[99]

3. Circumstantial Evidence

Knowledge of environmental crimes can be proved by circumstantial evidence. For example, in *Hayes International*, a corporation and one employee were charged with knowingly transporting hazardous waste to an unpermitted facility in violation of RCRA §3008(d)(1). The prosecution proved that the employee knew that the facility to which the paint waste was shipped derived no economic benefit from it, but failed to follow internal corporate procedures requiring disposal of wastes lacking resale value only at EPA-approved sites. Even though the government failed to present direct proof that the employee knew that the waste was not being recycled, the court held that this circumstantial evidence successfully proved guilty knowledge.[100] The court recognized, however, that the employee's good-faith belief that the material was being recycled, if proved, would be a valid affirmative defense.[101]

In particular, the knowing endangerment provisions of RCRA, the CAA, and the CWA expressly provide that in proving knowledge, circumstantial evidence may be used, including evidence that the defendant took affirmative steps to shield himself from relevant information.[102]

Other courts have permitted the inference of criminal knowledge to be based on what the accused would have known through the exercise of reasonable diligence, when the defendant had some affirmative duty to know the facts or to investigate the situation. For example, in *United States v. Dee*,[103] the Fourth Circuit found that knowledge could be inferred with respect to one of the defendants from evidence that he was informed by safety inspectors and employees of problems with stored chemicals. The defendant did not respond but merely "told staff to clean it up as best they could."[104] The court also found that knowledge could be inferred from evidence that the defendant was in charge of operations at the plant, had previously taken action with respect to the chemicals' storage, repeatedly ignored warnings, and took no actions to comply with RCRA.[105]

II. The Responsible Corporate Officer Doctrine

Where the prosecution has difficulty gathering evidence sufficient to satisfy the knowledge element of environmental offenses, the DOJ often will rely on the responsible corporate officer (RCO) doctrine as a substitute for proof of actual knowledge.[106] In rare instances, courts have accepted this RCO argument, i.e., that proof that an individual occupied a supervisory position in the offending corporation is sufficient

98. United States v. Hayes Int'l Corp., 786 F.2d 1499, 16 ELR 20717 (11th Cir. 1986). In *United States v. Pacific Hide & Fur Depot, Inc.*, however, the Ninth Circuit reversed a conviction under TSCA, where the trial court's instructions had allowed the jury to convict the defendant of knowing violations on the basis of mere reckless conduct. 768 F.2d 1096, 15 ELR 20851 (9th Cir. 1985). The court held that although liability for knowing violations of TSCA could be based on willful blindness, "[i]t is not enough that [the] defendant was mistaken, recklessly disregarded the truth, or negligently failed to inquire." *Id.* at 1098 (overruled in part by United States v. Heredia, 483 F.3d 913, 920 (9th Cir. 2007).

99. United States v. Hopkins, 53 F.3d 533, 542, 25 ELR 21178 (2d Cir. 1995) (citations omitted), *cert. denied,* Hopkins v. United States, 516 U.S. 107 (1996); *see also* United States v. Buckley, 934 F.2d 84, 88, 21 ELR 21113, 21115 (6th Cir. 1991).

100. *Hayes International*, 786 F.2d at 1506-07.

101. *Id.* at 1506.

102. 42 U.S.C. §6928(f)(2), ELR Stat. RCRA §3008(f)(2); *id.* §7413(c)(5)(B), ELR Stat. CAA §113(c)(5)(B); 33 U.S.C. §1319(c)(3)(B), ELR Stat. FWPCA §309(c)(3)(B).

103. United States v. Dee, 912 F.2d 741, 21 ELR 20051 (4th Cir. 1990), *cert. denied,* Dee v. United States, 499 U.S. 919 (1991).

104. *Id.* at 747.

105. *See, e.g.*, United States v. White, 766 F. Supp. 873, 22 ELR 20050 (E.D. Wash. 1991); United States v. Brittain, 931 F.2d 1413, 21 ELR 21092 (10th Cir. 1991).

106. Under the CWA and CAA, a person subject to the provisions of the Act is defined, for purposes of the criminal provisions, to specifically include a responsible corporate officer. 33 U.S.C. §1319(c)(6) (CWA); 42 U.S.C. §7413(c)(6) (CAA).

to impute criminal knowledge from a subordinate employee with guilty knowledge to a superior who was unaware of the violations.[107] In most cases, however, the courts have interpreted the RCO doctrine as providing an additional piece of circumstantial evidence with which the government may seek to satisfy the required knowledge element, but does not, by itself, provide a conclusive means of imputing guilty knowledge to senior officials.[108]

DOJ policy announcements appear to have accepted as a matter of charging policy this substantive limitation on the scope of the RCO doctrine. In each case, however, in which federal prosecutors rely on this approach to proving knowledge, prosecutors and defense counsel inevitably spar over the evidence that may be admitted in support of this theory of liability and the terms of the instruction concerning the circumstances on which the jury may take the individual defendant's corporate position into account in determining whether he is criminally liable.[109]

Recently, FDA officials have carried through on their announced intentions to utilize the RCO doctrine more aggressively.[110] For example, in *United States* v. *Purdue Frederick Co., Inc.*, three former senior corporate officers of a pharmaceutical company were convicted of RCO misdemeanors as a result of plea agreements. The company itself pleaded guilty to a felony charge of "misbranding OxyContin, a prescription opioid pain medication, with the intent to defraud or mislead . . ..."[111] The plea agreement asserted that company personnel had been involved in the false and misleading marketing of OxyContin for a period exceeding five years.[112] The executives—the chief scientific officer, the executive vice president and chief legal officer, and the president and chief executive officer— also pleaded guilty to misdemeanor misbranding charges under the RCO, even though they were not "charged with personal knowledge of the misbranding or with any personal intent to defraud."[113] The plea agreements provided for payment of $34.5 million to a state fund and no term of incarceration for the individuals.[114] The executives subsequently were excluded by the U.S. Department of Health and Human Services (HHS) from participating in any federal health care program for 12 years.[115]

A. *Origins of the Responsible Corporate Officer Doctrine*

The RCO doctrine evolved from two Supreme Court cases decided under the Federal Food, Drug, and Cosmetic Act (FDCA), a strict liability statute with misdemeanor penalties.

In *United States v. Dotterweich*,[116] the Supreme Court held that the president of a company could be convicted of illegally distributing adulterated drugs through acts committed by his subordinates. The Court held that no showing of mens rea was necessary to establish culpability under the FFDCA, which it characterized as a "public welfare statute." The Court recognized that when applied to individuals acting on behalf of a company, the statute might be read to "sweep . . . within its condemnation any person however

107. *See, e.g.*, *Brittain*, 931 F.2d at 1413.
108. *See, e.g.*, United States v. MacDonald & Watson Waste Oil Co., 933 F.2d 35, 21 ELR 21449 (1st Cir. 1991).
109. David G. Dickman et al., *Environmental Counselor,* Responsible Corporate Officers and Environmental Criminal Liability: More Court Opinions, More Court Confusion (Sept. 15, 2002); Joseph G. Block, *The Responsible Corporate Officer Doctrine—Can You Go to Jail for What You Don't Know?*, Envtl. L. Nw. Sch. Lewis & Clark Coll. (Sept. 1992).
110. *See, e.g.*, Letter from FDA Commissioner Margaret A. Hamburg, to Sen. Charles E. Grassley 2 (Mar. 4, 2010), http://webcache.googleusercontent.com/search?q=cache:HzPj_PSxOf0J:www.grassley.senate.gov/about/upload/FDA-3-4-10-Hamburg-letter-to-Grassley-re-GAO-report-on-OCI.pdf+&cd=1&hl=en&ct=clnk&gl=us (last visited June 4, 2013) (citing a committee recommendation to "increase the appropriate use of misdemeanor prosecutions, a valuable enforcement tool, to hold responsible corporate officials accountable"); Testimony of Lewis Morris, Chief Counsel, to the HHS IG, House Committee on Ways and Means, Subcomm. on Oversight (Mar. 2, 2011), http://oig.hhs.gov/testimony/docs/2011/morris_testimony_03022011.pdf (last visited May 28, 2013) ("We intend to use [exclusion authority] in a broader range of circumstances"); see HHS Guidance for Implementing Permissive Exclusion Authority (Oct. 2010), http://www.oig.hhs.gov/fraud/exclusions/files/permissive_excl_under_1128b15_10192010.pdf (last visited May 28, 2013); FDA Guidance for *Park* Doctrine Prosecutions (Jan. 26, 2011), http://www.fda.gov/ICECI/ComplianceManuals/RegulatoryProceduresManual/ucm176738.htm#SUB6-5-3 (last visited May 28, 2013).
111. United States v. Purdue Frederick Co., Inc., 495 F. Supp. 2d 569, 570 (W.D. Va. 2007).
112. *Id.* at 571.
113. *Id.* at 570-71.
114. *Id.* at 573.
115. Friedman v. Sibelius, 686 F.3d 813 (402 U.S. App. D.C. 15 (2012)), *rehearing, en banc, denied*, 2012 U.S. App. LEXIS 24631 (affirming HHS exclusion).
116. 320 U.S. 277 (1943).

remotely entangled in the proscribed shipment."[117] The Court, however, narrowed the range of individuals subject to liability to finding that "[t]he offense is committed . . . by all who [have] a responsible share in the furtherance of the transaction which the statute outlaws."[118] But the Court declined to define the scope of the term "responsible share," leaving this definition to "the good sense of prosecutors, the wise guidance of trial judges, and the ultimate judgment of juries."[119]

In *United States v. Park*,[120] the chief executive officer of a large national retail food operation was convicted of illegally distributing rodent-infested food, which had been discovered at a corporate warehouse. The evidence showed that the U.S. Food and Drug Administration had previously notified the officer of a similar problem at a different warehouse and that he had actual notice of the problem at the warehouse where the contaminated food was found. The prosecution also showed that one vice president was in charge of sanitation for both facilities and that the defendant had previously conferred with that subordinate, as well as other officers to ensure that corrective action would be taken.

The CEO did not participate in the acts causing the violation, but was nonetheless convicted under this strict liability provision. On appeal, he claimed that he was denied due process by being convicted without proof of wrongful action on his part. The Supreme Court held that the government could establish liability by demonstrating "that the defendant had, by reasons of his position in the corporation, responsibility and authority either to prevent in the first instance, or promptly to correct, the violation complained of, and that he failed to do so."[121] The Court found that the conviction was proper because the defendant was aware that the company's internal system for ensuring sanitary conditions was not working, but failed to restructure the system once notified that similar problems had arisen at two warehouses.[122] The Court recognized, however, that the officer could have raised an affirmative defense that he was powerless to prevent the violation, and that he could have sought a jury instruction requiring the government to prove beyond a reasonable doubt that he had been capable of preventing the violation.

Three Justices dissented. They argued that the jury was provided with no meaningful guidance as to what constituted a "responsible relation" to the offense, and could have convicted based solely on the defendant's corporate position.[123] The dissenters were particularly concerned that the decision imposed criminal liability on the officer for conduct of which he was unaware and in which he did not participate. They argued:

> The standardless conviction approved today can serve in another case tomorrow to support a felony conviction and a substantial prison sentence. However highly the Court may regard the social objective of the [FFDCA], that regard cannot serve to justify a criminal conviction so wholly alien to fundamental principles of our law.[124]

B. *The Polar Decisions Extending the Responsible Corporate Officer Doctrine to Environmental Cases*

The DOJ periodically seeks to apply the RCO doctrine to prove criminal liability under both misdemeanor (negligence) and felony (knowledge) statutes in which evidence of direct knowledge may be inadequate to convict. Prosecutors have justified this approach on two grounds. First, courts have held these provisions to be public welfare statutes, like the applicable statute in *Dotterweich* and *Park*. Second, the CAA and the CWA expressly include the term "responsible corporate officer" in their respective definitions of persons who can be liable. The statues, however, do not define the class of individuals who may be considered responsible corporate officers, and the legislative history does not provide any further guidance. Accordingly, courts have had difficulty translating the doctrine to the environmental area. Complications have

117. *Id.* at 284.
118. *Id.*
119. *Id.* at 285.
120. 421 U.S. 658 (1975).
121. *Id.* at 673-74.
122. *Id.* at 677.
123. *Park,* 421 U.S. at 679-80 (Stewart, J., dissenting).
124. *Id.* at 683.

arisen partly because federal environmental criminal provisions require a minimal showing of knowledge, and partly because of the ambiguous standards announced in *Dotterweich* and *Park.*

In practical terms, the critical question is whether the government may prove a corporate officer has guilty knowledge simply by showing that the person would have known that environmental violations were occurring had the officer been properly fulfilling his or her duties. The question also arises whether this characterization of the RCO doctrine could allow imposition of vicarious criminal liability for corporate negligence and mismanagement, thereby reading the requirement of criminal knowledge out of these laws insofar as applied to senior corporate officers.

Two cases serve as bookends that define the application of the doctrine in the environmental context. The case on which prosecutors tend to rely is *United States v. Brittain.*[125] The defendant, a city's public utilities director with general supervisory authority over the operation of its wastewater treatment plant, was charged with two misdemeanor counts under §§301(a) and 309(c)(1) of the CWA for unlawful discharges into navigable waters. The evidence showed that the staff had advised the director that pollutants were being discharged into a local creek in violation of permit limits. He also had personally observed the discharges on two occasions, but instructed the plant supervisor not to report them to the EPA, contrary to the city's permit requirement.

The trial court rejected the government's argument that the director could be held criminally liable for these violations under the RCO doctrine. Consequently, this theory of liability was not submitted to the jury due to the defendant's successful objection. The director nonetheless was convicted. On appeal, he argued that there was no evidence that he personally caused the unlawful discharge and that the only proof of his involvement with the discharge was his official relationship to the polluting entity. The director claimed that he could not be held liable under the Act's definition of an "individual," and could only be found liable if the government proved that he was the permittee or a responsible corporate officer—a charge that had not been submitted to the jury.

The Tenth Circuit affirmed the convictions, holding that the term "responsible corporate officer" in the CWA did not narrow the range of "individuals" subject to criminal liability. Although the evidence would have permitted the court to treat the case as one in which the defendant was directly involved in the violation, it chose to address the issue in terms of the RCO doctrine:

> We think that Congress perceived this objective [restoration of the integrity of the nation's waters] to outweigh hardships suffered by "responsible corporate officers" who are held criminally liable in spite of their lack of "consciousness of wrongdoing," . . .. Under this interpretation, a "responsible corporation officer," to be held criminally liable, would not have to "willfully or negligently" cause a permit violation. Instead, the willfulness or negligence of the actor would be imputed to him by virtue of his position of responsibility.[126]

Because the jury was charged on an actual knowledge theory, the broad language about imputation of willfulness or negligence is dictum. Further, the case involved misdemeanor convictions, not felonies, so its precedential significance arguably should be limited for environmental felony prosecutions. Nevertheless, Brittain is the strongest support for an aggressive interpretation of the RCO doctrine.

By contrast, defense counsel typically rely on *United States v. MacDonald & Watson Waste Oil Co.*[127] There, corporation and its president were convicted on two counts each of knowingly transporting hazardous waste to a facility that did not have a permit, in violation of §3008(d)(1) of RCRA. The evidence showed that hazardous waste had been illegally transported to an unpermitted site operated by the company, under the supervision of a corporate employee. The evidence further showed that the company president had participated in the day-to-day management of that site and had been warned on other occasions that his company had illegally disposed of hazardous waste. There was, however, no direct evidence that the president knew of the particular unlawful shipment charged in the indictment.

The trial court issued the following instruction on the RCO doctrine:

---

125. 931 F.2d 1413, 21 ELR 21092 (10th Cir. 1991).
126. *Id.* at 1419.
127. United States v. MacDonald & Watson Waste Oil Co., 933 F.2d 35, 21 ELR 21449 (1st Cir. 1993).

> When an individual defendant is also a corporate officer, the government may prove that individual's knowledge in either of two ways. The first way is to demonstrate that the defendant had actual knowledge of the act in question. The second way is to establish that the defendant was what is called a responsible officer of the corporation committing the act. In order to prove that a person is a responsible corporate officer three things must be shown.
>
> First, it must be shown that the person is an officer of the corporation, not merely an employee.
>
> Second, it must be shown that the officer had direct responsibility for the activities that are alleged to be illegal. Simply being an officer or even the president of a corporation is not enough. The government must prove that the person had a responsibility to supervise the activities in question.
>
> And the third requirement is that the officer must have known or believed that the illegal activity of the type alleged occurred.[128]

The First Circuit overturned the president's conviction, holding that the district court had improperly applied the RCO doctrine "as a substitute mean of proving the explicit knowledge element of this RCRA felony."[129] The court held that the charge was defective because it instructed the jury "that proof that [the president] was a responsible corporate officer would conclusively prove the element of his knowledge.[130] The court rejected the government's argument that the instruction merely permitted use of the doctrine to raise the inference of guilty knowledge, and observed that the instructions on willful blindness and circumstantial evidence:

> [W]ould have sufficed had it merely been the court's purpose to point out that knowledge could established by circumstantial evidence, although the court could, had it wished, have elaborated on the extent to which [the president's] responsibilities and duties might lead to a reasonable inference that he knew of the [illegal disposal].[131]

Thus, absent proof that the president had actual knowledge of the specific shipments charged in the indictment, the conviction was overturned.

MacDonald & Watson established that the RCO doctrine provides an additional piece of circumstantial evidence to prove criminal liability. This pathway does not, however, provide an independent means by which guilty knowledge may be imputed from an employee with direct responsibility for an environmental violation to a supervising employee or an officer at headquarters.

C. Application of the Responsible Corporate Officer Doctrine in Recent Environmental Cases

Brittain and *MacDonald & Watson* continue to define the outer boundaries within which federal prosecutors and defense counsel conduct their arguments about the strength of the evidence against an officer and the instructions that the trial judge should issue to guide the jury in applying the reasonable corporate officer doctrine. While issues involving application of the doctrine have been bitterly fought in a series of cases, the contours of the doctrine have not changed appreciably in recent years.

The most significant recent decisions include:

In *United States v. Iverson*,[132] the court held that a person qualifies as a responsible corporate officer if he "has the authority to exercise control over the corporation's activity that caused the illegal discharges, and that "[t]here" is no requirement that the officer in fact exercise such authority or that the corporation expressly vest a duty in the officer to oversee the activity."[133] On this basis, the officer could be convicted without proof that he personally had taken an affirmative act that actually caused the illegal discharges.

In *United States v. Hanousek*,[134] the court concluded that the defendant could be convicted under the RCO doctrine for a misdemeanor violation of the CWA "only on the basis of his own negligent conduct

---

128. *Id.* at 50-51.
129. *Id.* at 52.
130. *Id.*
131. *Id.*
132. 162 F.3d 1015, 29 ELR 20367 (9th Cir. 1998).
133. *Id.* at 1025.
134. 176 F.3d 1116, 29 ELR 21049 (9th Cir. 1999), *cert. denied*, 528 U.S. 1102 (2000).

and not on the basis of the negligence of others . . . ."[135] An officer thus may not be held vicariously liable for the negligence of his subordinates, but his own negligent acts must have contributed to an illegal discharge that was reasonably foreseeable from the failure to exercise due care.

In *United States v. Hong*,[136] the defendant was convicted under the RCO doctrine for misdemeanor violations of the CWA for negligent discharges of pollutants even though he was not formally an officer of the company. "The gravamen of liability as a responsible corporate officer is not one's corporate title or the lack thereof; rather the pertinent question is whether the defendant bore such a relation to the corporation it is appropriate to hold him criminally liable for failing to prevent the charged violation of the CWA."[137]

In sum, the current state of the law can be summarized as follows:

> A person may be found guilty as a "responsible corporate officer" if the government proves beyond a reasonable doubt that:
>
> (1) he had knowledge of the facts that gave rise to the violation;
>
> (2) he had the authority and capacity to prevent the violation; and
>
> (3) he failed to prevent the violation.[138]

D. Concluding Thoughts on the Responsible Corporate Officer Doctrine

In practical terms, the actual scope of the RCO doctrine as applied to corporate officials depends to an important degree on how aggressive the DOJ prosecutor wishes to be in a particular case. Under this doctrine, a corporate officer may not be held liable solely because of his position. But evidence of his position can constitute important circumstantial evidence that combined with more direct evidence of knowledge or participation, or an inference that his staff was likely to have informed an official of the existence of a risk that an illegal discharge might occur, could be sufficient to satisfy the prosecutor's duty to prove the requisite mental element required for conviction of an environmental offense.

Although there are legal and policy limits on the reach of RCO doctrine, it has nonetheless continued to play a critical role in environmental investigations. The government's ability to use the doctrine as circumstantial proof of actual knowledge reduces the quantum of evidence otherwise necessary to satisfy the knowledge element for officials at corporate headquarters. This threat to senior corporate officials constitutes a substantial weapon in the prosecutor's arsenal and creates a leverage opportunity for the prosecution in negotiations with a corporation that seeks a comprehensive resolution of all possible criminal charges.

III. Defense Strategies in Environmental Criminal Cases

With the diminution of the knowledge element, defense strategies in environmental cases tend to focus on difficulties in understanding how the complex regulatory schemes work and on challenges to the government's scientific proof. The following five cases stand out as examples of successful regulatory defenses.

- *United States v. Plaza Health Laboratories, Inc.*[139] The Second Circuit held that the key definitional term "point source" in the CWA is ambiguous. Applying the rule of lenity, the court held that a human being is not a point source and reversed criminal convictions under CWA §§301(a) and 309(c)(2) for disposing of vials containing tainted blood in navigable waters.
- *United States v. Heuer.*[140] The Ninth Circuit reversed a conviction under RCRA §3008(d)(2)(B) for illegal disposal of hazardous waste, holding that in order "to support [criminal] liability under [§3008(d)(2)(B)] a condition, express or implied, must be clear on the face of a permit."[141] The court

135. *Id.* at 1123.
136. 242 F.3d 528, 31 ELR 20509 (4th Cir. 2001), *cert. denied*, 534 U.S. 823 (2001).
137. *Id.* at 531.
138. Jury Instructions in United States v. McWane, Inc., No. 261-1, 2:04-cr-00199 (N.D. Ala. 2005), included hereto as Appendix 15.
139. 3 F.3d 643, 23 ELR 21526 (2d Cir. 1993), *cert. denied sub nom.* United States v. Villegas, 512 U.S. 1245 (1994).
140. 4 F.3d 723, 23 ELR 21357 (9th Cir. 1993), *cert. denied*, Heuer v. United States, 510 U.S. 1164 (1994).
141. *Id.* at 731.

found that there was no express provision in the facility's permit that prohibited it from burning wastes that were generated at other facilities, and this condition could neither be implied from prior course of dealings between the regulator and the permit holder nor deemed incorporated by reference.

- *United States v. Self.*[142] The Tenth Circuit found that EPA's RCRA regulations were ambiguous as to whether natural gas condensate burned as fuel was classified as a hazardous waste. The court interpreted the ambiguous language against the government and reversed several RCRA convictions predicated on this ground.

- *United States v. Goodner Bros. Aircraft.*[143] The Eighth Circuit overturned criminal convictions that were premised on the RCRA mixture rule, which the U.S. Court of Appeals for the District of Columbia Circuit had since invalidated based on EPA's failure to comply with the Administrative Procedure Act in promulgating the rule.[144]

- *Adamo Wrecking Co. v. United States.*[145] This case established a narrow exception to the CAA's preclusive review provision, which provides that the validity of EPA emissions standards may be challenged only by civil suits filed in the D.C. Circuit immediately after the rules are promulgated.[146] *Adamo* involved a CAA criminal prosecution in which the defendant challenged EPA's authority to issue a work practice standard for asbestos in place of a rule. The court of appeals held that the preclusive review provision barred the defense that EPA had authority only to issue an emissions standard, not a work practice standard. The Supreme Court reversed, holding that the defendant's objection that the work practice standard was invalid was not subject to the preclusive review provision, and that the district court had jurisdiction to entertain this objection to the indictment.[147]

Although several such approaches have worked, broader lessons can be drawn from the more common cases in which courts have rejected proffered defenses. For example:

- *United States v. Louisville Edible Oil Products, Inc.*[148] The Sixth Circuit rejected a double jeopardy argument that the federal government could not bring criminal charges against a company against which a local environmental agency had already imposed large fines for violations of the CAA and CERCLA.

- *United States v. Mills.*[149] The court rejected the defendants' argument that Congress had unconstitutionally delegated to an administrative agency the power under the CWA to define "waters of the United States" as including "wetlands."

- *United States v. Ellen.*[150] The Fourth Circuit rejected arguments that uncertainty over the definition of "wetlands" denied the defendant due process and violated the Ex Post Facto Clause.

- *United States v. Boldt.*[151] The First Circuit held that the CWA does not recognize a defense of economic or business necessity. Thus, the issue of whether the only alternative to noncompliance was closure of the plant could not be presented to the jury.

- *United States v. Marathon Development Corp.*[152] The First Circuit rejected arguments that provisions in the CWA authorizing states to impose more stringent water quality standards than those required by EPA denied criminal defendants equal protection of the law.

142. 2 F.3d 1071, 23 ELR 21301 (10th Cir. 1993).
143. 966 F.2d 380, 22 ELR 21201 (8th Cir. 1992), *cert. denied*, Goodner v. United States, 506 U.S. 1049 (1993).
144. *See* Shell Oil Co. v. EPA, 950 F.2d 741, 22 ELR 20305 (D.C. Cir. 1991, *amended* 1992).
145. 434 U.S. 275, 8 ELR 20171 (1978), *vacated without opinion*, United States v. Adamo Wrecking Co., 571 F.2d 582 (6th Cir. Mich. 1978).
146. 42 U.S.C. §7607(b), ELR Stat. CAA §307(b).
147. *Adamo*, 434 U.S. at 285.
148. 926 F.2d 584, 21 ELR 20690 (6th Cir. 1991), *cert. denied*, 502 U.S. 859 (1991).
149. 817 F. Supp. 1546, 23 ELR 21096 (N.D. Fla. 1993).
150. 961 F.2d 462, 22 ELR 21282 (4th Cir. 1992), *cert. denied*, 506 U.S. 875 (1992).
151. 929 F.2d 35, 21 ELR 20998 (1st Cir. 1991).
152. 867 F.2d 96, 19 ELR 20683 (1st Cir. 1989).

The defense of entrapment by estoppel, i.e., that the defendant acted in reliance on instructions or guidance from a state or federal official about how to comply with the environmental rules governing the conduct that was the subject of the indictment, has also been argued, but the authors are unaware of it ever being successful.

In sum, as long as environmental crimes continue to be subject to a de minimus knowledge requirement, defendants will have little hope of defeating the government at trial on the issue of intent. This harsh reality gives prosecutors substantial leverage to compel targets to enter into plea agreements, either at the completion of the criminal investigation or before trial. For the year 2012 (based on data from Oct. 1, 2011 to Sept. 30, 2012), the U.S. Sentencing Commission found that 97% of all environmental and wildlife cases concluded with a plea, and the remaining 3% went to trial.[153] Accordingly, in most cases, the best means of avoiding liability will be through successful defense of the investigation. It is in this arena that seasoned environmental crimes counsel can make a particularly significant difference in the outcome. Pretrial defense strategies are discussed in Chapters Five and Six.

153. *See* U.S. Sentencing Comm'n, Preliminary Quarterly Data Report Fiscal Year 2012, Guilty Pleas and Trials in Each Primary Offense Category 42, tbl. 22 (2012) (noting there were 198 "primary offense" environmental and wildlife cases in 2012).

Chapter 5: Grand Juries, Subpoenas, Document Production Issues in the Digital Age, Internal Investigation, and More

A common way for a company to learn that it is the subject of a government investigation is for an officer, employee, or former employee to report to management that he or she has been contacted by a law enforcement agent seeking an interview. This interview is often a precursor to the receipt of a subpoena commanding the employee's appearance before a grand jury and should be treated with the utmost seriousness. The company also may learn of the government's interest in its activities through receipt of a grand jury subpoena for documents or other evidence.

This chapter discusses the basics of grand juries and grand jury subpoenas, as well as common issues that arise in this area, including conducting an internal, i.e., shadow investigation, privilege and waiver, production of documents, protecting employee and company rights, strategy decisions (including whether to enter into a joint defense agreement and/or disclose the results of the company's internal investigation), disciplining employees, corrective actions, and global settlements.

I. Grand Jury

A. *The Basics*

The Fifth Amendment states in part: "No person shall be held to answer for a capital, or otherwise infamous crime, unless on a presentment or indictment of a Grand Jury, except in cases arising in the land or naval forces, or in the Militia when in actual service in time of War or public danger." Grand jurors are generally drawn from the same pool of potential jurors as are any other jury panels, and in the same manner; however, they are not screened for bias or other improper factors.

The original purpose of the grand jury was to act as a buffer between the king (and his prosecutors) and the citizens. Critics argue that this safeguarding role has been erased, and that a prosecutor today could "indict a ham sandwich" if he or she so chose. As the American Bar Association (ABA) has stated:

> The grand jury is independent in theory, and although the instructions given to the grand jurors inform them they are to use their judgment, the practical realities of the situation mitigate against it.
>
> The grand jury hears only cases brought to it by the prosecutor. The prosecutor decides which witnesses to call. The prosecutor decides which witnesses will receive immunity. The basic questioning is done by the prosecutor on a theory he or she articulates. The grand jury members are generally permitted to ask questions at the end of a witness's testimony. The prosecutor generally decides if he or she has enough evidence to seek an indictment. Occasionally the grand jurors may be asked whether they would like to hear any additional witnesses, but since their job is only to judge what the prosecutor has produced, they rarely ask to do so.
>
> The prosecutor drafts the charges and reads them to the grand jury. There is no requirement that the grand jury be read any instructions on the law, and such instructions are rarely given.[1]

---

1. ABA, *FAQs About the Grand Jury System*, http://www.abanow.org/2010/03/faqs-about-the-grand-jury-system (last visited May 28, 2013).

The primary function of the modern grand jury is to review the evidence presented by the prosecutor and determine whether there is probable cause to return an indictment. If the grand jury fails to return an indictment, the prosecutor can try again to obtain an indictment, i.e., double jeopardy does not apply.

An indictment normally consists of a short and plain statement of where, when, and how the defendant allegedly committed the offense. Each offense must be set out in a separate count. Indictments for complex crimes, such as environmental crimes, may consist of hundreds of pages.

For criminal environmental investigations, "long-term" grand juries will typically be impaneled. These grand juries generally sit fewer days each week, and their terms can be extended in six-month increments for up to three years. Should a grand jury "expire" before an indictment can be returned, the prosecutor need not re-present all of the evidence to the new grand jury. The new grand jury is provided with transcripts of previous proceedings for its review.

Rule 6(e) of the Federal Rules of Criminal Procedure prohibits grand jurors from disclosing what happened before the grand jury, unless they are ordered to do so in a judicial proceeding. Witnesses before a grand jury are not so prohibited, however. Thus, interviewing grand jury witnesses (should they be willing) on the substance of their testimony is a common component of a company's internal investigation, as will be discussed later.

While a witness may not have his or her lawyer present in the grand jury room, he or she may interrupt the testimony and leave the grand jury room to consult with counsel. A witness called before a grand jury under a grant of immunity may not refuse to testify based upon concerns about self-incrimination. The grant of immunity overcomes the witness' privilege against self-incrimination. This grant of immunity prohibits the prosecutor from using that testimony (or the "fruits" of such testimony) to bring charges against the witness. Should the prosecutor decide to pursue charges, she bears the burden of proving an independent source for the evidence. Notably, however, false testimony before a grand jury may result in the witness being separately prosecuted for perjury.

The target of a grand jury investigation has no right to present evidence in his or her defense. Generally, a target is not called before the grand jury unless it is essential for the prosecutor to do so. Many prosecutors will inform a witness if they are a target of the grand jury investigation, if asked. Nevertheless, only the U.S. Court of Appeals for the Second Circuit requires that such information be provided as a matter of law.[2] Thus, if your client is contacted by the government, it is important to determine his or her status (witness, subject or target) before consenting to an interview. Depending upon what the prosecutor divulges, it may be prudent to obtain some sort of immunity from prosecution for information shared by your client during the interview,[3] or to provide an attorney proffer. In extreme circumstances, it may be advisable for your client to avoid being interviewed through reliance on the Fifth Amendment's privilege against self-incrimination. Such a refusal, however, generally results in indictment.

B. *The Grand Jury Subpoena*

A grand jury has broad power to investigate, and the scope of its subpoena power is co-extensive. All relevant witnesses, non-privileged documents, and other physical evidence may be subpoenaed so long as the demand is not unreasonably burdensome on the recipient. The prosecutor may not use a grand jury subpoena to conduct a "fishing expedition"[4]; however, the low burden of "relevance" is easily met, and a subpoena is rarely invalidated on the basis that it sought information irrelevant to the grand jury's investigation. Subpoenas also may not be used to conduct civil investigations, trial discovery, or to harass or intimidate those subpoenaed. Showing misuse of a grand jury or its subpoena powers is a difficult burden for the defense to meet, however.

When responding to a subpoena *duces tecum*, i.e., for documents or other evidence, counsel should remember that the obligation to respond to the subpoena is a continuing one.[5] Thus, later-discovered mate-

2. United States v. Jacobs, 547 F.2d 772 (2d Cir. 1976), *cert. dismissed*, 436 U.S. 31 (1978).
3. This is often referred to as "Queen for the Day" immunity.
4. United States v. R. Enterprises, Inc., 498 U.S. 292 (1991); FTC v. American Tobacco Co., 264 U.S. 298, 305-06 (1924).
5. United States v. Barth, 745 F.2d 184, 189 (2d Cir. 1984), *cert. denied*, 470 U.S. 1004 (1985).

rials falling within the time frame of the subpoena must be produced to the government. The challenges of responding to a subpoena *duces tecum* in today's digital world will be discussed below.

II. Conducting an Internal (Shadow) Investigation

A. *Staffing the Investigation and Choosing the Right Counsel*

Once the decision is made to conduct in internal investigation, an immediate decision must be made as to who will conduct the investigation and how it will be staffed. While there may be occasions when the investigation does not require the involvement of attorneys, in the environmental area where the intent standard is reduced, and virtually any violation of an environmental law is potentially subject to criminal prosecution, having an attorney conduct the investigation, or at a minimum having company personnel conduct the investigation under the direction of attorneys should be a strong consideration. A major benefit also is that the involvement of attorneys will assist the company in asserting the attorney-client and work product protections for information obtained during the investigation. An important decision that corporate officers, directors, or general counsel must make shortly after learning of a government investigation is whether to retain outside counsel or to rely solely upon in-house attorneys to oversee the company's response.

In-house counsel must be involved in responding to any government investigation because their knowledge of the company is invaluable in identifying sources of information and assessing the allegations. On the other hand, outside counsel can provide the company with particular expertise in criminal matters. Further, if in-house counsel was in any way involved with the business decisions or corporate policies under investigation, the government may question the independence and validity of the results of his or her analysis and investigation. Outside counsel also may be perceived by prosecutors as more independent during negotiations.

There are several reasons why it is crucial to get criminal counsel involved at an early stage of defending an investigation. First, criminal counsel, and preferably environmental criminal counsel, is experienced in solving the many knotty, complex issues that inevitably are part of an environmental criminal case. Second, as stated above, virtually any violation of environmental laws is potentially subject to criminal prosecution. For this reason, in-house and/or civil counsel can initially underestimate the seriousness and the direction of the government's criminal investigation. Third, criminal enforcement is sufficiently different from civil enforcement—both in process and in tempo—that immediate involvement of criminal counsel is advisable as soon as the company understands that it may be the subject of any inquiry concerning environmental issues.

B. *Employee Rights Vis-à-Vis the Government*

Once a company becomes aware that it is being investigated—often as a result of a criminal search, a request to interview a current or former employee, or receipt of a grand jury subpoena for a witness or documents—the company should provide current and former employees, consultants, and contractors with a letter memorandum informing them that an investigation appears to be underway.[6] The letter memorandum should offer employees a brief overview of the matters that the government appears to be looking into, warn employees that government agents might contact them at home, and request employees to inform management if they are contacted. The letter also ought to inform employees of their rights vis-à-vis the government. These rights include the right to:

- consent to an interview;
- decline an interview;
- ask that questions be submitted in writing as an alternative to an interview;

6. We recommend that you create an advisory letter or memorandum, which creates a permanent record of what the employees were told and ensures the communication between the company and its employees will not be misconstrued.

- designate the time and place of an interview;
- be treated fairly, i.e., investigators should not employ intimidation or use express/implied threats;
- consult with a company attorney before and/or during an interview; and
- consult with a personal attorney before and/or during an interview.[7]

C. *Employee Rights Vis-à-Vis the Company*

Once they become aware that the government is investigating its actions, many companies decide to conduct an internal investigation of the events under review, often referred to as the "shadow investigation." Debriefing an employee is one of the most important ways to gather facts during the early stages of a government investigation. To ensure the debriefing is covered by the attorney-client privilege, it should be conducted by counsel, preferably outside counsel. As a part of that process, if the government has interviewed an employee, the company should ask that person to provide a debriefing. This is the best method by which to track the "evidence" that the government gathers from employee witnesses. Such information also is critical to understanding the government's theory of the case, as well as providing a springboard for the company's own investigation. Getting ahead of the government's investigation is often crucial to counsel's ability to resolve the investigation without prosecution. Thus, company counsel should debrief every individual who is interviewed by the government as soon as possible.

At the outset of any employee debriefing, before the company's attorney asks a single question, counsel should provide a brief memorandum to the employee explaining that (1) company counsel represents the company and not the employee, (2) the communications exchanged during the debriefing are privileged and confidential, and (3) the company controls the privilege and may at its own discretion choose to waive it.[8] If counsel does not provide this information to the employee in written form, he or she *must* do so orally before asking the employee the first question.[9] This communication is referred to as the *Upjohn* warning.[10]

In conducting the debriefing, counsel should ask the employee to recall the name(s), description(s), and affiliation(s) of the interviewing agent(s), the questions asked, the answers given, and what, if any, documents the employee was shown by, or gave to, the investigator(s).

When company attorneys interact with employees who have knowledge of the actions under investigation, the following "employee rights" issues should be kept in mind.

1. Targeted Individuals

Employees likely will require separate counsel when (1) the employee has been identified by the government as a "target" of the investigation, i.e., the employee is under investigation for potential individual criminal conduct, or (2) the employee appears to have taken an illegal action contrary to company policy.[11]

---

7. Whether the company will cover the fees for said attorney is an important consideration. Per the McNulty Memorandum, prosecutors are not to "take into account whether a corporation is advancing attorneys' fees to employees or agents under investigation and indictment," except in the "extremely rare case" where the company intended to impede the investigation. Deputy Attorney General Paul McNulty, Principles of Federal Prosecution of Business Organizations (Dec. 12, 2006).
8. Issues of privilege and waiver are discussed *infra* in Section D.
9. The purpose of providing the employee this information, which implicitly amount to a warning, is to clarify that counsel represents the corporation rather than the employee. *See* Upjohn v. United States, 449 U.S. 383, 391-92 (1981). Failure to provide an employee with a proper *Upjohn* warning could have severe consequences. For example, a federal district court found that as a result of inadequate *Upjohn* warnings, all statements made by the corporation's Chief Financial Officer to corporate counsel must be suppressed. *See* United States v. Nicholas, No. SACR 08-00139-CJC (C.D. Cal.) (No. 199-2, Apr. 1, 2009 Order Suppressing Privileged Communications). For more detailed analysis of the implications of the Nicholas ruling with respect to Upjohn warnings and some practical tips for warning witnesses, see David Kettle & Danette Edwards, *United States v. Henry T. Nicholas et al.*: Expanding the *Upjohn* Suppression Remedy, BNA White Collar Crime Rep. (May 22, 2009). In 2008, the ABA's White Collar Crime Committee formed a task force to recommend best practices when providing *Upjohn* warnings. Those recommendations were published in August 2008, and are available as Appendix 18.
10. *Upjohn,* 449 U.S. at 383.
11. If the need for individual counsel becomes apparent in the process of a debriefing, company counsel should consider ending the interview immediately to avoid receiving any statements that could be construed as admissions of illegal behavior, which could create eventual conflicts and waive privileges, and recommend independent counsel for the employee.

2. Whistleblowers

As a matter of law, companies cannot discipline or discharge employees for their involvement in bringing environmental violations to light.[12] Companies should have compliance mechanisms in place that encourage and facilitate internal communications of potential environmental problems.

3. Grand Jury Witnesses

Although grand jury secrecy requires the prosecutor and members of the grand jury to treat testimony as confidential, grand jury witnesses may voluntarily disclose their testimony. The company may not, however, compel such disclosure.

D. More on Interviewing Witnesses

Counsel should work with managers responsible for the company program, operation, or activity under investigation to generate a list of all current employees, former employees, and anyone else involved in the matters under investigation who may be sources of information. Once those persons have been identified, counsel and management should designate a single point of contact to serve as liaison between defense counsel and employees to contact potential interviewees and to set up appointments. Interviewees may be uncomfortable or unduly worried if the company's first contact about the matters under investigation comes from an attorney. At all costs, however, interviews should be scheduled promptly. Re-interviews should be conducted as needed. The sooner counsel is able to speak with potential witnesses (before memories and details fade), the better. In addition, a witness's recitation of past facts often supports the party who first reaches the witness.

When interviewing in the early stages of an internal investigation, counsel may not fully understand the implications of statements by witnesses. As counsel develops greater familiarity with the facts, further interviews may be necessary, especially with key individuals.

E. Collecting Documents

Counsel should follow the same approach to collecting documents as would be followed in responding to a subpoena (discussed below in Section F). During an internal investigation, documents are essential to uncovering the underlying facts. They often tell the tale themselves, can help to identify employees and other potential witnesses who should be interviewed, and can be used to refresh the memories of potential witnesses and/or to reconcile conflicting recollections.

To ensure that your company has the most complete and accurate information possible, the following steps may be necessary (if not already undertaken in response to a government subpoena):

a. initiate a fail-safe "document hold" or "litigation hold" system;

b. appoint a document custodian (generally a non-attorney). This should be a company employee *not* involved in the events underlying the government investigation;

c. request from employees the documents relevant to your investigation, and be diligent (if not tenacious) in following up your requests by meeting in person with all key individuals to review their files;

d. circulate additions and modifications to your requests in writing;

e. gather documents and other relevant information from all consultants, vendors, or other agents of the company who played a role in the activities under investigation; and

12. Most major federal environmental laws include specific provisions encouraging and protecting whistleblowers. *See, e.g.*, 33 U.S.C. §1367(a) (Clean Water Act); 42 U.S.C. §7622(a) (Clean Air Act); 42 U.S.C. §6971(a) (Resource Conservation and Recovery Act (RCRA)). Similarly, §806 of the Sarbanes-Oxley Act provides whistleblower protection for employees of publicly traded companies. *See* 18 U.S.C. §1514A. Moreover, courts uniformly have held that dismissals based on whistleblowing amount to wrongful discharges. *See, e.g.*, Phipps v. Clark Oil Ref. Corp., 408 N.W.2d 569, 571 (D. Minn. 1987).

f. track the source of all documents carefully, as an inability to provide documents that the government requests may lead the government to conclude that the company is not cooperating.

F. *Preventing Add-On Allegations*

Because the interests of the company may differ from those of its officers and employees (both current and former) during a criminal investigation, it is particularly important that the company do everything within its power to avoid even the appearance of obstruction, witness tampering, or harassment when dealing with them. To that end, the company's lawyer should keep in mind the following:

- You can advise employees that they have the right not to talk to the government, the right to talk to the government with assistance of counsel, and the right to control the terms of the interaction. But *never* instruct an employee not to answer government questions.
- When debriefing employees or other persons who have been interviewed by the government, you should have more than one company representative present. Because it is not advisable to record interviews verbatim, it is easy to end up in a "word against word" dispute over questions asked, things said, etc. Having a witness present during the interview minimizes the possibility of unfounded obstruction or witness tampering allegations, and provides a way to corroborate the recollection of the other interviewer regarding the employee's statements.
- Ask open-ended questions during interviews so as to avoid the appearance that you are leading employees to favorable recollections, interpretations, or conclusions. Where stories appear to be at odds among employees, follow up on discrepancies with care, preferably through counsel for those individuals (if they are represented) to avoid even the appearance of witness tampering. When it seems clear that an employee may be individually exposed to liability and can conceivably have interests at odds with those of the company, strongly advise that person of his or her right to individual counsel.
- Do not discipline uncooperative employees without first determining their potential role in the case and consulting a defense attorney with substantial experience in dealing with issues surrounding employee discipline in the context of an ongoing investigation.
- Do not attempt to compel disclosure of employee grand jury testimony through threat of disciplinary action.

G. *Issues of Privilege and Waiver*

1. The Basics

Issues of attorney-client privilege and work product protection arise repeatedly in the course of environmental criminal investigations. For example, a subpoena may seek production of internal investigative reports or documents generated by an expert retained after a search. Privilege issues are particularly important with respect to environmental consultants. Documents they prepare relating to compliance with environmental regulations at the facility will be submitted to the regulator and thus are not privileged. Other documents they prepare, however, may be directed toward defense of potential litigation and thus may be privileged. It is important for the company to understand from the outset how the attorney-client privilege and work product protections will apply to different classes of records.

In *Upjohn*,[13] the U.S. Supreme Court held that the attorney-client privilege applies to communications made by corporate employees to counsel for the company in the context of an internal investigation. There, the company's in-house and outside counsel had initiated an investigation after receiving reports that its foreign subsidiary was engaging in illegal conduct. The government subsequently sought production of documents generated in the course of that investigation. The court of appeals held that the privilege did not

13. 449 U.S. at 383.

attach to communications made by employees who were "not responsible for directing Upjohn's actions in response to legal advice" but only to officials in the "control group." The Supreme Court reversed, rejecting the "control group" test in favor of a broader rule that the privilege protects communications of even low-level employees.[14] The Court found that in order to qualify for the privilege, however, the disclosures must be made within the scope of the employees' duties, and the employees must be aware that they are being questioned "in order that the corporation [may] obtain legal advice."[15]

The work-product doctrine insulates from discovery an attorney's mental impressions, conclusions, opinions, or legal theories contained in materials prepared in anticipation of litigation.[16] Subject to disclosure on a showing of substantial need, the work-product doctrine protects the confidentiality of materials generated by attorneys and by non-attorneys hired by counsel, if such materials are prepared in anticipation of civil or criminal litigation.

To ensure the confidentiality of information generated as part of an internal investigation, implementation of a number of safeguards is advisable.[17] These include generating a formal corporate resolution which establishes that counsel will be conducting an investigation for the purpose of obtaining legal advice; marking all documents pertaining to the investigation as "privileged and confidential"; and ensuring that all outside experts and investigators are retained by and report directly to counsel. Finally, internal investigation reports should not be distributed beyond the senior management who are a part of the review process. Only a few copies of the reports should be made, and the copies should be numbered and their whereabouts known at all times.

Scientific experts increasingly play a critical role in criminal environmental cases. Investigations and prosecutions frequently turn on questions of scientific proof, such as the calibration of monitoring instruments, sampling protocols, averaging times for determining allowable pollution levels, testing protocols, and the accuracy of testing labs. Litigation consultants are encountering increased scrutiny by the government.[18] Aggressive advocacy regarding scientific arguments, which might be normal in an administrative or civil context, may be re-characterized by the government as obstruction of justice in a criminal investigation. The DOJ ECS established a Lab Fraud Task Force and Lab Fraud Initiative to survey the problem of fraudulent laboratory testing and to determine how best to tackle it. ECS attorneys prosecuted several nationally significant cases associated with the Initiative.[19] Further, criminal prosecutors have targeted consultants for prosecution based on claims of falsifying reports.[20]

H. Keeping the Investigation Privileged

Once a company becomes aware of a government investigation, management (or a committee composed of members of the board of directors) should meet with counsel to set the parameters for the scope of the company's internal investigation. At the outset, counsel should consider requesting formal written authorization from management (or from the board) to institute the internal investigation. That authorization should include:

- a clear statement identifying the client, e.g., the company or a committee of board members;
- a statement that a government investigation has been initiated;
- a broad definition of the scope of the investigation;
- a statement of the confidential nature of the investigation;

---

14. *Id.* at 394-95.
15. *Id.* at 394.
16. *See* Hickman v. Taylor, 329 U.S. 495 (1947), *cert. denied*, 336 U.S. 906 (1949).
17. *See generally* Richard Marmaro, *Protecting the Results of Internal Corporate Investigations*, 1 BNA White Collar Crime Rep. No. 4 (July/Aug. 1987).
18. *See* United States v. Eureka Labs., Inc., No. 94-262 (E.D. Cal. May 17, 1995) (chemists at an environmental testing lab convicted of providing federal agencies with false results on water, soil, and air sampling tests).
19. *See* U.S. DOJ, Env. & Nat. Resources Div. Laboratory Fraud, *available at* http://www.justive.gov/enrd/3397.htm (last visited Feb. 5, 2014).
20. *E.g.*, United States v. Fern, No. 94-322, 25 Env't Rptr. 2013 (S.D. Fla. Feb. 17, 1995).

- a statement that counsel has been retained to provide legal advice in anticipation of litigation (as opposed to mere business advice); and
- a directive requiring the cooperation of company personnel.

The company's internal investigation should cover at least the same ground as the government's investigation. Because the purpose of an internal investigation is to eliminate surprises, however, the company's investigation may need to exceed the scope of the government's inquiry. The investigation should focus on developing those facts that mark the case as one that merits anything but criminal prosecution.

1. Establish Attorney Supervision

The attorney-client privilege and work product doctrine are the keys to keeping the internal investigation confidential. To best establish and protect the privilege, all members of the investigative team should report to defense counsel, and any consultants hired to assist in the investigation or defense preparation should be engaged directly by defense counsel.[21]

When communicating with the client, counsel may integrate factual information and legal opinion (rather than segregating such information, as is usually the approach for most routine environmental compliance efforts). Counsel must be aware, however, that the company could decide to waive privilege as to those communications in an effort to demonstrate its cooperation with the government. Consequently, it behooves counsel to draft (and review) documents containing key facts, analysis of vital information, and discussion of legal advice while keeping in mind that they may be turned over to the government in the future. As appropriate, counsel should also consider communicating some information to the client orally rather than in writing.

2. Limit Circulation of Investigation Materials and Label Them Appropriately

Circulating materials to parties outside the company (other than the outside attorneys or consultants assisting the attorney who are involved in the internal investigation) constitutes a waiver of privilege.[22]

Even a circulation of materials *within* the company that is too broad can constitute a waiver. For example, blanket circulation of materials to all high-level company officials (including persons not involved in making decisions concerning the case) risks a finding of waiver. Similarly, including low-level managers and line workers beyond the degree necessary to gather facts and identify issues important to the case may violate the "in confidence" prong of the attorney-client privilege test.

With this in mind, counsel should consider taking the following protective measures:

- Mark all e-mails/hard copies with "Attorney-Client Privilege. Attorney Work Product. Do Not Disseminate." Counsel also should include a notation that the materials are "subject to joint defense agreement" if counsel has entered into such an agreement with counsel for related entities or individuals involved in the case.
- Direct persons that have access to privileged materials to avoid circulating copies or sharing information verbally beyond an expressly defined group of essential decision makers.
- Direct persons that are involved to keep all privileged materials in a secure location.

When submitting to the government a letter brief or "white paper" that sets forth legal and factual arguments in favor of not bringing a prosecution, counsel should minimize the possibility of inadvertently waiving privilege by:

---

21. *See, e.g.*, United States v. Torf (In re Grand Jury Subpoena), 357 F.3d 900 (9th Cir. 2004) (finding documents prepared by environmental consultant were protected by the work product doctrine because they were created at the direction of defense counsel in anticipation of litigation); United States v. Kovel, 296 F.2d 918, 922 (2d Cir. 1961) (allowing, in certain situations, lawyers to share privileged communications with outside agents who are "interpreting" complex information for them).
22. *Id. See, e.g.*, United States v. El Paso Co, 682 F.2d 530, 538 (5th Cir. 1982), *cert. denied*, 466 U.S. 944 (1984); DVI Financial Servs. Inc. v. Florida Heart, LLC., 2003 U.S. Dist. LEXIS 12205 (E.D. Pa. June 23, 2003).

- seeking a written agreement with the prosecutor that the communications will fall under Rule 11 of the Federal Rules of Criminal Procedure and Rule 410 of the Federal Rules of Evidence, and that the government will not argue that the submission constitutes a waiver of privilege[23]; and
- avoiding the inclusion of attachments that could reasonably be characterized as attorney work product.[24]

3. Handle Witness Interviews Carefully

In addition to the basic principles discussed above regarding the debriefing of employees already interviewed by the government, counsel should keep the following points in mind when recording information gathered during witness interviews.

- Prior to interviewing employees, the company's management should issue a written directive specifically authorizing the investigation and requesting the cooperation of company personnel. This directive sets the context for claiming privilege, and a copy should be provided to all persons who are expected to become involved in the investigation.
- Counsel should perform witness interviews. Interviews performed by managers within the company, private investigators, or other non-legal personnel may dilute or destroy a claim of privilege. If in-house counsel is even tangentially involved with the activities being investigated, outside counsel should handle the interviews to minimize the appearance of self-dealing and to avoid increasing the exposure of in-house counsel to allegations of obstruction, witness tampering, or harassment.
- Do *not*: (1) electronically record witness interviews; (2) use questionnaires to interview witnesses; (3) record witness interviews in verbatim or written form, or (4) ask witnesses to review and sign (or otherwise adopt) any documents summarizing their interviews. The government has a right to obtain copies of all "statements" of witnesses who testify at trial.[25]
- Remind the employee being interviewed that the conversation is privileged, that the privilege belongs to the company (not the employee), and that the employee should not disclose the information exchanged during the interview without company permission.
- When counsel writes up interview notes, preface the document with a brief paragraph identifying the information as privileged. The preface also should assert that the document is protected work product, and should set forth a short justification for such a claim. For example: "The following memorandum reflects my thoughts, impressions, and analyses, and it constitutes my opinion work product. It is not intended to provide a verbatim or substantially verbatim recital of [the employee's] statements. I have exercised my professional judgment in determining what information is included and how to characterize it. This memorandum is prepared in anticipation of litigation and for the purpose of advising [the company] in connection with the government's investigation of the [insert name] facility."

---

23. *See* Fed. R. Crim. R. 11(f) (discussions or statements in the course of plea negotiations are inadmissible); Fed. R. Evid. 410 (ruling inadmissible, subject to certain exceptions, "any statement made in the course of plea discussions with an attorney for the prosecuting authority which do not result in a plea of guilty or which result in a plea of guilty later withdrawn").
24. Whenever counsel reveals some of her investigatory material to the government, she risks a waiver of privilege, particularly if she presents the material in what could be called an "unfair" or "skewed" manner. *See, e.g.*, In re Martin Marietta, 856 F.2d 619, 623-26 (4th Cir. 1988), *cert. denied*, 490 U.S. 1011 (1989). In addition, third parties in a civil suit, derivative action, or a related proceeding may subsequently seek disclosure of confidential material by arguing that the company waived privilege and/or work product protection when it shared the information with the prosecutor. *See, e.g.*, Westinghouse Elec. Corp. v. Philippines, 951 F.2d 1414, 1426 n.12 (3d Cir. 1991). Arguments that the waiver to the government was a "limited waiver," "partial waiver," or "selective waiver" are generally unsuccessful. *See* Lawrence E. Jaffe Pension Plan v. Household Int'l, Inc., 244 F.R.D. 412 (N.D. Ill. 2006) (reviewing trends in the case law).
25. *See* Fed. R. Crim. P. 26.2(a) ("After a witness other than the defendant has testified on direct examination, the court, on motion of a party who did not call the witness, must order . . . the defendant and the defendant's attorney to produce, for the examination and use of the moving party, any statement of the witness that is in their possession and that relates to the subject matter of the witness's testimony."); *see also* Fed. R. Crim. P. 26.2(f) (defining "statement").

III. Responding to a Subpoena for Documents

A. *Basics of Document Subpoenas*

1. Receiving Service

To ensure that a subpoena served on the company is delivered immediately to in-house counsel, the company should have procedures in place for (1) greeting, identifying, and announcing visitors, and (2) identifying subpoenas received in the mail and immediately forwarding them to counsel. Upon receiving the subpoena, counsel should determine its scope, timing of production, and meet with the appropriate company officials to identify all the potential sources of responsive documents. It is imperative that company counsel takes the steps necessary to ensure that all potential responsive documents are preserved by arranging for issuance of a "litigation hold" notice to appropriate officers and employees.

2. Contact the Issuing Agency

Counsel should consider making an informal contact with the issuing agency to establish a reasonable timetable and method for compliance. Such contact may also lead to an agreement to limit or narrow an overly broad request for documents. It is important to attempt to find out at this point whether the company is viewed as the target of a criminal investigation or whether it is being subpoenaed as a witness or source of evidence for purposes of investigating another company.

B. *Protect Your Rights When Responding to a Subpoena for Documents*

1. Motion to Quash

A formal objection to a subpoena takes the form of a motion to quash. A motion to quash is appropriate if:

- the subpoena is not reasonable in scope or is not sufficiently particular;
- the timing of production required by the subpoena is unreasonable;
- the subpoena calls for production of privileged material;
- the subpoena calls for the production of purely personal papers that may be protected by the Fifth Amendment privilege against self-incrimination[26];
- the subpoena is issued to gather evidence for a criminal trial after an indictment has been returned; or
- a grand jury subpoena has been issued solely to gather information for a civil action.

Assuming that the company does not elect to move to quash the subpoena, here are some tips on how best to respond to it:

C. *Designate a Custodian of Record*

The company should designate a "custodian of record" to oversee the document production. The custodian must not be a potential witness or target in the matters under investigation. Having someone who is "detached" from the substantive issues serve as the custodian can help eliminate many of the risks of the allegations of obstruction or concealment that can result from production miscues. In addition, because the custodian likely will be called as a witness to testify to the source of specific documents, it is best if the custodian is not company counsel.

---

26. Only an individual may assert the Fifth Amendment privilege against self-incrimination. The privilege does not apply to entities such as corporations, partnerships, or even sole proprietorships. Braswell v. United States, 487 U.S. 99, 116 (1988).

D. *Set Up a Fail-Safe "Litigation Hold" or "Document Hold" System*

Identify all employees who may have discoverable records or electronically stored information relevant to the subpoena. Send a copy of the subpoena to each of those employees with clarifying instructions about the terms of the subpoena. Include a "litigation hold" notice that instructs the recipients to preserve, and to not destroy, any documents relevant to the subpoena. Contact the information technology (IT) support team for assistance. Because so much of a company's information is electronically stored, it is strongly recommend that the company's IT department be notified and requested to preserve for the custodian any and all back-up tapes or other back up memory that is potentially relevant to the subpoena. Have the IT department suspend temporarily the company's usual document destruction policies, and have that instruction issued in writing to document the policy. Work with IT to preserve all portable media, such as flash drives or other peripheral devices, which could contain relevant information.[27]

E. *Establish a System for Identifying Privileged Documents*

Put together a list of telltale signs that a document is privileged, such as that it is authored by the company's inside or outside counsel for use by those producing the document in response to the subpoena. In addition, the company must prepare a log of the privileged documents responsive to the subpoena that it intends to withhold.

F. *Track Evidence When Responding to a Subpoena for Documents*

1. Circulate the Subpoena with Clarifying Instructions

As stated above, counsel or the custodian of record should circulate an e-mail/memorandum to all persons who maintain potentially relevant documents that clarifies the scope of the government requests, urges a thorough response, and details logistical arrangements for the collection and production of the documents.

2. Follow Up With Employees in Person

The custodian of record should meet with most individual employees involved in producing documents regularly to make certain that they have considered all possible sources of responsive documents within their control.

3. Require Individuals to Certify Their Efforts

The custodian of record should have employees involved in producing documents sign a document certifying that the information provided is, to the best of their knowledge, all the responsive material that is within their possession.

4. Track the Sources of Documents to Be Produced

The custodian of record should track the source of each responsive document he or she receives. This is necessary so that company counsel can determine who was privy to the information in key documents.

---

27. Proper document retention in the digital age is an increasingly important issue. *See, e.g.*, W. Warren Hamel & Lowell M. Rothschild, "Coming Soon to a Grand Jury Near You: The Broader Implications of the New Civil Rules Relating to Electronically Stored Information for Environmental Enforcement." (ABA Envtl. L. Conf. Mar. 8, 2007).

5. Bates Stamp Responsive Documents, Index, or Systematize Produced Documents, and Create a Privilege Log

The company should number each page of all documents to be produced, so that each page has an unambiguous point of reference, and should generate an index that identifies each document by Bates number range and any other vital information, i.e., source, date, author(s), and so on. At a minimum, the company must create a log indexing the responsive documents that have been withheld as privileged. The index for production to the government should comply with any specific directions in the subpoena as to what information should be included in the index. A more detailed index, for instance one that identifies particularly important ("hot") documents, is often generated solely for internal use.

6. Re-Circulate the Subpoena With Clarifying Instructions

Oftentimes a "fresh read" of the subpoena will help employees recall material they had previously forgotten or prompt them to reconsider materials they had previously deemed to be non-responsive. It may be beneficial to re-circulate the subpoena after the initial round of documents have been collected (7-10 days after initial circulation) with clarifying instructions geared to issue-spotting. As noted above, the duty to respond to a subpoena is a continuing one. Although submission of late-discovered materials may draw the ire of the issuing attorney, the obligation is a strict one.

7. Keep a Complete Record of Your Production

Counsel should record the following points in writing: (1) delineating the company's interpretation of ambiguous subpoena requests; (2) documenting amendments and clarifications that are agreed upon with the prosecutor; (3) recording the specific protocol followed in carrying out the production; and (4) tracking materials with the date produced and delivered.

G. Prevent Add-On Allegations

A document production can affect the company's credibility with the prosecutor. When the prosecutor's confidence in the production is shaken, then allegations of obstruction and concealment tend to arise. To avoid such a situation, the company should abide by the following principles:

- never destroy, alter, or conceal a document that is arguably responsive to a subpoena request;
- always produce all responsive documents that each employee maintains, even though this may require producing numerous copies of what is essentially the same document;
- explain any gaps in Bates ranges;
- clarify ambiguities in subpoena requests in writing; and
- evaluate documents withheld as privileged and provide a privilege log of such documents.

IV. Electronic Discovery

In today's electronic world, responding to a subpoena *duces tecum* can be more burdensome (and expensive) than ever. *Zubulake v. USB Warburg*[28] is the groundbreaking (civil) case in the field of electronic discovery. In a series of decisions, the court established important practices relating to both the legal and technical aspects of electronic discovery, as the relevant communication among interested parties was in digital form. The main issues raised were:

28. 217 F.R.D. 309 (S.D.N.Y. 2003).

- the scope of a party's duty to preserve digital evidence during the course of litigation or even when it is first acknowledged that a chance of litigation exists;
- a lawyer's duty to monitor the client's compliance with electronic data preservation and production;
- data sampling, so that knowledge about costs and effectiveness of the recovering process are known in advance;
- the ability for the disclosing party to shift the costs to the requesting party of recovering "inaccessible" media; and
- the imposition of sanctions for the spoliation of digital evidence.

Spring boarding off the *Zubulake* decision, the 2006 amendments to the Federal Rules of Civil Procedure covered five related areas:

- definition of discoverable material;
- early attention to issues relating to electronic discovery, including the format of production;
- discovery of electronically stored information from sources that are not reasonably accessible;
- the procedure for asserting claims of privilege or work product protection after production; and
- a "safe harbor" limit on sanctions for the loss of electronically stored information as a result of the routine operation of computer systems.

Unlike in the civil context, only a few criminal cases have grappled with emerging issues of producing electronically stored information in response to grand jury subpoenas. As a basic starting point, the Fourth Amendment requires that all searches and seizures of private documents by the government be reasonable. This reasonableness standard applies to subpoenas *duces tecum*.[29] Nevertheless, the Supreme Court has suggested that this limitation, at most, prohibits indefinite descriptions of the documents to be produced.[30] Under the Federal Rules of Criminal Procedure, "the court may quash or modify the subpoena if compliance would be unreasonable or oppressive."[31] As the courts have provided little assistance in applying the reasonableness standard to grand jury subpoenas seeking electronic data, reaching a limiting agreement with the issuing attorney may be the most viable solution to overly burdensome subpoenas.

The primary interest of most clients is how to keep costs manageable in responding to a subpoena, especially where large volumes of electronic materials potentially are responsive. An attorney review of potentially relevant documents usually involves a significant cost, narrowing the field of electronic data to those most likely to be responsive on the front end will result in fewer documents needing to be reviewed on the back end. This may be achieved through electronic fields that screen for, among others: (1) search terms; (2) date limitations; and (3) key persons.

Providing a list of the proposed screening criteria to the issuing government attorney with an opportunity for his or her input can often result in an agreement as to which fields are reasonably likely to produce relevant documents. If no agreement can be reached, filing a motion to quash may be necessary.

The recipient of a subpoena always should be afforded sufficient time to review the electronic data being subpoenaed. This may require an agreement with the issuing attorney for an extension of time from the original subpoena production date. If no agreement can be reached, again, it may be necessary to file a motion to quash.

Because many companies routinely delete electronic data, and individual employees often have access to and the ability to destroy electronically stored data, it is particularly important in this "digital world" for the recipient to issue a document hold immediately upon receipt of a grand jury subpoena. Even an "innocent" destruction of data after receipt of a grand jury subpoena is likely to generate substantial ill will on behalf of the investigating attorney, even if no formal charges are filed for obstruction of justice.

29. *See* United States v. Bailey (In re Subpoena *Duces Tecum*), 228 F.3d 341, 347 (4th Cir. 2000).
30. Oklahoma Press Publishing Co. v. Walling, 327 U.S. 186, 208 (1946).
31. Fed. R. Civ. P. 17(c)(2).

Another important issue in the world of electronic data arises when the government seizes electronic storage devices, e.g., hard drives, laptop computers, cell phones, etc., and/or the subpoena *duces tecum* seeks physical production of storage devices, rather than specific data contained on such devices. Undoubtedly, storage devices will contain information that is irrelevant to the government's investigation. But what if they also contain privileged information or, worse yet, evidence of a crime of which the government was previously unaware? In order to address such concerns, the issuing authority should establish "taint teams," the purpose of which is to have government attorneys, unrelated to the investigation at hand, perform the initial review of the documents. Of course, the problem for the recipient is that such "taint teams" are not really unrelated, neutral parties, so their decisions regarding privilege are likely to favor disclosure. The government also is unlikely to ignore evidence of a crime, even if unknown at the time the subpoena was issued.

Thus, the counsel for the recipient should insist that the subpoena *duces tecum* apply only to relevant electronic data, not to electronic storage devices (just as a subpoena should seek files, not filing cabinets). If the issuing attorney will not agree to this limitation, it may be necessary for the company to file a motion to quash. The responding party also has a right to sufficient time to review potentially responsive materials for relevance and privilege. The motion to squash may raise this issue as well if the prosecution will not agree to reasonable terms.

Because the law governing responses to a subpoena *duces tecum* demanding production of electronic data is a rapidly evolving area, counsel must be familiar with recent developments and changes in the law within the jurisdiction in which the subpoenas are issued.

V. Other Issues That Commonly Arise During a Government Investigation

A. *Sampling and Testing*

If the government took samples from a facility, its counsel should insist on receiving split samples. Indeed, the company may have received split samples at the time of the search. Although EPA has taken the position that providing split samples is not required for all criminal searches, its policy is to furnish such samples.[32] If the company did not do so at the time of the search, however, counsel should attempt to determine what tests the government will perform (or has performed) on the samples, and attempt to obtain the results of such tests once they become available.

Once counsel obtains information about the government's sampling and testing, he should consider advising the company to hire a consultant to perform identical tests on the split samples, as well as any other tests that the consultant deems necessary to authenticate or to contest the government's methods or results. If the prosecutor views contamination or harm to the environment as a significant factor in deciding whether to file criminal charges, the company may want to hire a consultant to perform appropriate sampling and testing for these purposes as well.

B. *Taking Corrective Action*

An issue that often arises in the course of an internal investigation is whether the company should take voluntary corrective action—for example remediating contamination, implementing improved compliance measures to prevent future violations, or disciplining employees involved in wrongdoing. Corrective action is a double-edged sword. It does demonstrate good corporate citizenship and strong environmental values, and may thereby play an important role in encouraging the prosecutor not to file criminal charges against the company or its employees. On the other hand, taking action to clean up contamination may be viewed as an admission that the company is responsible for pollutants that may be attributable to others.

Unless there is substantial doubt that the company is responsible for the environmental contamination resulted from the company's compliance problems, it will almost always benefit from swift and voluntary remediation efforts. Such actions minimize the environmental impact of the contamination and thus mini-

32. Both RCRA (42 U.S.C. §6927(a)) and the Comprehensive Environmental Response, Compensation, and Liability Act (42 U.S.C. §9604(e)(4)(B)) require the government to provide split samples.

mize the company's potential liability going forward. Moreover, an environmental criminal investigation may last two or three years, or longer. It is important to convince the prosecutor, before he or she decides whether to file charges, that the company has "gotten the message" and has corrected any deficiencies. In all cases, however, the company should, whenever possible, involve defense counsel before taking corrective actions, to avoid making inadvertent and damaging admissions, and to make certain that the company's action will not be viewed adversely by the prosecutor.

C. *Disciplining Employees*

Disciplinary action is a particularly thorny form of corrective action. On the one hand, the government likely will expect a company under investigation to take disciplinary action when appropriate or required by company policy.[33] On the other hand, taking inappropriate disciplinary measures or taking disciplinary action against the wrong individual may result in: (1) the prosecutor's accusing the company of attempting to intimidate employees; (2) the company's seemingly, and perhaps unwittingly, identifying or labeling an employee as a "guilty party," when in fact he or she is not; (3) injured employees pursuing civil remedies against the company for violations of labor agreements or state employment laws; or (4) encouraging employees to cooperate with the government. Needless to say, the company should not take any disciplinary action without first consulting with defense counsel who is experienced in dealing with such issues in the context of a criminal investigation.

In general, however, while dismissal may be necessary in extreme cases—for instance, when employees engaged in culpable conduct or in fabrication or destruction of evidence—some form of suspension, paid administrative leave, or reassignment is often preferable. Keep in mind that firing an employee drastically diminishes the company's access to that person during the course of the investigation.

D. *Voluntary Disclosure*

Some violations do inevitably occur despite implementation of effective environmental compliance systems.. The Voluntary Disclosure Programs of the EPA, DOJ and the Coast Guard—attempt to encourage companies to blow the whistle on themselves by voluntarily reporting their violations.[34] These programs offer incentives for companies to self-police and to disclose to EPA environmental violations in exchange for potential enforcement leniency—but only if the disclosing entity satisfies specified conditions, such as prompt disclosure, remediation, correction, cooperation and the like.[35] In the context of internal investigations, if a company is considering the possibility of voluntarily disclosing violations, it must be remembered that the EPA and Coast Guard policies require the disclosure within 21 days of discovery of the violation.[36] This sets up a potential dilemma for the company and its counsel as, depending upon the complexity and scope of the underlying violation(s), the full extent of the violation may not be known within 21 days of initial discovery. Further, as one of the conditions of the programs is cooperation with the agencies in their investigations, an agency will often ask for a copy of any internal investigation conducted. Production of a written internal investigation report presents a substantial risk that all the privileges with respect to the

---

33. The U.S. Department of Justice's (DOJ's) policy treats internal company disciplinary programs as a significant factor when determining whether to prosecute a company. *See* Richard B. Stewart Memorandum re: "Exercise of Criminal Prosecutorial Discretion for Environmental Violations in the Context of Significant Voluntary Compliance or Disclosure Efforts by the Violator" (June 3, 1991). In addition, the *U.S. Sentencing Guidelines* treat internal company disciplinary programs as a potential mitigating or aggravating factor in determining the appropriate corporate sentence.

34. *See* Chapter 2, Section II.2. *supra.*

35. The EPA policy provides for potential reductions in civil penalties and for a non-recommendation for criminal prosecution. *See* U.S. EPA, Incentives for Self-Policing: Discovery, Disclosure, Correction, and Prevention of Violations, 65 Fed. Reg. 19618, 19625 (Apr. 11, 2000) [hereinafter EPA Voluntary Disclosure Policy]. The Coast Guard policy addresses only non-recommendation for criminal prosecution. *See* U.S. Coast Guard, *Maritime Law Enforcement Manual, App. V, sec. 4, Environmental Crimes: Voluntary Disclosure Policy* [hereinafter Coast Guard Voluntary Disclosure Policy], *available at* http://www.uscg.mil/foia/ docs/CH-4%20Appendix%20V.pdf (last visited May 28, 2013). The DOJ Policy states that disclosure will be viewed as mitigating factors in the exercise of the agency prosecutorial discretion. U.S. DOJ, Factors In Decisions On Criminal Prosecutions For Environmental Violations In The Context Of Significant Voluntary Compliance Or Disclosure Efforts By The Violator (July 1, 1991), *available at* http://www.justice.gov/enrd/3058.htm (last visited May 28, 2013)..

36. *See* EPA Voluntary Disclosure Policy, supra note 35, at 19626; Coast Guard Voluntary Disclosure Policy, *supra* note 35, at V.5.b

investigation will be deemed to be waived.[37] For these reasons, it is highly recommended that outside legal counsel familiar with these voluntary disclosure programs be consulted prior to making a disclosure to the government.

EPA's voluntary disclosure program is discussed at length in Chapter 2, Section A.

E. Identifying Whether Individual Employees Need Separate Counsel

Because a company can only act through its directors, officers, and employees, the conduct of individuals is always at issue in environmental criminal investigations. Therefore, corporate counsel must determine early on whether an employee's interests could potentially become adverse to those of the company. As a general rule, it is not advisable for the company's counsel also to represent employees, even if no conflict is foreseen at the inception of the investigation.

Employees (including former employees) *require* separate counsel when:

- the prosecutor has identified the employee as a "target" or "subject" of the investigation; or
- the employee appears to have taken action contrary to company policy or the directions of a supervisor.

Employees who are identified as "witnesses" are less likely to require separate counsel, unless facts known to the company suggest that an employee could eventually become a target or subject of the investigation. It often is appropriate to have one separate counsel (sometimes nicknamed "bullpen counsel") who can represent all employees who are in the "witness" category.

Even when there is no apparent conflict between the company and individual employees, there are still advantages to hiring separate counsel for employees. Among other benefits, separate counsel serves to demonstrate the company's commitment to protect employees from the personal risks of a criminal investigation, establishes a buffer between the company and recalcitrant or untrustworthy employees (thereby reducing inferences of corporate misconduct), and provides another voice to influence the prosecutor about the direction and scope of the government's investigation.

F. Deciding Whether to Join Forces With Employees' Counsel in a Joint Defense Agreement

Many environmental investigations cover activities that involve multiple corporations or multiple individuals. Often, each of those under scrutiny may gain an advantage by sharing information with the other potential targets through a joint defense agreement. These arrangements allow attorneys for various parties to exchange information without waiving the attorney-client or work product privileges. Pooling of information can allow potential defendants to extend their information gathering network, obtain factual and legal suggestions, and take advantage of each other's expertise, at a considerable savings in cost and time.

The joint defense privilege, contained in agreements among groups of defendants or subjects of investigations, has long been recognized by the courts.[38] Certain core elements are required in joint defense agreements to maintain the privileged status of the information exchanged. The parties must share a common interest; the information must have been exchanged in order to facilitate their representation; and the materials must still qualify as confidential at the time one attorney shares them with the group.[39] Although the agreement need not be written to be legally valid, a written arrangement clarifies each party's objectives, reduces the chances of conflicts of interest, and better protects against government challenges to the privilege.

---

37. *See infra* Section R. A majority of courts have held that disclosure of a report to a law enforcement agency waives privileges normally applicable to the report. *See, e.g.,* In re Subpoena Duces Tecum (Fulbright & Jaworski), 738 F.2d 1367 (D.C. Cir. 1984); United States v. Billmyer, 57 F.3d 31 (1st Cir. 1995); Westinghouse Elec. Corp. v. Repub. of the Philippines, 951 F.2d 1414 (3d. Cir. 1991); In re Martin Marietta Corp., 856 F.2d 619 (4th Cir. 1988), *cert. denied,* 490 U.S. 1011 (1989); In re Qwest Communications Int'l, Inc., 450 F.3d 1179 (10th Cir.), *cert. denied,* 549 U.S. 1031 (2006). *But see* Diversified Indus., Inc. v. Meredith, 572 F.2d 596 (8th Cir. 1977) (en banc) (holding that voluntary disclosure of an internal investigation report does not waive privileges otherwise applicable to the report).

38. *See, e.g.,* United States v. Schwimmer, 892 F.2d 237 (2d Cir. 1989), *cert. denied,* 489 U.S. 1083 (1991), *later proceeding at* 892 F.2d 237 (2d Cir. 1989), *cert. denied,* 493 U.S. 1071 (1990).

39. *E.g.,* Hunydee v. United States, 355 F.2d 183 (9th Cir. 1965); Continental Oil Co. v. United States, 330 F.2d 347 (9th Cir. 1964).

While each agreement must be tailored to the specific facts of a particular investigation, all joint defense agreements should cover both the attorneys and the clients. The arrangement should cover all shared materials, acknowledge that each lawyer's obligations to his or her client may prevent the sharing of all information, and provide for procedures for withdrawal from the agreement and return of documents. An agreement should extend to debriefing memoranda of witness interviews and work product generated during the investigation. It should preclude disclosure of any covered documents to the government by one party without the permission of all other parties. Finally, confidential protection should continue to apply to any material previously provided a member who later withdraws. The agreement also should preserve the right of cross-examination at trial if one of the persons covered later becomes a defendant and the others become witnesses.[40]

As each case is unique, and the considerations whether to enter into a joint defense agreement are tied inextricably to the facts of each case, there is no "one answer fits all" to the question of whether the corporation should enter into such an agreement in a specific environmental investigation. In general, though, a joint defense agreement may help the company by showing support for employees and improving the flow of potentially critical information among counsel for all of the likely targets in a criminal investigation. In addition, the existence of such an arrangement usually will ensure that the company is informed in advance if one of the individual parties to the agreement decides to cooperate with the government.

Such an agreement, however, also may create some difficulty for a corporation. Later in the investigation, the company may decide its best course is to cooperate with the government, and it would need to be free to act independently on the information that it receives. In addition, most prosecutors have very negative views of joint defense agreements.

G. *Protecting the Company From Parallel Proceedings*

Any company that becomes the subject of an environmental investigation faces a wide array of potential enforcement actions. Federal authorities may institute simultaneous or successive administrative, civil, or criminal enforcement actions arising out of a single set of facts. State authorities may do the same, even in the face of past or ongoing federal action(s) based upon the same facts. Finally, private litigants may bring an action based upon the same body of facts. This not only multiplies a company's potential liability for a single violation, but also creates some difficult strategic choices, notably how to deal with the risks potentially presented by parallel criminal and civil proceedings.

While a full discussion of the complex, often tangled issues arising with respect to parallel proceedings is beyond the scope of this deskbook, defense counsel's preferred goal often should be to stay any civil action pending resolution of the criminal matter. Because such an extreme measure is difficult to achieve, however, it may make more strategic sense to seek a stay of civil discovery until the government decides whether to indict. A more limited and likely more realistic option would be to seek a protective order precluding or limiting the civil authorities from sharing their discovery with criminal prosecutors.

Parallel proceedings are discussed in more detail, in Chapter 2, Section F.

H *Considering Collateral Consequences*

A criminal environmental violation may have more wide-ranging effects than simply spawning several legal actions. It also may result in important collateral consequences, including loss of government contracting rights (called "suspension" and "debarment") and loss of vital environmental permits. The important lesson is that a company cannot assume that its problems will remain confined to any one arena. It must be prepared to defend or negotiate on multiple fronts simultaneously.

Conviction of an environmental crime may have unexpected consequences beyond the obvious ones associated with monetary fines and jail terms. Federal and state agencies often bar convicted defendants from bidding for, or continuing to maintain, government contracts. In addition, a number of state laws

40. United States v. Anderson, 790 F. Supp. 231 (W.D. Wash. 1992) (defendant's participation in joint defense agreement which limited counsel's access to use confidential information on cross-examination did not present conflict of interest that required counsel's disqualification).

empower regulators to deny environmental permits or renewals to persons or organizations whose histories include past convictions. Thus, seeking some form of global resolution to a criminal enforcement matter is usually advisable. Consequences of a criminal environmental conviction are discussed in more detail in Chapter 8, section J through O.

I. Considering a Deferred Prosecution/Non-Prosecution Agreement

Deferred Prosecution Agreements (DPAs) and Non-Prosecution Agreements (NPAs) are a species of federal pretrial diversion.[41] Under a DPA, the prosecutor charges a corporation in a criminal investigation, but agrees to defer prosecution for a given period of time. If the corporation complies with the terms of the DPA, the prosecutor dismisses the charges at the end of the agreement. Under an NPA, the government agrees not to file a charging document, provided that the company adheres to the terms of the agreement. As discussed, in Chapter 2, Section G, these types of agreements, which have become increasingly common in several areas, cannot be entered into lightly.[42]

In determining whether a DPA or NPA is in the company's best interests, counsel must be forewarned that prosecutors wield great discretion in this realm. The agreement might place onerous demands on the company, and while staying or avoiding prosecution, it might nevertheless invite other substantial consequences, such as initiation of suspension and/or debarment proceedings. Suspension and debarment proceedings are discussed in more detail in Chapter 8, section L

J. Disclosing the Results of the Internal Investigation

At some stage of the internal investigation, counsel will request a meeting with the prosecutor to discuss its view of the case or to attempt to persuade the government that the client should not be charged with a criminal offense. Such pre-charging meetings are indispensable prerequisites to effective representation. Counsel cannot simply wait until the client is indicted to discover the government's case.

In conducting these meetings, defense counsel must walk a fine line between revealing too little, and failing to apprise the prosecution of problems with its case, and revealing too much, thereby eliminating the element of surprise and giving the prosecutor a road map to successful pursuit of the case. Disclosure of even part of an internal investigation report may constitute a waiver of the attorney-client privilege and work product doctrine for the entire investigation. Courts have held that once the company shares some of its investigatory material with the government, the privilege may be waived for all related materials, particularly if the information provided presents an unfair or skewed perspective.[43]

The leading case on waiver is *In re Martin Marietta Corporation*.[44] There, during a meeting with the government, company counsel quoted directly from a position paper that reflected materials compiled during an internal investigation, including statements of witnesses. The court ruled that by revealing the statements of its employees, counsel had waived the attorney-client privilege.

In light of *Martin Marietta*, if the entity under investigation elects to make a written submission to the government, counsel should, at a minimum, obtain a prior express agreement from the prosecutor that the submission will not waive the attorney-client privilege or work product protection for any material disclosed. If possible, the information should be presented orally, as written statements are more likely to be found to constitute a waiver and be admitted against the corporation at trial. Finally, counsel should attempt to bring all remarks under the protection of Rule 11(e)(6)(D) of the Federal Rules of Criminal Procedure, which generally prohibits the admission of statements made in the course of plea discussions.

---

41. U.S. Attorneys' Manual §9-22.010, at 712 (Criminal Resource Manual).

42. DPAs and NPAs have been applied in a wide variety of criminal cases, such as money laundering, public corruption, and the Foreign Corrupt Practices Act. They are especially common in fraud cases, such as bank fraud, securities fraud, tax fraud, and health care fraud. For application of DPAs and NPAs in the environmental criminal context, see Joseph G. Block & David L. Feinberg, *Look Before You Leap: DPAs, NPAs, and the Environmental Criminal Case*, *in* The 22nd Annual National Institute on White Collar Crime V-1 (ABA 2008).

43. *See* Westinghouse Elec. Corp. v. Republic of the Philippines, 951 F.2d 1414, 1426 n.13 (3d Cir. 1991) ("When a party discloses a portion of otherwise privileged materials while withholding the rest, the privilege is waived only as to those communications actually disclosed, unless a partial waiver would be unfair to the party's adversary.").

44. 856 F.2d 619 (4th Cir. 1988), *cert. denied*, 490 U.S. 1011 (1989).

In order arguably to qualify for this protection, counsel should at least mention to the prosecutor the possibility of a plea agreement as a means of resolving the investigation.

In addition, counsel should be aware of the risk that third parties in a derivative action or a related proceeding may subsequently seek disclosure of confidential material, by arguing that the company waived the attorney-client privilege and/or work product protection when it shared the information with the prosecutor.[45] For example, in *Westinghouse Electric Corporation v. Republic of the Philippines*,[46] the U.S. Court of Appeals for the Third Circuit held that disclosure of a privileged internal investigation report to the U.S. Securities and Exchange Commission and to DOJ waived the attorney-client privilege and work product protection, even though the federal agencies had agreed to maintain the confidentiality of the material submitted. The court indicated, however, that if the disclosure of the report to the government had been compelled, and the company had fully contested the subpoena in court, then there might not have been a waiver of the privilege upon release of the information.[47] Thus, after *Westinghouse,* the company's production of an internal investigation report, without contesting the subpoena, apparently would not be considered compulsory disclosure, and therefore may waive the privileges for private litigation as well.

K. *Global Agreements*

A company under environmental criminal investigation often finds it advantageous to seek a comprehensive settlement of its liabilities, both criminal and civil, simultaneously with both the federal and state governments. By resolving all potential obligations at the same time, a company may put the problems behind it and be able to focus on the future, with defined limits on its financial outlays and a compressed period of negative publicity. The decision whether to seek a global settlement calls for the exercise of fine judgment, especially when charges against individuals potentially are involved.

One of the most valuable functions environmental criminal counsel can serve is assessing the prospects for simultaneous settlement with all levels of government, on both the criminal and regulatory sides, and then successfully negotiating and managing the multiple independent settlements that are necessary to accomplish a complete resolution of the problem.

Whether to seek a global settlement is a strategic decision that the company must make, based upon its evaluation of its civil and criminal liability at the conclusion of a thorough internal investigation. The prosecutor will not affirmatively seek a global settlement; it must be initiated, negotiated, and closed by the corporate defendant. The window for negotiating such a resolution also is limited. The prosecutor will not agree to release any claims until the government has completed its investigation of all potential charges against the company and responsible individuals. Seeking a global solution at the wrong time may compel the prosecution to open up other areas it had no previous interest in investigating. Further, the government also is reluctant to waive its civil remedies and adamant about the corporation's obligation fully to remediate the effects of pollution.

A major impediment to achieving a global settlement is the number of governmental bodies with which the company must deal, each of which has its own interests and priorities. Left to their own devices, these agencies make little effort to coordinate their own actions. For example, criminal prosecutors typically are not the same persons as those responsible for civil penalty actions. On the regulatory side, the official dealing with air pollutions issues usually is not responsible for hazardous waste issues, and thus may have little understanding of how the Resource Conservation and Recovery Act (RCRA) works or how a solution that makes sense from a discrete "air" perspective may exacerbate hazardous waste problems. Further, different levels of government may be responsible for the judicial and regulatory parts of the problem. Indeed, there may be competition for primary jurisdiction, both among federal and state enforcement personnel and between federal and

---

45. In *United States v. Billmyer*, 57 F.3d 31 (1st Cir. 1995), the court of appeals held that disclosure to the government of the results of an internal investigation conducted by counsel waived the privilege and therefore compelled the company to produce the documents in response to a subpoena served by former corporate employees who were indicted based in part on that disclosure.
46. 951 F.2d 1414 (3d Cir. 1991).
47. *Id.* at 1427 n.15. The Third Circuit explicitly rejected the U.S. Court of Appeals for the Eighth Circuit's doctrine that voluntary disclosure to the government constitutes only a limited waiver of the attorney-client privilege. 951 F.2d at 1423-27 (citing to the Circuit's decision in Diversified Indus., Inc. v. Meredith, 572 F.2d 596 (8th Cir. 1978) (en banc)).

state regulators. Accordingly, the indispensable prerequisite for a successful global resolution is for the target to accept this fact of life and accept full responsibility for making the settlement happen.

In particular, during negotiations to resolve a criminal case, the target must address the question of civil liability. An admission of guilt may be used as evidence against the company in a subsequent civil case and may have conclusive collateral estoppel effects.[48] For example, a plea of guilty to the illegal disposal of hazardous waste in a criminal case may expose a company to significant costs in a subsequent civil case to clean-up or remediate the waste site, as well as to claims by citizens' groups for injunctive relief or injured employees for damages.

Prosecutors engaged in the negotiation of a criminal plea cannot formally agree to terms that would bind a federal civil regulator with jurisdiction over a facility. Individual prosecutors vary widely in the degree to which they are willing to attempt to interest the environmental regulator in a resolution acceptable to the company and the extent to which they are persuasive when they make the effort. Further, while a federal prosecutor may have good relations with state prosecutors and may be able to work out a resolution of all possible criminal charges at all levels, a federal prosecutor will have greater difficulty in helping a company close a deal with independent state environmental regulators.

The corporate target needs to understand that negotiations for a global settlement can be time consuming and expensive. The company must harmonize the priorities and bureaucratic interests of each government agency involved and sequence its activities carefully to bring each separate investigation to a simultaneous completion. There may be advantages in pursuing such an approach, because the environmental prosecutor may well consider reducing charges or not prosecuting in return for significant environmental cleanup commitments or agreements to install state of the art pollution control equipment enforced through a revised permit. Nevertheless, once the outline of a plea agreement is reached, the prosecutor may have little patience with the time necessary for the company to complete negotiations with administrative agencies. Civil regulators understand this fact and may not hesitate to exploit the enhanced leverage this gives them over the target. Counsel cannot expect the prosecutor to serve as the "closer" within the government, but must perform that function herself.

One example of a successful global settlement involving both the federal, state, and city governments is *United States v. Exxon Corporation,* involving the rupture of an oil pipeline that discharged 567,000 gallons of heating oil into New York harbor.[49] The states of New York and New Jersey joined the United States in a Memorandum of Agreement with the corporation. The agreement set out the fines that Exxon would pay to the three sovereigns following its guilty plea to a CWA violation. Exxon agreed to pay $15 million in criminal and civil fines and in restitution to the three governments. In return, New York and New Jersey agreed to bring no criminal charges against Exxon. In a separate plea agreement with the federal government alone, Exxon pleaded guilty to a single misdemeanor charge of negligent violation of the CWA.

L. *The Role of Alleged Victims*

The Federal Crime Victims' Rights Act (CVRA)[50] grants victims proximately harmed by criminal activity certain participatory rights in a criminal case, including the right to confer with the prosecutor. Recent cases applying the CVRA to environmental criminal cases demonstrate that this process may add an additional layer of litigation during sentencing, and the possible upset of negotiated resolutions between the defendant and the government.[51] The CVRA is discussed in detail in Chapter 8, Section I.

---

48. See Chapter 5, Subpart P *supra*, for additional discussion of possible collateral civil consequences of a criminal conviction.
49. United States v. Exxon Corporation, Civ. No. 91-1003 (D.NYJ. June 14, 1991)(Consent Order), *available at* http://www.gc.noaa.gov/gc-cd/exx2.pdf (last visited Feb. 6, 2014).
50. 18 U.S.C. §3771.
51. *See, e.g.*, United States v. BP Prods. N. Am., No. H-07-434, 2008 U.S. Dist. LEXIS 12893 **58-59 (S.D. Tex. Feb. 21, 2008), *mandamus denied in part*, In re Dean, 527 F.3d 391, 395 (5th Cir. 2008). *See also* Judson W. Starr et al., *A New Intersection: Environmental Crimes and Victims' Rights*, 23 Nat. Resources & Env't 41 (Winter 2009).

VI. Going to Trial

The decision whether to proceed to trial is inevitably intertwined with the possible penalty under the applicable guidelines, discussed *infra* in Chapter 8, Section B, and with whether a guilty plea would substantially reduce the possible sentence. Historically, if the government obtained an environmental conviction, it was likely that the convicted individual would be sentenced to at least some term of imprisonment. The mandatory *U.S. Sentencing Guidelines* in effect from 1987-2005 severely constrained the discretion of federal judges where environmental crimes were concerned, by requiring prison sentences for most convictions.

But, anecdotal evidence suggests that one effect of subsequent Supreme Court's rulings that the sentencing guidelines are advisory only, and that trial judges have discretion to impose sentences outside the recommended range of the guidelines, has been to increase the number of defendants who elect to proceed to trial in environmental criminal cases.[52]

The U.S. Sentencing Commission data shows that for all types of criminal cases, the ratio of pleas to trial steadily increased from 2006 to 2010.[53] According to the U.S. Sentencing Commission, based on data from Oct. 1, 2011, to Sept. 30, 2012, 97% of all environmental and wildlife cases concluded with a plea, and the remaining 3% went to trial.[54] For the period from Oct. 2, 2010, to Sept. 30, 2011, 93.6% of all environmental and wildlife cases concluded with a plea, and the remaining 6.4% went to trial.[55]

52. *See* United States v. Booker, 543 U.S. 220 (2005); Judson W. Starr & Gregory S. Braker, *Sentencing Guidelines for Corporate Environmental Crimes: Is It Fine Having No Fine Guidelines?*, Federal Bar Ass'n (Apr./May 1997).
53. *See* U.S. Sentencing Comm'n, 2010 Sourcebook of Federal Sentencing Statistics, fig. c (2010).
54. *See* U.S. Sentencing Comm'n, Preliminary Quarterly Data Report Fiscal Year 2012, 42, tbl. 22 (2012) (noting there were 198 "primary offense" environmental and wildlife cases in fiscal year 2012).
55. *See, e.g.*, Steven P. Solow & Anne M. Carpenter, *The State of Environmental Crime Enforcement: A Survey of Developments in 2012* (noting that of the 451 defendants that were involved in criminal environmental cases in 2012, 354 pleaded guilty and 48 proceeded to trial on their charges), http://www.kattenlaw.com/files/Publication/04515e8c-c19e-4848-8e89-001f5c23dff1/Presentation/PublicationAttachment/5a6a0b0b-0858-4f9f-9c7c-07f24762bd16/Daily%20Environment%20Report.pdf (last visited May 28, 2013).

Chapter 6:
Pre-Trial

From the first client interview or assignment of a new case, the diligent attorney is thinking about trial and trial strategy. Although the majority of environmental criminal cases eventually settle, many reach the pretrial stage. Discovery, depositions, motion practice, subpoenas, and familiarity with the Federal Rules of Criminal Procedure are therefore just a few of the areas in which a criminal environmental attorney must be competent, if not downright savvy. This chapter is intended to highlight a few nuances within these general areas.

I. Discovery

"There is no general constitutional right to discovery in a criminal case."[1] Unlike civil discovery, where some materials are automatically produced as a matter of right, in criminal prosecutions, the defendant must invoke the right to discovery.[2] Over time, a patchwork of statutory and judicial rules has evolved to govern this discovery. These rules include: (1) the Jencks Act[3]; (2) the Federal Rules of Criminal Procedure; (3) the Freedom of Information Act; (4) *Brady v. Maryland*[4]; and (5) *Giglio v. United States*, among others.[5] In 2010, the U.S. Department of Justice (DOJ) also issued a series of three guidance documents regarding the federal government's pretrial discovery obligations.

A. The Jencks Act

In *Jencks v. United States*,[6] the defendant appealed his conviction for filing an affidavit that falsely stated he was not a member of, or affiliated with, the Communist party. Crucial testimony against Jencks was provided by two undercover Federal Bureau of Investigation (FBI) agents, who testified that they had made regular oral or written reports to their superiors regarding the matters about which they had testified. Prior to trial, Jencks moved for production of these reports, in order to impeach the agents' testimony, but his motions were denied. The U.S. Supreme Court reversed, finding that the denial of Jencks' motions to produce the reports was reversible error, holding:

> Every experienced trial judge and trial lawyer knows the value for impeaching purposes of statements of the witness recording the events before time dulls treacherous memory. Flat contradiction between the witness' testimony and the version of the events given in his reports is not the only test of inconsistency. The omission from the reports of facts related at the trial, or a contrast in emphasis upon the same facts, even a

1. Weatherford v. Bursey, 429 U.S. 545, 559 (1977).
2. *Compare* Fed. R. Crim. P. 16(a)(1), *with* Fed. R. Civ. P. 26(a).
3. The *Jencks* Act requires prosecutors to turn over to the defense statements made by testifying witnesses if those statements are in the prosecutor's possession. *See* 18 U.S.C. §3500; Fed. R. Crim. P. 26.2.
4. 373 U.S. 83 (1963).
5. 405 U.S. 150 (1972).
6. 353 U.S. 657 (1957).

different order of treatment, are also relevant to the cross-examining process of testing the credibility of a witness' trial testimony.[7]

In response to this decision, Congress enacted the Jencks Act.[8] Under the statute, material relating to testimony by government witnesses is not subject to subpoena, discovery, or inspection by defense counsel until after the witness has testified.[9] Once the government's witness has testified, however, defense counsel may move the court to order the government to deliver all material in its possession relating to the witness' testimony.[10] The motion must be made at the close of the direct testimony of the specific witness concerning whom the documents are sought, not at the close of the prosecution's case. Denial of a Jencks motion is reversible error, but the trial court need not order the disclosure sua sponte.

Jencks material includes "any statement" of the witness. Under the Act, a "statement" is:

(1) A written statement made by the witness and signed or otherwise adopted or approved by him;

(2) a stenographic, mechanical, electrical, or other recording, or a transcription thereof, which is a substantially verbatim recital of an oral statement made by said witness and recorded contemporaneously with the making of such oral statement; or

(3) a statement, however taken or recorded, or a transcription thereof, if any, made by said witness to a grand jury.[11]

Typically, Jencks material consists of police notes, memoranda, reports, summaries, letters or verbatim transcripts, and grand jury transcripts. Under the plain language of the Act, rough drafts, even if substantially identical to the final version, should be produced.[12] Defense counsel should be prepared to challenge an attempt by the government to avoid production of documents covered by the Jenks Act, particularly interview notes, by asserting that they are exempt from disclosure under the attorney work product protection. The government is under no obligation to create a producible record, such as by transcribing oral statements, but must produce all covered documents that were generated.

The trial court has discretion to decide whether Jencks material should be delivered to the defendant before trial. Courts typically will order production beforehand in order to expedite a trial involving many witnesses, but usually only by a matter of days, not weeks.[13] Disclosure of Jencks material also may be required before trial under the *Brady* doctrine. The bar, however, against compulsory disclosure prior to the testimony of the witness cannot be circumvented by resort to the Freedom of Information Act or Rule 16 of the Federal Rules of Criminal Procedure. Pretrial disclosure of grand jury material is similarly governed by Rule 6(e) of the Federal Rules of Criminal Procedure.[14] As a result, the advantages of disclosure under Jencks pales in comparison to disclosure under Rule 16, as it is usually too little, too late, to be of much use to the defense.

The Jencks Act applies only to statements "in the possession of the United States,"[15] which courts have interpreted to mean in the possession of the federal prosecutor.[16] Thus, the Act does not reach materials in control of state agencies. It is also important to note that Jencks requests that are denied pretrial based on the prosecutor's representation that that "the material is not in the Government's possession" must be reasserted at trial. Otherwise, the court will consider the request to have been abandoned.[17]

In requesting Jencks materials, the defendant is required to have some reason to believe that the documents actually exist. Typically, this issue arises where the witness uses a document in testifying from, or testifies about the existence of, a document. If the government disagrees that production of the document is

7. *Id.* at 667.
8. 18 U.S.C. §3500.
9. *Id.* §3500(a).
10. *Id.* §3500(b).
11. *Id.* §3500.
12. *See, e.g.*, United States v. Sanchez, 635 F.2d 47 (2d Cir. 1980), *affirmed without opinion*, 647 F.2d 163 (2d Cir. N.Y. 1981).
13. *See, e.g.*, United States v. Narcisco, 446 F. Supp. 252 (1977).
14. *See, e.g.*, United States v. Anderson, 368 F. Supp. 1253 (1973).
15. *Id.*
16. *See, e.g.*, United States v. Trevino, 556 F.2d 1265 (5th Cir. 1977), *rehearing denied by*, 562 F.2d 1258 (5th Cir. Tex. 1977).
17. *See, e.g.*, United States v. McKenzie, 768 F.2d 602 (5th Cir. 1985), *cert. denied*, 474 U.S. 1086 (1986).

required under Jencks, the court may conduct a voir dire examination of the witness,[18]outside the presence of the jury to examine extrinsic evidence,[19] or examine the document in camera.[20] If the government elects not to produce a statement required by the Act, the court may exclude the witness's testimony or declare a mistrial pursuant to 18 U.S.C. §3500(d).

The primary provisions of the Jencks Act have been incorporated into Federal Rule of Criminal Procedure 26.2. The rule, however, extends the production requirement provisions of the Act to include any witness other than the defendant.

B. *Federal Rules of Criminal Procedure*

1. Rule 15 Depositions

Under Federal Rule of Criminal Procedure 15(a), "[a] party may move that a prospective witness be deposed in order to preserve testimony for trial"; and "[t]he court may grant the motion because of exceptional circumstances and in the interest of justice."[21] Rule 15 arguably may be used to "preserve" testimony for sentencing as well as trial.[22] The moving party bears the burden of proving exceptional circumstances.[23] In determining whether exceptional circumstances exist, the court considers: (1) the materiality of the testimony, and (2) the unavailability of the witness.[24]

Unlike in civil cases, Rule 15 depositions are not allowed merely for discovery purposes. In *United States v. Fei Ye*, the U.S. Court of Appeals for the Ninth Circuit noted that pursuant to Rule 15: "A party may move that a prospective witness be deposed in order to preserve testimony for trial, and that the court may grant the motion because of exceptional circumstances and in the interest of justice."[25] The U.S. Court of Appeals for the Fifth Circuit similarly stated in *In Re Eisenberg* that "[i]n criminal cases, depositions are not intended as discovery devices. They are in limited favor where a party's own witness is unable to attend trial."[26] Thus, deposing the government's witnesses will not be an option in most environmental crimes cases.

The "exceptional circumstances" finding turns on the physical absence of an important witness. For example, in *United States v. Fleet Management*, the U.S. District Court for the Eastern District of Pennsylvania found that "[a] substantial likelihood of unavailability can be found when the proposed deponent is beyond the subpoena powers of the United States and has declared his unwillingness to testify at trial, or even having declared willingness to testify cannot be subpoenaed if he changes his mind."[27] Thus, where counsel for two crewmembers of a vessel accused of illegally discharging oil in foreign waters and entering the United States with false oil record books wrote letters stating that their clients would not be willing to return to the United States from India to testify at trial, the court ruled that the witnesses were "unavailable" within the meaning of Rule 15. Counsel for the defendants therefore was permitted to depose the crewmembers in India.[28]

---

18. *See, e.g.,* United States v. Gallagher, 576 F.2d 1028 (3d Cir. 1978), *cert. denied,* 444 U.S. 1043 (1980).
19. *See, e.g.,* Campbell v. United States, 365 U.S. 85 (1961).
20. *See, e.g.,* United States v. Allen, 798 F.2d 985 (7th Cir. 1986).
21. Fed. R. Crim. P. 15(a)(1).
22. *See, e.g.,* United States v. Fei Ye, 436 F.3d 1117, 1123 (9th Cir. 2006).
23. United States v. Ismaili, 828 F.2d 153, 159 (3d Cir. 1987), *cert. denied,* 485 U.S. 935 (1988).
24. *Id.*
25. 436 F.3d 1117, 1123 (9th Cir. 2006).
26. In re Eisenberg, 654 F.2d 1107, 1113 n.9 (5th Cir. 1981) (citing United States v. Wilson, 601 F.2d 95, 97 (3d Cir. 1979); United States v. Rich, 580 F.2d 929, 933-34 (9th Cir. 1978), *cert. denied,* 439 U.S. 935 (1978)).
27. 2007 U.S. Dist. LEXIS 63213, *-3-4 (E.D. Pa. Aug. 28, 2007) (citing United States v. Ramos, 45 F.3d 1519, 1523 (11th Cir. 1995)). The court also permitted the government to take Rule 15 depositions of three other crewmembers prior to their departure from the United States. 2007 U.S. Dist. LEXIS 41279 (E.D. Pa. May 25, 2007). Of interest in this decision is that the witnesses were all material witnesses and had all expressed a desire to immediately leave the United States, but had all said they would be willing to return to the United States to testify at trial, if available, if it was possible to return, and if the government paid for the expenses of their return. However, the court noted that, upon their return to India, they would be beyond the subpoena power of the United States and there was no way for the court to ensure their return. The court thus found they were unavailable under Rule 15(a). Id. at *8. *See also* United States v. Drogoul, 1 F.3d 1546, 1553 (11th Cir. 1993) ("A potential witness is unavailable for purposes of Rule 15(a) . . . whenever a substantial likelihood exists that the proposed deponent will not testify at trial.").
28. 2007 U.S. Dist. LEXIS 63123 at *4-5. The court declined however, to require the government to pay the costs of such depositions. *Id.* at *5.

The contrast between Rule 15 depositions in criminal and civil cases is apparent in the context of parallel proceedings. During the civil case, defense counsel may be able to gain access to the testimony of government witnesses. Such pretrial and trial examination of government witnesses provides defense counsel with the prosecution's evidence—evidence which would not have been available but for the civil trial—well in advance of the criminal trial. Such testimony also may be used to impeach the government's witnesses at the criminal trial, should they attempt to offer inconsistent testimony.

2. Rule 16 Discovery

Rule 16 has been significantly expanded since the Federal Rules of Criminal Procedure were first adopted. It now imposes discovery obligations both on the government and the defense.[29] Rule 16 thus prevents criminal trials from becoming "a sporting contest in which the game of cat and mouse is acceptable."[30] "When defendants invoke Rule 16, they open themselves up to discovery to gain access to information held by the government; thus, they invariably give the government some inkling of the defense theory of the case. Through this process, prosecutors become more informed about their own case and the evidence in their possession."[31]

Pursuant to Rule 16, defense counsel is entitled to receive four basic pieces of information on behalf of the defendant: (1) his written or recorded statement; (2) a copy of his prior criminal record; (3) reports of any physical and mental evaluation or scientific experiments that are either material to the preparation of the defense or are intended for use at trial by the prosecutor, and (4) a written summary of any expert testimony the prosecutor intends to use, including the expert's qualifications, opinion and the basis for such opinion.[32] Environmental crimes cases almost always include a corporate defendant, which also brings into play Rule 16(a)(1)(C),[33] which entitles a corporate defendant to the grand jury testimony of present and former employees who will be called as witnesses at trial.

Rule 16(a)(1)(A) initially required only that the government turn over "the substance of any oral statement which the government intends to offer in evidence at the trial."[34] In 1991, the rule was amended to broaden the government's disclosure obligations. Rule 16(a)(1)(A) now requires the government to disclose "that portion of any written record containing the substance of any relevant oral statement made by the defendant whether before or after arrest in response to interrogation by any possible person then known to the defendant to be a government agent."[35] Thus, it may also be possible for a corporate defendant to obtain any statements corporate employees may have made to law enforcement officers.

While Rule 16(a)(1) delineates the scope of the government's production obligations, Rule 16(a)(2) expressly protects certain categories of work product documents from disclosure. Prior to 2013, this rule read:

> Except as Rule 16(a)(1) provides otherwise, this rule does not authorize the discovery or inspection of reports, memoranda, or other internal government documents made by an attorney for the government or other govern-

29. *See* Fed. R. Crim. P. 16(a) (Government's Disclosure); (b) (Defendant's Disclosure).
30. United States v. Howell, 231 F.3d 615, 626 (9th Cir. 2000), *cert. denied*, 534 U.S. 831 (2001); *see also* Berger v. United States, 295 U.S. 78, 88 (1935) ("The United States Attorney['s] . . . interest, therefore, in a criminal prosecution is not that it shall win a case, but that justice shall be done.").
31. *See* United States v. Fort, 478 F.3d 1099 (9th Cir. 2007) (Wardlaw, J., dissenting), *cert. denied*, 552 U.S. 948 (2007).
32. Fed. R. Crim. P. 16(a)(1)(A), (B), (D), (E), (F) & (G).
33. Fed. R. Crim. P. 16(a)(1)(C) provides:
    Upon defendant's request, if defendant is an organization, the government must disclose to the defendant any statement described in Fed. R. Crim. P. 16(a)(1)(A) and (B), if the government contends that the person making the statement (i) was legally able to bind the defendant regarding the subject of the statement because of that person's position as the defendant's director, officer, employee, or agent; or (ii) was personally involved in the alleged conduct constituting the offense and was legally able to bind the defendant regarding that conduct because of that person's position as the defendant's director, officer, employee, or agent.
34. *See* United States v. Crowell, 586 F.2d 1020, 1029 (4th Cir. 1978), *cert. denied*, 440 U.S. 959 (1979). In *Crowell*, which was decided prior to the 1991 Amendments, the U.S. Court of Appeals for the Fourth Circuit held that the government had not violated Rule 16 by failing to produce an agent's notes where the agent had testified at trial that "his report incorporated the entire contents of his notes except for those portions which did not relate to the investigation." Under those circumstances, the court of appeals concluded that the government had "furnished counsel all relevant statements in the possession of the government" and that the district court had not erred in refusing to strike the agent's testimony. *Id.*
35. *Id.*

ment agent in connection with investigating or prosecuting the case. Nor does this rule authorize the discovery or inspection of statements made by prospective government witnesses except as provided in 18 U.S.C. §3500.

A literal interpretation of Rule 16(a)(2)—if a document is subject to production under Rule 16(a)(1), then it cannot be withheld on the basis of Rule 16(a)(2)—potentially produced results that most courts refused to entertain. For instance, under a literal interpretation, pursuant to Rule 16(a)(1)€, which states that "[u]pon a defendant's request, the government must permit the defendant to inspect and to copy documents . . . if the item is within the government's possession, custody, or control and . . . the item is material to preparing the defense . . .," As a result, the proper resolution of the interplay between Rules 16(a)(1) and 16(a)(2) was the subject of some debate.[36]

In *United States v. Fort*,[37] the Ninth Circuit followed the interpretive theory first outlined by the U.S. District Court for the Northern District of Alabama in *United States v. Rudolph*,[38] and held that the first clause of Rule 16(a)(2) should be interpreted to mean: "Except as Rule 16(a)(1)(A), (B), (C), (D), (F), and (G) provide." Thus, while a defendant could obtain a copy of his own statement under Rule 16(a)(1)(A), he could not obtain under Rule 16(a)(1)(E) the internal government legal memorandum outlining the perceived weaknesses of his statement.[39] In 2013, Rule 16(a)(2) was amended to reflect the interpretation of this Rule in accordance with the holding in the *Fort* and *Rudolph* decisions, and Rule 16(a)(2) now reads "Except as permitted by Rule 16(a)(1)(A)-(D), (F), and (G) . . .."

Fort also is significant, in that the Ninth Circuit held that inculpatory (that is, non-*Brady*), non-public investigative reports made by a local police officer, and then turned over to prosecutors for use in a federal prosecution concerning the same acts by the same persons, are exempted from disclosure by Rule 16(a)(2), because the police officer is deemed an "agent" of the federal government. *Fort* thereby dramatically expanded the definition of a "federal agent" for purposes of Rule 16(a)(2).

Defense counsel should bear in mind that if police officers are federal agents for purposes of the work product protection afforded by Rule 16(a)(2), they also may be considered federal agents for disclosure purposes pursuant to Rule 16(a)(1) and *Brady/Giglio*.[40] Additionally, it should be remembered that once a defendant makes a Rule 16 discovery request and the government complies, the government is entitled to seek reciprocal discovery from the defendant.[41]

3. Rule 17 Subpoenas

Pursuant to Rule 17 of the Federal Rules of Criminal Procedure, a subpoena *ad testificandum* requires the witness to appear and testify before the grand jury, while a subpoena *duces tecum* requires "the witness to produce any books, papers, documents, data, or other objects the subpoena designates."[42] Upon a timely motion, "the court may quash or modify the subpoena if compliance would be unreasonable or oppressive."[43]

36. One such issue is whether the amended language of Rule 16(a)(1)(A) extends to the production of rough notes of agents and prosecutors, even where a final report (such as an FBI Form 302) has already been produced. *See, e.g.*, United States v. Molina-Guevara, 96 F.3d 698, 705 (3d Cir. 1996) (holding that Rule 16 requires disclosure of handwritten notes from which the agent prepared final report); United States v. Griggs, 111 F. Supp. 2d 551, 555 (M.D. Pa. 2000) (finding that "ordering disclosure of the notes is necessary to effectuate the purpose of Rule 16(a)(1)(A)"); United States v. Carucci, 183 F.R.D. 614, 615 (S.D.N.Y. 1999) (holding that "unambiguous and unequivocal language" of Rule 16(a)(1)(A) compelled the court to require the government to disclose the agent's notes of defendant's prior interview). *But cf.* United States v. Almohandis, 307 F. Supp. 2d 253 (D. Mass. 2004).
37. 472 F.3d 1106, 1107 (9th Cir. 2007).
38. 224 F.R.D. 503 (N.D. Ala. 2004).
39. *See* David E. Roth & Brian L. Flack, United States v. Fort, *The Ninth Circuit Clarifies the Relationship Between Federal Rules of Criminal Procedure 16(a)(1)(E) and (16)(a)(2)*, Envtl. Enforcement & Crimes Comm. Newsl. 13 (June 2007).
40. *See* United States v. Fort, 478 F.3d 1099 (9th Cir. 2007), *cert. denied*, 552 U.S. 948 (2007) (Wardlaw, J., dissenting) (predicting that *Fort* will vastly expand the kinds of materials that the federal government will have to produce during discovery).
41. *See* Fed. R. Crim. P. 16(b)(1).
42. *Id.* 17(c)(1).
43. *Id.* 17(c)(2).

a. Subpoena *Ad Testificandum*

Experienced criminal attorneys typically are wary of allowing their clients to appear and testify before a grand jury, and with good reason. Grand jury proceedings are secret, so the client must testify, if at all, unaccompanied by counsel. Counsel must carefully weigh beforehand the risk that a witness will incriminate himself or offer inconsistent or mistaken testimony that is later deemed to be perjurous, or that the prosecution will learn of new information through the testimony that furthers its investigation and later ensnares their client. Nevertheless, in certain circumstances, such as with a cooperating company or low-level employees and the appropriate assurances from the prosecutor, i.e., written assurance of non-target status or Queen for the Day immunity, the tactical decision may be to allow the client to testify.

If the client does testify, counsel should fully debrief him as soon as possible afterwards. Learning exactly what questions were asked often provides important insights into the prosecutor's theory of the case.

b. Subpoena *Duces Tecum*

Although a literal reading of Rule 17 might suggest that it bestows broad discovery powers upon defense counsel, district courts have significantly limited its reach, in reliance upon *United States v. Nixon*.[44] Under *Nixon*, the defendant must show that the subpoenaed material is: (1) relevant; (2) admissible as evidence; and (3) specifically identified.[45] Although some judges have occasionally found reason to impose a lesser showing of the defendant,[46] courts typically conclude that "[s]ubpoenas issued pursuant to Rule 17(c) are not discovery devices and may not be used to expand the scope of Rule 16 . . .."[47] Where subpoenas are deemed to be discovery devices, they will be quashed.[48]

C. *The Freedom of Information Act*

An integral part of environmental defense counsel's discovery practice should be a Freedom of Information Act (FOIA)[49] request, filed as soon as possible with the appropriate regulatory agency, to increase the chances of an agency response before trial.[50] Given the inherently regulatory basis of an environmental crimes case, FOIA requests often will produce pertinent information the government would otherwise resist providing to defense counsel. Policies developed and implemented by administrative agencies guide environmental testing methodology, inspection protocols, and even jurisdictional determinations. FOIA requests regarding these policies and procedures can reveal information that supports variances from standard operating procedures, or even agency bias toward a particular outcome.

FOIA provides a mechanism for individuals to obtain a broad range of information from the U.S. government.[51]

In addition to creating certain statutory exemptions,[52] Congress attempted to prevent criminal defendants from abusing FOIA by adopting Exemption 7.[53] It specifically exempts from production documents collected in connection with a law enforcement investigation:

---

44. 418 U.S. 683 (1974).
45. *Id.* at 700.
46. *See, e.g.*, United States v. Tucker, 249 F.R.D. 58 (S.D.N.Y. 2008) (relaxing the *Nixon* standard when applied to a defendant's subpoena issued to a third party shortly before the trial date).
47. *See* Order, United States v. Fletcher, No. 06 MJ 4314 PCT MEA (Oct. 25, 2006) (Magistrate Judge Asprey) (citing United States v. Brooks, 966 F.2d 1500, 1505 (D.C. Cir. 1992); United States v. Cuthbertson, 630 F.2d 139, 146 (3d Cir. 1980); United States v. Cherry, 876 F. Supp. 547, 552 (S.D.N.Y. 1995)).
48. *See id.* Order at 4.
49. 5 U.S.C. §552. FOIA was signed into law by President Lyndon B. Johnson in 1966.
50. Although information received after trial might form the basis for a new trial pursuant to *Brady v. Maryland*, 373 U.S. 83 (1963), this would likely be an uphill battle best avoided, if possible.
51. 5 U.S.C. §552(a)(2).
52. Such exemptions include information: "related solely to the internal personnel rules and practices of an agency;" "inter-agency or intra-agency memorandums or letters which would not be available by law to a party other than an agency in litigation with the agency;" and "geological and geophysical information and data, including maps, concerning wells." *Id.* §552(b).
53. *Id.* §552(b)(7).

> [R]ecords or information compiled for law enforcement purposes, but only to the extent that the production of such law enforcement records or information (A) could reasonably be expected to interfere with enforcement proceedings, (B) would deprive a person of a right to a fair trial or an impartial adjudication, (C) could reasonably be expected to constitute an unwarranted invasion of personal privacy, (D) could reasonably be expected to disclose the identity of a confidential source, including a State, local, or foreign agency or authority or any private institution which furnished information on a confidential basis, and, in the case of a record or information compiled by a criminal law enforcement authority in the course of a criminal investigation or by an agency conducting a lawful national security intelligence investigation, information furnished by a confidential source, (E) would disclose techniques and procedures for law enforcement investigations or prosecutions, or would disclose guidelines for law enforcement investigations or prosecutions if such disclosure could reasonably be expected to risk circumvention of the law, or (F) could reasonably be expected to endanger the life or physical safety of any individual.

Each agency has complete discretion in deciding whether to waive the exemption and release all documents covered by the law enforcement provision. Federal courts have repeatedly upheld an agency's refusal to waive an exemption.[54] Because each agency is charged with developing and implementing its own FOIA policies and procedures, defense counsel must first identify to which agency FOIA applications should be submitted and then review the particular agency's submission procedures. Most federal agencies have relatively easy-to-use FOIA guidelines on their internet sites.[55] Many states have also adopted their own FOIA laws.[56]

Time is of the essence in the FOIA process because many agencies typically lag well behind the statutory deadlines for responding to a request. The challenge is to determine what agency documents might be critical to the defense and then narrowly-tailoring a FOIA request that will expedite the process and reduce the agency's ability to assert that an extension of time is warranted (from the nominal twenty day limit for response) due to the need to produce voluminous documentation.[57] If a dispute regarding a FOIA request arises, it typically must be litigated through the established administrative and judicial processes.[58]

Counsel should be cautious, however, of tipping off the government as to the defense strategy through overly specific FOIA requests. For instance, counsel must assume that the Environmental Crimes Section (ECS) will quickly learn of a request submitted to the U.S. Environmental Protection Agency. Similar considerations would also apply before submitting a FOIA request to a state regulatory agency.

D. Brady *Material*

> Though not technically a rule of criminal discovery, *Brady [v. Maryland]* and its progeny play an important role in the process. Discovery decisions made by prosecutors must always be made with one eye on successful prosecution and the other on the potential for reversible error for failure to disclose information.[59]

"Generally, *Brady* violations first come before a court after the trial and the court may then consider the materiality of what was suppressed or omitted from disclosures made, in the context of the complete trial record."[60]

---

54. *See* Strout v. U.S. Parole Comm'n, 40 F.3d 136, 139 (6th Cir. 1994) (names and addresses of people who wrote to Parole Commission opposing a convict's parole are exempt from FOIA disclosure); Department of State v. Washington Post Co., 456 U.S. 595 (1982) (rejecting requests for information about private citizens as exempt under FOIA).
55. *See, e.g.*, http://www.epa.gov/foia/ (last visited May 28, 2013) (EPA FOIA procedures); http://www.usdoj.gov/oip/index.html (last visited June 4, 2013) (DOJ FOIA procedures); http://foia.fbi.gov/ (last visited May 28, 2013) (FBI FOIA procedures); http://www.dol.gov/dol/foia/main.htm (last visited May 28, 2013) (U.S. Department of Labor FOIA procedures).
56. *See, e.g.*, Ala. Code §36-12-40, Ga. Code Ann. §50-18-70, N.C. Gen. Stat. §§132-1 through 132-10.
57. *See* 5 U.S.C. §552(a)(6)(B)(iii)(II).
58. "[T]he discovery provisions of the Federal Rules of Criminal Procedure and the FOIA provide two independent schemes for obtaining information through the judicial process. Although information obtained through the FOIA may be useful in a criminal trial . . .. FOIA was not intended as a device to delay ongoing litigation or to enlarge the scope of discovery beyond that already provided by the Federal Rules of Criminal Procedure." United States v. Murdock, 548 F.2d 599, 602 (5th Cir. 1977); *see also* United States v. U.S. District Court, Central District of Cal., L.A., 717 F.2d 478 (9th Cir. 1983); United States v. Buckley, 586 F.2d 498 (5th Cir. 1978), *cert. denied*, 440 U.S. 982 (1979); Freuhaf Corp. v. Thornton, 507 F.2d 1253 (6th Cir. 1974).
59. United States v. Fort, 478 F.3d 1099 (9th Cir. 2007).
60. United States v. McVeigh, 954 F. Supp. 1441, 1449-50 (D. Colo. 1997), *cert. denied*, 526 U.S. 1007 (1999).

In *Brady v. Maryland*,[61] the state prosecuted Brady and his companion, Boblit, for murder. Brady admitted to being involved in the murder, but claimed that Boblit had done the actual killing. The prosecution withheld from Brady a written statement by Boblit, in which he confessed to having performed the murder by himself. Brady argued that his conviction violated the Due Process Clause of the Fourteenth Amendment because the prosecution had withheld this exculpatory evidence from him before trial. The Supreme Court agreed, holding "that the suppression by the prosecution of evidence favorable to an accused upon request violates due process where the evidence is material either to guilt or punishment, irrespective of the good faith or bad faith of the prosecution."[62]

Subsequent Supreme Court decisions have held that both federal and state prosecutors have an affirmative, constitutionally mandated duty to disclose exculpatory evidence to the defendant to help ensure his right to a fair trial under the Due Process Clauses of the Fifth and Fourteenth Amendments.[63] *Brady* thus requires that prosecutors fully disclose to the accused all exculpatory evidence in their possession. Although *Brady* did not define what constitutes "material" evidence, the standard has been interpreted to mean "when prejudice to the accused ensues . . . [and where] the nondisclosure [is] so serious that there is a reasonable probability that the suppressed evidence would have produced a different verdict."[64]

Supreme Court decisions following *Brady* expanded the prosecution's obligations to include the duty to disclose: (1) impeachment evidence[65]; (2) favorable evidence in the absence of a request by the accused[66]; and (3) evidence in the possession of government persons or organizations, e.g., the police.[67]

The *Brady* doctrine applies fully in environmental criminal cases. Besides more obvious inquiries, e.g., favorable witness statements, environmental crimes cases may warrant inquiries into: favorable regulatory inspections and compliance reports; favorable environmental testing results; and agency interpretations of regulations that are contrary to the prosecution's view.

E. Giglio *Material*

Exculpatory impeachment evidence is commonly referred to as *Giglio* material. It includes, but is not limited to: (1) specific instances of conduct of a witness for the purpose of attacking the witness' credibility or character for truthfulness; (2) evidence in the form of opinion or reputation as to a witness' character for truthfulness; (3) prior inconsistent statements; and (4) information that may be used to suggest that a witness is biased.

In *Giglio v. United States*,[68] the defendant was convicted of forgery based primarily on the testimony of an unindicted co-conspirator who testified that he had not received any promises of leniency in exchange for his testimony against *Giglio*. In fact, the prosecutor who presented the case to the grand jury had promised not to prosecute the co-conspirator in exchange for his testimony. The Supreme Court overturned the conviction and was not swayed by the trial prosecutor's claim that he was unaware of the deal. "When the reliability of a given witness may be determinative of guilt or innocence," the Court wrote, "nondisclosure of evidence affecting credibility falls within this general rule." The Court held that exculpatory evidence includes evidence affecting witness credibility, where the witness's "reliability" is likely "determinative of guilt or innocence."[69]

F. DOJ Guidance

In response to a series of high-profile cases, including one of the largest environmental prosecutions in DOJ's history (where a jury acquitted W.R. Grace & Company and three of its former executives of all

61. 373 U.S. 83 (1963).
62. *Id.* at 87.
63. *See* United States v. Bagley, 473 U.S. 667, 675 (1985) ("The *Brady* rule is based on the requirement of due process. Its purpose is not to displace the adversary system as the primary means by which truth is uncovered, but to ensure that a miscarriage of justice does not occur.").
64. Strickler v. Greene, 527 U.S. 263, 281 (1999).
65. Giglio v. United States, 405 U.S. 150 (1972).
66. United States v. Agurs, 427 U.S. 97, 107 (1976).
67. Kyles v. Whitley, 514 U.S. 419, 437 (1995).
68. 405 U.S. 150 (1972).
69. *Id.* at 154.

charges after more than two months of trial),[70] that highlighted concerns as to whether prosecutors were fairly discharging their obligation to produce exculpatory evidence (along with other prosecutorial misconduct), DOJ issued a series of three guidance memoranda regarding the federal government's pre-trial discovery obligations.

In the first, Deputy Attorney General David Ogden outlines a number of training initiatives and resources that "are intended to ensure that we have the resources, training and guidance to meet our obligations and that we thoroughly and thoughtfully evaluate our discovery obligations in every case in a manner that facilitates our sole function—to seek justice."[71]

The second,

> direct[s] the USAOs and each Department litigating component handling criminal matters to develop a discovery policy that reflects circuit and district court precedent and local rules and practices. This directive requires each office to establish a discovery policy with which prosecutors in that office must comply. The policy should also provide that specific, case-related considerations may warrant a departure from the uniform discovery practices of the office. Because it is expected that such considerations will sometimes justify a departure from the particular office practice, your policy must set forth procedures prosecutors are required to follow to obtain supervisory approval to depart from the uniform practices in an appropriate case.[72]

The third and most substantive guidance document, lays out four specific steps that will result in prosecutors being "more likely to meet all legal requirements, to make considered decisions about disclosures in a particular case, and to achieve a just result in every case."[73] In Step 1, Gathering and Reviewing Discoverable Information, the guidance states:

> It is the obligation of federal prosecutors, in preparing for trial, to seek all exculpatory and impeachment information from all members of the prosecution team. Members of the prosecution team include federal, state, and local law enforcement officers and other government officials participating in the investigation and prosecution of the criminal case against the defendant.
>
> Some factors to be considered in determining whether to review potentially discoverable information from another federal agency include:
>
> - whether the prosecutor and the agency conducted a joint investigation or shared resources related to investigating the case;
> - whether the agency played an active role in the prosecution, including conducting arrests or searches, interviewing witnesses, developing prosecutorial strategy, participating in targeting discussions, or otherwise acting as part of the prosecution team;
> - whether the prosecutor knows of and has access to discoverable information held by the agency;
> - whether the prosecutor has obtained other information and/or evidence from the agency;
> - the degree to which information gathered by the prosecutor has been shared with the agency;
> - whether a member of an agency has been made a Special Assistant United States Attorney;
> - the degree to which decisions have been made jointly regarding civil, criminal, or administrative charges; and
> - the degree to which the interests of the parties in parallel proceedings diverge such that information gathered by one party is not relevant to the other party.

---

70. Others include dismissal of charges against members of the Duke University lacrosse team, U.S. Senator Ted Stevens, and Blackwater security guards in Iraq.

71. David W. Ogden, Issuance of Guidance and Summary of Actions Taken in Response to the Report of the Department of Justice Criminal Discovery and Case Management Working Group (Jan. 4, 2010), *available at* http://www.justice.gov/dag/dag-memo.html (last visited June 4, 2013).

72. David W. Ogden, Requirement for Office Discovery Policies in Criminal Matters (Jan. 4, 2010), *available at* http://www.justice.gov/dag/dag-to-usas-component-heads.html (last visited June 4, 2013).

73. David W. Ogden, Guidance for Prosecutors Regarding Criminal Discovery (Jan. 4, 2010), *available at* http://www.justice.gov/dag/discovery-guidance.html (last visited May 28, 2013).

> Prosecutors are encouraged to err on the side of inclusiveness when identifying the members of the prosecution team for discovery purposes. Carefully considered efforts to locate discoverable information are more likely to avoid future litigation over *Brady* and *Giglio* issues and avoid surprises at trial.

Material within the possession or control of the prosecution team that must be reviewed by the prosecutor includes: (1) investigative agency files; (2) confidential informant, witness, and source files; (3) case investigation evidence and files; (4) evidence or documents in the possession of civil attorneys and regulatory agencies; (5) substantive case-related communications; (6) potential *Giglio* information relating to law enforcement witnesses; (7) potential *Giglio* information relating to non-law enforcement witnesses; and (8) information obtained in witness interviews.

In Step 2, Conducting the Review, the guidance notes that the prosecutor is ultimately the one responsible for compliance with the government's discovery obligations. Thus, while workload may require the prosecutor to delegate the identification of potentially discoverable information to other team members, the guidance cautions that ultimate *Brady* decisions may not be delegated, and rest squarely with the prosecutor. The guidance also notes that for voluminous productions by third parties, prosecutors may decide to simply provide defense counsel with access to all materials to avoid the possibility that the review process "fails to identify material discoverable evidence."

In Step 3, Making the Disclosure, with respect to actually producing discoverable evidence to defendants, the guidance notes "that Section 001 [of the U.S. Attorneys' Manual] details the Department's policy regarding the disclosure of exculpatory and impeachment information and provides for broader disclosures than required by *Brady* and *Giglio*. Prosecutors are also encouraged to provide discovery broader and more comprehensive than the discovery obligations." Nevertheless, in contemplating discovery in addition to that required, prosecutors are cautioned to consider any countervailing interests, such as the protection of witnesses and victims, the integrity of the investigation, privileged materials, and national security interests, among others. Exculpatory evidence is directed to be disclosed "reasonably promptly" after discovery. Impeachment evidence is directed to be disclosed "at a reasonable time before trial" to ensure the trial proceeds efficiently. The guidance also includes "reminders" that local court rules must be consulted and that a prosecutor's discovery obligation is a continuing one.

In Step 4, Making a Record, the guidance notes that "[p]rosecutors should make a record of when and how information is disclosed or otherwise made available. While discovery matters are often the subject of litigation in criminal cases, keeping a record of the disclosures confines the litigation to substantive matters and avoids time-consuming disputes about what was disclosed."

While the above guidance acknowledges that it cannot answer every question that will arise during discovery, and critics have pointed to the numerous instances where the prosecutor's discretion is relied upon, it serves as an important reminder that observance of the rules of pretrial discovery will facilitate the government's desired end result: a fair and just trial.

Notably, despite this series of guidance memorandum recommending broader pretrial discovery than that which is arguable required, the government has not indicated a willingness to expand the discovery provided in advance of a plea agreement, and indeed often requires the waiver of discovery rights as part of a plea agreement.[74] When combined with the fact that the vast majority of environmental criminal cases are settled via plea agreement,[75] the aforementioned DOJ guidance may be of little benefit to the vast majority of defendants.

II. Motion Practice

Motion practice is a basic component of effective legal representation, and an environmental criminal case is no exception. With more companies and individuals deciding in recent years to proceed to trial rather

74. *See, e.g.*, Ellen S. Podgor, *Pleading Blindly*, 80 Miss. L. Rev. 1633, 1633-34 (2011); Daniel Blank, *Plea Bargain Waivers Reconsidered: A Legal Pragmatist's Guide to Loss, Abandonment and Alienation*, 68 Fordham L. Rev. 2011 (2000) (noting requirements to waive discovery rights in plea agreements).

75. For 2012, based on data from Oct. 1, 2011, through Sept. 30, 2012, the U.S. Sentencing Commission found that 97% of all environmental and wildlife cases concluded with a plea, and the remaining 3% went to trial. *See* U.S. Sentencing Comm'n, Preliminary Quarterly Data Report Fiscal Year 2012 42, tbl. 22 (2012) (noting there were 198 "primary offense" environmental and wildlife cases in fiscal year 2012).

than plead to an environmental crime, litigators must be aware of how environmental crimes cases differ from other offenses and of the nuances required to fine tune normal principles to reflect the unique features of the offenses charged. The issues presented are usually complex, the indictments filed are often lengthy, and the dense statutory and regulatory frameworks frequently involved can quickly lead the unwary or inexperienced counsel astray.

These complexities also may seem daunting to the trial judge. They may make the court more willing than in other types of cases to defer to the prosecutor, who is typically supported by either the EPA or the state's environmental agency, or both, regarding interpretation of the statutory and regulatory framework. Motion practice is therefore a key opportunity for defense counsel to demonstrate that she also is capable of guiding the court through the complications that abound in untangling environmental issues. Pretrial motions also are essential in exposing the government's core theories, as well as identifying for the court the evidence on which the prosecutor actually intends to rely. A few "less standard" motions to keep in mind in any environmental crimes case include:

A. *Bill of Particulars*

The more complicated the indictment, the stronger the argument in favor of defense counsel filing a bill of particulars. The complexity of environmental indictments is perhaps rivaled only by tax indictments. Environmental indictments, however, typically omit key information the government would prefer to keep out of the defense's hands for as long as possible, such as:

(1) The specific dates and locations the alleged unlawful events occurred;

(2) The identity of the alleged participants in the crimes charged; and

(3) The identity of the alleged victims (in knowing endangerment cases).

This complexity should be highlighted for the judge, and a bill of particulars may provide an effective tool to defense counsel in identifying weaknesses in the government's case.

Although the success rate of such motions should naturally be considered where resources are limited, several courts have required the government to provide additional information in response to a bill of particulars.[76]

B. *Motion in Limine*

A successful motion *in limine* can reduce the workload of defense counsel by limiting in advance the evidence the government may present at trial. Uniquely to the practice of environmental law, counsel should consider filing a motion in limine that seeks to preclude the government's ability to present evidence of environmental harm. As environmental harm is often not an element of the offense charged, such motions typically focus on the lack of relevance as opposed to the likelihood of prejudice to the defendant posed by such evidence.

---

76. *See, e.g.,* United States v. Odfjell Westfal-Larsen, No. H-87-220 (S.D. Tex. 1987) (alleging unlawful storage and disposal of hazardous wastes under RCRA). The government was required to provide in a Bill of Particulars:

(1) "the specific occasions on which there was disposal, and for each, identify the date, time, who personally did the disposal, and the nature of the alleged 'hazardous wastes."
(2) "the names of all alleged co-conspirators presently known to the government, whether indicted or unindicted herein, and the times of their alleged participation in the alleged conspiracy."
(3) "when and what hazardous wastes were generated."
(4) "the name of the person or persons who were allegedly placed in imminent danger of death or serious bodily injury, where each said person was located . . ., and the nature and degree of the imminent danger to each said person."
(5) "any overt acts not enumerated or incorporated by reference in Count 1, concerning which acts the government intends to offer evidence upon trial of the Indictment herein."

See also United States v. Laughlin, 768 F. Supp. 957, 967 (N.D.N.Y. 1991) (prosecution was required to identify in a bill of particulars the precise hazardous wastes upon which it intended to rely); United States v. White, 766 F. Supp. 873 (E.D. Wash. 1991) (prosecution required in a knowing endangerment case to provide the identity of the persons allegedly endangered and the injuries allegedly suffered).

All efforts to minimize or prevent reference to environmental harm are worthwhile in defending an environmental crimes case. The less jurors feel personally affected by the alleged conduct of the defendant, individual(s) or corporation, the more likely they are to believe the case should have been brought in a civil forum, if at all. Even where such a motion is ultimately denied, it may have indirect benefits. The judge likely will gain new appreciation for the limits of relevance offered by such evidence, as well as being sensitized to its propensity for unfair prejudice by inflaming the jury. The motion also will put the prosecution on notice that any questions related to environmental harm, as well as any resulting witness testimony, will be closely scrutinized by defense counsel.

Given the ECS's recent initiative to insert health and safety issues into what are fundamentally environmental crimes cases, a motion *in limine* to exclude such evidence, particularly of gruesome or graphic workplace injuries, also should be considered by defense counsel for reasons similar to those for seeking to exclude or limit evidence of environmental harm.

On the flip side, in environmental crimes cases where there is no evidence of environmental harm, defense attorneys should be prepared for the likelihood that the government will file a motion *in limine* seeking to prevent the defense from highlighting this to the jury.[77]

C. *Motion to Suppress*

The existence of Fourth Amendment issues must be considered in an environmental crimes case, and a motion to suppress filed when appropriate. Particular consideration should be given to whether the initial governmental search was conducted pursuant to a statute authorizing warrantless searches. These statutes, which may authorize searches without requiring a high level of suspicion, may be particularly vulnerable to constitutional challenge, especially where the statute gives the state agency unbridled discretion.78 Whether a state regulatory inspection was simply a pretext for an ongoing criminal investigation also may be an important consideration.

---

77. United States v. Linden Beverage Co., 1996 WL 455845 (W.D. Va. 1996) (prosecutors successfully filed pretrial or in limine motions to prevent the defendants from showing the jury that the nearby stream was not harmed). Despite the fact that the Devaney Memorandum seemingly limits criminal investigations to cases where there is both significant environmental harm and a high degree of culpability, the Memorandum is ignored in cases where there is little or no environmental harm. *See, e.g., id. See also* Earl Devaney, Director of EPA's Office of Criminal Enforcement Issues a Memorandum, The Exercise of Investigative Discretion.

Chapter 7:
Trial

This chapter describes aspects of the trial process that have proved significant in prior environmental criminal prosecutions.

I. Evidence

"Evidence," in its most general sense, includes everything that is used to determine or demonstrate the truth of an assertion. Testimonial evidence covers what witnesses say under oath or affirmation. Real evidence includes all types of tangible objects. Lawyers also may stipulate to facts upon which they agree, and courts may take judicial notice of facts that are common knowledge.

The law further distinguishes between direct evidence and circumstantial evidence. Direct evidence proves the point without the need to draw any conclusions, while circumstantial evidence requires the trier of fact to draw a conclusion that some relevant fact occurred.

In most environmental crimes cases, the government bears the burden of proving that the defendant is guilty beyond a reasonable doubt.[1] The burden of proof is often associated with the latin maxim *semper necessitas probandi incumbit ei qui agit*, which can be translated as: "the necessity of proof always lies with the person who lays charges."

The U.S. Supreme Court held in *Jackson v. Virginia* that the U.S. Constitution requires enough evidence to justify a rational trier of fact in finding guilt beyond a reasonable doubt.[2] This type of "legal burden" or "burden of persuasion" remains on the government for the duration of the trial. Thus, the government must introduce sufficient evidence of a crime to overcome the presumption that the defendant is innocent. If the government is able to meet its burden to the satisfaction of the trier of fact, the defendant will be found guilty.

In contrast, an "evidentiary burden" or "burden of production" shifts between the parties over the course of the trial. If one party submits evidence that the court will consider a prima facie showing of some element of the crime, the burden shifts to the other party to present evidence to refute that presumption.

The frequent absence of smoking gun, i.e., direct, evidence in environmental crimes cases often results in prosecutors having to rely on expert witness testimony and circumstantial evidence to demonstrate the severity of the environmental offense and to link the defendant to the crime. This can be beneficial to defense counsel, as such evidence is more susceptible to attack.

Of course, not all evidence—smoking gun or otherwise—is admissible. In federal court, evidence is admitted or excluded based upon the Federal Rules of Evidence, which attempt to safeguard the parties against injustice.

---

1. "Reasonable doubt" is the standard required in most criminal cases and constitutes the highest level of the burden of persuasion. It requires that the proposition being presented by the government must be proven so that no reasonable doubt remains in the mind of a reasonable person that the defendant is guilty. This standard leaves room for doubt, but only to the extent that it would not affect a reasonable person's belief that the defendant is guilty. Jury instructions typically explain that a reasonable doubt is a doubt based on reason and common sense. *See, e.g.*, Jackson v. Virginia, 443 U.S. 307 (1979).
2. 443 U.S. 307 (1979).

A. *Rules of Evidence*

The rules of evidence are the principles by which a court determines whether evidence is admissible at trial. Federal courts follow the Federal Rules of Evidence, while state courts generally follow their own rules. State rules of evidence are usually imposed by the state legislature upon the state courts.

In establishing what evidence is admissible, many rules of evidence concentrate first on the relevancy of the offered evidence. For example, Rule 402 of the Federal Rules of Evidence states: "All relevant evidence is admissible, except as otherwise provided by the Constitution of the United States, by Act of Congress, by these rules, or by other rules prescribed by the Supreme Court pursuant to statutory authority. Evidence which is not relevant is not admissible."

Rules of evidence also address privileges, witnesses, opinions and expert testimony, hearsay, competency, authentication and identification, contents of writings, recordings and photographs, and various other topics.

Although the majority of the Federal Rules of Evidence apply equally to civil and criminal proceedings, certain rules are tailored to criminal cases.[3]

B. *Rules of Criminal Procedure*

The Federal Rules of Criminal Procedure are the procedural principles that govern how criminal prosecutions are conducted in federal courts. From pre-indictment through post-conviction, the rules guarantee constitutional due process to those individuals charged with a crime. While several good digests of the rules are available,[4] they still pale in comparison to a practitioner's thorough and periodic review of the actual rules.

The Federal Rules of Criminal Procedure are promulgated by the Supreme Court pursuant to its statutory authority under the Rules Enabling Act.[5] The first set of rules was adopted by order of the Court on Dec. 26, 1944, and took effect on Mar. 21, 1946. Nowadays, the Supreme Court must transmit a copy of its rules to Congress no later than May 1 of the year in which they are to go into effect, and the new rules can then become effective no earlier than December 1 of that year. Congress retains the power to reject the proposed rules or amendments, to modify them, or to enact rules or amendments itself. Congress, however, has rarely rejected the Court's proposed amendments, but it has frequently adopted its own.

The Federal Rules of Criminal Procedure are organized into nine sections:

- Section I covers rules of applicability and interpretation (Rules 1-2);
- Section II addresses preliminary proceedings, from the arrest and filing of the complaint (charging document) through the preliminary hearing (Rules 3-5);
- Section III addresses the process surrounding the grand jury and the return of an indictment (the formal charging document returned by the grand jury) or information (formal charging document returned by the prosecutor) (Rules 6-9);
- Section IV addresses arraignment and preparation for trial, including the entering of a guilty or not guilty plea and discovery (pretrial exchange of information between the parties) (Rules 10-17);
- Section V covers the venue for the case and possible transfer from one district to another (Rules 18-22);
- Section VI addresses the trial procedures, including the calling of jurors, argument by counsel, and jury instructions (there is a separate code of evidence) (Rules 23-31);
- Section VII addresses post-conviction procedures, including sentencing and post-trial motions (Rules 32-39);

---

3. *See, e.g.*, Rule 404(a)(1) "Character of accused."
4. *See, e.g.*, Lucien B. Campbell, The Federal Rules of Criminal Procedure: Application and Practice (2001), *available at* http://www.google.com/url?sa=t&rct=j&q=&esrc=s&frm=1&source=web&cd=1&ved=0CDEQFjAA&url=http%3A%2F%2Fnj.fd.org%2FCJASupport%2Ffrcp0301.pdf&ei=plSmUYbPFbTJ4AOI64DQCQ&usg=AFQjCNGXXB1WKj-_xPQ7oAO1CvCa7jyZcQ&sig2=vx72BK-qqMEiykRU-2-ofQ&bvm=bv.47008514,d.dmg (last visited May 29, 2013).
5. 28 U.S.C. §§2072, 2074.

- Section VIII addresses supplementary and special proceedings such as arrest for failing to appear in another district and the procedure for obtaining search warrants (Rules 40-42); and
- Section IX addresses general provisions such as when a defendant's presence in court is required, the right to appointed counsel, the computation of time under the rules, and the use of cameras in the courtroom (Rules 43-60).[6]

The jury instructions delivered by U.S. District Judge Donald Molloy in the widely publicized case of *United States v. W.R. Grace & Co.*,[7] highlights the obligations placed on the prosecution by the Federal Rules of Criminal Procedure.

> The rules of criminal procedure place an obligation on the government and its agents, to produce certain kinds of evidence or proof if it is requested by the defendants or ordered by the court. The suppression by the prosecution of evidence favorable to an accused violates the due process of the law where the evidence is material to the question of guilt, irrespective of the good faith or bad faith of the prosecution. Prosecutors have an affirmative duty to comply with the Constitution, the Federal Rules of Criminal Procedure and the orders of the court. That duty includes the affirmative responsibility to learn of any evidence favorable to the accused and to disclose such evidence in a timely manner so that it can be effectively used by the accused.[8]

Judge Molloy's jury instructions further discussed the consequences that may befall those who fail to afford the rules their proper deference:

> The government has violated its solemn obligation and duty in this case by suppressing or withholding material proof pertinent to the credibility of Robert Locke. As a sanction for this inexcusable dereliction of duty the Court has entered an order that prohibits consideration of any proof offered by Robert Locke in the case brought against Robert Bettacchi . . .. [The jury] will have to decide what weight to give to Locke's testimony if any but [it] should be very cautious about making a determination of criminal liability for any defendant based upon his proof.[9]

The jury later acquitted W.R. Grace & Co. and three executives on charges that they had knowingly contaminated residents of Libby, Montana, with asbestos and then had conspired to cover up the offense. Judge Malloy's severe reprimand of the government also reverberated throughout the legal community, and caused many to speculate that the government would, at least for a time, be more inclined to produce any evidence even arguably favorable to the accused. As discussed earlier, the *W.R. Grace & Co.* case, among others, prompted the U.S. Department of Justice (DOJ) to issue a series of guidance documents detailing prosecutors' pretrial discovery obligations pursuant to Rule 16 of the Federal Rules of Criminal Procedure.

Judge Molloy's jury instructions serve the critical function of underscoring the need for all criminal law practitioners to be as familiar with the Federal Rules of Criminal Procedure as they are with the Federal Rules of Evidence, and to carefully obey all the mandates contained therein.

C. *Expert Witnesses*

In 1923, in *Frye v. United States*, the U.S. District Court for the District of Columbia Circuit established a test governing the admissibility of scientific evidence.[10] The court held that testimony "must be sufficiently established to have gained general acceptance in the particular field in which it belongs."[11] For 70 years, this "general acceptance" test was used by the majority of courts in determining whether scientific evidence was admissible at trial.[12]

---

6. Notes on Criminal Procedure in the U.S. and on the Federal Rules of Criminal Procedure (Sept. 15, 2005), *available at* www.law.cam.ac.uk/faculty-resources/10006371.pdf (last visited June 4, 2013).
7. United States v. W.R. Grace, No. 05-CR-7, Jury Instruction No. 13 (D. Mont. May 6, 2009).
8. *Available at* http://www.google.com/url?sa=t&rct=j&q=&esrc=s&frm=1&source=web&cd=8&cad=rja&ved=0CGAQFjAH&url=http%3A%2F%2Fwww.nacdl.org%2FWorkArea%2Flinkit.aspx%3FLinkIdentifier%3Did%26ItemID%3D17618&ei=8MNcUb3HJpO24APk-4CwCA&usg=AFQjCNHNu6_WF17Hz_8_Ac2cs5Nu7SCQBg&sig2=H3DLXG5wbcshzZk4pdterQ&bvm=bv.44770516,d.dmg (last visited May 28, 2013).
9. *Id.*
10. 293 F. 1013 (D.C. Cir. 1923).
11. *Id.* at 1014.
12. *See* Daubert v. Merrell Dow Pharmaceuticals, Inc., 509 U.S. 579, 585, 23 ELR 20979 (1993).

In 1993, the Supreme Court unanimously held in *Daubert v. Merrell Dow Pharmaceuticals, Inc.*, that the *Frye* general acceptance test had been superseded by Rule 702 of the Federal Rules of Evidence,[13] which contains no language requiring "general acceptance as an absolute prerequisite to admissibility." Based on the language of Rule 702, the Court instead developed a two-prong test, requiring trial judges "to determine at the outset, pursuant to Rule 104(a),[14] whether the expert is proposing to testify to (1) scientific knowledge that (2) will assist the trier of fact to understand or determine a fact in issue."

The Court enumerated four factors that trial judges may consider in determining whether a theory or technique constitutes "scientific knowledge":

> (1) whether the underlying methodology and the expert's theory has, or could, be tested; (2) whether the theory or technique has been subjected to peer review and publication; (3) whether the theory or technique has a "known or potential rate of error"; and (4) whether the theory or technique has been generally accepted in the scientific community."[15]

In establishing these principles, the Court rejected the argument that this more liberal standard would have negative consequences, noting that "[v]igorous cross-examination, presentation of contrary evidence, and careful instruction on the burden of proof are the traditional and appropriate means of attacking shaky but admissible evidence."[16]

In *Kuhmo Tire Co. v. Carmichael*, the Supreme Court subsequently held that "*Daubert's* general holding—setting forth the trial judge's general gatekeeping obligations—applies not only to testimony based on scientific knowledge, but also to testimony based on technical or other specialized knowledge."[17] *Kuhmo* also clarified that a trial judge may consider one of more of the *Daubert* factors, but that the factors do not constitute a "definitive checklist or test."[18] As the Court recognized: "The factors identified in *Daubert* may or may not be pertinent in assessing reliability, depending on the nature of the issue, the expert's particular expertise, and the subject of his testimony."[19]

I. Application of *Daubert* and Its Progeny in Environmental Crimes Cases

In *United States v. John Morrell & Co.*, the defendant, a slaughterhouse company, pled guilty to six felony counts of conspiracy, illegal dumping of pollutants into the Big Sioux River and the filing of false reports with the U.S. Environmental Protection Agency (EPA) to conceal the criminal offenses. The evidence showed that the company's NPDES discharge monitoring reports had been falsified to indicate compliance with its discharge permit. One set of books indicated the real numbers from the testing, while the other was fabricated for reporting to EPA. The company was sentenced to pay a criminal fine of $2 million and to pay an additional $1 million to establish an environmental cleanup fund for the company's criminal violations of the Clean Water Act (CWA).[20]

In a *Daubert* hearing, the defendant challenged its own chemist and data, arguing that the chemist's methodology was unreliable and that the sampling data could be higher or lower.[21] The company also argued that the chemist was incompetent and unreliable and had used no quality control measures. The government's expert, who the defendant also challenged, had examined the company's data and offered the

13. Rule 702 provides: "If scientific, technical, or other specialized knowledge will assist the trier of fact to understand the evidence or to determine a fact in issue, a witness qualified as an expert by knowledge, skill, experience, training, or education, may testify thereto in the form of an opinion or otherwise."
14. Rule 104(a) provides: "Preliminary questions concerning the qualification of a person to be a witness, the existence of a privilege, or the admissibility of evidence shall be determined by the court . . .. In making its determination it is not bound by the rules of evidence except those with respect to privileges."
15. *Daubert,* 509 U.S. at 593, 594.
16. *Id.* at 596.
17. 526 U.S. 137, 141, 29 ELR 20638 (1999).
18. *Id.* at 150 (citing *Daubert,* 509 U.S. at 593).
19. *Id.* at 150.
20. U.S. EPA, South Dakota Slaughterhouse Company Fined $2 Million (May 31, 1996), *available at* http://yosemite1.epa.gov/opa/admpress.nsf/6427a6b7538955c585257359003f0230/12ba49958ef743958525646c0050ee01!OpenDocument&Start=2.1&Count=5&Expand=2.1 (last visited May 28, 2013).
21. U.S. EPA, 13th INTERPOL Forensic Science Symposium D3-154 (Oct. 16-19, 2001), *available at* http://www.interpol.int/public/Forensic/IFSS/meeting13/Reviews/Environmental.pdf (last visited Mar. 30, 2013).

opinion that the data was of sufficient quality to prove permit violations. The court rejected the defendant's challenge and accepted the company's data for use in the trial.[22]

In *United States v. Hansen*,[23] the defendant owned and operated an industrial plant that generated hazardous waste. Following an investigation by EPA, Hansen and others were found guilty of violating the CWA, the Resource Conservation and Recovery Act (RCRA), the Comprehensive Environmental Response, Compensation, and Liability Act (CERCLA), and the Endangered Species Act (ESA).[24] On appeal, Hansen argued that the district court had erred in admitting the testimony of Daniel Teitelbaum and Christopher Reh, both expert witnesses for the government.[25] Before trial, Hansen had requested a *Daubert* hearing to exclude their testimony regarding scientific conclusions and exhibits. The district court rejected his motion, stating that the motion did "not identify the source, the substance, or most importantly, the methodology of this testimony" and that, as a result, there was "no underlying methodology or reasoning for the court to assess."[26] At trial, when the government moved to present Teitelbaum as an expert, Hansen failed to object to this designation or Teitelbaum's testimony, and failed to cross-examine him.

The U.S. Court of Appeals for the Eleventh Circuit held that the district court had not erred in admitting Teitelbaum's testimony, noting that

> Hansen's motion for a *Daubert* hearing was neither addressed to the charges to which Teitelbaum testified, his testimony in general, nor supported by the source, substance, or methodology of the challenged testimony. Teitelbaum's testimony was based on his review of biological samples, interviews, and documents, and assisted the trier of fact in understanding the potential injuries that could result from the conditions of the plant. The district judge did not abuse his discretion by denying the motion or by admitting the testimony.[27]

The Eleventh Circuit similarly held that Reh's testimony was properly admitted.

In *United States v. Cunningham*,[28] the defendant operated a chemical company, which sold a machine to electroplating companies that removed hexavalent chromium from their wastewater through the addition of a barium compound. The removal process generated a yellow sludge, which the company instructed its customers should be stored in 55-gallon drums and stated would be collected by the company.[29] The Ohio EPA subsequently found 496 55-gallon drums of the sludge on the Cunningham family farm. The majority of the drums were leaking onto the ground, and some were missing tops. After being informed by the agency that the sludge was a hazardous waste, Cunningham moved some of the drums to the parking lot of the Rose Lab Company, which did not have a permit to treat, store, or dispose of hazardous waste.

Cunningham was convicted of conspiring to transport hazardous waste, illegally transporting hazardous waste, and illegally disposing of hazardous waste. On appeal, Cunningham argued that the district court had erred by refusing to allow him to question Rose Lab's plant manager.[30] Cunningham's attorney established that the manager had an undergraduate degree in chemistry, but when he asked whether the manager believed the yellow sludge was hazardous, the government objected. Cunningham was permitted to make a proffer as to the manager's testimony. He stated that because the sludge could not be dissolved in hydrochloric acid, it was not hazardous. He also stated, however, that he did not take any other factors into account in determining that the sludge was not hazardous.[31] The district court subsequently sustained the government's objection and excluded the manager's testimony as to the hazardous nature of the sludge.

The Eleventh Circuit found that the district court had not abused its discretion in limiting the testimony, concluding that "Cunningham failed to establish the reliability of the manager's proffered testimony under the standards laid out by the Supreme Court in [*Daubert*] and [*Kuhmo*]."[32] He failed to demonstrate that the manager's opinion was "scientifically valid," as it was based on an "unproven testing method," and

22. *Id.*
23. 262 F.3d 1217 (11th Cir. 2001), *cert. denied*, 535 U.S. 1111 (2002).
24. *Id.* at 1231.
25. *Id.* at 1232.
26. *Id.* at 1233.
27. *Id.* at 1234.
28. 194 F.3d 1186, 30 ELR 20202 (11th Cir. 1999), *cert. denied*, 531 U.S. 831 (2000).
29. *Id.* at 1190.
30. *Id.* at 1196.
31. *Id.*
32. *Id.* at 1197.

the manager was unfamiliar with the relevant regulations and disagreed with the EPA's regulatory determination that barium was a hazardous waste.[33]

In *United States v. Elias*,[34] the U.S. Court of Appeals for the Ninth Circuit held that the district court did not abuse its discretion in admitting testimony from a government expert witness and denying a *Daubert* hearing on admission of his testimony. The defendant was convicted of knowingly endangering his employees by exposing them to cyanide waste, after a criminal investigation by EPA revealed that an employee was sent into a storage tank to clean out cyanide sludge without the required protective equipment. At trial, the government developed a model to demonstrate that the waste material in the storage tank was capable of generating toxic gases in harmful levels. The defense made a *Daubert* challenge, arguing that the tank model and the waste sample collected from the storage tank on the premises were not representative of the actual circumstances at the time of the alleged offense.[35] The court denied the request for a hearing, and the government expert was permitted to offer his opinion that the waste was hazardous and explained how the evidence (sample analyses, medical records, etc.) supported his opinion.[36]

Although there are few reported decisions regarding successful *Daubert* challenges in environmental criminal cases, practitioners should not hesitate to challenge an expert witness offered by the government, and should be prepared to have their experts challenged in turn. Several commentators have noted that although *Daubert* was intended to simplify questions of admissibility of expert testimony, judicial decisions are inconsistent from one court to the next.[37] As a result, it is often difficult to predict the outcome of a *Daubert* challenge.

II. Confrontation Clause

The Confrontation Clause of the Sixth Amendment of the Constitution provides that "in all criminal prosecutions, the accused shall enjoy the right . . . to be confronted with the witnesses against him." The Confrontation Clause has its roots in both English common law,[38] which protected the right of cross-examination, and Roman law, which guaranteed persons accused of a crime the right to look their accusers in the eye.[39] The Bill of Rights originally functioned only as a restriction against the federal government, but was extended by the Supreme Court in the 1960s to apply to the states under the Incorporation Doctrine.[40] Two fundamental Confrontation Clause decisions address issues that often arise in environmental criminal cases, particularly where large numbers of persons are involved and "testimony" is provided in various forums and formats to government officials.

A. Crawford v. Washington

Prior to 2004, hearsay statements could withstand a Confrontation Clause challenge if the unavailable declarant's out-of-court statement bore adequate "indicia of reliability," or "particularized guarantees of trustworthiness."[41] Under *Ohio v. Roberts*, this standard could be satisfied: (1) if the statement fell within a "firmly rooted hearsay exception"; or (2) if the statement bore a "particularized guarantees of

33. *Id.* (citing *Daubert*, 509 U.S. at 592-93).
34. 269 F.3d 1003 (9th Cir. 2001).
35. *See supra* note 21.
36. *Id.*
37. *See, e.g.*, Craig L. Montz, *Trial Judge as Scientific Gatekeepers After* Daubert, Joiner, Kuhmo Tire, *and Amended Rule 702: Is Anyone Still Buying This?*, 33 UWLA L. Rev. 87, 103 (2001).
38. 1 J. Stephen, History of the Criminal Law of England 326 (1883).
39. According to Acts of the Apostles 25:16, the Roman governor Porcius Festus, discussing the proper treatment of his prisoner Paul, stated: "It is not the manner of the Romans to deliver any man up to die before the accused has met his accusers face-to-face, and has been given a chance to defend himself against the charges." *See also* Coy v. Iowa, 487 U.S. 1012, 1015-16 (1988); Herrmann & Speer, *Facing the Accuser: Ancient and Medieval Precursors of the Confrontation Clause*, 34 Va. J. Int'l L. 481 (1994).
40. *See, e.g.*, Smith v. Illinois, 390 U.S. 129 (1968) (where the state would not produce the witness in person because it said that revealing his identity would undermine the secretive nature and strategies used by the police department, the defendant's Sixth Amendment right was violated); Bruton v. United States, 391 U.S. 123 (1968) (the admission of a statement of one person against another person who were tried in a joint trial, neither of whom took the stand, violated the defendant's right to confront his accuser).
41. 448 U.S. 56, 66 (1980).

trustworthiness."[42] Courts generally concluded that, with respect to the "firmly rooted hearsay exception" standard, the "hearsay rules and the Confrontation Clause are generally designed to protect similar values."[43] Whether a statement of an unavailable declarant bore "particularized guarantees of trustworthiness" was determined by the court's weighing of certain substantive factors.[44]

In 2004, in *Crawford v. Washington*,[45] the Supreme Court held that the defendant's Sixth Amendment right to confront his accusers could not be taken away in cases where the judge determined that testimonial hearsay evidence was reliable. Writing for the majority, Justice Antonin Scalia stated: "Where testimonial statements are involved, we do not think the Framers meant to leave the Sixth Amendment's protection to the vagaries of the rules of evidence, much less to amorphous notions of 'reliability.'"

In *Crawford,* the defendant had prevented his wife from testifying at trial on the grounds that Washington State's marital-privilege statute[46] bars a spouse from testifying adversely without the other spouse's consent.[47] The prosecution maintained that the wife's out-of-court tape-recorded statement was admissible under the hearsay exception for statements against penal interest.[48] Applying *Roberts*, the trial court found that the wife's statement to the police bore "particularized guarantees of trustworthiness" and was admissible,[49] and its decision ultimately was affirmed by the highest state court.[50]

The Supreme Court granted review and reversed, holding that Crawford's Sixth Amendment rights had been violated, as only the constitutionally-mandated tool of cross-examination was permissible in assessing reliability.[51] It concluded that the Sixth Amendment not only requires reliability, but also mandates how reliability is to be determined.

Following *Crawford,* "testimonial statements of a declarant are not admissible against the accused unless: (1) the prosecution calls the declarant as a witness, thus giving the accused a present opportunity for cross-examination; (2) the declarant is now unavailable, and the accused had a prior opportunity to cross-examine him or her; or (3) the accused has wrongfully procured the declarant's unavailability."[52]

Crawford left certain questions unanswered, including what constitutes sufficient opportunity for cross-examination. It "le[ft] for another day any effort to spell out a comprehensive definition of "testimonial,'" but noted that "[w]hatever else the term covers, it applies at a minimum to prior testimony at a preliminary hearing, before a grand jury, or at a former trial; and to police interrogations."[53]

As environmental criminal cases are often complex with extensive grand jury proceedings prior to indictment, and routinely involve government interviews of corporate employees, *Crawford* was an important step towards guaranteeing defendants the right to confront their accuser.

B. Melendez-Diaz v. Massachusetts

In *Melendez-Diaz v. Massachusetts*,[54] the defendant was charged with distributing cocaine and with trafficking in cocaine. At trial, the prosecution introduced several bags seized from the police cruiser in which Melendez-Diaz had been transported to the police station. It also submitted three "certificates of analysis" showing that the forensic analysis performed on the seized substances had determined them to be cocaine. "The certificates were sworn to before a notary public by analysts at the State Laboratory Institute of the Massachusetts Department of Public Health, as required under Massachusetts law[,]" but the analysts did not appear to testify.[55] Melendez-Diaz objected to the admission of the certificates, arguing that the Con-

42. *Id.*
43. California v. Green, 399 U.S. 149, 155 (1970).
44. *See, e.g.*, State v. Crawford, No. 25307-1-II, 2001 Wash. App. LEXIS 1723 (Wash. Ct. App. July 30, 2001) (utilizing a nine-factor test).
45. 541 U.S. 36 (2004).
46. Wash. Rev. Code §5.60.060(1) (1994).
47. *Crawford*, 541 U.S. at 40.
48. *Id.*
49. Superior Court of Thurston County. Docket No: 99-1-01205-8. Date filed: 11/19/1999.
50. State v. Crawford, 54 P.3d 656, 662 (Wash. 2002).
51. Crawford, 541 U.S. at 68.
52. Ralph Ruebner & Timothy Scahill, Crawford v. Washington, *the Confrontation Clause, and Hearsay: A New Paradigm for Illinois Evidence Law*, 36 Loy. U. Chi. L.J. 704, 714 (2005).
53. *Crawford*, 541 U.S. at 68.
54. 557 U.S. 305 (2009).
55. *Id.* at 308.

frontation Clause and the Supreme Court's decision in *Crawford* required that the analysts be present. The objection was overruled, the certificates were admitted as prima facie evidence of the composition of the narcotic, and Melendez-Diaz was subsequently convicted.

On appeal, Melendez-Diaz argued that his Sixth Amendment rights had been violated through admission of the certificates. The Supreme Court, in another opinion by Justice Scalia, held that "[t]he Sixth Amendment does not permit the prosecution to prove its case via *ex parte* out-of-court affidavits, and the admission of such evidence against Melendez-Diaz was error."[56] As the Court explained: *Crawford* guarantees a defendant's right to confront those "who 'bear testimony' against him."

> Various formulations of this core class of testimonial statements exist: ex parte in-court testimony or its functional equivalent—that is, material such as affidavits, custodial examinations, prior testimony that the defendant was unable to cross-examine, or similar pretrial statements that declarants would reasonably expect to be used prosecutorially; extrajudicial statements . . . contained in formalized testimonial materials, such as affidavits, depositions, prior testimony, or confessions; statements that were made under circumstances which would lead an objective witness reasonably to believe that the statement would be available for use at a later trial.[57]

The Court was quick to note:

> [t]here is little doubt that the documents at issue in this case fall within the "core class of testimonial statements" thus described . . .. [W]hile denominated by Massachusetts law [as] "certificates," [the documents at issue] are quite plainly affidavits: "declaration[s] of facts written down and sworn to by the declarant before an officer authorized to administer oaths . . ." [N]ot only were the affidavits "made under circumstances which would lead an objective witness reasonably to believe that the statement would be available for use at a later trial," *Crawford, supra*, at 52, . . ., but under Massachusetts law the *sole purpose* of the affidavits was to provide "prima facie evidence of the composition, quality, and the net weight" of the analyzed substance . . .."[58] [T]he analysts were aware of the affidavits' evidentiary purpose, since that purpose—as stated in the relevant state-law provision—was reprinted on the affidavits themselves.[59]

The Court therefore held that "[a]bsent a showing that the analysts were unavailable to testify at trial *and* that petitioner had a prior opportunity to cross-examine them, petitioner was entitled to 'be confronted with' the analysts at trial."[60]

As environmental criminal cases routinely involve samples, lab reports, and other technical analytical information, *Melendez-Diaz* was another critical step toward assuring defendants of their right to confront their accusers.

III. Jury Instructions

Following the presentation of all the evidence, there remain two key steps in any trial: closing arguments and jury instructions. Jury instructions are the set of legal rules that jurors must follow when deciding whether the defendant is innocent or guilty. These instructions are delivered to the jury by the judge, who often reads them aloud. The instructions are often broken down into what verdict the jurors should deliver, based on what facts they determine to be true. The instructions also define key terms such as "reasonable doubt" and "knowingly."

With the exception of Texas and West Virginia, all states have a basic set of jury instructions that are used to provide the framework for the charge to the jury.[61] Certain federal courts also provide pattern criminal jury instructions.[62] Both sides, the prosecution and the defense, however, are typically afforded an opportunity to offer their own jury instructions. The proposed instructions are usually taken from model instructions or crafted by counsel based on prior court decisions. During a conference, the judge reviews

56. *Id.* at 329.
57. *Id.* at 310 (citing *Crawford*, 541 U.S. at 51-52 (internal quotation marks and citations omitted)).
58. *Id.* at 310-11 (citing Black's Law Dictionary 62 (8th ed. 2004)).
59. *Id.* at 311 (emphasis in original).
60. *Id* (emphasis in original).
61. *See, e.g., Florida Standard Criminal Jury Instructions*, http://www.floridasupremecourt.org/jury_instructions/instructions.shtml (last visited June 4, 2013).
62. *See, e.g., Sixth Circuit Pattern Jury Instructions*, http://www.ca6.uscourts.gov/internet/crim_jury_insts.htm (last visited June 4, 2013).

the instructions requested by both sides. If they agree, the instruction will be provided to the jury. If one side objects to another's request, or the language differs between their proposed instructions, the judge will hear arguments from both sides and make a ruling. It is the judge's responsibility to ensure key instructions are included, even if not requested by either side.[63]

The importance of jury instructions cannot be overstated, as "[j]urors frequently misunderstand instructions from the judge on legal issues, fail to recall critical evidence, and suffer from boredom and apathy during trials[.]"[64] Amazingly, a study conducted in the 1970s found that only half of the jurors surveyed understood that the defendant did not have to present evidence of his innocence, despite an explicit instruction on the presumption of innocence.[65] More recent studies have reaffirmed that many jurors do not understand the jury instructions they are given.[66] Naturally, such problems are compounded by complex legal issues, such as those typically present in environmental criminal procedures.

Efforts to reform the process of instructing the jury, including the timing and manner in which the instructions are delivered, have not been met with widespread enthusiasm. "Even those lawyers who do recognize that juries are confused may resist any efforts to correct this confusion if they believe the confusion benefits their clients."[67]

IV. Jury Deliberations

The judge will instruct the jury regarding the selection of a foreperson, the importance of discussing all the evidence before voting on any of the charges, and voting on each charge separately. Exhibits introduced during trial are typically sent to the jury room for use during deliberations. No one is permitted in the jury room during deliberations except the jurors. If the jurors have a question, it will be answered by the judge in the courtroom with all parties present.

Although environmental crimes trials often last for weeks, juries may return a verdict within a day or two of beginning deliberations. There is no time limit, however, and juries that cannot reach a decision will so inform the judge. A jury that cannot reach a decision is referred to as a "hung jury." Defense counsel should ask that the charges be dismissed where a hung jury results; however, this request usually will be denied, and the prosecutor will be allowed to re-file the charges.

V. Verdict

Once the jury has reached a decision, the foreperson notifies the judge. All parties will return to the courtroom for a reading of the verdict. Each charge and the corresponding verdict is then read. Once the jury has returned its verdict, but before it has been retired, either side has the right to request that the jury be "polled." The court must accept this request and poll the jury. When polling the jury, each juror will be asked whether he or she agrees with the verdict. The judge will typically frame the question for the jurors. If there appears, however, to be hesitation on the part of any juror, counsel may request that the judge ask follow up questions. Failure to make a complete record will waive the issue for appeal. Should any juror disavow the verdict, the judge will typically instruct the jury to return to deliberations, although, in rare instances, he or she may also dismiss the jury.

A request to poll the jury is of particular importance in an environmental criminal case due to the complexity of these offenses and the enhanced possibility that an individual juror may not agree with the verdict.

---

63. *See* Judy Hails, Criminal Evidence 44 (2009).
64. Ellen Chilton & Patricia Henley, *Jury Instructions: Helping Jurors Understand the Evidence and the Law*, http://gov.uchastings.edu/public-law/docs/plri/juryinst.pdf. (last visited June 4, 2013).
65. Strawn & Buchanan, *Jury Confusion: A Threat to Justice*, 59 Judicature 478 (1976).
66. Reid Hastie et al., Inside the Jury (1983); Robert F. Forston, *Sense and Non-Sense: Jury Trial Communication*, 1975 B.Y.U. L. Rev. 601; Amiram Elwork et al., *Judicial Decisions: In Ignorance of Law or in Light of It,* 1 Law & Hum. Behav. 163 (1970); Walter W. Steele Jr. & Elizabeth G. Thornburg, *Jury Instructions: A Persistent Failure to Communicate*, 67 N.C. L. Rev. 77 (1988).
67. *See supra* note 64.

Chapter 8: Sentencing

I. Consequences of an Environmental Criminal Conviction

Once the accused has been found guilty of committing a crime, whether through a plea agreement or jury verdict, punishment will be determined in the sentencing phase. In environmental crimes cases, the judge usually receives input from the prosecutor, the defense, and the probation department (which prepares the "pre-sentencing report") before sentencing the defendant. Thus, entry of a judgment of guilty does not end the defendant's ordeal or counsel's responsibilities. In many respects, a determination of guilt represents only the mid-point in the judicial process.

The consequences of conviction are potentially severe, in terms of the sentence that may be imposed, the costs of the remedial obligations, and the collateral effects on corporate defendant's ability to conduct business in the future. Prosecutors are well aware of the stringency of the available penalties, and they do not hesitate to use them as leverage to persuade environmental violators to enter into plea agreements. Indeed, approximately 90% of criminal defendants enter plea agreements rather than stand trial.[1]

A. Remedial Obligations and Negotiated Pleas

An entity that is found guilty of an environmental crime likely will be compelled to cleanup any remaining pollution from the violation and remediate any damages. The costs of remediation frequently exceed the amount of fines imposed, often by substantial multiples. The recent BP settlement resulting from the explosion and fire on the Mobile Offshore Drilling Unit Deepwater Horizon and the blowout of the well it was drilling on the Gulf of Mexico, which provides for the largest criminal environmental fine in history ($4.5 billion), demonstrates this dynamic.[2] A corporation inevitably will be required to make large outlays upon conviction, whether as part of the criminal sentence or as a consequence of a subsequent civil suit. This consideration often plays a substantial role in the company's decision whether to seek a plea agreement and in the prosecutor's charging decisions.

During an environmental investigation, the government likely will seek evidence of all pollution generated or disposed of by the polluter. Both the prosecutor and the regulatory agency will be interested in making certain the violator cleans up all the contamination detected, whether it factors into the actual criminal charges or not. Further, an environmental prosecutor, as distinguished from a conventional prosecutor, may seek to maximize the combination of criminal penalties and cleanup benefits, rather than focusing strictly on the length of sentences and fines. Accordingly, an environmental prosecutor may be

1. *See generally Guide to the Federal Judicial System*, http://www.justice.gov/usao/mow/guidebook/civil.html (last visited May 28, 2013).
2. "Under the settlement, BP will pay about $4 billion in penalties over five years. That amount includes $1.256 billion in criminal fines, $2.394 billion to the National Fish and Wildlife Foundation for remediation efforts and $350 million to the National Academy of Sciences. The criminal fine is one of the largest against a corporation. *See "BP to Pay 4.5M in Fines,"* http://fishery.about.com/od/Catastrophicevents/a/Bp-To-Pay-4-5-Billion-In-Fines.htm (last visited May 28, 2013). BP also agreed to pay $7.8 billion to settle civil economic-loss claims, and had paid out an estimated $26 billion for clean-up and other damage claims. Civil penalty and other civil claims by the federal and state governments and others remain pending. Paul M. Barrett, *Appeals Court Blesses BP Spill Settlement but the Legal Battle Drags On*, Bloomberg Businessweek (Jan. 13, 2014), *available at* http://www.businessweek.com/articles/2014-01-13/bp-gulf-oil-spill-settlement-upheld-but-legal-battle-drags-on (last visited Feb. 7, 2014)..

willing to trade a significantly greater cleanup commitment than could be required by law, in return for foregoing possible criminal charges against the entity, foregoing criminal charges against individuals, or reducing the severity or number of counts filed. Accordingly, corporations faced with the inevitability of cleaning up their pollution may seek a negotiated resolution, based on their willingness to undertake a comprehensive remediation program.

The prosecutor may be attracted to such a resolution, because it benefits the environment directly, through prompt elimination of contaminants, rather than indirectly through deterrence of potential future violators. The large dollar amount involved also may generate favorable publicity for the prosecutor's office. The prosecutor does not act with a free hand, however, and may need the concurrence of federal and state civil regulators on many of the cleanup terms that have critical cost implications.

For the polluter, the principal attraction of a negotiated resolution, besides the possibility of reduced charges, is the greater flexibility that may be afforded in a plea agreement on such vital terms as the level of cleanup required, the permissible remediation techniques, the timetable, and post-cleanup obligations. A plea agreement provides opportunities for substantial cost savings in these areas compared to those that would be incurred in an adverse judgment entered after trial. Further, with the prosecutor's cooperation, a company may be able to structure the agreement in a manner that makes some of the out-of-pocket costs tax deductible. A plea entered into pursuant to Rule 11(c)(1)(c) provides the defendant with the added comfort that the plea must be accepted as agreed to or, if not accepted, the court must allow the defendant to withdraw his plea and proceed to trial. In entering into these discussions, the company must realize that all aspects of its environmental performance will be in play, including prior disposals that are not included in the contemplated changes, other operations besides those implicated in the criminal complaint, and discharges to other media in addition to those involved in the criminal violation.

The degree of cooperation demonstrated by the company during the investigative process may affect significantly the willingness of the prosecutor to consider a consensual resolution. None of these benefits is likely to be achieved unless the prosecutor is convinced of the company's good faith and the regulatory agency has confidence in the company's reliability. Effective environmental criminal counsel therefore, must understand the difficult balancing act he or she must play in conducting the defense of the investigation to address all these problems simultaneously. Counsel must organize the defense in a manner that fully presents the company's position on the merits, without turning either the prosecutor or the regulator against it. More so than in most other types of criminal cases, relations with government prosecutors and enforcement personnel in environmental cases must not be cast in an adversarial, scorched-earth tone, for fear of precluding later opportunities to turn the discussions toward negotiations over the scope of the cleanup and the terms of permits governing future operations. The regulated entity has a long-term, involuntary relationship with its regulator that can significantly affect the future cost of doing business and thus its ability to compete.

Finally, since settlement must be reached with all federal and state criminal and regulatory agencies, counsel must eliminate the risk that the cleanup resolution may later be undone by another sovereign entity with overlapping enforcement authority initiating proceedings on the same issues.[3]

B. *Federal Sentencing Guidelines*

In 1984, Congress passed the Sentencing Reform Act in an effort to alleviate sentencing disparity, which was prevalent in the federal sentencing system. The statute reformed the sentencing system by: "(1) dropping rehabilitation as one of the goals of punishment; (2) creating the United States Sentencing Commission and charging it with establishing Sentencing Guidelines; (3) making all federal sentences determinate; and (4) authorizing appellate review of sentences."[4] In accordance with Act, the U.S. Sentencing Commission promulgated the *U.S. Sentencing Guidelines*[5] [hereinafter Sentencing Guidelines or Guidelines]. The

3. *See* Chapter 2, Section G, Parallel Proceedings, *supra*.
4. Lisa M. Seghetti, CRS Report to Congress, Federal Sentencing Guidelines: Background, Legal Analysis, and Policy Options (June 2007), *available at* http://www.fas.org/sgp/crs/misc/RL32766.pdf (last visited May 28, 2013).
5. United States Sentencing Comm'n, Guidelines Manual (Nov. 2013) [hereinafter Sentencing Guidelines], *available at* http://www.ussc.gov/Guidelines/2013_Guidelines/index.cfm (last visited Feb. 10, 2014)

Guidelines set out a uniform sentencing policy for individuals and organizations convicted of felonies and serious (Class A) misdemeanors.

Pursuant to the Sentencing Reform Act, federal district judges originally were required to impose a sentence within the range specified by the Guidelines. This remained the law until the U.S. Supreme Court's 2005 decision in *United States v. Booker*,[6] which held that the SentencGuidelines are advisory only. Notwithstanding, *Booker*, however, the majority of defendants continue to be sentenced within the ranges specified by the guidelines. Accordingly, environmental criminal counsel must be comfortable navigating them.

Notably, in a recent U.S. Supreme Court case, the Court held that the Sentencing Guidelines in effect at the time the crime is committed, as opposed to those in effect at the time the defendant is sentenced, are controlling.[7] To hold otherwise, the Court concluded, would violate the *ex post facto* clause, which prohibits a defendant from being sentenced under guidelines promulgated after the criminal act was committed where the new version provides a higher sentencing range than the version in place at the time of the offense.

C. *Criminal Sentencing for Individuals*

Chapter Two of the Sentencing Guidelines for individuals provide for assignment of a numeric value to an environmental crime through a three-step process considering: (1) the base offense level; (2) specific offense characteristics; and (3) adjustments for other factors. Once the process laid out in that chapter is completed, further modification to the "offense number" can be made based upon additional factors (not specific to environmental crimes) considered in Chapters Three and Four of the Sentencing Guidelines.

1. Base Offense Level

The first step in determining the sentence is to select the most appropriate offense category and its associated base offense level. There are six general types of offenses listed for environmental crimes, only three of which are broadly applicable[8]:

- Knowing endangerment resulting from mishandling hazardous or toxic substances, pesticides or other pollutants: Base offense level 24[9];
- Mishandling of hazardous or toxic substances or pesticides: recordkeeping, tampering, and falsification: Base offense level 8[10]; and
- Mishandling of other environment pollutants: recordkeeping, tampering, and falsification: Base offense level 6.[11]

For example, if the offense involved illegal disposal of polychlorinated biphenyls (PCBs), a hazardous substance, the base offense level would be eight, the level prescribed under §2Q1.2 of the Guidelines for violations involving hazardous or toxic substances or pesticides. If, on the other hand, the offense involved the illegal disposal of oil or petroleum byproducts, the base offense level would be six, as prescribed under §2Q1.3 of the Guidelines for mishandling of "other pollutants."

---

6. 543 U.S. 220 (2005).
7. Peugh v. United States, 133 S. Ct. 594 (2013).
8. The other three offenses are: tampering or attempted tampering with public water system; threatened tampering with public water system; and hazardous or injurious devices on federal lands.
9. Sentencing Guidelines *supra* note 5, §2Q1.1.
10. *Id.* §2Q1.2.
11. *Id.* §2Q1.3.

2. Specific Offense Characteristics

The base offense level is then increased if there are "specific offense characteristics"—that is, aggravating circumstances. These characteristics include ongoing, continuous or repetitive discharges of the substance[12]; substantial likelihood of death or serious bodily injury as a result of the wrongdoing[13]; the requirement of a substantial expenditure for cleanup[14]; or the failure to obtain a permit.[15] For example, if a person convicted of mishandling hazardous wastes is found to have created a substantial likelihood of death or serious injury, the offense level would be increased by nine, which could translate into an increase of several months in the recommended sentence range.[16]

3. Adjustments

After the base offense level is calculated and any specific offense characteristic points are added, the Guidelines recommend downward or upward "departures" from the offense level. For example, where the violation resulted from negligent rather than knowing behavior, the Guidelines recommend a downward departure[17]; where the offense involved highly hazardous substances, the Guidelines recommend an upward departure[18]; and where the offense resulted in a substantial expense for cleanup, the Guidelines recommend an upward departure.[19] In addition, the Guidelines recommend a downward departure upon motion of the government stating that the defendant provided substantial assistance in pursuing other persons who committed a crime.[20]

Once these adjustments set forth in Chapter Two of the Guidelines are applied, additional modifications remain to be made. Chapter Three provides for adjustments to the offense level to take into account other factors applicable to all criminal offenses, and not specific to environmental crimes. These mechanisms account for the defendant's role in the offense. The sentence is adjusted depending on whether the defendant was an organizer or leader of the offense; whether he impeded the investigation, prosecution, or sentencing of the offense; and whether he accepted responsibility for his actions.[21] The base offense level, specific offense characteristics, and any adjustments are then totaled to arrive at a final offense number.

Next, pursuant to Chapter Four, the defendant's criminal history must be determined. There are six criminal history categories, each of which is associated with a range of criminal history points. As most defendants convicted of an environmental crime are first time offenders, typically they fall within the 0-1 range.

Once the offense number and criminal history range have been determined, the Sentencing Table[22] the Guidelines shows the relationship between these two factors. Where the offense and criminal history factors intersect, the grid specifies a confinement range, expressed in a number of months.

The Sentencing Table also specifies four sentencing zones: A, B, C, and D. Zone A and Zone B defendants are eligible for probation, once they have satisfied at least one month of their sentence by imprisonment. Zone C defendants must serve at least half of their sentence in prison before they are eligible for

12. *Id.* §2Q1.2(b)(1)(A) (hazardous waste); *id.* §2Q1.3(b)(1)(A) (non-hazardous waste). *See* United States v. Suarez, 15 F.3d 1094 (9th Cir. 1994) (trial court required to impose either a six-level increase under §2Q1.3(b)(1)(A) for an "ongoing, continuous, or repetitive discharge," or a four-level increase under §2Q1.3(b)(1)(B) "if the offense otherwise involved a discharge").
13. Sentencing Guidelines; *supra* note §§2Q1.2(b)(2), 2Q1.3(b)(2).
14. *Id.* §§2Q1.2(b)(3), 2Q1.3(b)(3).
15. *Id.* §§2Q1.2(b)(4), 2Q1.3(b)(4).
16. *Id.* §2Q1.2(b)(2).
17. *Id.* §2Q1.2, Application Note 4.
18. *Id.* §2Q1.2, (b)(1)(B)
19. *Id.* §2Q1.2, (b)(3)
20. *Id.* §5K1.1.
21. *Id.* §3B1.1. In United States v. Booker, 543 U.S. 220 (2005), the Supreme Court held that a defendant's Sixth Amendment right to jury trial requires that other than a prior conviction, only facts admitted by a defendant or proved beyond a reasonable doubt to a jury can be used by the sentencing judge to calculate a sentence under the Guidelines. Thus, any enhancement factor that would be a basis for an upward departure under the Sentencing Guidelines would have to have been proven by the government to a jury beyond a reasonable doubt. Until the *Booker* decision, sentencing judges could make findings of such facts on their own and only needed to have found such facts under a "preponderance of the evidence" standard. See discussion of *Booker* decision in Section F, *infra.*
22. United States Sentencing Comm'n, Sentencing Table (Nov. 2013), *available at* http://www.ussc.gov/Guidelines/2013_Guidelines/Manual_PDF/Sentencing_Table.pdf (last visited Feb. 10, 2014).

probation while Zone D defendants, whose sentencing ranges are 12 months or greater, are required to be imprisoned for the minimum period of their sentence.

A similar Fine Table[23] determines the nature of the criminal fine that is to be imposed upon the defendant, which is also calculated from the base offense level as adjusted.[24]

D. *Criminal Sentencing for Organizations*

In 1991, a new Chapter Eight was added to the Sentencing Guidelines to address situations in which restitution,[25] fines,[26] and probation[27] appropriately may be applied to corporations convicted of criminal offenses. These Organizational Guidelines specifically exempted environmental crimes from their financial penalty provisions, because the Sentencing Commission needed to give further consideration to the problems of adapting its neutral sentencing principles to this context.[28] Although two decades have now passed, the Sentencing Commission has never adopted Organizational Guidelines for environmental offenses. However, the parts, of the Organizational Guidelines concerning restitution, remediation, community service, and notice to victims have been made applicable to companies convicted of environmental crimes.[29]

In addition, the financial penalty section of the Organizational Guidelines is applicable to convictions for false statements, conspiracy, and mail or wire fraud, which may be charged in conjunction with or in lieu of environmental offenses. Further, the Guidelines allow the sentencing court to impose, as a condition of probation that may last for up to five years[30]; a requirement that the organization publicize the nature of its offense[31] periodically submit information regarding remedial programs to the court[32]; assign probation officers to monitor the organization's operations[33]; require the organization to develop a compliance program[34]; submit to regular or unannounced examinations of its books, records, and premises[35]; and perform community service.[36]

The Organizational Guidelines also place substantial emphasis on a corporation's development of an effective compliance program.[37] Indicators of an effective compliance program include: compliance standards and procedures reasonably capable of reducing the prospect of criminal conduct; assignment of a high-level employee with responsibility to oversee these standards; steps to effectively communicate standards and procedures; and consistent enforcement of those standards.[38] An effective compliance program is of particular importance in the environmental crimes area, because the existence of such a program may substantially mitigate any potential fine that might be imposed.

In 2010, Chapter Eight of the Sentencing Guidelines was amended, including the section dealing with compliance programs.[39] Previously, the Guidelines provided for a downward departure if the offense occurred even though a company had in place at the time of the offense an effective compliance and ethics program,[40] but set up a rebuttable presumption that a company did not have an effective compliance

---

23. United States Sentencing Comm'n, Fine Table (Nov. 2013), *available at* http://www.ussc.gov/Guidelines/2013_Guidelines/Manual_PDF/Fine_Table.pdf.
24. Sentencing Guidelines, *supra* note 5, §5E1.2.
25. Sentencing Guidelines, *supra* note 5, §8B1.1.
26. *Id.* §8C.
27. *Id.* §8D.
28. *See* Ilene H. Nagel & Winthrop M. Swenson, "*The Federal Sentencing Guidelines for Corporations: Their Development, Theoretical Underpinnings, and Some Thoughts About Their Future,*" 71 Wash. U. L.Q. 205, 256 (1993).
29. See Sentencing Guidelines, *supra* note 5, §8B1.
30. *Id.* §8D1.2.
31. *Id.* §8D1.4(a).
32. *Id.* §8D1.4(b)(3).
33. *Id.* §8D1.4(b)(3), (4).
34. *Id.* §8D1.4(b)(1).
35. *Id.* §8D1.4(b)(5).
36. *Id.* §8D1.3(b).
37. Development of an effective compliance program is discussed in Appendix 19 of this Deskbook. *See also* Sentencing Guidelines, *supra* note 5, §8B.2.1.
38. Sentencing Guidelines, *supra* note 5, §8A1.2.
39. Amendment 744 to U.S. Sentencing Guidelines (Effective date Nov. 1, 2010), *available at* http://www.ussc.gov/Guidelines/2010_guidelines/Manual_PDF/Appendix_C_Supplement.pdf (last visited Feb. 10, 2014).
40. U.S. Sentencing Guidelines, §8C2.5(f)(1) (2009) [hereinafter 2009 Guidelines], *available at* http://www.ussc.gov/Guidelines/2009_guidelines/Manual/CHAP8.pdf (last visited Feb. 10, 2014)

and ethics program if "an individual (i) within high-level personnel of a small organization; or (2) within substantial authority personnel, but not within high-level personnel, of any organization participated in, condoned, or was willfully ignorant of the offense."[41] The 2010 amendments added an additional provision which stated that this rebuttable presumption provision would not apply, and a downward departure would still be authorized, if the following four criteria are met:

- the highest level personnel with operational responsibility for the compliance program "have direct reporting obligations to the governing authority or an appropriate subgroup thereof";
- the problem was discovered by the compliance program before it was discovered from outside the company or "before such discovery was reasonably likely";
- the company "promptly reported the offense to appropriate governmental authorities"; and
- "[n]o individual with operational responsibility for the compliance and ethics program participated in, condoned, or was willfully ignorant of the offense."[42]

Regarding criteria for an effective compliance and ethics program, the Guidelines provide: "After criminal conduct has been detected, the organization shall take reasonable steps to respond appropriately to the criminal conduct and to prevent further similar criminal conduct, including making any necessary modifications to the organization's compliance and ethics program."[43] This 2010 Amendments further explained what an appropriate response entails by providing:

> First, the organization should respond appropriately to the criminal conduct. The organization should take reasonable steps, as warranted under the circumstances, to remedy the harm resulting from the criminal conduct. These steps may include, where appropriate, providing restitution to identifiable victims, as well as other forms of remediation. Other reasonable steps to respond appropriately to the criminal conduct may include self-reporting and cooperation with authorities.
>
> Second, the organization should act appropriately to prevent further similar criminal conduct, including assessing the compliance and ethics program and making modifications necessary to ensure the program is effective. The steps taken . . . may include the use of an outside professional advisor to ensure adequate assessment and implementation of any modifications.[44]

By suggesting the use of an outside professional, the guidelines appear to be echoing the sentiment of recent years, largely in non-environmental cases, where the U.S. Department of Justice (DOJ) has suggested the use of independent outside monitors as a condition of a Deferred Prosecution Agreement (DPA) with a corporate defendant.

E. *The Failed Attempt to Adopt Comprehensive Organizational Guidelines for Environmental Crimes*

In December 1991, after several failed attempts to formulate appropriate Organizational Guidelines for environmental crimes, the Sentencing Commission appointed an Advisory Working Group to consider how general principles governing criminal punishment could be modified and applied in this specific area.

Three major policy problems had made it difficult for the Sentencing Commission to determine the amount of the fine that should be imposed on a corporation convicted of an environmental offense. First, defining and computing the amount of loss, a key factor in assessing the seriousness of an offense under the Organizational Guidelines, is extremely difficult for environmental crimes. Unlike other white collar crimes such as securities fraud, there is no necessary correlation between the gain to the defendant and the loss to society. The economic rationale for regulation of pollution is based on externalities—that is, the

41. *Id.* §8C2.5(f)(3)(B). A "small organization" for purposes of this guideline is one that had fewer than 200 employees at the time of the offense. *See id.*, Application Note 1.
42. Amendment 744 to U.S. Sentencing Guidelines, *supra* note 39 (adding §8C2.5(f)(3)(C)).
43. Sentencing Guidelines, §8B2.1(b)(7).
44. Amendment 744 to U.S. Sentencing Guidelines, *supra* note 39 (redesignating then existing Application Note 6 to §8B2.1 as Note 7 and adding new Note 6 titled "Application of Subsection (b)(7)")..

costs that pollution imposes on the society that are not reflected in the cost of the product to its owner. Externalities dominate the penalty calculus as well. Environmental violations that produce small economic gains to the defendant may result in large harm to the public. The costs of remediating an illegal discharge often are many times what it would have cost the defendant to dispose of the waste lawfully. Accordingly, the general principles break down in the face of these environmental externalities.

Second, as discussed in Chapter Four, the degree of knowledge needed for an environmental criminal conviction is *de minimis*. The Guidelines ordinarily consider intent to be an important factor in determining the appropriate amount of a fine for an organization. Nevertheless, the environmental harm caused by a violation is often disproportionate to the mental state of the defendant. A negligent violation such as the 1989 *Exxon Valdez* oil spill can cause massive environmental degradation, while a willful violation may not result in any environmental harm at all.

Third, environmental crimes are subject to overlapping enforcement schemes and greater collateral sanctions than other areas of law. An extensive system of civil enforcement for violations exists at both the state and federal levels, which attempts to capture directly, through the "economic benefit to the violator" part of the civil penalty calculus, the monetary gain the polluter realized from failing to comply with the law. Further, because the government can obtain extensive remedial relief, including money damages, the harm to the environment can often be largely corrected through civil enforcement. Since the cost of cleanup may greatly outweigh the initial cost of compliance, the threat of civil liability works as an effective deterrent in the environmental area. Finally, unlike other areas, the collateral consequences of an environmental conviction are substantial and contribute to the effective degree of deterrence and punishment.

Despite these obstacles, on Mar. 5, 1993, the Advisory Working Group released draft Organizational Guidelines for environmental crimes. After extensive public comment, the Advisory Working Group released a second draft on Nov. 16, 1993, which was sent to the full Commission for consideration.[45] The commission, however, was unable to resolve the policy issue presented and has never issued final guidelines.

> The existing Guidelines do apply to organizational environmental crimes with respect to *restitution, remediation, community service, notice to victims,* and *probation.* Thus, many of the sentencing options best suited to ensuring future organizational compliance and to rectifying any harm caused by a violation have been governed by the Sentencing Guidelines for Organizations since November 1, 1991.[46]

As for the imposition of fines, without the publication of final Environmental Organizational Guidelines, courts were left to do much as they had done before. "Where harms can be roughly quantified, fines often tend to be based on a rough approximately of damages . . ..Where harms cannot be reasonably quantified, fines necessarily are less predictable and focus more on punishing the defendant corporation in rough correlation with the egregiousness of the behavior at issue."[47]

The Draft Environmental Organizational Guidelines, proposed as a new Chapter 9 of the existing sentencing guidelines, contain both fine and probation sections.[48] The proposed fine provisions were completely new, while the proposed probation provisions would replace the existing probation provisions in Chapter 8 for crimes committed by organizations.

The Draft Environmental Organizational Guidelines use the maximum statutory fine as the starting point to determine the criminal fine and then provide for possible downward adjustment, depending on the elements and the characteristics of the offense and the presence of any aggravating or mitigating factors. Much of the procedure to determine fines under the Draft Environmental Organizational Guidelines closely follows that of Chapter 2 of the current Sentencing Guidelines.

---

45. The Draft Environmental Organizational Guidelines [hereinafter Draft Environmental Guidelines] *are available at* http://www.ussc.gov/Research/Working_Group_Reports/Miscellaneous/19931206_Environmental_Sanctions.pdf (last visited Feb. 10, 2014).
46. Judson W. Starr & Gregory S. Braker, *Sentencing Guidelines for Corporate Environmental Crimes: Is it Fine Having No Fine Guidelines?* 1 (April 30-May 2, 1997) (unpublished article presented at the Sixth Annual Federal Sentencing Guidelines Seminar, Federal Bar Ass'n, (Tampa Bay Chapter)), *available at* http://www.venable.com/files/Publication/e303d7e9-23b4-4762-ac70-f56346cf23bd/Presentation/PublicationAttachment/213ad161-f11f-4507-b74c-99ec15d9bf45/519.pdf (last visited Feb. 10, 2014)
47. *Id.* at 24-25.
48. Draft Environmental Guidelines, *supra* note 45, §§9E and F.

Under the Draft Environmental Organizational Guidelines, in general the first step is to determine the primary offense level.[49] This is done by determining the type of environmental offense.[50] As in Chapter 2 of the current Sentencing Guidelines, numerical values, or levels, are assigned to types of offenses and to the specific offense characteristics. The facts of each offense determine how these levels will be added. The level assigned to the types of offenses is referred to as a "base offense level." For example, the base offense level for the mishandling of hazardous or toxic substances is eight.[51] The numerical values of specific offense characteristics may change, depending on the type of violation, and certain specific offense characteristics do not apply to all types of offenses.

Once the primary offense level has been determined, courts could apply culpability factors, which would include both aggravating and mitigating factors.[52] This part of the calculation assigns numerical values that are added to or subtracted from the primary offense level. Aggravating factors include management involvement in the offense; an organization's prior criminal history; an organization's prior civil compliance history; violation of orders; concealment; and the absence of a corporate compliance program or other organized effort to comply with environmental requirements.[53] Mitigating factors include a corporate commitment to environmental compliance; cooperation and self-reporting of the violation; and remedial assistance.[54]

Application of aggravating and mitigating factors to the primary offense level determines the offense level for the violation. To calculate the fine, the Draft Environmental Organizational Guidelines set up an offense level fine table.[55] According to this grid, each offense level corresponds to a percentage of the maximum statutory fine. For example, the court could sentence an organization whose conduct resulted in an offense level of 20 to between 70% and 90% of the maximum statutory fine. The Draft Environmental Organizational Guidelines, however, generally limit mitigation to 50% of the offense level.[56]

The Probation section of the Draft Environmental Organizational Guidelines largely mirrors that of the current Organizational Guidelines. The Draft Environmental Organizational Guidelines, however, allow courts to impose more stringent and detailed remedial programs than currently allowed and permit courts to order violating organizations to publicize their offense and the punishment imposed.[57]

The Sentencing Commission has not acted on the Draft Environmental Organizational Guidelines in more than 20 years since the draft was published. It seems unlikely that the commission will do so in the near future, particularly given the intervening Supreme Court rulings that make the guidelines advisory rather than mandatory. Although some believe the Draft Environmental Organizational Guidelines would have "dramatically increase[d] the level of fines imposed upon corporations convicted of environmental crimes,"[58] as the recent BP $4.5 billion corporate plea and settlement for the Gulf Oil Spill demonstrate, courts are able to impose significant criminal environmental fines against corporations without reliance on the Guidelines. Whether these fines are ultimately sufficient to ensure that corporate violators clean up their acts is a matter of constant debate.[59]

---

49. *Id.* §9A1.2(a)(2). If the organization is operated primarily for a criminal purpose or primarily by criminal means, courts should not apply offense levels and should determine a fine sufficient to divest the organization of all of its net assets. *Id.* §§9A1.2(a)(1) and 9B1.1.
50. *Id.* §9B2.1(a).
51. *Id.* §9B2.1(b)(2)(A). This same base offense level applies to mishandling of hazardous or toxic substances under the Sentencing Guidelines §2Q1.2.
52. Draft Environmental Guidelines, *supra* note 45, §9C.
53. *Id.* §9C1.1.
54. *Id.* §9C1.2. Proposed §9D1.1 details the seven factors that determine environmental compliance. To grant mitigation under Proposed §9C1.2(a) for environmental compliance, the sentencing court must conclude that each of the seven factors was substantially satisfied. These factors, include: (1) line management attention to compliance; (2) integration of environmental policies, standards, and procedures; (3) auditing, monitoring, reporting, and tracking systems; (4) regulatory expertise, training, and evaluation; (5) incentives for compliance; (6) disciplinary procedures; and (7) continuing evaluation and improvement. An organization can obtain additional mitigation if, in addition to meeting the preceding seven factors, it has implemented additional programs or components that demonstrate its commitment to environmental compliance
55. *Id.* §9E1.1.
56. *Id.* §9E1.2(b).
57. *Id.* §9F.
58. Starr & Braker, *supra* note 46, at 26.
59. Carrie C. Boyd, *Expanding the Arsenal for Sentencing Environmental Crimes: Would Therapeutic Jurisprudence and Restorative Justice Work?*, 32 Wm. & Mary Envtl. L. & Pol'y Rev. 483 (2008), *available at* http://scholarship.law.wm.edu/wmelpr/vol32/iss2/6 (last visited May 29, 2013).

F. The Sentencing Guidelines Are Discretionary, Not Mandatory

There has been a fundamental change in the nature and effect of the sentencing guidelines as a result of two Supreme Court decisions. In *United States v. Booker*,[60] the Court held that the defendant's Sixth Amendment right to a jury trial had been violated by the sentencing judge's conclusion that application of guidelines was mandatory. Booker had been arrested after police officers found 92.5 grams of crack cocaine in his duffle bag, and he later admitted to selling an additional 566 grams. The jury found Booker guilty of possession with intent to distribute at least 50 grams of cocaine. The guidelines provided for a statutory minimum sentence of 10 years in prison, with a maximum sentence of life imprisonment. At sentencing, however, the judge found that Booker had distributed the additional 566 grams and also had obstructed justice. Under the guidelines, as a result of the increased distribution and obstruction of justice findings, the judge increased Booker's base offense level from 32 to 36, which made Booker's sentencing range 30 years to life.

Booker appealed to the U.S. Court of Appeals for the Seventh Circuit, arguing that application of the guidelines violated his Sixth Amendment rights because the judge had found facts that affected his sentencing range which had not been found by the jury. The Seventh Circuit agreed and reversed Booker's sentence. The Supreme Court affirmed. It held that a defendant's Sixth Amendment right to jury trial requires that other than a prior conviction, only facts admitted by a defendant or proved beyond a reasonable doubt to a jury can be used by the sentencing judge to calculate a sentence. In order to remedy the constitutional violation, in a split-majority ruling, the Court struck down the provision of the federal sentencing statute that required federal district judges to impose a sentence within the guidelines. The Court also struck down the provision that deprived federal appeals courts of the power to review sentences imposed outside of the guidelines' range.[61]

In *Gall v. United States*,[62] the Supreme Court further held that the federal appeals courts may not presume that a sentence falling outside the range recommended by the guidelines is unreasonable. Applying this rule, the Court upheld Gall's sentence of 36 months' probation, despite the guidelines' recommended sentence of 30 to 37 months imprisonment.

In *Kimbrough v. United States*, the Court expanded upon *Gall*, finding that there need not be something factually unusual about a case in order to justify a variance from the guidelines.[63] A sentencing judge may lawfully grant a variance even if she simply disagrees with a policy choice embodied in a guideline.

The net effort of these three decisions has been to embolden, if not downright encourage, judges to exercise their discretion in determining appropriate sentences, notwithstanding the range recommended the guidelines. According to EPA: "As in past years, the total level of incarceration [in EPA criminal cases] in FY 2010 [] was reduced by Supreme Court decisions which made the U.S. federal sentencing guidelines discretionary rather than mandatory for use by federal district court judges. Mandatory sentences would have included 26 additional years of jail time."[64]

G. Criminal Fines, the Alternative Fines Act, and the Southern Union Case

Criminal fines in environmental cases can be determined three different ways, with the maximum fine in a case involving a company based on the greater of fines derived from: (1) the statute of conviction, which may provide a fixed maximum fine or a fine per day of violation;[65] (2) 18 U.S.C. §3571(c), which provides a maximum fine for organizations of $500,000 for felonies or $200,000 for misdemeanors; or (3) the Alternative Fines Act, which authorizes fines of up to twice the pecuniary gain or pecuniary loss resulting from

60. 543 U.S. 220 (2005).
61. *Id.* at 260.
62. 552 U.S. 38 (2007).
63. *Id.* at 85, 109 (2007).
64. U.S. EPA, *Criminal Enforcement Annual Results FY 2010,* http://www.epa.gov/compliance/resources/reports/endofyear/eoy2010/criminal/index.html (last visited May 29, 2013). "In FY 2010, individual criminal defendants [in EPA cases] were sentenced to a total of 72 years of jail-time (down from 76 years in FY 2009)." *Id.*
65. *See, e.g.,* Clean Water Act, 33 U.S.C. §1319(c) (providing for a fine of not less than $2,500 nor more than $25,000 per day of negligent violation, or a fine of not less than $5,000 nor more than $50,000 per day of knowing violation).

the offense(s).[66] The government thus can exercise significant discretion in determining what type of fine to seek and the basis for that fine, and it may seek fines well above the statutory cap by either relying on the per day of violation theory and accumulating a large fine amount by seeking the maximum fine per day, or using the alternative fine provision, particularly if there is extensive damages or economic losses to third parties resulting from the pollution.

Prosecutors in environmental cases have frequently charged companies in indictments involving a single count, such as violation of the CWA, but alleged the violation occurred over a period of time. In the case of the CWA, which provides for a fine for a knowing violation of up to $50,000 per day of violation,[67] prosecutors could therefore seek penalties based on the number of days during that period over which the violation was alleged to have occurred.[68] Further, prosecutors were free to ask courts to assess penalties above the statutory maximum for a single count without ever having to present facts to a jury supporting the full amount of the fine as long as the sentencing court found that the necessary facts existed by a preponderance of the evidence.[69]

In 2012, in *Southern Union Co. v. United States,* the Supreme Court significantly circumscribed prosecutors' ability to charge cases and seek criminal fines in this manner, or through reliance on pecuniary gains or losses under the Alternative Fines Act.[70] The defendant, Southern Union, had a subsidiary company that stored liquid mercury at a facility. Vandals broke into the facility and spread mercury around the facility and neighboring areas. The company was charged with a single count of illegal storage of hazardous waste in violation of RCRA over approximately a two-year period. At trial, the jury found the company guilty of the violation of RCRA, but the court did not require the jury to identify the dates of violation; instead the jury was only required to find that the illegal storage had occurred for at least one day during the time period alleged. Based on a finding by the jury that a single violation of RCRA happened at some time during the date range in the indictment, the potential existed for the trial judge to award a fine of over $38 million, and the fine actually awarded was $6 million.[71]

On appeal, Southern Union argued that the criminal fine awarded violated the Sixth Amendment as interpreted in *Apprendi v. New Jersey,* which held in a case involving a sentence of confinement that any fact other than a prior conviction "that increases the penalty for a crime beyond the prescribed statutory maximum must be submitted to a jury, and proved beyond a reasonable doubt."[72] Because all the jury found was that a violation of RCRA had occurred, Southern Union argued that only the statutory maximum fine for a single violation, $50,000, could be awarded, and that any fine amount in excess of $50,000 would had to have been based on proof beyond a reasonable doubt found by the jury as to each date of additional violation.[73] The Supreme Court agreed, holding that there was "no principled basis under *Apprendi* for treating criminal fines differently" than sentences to imprisonment.[74] The decision applies to more than just per-day penalties as the Court stated that "[s]ometimes, as here, the fact is the duration of the statutory violation; under other statutes it is the amount of the defendant's gain or the victim's loss, or some other factor."[75] In any of these situations, the Court held that any fact that increases a defendant's criminal fine above the statutory maximum must, to be constitutionally valid under the Sixth Amendment, be found by a jury beyond a reasonable doubt.

Going forward, the *Southern Union* decision will have an effect not just on sentencing, but on how cases are charged, particularly against organizations, and likely on negotiation of plea agreements. Prosecutors will have to be specific in detailing the facts that will lead to increased penalties in charging documents, and in plea negotiations, defendants have more leverage in terms of requiring specificity from the gov-

66. 18 U.S.C. §3571(d).
67. 33 U.S.C. §1319(c)(2).
68. *See, e.g.,* U.S. v. Chemetco Co., 274 F.3d 1154 (7th Cir. 2001) (charging company with one count of violating CWA over a ten-year period).
69. The Sentencing Guidelines do not establish the standard of proof for determining factual issues under the Guidelines. Most courts held that the standard of proof was a preponderance of the evidence, *See* McMillan v. Pennsylvania, 477 U.S. 79, 92 (1986).
70. 567 U.S. ____, 132 S. Ct. 2344 (2012).
71. *Id.* at 2349. The company was also sentenced to a community service obligation of $12 million. *Id.*
72. 530 U.S. 466, 490 (2000).
73. *Southern Union,* 132 S. Ct. at 2349.
74. *Id.* at 2350.
75. *Id.* at 2350-51.

ernment regarding days of violations and/or proof of pecuniary gains or losses on which potential fine amounts can be based.

H. Statistics Concerning Criminal Environmental Sentences

From 1996 to 2007, "only a little more than one third of environmental defendants received prison terms," which is "far lower than was the norm for federal defendants generally (81.6 percent in 1996–2001 42 and 87.1 percent in 2004–2007)."[76] Of those receiving prison terms, "[t]he overwhelming majority [] received prison terms of two years or less."[77] In contrast, during the same time period, most federal defendants received prison terms of greater than two years.

In addition, "more than 85 percent of environmental defendants sentenced within the guidelines range receive the very lowest possible sentence in that range," which suggests that "judges may still think the guidelines are on the harsh side for environmental defendants."[78] Some observers go even further and suggest that minimal sentences for environmental offences is a result of judicial bias against environmental crimes, i.e., the belief that environmental crimes are not "real crimes," particularly where there is no harm to individuals or the environment.[79]

Whatever the cause, in determining whether to proceed to trial or reach a plea agreement, defense counsel often factor into that decision the likelihood that the sentencing judge may award a relatively light sentence even if the defendant is convicted. There are no guarantees, however, that the court will act consistently with counsel's risk calculus. For example, in *United States v. McWane Cast Iron Pipe Co.*, a jury convicted the company and three individuals of numerous violations including, conspiracy, false statements, and violations of the Clean Water Act (CWA).[80] A senior district court judge in Alabama later sentenced the individuals to fines and probation, despite the guidelines' recommendation of many months of incarceration.[81] Individuals convicted of similar environmental crimes at a sister facility in New Jersey, however, received sentences within the guidelines, ranging from 6 to 70 months in prison, which were upheld by the U.S. Court of Appeals for the Third Circuit.[82]

I. Factors to Be Considered in Imposing a Sentence

Under governing law, the sentencing court is required to impose a sentence sufficient, but no greater than necessary, to comply with the purposes set forth in 18 U.S.C. §3553(a)(2).[83]

The relevant factors set forth in §3553(a) include:

(1) the nature and circumstances of the offense and the history and characteristics of the defendant;

(2) the need for the sentence imposed—

(A) to reflect the seriousness of the offense, to promote respect for the law, and to provide just punishment for the offense;

(B) to afford adequate deterrence to criminal conduct;

76. Michael M. O'Hear, *Bark and Bite: The Environmental Sentencing Guidelines After* Booker, 4 Utah L. Rev. 1151, 1157 (2009), *available at* http://epubs.utah.edu/index.php/ulr/article/viewFile/262/225 (last visited May 29, 2013).
77. *Id.*
78. *Id.* at 1158.
79. *See, e.g.,* Donald J. Rebovich, *Prosecutorial Decision Making and the Environmental Prosecutor: Reaching a Crossroads for Public Protection, in* Environmental Crime And Criminality: Theoretical And Practical Issues 77, 86 (Sally M. Edwards et al. eds.1996) (stating that "For judges, part of the problem of accepting a criminal connotation for environmental offenses can be traced to a natural comparison of environmental offenses to other offenses that these judges are routinely exposed to. These other offenses may be ones which entail elements of traditional person-to-person violence and involve individual victims who have incurred injuries from the violent acts . . ..").
80. *See* DOJ, Press Release, *available at* http://www.justice.gov/opa/pr/2005/December/ (last visited May 29, 2013). AAfter the convictions were overturned by the U.S. Court of Appeals for the Eleventh Circuit and the case was remanded to the district court for trial, the case was resolved in a plea agreement. *See* U.S. EPA, *McWane Convictions Summary*, http://dss.ucsd.edu/-ecomisso/philo28/documents/DOJMcWane. pdf. *See also* United States v. McWane Cast Iron Pipe Co., (Opinion of Judge Hull), D.C. Docket No. 04-00199-CR-2-RBP-RRA (11th Cir. filed Oct. 24, 2007).
81. *Id.*
82. Third Circuit Opinion *available at* http://www.ca3.uscourts.gov/opinarch/092305p.pdf (last visited May 29, 2013).
83. *See* 18 U.S.C. §3553(a).1.

(C) to protect the public from further crimes of the defendant; and

(D) to provide the defendant with needed educational or vocational training, medical care, or other correctional treatment in the most effective manner;

(3) the kinds of sentences available;

(4) the kinds of sentence and the sentencing range established [by the Federal Sentencing Guidelines] . . .;

(5) any pertinent policy statement [issued by the Sentencing Commission];

(6) the need to avoid unwarranted sentence disparities among defendants with similar records who have been found guilty of similar conduct; and

(7) the need to provide restitution to any victims of the offense.

On appeal, a sentence is reviewed for reasonableness under a deferential abuse-of-discretion standard, with the party challenging the sentence bearing the burden of demonstrating unreasonableness.[84] The reviewing court will first determine whether the district court "committed any significant procedural error, such as miscalculating the advisory guidelines range, treating the guidelines range as mandatory, or failing to consider the 18 U.S.C. §3553(a) factors."[85] Thereafter, the appellate court will review the sentence for substantive reasonableness in light of the record and the §3553(a) factors.[86] Nevertheless, the weight given to any specific §3553(a) factor is within the discretion of the district court.[87]

J. The Crime Victims' Rights Act

The Crime Victims' Rights Act (CVRA) of 2004 extends to the victim of any federal crime the rights afforded under Rule 32 of the Federal Rules of Criminal Procedure.[88] Any victim of a crime of violence or sexual abuse who is present at sentencing must be permitted to be heard before the sentence is imposed.[89]

Specifically, the CVRA gives crime victims: (1) the right to be reasonably protected from the accused; (2) the right to reasonable, accurate, and timely notice of any public court or parole proceeding involving the crime; (3) the right not to be excluded from any such public court proceeding, except in certain limited circumstances; (4) the right to be reasonably heard at any public proceeding in the district court involving release, plea, sentencing, or any parole proceeding; (5) the reasonable right to confer with the government attorney in the case; (6) the right to full and timely restitution as provided in law; (7) the right to proceedings free from unreasonable delay; and (8) the right to be treated with fairness and with respect.[90]

"[U]nlike previous reforms, the CVRA gives crime victims direct standing to vindicate their procedural and substantive rights in criminal cases independently of prosecutors . . . and also imposes on the judiciary an affirmative obligation to 'ensure' that those rights are 'afforded.'"[91] If the district court denies the relief sought, crime victims may petition for a writ of mandamus from the court of appeals. The CVRA further requires that the appellate court "take up and decide such application forthwith within 72 hours after the petition has been filed."[92] Nevertheless, despite the CVRA's assurance that "[i]n no event shall proceedings be stayed or subject to a continuance of more than five days for purposes of enforcing this chapter,"[93] the initial cohort of cases make clear that CVRA claims can extend proceedings by far longer.[94]

Violation of a victim's CVRA rights does not provide the defendant grounds for a new trial. It allows a victim's motion to reopen a plea or sentence only where: (1) the victim asserts the right to be heard before

84. *See, e.g.*, United States v. Sarras, 575 F.3d 1191, 1219 (11th Cir. 2009).
85. *Id.*
86. United States v. Beckles, 565 F.3d 832, 845 (11th Cir. 2009), *cert. denied*, 558 U.S. 906 (2009).
87. United States v. Amedeo, 487 F.3d 823, 832 (11th Cir. 2007), *cert. denied*, 552 U.S. 1049 (2007).
88. 18 U.S.C. §3771.
89. Fed. R. Crim. P. 32(i)(4)(B).
90. 18 U.S.C. §3771(a).
91. United States v. Turner, 367 F. Supp. 2d 319, 322 (E.D.N.Y. 2005).
92. 18 U.S.C. §3771(d)(3).
93. *Id.*
94. *See, e.g., In re Dean*, 527 F.3d 391, 393 (5th Cir. 2008) (final decision denying the crime victims, writ of mandamus was not issued for six weeks following the initial appeal from the district court's opinion, which had rejected the victims' allegations that their rights under the CVRA were violated. Another two months passed before the district court took further action.).

or during the proceeding and is denied; (2) the victim petitions the court of appeals for a writ of mandamus within ten days of the denial; and (3) in the case of a plea, the accused has not pled to the highest offense charged.[95]

Importantly, for criminal environmental purposes, the CVRA defines a "crime victim" as "a person directly and proximately harmed as a result of the commission of a federal offense."[96] Determining who has been "directly and proximately harmed," however, is not nearly as clear in an environmental crimes case as it is with more traditional crimes, such as assault or robbery. Indeed, an environmental crimes case in Texas demonstrates just how large the potential CVRA victim list may become.

At the 2007 trial of CITGO Petroleum Corporation (CITGO), a witness testified that a foul-smelling odor from the defendant's tanks was present in neighboring communities. CITGO was later convicted of operating oil/water separator tanks without the required emission control equipment, in violation of the Clean Air Act (CAA).[97] In preparation for sentencing, and to meet its obligations under the CVRA, the government held community meetings to determine the possible victims of CITGO's illegal conduct. The government later argued that "it has an affirmative duty to advocate on behalf of these crime victims who were exposed to these emission events," suggesting that all residents exposed to odors might qualify as victims under the CVRA.[98]

"Four years after the conviction, but prior to sentencing of CITGO, a pro bono attorney representing 300 citizens in the Corpus Christi area sued for compensation under the CVRA. The federal district court denied status under the Crime Victims Act since the case was not brought until four years after the conviction and because the alleged victims could show no causal connection between their alleged injuries and the acts of Citgo."[99] The U.S. Court of Appeals for the Fifth Circuit reversed, holding that "[t]he CVRA does not contain a time limit within which putative crime victims must seek relief in the district court" and granted the Community Members' mandamus petition "to the extent that the district court must hear all new victim status arguments being submitted pre-sentencing by pro bono counsel."[100] As a result, the district court reversed its prior decision and held that citizens harmed by Citgo's CAA violation qualify as crime victims under the CVRA based on the fact that they had breathed the fumes from the tanks.[101] "The District Court further held that, as crime victims, the affected citizens could provide victim impact statements at sentencing and could claim reasonable financial restitution for the harms that resulted from CITGO's criminal actions.[102] The citizens now seek almost $30 million in restitution."[103]

Given the potential for hundreds of "victims" in the environmental crimes context, the most troubling of the CVRA's provisions may be the Act's guarantee of a victim's "reasonable right to confer" with the government attorney. Clearly, were hundreds of victims entitled to access to the government attorney at every stage of the judicial process, it would be nearly impossible for the government to prosecute a case in a timely fashion. Fortunately, the Act itself puts a limit on the victim's rights by inserting the word "reasonable" before "right to confer." Thus, while there is still relatively little case law interpreting the provision, it seems likely that so long as the government attorney allows potential victims some sensible opportunity to confer, he or she need not do so at every juncture.[104]

The CVRA's guarantee to victims of "the right to be reasonably heard at any public proceeding in the district court involving release, plea, sentencing, or any parole proceeding"[105] would be equally problematic

---

95. 18 U.S.C. §3771(d)(5).
96. *Id.* §3771(e).
97. United States v. CITGO Petroleum Corp., Crim. No. CR-06-563 (S.D. Tex. June 27, 2007).
98. *Id.* Gov't's Memo. in Support of a Finding That the Representative Victim/Witnesses Are Crime Victims Pursuant to the CVRA at 4.
99. Jackson Kelly, *Use of Crime Victims' Rights Act Based on Clean Air Act Violation*, http://eem.jacksonkelly.com/2013/02/use-of-crime-victims-rights-act-based-on-clean-air-act-violation-.html (last visited May 29, 2013).
100. *In re:* Jewell Allen *et al*, 701 F.3d 734, 735 (5th Cir. 2012)
101. United States v. CITGO Petroleum Corp., 893 F.Supp.2d 848, 853-54 (S.D. Tex. 2012).
102. *Id.* at 854-55
103. Jackson Kelly, *A Recent Court Decision Opens Door for "Crime Victims" of Statutory Violations*, http://govtcontractsmonitor.jacksonkelly.com/2013/02/a-recent-court-decision-opens-door-for-crime-victims-of-statutory-violations.html (last visited May 29, 2013).
104. *See* Judson Starr et al., *A New Intersection: Environmental Crimes and Victims' Rights*, 23 Nat. Resources & Env. No. 3 (Winter 2009) (discussing several pioneer environmental crimes cases that address the CVRA), *available at* http://www.venable.com/files/Publication/7beef7a3-c08b-4ca6-8821-1aeba7c5e942/Presentation/PublicationAttachment/77f449c0-c181-4536-90cb-19eeb0df6c2d/01_09_Starr_Flack_Foley.pdf (last visited Feb. 18, 2014).
105. 18 U.S.C. §3771(a)(4).

in cases with hundreds of victims without inclusion of the term "reasonably" before "heard." However, it remains to be determined how courts will interpret what the CVRA means by using the term "heard," *i.e.*, whether the victim's rights can be satisfied by the submission of a written statement, or whether each victim must be afforded an opportunity to speak in open court.

While the full impact of the CVRA on environmental crimes cases remains to be determined, at least one conclusion seems certain: the defense, prosecution, and victims of the alleged crime are unlikely to agree as to what level of participation by victims in such cases is deemed "reasonable."

II. Collateral Consequences of Environmental Crimes Convictions

Consequences collateral to an environmental conviction may have more significant adverse effects on a corporation than the criminal penalties, particularly for companies that have contracts with the federal government. A corporation charged with an environmental crime must consider the potential adverse effects of conviction in several areas, including: mandatory blacklisting for future federal contracts; suspension and debarment from government contracts; federal tax consequences; SEC disclosure obligations; and potential disqualification from holding environmental operating licenses under state "bad actor" statutes.

These impacts can be so devastating to the future conduct of a business that prosecutors have substantial leverage in compelling companies to accept a criminal plea, in the hopes of receiving favorable exercise of discretion on these matters. A corporation defending against an environmental crime should keep these potential collateral effects in mind from the very beginning of the investigation and should look for opportunities to minimize their adverse effects.[106]

A. *Mandatory "Listing" of a Facility Under the CWA and the CAA*

The CWA and the CAA prohibit federal agencies from entering into new contracts with, or issuing any grants that will be performed or used at, the facility that gave rise to a conviction under those statutes.[107] This "listing" applies for an indefinite period of time and operates prospectively, not retroactively. Accordingly, a criminal conviction under these statutes does not require cancellation of contracts, grants, or other forms of assistance already awarded to the facility. But it does preclude federal agencies from entering into new arrangements, including the renewal or extension of contracts or grants, until the convicted entity can demonstrate to EPA that the conditions giving rise to the conviction have been corrected.

Specifically, §508(a) of the CWA, prohibits all federal agencies from entering into any contract with any person who has been convicted of a criminal offense under §309(c) "if such contract is to be performed at *any facility* at which the violation which gave rise to such conviction occurred, and if such *facility* is owned, leased, or supervised by such person. . .."[108] Listing under §508(a) applies only to the particular facility involved, and not to the entire subsidiary or company to which the facility belongs.

Section 306 of the CAA contains a similar provision, which requires mandatory listing for a criminal conviction under §113(c).[109] The 1990 Amendments of the CAA give EPA discretion to extend the listing beyond the facility at which the violation occurred to include other facilities owned or operated by the convicted person or entity.[110]

The listing program is administered by the EPA Suspension and Debarment Official (SDO),. EPA regulations implementing the CWA and the CAA[111] provide for maintenance of a List of Violating Facilities (the List), which is published in the *Federal Register* and disseminated to all federal agencies. A separate

---

106. *See generally* David T. Buente Jr. et al., "The Civil Implications of Environmental Crimes," ALI-ABA Criminal Enforcement of Environmental Laws 395 (1994).
107. 33 U.S.C. §1368(a) (CWA); 42 U.S.C. §706 (CAA).
108. 33 U.S.C. §1368(a), CWA §508(a) (emphasis added). This provision also prohibits participation in any federal loan, loan guarantee, grant, or other assistance program.
109. 42 U.S.C. §7606, CAA §306.
110. *Id.* §7606(a). CAA §306(a). The term "facility" is defined expansively in 40 C.F.R. §15.4 to give EPA Suspension and Debarment Official (SDO) authority to consider all operations at one location or site that are part of the same facility. EPA has not issued a regulation to define how and when it will exercise its authority under the CAA to extend listing beyond the particular facility involved in a violation.
111. 40 C.F.R. pt. 15.

listing for excluded parties and facilities is maintained under the System for Award Management (SAM) (formerly the Excluded Parties List System (EPLS)), which is maintained by the General Services Administration and contains information from various federal procurement systems.[112] Publication as a violating facility on the List or identification as an excluded facility in the SAM bars the facility or, if applicable, its parent or affiliated entities, from being awarded any new federal contract, grant or other federal assistance. This exclusion is administered under the Federal Acquisition Regulation (FAR),[113] the Non-Procurement Rule,[114] and other agency regulations that require each bidder for a contract or applicant for a federal grant or other assistance to certify, subject to the provisions of the False Statements Act,[115] that the bidder is not ineligible to receive the award.[116]

In order to remove a facility or entity from the List, the SDO must certify that remedial actions have been taken to correct the conditions giving rise to the violation.[117] A removal action may be initiated by the company or by the listing official.[118] After receiving a delisting request, the SDO will request a review and recommendation from the EPA Regional Office before making a final decision. If the listing official refuses to remove the facility from the List, the owner or operator of the facility may request a removal hearing, at which it must demonstrate by a preponderance of the evidence that the condition giving rise to the listing has been corrected.[119]

Under a 1991 EPA policy statement, correction of the "conditions giving rise to the violation" requires the adoption of an appropriate "corporate attitude" toward future compliance with environmental laws and regulations. EPA identified several criteria it will consider in determining whether such an attitude exists, including:

- The existence of written procedures defining the company's environmental standards, which are consistently enforced through disciplinary mechanisms.
- An effective program to apply these standards, such as a monitoring and auditing system, and methods by which employees can report environmental problems without retribution.
- A program for prevention and immediate correction of future environmental problems, which may include an independent environmental audit to ensure there are no other problems at the facility.[120]

Through these "attitude adjustment" factors, EPA seeks to assure, as consideration for release from the List, that the violator will adopt prospective environmental practices that are more stringent than EPA could require under its direct statutory powers.

A company facing a CWA or CAA criminal charge must consider the practical consequences if the facility involved cannot receive future federal contracts or grants for a period of time. This concern may play an instrumental role in any plea negotiations. In particular, a company contemplating a plea will want to determine if EPA will discuss how the "facility" subject to mandatory listing would be defined. The company also should determine whether EPA will forego exercise of its discretion to extend the listing beyond the offending facility.

---

112. *See* System for Award Management, https://www.sam.gov/portal/public/SAM/#1 (last visited Feb. 18, 2014).
113. 48 C.F.R. Parts 1-51, *available at* http://www.acquisition.gov/far/current/pdf/FAR.pdf (last visited Feb. 18, 2014).
114. 2 C.F.R. Part 180, *available at* http://www.ecfr.gov/cgi-bin/text-idx?SID=7e457a35adb3fe949481def7267b95d7&node=2:1.1.1.1.9&rgn=div5 (last visited Feb. 26, 2014).
115. 18 U.S.C. §1001.
116. 48 C.F.R. §52.209-5 (Certification Regarding Responsibility Matters). EPA's rules explicitly apply the listing sanction to subcontracts as well. 40 C.F.R. §15.4. Federal agency heads have authority to exempt certain contracts or grants from the listing disqualification, based on the "paramount" interests of the United States. Id. §15.51(c)(2). Such exemptions are rare and must be reported to Congress.
117. 40 C.F.R. §§15.20, 15.22(b).
118. *Id.* §15.22(a).
119. *Id.* §15.24. Even if the conditions creating the violations have been completely corrected by the time of conviction, from a practical standpoint the facility will be listed for some period of time while EPA considers the petition for removing the facility or entity from the List. As a matter of policy, EPA has refused to entertain any request to be removed from the List, or to review corrective actions regarding the violation, prior to placing the facility on the List.
120. EPA Policy Regarding the Role of Corporate Attitude, Policies, Practices, and Procedures in Determining Whether to Remove a Facility From the EPA List of Violating Facilities Following a Criminal Conviction, 56 Fed. Reg. 64785 (1991).

B. *Suspension and Debarment of a Company From Future Government Contracts*

The FAR and Non-Procurement Rule provide that government agencies may only contract or do business with responsible companies.[121] Federal agencies have authority to suspend and debar companies from receiving future contracts and grants when the contractor is determined to be non-responsible. A conviction at trial for a guilty plea to an environmental criminal offense, likely will cause a federal agency to question the responsibility of the contractor.[122] The FAR specifically provides that a conviction of a criminal offense in "[p]erforming a public contract or subcontract," or "[c]ommission of any other offense indicating a lack of business integrity or business honesty that seriously and directly affects the present responsibility of a Government contractor or subcontractor" serves as a basis for suspension and debarment.[123] Thus, any environmental violation potentially can have a significant adverse economic effect on a government contractor over and above any criminal or civil fines or penalties.

Suspension is an interim prohibition to deal with a contractor, pending receipt of further information. It temporarily disqualifies the contractor from receiving new government contracts or having existing contracts renewed or extended until the basis for the suspension is resolved. Although it is typically based on the return of an indictment, suspension can occur whenever adequate evidence exists to believe that a contractor has committed an offense which may give rise to debarment and that there is an immediate need for the government to take action to protect the public interest.[124]

Debarment is the disqualification of a contractor for a set period of time—typically from one to three years. The decision to debar and the length of the sanction are within the discretion of the debarring official. The length is based on the nature of the basis for debarment, any mitigating circumstances, and any remedial actions that the contractor has taken.[125]

If a company is convicted of an environmental crime, it likely will be proposed for debarment. If a company has not already been suspended, the notice of the proposed debarment may automatically bar the company from receipt of contracts until a final decision is made by the debarring official.[126] Debarment may apply to all of the company's activities, not just to those performed at the offending facility.

Suspension and debarment are discretionary administrative procedures to protect the public interest from undesirable contractors, by excluding these entities from receiving new federal contracts or participating in federal assistance programs based on evidence that the contractor lacks "present responsibility."[127] To effectuate this policy, the FAR and other agency procurement regulations require contracting officers to review the present responsibility of potential awardees before the award of every contract.[128]

The Clean Contracting Act,[129] signed into law in October 2008, has stimulated increased suspension and debarment activity throughout the federal government. In particular, Section 873 of the Act requires the Interagency Committee on Debarment and Suspension to submit to Congress an annual report "on member agencies' active participation in the committee's work" and "a summary of each agency's activities and accomplishments in the government-wide debarment system." In light of this increased scrutiny by

121. *See, e.g.,* 48 C.F.R. §9.103 (FAR 9.103).

122. Under the FAR, "conviction" means "a judgment or conviction of a criminal offense by any court of competent jurisdiction, whether entered upon a verdict or a plea, and includes a conviction entered upon a plea of nolo contendere." *Id.* §2.101.

123. *Id.* §§9.407-2, 9.406-2.

124. *See id.* §§9.407-2, 9.407-4.

125. *Id.* §9-406-4.

126. The suspension and debarment regulations apply government-wide and have been bifurcated by procurement and non-procurement, e.g., grants, federal assistance, etc., activities. *Id.* Subpart 9.4 (procurement suspension and debarment regulations (the FAR Rule)); 2 C.F.R. Part 180 (non-procurement suspension and debarment regulations (the "Common Rule")). For the most part, these regulations mirror one another; however, they differ in at least one material respect—a proposed debarment under the FAR Rule imposes an immediate exclusion, akin to suspension. On the other hand, a proposed debarment under the Common Rule has no practical effect. Rather it merely starts the clock on the debarment process, but continues to allow federal agencies to enter into new contracts or award new grants to the entity. EPA typically follows the Common Rule.

127. 48 C.F.R. §9.104-1(d). There are other potential collateral consequences from suspension or debarment. For instance, a contractor may lose its security clearance or specialty license, which would not allow the person or business to qualify for certain contracts ever after the suspension or debarment period expires. Additionally, a federal suspension or debarment may also disqualify a company from competing for many local and state contracts, or even result in automatic suspension or debarment by a state or local government. *See, e.g.,* City of Cleveland, Ohio, *Vendor Debarment and Suspension Policy* (July 20, 2011) at 3 (stating the City will not accept or approve a bid, or enter into any contract for goods or services, with a contractor, person or firm that is debarred or suspended by the City, the state of Ohio, or the federal government).

128. *See, e.g., id.* §9.104-1.

129. 129. Pub. L. No. 110-417, Title VIII, Subtitle G, 2008 U.S.C.C.A.N. (122 Stat.) 4546.

Congress, agencies that were previously dormant in the area of suspension and debarment have become increasingly active.

Suspension and debarment by any one agency is effective throughout the federal government, and results in the entity's disqualification from any new federal awards by all agencies during the period the adverse action is in effect.[130] The contractor's name is placed on a consolidated list that is available to all federal agencies and the public—the SAM (formerly the EPLS).[131] The prohibition against award of a new contract, grant or cooperative agreement; consenting to a subcontract or subaward; or renewing or extending an existing contract, grant or cooperative agreement with the disqualified entity is enforced through two primary mechanisms: (1) the cognizant contracting officer must consult SAM prior to taking one of these actions to determine if the prospective contractor or grantee is listed;[132] and (2) certification requirements.[133]

The FAR and the EPA suspension and debarment regulations recommend that where multiple agencies have an interest in a particular company, one agency should be designated as the lead agency to consider suspension or debarment action.[134] There are no set rules for determining which agency will take the lead in a particular suspension or debarment. Normally, considerations such as the agency with the largest contract (by dollar value), primary contacts, either through contracts or federal assistance programs with a particular federal agency, or a particular interest arising out of the underlying actions giving rise to the potential suspension or debarment, play a role in designating the lead agency. If the violation does not arise out of a particular government contract or government program, but exclusively concerns the violation of an environmental law or regulation, EPA has consistently taken the lead agency role. In such circumstances, other federal agencies will typically defer to EPA's SDO.

While the effect of a suspension or debarment action is government-wide, its scope may be limited to a particular organizational element, or it may extend to the entire company, depending upon the facts and the policy of the agency taking the action.[135] The debarring agency may limit the scope of the sanction to the organizational element responsible for the misconduct, unless the evidence shows that other elements or corporate headquarters were involved in the events leading to debarment. If other elements of the corporation remain eligible to receive contracts, however, they may not contract with the debarred component.

The company may present arguments and evidence in opposition to the proposed debarment before a decision is reached. A final agency decision to debar may be reviewed in federal court, although judi-

---

130. Suspension and debarment apply to both a company's procurement and non-procurement relationships with the federal government. Pursuant to 48 C.F.R. Subpart 9.4, EPA has suspension and debarment authority regarding federal procurement programs. Pursuant to 40 C.F.R. Part 32, EPA also has suspension and debarment authority for nonprocurement programs.

131. 48 C.F.R. §9.404.

132. *Id.* §9.405(d)(1).

133. *Id.* §52.209-5. FAR 9.405(d)(2) (48 C.F.R. §9.405(d)(2)) requires an agency to reject the bid of a entity listed in the SAM Exclusions unless "the agency head determines in writing that there is a compelling reason to consider the bid."

134. *Id.* §§9.402(c), (d); 40 C.F.R. §32.115(c). While a determination by the lead agency to forgo suspension or debarment action is followed by other agencies in the vast majority of cases, a contracting agency still has the responsibility to make a determination as to the present responsibility of the bidding company. In *OSG Product Tankers LLC v. United States,* 82 Fed. Cl. 570 (Ct. Fed. Cl. 2008), Overseas Shipholding Group (OSG), the parent company of OSG Product Tankers, had pleaded guilty to various environmental-related violations and had negotiated a settlement agreement with the Maritime Administration (MarAd), which had been designated the lead agency for suspension and debarment purposes, in lieu of debarment. Under the settlement agreement, as long as OSG complied with the terms of its plea agreement in the criminal case, which included the implementation of a comprehensive environmental compliance plan, MarAd agreed to forgo debarment on behalf of the government. OSG Product Tankers subsequently bid on a contract solicited by a separate agency, the Military Sealift Command (MSC). In considering the bid, the MSC contracting officer found that OSG Product Tankers was not presently responsible based primarily on the criminal plea entered into by OSG and the facts of that case, even though OSG Product Tankers had submitted the lowest bid and was otherwise qualified, and MSC awarded the contract to another bidder. OSG Product Tankers appealed the decision to the Federal Court of Claims, arguing that "the contracting officer lacked authority to issue a non-responsibility determination based on integrity and business ethics" because "the Government resolved that issue during the debarment proceedings against its parent company, OSG." *Id.* at 573. Regarding this issue, the court held:

> Plaintiff's case depends on its argument that a contracting officer may not disqualify a bidder on the same grounds that a separate government agency thought insufficient to warrant debarment. Procurement officials are obligated by law to make their own responsibility determinations, however. This contracting officer was not bound by rulings made by other agencies for purposes unrelated to plaintiff=s responsibility as a bidder. MarAd's debarment decision did not preempt, control, or prohibit her responsibility decision; she evaluated that information with the same weight as other facts, as she was legally required to..

Id. at 584.

135. FAR 9.406-1(b) (48 C.F.R. §9.406-1(b)) provides that these sanctions apply to "all divisions or other organizational elements of the contractor, unless the . . . decision is limited by its terms to specific divisions, organizational elements, or commodities." EPA, like many other agencies, has shown a preference for taking action against the lowest possible operating unit or division involved in the criminal action.

cial relief is subject to the deferential rational basis standard and therefore rarely granted. In certain circumstances, the agency may entertain a petition to reduce the length of a debarment.[136] For example, a post-violation change in ownership of a facility responsible for the wrongdoing is an accepted ground for discretionary reduction of the term of debarment.[137]

A company facing an environmental criminal charge should consider carefully the effects of suspension and debarment on its business. The government may be willing to forego suspension and debarment procedures if it is assured of the company's present responsibility through other means, such as a settlement agreement which imposes conditions on the business. The lead agency may require the company to agree to operating restrictions, removal, or discipline of those responsible for the wrongdoing, and/or training and compliance programs. Consequently, settlement discussions in the criminal case and the debarment action may proceed on separate tracks. Moreover, a company may want to consider making a proactive submission to the lead agency SDO in advance of, or contemporaneously with, plea or settlement discussions in order to attempt to convince the agency that the situation that gave rise to the violations has been corrected and that the company is otherwise a "responsible" contractor such that suspension or debarment proceedings are unnecessary. However, many settlement discussions begin only after a post-indictment suspension has been imposed, which significantly reduces the company's bargaining leverage.

C. Federal Tax Consequences

A criminal fine, including a fine paid pursuant to a plea of *nolo contendere*, is not deductible from gross income as an ordinary and necessary business expense under Section 162(a) of the Internal Revenue Code (IRC).[138] Federal tax regulations, however, provide that amounts paid to the government as "compensatory damages" do not constitute fines or penalties and thus may be deducted.[139]

The case law provides conflicting guidance on the factors that allow a restitution payment in a criminal case to be treated as tax deductible. Determinations of deductibility are fact-specific and depend on whether the restitution payment is characterized primarily as punitive or compensatory. Thus, the fact that a payment is denominated as "restitution" does not necessarily qualify it as a restitution payment that is deductible under §165(c)(2) of the IRC. For example, a deduction is not permitted where the payments are made in satisfaction of criminal liability to the state even if the payments are described as restitution.[140] In *Waldman v. Commissioner*, the court noted that where a payment serves both a law enforcement function and a compensatory function, it must be determined which purpose the payment was designed to serve. To make this determination, the *Waldman* court looked to state law and concluded that the payment was not deductible as it was in satisfaction of a criminal liability.[141]

In *Allied-Signal, Inc. v. Commissioner*,[142] the Tax Court held that a restitutionary payment made before sentencing, with a firm expectation of a lower sentence as quid pro quo, was not tax deductible. Prior to sentencing, the defendant, which had pleaded nolo contendere without a plea agreement, made a multimillion-dollar contribution to an environmental fund that benefitted the state. It argued that the payment should be deductible because the payment was voluntary and was made primarily to compensate the state rather than to punish the defendant. The Tax Court rejected the arguments, holding that the payment was involuntarily made as a *quid pro quo* for a lower fine, and that its primary purpose was punishment.[143]

---

136. *Id.* §9.406-4(c)(3).
137. *See* EPA Policy Statement, *supra* note 119, 56 Fed. Reg. at 64787.
138. 26 U.S.C. §162(f); Treas. Reg. 1.162-21(b)(1)(i). A nondeductible "fine or similar penalty" includes an amount paid as a civil penalty, or paid in settlement of actual or potential liability for a fine or penalty. Treas. Reg. §1.162-21(b)(1)(ii),(iii). *See* True v. United States, 894 F.2d 1197 (10th Cir. 1990) (CWA civil penalties nondeductible); Colt Indus. Inc. v. United States, 11 Cl. Ct. 140 (1986), *aff'd*, 880 F.2d 1311 (Fed. Cir. 1989).
139. Treas. Reg. §1.162-21(b)(2).
140. Kraft v. United States, 991 F.2d 292 (6th Cir. 1993), *cert. denied*, 510 U.S. 976 (1993); *see also* Bailey v. Commissioner, 756 F.2d 44 (6th Cir. 1985) (restitution payment connected with a sentence was disallowed as a deduction, even though the fine was applied as restitution in a settlement of a multidistrict class action then pending against the taxpayer corporation and its officers).
141. Waldman v. Commissioner, 88 T.C. 1384 (1987), *aff'd*, 850 F.2d 611 (9th Cir. 1988).
142. 63 T.C.M. (CCH) 2672 (1992), *aff'd*, 54 F.3d 767 (3d Cir. 1995).
143. *Id.* at 2681-83.

In *Colt Industries Inc. v. United States*,[144] the court rejected an argument that an environmental payment was tax deductible. The court first noted that the defendant had not articulated how its payments of $1.6 million to the Pennsylvania Clean Air and Clean Water Fund, administered by the Pennsylvania Department of Environmental Resources, would compensate the government. The court then went even further, stating that neither the CWA nor the CAA authorized the EPA to seek compensatory damages.[145]

In 2008, a coordinated issues paper issued by the Internal Revenue Service's Large and Mid-Size Business Division also cast serious doubt on whether companies could claim a deduction or amortization for the costs of a Supplemental Environmental Project (SEP).[146] The use of SEPs as a settlement vehicle has risen dramatically, and is often encouraged by the EPA as a means of achieving environmentally beneficial projects that cost more than the equivalent of the fine that might otherwise be imposed on the offending company. The IRS noted, however, that "because §162(f) represents a codification of the public policy doctrine, the analyses used by the courts and the Service in determining whether certain expenses meet the definition of a fine or similar penalty for purposes of §162(f) are relevant for determining whether any [SEP] expenditure, or a portion thereof, constitutes a fine or penalty whose allowance as a tax benefit would frustrate public policy."[147] As a result of this policy, it is important that any such settlement should specify which portion of the SEP is intended to be compensatory and/or beyond the amount that would otherwise be paid in a civil or criminal penalty.[148] Such a statement may determine whether the compensatory portion may be deemed remedial and deductible or whether it has to be capitalized and recovered as a depreciation or amortization expense in the future.

As the terms of a plea agreement or sentence may affect the deductibility of a restitution payment, with the cooperation of the prosecutor, the defendant may be able to structure a restitution payment to increase the likelihood that the payment will be deductible.[149] A defendant considering such a plea agreement should consult carefully with an experienced tax attorney on this issue.

D. SEC Disclosure Obligations

"Over the years, SEC and EPA have made sporadic efforts to coordinate on improving environmental disclosure; currently, EPA periodically shares limited information on specific, environment-related legal proceedings, such as those involving monetary sanctions."[150] However, the SEC and EPA do not have a formal agreement to share relevant information.

A public company's duty to disclose environmental liabilities to the public in its SEC filings arises from two main sources: periodic disclosure requirements and general anti-fraud provisions. While some believe the SEC's requirements for environmental disclosure are too flexible and too narrow in scope, others, primarily in the regulated industry, believe the flexibility is necessary and the scope appropriate. Perhaps due to the nature of the regulations, "an SEC review of annual filings from Fortune 500 companies in 2002 found relatively few problems with environmental disclosure overall, compared with other types of disclosure."[151]

The SEC's reporting system is centered around Regulation S-K, which lists reporting requirements for registrants.[152] The provisions of Regulation S-K most relevant to environmental matters are: Item 101, which requires a description of business; Item 103, which requires disclosure of material legal proceedings; Item 303, which is management's discussion and analysis (MD&A) of financial condition and results

144. 880 F.2d 1311 (Fed. Cir. 1989).
145. *Id.* at 1314.
146. IRS Issue Paper LMSB-04-0608-036 (July 9, 2008)
147. *Id.*
148. George J. Schutzer & Ora R. Sheinson, *Curtailing Environmental Settlement Deductibility*, LAW 360, (Dec. 1, 2008), *available at* http://www.law360.com/articles/78584/curtailing-environmental-settlement-deductibility (last visited Feb. 19, 2014).
149. The *Exxon Valdez* plea agreement, for example, was designed to take advantage of the tax deductibility of compensatory payments. The restitution was expressly stated to be "exclusively remedial, compensatory, and non-punitive, and . . . separate and distinct from the fines . . .." Plea Agreement, United States v. Exxon Corp., No. A90-015 (Sept. 26, 1991) at 9.
150. U.S. GAO, REPORT TO CONGRESSIONAL REQUESTERS, ENVIRONMENTAL DISCLOSURE: SEC SHOULD EXPLORE WAYS TO IMPROVE TRACKING AND TRANSPARENCY OF INFORMATION (July 2004), *available at* http://www.gao.gov/new.items/d04808.pdf (last visited May 29, 2013).
151. *Id.* at 4.
152. 17 C.F.R. §§229.10 to 229.915 (1994).

of operations; and Item 503, which is a discussion of the most significant factors that make the offering speculative or risky.

Under Regulation S-K Item 101, the registrant must provide a general description of its business and disclose material effects that compliance with federal, state and local environmental laws may have upon its capital expenditures, earnings, and competitive position.[153]

Item 103 generally requires that the company describe any material pending legal proceedings, "other than ordinary routine litigation incidental to the business."[154] Instruction 5 to Item 103, however, specifically provides that litigation "arising under any federal, state or local provisions that have been enacted or adopted regulating the discharge of materials into the environment or primar[il]y for the purpose of protecting the environment" shall not be deemed "ordinary routine litigation incidental to the business." The Instruction requires that three different types of environmental litigation must be disclosed:

- any administrative or judicial proceeding which is material to the registrant's business or financial condition;
- any administrative or judicial proceeding which is primarily a claim for damages, or concerns potential monetary sanctions, capital expenditures, deferred charges or charges to income, and the amount involved exclusive of interest and costs exceeds 10% of the current assets of the registrant and its subsidiaries on a consolidated basis; or
- any administrative or judicial proceeding which involves a governmental authority as a party and involves potential monetary sanctions, unless the registrant reasonably believes that the proceeding will result in no monetary sanctions which, exclusive of interest and costs, are less than $100,000.

In a 1979 Interpretive Release, the SEC explained that environmental "proceedings" may take the form of informal or formal notices of violation, administrative orders, civil suits, or criminal prosecutions.[155] At least one court has disagreed, however, with the SEC's position that a notice of violation constitutes a reportable" "proceeding."[156]

A company considering entering a plea to an environmental crime should discuss with its securities counsel whether, based on its knowledge of contemplated proceedings by the government, the company is required to make public disclosure pursuant to the instructions to Regulation S-K Item 103.[157] "In addition to possibly preparing and disclosing cost estimates, it may also be necessary for the company to set forth the basis for its estimates, the assumptions and methods used in reaching such estimates, and the extent of uncertainty that projected future costs may be expended in order for the disclosure not to be misleading."[158]

Under Item 303, the management's decision an analysis (MD&A) narrative discussion of the registrant's financial condition should include those "material events and uncertainties known to management that would cause reported financial information not to be necessarily indicative of future operating results or future financial condition."[159] The MD&A Interpretive Release expands the disclosure requirement to include disclosure of known uncertainties unless management can determine in an objectively reasonable assessment that a material effect is not reasonably likely to occur.[160]

In 2006, the SEC's Division of Corporate Finance noted that, in disclosing loss contingencies under Item 303, a company may need to disclose environmental contamination even before accounting recogni-

153. *Id.* §229.101.
154. *Id.* §229.103.
155. *See* Environmental Disclosure Requirements, Securities Act Release No. 6130, Fed. Sec. L. Rep. (CCH) ¶ 23507B, at 17203-06 n.14 (Sept. 27, 1979).
156. Crouse-Hinds Co. v. Internorth, Inc., 518 F. Supp. 416, 474-75 (N.D.N.Y. 1980).
157. One consideration will be the "materiality" of the proceeding. *See, e.g.*, Wielgos v. Commonwealth Edison Co., 892 F.2d 509 (7th Cir. 1989) (shareholder alleged that the company violated Item 103 by failing to disclose that it had an application to operate a nuclear power plant pending before the Atomic Safety Licensing Board (ALSB). When the ALSB denied the application, the company's stock fell.).
158. Davis Polk & Wardwell, Environmental Disclosure in SEC Filings 5 (2009), ***available at*** http://www.davispolk.com/1485409/clientmemos/01.21.09.env.disclosure.sec.filings.pdf (last visited May 29, 2013) (citing Environmental Disclosure Requirements, Securities Act Release No. 6130, Fed. Sec. L. Rep. (CCH) ¶ 23507B, at 17203-5 (Sept. 27, 1979)).
159. 17 C.F.R. §229.303, Instruction at 3.
160. *See* Release Nos. 33-6835, 34-26831 (May 18, 1989), 54 Fed. Reg. 22427 (May 24, 1989).

tion of such contingency, if such contamination creates a reasonable likelihood that its financial condition or results of operations will be materially affected.[161]

Under Regulation K-K Item 503(c), environmental risks must be disclosed if significant to the company or offering. "Depending on a company's particular situation, it may need to disclose risks related to climate change, contamination and remediation liabilities, compliance with environmental laws (including enforcement actions and permitting matters), environmental litigation and hazardous material exposure issues (including toxic tort and asbestos claims)."[162]

Beyond specific periodic disclosures, the general antifraud provisions of the Securities Act and the Securities Exchange Act of 1934 prohibit the inaccurate representation of a registrant's environmental record.[163] The SEC has stated:

> The Commission's general reporting rules require disclosure of any additional material information, beyond that for which disclosure is required by specific Commission rule, necessary to make required statements not misleading. In the context of its environmental releases, the Commission has interpreted these rules as requiring disclosure of "all other environmental information of which the average prudent investor might reasonably be informed."[164]

In *United Paper Workers International Union v. International Paper Co.*,[165] a shareholder suit, the court found that the company committed a proxy rule violation by materially misrepresenting its environmental record, by failing disclose that it had been accused of numerous environmental offenses, had pleaded guilty to felonies, had agreed to pay large fines, and had been the target of numerous administrative complaints.

The requirements of Form 20-F, addressing foreign private issuers, filing annual reports or registration statements pursuant to the Securities Act or the Exchange Act, also may give rise to a duty to disclose actual or potential environmental liabilities in SEC filings. Item 4.D of Form 20-F requires issuers to provide "information regarding any material tangible fixed assets, including leased properties," and including a description of "any environmental issues that may affect the company's utilization of the assets." Other provisions of Form 20-F also may require a foreign private issuer to disclose environmental liabilities.

E. State "Bad Actor" Provisions

A "bad actor" provision is a statute or regulation that denies a license, permit, or other benefit to a person or company based on a poor regulatory compliance history. A person or company facing an environmental criminal charge should carefully review whether its operations are covered by federal or state licensing or regulatory statutes that impose sanctions if the regulated entity, its owners, its key employees, or its affiliates are convicted of a crime.

Virtually all adverse "bad actor" consequences are imposed at the state level.[166] A majority of states have enacted statutes under which a history of poor environmental compliance, particularly an environmental criminal conviction, can jeopardize the person's right to hold operating permits. These provisionally apply especially if the permit holder or applicant does not make a substantial effort to correct the condition that led to the violation.[167] These provisions arise primarily in the hazardous waste area, as a result of initiatives to address the penetration of organized crime into solid waste disposal. To enforce these restrictions, several

161. Current Accounting and Disclosure Issues in the Division of Corporation Finance, Prepared by Accounting Staff Members in the Division of Corporation Finance, November 30, 2006, *available at* http://www.sec.gov/divisions/corpfin/cfacctdisclosureissues.pdf (last visited May 29, 2013).
162. Davis Polk & Wardwell, Environmental Disclosure in SEC Filings 15 (2009), *available at* http://www.davispolk.com/1485409/clientmemos/01.21.09.env.disclosure.sec.filings.pdf (last visited May 29, 2013).
163. Sections 11 and 12 of the Securities Act and Section 10 of the Exchange Act comprise the "general antifraud provisions" of the securities laws.
164. *In re Occidental Petroleum Corp.*, Exchange Act Release No. 16950, Fed. Sec. L. Rep. (CCH) ¶ 82622, at 83356. 1980 SEC LEXIS 1158 (July 2, 1980) (citing a variety of SEC releases).
165. 985 F.2d 1190 (2d Cir. 1993).
166. There is a narrow federal bad actor provision under TSCA. Under §6(e)(1), 15 U.S.C. §2605(e)(1), poor environmental compliance of the applicant, its principals or its key employees may lead to the denial of an application to store PCBs for disposal. 40 C.F.R. §761.65(d), as amended by 58 Fed. Reg. 59372 (Nov. 9, 1993).
167. Other states, such as New Mexico, continue to wrestle with the topic. *See* Trip Jennings, *"Bad Actor" Legislation Dies on House Floor*, New Mexico Independent (Feb. 10, 2010), *available at* http://drillingsantafe.blogspot.com/2010/02/bad-actor-legislation-hb-276-dies-on.html.

states, including Indiana, New Jersey, and Ohio,[168] require affirmative disclosure of compliance history by a hazardous waste license applicant. Failure to disclose compliance history properly can provide independent grounds in some states for denial or revocation of hazardous waste permits.

Denial of a crucial permit under a bad actor provision could effectively put a party out of business. Therefore, the target of a criminal investigation has significant incentives to structure the plea in a manner that minimizes the adverse effects on its qualifications to do business prospectively. Because disqualification is generally discretionary, permit holders are well advised to attempt to discuss the likely consequences with civil regulators well in advance of agreeing to any criminal plea.

168. West's AIC §13-7-10.2-3(b); N.J. Stat. §13:1E-127(e); Ohio Rev. Code §3734.41(D).

Part Three: Statutes and Cases

Chapter 9:
Specific Environmental Statutes

At the heart of environmental criminal law are several, sector-specific statutes that criminalize certain violations of environmental laws and regulations. Issues related to voluntary disclosures, government investigations, prosecution decisions, trial strategy, and sentencing all revolve around the primary question of whether the defendant's conduct violated a specific statutory prohibition.

The most important environmental statutes that provide for criminal prosecution in appropriate circumstances include: the Clean Water Act (CWA); the Clean Air Act (CAA); the Convention on International Trade in Endangered Species of Wild Fauna and Flora (CITES); the Endangered Species Act (ESA); the Federal Insecticide, Fungicide, and Rodenticide Act (FIFRA); the Lacey Act; the Migratory Bird Treaty Act (MBTA); the Act to Prevent Pollution From Ships; the Ocean Dumping Act; the Oil Pollution Act (OPA); the Resource Conservation and Recovery Act (RCRA); the Safe Drinking Water Act (SDWA); and the Toxic Substances Control Act (TSCA).

When the government brings an indictment under these statutes directly, it often also charges various offenses under Title 18 of the U.S. Code, including conspiracy, obstruction of justice, destruction of evidence, or false statements to the government. In some situations, these Title 18 violations have the potential to criminalize conduct under other environmental statutes, which do not themselves provide independent criminal penalties, such as the Comprehensive Environmental Response, Compensation, and Liability Act (CERCLA or Superfund). The Environmental Crime Section's (ECS') Worker Endangerment Initiative similarly is geared toward using the criminal provisions of environmental statutes to punish corporations that violate worker safety regulations, because the Occupational Safety and Health Act does not contain a provision that punishes as a felony acts by corporations or managers that threaten worker safety. There are other synergies as well, such as criminal sanctions associated with laws that govern the transportation of hazardous chemicals and pollutants, and, in the current absence of more specific regulations, utilization of the CWA in hydraulic fracturing ("fracking") cases.

The following sections are an overview of each of these statutes, highlighting the nuances as they apply to environmental criminal cases, and discussing significant decisions. The case law discussion is not intended to be exhaustive, but simply to provide a flavor for the types of prosecution typically brought under the different statutes. For a more comprehensive discussion of case law specific to each statute, see Appendix 1 at www.eli.org/environmental-crimes-second-edition.[1]

I. The Clean Water Act

A. *Overview*

The CWA prohibits discharges of pollutants into the waters of the United States without a permit. Covered pollutants include most substances that can be harmful to aquatic functions and values. Most waters are covered, including all interstate waters, their tributaries, and adjacent wetlands.

1. Other sources include the websites of the U.S. Environmental Protection Agency (EPA) and the U.S. Department of Justice (DOJ) and Steve Solow's annual surveys of developments in environmental crime enforcement, http://www.kattenlaw.com/steve-solow/ (last visited May 29, 2013).

Prohibited discharges take two main forms: point source and nonpoint source emissions. Point source discharges are discrete discharges from the end of a pipe or channel, a shovel blade, or similar source. Nonpoint source discharges are generally stormwater discharges flowing from developed or undeveloped property, city streets, suburban lawns, and farm fields.[2]

With some exceptions, the civil aspects of the CWA are implemented and enforced by the U.S. Environmental Protection Agency (EPA). The principal exception is the CWA's statute's prohibition against filling wetlands, which falls under the regulatory authority of the U.S. Army Corps of Engineers (the Corps), with oversight by EPA. This division of regulatory authority significantly complicates enforcement of the law.[3]

B. *Prohibitions*

The CWA[4] prohibits "the discharge of any pollutant by any person," except in compliance with its terms.[5] This broad prohibition is somewhat narrowed by the defined terms in this phrase, but each of those terms contains multiple defined and circular references. Ultimately, the CWA's scope—and thus the scope of the U.S. Department of Justice's (DOJ's) potential criminal jurisdiction—is broad. To aid the reader in understanding the reach of this phrase, the defined terms appear in bold in the following discussion.

The term **"person"** is inclusive and does not limit the scope of the CWA. It refers to "an individual, corporation, partnership, association, [s]tate, municipality, commission, or political subdivision of a [s]tate, or any interstate body."[6] The definitions of "state" and "municipality" are equally broad. **"State"** refers to "a [s]tate, the District of Columbia, the Commonwealth of Puerto Rico, the Virgin Islands, Guam, American Samoa, the Commonwealth of the Northern Mariana Islands, and the Trust Territory of the Pacific Islands."[7] A **"municipality"** is

> a city, town, borough, county, parish, district, association, or other public body created by or pursuant to [s]tate law and having jurisdiction over disposal of sewage, industrial wastes, or other wastes, or an Indian tribe or an authorized Indian tribal organization, or a designated and approved management agency under section 1288 of the CWA.[8]

Other defined terms place some limits on the expansive reach of the law. For example, **"discharge of a pollutant"** is defined as "any addition of any pollutant to navigable waters from any point source" or "any addition of any pollutant to the waters of the contiguous zone or the ocean from any point source other than a vessel or other floating craft."[9]

The phrase **"point source"** is defined in turn to cover "any discernible, confined and discrete conveyance, including but not limited to any pipe, ditch, channel, tunnel, conduit, well, discrete fissure, container, rolling stock, concentrated animal feeding operation, or vessel or other floating craft from which pollutants are or may be discharged."[10] A **"pollutant"** is defined as "dredged spoil, solid waste, incinerator residue, sewage, garbage, sewage sludge, munitions, chemical wastes, biological materials, radioactive materials,

---

2. At the time the CWA was first passed, point source discharges from industrial or municipal solid waste treatment facilities constituted 85% of all water pollution and were of significantly greater concern to Congress than nonpoint source discharges. *See* William Ruckelshaus, *A New Shade of Green*, www.wsj.com/article/SB10001424052702303410404575151640963114892.html (last visited May 29, 2013). As a result, the CWA establishes a fairly strict regime for point source discharges but largely leaves control of nonpoint source discharges to the states. As a result, there are few criminal prosecutions related to nonpoint source discharges, and this chapter does not discuss them in detail.
3. For a more complete discussion of this complexity, see Margaret Strand & Lowell Rothschild, Wetlands Deskbook, (3d Ed., 2009). In addition, the United States Coast Guard has a role in enforcement of the CWA, primarily as it applies to vessels and marine-transportation-related facilities, as well as in the coastal zone of the United States. The definition of transportation-related facility is established under a Memorandum of Understanding between the Secretary of Transportation and the Administrator of the EPA. 40 C.F.R. pt. 112, app. A. The definition of coastal zone is in the National Contingency Plan, 40 C.F.R. §300.5
4. 33 U.S.C. §1251.
5. *Id.* §1311(a), CWA §301(a). As described below, the primary avenue for lawful discharges is through the CWA permit system. However, Section 311 of the CWA (33 U.S.C. §1321) specifically prohibits the discharge of oil and hazardous substances into (1) the navigable waters of the United States, (2) the U.S. contiguous zone, and (3) the U.S. Exclusive Economic Zone (EEZ). For a more detailed discussion of this provision of the CWA, *see infra* Section II.D.3 of this Chapter.
6. *Id.* §1362(5), CWA §502(5).
7. *Id.* §1362(3), CWA §502(3).
8. *Id.* §1362(4), CWA §502(4).
9. *Id.* §1362(12), CWA §502(12).
10. *Id.* §1362(14), CWA §502(14).

heat, wrecked or discarded equipment, rock, sand, cellar dirt and industrial, municipal, and agricultural waste discharged into water."[11]

The most significant limitation on the government's jurisdiction under the CWA has developed from this secondary set of definitions. In particular, the term **"navigable waters,"** has been the centerpiece of much civil and criminal litigation and agency guidance. As defined in the CWA, the term "means the waters of the United States, including the territorial seas."[12] But the courts often have been asked to apply this term to "waters" that do not fit the common sense notion of "navigable."

In sum, the language of the CWA prohibits anyone and everyone from using any discernible, confined, and discrete conveyance to add almost any type of waste to a water of the United States, unless specifically allowed under the CWA. EPA's rules and guidance have provided some clarification of this prohibition.

C. Penalties

The government is authorized to enforce noncompliance with the CWA through administrative,[13] civil,[14] or criminal penalties.[15] Criminal penalties attach to both negligent[16] and knowing[17] violations of the CWA. For both categories of offenses, the penalties may be doubled for repeat violations.[18]

- Negligent violations are punishable by a fine of between $2,500 and $25,000 per day of violation and/or up to one year of imprisonment.[19] Subsequent negligent violations carry a penalty of between $2,500 and $50,000 per day of violation and/or up to two years' imprisonment.[20]
- Knowing violations are punishable by a fine of between $5,000 and $50,000 per day of violation and/or up to three years of imprisonment.[21] Subsequent repeat violations carry a penalty of between $5,000 and $100,000 per day of violation and/or up to six years of imprisonment.[22]
- Knowing violations carry enhanced penalties if the violator knows at the time of the violation that another person is being placed in imminent danger of death or serious injury by the action.[23] Individuals committing such violations are subject to a maximum penalty of $250,000 and 15 years of imprisonment,[24] and organizations to a maximum penalty of $1 million.[25] Repeat violators are subject to doubling of these penalties.[26]

Maximum penalty calculations are relatively straightforward—the number of violations is multiplied by the maximum penalty. One wrinkle results from the fact that in the civil enforcement context, violations of the CWA prohibition against the filling of wetlands are often charged on a "continuing" basis. Under the "continuing violation" theory, the illegal filling may occur over a discrete period of days, but every day the illegal fill remains in place is calculated as a new "day of violation."[27] While it is possible to consider discharges into waters other than wetlands in violation of a permit as a continuing discharge, historically, discharges into non-wetland waters are treated as one-time violations in both the civil and criminal

11. *Id.* §1362(6), CWA §502(6).
12. *Id.* §1362(7), CWA §502(7). The territorial sea is specifically defined to extend three (3) nautical miles seaward from the line of ordinary low water along the coast. *Id.* §1362(8). This is important because the United States, for the application of most other statutes, has adopted a territorial sea extending seaward out to 12 nautical miles. *See, generally*, discussion *infra* at Section II,B. of this Chapter.
13. *Id.* §1319(g), CWA §309(g).
14. *Id.* §1319(b), CWA §309(b).
15. *Id.* §1319(c), CWA §309(c).
16. *Id.* §1319(c)(1), CWA §309(c)(1).
17. *Id.* §1319(c)(2), CWA §309(c)(2).
18. *Id.* §1319(c)(1) and (2), CWA §309(c)(1) and (2).
19. *Id.* §1319(c)(1), CWA §309(c)(1).
20. *Id.*
21. *Id.*
22. *Id.*
23. *Id.* §1319(c)(3)(A), CWA §309(c)(3)(A).
24. *Id.*
25. *Id.*
26. *Id.*
27. *See, e.g.*, United States v. Reaves, 923 F. Supp. 1530, 26 ELR 21394 (M.D. Fla. 1996); Strand & Rothschild, *supra* note 3, at 120-21.

contexts, with each discharge being a separate day of violation. With the Supreme Court decision in the Southern Union case, it is most likely that this will continue to be the situation.[28]

D. Permits and Permit Requirements

The primary avenue for legal discharges under the CWA is a permit system, the national pollutant discharge elimination system (NPDES).[29] Each NPDES permit limits the amount of a pollutant or pollutants that a permittee may discharge. These "effluent limitations" are often based on the implementation of particular technological control technology. They provide a numerical ceiling on the quantity of pollutant that permittees may discharge. NPDES permits come with a myriad of conditions and requirements, the violation of any one which may result in imposition of civil and criminal penalties.

One of the most significant permit conditions is that permittees must periodically monitor their effluent discharges and self-report the results to the relevant regulatory agency (usually the local state EPA). The permit holder must certify as to the accuracy of these discharge monitoring reports (DMRs). As a result, DMRs are a prime source of evidence used in civil and criminal proceedings, when they show that effluent standards have been exceeded. Sometimes DMRs show that effluent limits have been exceeded time and time again, providing evidence of a knowing violation of the law. On occasion, rather that submit a DMR showing such an exceedence, a violator will submit an altered DMR showing no violation and, thereby, makes a false statement to the government.

Other conditions, such as sampling intervals and protocols are commonly included in NPDES permits. Violations of these terms can form the basis for enforcement actions separate and apart from exceeding the basic effluent limitations.

E. Jurisdictional Considerations

Despite the broad scope of the CWA, there are several significant jurisdictional limitations on its application.

1. Statutory Jurisdiction

The statute itself establishes several jurisdictional limitations. For example, "agricultural stormwater discharges and return flows from irrigated agriculture" are excluded from the definition of "point source."[30] The definition of "pollutant" explicitly excludes:

> (A) sewage from vessels or a discharge incidental to the normal operation of a vessel of the Armed Forces within the meaning of section 1322 of this title; [and] (B) water, gas, or other material which is injected into a well to facilitate production of oil or gas, or water derived in association with oil or gas production and disposed of in a well, if the well-used either to facilitate production or for disposal purposes is approved by authority of the State in which the well is located, and if such State determines that such injection or disposal will not result in the degradation of ground or surface water resources.[31]

2. EPA Rules and Guidance

As described above, one of the main limitations on the scope of the CWA is that it applies only to discharges into "navigable waters," which are defined as "the waters of the United States, including the territorial seas."[32] Over the years, however, EPA and the Corps have further refined this limitation by defining "waters of the United States." EPA and the Corps currently follow the same definition of the term, which includes:

---

28. For a more detailed analysis of he contining violation issue in the context of Clean Water Act cases, see Susan F. Mandiberg, *Fault Lines in the Clean Water Act: Criminal Enforcement, Continuing Violations and Mental State*, 33 Envtl. L. 173, 181-190 (2003). Discussion of the Southern Union case is *supra* at Chapter 8, Section I.G.
29. 33 U.S.C. §1342, CWA §402.
30. *Id.* §1362(14), CWA §502(14).
31. *Id.* §1362(6), CWA §502(6).
32. *Id.* §1362(7), CWA §502(7).

- all traditionally navigable waters;
- all interstate waters, including interstate wetlands;
- all waters, including wetlands, the use, degradation, or destruction of which could affect interstate commerce;
- the territorial seas; and
- wetlands adjacent to, and tributaries and impoundments of, other waters within the definition.[33]

The scope of these regulations has been significantly affected by a series of U.S. Supreme Court decisions.

3. Case Law Interpretation

The primary CWA jurisdictional controversy relates to the scope of federal jurisdiction over "isolated" waters, i.e., those removed from interstate waters and those traditionally used for interstate commerce. The last decade has seen a steady shift from a fairly expansive, but well-defined jurisdiction over such waters to a somewhat more limited, but much more confounding one.

In 1985, following internal discussions among the interested federal agencies, the EPA General Counsel issued an opinion concluding that the CWA's jurisdiction extended to isolated waters that were or could be used by migratory birds or endangered species.[34] In 1986, several environmental groups sued the Corps to compel a change in its practices and force it to extend its jurisdiction to such waters.[35] During the course of that litigation, the Corps announced that it concurred in EPA's view[36] and issued confirming memoranda to its districts.[37]

Following this development, multiple courts considered and divided over the validity of the Migratory Bird Rule as a basis for CWA jurisdiction. For example, the U.S. Court of Appeals for the Fourth Circuit refused to recognize EPA's jurisdiction,[38] and the U.S. Court of Appeals for the Sixth Circuit questioned this basis for asserting federal authority.[39] By contrast, the U.S. Court of Appeals for the Ninth Circuit and numerous district courts concluded that the CWA did extend to isolated waters used or subject to use by migratory birds.[40]

In 2001, the Supreme Court resolved this split among the circuits in the *Solid Waste Agency of Northern Cook County (SWANCC) v. U.S. Army Corps of Engineers* case, which concerned the application of the

---

33. 33 C.F.R. §328.3(a), 40 C.F.R. §230.3(s). While the CWA has only one definition of "waters of the United States," different federal agencies use different approaches to evaluate jurisdiction under the CWA. For instance, the Corps of Engineers typically performs a jurisdictional determination for a specific water body prior to issuing a permit under Section 404 of the CWA. On the other hand, jurisdictional evaluations of water bodies under Section 402 (NPDES), Section 303 (Water Quality Standards), and Section 311 (Oil and Hazardous Substances) are typically done as part of enforcement actions. As a result, most CWA jurisdiction determinations are made by the Corps of Engineers, which has estimated it may make over 100,000 such determinations annually. *See* Donna M. Downing, *Scope of "The Waters of the United States" Protected by the Clean Water Act,* in The Clean Water Act Deskbook at 11, 20 (Mark A. Ryan ed., 3d Ed. 2011).
34. Memorandum from Francis S. Blake, General Counsel, U.S. EPA, to Richard E. Sanderson, Acting Ass't Administrator, Office of External Affairs, U.S. EPA (Sept. 12, 1985) (CWA jurisdiction over isolated waters).
35. National Wildlife Fed'n v. Laubscher, No. G-86-37, 17 ELR 20891 (S.D. Tex. 1987) (magistrate's opinion); 662 F. Supp. 548, 17 ELR 20892 (S.D. Tex. 1987) (court opinion).
36. 51 Fed. Reg. 41206, 41217 (Nov. 13, 1986).
37. Memorandum from Brigadier General Patrick J. Kelly, Deputy Director of Civil Works, U.S. Army Corps of Engineers, Corps Field Offices (Nov. 8, 1985) (EPA memorandum on Clean Water Act jurisdiction over isolated waters); Memorandum from Brigadier General Patrick J. Kelly, to Commander, Southwestern Division, U.S. Army Corps of Engineers (Feb. 11, 1986) (Commerce Clause jurisdiction over isolated waters).
38. *See, e.g.*, Tabb Lakes Ltd. v. United States, 715 F. Supp. 726, 19 ELR 20672 (E.D. Va. 1988), *aff'd without opinion*, 885 F.2d 866, 20 ELR 20008 (4th Cir. 1989) (questioning jurisdiction based upon migratory bird usage without Corps having promulgated a formal rule to this effect).
39. Hoffman Homes, Inc. v. United States EPA, 961 F.2d 1310, 22 ELR 21148 (7th Cir. 1992) (denying jurisdiction under the CWA based upon migratory bird usage), *vacated without opinion*, 975 F.2d 1554, 22 ELR 21547 (7th Cir. 1992).
40. Leslie Salt Co. v. United States, 660 F. Supp. 183, 22 ELR 20361 (N.D. Cal. 1987), *judgment for plaintiffs*, 700 F. Supp. 476, 19 ELR 20420 (N.D. Cal. 1989), *rev'd and remanded*, 896 F.2d 354, 20 ELR 20477 (9th Cir. 1990), *cert. denied*, 498 U.S. 1126 (1991), *on remand*, 820 F. Supp. 478 (N.D. Cal. 1992), *reh'g denied*, 820 F. Supp. 478 (N.D. Cal. 1992), *aff'd*, 55 F.3d 1388, 25 ELR 21046 (9th Cir. 1995), *cert. denied sub nom.* Cargill, Inc. v. United States, 516 U.S. 955, 26 ELR 20001 (1995). *See also* United States v. Hallmark Constr. Co., 14 F. Supp. 2d 1069, 29 ELR 20168 (N.D. Ill. 1998) (supporting jurisdiction based upon migratory bird usage without need for regulatory promulgation to that effect); United States v. Suarez, 846 F. Supp. 892 (D. Guam 1994) (wetland violator not denied effective counsel where attorney failed to raise jurisdictional defense as wetlands were adjacent, not isolated).

CWA to a truly isolated water—open water filling a former mining pit.[41] The Court determined that where intrastate waters are "isolated," the Migratory Bird Rule is insufficient as the sole basis for establishing jurisdiction. In reaching its decision, the Court focused heavily on the statutory term "navigable":

> We said in *[United States v.] Riverside Bayview Homes* that the word "navigable" in the statute was of "limited effect" and went on to hold that §404(a) extended to nonnavigable wetlands adjacent to open waters. But it is one thing to give a word limited effect and quite another to give it no effect whatever . . ..
>
> Where an administrative interpretation of a statute invokes the outer limits of Congress' power, we expect a clear indication that Congress intended that result . . .. This concern is heightened where the administrative interpretation alters the federal-state framework by permitting federal encroachment upon a traditional state power.[42]

The Court also identified, but did not resolve, the question whether the Commerce Clause would support federal authority over isolated, wholly intrastate waters.[43]

After the *SWANCC* decision, EPA and the Corps abandoned the Migratory Bird Rule as a basis for CWA jurisdiction and relied instead primarily on the tributary system of the water. Since all navigable waters and their tributaries, as well as adjacent wetlands, are subject to federal jurisdiction, the agencies attempted to follow the water downstream from the site of the conduct at issue to a navigable water. These linkages often took fairly circuitous routes.[44]

In 2006, the Supreme Court attempted to clarify the issue in *Rapanos v. United States*, but only muddied the matter further.[45] The Court reached consensus only on the conclusion that the lower court decision should be overturned, but issued no majority opinion. It split 4-1-4 and provided three different views as to the appropriate limits of jurisdiction under the CWA. The plurality opinion, authored by Justice Antonin Scalia (joined by Justices John Roberts, Samuel Alito, and Clarence Thomas), took the position that "waters of the United States" required, at a minimum, "relatively permanent water."

> On its only plausible interpretation, the phrase "waters of the United States" include only those relatively permanent, standing or continuously flowing bodies of water "forming geographic features" that are described in ordinary parlance as "streams [,] . . . oceans, rivers, [and] lakes." See Webster's Second 2882. The phrase does not include channels through which water flows intermittently or ephemerally, or channels that periodically provide drainage for rainfall.[46]

Justice Anthony Kennedy, concurring in the judgment, established an entirely different standard for defining "waters of the United States." "Jurisdiction . . . depends upon the existence of a significant nexus between the wetlands in question and navigable waters in the traditional sense."[47] Drawing on the purposes of the CWA, he concluded that criteria other than water level and flow could constitute a "significant nexus" between a wetland or tributary and traditionally navigable waters. Accordingly, he found that "wetlands possess the requisite nexus, and thus come within the statutory phrase 'navigable

---

41. 531 U.S. 159, 31 ELR 20382 (2001) (SWANCC).
42. *Id.* at 172-73 (citing United States v. Riverside Bayview Homes 474 U.S. 121, 16 ELR 20086 (1985)).
43. *Id.* at 173.
44. *See, e.g.*, United States v. Buday, 138 F. Supp. 2d 1282 (D. Mont. 2001) (wetlands adjacent to a creek that flows to another creek that flows into a navigable-in-fact river were jurisdictional); California Sportfishing Ass'n v. Diablo Grande, 209 F. Supp. 2d 1059 (E.D. Cal. 2002) (a creek is "jurisdictional" because it flows into a navigable-in-fact river, despite flowing through an underground pipeline along the way); Idaho Rural Council v. Bosma, 143 F. Supp. 2d 1169 (D. Idaho 2001) (a discharge into a spring was regulated by the CWA where the spring ran into a pond, "across a pasture," into a canal and into a creek that is a water of the United States); In the Matter of Mr. C.W. Smith, EPA Docket No. CWA-04-2001-1501, 2004 WL 1658484 (EPA July 15, 2004) (property was jurisdictional because it has a creek running through it which flows into another creek, into a river, into a lake, and into a navigable-in-fact river. Jurisdiction also existed because interstate travelers fished in the pond.); United States v. Deaton, 332 F.3d 698, 33 ELR 20223 (4th Cir. 2003), *cert. denied*, 541 U.S. 972 (2004) (wetlands were jurisdictional where they were adjacent to a ditch that connected to a roadside ditch, to a culvert, under a road, to another ditch, to a creek, to another creek and to a navigable-in-fact river); United States v. Rueth Dev. Co., 189 F. Supp. 2d 874 (N.D. Ind. 2001), *aff'd*, 335 F.3d 598, 33 ELR 20238 (7th Cir. 2003), *cert. denied*, 540 U.S. 1050 (2003) (jurisdiction existed where the wetlands were adjacent to a ditch that led to another ditch that led to a navigable water. The court stated that a drop of rainwater at the wetlands would certainly intermingle with water in the navigable waterway. Elsewhere it stated that a "molecule of water" could flow toward and mix with the navigable waterway. Following the signing of a consent decree by the defendant, the finding of adjacency was vacated by the court.).
45. 547 U.S. 715, 36 ELR 20116 (2006).
46. *Id.* at 739.
47. *Id.* at 779.

waters,' if the wetlands, either alone or in combination with similarly situated lands in the region, significantly affect the chemical, physical and biological integrity of other covered waters more readily understood as 'navigable.'"[48]

The four dissenters (Justices Stevens, Souter, Ginsberg, and Breyer) would have upheld the broad jurisdictional theory on which the government regulations were based.

The *Rapanos* decision has created great difficulties for the agencies in implementing the CWA. The courts also have struggled with whether the appropriate jurisdictional test is the plurality's conclusion or is Justice Kennedy's unique interpretation of CWA jurisdiction. The government has argued that either test is sufficient, while the regulated community often submits that the "significant nexus" test applies. To date, the circuits have divided on this question, and the Supreme Court has not resolved the conflict.[49] The resulting confusion among the courts has confounded prosecutors in deciding whether to file criminal charges under the CWA.

In the criminal context, the most significant decision addressing the jurisdictional question post-*Rapanos* is *United States v. Robison*.[50] The U.S. Court of Appeals for the Eleventh Circuit overturned criminal convictions for discharging pollutants to a water of the United States, holding that the trial court had failed to issue a jury instruction on the question of federal jurisdiction that followed the *Rapanos* decision (which was handed down after the convictions).

The obvious problem resulting from *Rapanos* is how the agencies and regulated entities can determine what constitutes a "significant nexus" to navigable waters, given that the term is not defined in the statute or the regulations and that Justice Kennedy provided few guidelines upon which to make the requisite connection. The agencies have issued guidance regarding their interpretation, but a decade later the courts have not resolved the question.

4. Federal Agency Response

None of the federal regulations defining "waters of the United States" has been amended since *SWANCC*. In 2003, EPA and the Corps issued an Advanced Notice of Proposed Rulemaking, requesting public comments on what wetlands or waters should be subject to federal jurisdiction in light of *SWANCC*.[51] They subsequently abandoned the effort to modify their regulations.[52] Instead, the agencies have issued several guidance documents.

On January 15, 2003, EPA and the Corps published a joint legal opinion stating that they would continue to assert jurisdiction over wetlands to the full extent of their authority, but would not use the Migratory Bird Rule.[53] In June 2007, the EPA and the Corps issued a joint Legal Memorandum discussing jurisdiction.[54] Following public comment, the memorandum was supplemented in December 2008 with additional information regarding the meaning of the terms "traditional navigable water" and "adjacent." The guidance includes a Memorandum of Agreement that established a coordination mechanism between EPA and the Corps regarding jurisdictional determinations.[55]

48. *Id.* at 780.
49. United States v. Gerke Excavating, Inc., 464 F.3d 723 (7th Cir. 2006), *pet. for reh'g denied* (Dec. 1, 2006) (Justice Kennedy's standard governs), *cert. denied*, 552 U.S. 810 (2007); United States v. Johnson, 467 F.3d 56 (1st Cir. 2006), *cert. denied*, 552 U.S. 948 (2007) (the government may use either the standard articulated by the plurality or the standard articulated by Justice Kennedy); San Francisco Baykeeper v. Cargill Salt Div., 481 F.3d 700, 707 (9th Cir. 2007) (Justice Kennedy's test was controlling).
50. 505 F.3d 1208 (11th Cir. 2007), *motion for reh'g en banc denied*, 521 F.3d 1319 (11th Cir. 2008), *cert. denied*, 555 U.S. 1045 (2008) (the Justice Kennedy opinion establishes the governing standard).
51. 68 Fed. Reg. 1991 (Jan. 15, 2003) *available at* http://www.epa.gov/owow/wetlands/pdf/ANPRM-FR.pdf (last visited Feb. 25, 2014).
52. EPA Press Release, EPA and Army Corps Issue Wetlands Decision (Dec. 16, 2003), available at http://yosemite.epa.gov/opa/admpress.nsf/e51aa292bac25b0b85257359003d925f/540f28acf38d7f9b85256dfe00714ab0!OpenDocument (last visited Feb. 25, 2014). 68 Fed. Reg. 1995 (Jan. 15 2003), *available at* http://water.epa.gov/lawsregs/guidance/wetlands/upload/2003_12_19_wetlands_Joint_Memo.pdf.
53. 68 Fed. Reg. 1995 (Jan. 15 2003), http://water.epa.gov/lawsregs/guidance/wetlands/upload/2003_12_19_wetlands_Joint_Memo.pdf.
54. U.S. EPA & U.S. Army Corps of Engineers, Clean Water Act Jurisdiction Following the U.S. Supreme Court's Decision in *Rapanos v. United States* & *Carabell v. United States* (June 5, 2007), *available at* http://water.epa.gov/lawsregs/guidance/wetlands/upload/2007_6_5_wetlands_RapanosGuidance6507.pdf (last visited Feb. 25, 2014).
55. U.S. EPA & U.S. Army Corps of Engineers, Clean Water Act Jurisdiction Following the U.S. Supreme Court's Decision in *Rapanos v. United States* & *Carabell v. United States* (Dec. 2, 2008), *available at* http://water.epa.gov/lawsregs/guidance/wetlands/upload/2008_12_3_wetlands_CWA_Jurisdiction_Following_Rapanos120208.pdf (last visited Feb. 25, 2014).

On May 3, 2011, EPA and the Corps published "Draft Guidance on Identifying Waters Protected by the Clean Water Act," which extends Justice Kennedy's significant nexus test in *Rapanos* to "other waters," *i.e.,* not just to wetlands.[56] The draft guidance would allow aggregation of waters that are "physically proximate" within a watershed.. However, EPA withdrew the Draft Guidance (at least in part) and the agencies announced that they plan to promulgate regulations rather than finalize the draft guidance.

EPA and the Corps have prepared a draft rule to clarify the jurisdiction of the CWA and sent it for federal regulatory review. This draft rule takes into consideration the latest peer-reviewed science reflected in a draft science report titled: Connectivity of Streams and Wetlands to Downstream Waters.[57] According to EPA, the report provides "[a] scientific basis needed to clarify Clean Water Act jurisdiction, including a description of the factors that influence connectivity and the mechanisms by which connected waters affect downstream waters. Any final regulatory action related to the jurisdiction of the Clean Water Act in a rulemaking will be based on the final version of this scientific assessment, which will reflect EPA's consideration of all comments received from the public and the independent peer review."[58] The proposed rule is supposed to clarify the status of the network of smaller waters that feed into larger ones and of wetlands, and will not change existing regulatory exemption and exclusions.[59]

5. Proposed Legislative Response to Changes in Federal Jurisdiction

Starting in 2007, bills were introduced in Congress to restore federal jurisdiction over the waters that were affected by the *SWANCC* and *Rapanos* decisions. At the state level, some states responded to *SWANCC* by taking steps to protect isolated waters.[60]

6. Other Jurisdictional Issues

Several other jurisdictional issues have emerged since *Rapanos*. Indeed, some questions thought to have been resolved prior to *Rapanos* have reemerged. Some of the cases discussed below therefore are no longer of historic interest only, but now may have new life.

a. Man-Made Hydrologic Connections

Both before and after *SWANCC*, courts generally held that man-made and/or intermittent connections to otherwise jurisdictional "waters of the United States" are sufficient to establish CWA jurisdiction.[61] *Rapanos* has reopened the question whether man-made conveyances or ditches provide a sufficient basis for federal jurisdiction.

While the plurality opinion in *Rapanos* criticized decisions that had upheld jurisdiction over wetlands adjacent to roadside ditches that carried only intermittent or ephemeral water flow,[62] it did not suggest that

56. U.S. EPA & U.S. Army Corps of Engineers, Draft Guidance on Identifying Waters Protected by the Clean Water Act (May 3, 2011), *available at* http://www.epa.gov/tribal/pdf/wous_guidance_4-2011.pdf (last visited Feb. 25, 2014).
57. U.S. EPA, *Connectivity of Streams and Wetlands to Downstream Waters: A Review and Synthesis of the Scientific Evidence* (September, 2013 External Review Draft, EPA/600/R-11/098B), *available at* http://yosemite.epa.gov/sab/sabproduct.nsf/fedrgstr_activites/7724357376745F48852579E60043E88C/$File/WOUS_ERD2_Sep2013.pdf (last visited Feb. 25, 2014).
58. U.S. EPA, Clean Water Act Definition of "Waters of the U.S.", http://water.epa.gov/lawsregs/guidance/wetlands/CWAwaters.cfm (last visited Feb. 25, 2014).
59. Examples of federal legislation that sought to amend the CWA's jurisdictional scope are the Clean Water Restoration Act of 2007. H.R. 2421, 110th Cong. (2007); the Clean Water Restoration Act, S.787, 111th Cong. (2009); and the America's Commitment to Clean Water Act, H.R. 5088, 111th Cong. (2010). The Association of State Wetland Managers maintains current information and links to state wetland programs at http://www.aswm.org/iam/ lost-sitemap (last visited May 29, 2013).
60. The Association of State Wetland Managers maintains current information and links to state wetland programs at http://www.aswm.org/iam/lost-sitemap (last visited May 29, 2013).
61. United States v. TGR Corp., 171 F.3d 762, 29 ELR 21059 (2d Cir. 1999) (a brook channeled through passageways built by developers is a jurisdictional tributary); Headwaters, Inc. v. Talent Irrigation Dist., 243 F.3d 526, 31 ELR 20535 (9th Cir. 2001) (irrigation canals are subject to CWA jurisdiction, even though the canals are separated from natural streams by a system of closed gates); Leslie Salt Co. v. United States, 896 F.2d 354, 20 ELR 20477 (9th Cir. 1990), *cert. denied*, 498 U.S. 1126 (1991) (ditches, road beds, and culverts that are hydrologically connected to jurisdictional surface waters are sufficient to establish CWA jurisdiction); United States v. Eidson, 108 F.3d 1336, 27 ELR 20853 (11th Cir. 1997), *cert. denied*, 522 U.S. 899 (1997) (man-made drainage ditches and canals that flow intermittently into a jurisdictional creek qualify as "tributaries").
62. 547 U.S. at 726-27.

the question of jurisdiction turned on whether a waterbody is man-made or natural. Under the plurality opinion, if permanent water flows, the non-navigable water body can be jurisdictional; and under the concurring opinion, if there is a significant nexus with navigable waters, the non-navigable water body can be jurisdictional. Neither test inquiries into the nature of the channel through which the water flows, *e.g.*, how it was formed. Nevertheless, the plurality opinion rests in part on distinguishing between "waters of the United States" and "point sources." Because ditches and other conveyances are defined as "point sources," the plurality opinion indicates that they would not constitute "waters of the United States." Thus CWA jurisdiction over man-made conveyances and ditches will likely remain highly controversial and a persistent source of litigation.

b. Groundwater Connections

Groundwater is not regulated under the CWA. The Corps has argued in court that groundwater is not a "water of the United States."[63] EPA also has made similar statements,[64] and numerous courts have reached the same conclusion.[65] It is possible, however, that the "significant nexus" test of Justice Kennedy's concurrence in *Rapanos* could be satisfied where water flowed in part through groundwater but still impacted navigable waters. It remains to be seen how groundwater ultimately will be classified.

Some courts and academics have distinguished between "isolated groundwater" (that which lacks a hydrological connection to jurisdictional surface waters) and "tributary groundwater" (that which has such a connection).[66] They argue that a finding that fails to address discharges that directly impact the integrity of CWA jurisdictional waters will ultimately undo the very purpose of the CWA: *i.e.,* "[T]o restore and maintain the chemical, physical, and biological integrity of the Nation's waters."[67] Where surface water has been diverted through culverts or pipes, it is generally not considered to be groundwater but rather man-made conveyances hydrologic connections.[68]

Most of the cases examining the issue of jurisdiction established by groundwater hydrology are citizen suits. Few involve enforcement actions by the federal agencies themselves, and the assertion of jurisdiction often has been contrary to express government positions.

F. *Proposals to Expand Restitution and Increase Sanctions Under the CWA*

Legislation introduced in the Senate following the failure of the Macondo well in the Gulf of Mexico in 2010, resulting in the largest oil spill in U.S. history, would have mandated that a judge order restitution to victims of environmental crimes, resulting from criminal violations of the CWA.[69] Currently, judges may

---

63. Town of Norfolk v. Corps of Eng'rs, 968 F.2d 1438, 1450-51, 22 ELR 21337 (1st Cir. 1992) ("The Corps has interpreted this definition to rely only to surface waters." "[W]e agree with the Corps . . ..").
64. "[T]he Clean Water Act does not give EPA the authority to regulate groundwater authority through NPDES permits." 62 Fed. Reg. 20177, 20178 (Apr. 25, 1997).
65. Village of Oconomowoc Lake v. Dayton Hudson Corp., 24 F.3d 962, 965, 24 ELR 21080 (7th Cir. 1994), *cert. denied*, 513 U.S. 930 (1994) ("Neither the Clean Water Act nor the EPA's definition [of "waters of the United States"] asserts authority over ground waters."); Rice v. Harken Exploration Co., 250 F.3d 264, 269, 31 ELR 20599 (5th Cir. 2001) ("The law in this Circuit is clear that ground waters are not protected waters under the CWA."); Patterson Farm v. City of Britton, 22 F. Supp. 2d 1085, 1091 (D.S.D. 1998).
66. *See* Philip M. Quatrochi, *Groundwater Jurisdiction Under the Clean Water Act: The Tributary Groundwater Dilemma*, 23 B.C. Envtl. Aff. L. Rev. 603, 619 (Spring 1996); Northern California River Watch v. City of Healdsburg, 496 F.3d 993 (9th Cir. 2007) (an abandoned sand and gravel pit that lacked a surface water connection to a nearby navigable river, but was adjacent to the river, fell within CWA jurisdiction). *See also, e.g., Rice*, 250 F.3d at 272; Quivira Mining Co. v. EPA, 765 F.2d 126, 130, 15 ELR 20530 (10th Cir. 1985), *cert. denied*, 474 U.S. 1055 (1986); Idaho Rural Council v. Bosma, 143 F. Supp. 2d 1169, 1180 (D. Idaho 2001); Washington Wilderness Coalition v. Hecla Mining Co., 870 F. Supp. 983, 990, 25 ELR 20661 (E.D. Wash. 1994); McLellan Ecological Seepage Situation v. Weinberger, 707 F. Supp. 1182, 1196, 19 ELR 20124 (E.D. Cal. 1988), *rev'd on other grounds*, 47 F.3d 325, 25 ELR 20628 (9th Cir. 1995), *cert. denied*, 516 U.S. 807 (1995); Aiello v. Town of Brookhaven, 136 F. Supp. 2d 81 (E.D.N.Y. 2001); Williams Pipeline Co. v. Bayer Co., 964 F. Supp. 1300 (S.D. Iowa 1997). *But see* Umatilla Waterquality Protective Ass'n v. Smith Frozen Foods, Inc., 962 F. Supp. 1312, 1318, 27 ELR 21411 (D. Ore. 1997); Kelley ex rel. Michigan v. United States, 618 F. Supp. 1103, 16 ELR 20080 (W.D. Mich. 1985).
67. 33 U.S.C. §1251(a).
68. *See, e.g.,* United States v. TRG Corp., 1998 U.S. Dist. LEXIS 9354 (D. Conn. 1998); California Sportfishing Protection Alliance v. Diablo Grande, Inc., 209 F. Supp. 2d 1059 (E.D. Cal. 2002).
69. Environmental Crimes and Enforcement Act of 2011, S. 350, 112th Cong. (2011) (proposing to amend 18 U.S.C. §3663A(c)(1)(A)).

impose restitution to an identified victim of an environmental crime, but not, for instance, for harm caused to natural resources.[70] The legislation died in the U.S. Senate.[71]

G. *Criminal Enforcement of the CWA*

As with violations of other environmental statutes, the United States tends to reserve criminal enforcement of the CWA for either intentional violations or those that cause extremely significant environmental impacts.

After capturing the attention of the nation, in January 2013, a federal judge in the U.S. District Court for the Eastern District of Louisiana approved a plea agreement entered into by BP for violations arising from the release of oil from the Macondo well in the Gulf of Mexico in 2010.[72] The Macondo well was operated by BP, and had been drilled by the Mobile Offshore Drilling Unit (MODU) *Deepwater Horizon*, owned and operated by a subsidiary of Transocean Deepwater, Inc., a subcontractor of BP. The well failed; eventually releasing between 4.5 and 5.5 million barrels of oil into the Gulf of Mexico. This was the worst oil discharge in U.S. history. In addition, gas discharged from the well enveloped the *Deepwater Horizon* and caused an explosion, which led to the sinking of the *Deepwater Horizon* and the loss of 11 crewmembers. BP pled guilty to 14 criminal counts, which included 11 counts under the maritime manslaughter statute, 1 count of obstruction of Congress, 1 misdemeanor count of violating the CWA provisions prohibiting the negligent discharge of oil, and 1 count under the MBTA.[73] BP was sentenced to pay $4 billion in criminal fines and recoveries as provided in the plea agreement.[74] In addition, Transocean agreed to plead to a single count of violating the CWA provisions prohibiting the negligent discharge of oil, and to pay $400 million in criminal fines and recoveries.[75]

In *United States v. Vierstra*,[76] the defendant was charged with three counts of negligently violating the CWA for discharging process wastewater from a concentrated animal feeding operation into a local canal in Idaho. Defendant moved for dismissal, arguing that the man-made canal was not within the CWA's jurisdiction. The Court disagreed, ruling that the canal was a "water of the United States" under the CWA, and that "federal CWA jurisdiction attaches, whether the channel is carrying water or dry." Relying on *Rapanos v. United States*,[77] the court determined the canal met both the "relatively permanent" and "significant nexus" standards to be considered a water of the United States because it was a tributary that connected to the Snake River, a navigable water. The court noted the "seasonal, [] recurring, regular, perennial, and substantial" nature of the river's flow to determine that is was "relatively permanent" within the *Rapanos* definition.

Defendant also argued that discharges into a dry creek bed were not violations of the CWA because there was no evidence that the pollutants were carried downstream because the creek bed was dry. The court rejected defendant's argument, holding that the creek bed was a "water of the United States" and therefore within the purview of the CWA.

In *United States v. United Water Environmental Services*, the defendants were charged with 26 counts of violations of the CWA, including conspiracy to defraud the government by hampering the functions

70. *See* 18 U.S.C. §§3553, 3663.
71. *See* http://www.congress-summary.com/B-112th-Congress/Senate_Bills_112th_Congress_A.html (last visited June 4, 2013).
72. *See* Reasons for Accepting Plea Agreement, U.S. v. BP Exploration and Prod., Inc., Crim. Case No. 2:12-cr-00292-SSV-DEK (E.D. La., Jan. 29, 2013), *available at* http://www.justice.gov/criminal/vns/docs/2013/01/2013-01-30-bp-exploration-reasons-for-accepting-plea-agreement.pdf (last visited Feb. 25, 2014).
73. Guilty Plea Agreement, U.S. v. BP Exploration and Prod., Inc., Crim. Case No. 2:12-cr-00292-SSV-DEK (E.D. La., Nov. __, 2012), *available at* http://www.justice.gov/criminal/vns/docs/2012/11/2012-11-15-BP-Guilty-Plea-Agreement.pdf (last visited Feb. 26, 2014).
74. Order, Doc. 66-3, U.S. v. BP Exploration and Prod., Inc., Crim. Case No. 2:12-cr-00292-SSV-DEK (E.D. La., Jan. 29, 2013), *available at* http://www.justice.gov/criminal/vns/docs/2013/01/2013-01-29-bp-exploration-order.pdf (last visited Feb. 26, 2014).
75. Cooperation Guilty Plea Agreement, U.S. v. Transocean Deepwater Inc., Case No. 13-cr-001 (E.D. La., Jan. 3, 2013), *available at* http://www.justice.gov/opa/documents/transocean-plea-agreement.pdf. (last visited Feb. 26, 2014). A third corporation, Halliburton Energy Services, Inc., another subcontractor of BP that was involved with the well drilling effort, pleaded guilty to destroying evidence in the case, and was fined the statutory maximum ($200,000). See U.S. Dept. of Justice, Press Release, *Halliburton Pleads Guilty to Destruction of Evidence in Connection with Deepwater Horizon Disaster and Is Sentenced to Statutory Maximum Fine*, (Sept. 19, 2013), *available at* http://www.justice.gov/opa/pr/2013/September/13-crm-1046.html (last visited Feb. 26, 2014).
76. 803 F. Supp. 2d 1166 (D. Idaho 2011), *decision reached on appeal*, 492 Fed. Appx. 738 (9th Cir. Idaho 2012).
77. 547 U.S. 715 (2006).

of EPA. Defendants were also charged with violating the CWA for tampering with a monitoring method required by the CWA. Defendants moved to dismiss the case against them, arguing the indictment was insufficient because the acts it charged were not illegal. Defendants argued that

> because, as the parties agree, it is not a crime to raise the level of chlorine added to the effluent and it is not a crime to take a grab sample, it cannot be a crime to raise the chlorine before taking the sample and lower it afterward unless it is alleged that the conduct was undertaken with consciousness of wrongdoing, in furtherance of, or to conceal other violations." The court denied the motion, determining that the question of whether or not Defendants actually tampered with the monitoring method was a question of fact that the jury had to decide.[78]

In *United States v. Agosto-Vega*,[79] defendants Agosto and his brother used their employees and a truck registered to their car dealership to drain raw sewage from a housing development and empty it into storm drains leading to a nearby creek basin. Defendants were convicted of conspiracy to violate the CWA and for aiding and abetting the discharge of raw sewage into U.S. waters. On appeal of their convictions, defendants argued that the public, namely their family members, should have been allowed into the courtroom during jury selection and that their Sixth Amendment rights to a public trial had been denied. The court agreed that under *Presley v. Georgia*,[80] the public should have been admitted. The court therefore vacated the convictions and granted the motion for a new trial.

Defendant Agosto also challenged the sufficiency of the evidence for his conviction under the CWA, arguing that the government had not proven he knew of the discharges made by truck. The court disagreed and held that the circumstantial evidence sufficient supported a finding of a knowing violation. The court reasoned that as Agosto was an experienced businessman who had instructed employees to take care of the sewage problem and provided them with a truck and as several eye witnesses had seen the truck dumping sewage into the drains, a jury could reasonably find that Agosto knew of the truck's activities. Defendants also argued that the government had failed to prove that the creek was "a water of the United States" under the CWA, but the court held that the government had shown that the creek was significantly connected to other bodies of water, meeting the standards in *Rapanos*.[81]

In *United States v. Moses*,[82] the defendant rerouted and reshaped the flow of three rivers without a permit, although he was consistently warned by the government against this activity. He was convicted for violating the CWA, and appealed. His arguments on appeal were that the river was seasonal, so it was not a water of the United States. Since much of his reconstruction involved moving the earth when the water was not flowing, he argued this was not the discharge of pollutants. The court held that even an intermittent waterway was one of the United States, and the fact that the pollutants were discharged when the river was dry was immaterial. The court noted that this analysis was in agreement with Kennedy's plurality opinion in *Rapanos*, an opinion the court found to be the controlling rule of law. The court also found the defendant's characterization of his massive reconstructive work as an "incidental fallback" to be ludicrous. The defendant's conviction was affirmed.

In *United States v. Perez*,[83] a company and its owner were convicted of unpermitted filling activity that took place on 17 acres of federally protected wetlands. The individual was sentenced to 36 months of imprisonment and 3 years of supervised release, an enhancement over the base level offense called for in the Sentencing Guidelines, upon finding the offense had resulted in an ongoing, continuous or repetitive discharge of a pollutant, and that the offense involved a discharge without a permit. Perez argued that the enhancement for an ongoing, continuous or repetitive discharge of a pollutant was improper because the trial court did not require the government to prove actual environmental contamination, and the enhancement for failing to obtain a permit was improper because the base offense level already accounted for the failure to obtain a permit. The court held that the enhancement for continuing discharge of a pollutant

78. 2011 U.S. Dist. LEXIS 94721, *10 (N.D. Ind. Aug. 24, 2011).
79. 617 F.3d 541 (1st Cir. 2010).
80. 558 U.S. 209 (2010).
81. 617 F.3d at 551.
82. 496 F.3d 984 (9th Cir. 2007).
83. 336 F.3d 1178 (11th Cir. 2004).

was proper because the Guideline applied to pollutants and the pollutant did not have to be designated as hazardous as the Guideline assumes actual environmental contamination; therefore, application of the Guideline was proper as the government proved Perez had engaged in repeated, unlawful dumping of pollutants in federally protected wetlands without a permit.[84] The court also ruled the enhancement for failure to obtain a permit was proper because the base offense level applies to a variety of CWA violations that do not involve the failure to obtain a permit, and, thus, the enhancement did not punish the defendant twice for the same offense.[85]

In *United States v. Lucas,* the defendants sold house lots and designed and certified septic systems on wetlands, but represented the lots as dry." This activity continued over the course of several years, notwithstanding their receipt of several cease and desist orders.[86] As a result of the illegal activity, "[s]eptic systems on the lots failed, causing waste discharges." The government charged the corporate developer and various individuals with CWA violations, mail fraud, and conspiracy to commit mail fraud and to violate the CWA.[87] The jury convicted the defendants on all counts. The court "[s]entenced Lucas to 108 months' imprisonment and three years' supervised release and fined him $15,000. It sentenced both Wrigley and Thompson to 87-month sentences with 3 years' supervised release and assessed $15,000 in fines against each of them. It fined BHA, Inc., $4.8 million and Consolidated Investments $500,000, and assessed [$1,407,400 million] in restitution against each Defendant."[88] The convictions and sentences were upheld on appeal.[89]

In *United States v. Pozsgai,*[90] the defendant filled wetlands on his property and continued to do so despite repeated warnings from the Corps that his acts were illegal. After he was served with a cease and desist order, and even after a court imposed a temporary restraining order. Upon conviction, he was sentenced to three years imprisonment and five years' probation, followed by one year of supervised release, and fined $200,000.[91] In addition, the government filed a civil action seeking restoration of the wetlands.[92]

Several important decisions have confirmed, however, that the government has an expansive criminal reach under the CWA, and need not limit its charging decisions to cases involving intentional violations of the law or those that cause extremely significant environmental impacts.

In *United States v. Hanousek,*[93] a backhoe operator who spilled oil into the navigable Skagway River was charged with one count of negligent discharge in violation of the CWA and one count of conspiracy to provide false information to U.S. Coast Guard officials who investigated the accident.[94] "Over Hanousek's objection, the district court instructed the jury that the government was required to prove only that Hanousek acted negligently, which the district court defined as 'the failure to use reasonable care.'"[95] On appeal, the Ninth Circuit affirmed, concluding that (1) Congress intended that a person who acts with ordinary negligence in violating 33 U.S.C. §1321(b)(3) may be subject to CWA criminal penalties[96]; and (2) given "that the criminal provisions of the CWA constitute public welfare legislation, and the fact that a public welfare statute may impose criminal penalties for ordinary negligent conduct without offending due process." Section 1319(c)(1)(A) "does not violate due process by permitting criminal penalties for ordinary negligent conduct."[97]

---

84. *Id.* at 1183.
85. *Id.* at 1184-85.
86. 516 F.3d 316, 322 (5th Cir. 2008).
87. *Id.* at 322 n.2.
88. *Id.* at 350.
89. *Id.* at 351.
90. 757 F. Supp. 21, 22 Envtl. L. Rep. (Envtl L. Inst.) 20536 (E.D. Pa. 1991), *aff'd in part, rev'd in part,* 947 F.2d 938, 22 Envtl. L. Rep. (Envtl L. Inst.) 20353 (3d Cir. 1991), *on remand,* 22 Envtl. L. Rep. (Envtl L. Inst.) 20772 (E.D. Pa. Jan. 23, 1992).
91. This penalty was later reduced to $5,000 based on the defendant's limited ability to pay a fine. United States v. Pozsgai, 22 Envtl. L. Rep. (Envtl L. Inst.) 20772 (E.D. Pa. Jan. 23, 1992).
92. United States v. Pozsgai, 999 F.2d 719, 23 Envtl. L. Rep. (Envtl L. Inst.) 21012 (3d Cir. 1993).
93. 176 F.3d 1116, 29 Envtl. L. Rep. (Envtl L. Inst.) 21049 (9th Cir. 1999), *cert. denied,* 528 U.S. 1102 (2000).
94. *Id.*
95. *Id.* at 1120.
96. *Id.* at 1121.
97. *Id.* at 1122. In the Supreme Court denial of certiorari, Justice Thomas, joined by Justice O'Connor, took the unusual step of dissenting from the denial, focusing in part on the issue of whether the CWA was properly characterized as public welfare legislation. Justice Thomas stated that while the CWA does regulate some dangerous activities and substances, it also "imposes criminal liability for persons using standard

Hanousek exemplifies the broad reach of the CWA's criminal provisions. The defendant was simply the supervisor of the project and was not even present at the time of the conduct that caused the spill. While the court concluded that he could not be held criminally liable on the basis of *respondeat superior* ("the district court's instructions adequately explained to the jury that Hanousek could be convicted only on the basis of his own negligent conduct and not on the basis of the negligence of others. . ."),[98] the decision is notable for imposing criminal sanctions for negligent supervision of activities, even if not directly involved in the activities..

In *United States v. Ortiz*,[99] the operator of a chemical distillation facility was convicted of violating the CWA by negligently discharging pollutants into the Colorado River by flushing them down the toilet.[100] The district court granted a post-trial acquittal, ruling that "an individual is not guilty of negligently discharging a pollutant unless he knows that the pollutant's path terminates in protected water."[101] The U.S. Court of Appeals for the Tenth Circuit reversed and reinstated the jury's verdict, holding that the CWA "criminalizes any act of ordinary negligence that leads to the discharge of a pollutant into the navigable waters of the United States," even if the responsible individual does not know that the pollutant's ultimate destination in such waters.[102]

In *United States v. Lippold*, the defendant moved to dismiss on the ground that the terms "waters of the United States" and "pollutant" were so vague that they violated the Due Process Clause of the Fifth Amendment when used as the basis for a criminal prosecution.[103] The court denied the motion, finding that the term "waters of the United States" had been sufficiently interpreted judicially, to at the very least include permanently flowing streams, and under the U.S. Court of Appeals for the Seventh Circuit analysis, to include intermittent waters as well.[104] It further found that even under Justice Kennedy's concurring opinion in *Rapanos*, as long as the government could establish that the streams the defendant allegedly polluted possessed a significant nexus to the main river, a conviction would not violate due process.[105]

Under these broad legal principles, DOJ has obtained a series of important convictions under the CWA including:

In *United States v. Exploration (Alaska), Inc.*,[106] BP experienced two different leaks from its oil pipelines. The first, which resulted in 200,000 gallons of oil spilling on the ground and eventually reaching a lake, was the largest ever on Alaska's North Slope. The second was much smaller but interfered with Prudhoe Bay oil production operations. The government alleged that BP ignored numerous indications that the pipeline had corroded internally. BP pled guilty and its sentencing included a $12 million fine, a $4 million community service payment, and $4 million in restitution.

In *United States v. Exxon Corp.*,[107] the government prosecuted the company for the discharge of 11 million gallons of crude oil from the *Exxon Valdez* into Prince William Sound, Alaska, which caused

equipment to engage in a broad range of ordinary industrial and commercial activities. This fact strongly militates against concluding that the public welfare doctrine applies." 528 U.S. at 1103 (Thomas, J. dissenting).

98. *Hanousek*, 176 F.3d at 1123. For a more detailed discussion of the *Hanousek* case and its impact in criminalizing "accidents," *see* Brigid Harrington, *A Proposed Narrowing of the Clean Water Act's Criminal Negligence Provisions: It's Only Human?*, 32 B.C. Envtl. Aff. L. Rev. 643 (2005).
99. 427 F.3d 1278 (10th Cir. 2005).
100. *Id.* at 1279-81.
101. *Id.* at 1279.
102. *Id.*
103. 2007 U.S. Dist. LEXIS 80513, No. 06-30002 (C.D. Ill. Oct. 31, 2007).
104. *Id.* at **9-10.
105. *Id.* at **13-15.
106. Crim. No. 3:07-cr-00125-RRB (D. Alaska), *plea entered* Nov. 29, 2007. The government alleged that the pipeline had been partially clogged with sediment and that BP had failed to run a cleaning device through the line for eight years. At the plea hearing, the court stated that "the failure to do what is considered standard pipeline maintenance made the violation especially bad." *BP Exploration Pleads Guilty to Violation of Clean Water Act for Prudhoe Bay Spill*, 38 Env't Rep. (BNA) No. 48, at 2613-14 (Dec. 7, 2007).
107. Plea Agreement, United States v. Exxon Corp., No. A90-015 CR (D. Alaska Sept. 26, 1991). While Exxon did plead guilty to a violation of the CWA, it was not to a violation of §311 of the Act (33 U.S.C. §1321), which addresses discharges of oil, because at the time of the Exxon Valdez incident, the enforcement provisions for that section only included civil penalties, Instead, Exxon pleaded guilty to a violation of §301 of the Act (33 U.S.C. §1311), which prohibits the discharge of any pollutant by any person without a permit. The fact that at the time the prohibition of discharges of oil in §311 of the Act did not carry criminal sanctions resulted in the amendment of the CWA by the Oil Pollution Act of 1990, §4301, Pub. L. No. 101-380, 104 Stat. 484 (1990), to apply to criminal sanctions in §309 of the CWA (33 U.S.C. §1319) to such discharges.

enormous damage to natural resources and wildlife. In October 1991, the parent its a subsidiary shipping corporation pleaded guilty to charges under the CWA, the MBTA, and other statutes. Exxon's sentence included a $25 million criminal fine and $125 million in restitution.

In *United States v. George*,[108] the government brought a prosecution under the CWA and RCRA against the executive vice president of a hazardous waste treatment facility and the plant manager for instructing employees to illegally dump large quantities of untreated hazardous and non-hazardous liquid wastes into the sewer system. After pleading guilty, the executive vice president was sentenced to 27th months confinement and to pay a $60,000 fine. The plant manager was sentenced to 12 months confinement and to pay a $60,000 fine. The company pleaded guilty and paid a $4.5 million fine and $1 million in community service obligations.

In *United States v. Puerto Rico Aqueduct & Sewer Authority*,[109] the government prosecuted a public for illegally discharging pollutants, in violation of its CWA permit at nine sanitary wastewater treatment plants and five drinking water treatment plants over a 25-year period. The authority pleaded guilty to 15 CWA violations and agreed to pay a fine of $9 million, to complete capital improvements to the nine wastewater treatment systems for nearly $109 million, to spend $10 million to correct the discharges, and to serve a five-year term of probation. As part of its probation, it also was required to comply with the terms of a consent decree that it negotiated separately to address civil actions, which required the authority to spend approximately $1.7 billion in capital improvement projects and other remedial measures that encompassed all of its 61 plants.[110]

In *United States v. Sinskey & Kumm*,[111] a plant manager and plant engineer at a large meat packing plant were found guilty by a jury of knowingly rendering an inaccurate monitoring method required to be maintained under the CWA and states in amounts exceeding CWA permit limitations. The court of appeals affirmed the convictions and confirmed that for a "knowing" violation of the CWA, the government was not required to prove that the defendant knew that his acts violated either the CWA or the NPDES permit, but merely that he was aware of the conduct that resulted in the permit's violation.[112]

II. Ocean and Vessel Pollution

In the mid-1990s, the federal government prosecuted Royal Caribbean Cruises, Ltd. for discharges of oil from the operation of one of its vessels. This case led to a major shift in the focus of criminal enforcement efforts involving the marine industry. The handling and disposal of all waste streams generated by vessels at sea and in port became the focus of aggressive enforcement efforts. Long-standing legislation, which contained criminal sanctions but had not previously been enforced criminally was resuscitated and applied in a criminal enforcement setting—arguably, in ways never envisioned by Congress. The DOJ's ECS developed a Vessel Initiative and began to work more closely with the Coast Guard and other agencies to investigate pollution from ships. Over the years, this Initiative led to many convictions and payment of large criminal fines.

Most of the world's vessels are flagged outside of the United States and are subject to administration and inspection by maritime administrations of the foreign countries where the vessels are flagged. Most of the world's seamen are non-U.S. citizens. Vessels and their operation customarily have been regulated through international conventions and treaties. The United States has been a primary proponent for adoption of strong environmental and safety standards for vessels as a member of International Maritime Organization,

---

108. *See* U.S. DOJ, United States v. George (E.D. Mich. 2005), http://www.justice.gov/enrd/3494.htm (last visited June 24, 2013); U.S. DOJ, Press Release, *Vice President of Detroit Hazardous Waste Firm Sentenced to 27 Months Imprisonment for Environmental Crimes* (Mar. 16, 2005), *available at* http://www.justice.gov/opa/pr/2005/March/05_enrd_125.htm (last visited Feb. 26, 2014).

109. *See* U.S. DOJ, United States v. Puerto Rico Aqueduct & Sewer Authority (D.P.R. 2007), http://www.justice.gov/enrd/3477.htm (last visited June 4, 2013); U.S. DOJ, Press Release, *Puerto Rico Aqueduct and Sewer Authority Indicted for Environmental Crimes; Will Pay $10 Million in Criminal and Civil Fines and Spend $1.7 Billion Improving Wastewater Treatment* (June 22, 2006), *available at* http://www.justice.gov/opa/pr/2006/June/06_enrd_382.html (last visited Feb. 25, 2014).

110. U.S. DOJ, Press Release, *Puerto Rico Aqueduct and Sewer Authority Indicted for Environmental Crimes; Will Pay $10 Million in Criminal and Civil Fines and Spend $1.7 Billion Improving Wastewater Treatment* (June 22, 2006), *available at* http://www.justice.gov/opa/pr/2006/June/06_enrd_382.html (last visited Feb. 25, 2014).

111. *See* U.S. DOJ, United States v. Sinskey & Kumm, http://www.justice.gov/enrd/3471.htm (last visited June 4, 2013).

112. 119 F.3d 712, 715-16 (8th Cir. 1997)119 F.3d 712, 715-16 (8th Cir. 1997).

the U.N. body that develops environmental and safety regimes to ensure that ships operate safely and in an environmentally sound manner wherever they are in the world. The member states that parties to these conventions then implement these international standards through domestic legislation.

Historically, the primary enforcement of these international standards was the responsibility of the flag states for vessels registered in those states. Beginning in the 1990's, port and coastal states, led by the United States, became more aggressive in the criminal enforcement of these standards against foreign vessels, corporate vessel owners, and crew members. In late 2009, representatives of the ECS estimated that the vessel cases comprised up to 30% of their total case load. Further, since 1999, convictions in vessel cases, primarily for false recordkeeping, have resulted in assessment of more than $200 million in fines. Those cases thus account for the vast majority of all criminal fines obtained by federal prosecutors in environmental cases.[113]

A. *Jurisdiction to Enforce Environmental Laws—Defining the Interests*

In order to fully appreciate the complex relationship among the various sovereign interests involved when the United States seeks to exercise criminal enforcement jurisdiction over foreign-flagged vessels, one must first understand the terms that defines these interests.

1. Flag State

A ship has the nationality of the state that registered it and authorized it to fly that state's flag (the flag state). Under customary international law, the flag state determines the conditions under which it will grant its nationality to a ship, thereby accepting responsibility for it and acquiring authority over it.[114] A ship "is deemed to be a part of the territory of that sovereignty whose flag it flies, and not to lose that character when in navigable waters within the territorial limits of another sovereignty."[115]

The Supreme Court has long held that the law of the flag state supersedes the authority of the state in whose waters the ship was operating, as long as the ship's activities did not affect the peace and good order of that state. "[A]ll matters of discipline and all things done on board which affected only the vessel or those belonging to her, and did not involve the peace or dignity of the country, or the tranquility of the port, should be left by the local government to be dealt with by the authorities of the nation to which the vessel belonged."[116] In general then, the flag state may exercise jurisdiction to prescribe, to adjudicate, and to enforce with respect to the ship and any conduct that takes place on it wherever the ship is operating.

2. Port State

The port state is that sovereignty in whose port a foreign flag vessel operates for loading or offloading cargo and embarking or disembarking passengers. In most cases, port state jurisdiction reaches to acts that occur in the internal waters of that sovereignty, including its ports and harbors. Generally speaking, "in time of peace, commercial ports must be left open to international traffic," and "liberty of access to ports granted to foreign vessels implies their right to load and unload their cargoes; embark and disembark their passengers."[117] Ordinarily, the general principle of open ports is confirmed through bilateral trade and friendship agreements between countries.

The port state may condition the entry of foreign ships into its ports on compliance with specified laws and regulations. Once a foreign flag commercial vessel voluntarily enters the port of a state, it becomes subject to that sovereignty jurisdiction. The port state may choose to forego assertion of its jurisdiction or limit it, within its sole discretion.[118] If crimes are committed on board a foreign vessel that are of a character that

113. Robert G. Edmonson, *Enforcement's Murky Waters*, J. Comm., Sept. 7, 2009, at 30. The fines and penalties for vessel cases arguably make up an even larger part of the DOJ enforcement program than any other types of environmental violations.
114. Lauritzen v. Larsen, 345 U.S. 571, 584 (1953).
115. *Id.* at 585 (quoting United States v. Flores, 289 U.S. 137 (1933)).
116. *Wildenhus's Case*, 120 U.S. 1, 12 (1887).
117. Constantine J. Colombos, The International Law of the Sea (6th ed. 1967).
118. Cunard S.S. Co. v. Mellon, 262 U.S. 100, 124 (1923).

disturbs the peace and tranquility of the port, then international law has long recognized the ability of the port state to assert its authority.[119] Under international law, pollution of the waters of the port in violation of local laws is the type of violation that disturbs the peace and tranquility of the port.

3. Coastal State

The coastal state is the sovereignty that exercises jurisdiction over waters off of its coast. International treaties regarding the ocean have attempted to establish the ability of states to prescribe through laws and regulations activities of foreign flag vessels operating in waters off of their coasts relating to safety, the environment, and the exploitation of natural resources. These treaties also have sought to establish the rights and duties of the coastal states to enforce those laws and regulations.[120]

Generally speaking, the authority of the flag state and the port state to enforce laws against vessels is concurrent. It is only in the interest of comity that a port state would defer to the flag state to deal with a violation of law by a foreign flag vessel that occurred in its port. The ability of the coastal state to enforce its laws is in competition with the right of vessels to exercise freedom of navigation. The best example of this is the long-standing international right of innocent passage—the right of a foreign vessel to pass through the territorial sea in the normal course of navigation without interference from the coastal state. Passage is innocent so long as it is not prejudicial to the peace, good order or security of the coastal state.[121]

B. Lines in the Water—Geographic Jurisdiction

Historically, the ability of a coastal state to address violations of national laws by vessels was determined by the extent to which that state could exercise territorial jurisdiction over the vessel. Vessels flying the U.S. flag in general are subject to the environmental laws of the United States based on the legal principle that the vessel is subject to the jurisdiction of the state whose flag it is flying, no matter where in the world it happens to be operating. Under U.S. law, jurisdiction is asserted either via specific statutes that apply to U.S. flag vessels no matter where they are operating,[122] or because a U.S. flag vessel is considered to be within the special maritime and territorial jurisdiction of the United States.[123] The "special maritime and territorial jurisdiction" is a statutorily created jurisdiction that establishes federal jurisdiction over specific crimes that occur in federal enclaves or in areas over which the United States exercises sovereignty outside the jurisdiction of the 50 states or foreign countries.

Jurisdiction over foreign flag vessels was more complicated, and the ability of a particular state to exercise jurisdiction depended upon where the vessel happened to be operating when the violation occurred. Generally, international law recognized the right of vessels to freely navigate on the high seas, *i.e.,* those waters beyond any national jurisdiction, and to operate without being subject to the jurisdiction of any state except the nation state whose flag it was flying.[124] This status has changed over the years such that in certain instances, a state may exercise jurisdiction over a foreign flag vessel on the high seas if that vessel poses a threat to the peace and good order of the state, such as when the vessel is involved in smuggling drugs or when an oil or chemical spill from a vessel threatens the coasts or waters of a state. States may also

---

119. *Wildenhus's Case*, 120 U.S. at 12.

120. *See, e.g.*, U.N. Convention on the Law of the Sea, *opened for signature* Dec. 10, 1982, U.N. Doc. A/CONF.62/122 (1982), *reprinted in* 21 I.L.M. 1261 [hereinafter UNCLOS]. The United States is not a party to the UNCLOS, but has stated that it is was prepared to accept and act in accordance with the balance of interests in UNCLOS, and would recognize the rights of other nations in the waters off of their coasts as reflected in the Convention. *See* Pres. Ronald Reagan, Statement on United States Ocean Policy, 19 Weekly Comp. Pres. Doc. 383 (Mar. 10, 1983).

In 1996, Congress enacted the Antiterrorism and Effective Death Penalty Act (AEDPA), which stated that "The Congress declares that all the territorial sea of the United States, as defined by Presidential Proclamation 5928 of Dec. 27, 1988, [the 12-nautical-mile territorial sea] for purposes of Federal criminal jurisdiction is part of the United States, subject to its sovereignty, and is within the special maritime and territorial jurisdiction of the United States for the purposes of title 18, United States Code." §901(a), Pub. L. No. 104-132, 110 Stat. 1214 (1996).

121. *See* UNCLOS, arts. 19, 21.

122. *See, e.g.*, Act to Prevent Pollution From Ships, 33 U.S.C. §1902(a)(1).

123. 18 U.S.C. §7.

124. *See, e.g.*, art. 87, UNCLOS.

exercise enforcement jurisdiction over foreign vessels on the high seas with the consent of the flag state, or if the vessel is under hot pursuit based on violations committed within the territory of the state.

Other than for navigation on the high seas, the ability of a state to enforce its laws on foreign flag vessels traditionally depended upon whether the waters seaward of its coastline were determined to be subject to the jurisdiction of that state, and for what purposes. In general, the further from the coast a foreign flag vessel was operating, the less the international community was willing to recognize the exercise of jurisdiction of any state other than the flag state over foreign vessels. This has resulted in the recognition of concentric zones of jurisdiction under international law. For purposes of enforcing federal environmental laws, the important zones are the internal and navigable waters of the United States, the territorial sea, the contiguous zone, and the exclusive economic zone (EEZ).

1. Internal and Navigable Waters of the United States

The "internal waters" of the United States are composed of all waters inside the baseline, which is typically the low water line along the coast of the United States. A foreign vessel voluntarily within the internal waters of the United States is subject to the prescriptive and enforcement authority of the United States for purposes of enforcing all laws applicable to the vessel. For all intents and purposes, there is no distinction between the jurisdiction of the United States to enforce its environmental and other laws on foreign vessels that are operating on the internal waters of the United States and its authority over persons on land.

In most environmental statutes, the internal waters and the territorial sea together are referred to as "the navigable waters" of the United States. Nevertheless, there are variations among statute. For example, the term "navigable waters of the United States" means different waters depending upon whether the statute at issue is the Refuse Act, the Act to Prevent Pollution From Ships, or the CWA.[125]

2. Territorial Sea

The "territorial sea" is considered part of the territory of the United States over which it exercises sovereignty. Federal jurisdiction to enforce its environmental laws over foreign vessels within the territorial sea is the same as its jurisdiction within internal waters, subject only to the right of innocent passage.

Starting in 1793, the United States consistently had claimed a territorial sea that extended three nautical miles from the baseline, which typically was the low water mark along the coast. This changed on Dec. 27, 1988, when President Ronald Reagan declared a 12-nautical-mile territorial sea in response to national security threats posed by Soviet spy ships operating off our coast. Nevertheless, the proclamation specifically limited the declaration to international legal issues, and specifically stated that the territorial sea remained the same for application of all domestic laws.[126]

3. Contiguous Zone

Until 1999, the United States had followed the provisions of the Convention on the Territorial Sea and Contiguous Zone, which established a "contiguous zone" of 12 nautical miles. In 1999, President Bill Clinton issued a proclamation that extended the contiguous zone of the United States to 24 nautical miles from the baseline of the United States.[127] Part of the justification for the extension of the contiguous zone was to assist the United States in enforcing its pollution laws.

125. "Navigable waters" for purposes of the Refuse Act, 33 U.S.C. §407, are those that meet the historical Commerce Clause definition of navigable waters applicable to most marine safety statutes. See 33 C.F.R. §2.36(a). As noted in Chapter 9, Part I, under the CWA, 33 U.S.C. §1251, the term is broader and has been interpreted to include some waters that would not be deemed navigable under the historical Commerce Clause definition. See 33 C.F.R. §2 36(b).

126. Presidential Proclamation No. 5928 (Dec. 27, 1988), *reprinted at* 54 Fed. Reg. 777 (Jan. 9, 1989). The territorial sea under the CWA is defined as extending three miles from the ordinary low water along the coast. 33 U.S.C. §1362(7). However, for purposes of the Act to Prevent Pollution from Ships, which implements the International Convention for the Prevention of Pollution from Ships or MARPOL, the territorial sea (and the navigable waters of the United States) extend to 12 nautical miles from the territorial sea baseline (typically the mean low water line) along the coast. 33 U.S.C. §1901(a)(7).

127. Presidential Proclamation No. 7219 (Aug. 2, 1999), *reprinted at* 64 Fed. Reg. 48701 (Aug. 9, 1999). Twenty-four nautical miles is the limit of the contiguous zone as recognized in the U.N. Convention on the Law of the Sea, art. 33. However, for purposes of the Clean Water Act,

Vessels in the contiguous zone are subject to the prescriptive and enforcement jurisdiction of the United States to prevent the infringement of its customs, fiscal, immigration and sanitation laws and regulations. The United States has taken the position that it has jurisdiction over foreign vessels in order to enforce its vessel-discharge requirements in the contiguous zone.

4. Exclusive Economic Zone

In 1983, the United States declared an exclusive economic zone of 200 nautical miles.[128] In proclaiming the 200 nautical mile EEZ, the United States declared that it would exercise its sovereign rights and jurisdiction in the zone in accordance with the rules of international law. In the policy statement accompanying the proclamation establishing the EEZ, President Reagan stated that the rules of international law applicable in its EEZ were those of United Nations Convention on the Law of the Sea (UNCLOS), which was enacted in 1983.[129]

C. International Environmental Law Applicable to Vessels

In 1973, international standards for the prevention of pollution originating from ships were enacted by the International Maritime Organization. These standards were established in the International Convention for the Prevention of Pollution From Ships, more commonly known as MARPOL.[130] The primary purpose of MARPOL was to prevent pollution of the oceans by focusing on the operational and accidental discharges of oil and other pollutants from vessels.

To achieve this purpose, MARPOL establishes construction, design, equipment and operational requirements to be met by vessels. Annex I of MARPOL addresses pollution by petroleum, Annex II by noxious liquid substances, Annex III by packaged hazardous substances, Annex IV by sewage, Annex V by garbage, and Annex VI by air.

The enforcement regime of MARPOL relies primarily on flag states to enact domestic laws to implement the standards and requirements of the Convention and to provide sanctions for violations of those standards and requirements by its vessels.[131] MARPOL was one of the earliest international instruments to also establish a role for port states that are parties to the convention in ensuring that all vessels met the requirements of the convention. All parties to the convention are required to cooperate in the detection of violations and the enforcement of the convention. If a violation is detected that occurred within the jurisdiction of the port state, that state may either take enforcement action under its own law or refer the case to the flag state.[132]

D. Federal Environmental Statutes Addressing Ocean and Vessel Pollution

United States regulation of ocean and vessel-source pollution is accomplished under a number of environmental statutes. The interaction of these statutes, and their interrelationship with the provisions of environmental enforcement under international law, present important issues for the marine industry, as the United States aggressively seeks to a prosecute violations of environmental laws by the marine industry in general and both U.S. and foreign flag vessels.

---

the contiguous zone remains as defined by the Convention on the Territorial Sea and the Contiguous Zone, *i.e.,* 12 nautical miles. 33 U.S.C. §1362(9).

128. Presidential Proclamation 5030 (Mar. 10, 1983), *reprinted at* 48 Fed. Reg. 10605 (Mar. 14, 1983); *see also* 33 C.F.R. §2.30

129. *See* UNCLOS *supra* note 119 Pres. Ronald Reagan, Statement on United States Ocean Policy, *supra* note 119.

130. 12 I.L.M. 1319 (1973) and its 1978 Protocol, 17 I.L.M. 546 (1978) [hereinafter MARPOL]. The 1973 MARPOL Convention was never ratified by the United States or by sufficient other states necessary for it to enter into force. It was, however, later modified by and incorporated into the 1978 Protocol, which was ratified by the Senate on July 2, 1980. H.R. Rep. No. 1224, 96th Cong. 3 (1980), *reprinted in* 1980 U.S.C.C.A.N. 4849, 4850.

131. MARPOL, art. 4.

132. *Id.* art. 6.

1. Act to Prevent Pollution From Ships, as Amended by the Marine Plastic Pollution Research and Control Act of 1987

The Act to Prevent Pollution from Ships (APPS) originally enforced Protocols I and II and Annexes I (petroleum) and II (noxious liquid substances) of MARPOL.[133] In 1987, the APPS was amended by the Marine Plastic Pollution Research and Control Act,[134] which implemented Annex V of MARPOL governing discharges of garbage from vessels.

For purposes of implementing Annex I and Annex II of MARPOL, the APPS applies to all U.S. flag seagoing ships anywhere in the world, and to all foreign flag seagoing ships while they are operating in the navigable waters of the United States or at a port or terminal under the jurisdiction of the United States.[135] The Coast Guard has promulgated regulations to implement the provision of Annexes I and II of MARPOL and the APPS.[136] These regulations limit discharges of oil and noxious liquid substances by imposing operational requirements on vessels, establishing reporting requirements for noncompliant discharges, and establishing specific requirements for monitoring equipment and record keeping applicable to discharges from vessels.

The APPS provisions implementing MARPOL Annex V (garbage) apply to all foreign flag vessels, whether they are seagoing vessels or not, not just while operating in the navigable waters of the United States (as do the petroleum and noxious liquid substances provisions), but also while they are operating in the EEZ of the United States.[137] The APPS provisions implementing Annex V of MARPOL apply to U.S. flag vessels wherever they are located.[138] Under MARPOL Annex V and the APPS, the discharge of plastics of any kind into the water is completely prohibited.[139] Further, the discharge of garbage from vessels into the navigable waters of the United States is also completely prohibited.[140] All other discharges of garbage must be conducted in compliance with specific operational requirements, which differ based on the distance of the vessel from the nearest land. As with petroleum, all vessels are required to keep records of garbage discharges and disposal.[141]

The APPS establishes felony criminal sanctions for knowing violations of the APPS, MARPOL, and Coast Guard implementing regulations. The APPS also provides a bounty of up to one-half of any criminal fine or civil penalty assessed for a violation to be paid to any person giving information leading to criminal conviction or assessment of a civil penalty.[142] Importantly, the APPS states that any action taken under the authority of the APPS, including enforcement, "shall be taken in accordance with international law."[143]

2. Ocean Dumping Act

Title I of the Marine Protection, Research, and Sanctuaries Act (the Ocean Dumping Act)[144] prohibits any vessel from transporting from the United States, or U.S. flag vessels from transporting from any location

133. Pub. L. No. 96-478, 96 Stat. 2297 (1980) (codified at 33 U.S.C. §§1901-1915). Noxious liquid substances are identified in Annex II of MARPOL, and defined by the Coast Guard in regulations at 33 C.F.R. §151.05.
134. *Id.* 100-220, tit. II, 101 Stat. 1460 (1987).
135. 33 U.S.C. §1902(a). Navigable waters are defined to include a territorial sea extending seaward to 12 nautical miles from the territorial sea baseline (typically the mean low water line) along the coast.
136. 33 C.F.R. pts. 151, 157.
137. 33 U.S.C. §1902(a)(3). The definition of garbage under MARPOL Annex V and the APPS is very broad, and encompasses essentially the discharge of any vessel-generated wastes that are not specifically covered by other MARPOL Annexes. Garbage includes traditional galley and habitation space solid wastes, maintenance wastes (such as rags and deck sweepings), and operational wastes (such as cargo residues or cargo-loading materials, e.g., pallets or dunnage)). 33 C.F.R. §151.05.
138. 33 U.S.C. §1902(a)(1).
139. *Id.* at §1902(b)(3)(B)(i); 33 C.F.R. §151.67.
140. 33 U.S.C. §§1902(b)(2)(B)(ii), (C), (D); 33 C.F.R. §§151.66. 151.69. The definition of garbage under MARPOL Annex V and the APPS is very broad, and encompasses essentially the discharge of any vessel-generated wastes that are not specifically covered by other MARPOL Annexes. Garbage includes traditional galley and habitation space solid wastes, maintenance wastes (such as rags and deck sweepings), and operational wastes (such as cargo residues or cargo-loading materials, e.g., pallets or dunnage). 33 C.F.R. §151.05.
141. *Id.* §151.55.
142. 33 U.S.C. §1908(a).
143. *Id.* §1912.
144. Pub. L. No. 92-532, 86 Stat. 1052 (1972) (codified at 33 U.S.C. §1401) *et seq.*). The Ocean Dumping Act implements the provisions of the Convention on the Prevention of Pollution by Dumping of Wastes and Other Matter, Dec. 29, 1972, 26 U.S.T. 2403, 1046 U.N.T.S. 120 (also known as the London Convention).

in the world, any material for the purpose of dumping it into ocean waters, except as may be authorized by a permit.[145] The law also prohibits the dumping[146] of material[147] transported from a location outside the United States into the waters of the territorial sea or contiguous zone[148] without a permit.[149]

The Ocean Dumping Act establishes felony criminal sanctions for any knowing violation of the statute, regulations, or terms of a permit.[150] The statute also provides that "each day of a continuing violation shall constitute a separate offense as shall the dumping from each of several vessels, or other sources."[151]

While the legislative history of environmental statutes rarely contains any indication regarding what constitutes a "knowing violation," the Ocean Dumping Act is an exception. The Senate Report accompanying the Act provides that the term "refers to a conscious act or conscious omission . . . which amounts to a violation of law, regulation or permit."[152] On this basis, courts have held that a convicting under the Ocean Dumping Act requires proof the defendants consciously engaged in the illegal action, and not proof that the defendant had knowledge of the relevant statutory provision that was violated.[153]

3. Clean Water Act, as Applied to Vessel and Ocean Pollution Cases

The CWA prohibits the discharge of a pollutant from a point source into a navigable water of the United States without a permit.[154] Under the CWA, a "point source" is specifically defined to include a vessel or other floating craft.

The EPA regulations implementing the NPDES permitting provisions of the CWA excluded "any discharge [of a pollutant] incidental to the normal operation of a vessel" from the permitting requirements. This provision was in effect for decades since the initial publication of the NPDES regulations.[155] However,

---

145. Ocean waters are defined as waters of the open sea lying seaward of the baseline from which the U.S. territorial sea is measured. 33 U.S.C. §1401(b).

146. Dumping is defined as the disposition of material, but does not include "a routine discharge of effluent incidental to the propulsion of, or operation of motor driven equipment on, vessels . . .." It also does not include disposition of material from any outfall structure that is regulated by the CWA, the Atomic Energy Act, or the Refuse Act, the construction of any fixed or artificial island or the intentional placement of any device in open waters if such construction or placement is otherwise regulated by federal or state law; and the deposit of materials, such as oyster shells, when made for the purpose of developing, maintaining, or harvesting fisheries resources or that its otherwise regulated by federal or state law. *Id.* §1402(f)..

147. "Material" is broadly defined as:

> Matter of any kind or description, including, but not limited to, dredged material, solid waste, incinerator residue, garbage, sewage, sewage sludge, munitions, radiological, chemical, and biological warfare agents, radioactive materials, chemicals, biological and laboratory waste, wreck or discarded equipment, rock, sand, excavation debris, and industrial, municipal, agricultural, and other waste; but such term does not mean sewage from vessels within the meaning of [33 U.S.C.] §1322 . . . Oil within the meaning of [33 U.S.C.] §1321 . . . shall be included only to the extent that such oil is taken on board a vessel or aircraft for the purpose of dumping.

Id. at §1402(c).

148. The territorial sea and the contiguous zone are defined in the same manner as those terms are defined for purposes of the CWA in 33 U.S.C. §1362. *See* 40 C.F.R. §220.2(c).

149. 33 U.S.C. §1401(c).

150. *Id.* §1415(b).

151. *Id.* §1415(c).

152. S. Rep. No. 451, 92d Cong., 1st Sess. (1971), *reprinted in* 1972 U.S.C.C.A.N. 4234, 4249.

153. United States v. Reilly, 827 F. Supp. 1076, 107, 24 ELR 20097 (D. Del. 1993), *aff'd*, 33 F.3d 1396 (3d Cir. 1994). *In Reilly*, the dumping of toxic ash into the Indian Ocean from an incinerator in Philadelphia, Pennsylvania, by the vessel KHIAN SEA led to the conviction of the Vice-President of Coastal Carriers Corporation, the operator of the KHIAN SEA. Even though the ship was registered in Liberia, the fact that the waste originated within the United States provided jurisdiction.

In United States v. Cook (D.C. Cir. 2003), the defendant, a Canadian citizen, was hired to oversee the demolition of sections of a U.S. flag ferry that was being turned into a gaming vessel. As the vessel transited from San Diego, through the Panama Canal and then to Mobile, Alabama, hundreds of bags of plastic garbage bags containing asbestos-contaminated demolition debris were dumped into the ocean. Canada extradited the defendant and trial was held in the District of Columbia District Court because the dumping occurred in international waters and the defendant was not a U.S. citizen. The defendant was charged with violations of the Ocean Dumping Act, the APPS (for discharging plastics), and for conspiracy. He was sentenced to 24 months confinement and three years of supervised release. See U.S. DOJ, Press Release, *U.S. Announces Sentencing of "Captain" Cook for Illegally Dumping Asbestos Into the Sea* (Ag. 27, 2003), *available at* http://www.justice.gov/opa/pr/2003/August/03_enrd_467.htm (last visited Feb. 27, 2014).

In United States v. Kinder Morgan Bulk Terminals, Inc., Case No. 3:08-CR-00185 (D. Ore. Aug. 13, 2008), defendant Kinder Morgan pleaded guilty to violation of the Ocean Dumping Act. The terminal had loaded an off-specification load of potash onto a cargo vessel and, after it was discovered that the potash was contaminated and not fit for sale, the defendant paid the ship's master to store the contaminated product on deck and discharge it at sea. The defendant was sentenced to a fine of $240,000. U.S. DOJ, Environmental Crimes Monthly Bulletin (Sept. 2008) at 12, *available at* http://www.justice.gov/enrd/2008/LPS-190687-v1-ECS_Bulletin_2008_09_Block.PDF (last visited Feb. 27, 2014).

154. 33 U.S.C. §1311. Permits are typically issued under Section 402 (33 U.S.C. §1342), the National Pollution Discharge Elimination System (NPDES), or under Section 404 (33 U.S.C. §1344), the dredge and fill requirements. *See generally* Part I of this Chapter.

155. *Id.* at §1362(14).

in 2005, this provision was ultimately challenged and it was ruled that this exclusion violated the requirements of the CWA.[156] As a consequence, a general permit under the NPDES provisions was issued by EPA to address discharges incidental to the normal operation of a vessel. The so-called Vessel General Permit (VGP) requires implementation of best management practices aboard United States flag and foreign vessels operating in U.S. navigable waters to address such discharges.[157]

The CWA also addresses pollution from vessels and facilities resulting from oil and hazardous substances. These provisions state:

> The discharge of oil or hazardous substances (i) into or upon the navigable waters of the United States, adjoining shorelines, or into or upon the waters of the contiguous zone, or (ii) in connection with activities . . . which may affect natural resources belonging to, appertaining to, or under the exclusive management authority of the United States . . . in such quantities as may be harmful . . . is prohibited, except . . . in the case of such discharges into the waters of the contiguous zone or which may affect natural resources belonging to, appertaining to, or under the exclusive management authority of the United States . . . where permitted under the Protocol of 1978 Relating to the International Convention for the Prevention of Pollution from Ships, 1973 [MARPOL] . . ..[158]

Thus, the CWA applies to the discharge by vessels of all pollutants into the navigable waters of the United States, and to the discharge of oil and hazardous substances into the navigable waters, the contiguous zone, and the EEZ. With regard to the prohibition against discharges of oil and hazardous substances in the contiguous zone and the EEZ of the United States, there is an exclusion for such discharges if they comply with MARPOL.

Until 1990, the section of the CWA applicable to oil and hazardous substance discharges provided for only civil penalties to enforce the prohibition against discharges. The public outcry resulting from the dramatic television footage of the discharge of over 11 million gallons of crude oil into the pristine waters of Prince William Sound caused by the grounding of the *Exxon Valdez* in 1989, and the perceived inadequacy of existing laws to deal with that incident, led Congress to enact the Oil Pollution Act of 1990 (OPA).[159] Among those laws determined to be inadequate were the available penalties for violations of the discharge prohibition, especially when compared to the criminal and civil penalties authorized to enforce other provisions of the CWA. Thus, the OPA amended the enforcement provisions of the CWA to cover violations of the oil and hazardous substances provisions of the CWA, thus providing criminal penalty sanctions as a means of enforcing those provisions.[160]

---

156. Northwest Envtl. Advocates v. United States EPA, 2005 U.S. Dist. LEXIS 5373 (N.D. Cal. 2005), *aff'd*, 537 F.3d 1006 (9th Cir. 2008). The primary focus of the legal challenge was the exclusion of ballast water discharges from regulation by the EPA under the NPDES provisions. These discharges, which were one of the primary causes of the introduction of non-indigenous organisms and species, such as the zebra mussel, into United States waters, had historically been regulated by the Coast Guard under separate legislation.
157. The original VGP was issued in 2008. 73 Fed. Reg. 79493 (Dec. 29, 2008). The final VGP for the states of Alaska and Hawaii was issued separately. 74 Fed. Reg. 7042 (Feb. 12, 2009). The first VGP was effective until December 19, 2013. On March 28, 2013, EPA re-issued the VGP for another five years. That reissued permit, the 2013 VGP, took effect December 19, 2013, and superseded the 2008 VGP at that time. 78 Fed. Reg. 21938 (Apr. 12, 2013). The 2013 VGP is available at http://www.epa.gov/npdes/pubs/vgp_permit2013.pdf (last visited Feb. 26, 2014). Vessels greater than or equal to 300 gross tons or that have the capacity to hold or discharge more than 8 cubic meters (2,113 gallons) of ballast water must submit a signed and certified, complete and accurate Notice of Intent (NOI) indicating the intent to be covered by the VGP. Owners and operators of vessels that meet the eligibility for permit coverage but are not required to submit an NOI are automatically authorized to discharge according to permit requirements. However, under the 2013 VGP, owners and operators not required to submit an NOI are now required to complete and keep a Permit Authorization and Record of Inspection (PARI) form onboard their vessel at all times, the purpose of which is to certify that the owner or operator has read and agreed to comply with the VGP.
158. 33 U.S.C. §1321.
159. Pub. L. No. 101-380, 104 Stat. 484 (1990).
160. 161. Id. §4301, In United States v. Fleet Management Limited, Case 3:08-cr-00160 SI, (N.D. Cal., 2009), the operator of the cargo ship Cosco Busan, Fleet Management, agreed to plead guilty to a negligent violation of the CWA as amended by the Oil Pollution Act of 1990 (OPA), to making a false statement in violation of 18 U.S.C. § 1001, and to obstruction of justice in violation of 18 U.S.C. §1519. The Cosco Busan had departed Oakland, California in a heavy fog in November 2007 and, hit the San Francisco – Oakland Bay Bridge. As a result, approximately 53,000 gallons of fuel oil was discharged into the San Francisco Bay., causing significant environmental damage, including the loss of over 2,000 migratory birds. Fleet Management agreed to pay an $8 million criminal fine, to pay a $2 million community service payment, and to serve 3 years on probation, one of the condition of which was to develop and implement an enhanced compliance program $7 million of the total criminal fine was imposed as a result of the CWA violation based on the Alternative Fines Act authorizing a fine of double the losses attributable to the violation. *See id.,* Plea Agreement, Doc. 328 (filed Aug. 13, 2009). The court subsequently sentenced the company in accordance with the Plea Agreement. *See* U.S. DOJ, Press Release, Shipping Firm Sentenced to Pay $10 Million for Causing Cosco Busan Oil Spill and Coverup (Feb. 19, 2010), *available at* http://www.justice.gov/opa/pr/2010/February/10-enrd-168.html (last visited Feb. 28, 2014).

    In addition, Captain John Cota, a California State and federally-licensed bar pilot who was on the Cosco Busan, pleaded guilty to a negligent violation of the CWA as amended by the OPA, and to a violation of the Migratory Bird Treaty Act.. He was sentenced to confinement

E. *Issues Unique to Vessel and Ocean Pollution Prosecutions*

1. Vessel and Crew Detentions

Vessels are mobile, and there are legitimate enforcement concerns regarding the ability of vessels to leave United States jurisdiction before criminal charges can be brought, or even before a complete investigation can be conducted. Thus, several statutes that seek to regulate pollution from vessels provide that if the government has reasonable cause to believe that a vessel, or its owner, operator or person in charge has violated the statute and may therefore be subject to a fine or civil penalty, then the Coast Guard may ask that the vessel's customs clearance be refused or revoked. Nevertheless, the required clearance may be granted "upon the filing of a bond or other surety satisfactory to [the Coast Guard]."[161] This ability to withhold or revoke required vessel customs clearances provides the government a great deal of leverage in vessel environmental cases.[162] Vessel owners and operators can suffer significant monetary losses, as well as losses of customer good will, if the passengers and cargoes their vessels are carrying are significantly delayed for any reason. Therefore to avoid undue delays to their vessels, most vessel owners will want to post a surety or bond during a pollution investigation, which could take months or years to complete.

The leverage exercised by the Coast Guard, in negotiations over terms of bonds or other surety often results in inclusion of terms over and above those necessary to ensure payment of any fines or penalties that may arise out of the alleged violations. In addition to a promise to pay any fine or penalty and the filing of security for such payment, such agreements may include such terms as submission to the jurisdiction of the court; access to witnesses; production of documents and evidence; and numerous other conditions related to crew members who may be held in the United States as witnesses or even suspects.[163]

Judicial challenges to the terms of sureties required by the Coast Guard have been made by the vessel owners and operators, but have been largely unsuccessful. For instance, in *Guiseppe Bottiglieri Shipping Co. S.P.A. v. United States*,[164] the Coast Guard conducted a boarding of a vessel and interviewed the ship's master and crew members, during which interviews the Coast Guard officials were allegedly informed that the vessel was equipped with a magic pipe that was used to conduct illegal discharges.[165] Based on these alle-

---

for 10 months. *See* U.S. DOJ, Press Release, Prison Sentence for Cosco Busan pilot (July 17, 2009), *available at* http://www.justice.gov/opa/pr/2009/July/09-enrd-698.html (last visited Feb. 28, 2014).

161. *See, e.g.*, APPS, 33 U.S.C. §1908(e); CWA, 33 U.S.C. §1321(b)(12) (provisions related to discharges of oil and hazardous substances).

162. The government has taken the position in litigation that "'surety satisfactory' is that which is designed to put the government in the same position it would have been had the vessel not departed." *See* Respondents' Memorandum in Opposition to Petitioner's Emergency Motion to Release Motor Tanker Triton, Kriton Maritime, S.A. v. United States, Case No. 3:07CV461(WWE) (D. Conn. Mar. 27, 2007), Doc. 5, at 19.

163. *See, e.g.*, Mercator Lines Ltd. (Singapore) et al. v. M/V Gaurav Prem Re: Material Witness Prastana Taohim, 2011 U.S. Dist. LEXIS 153429, Misc. No. 11-00024-CG-C, Crim. No. 11-mj-00203-N (S.D. Ala. Oct. 25, 2011), at **6-15, *aff'd*, Misc. No. 11-00024-GC-C (S.D. Ala. Nov. 18, 2011), Doc. 40 (quoting language from security agreement between vessel owner and operator and Coast Guard). The crewmembers were removed from vessel in light of allegations of violations of the Act to Prevent Pollution From Ships. The agreement required the vessel owner and operator to:
    - facilitate interviews of any officer or crewmember employed by owner or operator;
    - cooperate with the United States to arrange for testimony of such officer or crew member;
    - assist the United States in effecting proper service of process related to alleged violations for such officer or crewmember not in the United States at the time the subpoena was issued;
    - encourage officers and crewmembers to cooperate with the United States in carrying out its investigation and in appearing for scheduled testimony;
    - provide reasonable lodging, a stated meal allowance, and health coverage to named officers and crewmembers who were removed from the vessel and detained in the United States;
    - obtain the necessary immigration status for the named officers and crewmembers that would allow them to remain in the United States for the duration of the agreement;
    - continue to employ and pay total wages to the named officers and crewmembers in a timely manner until such time as the United States advised that their presence was no longer necessary;
    - upon being informed their presence was no longer necessary, repatriate the named officers and crewmembers to their home country or another port to complete their employment contract;
    - request that the named officers and crewmembers surrender their passports;
    - request that the named officers and crewmembers remain in the court's jurisdiction; and
    - provide the named officers and crewmembers with reasonable transportation to all places of testimony and all meetings with the Department of Justice attorneys and law enforcement agents.

164. 843 F. Supp. 2d 1241 (S.D. Ala. 2012).

165. *Id.* at 1243. A "magic pipe" is a term for illegal piping that is used to discharge oily bilge water or other oily effluents directly overboard, bypassing mandated pollution prevention and monitoring equipment.

gations, the Coast Guard requested that the vessel's departure clearance be withheld.[166] The vessel owner then attempted to negotiate a security agreement with the Coast Guard. The primary provisions at issue during the negotiations were the amount of a monetary bond to be posted, and the provisions related to the owner's financial responsibilities for are and maintenance of eight foreign crew members that the Coast Guard required to remain in the United States for purposes of the investigation of the pollution violations if the vessel were to be cleared to depart the United States.[167] The vessel owner brought an action under the Administrative Procedure Act (APA) challenging the amount of the bond mandated by the Coast Guard and the length of time that the Coast Guard required the owner to pay for the crew members' wage and expenses for their stay in the United States.[168]

The vessel owner argued that the Coast Guard had "arbitrarily, capriciously, and purposefully refused to negotiate in good faith and [had] failed to accept to accept a reasonable bond or other form of surety in accordance with the clear statutory requirements of [the APPS]."[169] After determining that the Coast Guard's "final, non-negotiable, take-it-or-leave-it" demand constituted final agency action for purposes of the APA,[170] the court determined that no review under the APA was available because the Coast Guard's actions in determining what terms of a bond or other surety under the APPS provisions are committed to its discretion under the law, and as such there is no law to apply and no meaningful standard against which to judge the exercise of its discretion.[171]

Challenges have also been brought by vessel owners and operators under other theories, such as under admiralty and based on the terms of the APPS itself. Again, the courts have found no jurisdiction to examine the reasonableness of the terms of the surety agreements that the Coast Guard has insisted be included.[172]

Even more problematical is the issue of detention of crewmembers who are foreign citizens. These crewmembers may be witnesses to illegal activity aboard a vessel prior to its port call in the United States, and prosecutors may desire to secure their presence in the United States for the investigation, for possible grand jury appearances, or for trial. Once foreign citizen crew members leave the jurisdiction of the United States, they are not subject to subpoena power, and may decide that they will not voluntarily appear in court or return to the United States to be interviewed or to testify before a grand jury or at trial. Thus, prosecutors face significant risks in their ability to make their case if they allow foreign crew members to depart the United States before trial.[173]

---

166. *Id.* at 1244.
167. *Id.* at 1244-45.
168. The owner had proposed to pay wages and expenses for the eight crew members for 60 days, while the government stated it would accept no period less than 180 days. *Id.* at 1245.
169. *Id.* at 1248.
170. *Id.* at 1247. The APA provides for judicial review of a "final agency action." 5 U.S.C. §704. In other cases, vessel owners had sought review under the APA challenging the Coast Guard's terms for surety agreements under the APPS provisions. The court determined that no review under the APA was available because no final agency action had occurred as at the time the action was brought, as the parties were still in negotiations over the terms of the security agreement. *See, e.g.*, Wilmina Shipping AS v. United States, 2010 WL 2079905 (S.D. Tex. 2010).
171. *Bottiglieri Shipping*, 843 F. Supp. 2d at 1248-49.
172. *See* Nimrich & Prahm Reederei Gmbh & Co. v. United States, 2012 U.S. Dist. LEXIS 65101, Civ. No. H-12-1142 (S.D. Tex. May 9, 2012). In *Nimrich*, the owner of a vessel that had its departure clearance withdrawn based on alleged violations of the APPS brought an "Emergency Motion to Fix Security" after negotiations between the vessel owner and the Coast Guard over the terms of a surety agreement to have the vessel released reached an impasse. The court found no jurisdiction under admiralty law because withholding of the clearance was not an *in rem or quasi in rem* attachment, which would be the action at issue under admiralty but was instead an administrative action pursuant to statutory authority. *Id.* at **6-8.

    The challenge based on APPS also failed. The APPS provides for persons to bring an action on their own behalf "against any person alleged to be in violation of the provisions of [APPS] or regulations issued [under the APPS]." 33 U.S.C. §1910(a)(1). It also provides, however, that such an action could not be brought prior to 60 days after the adversely affected party had given notice in writing and under oath to the alleged violator (*i.e.,* Coast Guard), the Secretary of Homeland Security, and the Attorney General. The vessel owner had not done so prior to filing the emergency motion challenging the Coast Guard's position as to the terms of an acceptable surety to have the vessel released. *Nimrich*, 2012 U.S. Dist. LEXIS 65101 at **8-9.
173. This risk may be further aggravated by the Supreme Court's holding that the use of recorded grand jury testimony is prohibited when a witness is unavailable. Crawford v. Washington, 541 U.S. 36 (2004). *See also* United States v. Petraia Maritime Ltd., 489 F. Supp. 2d 90 (D. Me. 2007) (crew members who entered into cooperation and immunity agreements with the government were no longer considered to be employees whose statements would be admissible under Rule 801(d)(2)(D) of the Federal Rules of Evidence as vicarious admissions of a party opponent as their interests had diverged from that of the vessel owner and thus there was not the required agency relationship necessary for admission of statements at trial under Rule 801(d)(2)(D). Further, because the witnesses' testimonies were not preserved via depositions or other means, the statements could not be used at trial when the witnesses were released and their presence could not be secured for trial, as admission of their hearsay statements at trial would violate the Confrontation Clause of the U.S. Constitution).

One means that has been used to secure the presence of foreign crew members in vessel cases is through material witness warrants.[174] Such warrants provide prosecutors with the power to detain individuals who are witnesses to a crime if it is impractical to secure their presence for trial or grand jury testimony by subpoena.[175] Problems arise in vessel cases because the crew members have no place to reside in the United States pending their appearance. Judges then have little choice but to detain the witnesses, many of whom are not themselves culpable for the crime, including potentially in federal correctional facilities. Needless to say, treatment of non-culpable witnesses as criminals in such instances causes both practical problems for prosecutors, *i.e.,* witnesses may become less likely to cooperate with the prosecutors who have had them confined, sometimes for months; and diplomatic problems for the United States with the governments of the countries of which these crew members are citizens. The only other alternative available is for the federal government to pay for quarters and subsistence for the foreign crew members while they are held in the United States, which can become very expensive if the investigation and trial are not concluded expeditiously.

In order to avoid the problems associated with material witness warrants, and the costs to the government of paying the expenses of detained crew members, the Coast Guard has insisted that surety agreements used to obtain release of vessels that have had their customs departure clearance withheld based on alleged violations of APPS or the CWA must include a clause that requires the owner or operator of the vessel to hold relevant crew members in the United States and to pay for their housing and subsistence.

Seafarers can suffer significant adverse effects from these surety agreements, whose terms they have no ability to negotiate. Sometimes, the vessel owner is required to hold the passports of detained crew members until they are released by the United States.[176] This means that the mariners are held far away from their families, perhaps for months at the time and cannot work or travel easily; and may suffer further isolation if they do not speak English well. Moreover, the crew members may be detained in small town motels, with no transportation except for official interviews or meetings with attorneys.[177]

Detained crew members have successfully challenged the ability of the government to hold them for prolonged periods of time. For example, in *In re Grand Jury Proceedings; Re: Investigation of Blow Wind Shipping, S.A.*[178] several crewmembers had been detained as material witnesses and were being housed, fed, and paid wages subject to a surety agreement between the vessel owner and the Coast Guard. The court was receptive to their arguments that the government should be required to take their depositions so that they could be released. The court flatly rejected the government's argument that the crew members were not detained for purposes of the material witness statute because they were not incarcerated.[179] The court noted that "this contention, carried to its logical extreme, would permit the government to prevent foreign nationals from leaving this country indefinitely," and means "in practical terms, that such material wit-

174. The statutory provision providing for the arrest of material witnesses provides:

> No material witness may be detained . . . if the testimony of such witness can adequately be secured by deposition and if further detention is not necessary to prevent a failure of justice. Release of a material witness may be delayed for a reasonable period of time until the deposition . . . can be taken . . ..

18 U.S.C. §3144. Fed. R. Crim. P. 15(a)(2) provides that "A witness who is detained under 18 U.S.C. §3144 may request to be deposed by filing a written motion and giving notice to the parties. The court may then order that the deposition be taken and may discharge the witness after the witness has signed under oath the deposition manuscript."

175. To obtain a material witness warrant, the prosecutor must submit an affidavit to a federal judge or magistrate, who may issue the warrant after finding that a person is material in a criminal proceeding and that it may become impracticable to secure the present of the person by subpoena. Once the warrant is issued, the witness is arrested and brought before the judge or magistrate, who decides whether to release the witness or detain him or her pending testimony to a grand jury or at trial. *See* 18 U.S.C. §3144 (requiring that the person be treated in accordance with the provisions of 18 U.S.C. §3142, which provides for such hearing).

176. *See supra* note 164 (example of surety agreement in which vessel owner is required to request that detained crewmembers surrender their passports).

177. For examples of the impacts on seafarers detained under surety agreements, *see, e.g.,* Solomon Moore, *Ship's Woes Leave 13 Stranded,* L.A. Times, Dec. 11, 2004, at B1; Corey Kilgannon, *Weeks of Waiting in Limbo Over a Dumping Case,* N.Y. Times, Jan. 22, 2005, at B1; *Seafarers Left Stranded by Regulatory Oversight,* Lloyd's List, Jan. 7, 2010, at 7.

178. 2010 U.S. Dist. LEXIS 14359, No. 10-mj-57-P-JHR (D. Me. Apr. 16, 2010).

179. Other courts also have found this argument to be unpersuasive. *See* United States v. Delnave Navigation, 2009 WL 743100, Crim. No. 09-130 (D.N.J. Mar. 18, 2009) at **1-2 (holding in a case involving alleged violations of the APPS that foreign crewmembers held as material witnesses in the United States against their will for over six months, with little end in sight, even though they had done nothing wrong, and whose passports were being held by the government, were "functionally detained" for purposes of 18 U.S.C. §3144, and ordering that they be deposed and released after the deposition); Mercator Lines Limited (Singapore) PTE. LTD v. M/V Gaurav Prem Re: Material Witness Prastana Taohim, 2011 U.S. Dist. LEXIS 153429, Misc. No. 11-00024-CG-C, Crim. No. 11-mj-00203-N (S.D. Ala., Oct. 25, 2011) at **25-26.

nesses could be kept away from their homes, in a foreign country where they do not speak the language and have no social connections and no way to engage in the line of work in which they are experienced, or any remunerative work, for periods of well over a year."[180] It further observed that the argument "also means that a material witness who is jailed would be able to seek discharge through deposition, while a material witness subject to a warrant, yet able to stay in a motel and walk to a grocery store or recreation, would not have that option."[181]

The government also argued unsuccessfully that the material witnesses were not innocent bystanders, but failed to indicate that they were targets of the grand jury investigation. The court stated that "[t]he interests of justice . . . cannot be fashioned from the government's ipse dixit; the material witnesses have a liberty interest in avoiding continued detention, and it is the duty of the United States attorney to consider the rights of the material witnesses."[182] The court granted the material witnesses' petition and ordered that the depositions of the witnesses be taken within 30 days.[183]

2. Whistleblower Bounties

Another area in which vessel pollution cases differ materially from land-based pollution cases is that some statutory provisions provide for significant financial bounties to crewmembers who report vessel pollution violations. The Act to Prevent Pollution from Ships authorizes the award of up to one-half of any fine or penalty imposed for violations of MARPOL, the APPS itself, or Coast Guard implementing regulations to any person giving information leading to a conviction or the assessment of civil penalties.[184] One federal prosecutor has stated: "I want every chief engineer in every ship in the world wondering if they [the crew] are trying to get rich off him."[185] With the number and size of the bounties that have been awarded, crewmembers aboard vessels have become aware that they may receive substantial compensation if they report violations of the pollution prevention laws to the United States.[186]

One potential problem with the bounty system is that crew members may not report the illegal conduct to vessel owners or operators so that it can be addressed immediately. Crewmembers, aware of the possibility that they may be eligible for hundreds of thousands, or even millions of dollars in awards may have a perverse incentive to avoid reporting illegal conduct to vessel operating companies or, at a minimum, to delay reporting such conduct until the vessels reach United States ports, thereby potentially aggravating any adverse environmental impacts of the illegal discharges. Some crew members have even hired attorneys to represent them for purposes of obtaining bounties in criminal cases against vessel operating companies.[187]

---

180. *Blow Wind Shipping*, 2010 U.S. Dist. LEXIS 14359 at **5-6.
181. *Id.* at *6.
182. *Id.* at *10.
183. *Id.* at **12-13.
184. 33 U.S.C. §1908(a).
185. *Whistleblower Gets $250,000 Award for Reporting Oil Infractions*, Professional Mariner, Apr./May 2004.
186. Examples of bounties paid to whistleblowers in vessel cases under 33 U.S.C. §1908(a) include: United States v. Rowan Companies, Inc., No. 2:07-CR-00298 (E.D. Tex. 2007) (court awarded $1 million bounty to offshore oil rig worker who reported illegal discharges from the rig) *available at* http://www.google.com/url?sa=t&rct=j&q=&esrc=s&frm=1&source=web&cd=3&cad=rja&ved=0CDcQFjAC&url=http%3A%2F%2Fwww.justice.gov%2Fenrd%2F2007%2FLPS-190712-v1-ECS_Bulletin_2007_11_Block.PDF&ei=y21UUuXPNbKi4AO-u4DIAg&usg=AFQjCNH0bvsGAl-2su5NbgZMk4mRNIVBDA&sig2=VfU9qwTv6b8DrmjjNdP8tw; United States v. Overseas Shipholding Group, Inc., 672 F. Supp. 2d 188 (D. Mass. 2010) (court awarded $5.25 million dollars to be split equally among 12 crew members from different ships who reported pollution and recordkeeping violations directly to the government, or to the company which then self-disclosed to the government); United States v. Irika Maritime, S.A. No. 3:06-CR-05661 (W.D. Wash. 2007) (court awarded one-half of $500,000 criminal fine to second engineer who reported illegal discharges and falsified records to Coast Guard); United States v. Wallenius Ship Management Pte., No. 2:06-CR-00213 (D.N.J. 2006) (court awarded one-half of a $5 million fine to be divided among four crewmembers who sent a fax to an international seafarers' union alleging that they were being ordered to engage in acts of pollution); United States v. Sun Ace Shipping Co., No. 2:06-CR-00599 (D.N.J. 2006) (court awarded half of $200,000 fine to be divided among three whistleblowers who lodged complaints with a religious organization that they were being forced to bypass pollution control equipment); United States v. MK Shipmanagement Co., Ltd., No. 2:06-CR-00307 (D.N.J. 2006) (court awarded half of a $200,000 fine to be split between two crew members who presented photos and records of illegal discharges to the government); United States v. OMI (D.N.J. 2004) (court awarded one-half of a $4.2 million dollar fine to a second engineer who reported illegal discharges and falsified records); United States v. Sabine Transp. (D. Iowa 2004) (court awarded one-half of $2 million fine to three employee whistleblowers for reporting information about pollution violations).
187. In the case of *United States v. Overseas Shipholding Group, Inc.*, 547 F. Supp. 2d 75 (D. Mass. 2008), two foreign crew members who had provided information to the government about illegal discharges aboard their vessel entered into a contingency fee arrangement providing an attorney with one-third of their recovery to represent their interests regarding shares of the bounty arising from the guilty plea of the company to illegal discharges and false recordkeeping from several of its vessels. The court ultimately awarded each whistleblower a bounty in the amount of $437,500. When the government learned of this development, it petitioned the court to not approve any fee agreement in excess

3. Warrantless Searches

The United States Coast Guard is the primary law enforcement agency for laws related to vessels and the marine industry. It has the responsibility to enforce and assist in the enforcement of all applicable federal laws on, under, and over the high seas and all waters subject to the jurisdiction of the United States.[188] To assist in the enforcement of the federal laws, the Coast Guard is given the authority to make inquiries, examinations, inspections, searches, seizures, and arrests upon the high seas and waters over which the United States has jurisdiction. Coast Guard officers are authorized to board any vessel subject to the jurisdiction or operation of any law of the United States to address inquiries to those on board, to examine the ship's documents and papers, and to examine, inspect, and search the vessel for violations of federal laws.[189] These courts have deemed this authority to be plenary.[190]

In addition to this general authority to board vessels without a warrant, the Coast Guard also has specific statutory authorities to board vessels related to the enforcement of various statutes. For example, the APPS authorizes the Coast Guard to board vessels and conduct inspections to determine whether the vessel has discharged oil or other regulated substances in violation of that statute or MARPOL.[191]

A recent case addressed the question whether the Coast Guard may utilize its general boarding authority to board vessels without a warrant if a whistleblower has contacted it before the vessel calls in a *United States* port and alleged that the vessel was discharging oil or other pollutants illegally. In *Overseas Shipholding Group, Inc.*, the vessel owner sought to suppress evidence obtained during a boarding of a vessel that occurred specifically because the Coast Guard had been informed by a whistleblower that illegal discharges had occurred while the vessel was operating outside of U.S. jurisdiction. In seeking to suppress the evidence, the vessel owner argued that the subsequent boarding, which the Coast Guard had told the crew was a "non-priority" regulatory compliance examination, was pre-textual, i.e., the government was using its administrative authority to board vessels in order to gather evidence for a criminal prosecution, and the boarding therefore violated the Fourth Amendment.[192]

---

of $10,000, citing concerns that payment of a contingency fee would undermine the purpose of the statute by providing disproportionate payment to counsel in lieu of the witnesses. When the attorney sought authorization from the court to obtain the agreed upon fees, the court applied a deferential standard to the contingent fee arrangement. Although both crew members informed the court that they were aware of the terms of the agreement they had signed and thought that the agreement should be authorized, the court found that that contingent fee arrangement was unethically excessive under the circumstances, and awarded a fee of $50,000 total.

In *United States v. Rowan Cos.*, No. 2:07-CR-00298 (E.D. Tex. 2007), an offshore oil rig worker observed illegal discharges of hydraulic fluids and other pollutants and reported them to the company. When his complaints went unheeded, he began documenting the discharges on videotape and collected samples. After the employee was terminated, he hired an attorney to file a *qui tam* action and presented the case to the DOJ. After the *qui tam* suit was dismissed by the court, Rowan pleaded guilty to violations of APPS for illegally discharged oil and garbage from the oil rig, and for false recordkeeping. The whistleblower ultimately was awarded a bounty of $1 million from a total criminal fine of $7 million assessed against the rig owner.

188. 14 U.S.C. §2.

189. *Id.* §89(a).

190. United States v. Ricardo, 619 F.2d 1124, 1129 (5th Cir.), *cert. denied*, 449 U.S. 1063 (1980). *But see* United States v. Warren, 550 F.2d 219, 224 (5th Cir. 1977), *overruled on other grounds en banc*, 578 F.2d 1058 (1978) (14 U.S.C. §89(a) "with its broad granting of power, is subject to serious constitutional attack if implemented without caution and restraint").

191. 33 U.S.C. §1907(c). *See also* United States v. Royal Caribbean Cruises, Ltd., 11 F. Supp. 2d 1358, 1367 (S.D. Fla. 1998) ("MARPOL authorizes, inter alia, a port state to inspect a ship to verify a discharge in violation of MARPOL . . .").

192. United States v. Overseas Shipholding Group, Inc., No. 1:06-CR-65(2), 2006 U.S. Dist. LEXIS 95813 at *9, (E.D. Tex. Oct. 4, 2006), *order adopting recommendation on motion to suppress* 2006 U.S. Dist. LEXIS 76386 (E.D. Tex. 2006). To guard against abuse of the administrative search rationale, the Supreme Court has held that the government may not use an administrative inspection scheme to search for evidence of criminal violations. New York v. Burger, 482 U.S. 691, 724 (1987) (Brennan, J., dissenting); *see* Michigan v. Clifford, 464 U.S. 287 (1984). *See also* Abel v. United States, 362 U.S. 217, 226, (1960) ("[t]he deliberate use by the Government of an administrative warrant for the purpose of gathering evidence in a criminal case must meet stern resistance by the courts.").

In *United States v. Overseas Shipholding Group*, a whistleblower reported to the Coast Guard that the chief engineer had bypassed required pollution prevention equipment while discharging from the bilge of the vessel. The whistleblower also stated he may be concerned for his safety due to the reporting. The ship was in port when the whistleblower made the report. *Overseas Shipholding*, 2006 U.S. Dist. LEXIS 95813 at **4-5. The local Coast Guard unit, which was responsible for conducting regulatory compliance inspections, was contacted by both Coast Guard legal officers and criminal investigators. The local unit was informed of the whistleblower's report, but told just to conduct a normal regulatory compliance boarding, even though the vessel was not scheduled for such a boarding. They were also told not to tip off the vessel's crew that there had been a report of an illegal discharge, and to look as normal as they could through the inspection. *Id.* at **3-4.

The Coast Guard team boarded the vessel and told the master and the crew that they were there to conduct a non-priority vessel inspection, including a review of vessel documents, the oil record book, and an inspection of the engineering spaces. The inspectors specifically examined the vessel's pollution prevention equipment that was alleged to have been bypassed and other pollution prevention equipment in the engine room. At the end of the inspection, no deficiencies were noted. The Coast Guard team issued a boarding report indicating no deficiencies and

In ruling on the motion to suppress, the magistrate judge initially addressed whether the vessel owner had a reasonable expectation of privacy in the areas searched. Based on the fact that the inspectors examined the ship's records, the engineering spaces, and the oil record book, which is required to be kept on the vessel and to be provided for examination by port state officials, the court concluded that the vessel owner did not have a reasonable expectation of privacy in any of the areas or items searched or inspected by the Coast Guard boarding team.[193]

In considering whether the search was pre-textual, the magistrate judge focused on the plenary authority of the Coast Guard under 14 U.S.C. §89 to stop and board vessels to inspect for safety, documentation, and customs violations. He concluded that these inspections are not covered by the general administrative search exception to the warrant requirement, but instead fall under the rubric of searches on the high seas or in U.S. territorial waters. He noted "[t]hat criminal activity might be suspected is immaterial to the issue of the reasonableness *vel non* of the search."[194] Finally, the court observed that the Supreme Court had "flatly dismissed the idea that an ulterior motive (for a boarding) might serve to strip the agents of their legal justification."[195] It held that the search was not pre-textual and that the Coast Guard had no duty to inform any crew members who may have committed a crime before boarding and conducting an inspection, particularly since this could cause repercussions for individuals on the vessel who informed the Coast Guard of the violations.[196]

F. *Vessel and Ocean Pollution Prosecutions*

To permit enforcement of their provisions international and domestic standards require that vessels maintain records related to the discharge, disposal, and transfer of various pollutants generated aboard the vessel, or carried as cargo aboard the vessel in instances in which the cargo can be a pollutant if intentionally or accidentally discharged into the water. Historically, these recordkeeping requirements have applied to oil, noxious liquid substances, garbage, sewage, and other such pollutants. More recently, international standards and domestic laws have been enacted to require recordkeeping related to air pollution from ships, control of non-indigenous species and organisms through discharges of ballast water, and pollutants generated by normal operation of the vessel.

The United States has sought to address pollution from ships, including foreign ships that call in its ports, by focusing on criminal prosecutions of recordkeeping violations. It does so using both environmental statutes meant to address pollution in U.S. waters or by U.S. flag vessels, and traditional Title 18 crimes such as false statements, obstruction of justice and conspiracy. Prosecutions based on these provisions are at the heart of DOJ's Vessel Initiative.

Recordkeeping violations may be based on alleged discharges of pollutants by foreign flag vessels that occurred outside the navigable waters of the United States or other waters subject to U.S. jurisdiction. DOJ has convinced federal courts that the records do not have to be presented to agents of the U.S. government in order to support criminal convictions for false recordkeeping. It is sufficient that the false records are aboard the vessel when it calls in a U.S. port on the basis that the vessel is required to maintain accurate records, and entering U.S. waters with false or inaccurate records is therefore in and of itself a violation.

The following cases highlight the principal legal issues that have been addressed in criminal prosecutions for vessel and ocean pollution violations.

1. *United States v. Royal Caribbean Cruise, Ltd.*[197]

The defendant, the owner and operator of a cruise ship, challenged the assertion of federal criminal enforcement jurisdiction for false statements in the oil record book related to a discharge of bilge water that had

indicating that the boarding had been a random, non-priority vessel inspection. *Id.* at **6-8. The vessel owner subsequently was charged with presenting a false oil record book to the Coast Guard team that boarded the vessel. *Id.* at *8, n.6.

193. *Id.* at **13-17.

194. *Id.* at *18 (citing United States v. Royal Caribbean Cruises, Ltd., 24 F. Supp. 2d 155, 164 (D.P.R. 1997)).

195. *Id.* at *19 (quoting Whren v. United States, 517 U.S. 806, 812 (1996)).

196. *Id.* at **20-21.

197. 11 F. Supp. 2d 1358 (S.D. Fla. 1998).

occurred in Bahamian waters.[198] The U.S. Department of State initially referred the violation to Liberia, the flag state of the vessel, and provided the evidence of an illegal discharge that had been gathered in an investigation conducted by the Coast Guard. Liberia determined that there was reasonable doubt that the vessel had violated MARPOL.

Thereafter, federal prosecutors charged Royal Caribbean Cruises, Ltd (RCCL) with knowingly and willfully using a false writing, *i.e.,* the oil record book, and presenting it to the Coast Guard in violation of 18 U.S.C. §1001. The indictment alleged that RCCL knew that the oil record book contained a false entry because it represented that all of the discharges from the machinery space bilges of the vessel were discharged through oily water separating equipment (OWS), as is required to be done by MARPOL, when in fact the OWS on the ship had been bypassed at the time of the discharge at issue.

RCCL moved to dismiss the indictment under both federal and international law because the discharge had occurred outside the jurisdiction of the United States. In examining the issue under international law, the court focused on the provisions in MARPOL that required the ship to keep an oil record book, to enter oil discharges in it, and to make it available for inspection by authorized port state officials. The court noted that while MARPOL authorizes the competent authority of a port state that is signatory to the convention, such as the Coast Guard of the United States, to inspect the oil record book and to investigate discharge violations, it requires violation reports related to incidents outside of port state jurisdiction to be referred to the flag state. The court also noted that MARPOL was not a self-executing treaty and was implemented in the United States through the APPS.[199] As such, APPS limits the application of Annex I of MARPOL, which contains the oil record book requirements, to foreign flag vessels only while they are in the navigable waters of the United States or while at a port or terminal under the jurisdiction of the United States. Despite these limitations, the court stated:

> If the policy goal of a comprehensive regime of anti-pollution measures is to be achieved, it is necessary that domestic and international law work together to the extent possible to maximize enforcement. The discharge of oil in an improper manner is one crime; the failure to keep an Oil Record Book as required under MARPOL/APPS is another; and the deliberate presentation of a false material writing to the U.S. Coast Guard is another.[200]

The court held that referral to the flag state may be proper in one instance and prosecution under U.S. law appropriate in another, and that ultimately the decision as to what violations to prosecute is within the discretion of the executive branch, not the courts.[201]

Addressing the issue under U.S. domestic law, the court noted that the Coast Guard had duties under MARPOL and other laws and treaties to board foreign flag vessels in port, and to pursue appropriate measures for violations of applicable laws and treaties when they were found. The court further concluded that such boardings and inspections were part of the regularly conducted activities of the Coast Guard and that false statements made in connection with those activities fall within the scope of §1001. The court held that the issue of U.S. jurisdiction over either the discharge or the attendant entries in the oil record book had no bearing on the question of its jurisdiction to enforce its laws regarding false statements to a government agency performing regular and proper duties in a U.S. port.[202] The court, therefore, denied the motion to dismiss.

---

198. MARPOL Annex I requires that a vessel subject to the convention be provided by the flag state with an oil record book. At the time of the RCCL case, the convention required that specifically listed operations involving oil and oily mixtures on board the vessel, including any discharges overboard of bilge water, be fully recorded without delay in the oil record book. The oil record book was required to be kept in a place aboard the vessel so that it was readily available for inspection at all reasonable times by the competent authority of any signatory party to the convention. MARPOL, Annex I, Regulation 20 (2003).

199. A treaty is self-executing if it both requires no implementing legislation and provides a specific private right of action. Haitian Refugee Center v. Baker, 949 F.2d 1109, 1110 (11th Cir. 1991).

200. *Royal Caribbean,* 11 F. Supp. 2d at 1368.

201. *Id.* at 1369.

202. *Id.* at 1366. RCCL also argued that specific safeguards in the UNCLOS precluded the United States from taking criminal action in this case. The court ruled that there was no specific private right of action under UNCLOS and, therefore, RCCL did not have standing to litigate these issues. In dicta, the court noted that even assuming RCCL did have standing, the UNCLOS safeguards did not apply because the false statement violation occurred while the vessel was in a United States port. *Id.* at 1374.

2. *United States v. Abrogar*[203]

The defendant was a foreign citizen who served as chief engineer on a foreign flag vessel. He agreed to plead guilty to "knowingly failing to maintain an accurate ORB in U.S. waters," in violation of the APPS.[204] When the guilty plea was entered, the Pre-Sentence Report recommended that the base offense level under the federal *Sentencing Guidelines*, §2Q1.3, should be enhanced by six levels because the offense resulted in an ongoing, continuous, or repetitive discharge into the environment. The trial judge agreed and, based on the enhanced offense level, sentenced the defendant to 12 months and 1 day of imprisonment followed by 3 years of supervised release.[205]

On appeal, the U.S. Court of Appeals for the Third Circuit vacated the sentence and remanded for re-sentencing. It found that, under the Sentencing Guidelines, an offense is defined as "the offense of conviction and all relevant conduct . . ..."[206] "Relevant conduct," the court noted, included "all acts and omissions committed, aided, abetted, counseled, commanded, induced, procured, or willfully caused by the defendant; and . . . that occurred during the commission of the offense of conviction, in preparation for that offense, or in the course of attempting to avoid detection or responsibility for that offense."[207]

To determine the defendant's relevant conduct, the court first considered the offense of conviction, which was a violation of the APPS. The court found that Congress had made the APPS criminal provisions applicable only to U.S. ships, wherever located, and to foreign ships in three specific instances: (1) when they are in the navigable waters of the United States; (2) while they are in the EEZ with respect to the requirements of MARPOL Annex V (Garbage); and (3) when at a port or terminal of the United States.[208] The court stated that the government in fact was arguing that the offense of conviction—failure to maintain an accurate ORB—occurred for offense-defining purposes not only in U.S. waters, but during the whole of Abrogar's tenure aboard the ship, or at least from the moment he made the first false entry.[209] The court stated, however, that the terms of the APPS and its implementing regulations exclude from criminal liability the "failure to maintain an accurate oil record book" by foreign vessels outside U.S. waters. The court felt this point was particularly significant analytically because it did not just implicate jurisdiction, but also whether MARPOL violations even constituted crimes under U.S. law.[210]

The court then stated that Abrogar's offense of conviction was the knowing failure to maintain an accurate oil record book within U.S. waters. Nevertheless, because the underlying discharges did not take place in U.S. waters, the discharges neither occurred during the commission of the offense of conviction, nor during the preparation for that offense, nor in the course of attempting to avoid detection or responsibility for maintaining a false ORB while in U.S. waters. Therefore, the court concluded that the discharges were not "relevant conduct" as defined by the *U.S. Sentencing Guidelines* thus, they could not be considered part of the offense under the guidelines and could not justify applying the six-level sentencing enhancement.[211]

The government also argued that the guidelines "reflect a general policy of enhancing sentencing for recordkeeping offenses to account for damage wrought by the underlying substantive offense."[212] The court rejected this structural argument for two reasons. First, it concluded that because criminal liability for MARPOL violations by a foreign vessel does not attach until the vessel enters U.S. waters, the

---

203. 459 F.3d 430 (3d Cir. 2006).

204. *Id.* at 432-33. In *Abrogar*, the defendant admitted to making false entries in the vessel's oil record book that were examined by the Coast Guard during a boarding. *Id.* at 433. In this regard, he was charged with essentially the same conduct as was the company in the RCCL case, making false statements to Coast Guard boarding team members when the vessel was in a U.S. port. However, the prosecutor chose to charge the defendant under APPS, instead of the false statements statute. *See also* United States v. Ionia Mgmt. S.A., 498 F. Supp. 2d 477 (D. Conn. 2007), *decision reached on appeal*, 555 F.3d 303 (2009) (defendant charged under APPS with failure to maintain an accurate ORB by failing to disclose exceptional discharges of oil-contaminated waste made through a bypass hose during a U.S. Coast Guard compliance inspection); United States v. Petraia Maritime, Ltd., 483 F. Supp. 2d 34 (D. Me. 2007) (defendant charged under APPS with failure to maintain an accurate ORB arising out of a Coast Guard inspection).

205. *Id.*

206. *Id.* at 434 (quoting *U.S. Sentencing Guidelines* §1B1.1, Application Note 1(H)).

207. *Id.* (quoting *U.S. Sentencing Guidelines* §1B1.3(a)(1)).

208. *Id.* at 434-35 (citing 33 U.S.C. §1902).

209. *Id.* at 435.

210. *Id.* at 435, n.3.

211. *Id.* at 436.

212. *Id.*

improper discharges, all of which occurred outside U.S. waters, did not constitute a substantive environmental offense under U.S. law, any more than the failure to maintain an accurate ORB outside U.S. waters constitutes a recordkeeping offense under U.S. law.[213] Second, the court reasoned that the plain meaning of the guidelines and the statutory provisions at issue militated against the government's position.[214] Any policies reflected in the guidelines were subordinate to the scope of liability and applicability in the APPS as established by Congress, and criminal liability in this case was clearly limited by the provisions of the APPS.[215] For these reasons, the Third Circuit held that the district court erred in applying the six-level sentencing enhancement.

3. *United States v. Jho*[216]

Although it was a sentencing case, *Abrogar* arguably indicated that failures to maintain an accurate ORB concerning discharges that occurred outside of U.S. jurisdiction could not be criminally prosecuted in the United States under the APPS, as opposed to the False Statements Acts, even when the Coast Guard had examined the ORB in port.

In *Jho*, the government successfully pushed the envelope to make vessel owners, operators, and crewmembers on foreign flag vessels criminally liable under the APPS for false entries in an ORB related to discharges that occurred outside of U.S. jurisdiction, if these vessels entered U.S. navigable waters with a false ORB, even if the vessels were never boarded by the Coast Guard and the ORBs were never inspected.

A vessel owner and the Chief Engineer on a foreign flag vessel that made frequent port calls in the United States were charged under a ten count indictment. One count alleged that the defendants conspired to violate the APPS by failing to maintain an accurate ORB, to obstruct justice in violation of 18 U.S.C. §1505 by using a false ORB during a Coast Guard boarding, and to make a false statement to the Coast Guard in the form of the oil record book in violation of the false statements statute. The second charge alleged a violation of §1001, for presenting a false ORB to the Coast Guard during a boarding. The remaining eight counts alleged that the defendants violated the APPS during eight separate port calls in the United States by failing to maintain an accurate ORB. The vessel actually was boarded by the Coast Guard on only one of the port calls, and that boarding also was the basis for the false statement statute count.

The defendants moved to dismiss the Indictment by challenging the jurisdiction of the United States over all alleged violations, but focusing primarily on the eight APPS counts. The court dismissed the APPS counts and that part of the conspiracy count that alleged a conspiracy to violate APPS.[217] While noting that both criminal and civil penalties are authorized by APPS, it concluded that the scope of the enforcement authority must be read in light of another APPS provision, which states that "any action taken under [APPS] shall be taken in accordance with international law."[218]

The court also acknowledged that under the UNCLOS, a coastal state has jurisdiction to enforce international pollution rules when the foreign vessel pollutes within the coastal state's territorial sea, exclusive economic zone, or continental shelf.[219] Nevertheless, UNCLOS limits the type of penalty that can be levied against foreign flag vessels to monetary penalties in this instance.[220]

---

213. *Id.*
214. *Id.* at 436-37.
215. *Id.* at 437.
216. United States v. Jho, 465 F. Supp. 2d 618 (E.D. Tex. 2006), *rev'd*, 534 F.3d 398 (5th Cir. 2008).
217. 465 F. Supp. 2d at 622.
218. *Id.* at 624 (quoting 33 U.S.C. §1912).
219. *Id.* at 625 (citing art. 16, UNCLOS). The court found that the UNCLOS codifies customary international law, and although UNCLOS had not been ratified by the Senate, it was appropriate to consider the UNCLOS jurisdictional provisions because pending a treaty's ratification by the Senate, "the United States is bound to uphold the purposes and principles of the agreement." *Id.* at 624 (quoting United States v. Royal Caribbean Cruises, Ltd., 24 F. Supp. 2d 155, 159 (D.P.R. 1997)). In examining the jurisdictional provisions of UNCLOS, the court noted that the flag state has primary responsibility for the enforcement of marine pollution laws under "the law of the flag rule." *Id.* at 625 (citing Lauritzen v. Larsen, 345 U.S. 571 (1953)).
220. *Id.* (citing art. 230(2), UNCLOS). Article 230(2) of UNCLOS states:

    Monetary penalties only may be imposed with respect to violations of national laws and regulations or applicable international rules and standards for the prevention, reduction and control of pollution of the marine environment, committed by foreign vessels in the territorial sea, except in the case of a willful and serious act of pollution in the territorial sea.

The court ultimately determined that the government was criminally prosecuting a foreign flag ship for alleged violations of U.S. Coast Guard regulations that had occurred aboard the ship while it was operating outside U.S. waters, and that because the defendants were not charged with an act of pollution in U.S. waters, the government could pursue only civil penalties for the violations of those regulations. Under these circumstances, the criminal prosecution ran afoul of well-established law of the flag principles that seek to ensure uniformity, comity and reciprocity among sea-faring nations. The court accordingly held that the APPS counts for failure to maintain an accurate oil record book, and that part of the conspiracy count alleging the defendants conspired to violate the APPS should be dismissed.[221]

On appeal, the Fifth Circuit reversed and held that the trial judge had erred in finding that the criminal conduct occurred outside U.S. waters. It concluded that the eight knowing failures to maintain an oil record book each occurred entirely within the ports of the United States.[222]

The court stated that accurate oil record books are necessary to carry out the goals of MARPOL and APPS, and that if the oil record books did not have to be "maintained" while in the ports or waters of the United States, then a foreign flag vessel could simply avoid application of the record book requirements by falsifying all of its record book information before entering port. This would severely hinder the Coast Guard's ability to conduct investigations against foreign flag vessels.[223]

In distinguishing *Abrogar*, the court noted that the defendant there did not dispute the content of the charge, which was failing "to maintain an accurate oil record book *while in the navigable waters of the United States*."[224] The indictment in *Jho* similarly, alleged that the violations occurred while the vessel was in port. On this basis, the court rejected any international law limitations on government efforts to enforce violations of domestic law.

The court found that it had been long established that a state has power to prosecute violations of its laws committed by foreign flag vessels in its ports, and that UNCLOS had broadened that traditional rule when it gave port states power to pursue violations of marine pollution laws beyond those that occurred in its ports.[225] The court therefore held that none of the UNCLOS provisions cited by the trial court "limits the power of a state to prosecute violations of its criminal laws that occur after a ship has voluntarily entered its port."[226] It reversed the dismissal of the indictment.

G. *The Current State of the Law in Prosecutions*

The vast majority of vessel-related prosecutions result in guilty pleas by vessel-owning or operating corporations and/or culpable crew members. Particularly for companies that operate fleets of vessels that call regularly on the United States, the ability of the Coast Guard to board that company's vessels at will and to rapidly expand investigations to other jurisdictions, where the vessel being investigated might have inspected by the Coast Guard in the past creates significant pressure to make business decisions to reduce the impact on vessel operations and resources that may be impacted by a long-term investigation. Similarly, foreign crew members who are targets of criminal investigations face prolonged detention in the United States, away from family and familiar surroundings. They thus frequently look to negotiate plea agreements as opposed to waiting for trial and sentencing hearings.[227]

Royal Caribbean demonstrated that if false records are presented to Coast Guard boarding officers while a foreign flag vessel is in a U.S. port, the False Statements Act can be utilized to prosecute criminally vessel owners and crewmembers responsible for making those false statements. Section 1001 is one of the most common criminal statutes charged in environmental prosecutions. It protects governmental functions, by

221. 465 F. Supp. 2d at 625.
222. 534 F.3d 398, 402-03 (5th Cir. 2008).
223. *Id.* at 403.
224. *Id.* at 404 (quoting *Abrogar*, 459 F.3d at 435).
225. *Id.* at 408-09.
226. *Id.* at 409.
227. *See, e.g.*, Bob Rust, *"Godspeed" to Chief Engineer*, TradeWinds (Aug. 31, 2006) (in case in which the chief engineer on a vessel pled guilty to one count of making a false entry in vessel's oil record book after having been detained in the United States by the government for eight months, the court sentenced defendant to one year's unsupervised probation, and he was allowed to return home after judge stated that his detention in United States amounted to "a form of incarceration").

ensuring that federal officials can carry out their duties and responsibilities based on accurate information. Nevertheless, the DOJ, as part of its Vessel Initiative, has become more aggressive in trying to pursue false or misleading statement claims in vessel cases under the APPS. That statute is particularly appealing to prosecutors because of its bounty provisions and because the APPS, as an environmental statute, required only proof of general knowledge as opposed to the higher specific intent standard required to be shown to convict under Section 1001.

The government's position is that false entries in the ORB, a document required by MARPOL to be on the vessel and in which all transfers, discharges or disposals of oil in machinery spaces of the vessel are required to be recorded, are violations of Coast Guard regulations implementing MARPOL and APPS. Under Coast Guard regulations, vessels are required to "maintain" an oil record book. The government's theory is that, the word "maintain" necessarily means that all entries in the oil record book are required to be accurate. Further, it did not matter where the discharge had occurred and whether it was subject to United States jurisdiction. Prosecutors claim that if a foreign flag vessel enters U.S. navigable waters and there is a false entry in the oil record book when the vessel is inspected by the Coast Guard, this constitutes a violation of the Coast Guard regulations that could be criminally prosecuted under APPS if the failure to maintain an accurate book was done "knowingly."

The *Jho* decision allows the government to take this theory farther, and the implications are potentially very significant, particularly for vessel owners and operators. The court of appeals upheld a charging theory under which the defendants allegedly committed a distinct criminal act each time the vessel entered a port of the United States with an oil record book that was known to be inaccurate.[228] Further, the court determined that a failure by part foreign vessel to maintain an accurate oil record book while in U.S. waters severely hindered the Coast Guard's ability to enforce MARPOL, regardless of whether the Coast Guard actually boarded the vessel. Finally, the mental element required for conviction on these charges is the relaxed, general knowledge standard—all that must be shown is knowledge of a requisite act, and under the *respondeat superior* doctrine, the vessel owner or operator may be liable based on the knowledge of its crew members.

Thus, under the theory in *Jho*, each entry into U.S. navigable waters with a false oil record book is a separate offense.[229] Vessels may call in multiple U.S. ports on a single voyage, or return to U.S. ports frequently with the same oil record book aboard. Separate indictments can be brought by local prosecutors in each jurisdiction. The potential for proliferation of charges puts tremendous pressure on vessel owners or operators to enter into plea bargains early in order to avoid increases in the number of charges or the increased costs associated with having to defend in multiple jurisdictions.

Recently, international and U.S. laws addressing vessel pollution have been expanded to include standards for air pollution, ballast water discharges, and other discharges incidental to vessel operations. Most of these standards similarly require that the vessel maintain records establishing compliance with the standards. These records also are subject to inspection by the Coast Guard and other government agencies whenever a foreign vessel calls in a United States port, and for U.S. vessels, wherever they operate. Thus, the potential exposure to criminal liability for vessel owners, operators and crew members based on the need to "maintain" accurate records is increasing rapidly.

228. *Jho*, 534 F.3d at 404. For a discussion of the issues that arise when vessels that call with an inaccurate oil record book in multiple ports and thus are subject to prosecutions in multiple-jurisdictions, *see* John F. Cooney, *Multi-Jurisdictional and Successive Prosecutions of Environmental Crimes: The Case for a Consistent Approach*, 96 J. Crim. L. & Criminology 435 (2006).

229. By rule, the oil record book must be kept aboard the vessel and subject to inspection for at least three years. 33 C.F.R. §151.25(k). Thus, potentially, under the government's theory, if a foreign vessel failed to log or falsely logged a discharge or transfer of oil or oily bilge water sometime during the three-year period prior to its entry into U.S. waters, even if that discharge or transfer occurred in the waters of another state or on the high seas, the owner and/or operator of the vessel is in violation of the APPS. Further complicating the issue is the fact that the crewmembers who failed to accurately make the required entry may not be on the vessel at the vessel enters the United States. as crew members usually serve for a period of months and then are replaced. In these instances, the crew on board at the time that the vessel calls in the United States may not even be aware of the inaccuracy.

III. The Clean Air Act

A. *Legislative History*

Often considered the most technical of the environmental statutes,[230] prosecution under the Clean Air Act (CAA)[231] has historically been disfavored in comparison to other environmental statutes such as the CWA.

The first federal regulatory legislation addressing air pollution was the Clean Air Act of 1963,[232] which set certain emission standards for stationary sources. The Air Quality Act of 1967[233] expanded federal activities into the areas of enforcement, ambient monitoring studies, and stationary source inspections.

The Clean Air Act Extension of 1970[234] resulted in a major shift in the federal government's role in air pollution control by authorizing the development of comprehensive federal and state regulations to limit emissions from both stationary and mobile sources. The focus of the law was remediating existing problems in noncompliance areas. Also, it was the first major environmental law to include a provision for citizen suits. Four important regulatory programs affecting stationary sources were created in 1970: the national ambient air quality standards (NAAQS),[235] state implementation plans (SIPs),[236] new source performance standards (NSPS),[237] and national emission standards for hazardous air pollutants (NESHAPs). The government's enforcement authority also was substantially expanded under the Act.

The CAA was substantially amended again in 1977, among other things, to add prevention of significant deterioration (PSD) permitting requirements for major new stationary sources and major modifications to exisiting major stationary source in areas attaining the NAAQS, as well as permitting requirements pertaining to major new sources and major modifications of existing major sources in non-attainment areas.[238]

The CAA was amended in 1990.[239] The 1990 Amendments increased the authority and responsibility of the federal government. New regulatory programs were added to address acid rain, which is largely generated by coal-fired power plants; ozone pollution; and the issuance of operating permits for major stationary sources. The program for controlling toxic air pollutants was expanded, and the NESHAPs were incorporated within it. The provisions for attainment and maintenance of NAAQS were substantially modified and expanded. Finally, provisions regarding increased enforcement authority and expanded research programs were added. Subsequent legislation has made only minor changes to the statute.

B. *The CAA Regulatory Regime*

The CAA essentially is divided into two regulatory schemes, one for mobile emission sources and one for stationary emission sources. Mobile sources, i.e., vehicles, are primarily regulated through federal regula-

---

230. Criminal attorneys should take heed, and appropriately consult with an air expert on any technical or substantive issues related to the Clean Air Act.
231. 42 U.S.C. §§7401 et seq.
232. 77 Stat. 401, Pub. L. No. 88-206.
233. 81 Stat. 485, Pub. L. No. 90-148.
234. 84 Stat. 1676, Pub. L. No. 91-604. The 1970 Extension was adopted at approximately the same time as the National Environmental Policy Act (NEPA), which established the U.S. Environmental Protection Agency (EPA). EPA was created on May 2, 1971, in order to implement the various requirements included in the Clean Air Act of 1970.
235. National ambient air quality standards (NAAQS) for each criteria pollutant are required to be adequate to protect human health and allow an adequate margin of safety. EPA may not consider the costs of control in establishing the NAAQS, but may consider whether the science is uncertain. Whitman v. American Trucking Ass'ns, 531 U.S. 457 (2001). NAAQS were supposed to have been met nationwide by 1975 and are to be reviewed every five years.
236. The CAA established a federal state partnership. EPA has responsibility for establishing air quality standards and for designating which areas meet the standards (attainment areas) and which areas do not meet the standards (nonattainment areas). The CAA requires states to submit to EPA for approval SIPs for coming into attainment, or continuing to attain the NAAQS. 42 U.S.C. §7410. Failure to submit an approvable SIP or failure to implement an approved SIP can result in federal highway funding restrictions, creation of a federal implementation plan, increased offsets, and refusal by EPA to approval construction permits.
237. NSPS decreased in significance, however, as requirements for best available control technology (BACT) and lowest achievable emission rate (LAER) technology to control criteria pollutants emerged.
238. Clean Air Act Amendments of 1977, 91 Stat. 685, Pub. L. No. 95-95. A "non-attainment" area is a geographic area that does not meet one or more of the federal air quality standards.
239. 104 Stat. 2399, Pub. L. No. 101-549.

tions on engines and fuel and through SIPs. In general, they are not prone to criminal enforcement. This chapter accordingly will focus on stationary sources.[240]

EPA regulates two types of emissions from stationary sources: approximately 190 hazardous air pollutants (HAPs) and seven criteria pollutants: ozone (smog); carbon monoxide; sulfur dioxide; nitrogen dioxide; lead; particulate matter (total particulate and fine particulate); and greenhouse gases (GHGs)).

For hazardous air pollutants,[241] sources that have the potential to emit 10 tons/year or more of a listed pollutant or 25 tons/year or more of a combination of listed pollutants are considered major sources[242] and are subject to emission standards, which are known as maximum achievable control technology (MACT) standards. For criteria pollutants, pollution controls can be required through two avenues. First, the facility could be a major stationary source (or a major modification to an existing major stationary source) subject to emission limitations through a PSD or nonattainment area construction permit. Also, a facility can be subject to emission standards through federal NSPS or through state regulations included in the SIP. In an attainment area, a new source is required to obtain a PSD permit if it will emit 250 tons or more per year, or 100 tons or more per year for certain listed sources. "To determine which threshold is relevant for a particular facility, EPA determines what source category it belongs to and what Standard Industrial Classification (SIC) code applies to it. . . . If the source falls within one of 27 source categories listed in the NSR regulations, then the 100 tons per year threshold applies. Otherwise, the 250 tons per year threshold is applicable."[243]

PSD permits for major stationary sources or major modifications to existing major sources must include emission limitations based on the use of the best available control technology (BACT). To establish BACT for each applicable pollutant, the permit-issuing authority must consider energy, environmental, and economic impacts and select an emissions limit that reflects the best available control technology, including fuel switching, add-on control technology, or other means.[244] Construction permits for major stationary sources or major modifications to existing major sources located in non-attainment areas must include emission limitations based on the "lowest achievable emissions rate," which is the most stringent emissions limit in any SIP for the class or category of the proposed facility, or the most stringent emissions limit achieved in practice by such class or category of stationary sources.[245]

Regardless of the type of emission and the corresponding control technology, criminal cases tend to follow a common fact pattern—a company and/or individual is accused of: (1) using "creative" arithmetic to keep emission numbers below threshold quantities; (2) receiving a permit based on a promise to run the facility at less than full time or at less than full capacity (thus, avoiding a threshold trigger), and then exceeded those permitted numbers; (3) making a "major modification" (which requires the installation of enhanced pollution control equipment) but characterizing it as "routine maintenance"[246]; and/or (4) submitting false information in response to mandatory permit reporting requirements. These types of violations are amenable to criminal prosecution.

The CAA is currently an area of great activity. EPA is continuing to implement the 1990 CAA Amendments and is also, pursuant to the Supreme Court's opinion in *Massachusetts v. U.S. Environmental Protec-*

---

240. 42 U.S.C. §7412(a)(3) states that a "stationary source" for purposes of the regulation of hazardous air pollutants has the same meaning as that term is defined for purposes of 42 U.S.C. §7411. Section 7411(a)(3) defines a stationary source as "any building, structure, facility, or installation which emits or may emit any air pollutant."

241. Hazardous air pollutants are listed at 42 U.S.C. §7412(b)(1). The CAA requires that the EPA periodically review the list established in the statute and, when appropriate, to revise the list by adding pollutants "which present, or may present, through inhalation or other routes of exposure, a threat of adverse human health effects . . . or adverse environmental effects, whether through ambient concentrations, bioaccumulation, deposition, or otherwise." *Id.* at §7412(b)(2).

242. *Id.* at §7412(a)(1).

243. U.S. EPA, *Fact Sheet—Proposed Changes to Treatment of Corn Milling Facilities Under Clean Air Act Permitting Programs*, http://www.epa.gov/nsr/fs20060228.html (last visited May 29, 2013).

244. 40 C.F.R. §52.21(b)(12).

245. *Id.* at §51.165(a)(1)(xiiii).

246. New or modified stationary sources must install "best adequately demonstrated technology." Technology is assessed on a categorical basis, as set forth in 40 C.F.R. pt. 60. New or modified sources also must obtain a preconstruction permit. Perhaps assuming the definition would be obvious, "new sources" is not defined. Modified sources include a physical change or change in the method of operation that result in a significant net emissions increase.

tion Agency,[247] establishing emission standards for the greenhouse gases. EPA has issued final rules for both mobile and stationary sources.[248]

C. *Permitting*

The CAA Amendments of 1990 established the "Title V" program, which created an operating permit program for significant stationary sources.[249] Under the prior program, one facility could have multiple permits, which often had inconsistent permit requirements. Title V created a comprehensive program in which the permit must include information on all types of regulated pollutants being released from the facility, the quantities that may be released, and what actions the source's owner or operator is required to take to reduce the pollution. The permits also must include plans to measure and report the air pollution emitted.

The goal of the Title V program was easier enforcement, consistency with other media programs, gathering of information (SIPs, trading, offsets), and having a "one-stop" source for determining all the sources air emission obligations. Covered sources include: acid rain program sources, major stationary sources, major sources of HAPs, sources subject to HAP regulation, NSPS sources, and PSD sources.

D. *Enforcement Under the CAA*

The first modern provision authorizing criminal prosecution of pollution was Section 113(c) of the CAA of 1970,[250] which punished violations of the Act as a misdemeanor. The statute, however, proved substantially unenforceable.[251] Enforcement was not based on a permitting system, so there was no clear delineation of the particular legal obligations applicable to the source. In addition, because there were few reporting and recordkeeping obligations, enforcement authorities could not routinely and cost effectively review whether an individual source had violated its obligations.

In creating the permitting program for larger industrial and commercial sources in 1990, Congress expressly intended to facilitate more aggressive enforcement of the CAA.[252] Few criminal cases previously had been initiated because prosecutors faced a difficult challenge in proving that an emissions violation at one plant had caused an entire area to exceed levels established by the governing SIP. The 1990 Amendments also upgraded CAA violations from misdemeanors to felonies, bringing air pollution crimes to parity with criminal violations of the other major environmental statutes, expanded false-statement crimes to include knowing omissions, concealment and failure to file required reports, and added criminal sanctions for knowingly failing to pay a fee regarding CAA program requirements.[253] In addition to increasing the deterrent effect of the Act, this amendment significantly increased the likelihood that DOJ would spend more of its limited environmental enforcement budget on prosecution of air pollution violations.

Under Section 113(c)(1) of the CAA, any person who knowingly violates an applicable implementation plan or various other requirements of the statute may be subject to imprisonment for up to five years.

---

247. 549 U.S. 497 (2007).

248. For example, since January 2011, by EPA rule sources emitting more than 75,000 tons per year of GHGs have acquired a Title V operating permit for all such sources and a PSD permit if any such source is modified. Similarly, as of July 1, 2011, stationary sources of GHGs emitting 100,000 tons per year were required to obtain GHG permits, even if they were not previously subject to regulation under the CAA. Approximately 550 facilities were required to obtain a first CAA operating permit, mostly solid waste landfills and large industrial facilities. Under the "tailoring rule" ultimately the GHG permit programs will be extended to major sources emitting over 25,000 tons of GHGs per year. 75 Fed. Reg. 31514 (June 3, 2010).

249. 42 U.S.C. §§7661a-7661f.

250. Pub. L. No. 91-604, 84 Stat. 1676, §113(c) (1970).

251. *See* James Miskiewicz & John S. Rudd, *Civil and Criminal Enforcement of the Clean Air Act After the 1990 Amendments,* 9 Pace Envtl. L. Rev. 281 (1992). Most successful prosecutions under this provision have been for violations of the work rules under the asbestos national emissions standard for hazardous air pollutants, rather than for core air pollution violations. *See, e.g.,* United States v. Buckley, 934 F.2d 84, 21 Envtl L. Rep. (Envtl. L. Inst.) 21113 (6th Cir. 1991).

252. Miskiewicz & Rudd, supra note 252, at 286 ("The Amendments were also driven by an obvious need to craft legislation that could be rationally and stringently enforced.")

253. Sec. 701, Pub. L. No. 101-549, 104 Stat. 2399, 2672 (codified at 42 U.S.C. §7413), The criminal sanctions for failure to pay a required fee do not apply to any fees under Title II of the CAA's mobile source program. Apparently, the rationale for including the criminal sanction for failure to pay fees was because fee-based economic incentive programs, such as the allowance program for acid rain, could not otherwise be enforced. *See* Michael S. Alushin, *Enforcement of the Clean Air Act Amendments of 1990,* 21 Envtl. L. 2217, 2219 (1991).

Any person who knowingly releases a listed hazardous air pollutant, and knows at the time that he or she thereby places another person in imminent danger of death or serious bodily injury, may be subject to imprisonment for up to 15 years.[254] A negligent release that places another in imminent risk is punishable by imprisonment of one year.[255] False statements and tampering with monitoring equipment carry a maximum term of imprisonment of two years.[256] Knowing failure to pay a required fee is a misdemeanor subject to imprisonment for up to one year.[257] Repeat convictions generally subjects the offender to a doubling of both the maximum fines and imprisonment allowed under the statute.[258]

The typical fact-pattern in most environmental crimes cases filed under the CAA, involves repeated exceedance of permit limits and/or a failure to accurately report air pollution information to the EPA or state regulatory agency. Due to the associated permit reporting obligations, Title 18 charges, such as false statements and conspiracy, also are common.[259]

EPA public information includes mapping the locations of HPVs, of which 1,501 exist across the United States in early 2013.[260]

Per EPA's OECA's April 2012 National Program Manager Guidance, petroleum refineries and chemical, petrochemical, and polymer manufacturers may be increasingly scrutinized:

> Industrial facilities emit significant amounts of hazardous air pollutants (HAPs). Causes include noncompliance with regulations intended to prevent the incomplete combustion of HAPs in steam-assisted flares due to low heat content and over-steaming. EPA has determined that these problems are particularly likely to occur at petroleum refineries and chemical, petrochemical, and polymer manufacturers. Under the Air Toxics National Enforcement Initiative (NEI), the Regions are targeting compliance evaluations (including CAA Section 114 information requests) at facilities in these sectors. The goal of the flaring enforcement enhancements are to improve EPA's efficiency and effectiveness in targeting, enforcing against, and reducing illegal emissions of HAPs from flares. We will do so by piloting innovative, efficient enforcement approaches, i.e., a flaring efficiency enforcement alert combined with individual-facility flaring notices, and using HQ contractor resources to enhance the Regions' ability to evaluate facilities' compliance based on their 114 responses, respond to violations, and meet existing ACS commitments more efficiently. In addition, we will use the results to demonstrate compliance and pollution control impacts beyond individual flaring enforcement actions to show general deterrence.[261]

Other areas, however, such as asbestos enforcement, may see a declining rate of criminal prosecutions:

> In light of budget constraints expected in FY13, EPA will maintain a limited national presence for asbestos NESHAP enforcement, with a focus on high-priority federal activities such as assessing, advising, and supporting state and local emergency response and recovery after catastrophic situations, e.g., earthquakes, hurricanes, and tornadoes, where structures with asbestos containing materials have been destroyed and normal procedures for abating asbestos before demolition are not feasible. Headquarters' development of new regulatory applicability determinations will be limited to requests that pose issues of first impression that are of national importance. Criminal enforcement will continue to be a viable and robust tool to address criminal violations of the Asbestos NESHAP regulations. Delegated state programs will continue to conduct the day-to-day activities associated with the receipt of notifications and related compliance monitoring and enforcement activities.[262]

---

254. 42 U.S.C. §7413(c)(5(A).
255. *Id.* at §7413(c)(4).
256. *Id.* at §§7413(c)(2(A) & (C).
257. *Id.* at §7413(c)(3).
258. *See, e.g., id.* at §§7413(c)(1), (2) &(3).
259. *See, e.g.,* United States v. Mathis, 738 F.3d 719 (6th Cir. 2013), reh'g denied en banc, 2014 U.S. App. LEXIS 1966 (2014)(conspiracy and false statements under Title 18); United States v. Starnes, 583 F.3d 196 (3d Cir. 2009) (false statements under Title 18; United States v. Shaw, 150 Fed. Appx. 863 (10th Cir. 2005), *cert. denied,* 547 U.S. 1130 (2006) (conviction of false statements under 18 U.S.C. §1001 upheld because CAA false statement provision was not the sole and exclusive means by which the Government could prosecute the making of a false statement to the EPA in violation of the CAA).
260. U.S. EPA, Enforcement and Compliance History Online, http://www.epa-echo.gov/echo/compliance_report_air.html (last visited May 29, 2013).
261. U.S. EPA, OECA, FY 2013 National Program Manager Guidance 15-16 (Apr. 20, 2012), *available at* http://nepis.epa.gov/Exe/ZyPDF.cgi?Dockey=P100F6FG.PDF.
262. *Id.* at p. 32.

E. Cases Involving the CAA

In *United States v. Bragg*,[263] three individuals were prosecuted for multiple CAA asbestos work practice and worker identification violations at an asbestos-abatement project.[264] The defendants had conspired to recruit untrained homeless men, obtained fraudulent asbestos training identification cards using false social security numbers, and directed the men to strip asbestos pipe insulation without first wetting the material. As a result, the workers were exposed to the severe health risks associated with asbestos inhalation.[265] The defendants were sentenced to prison for terms of between 24 and 33 months.[266] Their prosecution helped prompt the ECS to launch a nationwide project with EPA and the National Coalition for the Homeless to halt the exploitation of homeless and itinerant workers for illegal asbestos work.

In *United States v. Louisiana Pacific Corp.*,[267] a major manufacturer of oriented strand board (a material similar to plywood) used in home construction and two employees were charged with multiple counts of conspiracy to violate the CAA, tampering with a monitoring device and method in violation of the CAA, and false statements in violation of the CAA, all related to pollution control technology used to filter out particles before discharging the emissions into the atmosphere as required under a state-issued air emissions permit. In addition to CAA violations, the defendants also were charged with wire fraud and mail fraud for misrepresentations to costumers related to quality control standards. Ultimately, the company to 18 felonies and agreed to pay $37 million in penalties, $5.5 million of which represents the largest criminal fine ever for a CAA violation. "As part of its guilty plea, the company admitted that between 1989 and 1994, its employees conspired to violate the CAA; tampered with the mill's air pollution monitoring equipment on numerous occasions; and made false statements to the Colorado Department of Health regarding the number of times the mill violated limits set forth in its pollution permits." The former mill superintendent and the former mill manager also pled guilty to conspiracy to violate the CAA, and were sentenced to six months home detention and a $10,000 fine; and five months imprisonment, five months home detention, and a $15,000 fine, respectively.[268]

In *United States v. Anwar*,[269] the defendant was a licensed on-board diagnostic inspector and owner-operator of an auto repair shop. From January 2010 through May 2011, the defendant clean scanned 1,008 vehicles using surrogate vehicles to falsely pass cars that would have otherwise failed emissions inspections. He illegally profited in excess of $50 per vehicle in exchange for the false passing results. The defendant pled guilty to conspiracy to violate the CAA, and was sentenced to 4 months in prison and 4 months of home confinement, and was ordered to serve 50 hours of community service. He was also prohibited from conducting vehicle inspections in the future.

In *United States v. Mathis*,[270] the defendants were the owner of an unused factory site and the owner of a company hired to conduct salvage and demolition activities at the former Standard Coosa Thatcher plant and entered into a year-long scheme in which the plant was illegally demolished while still containing extensive amounts of asbestos. Additionally, the defendants hired day laborers and paid them low wages to improperly remove asbestos-containing materials without following federal regulations that were intended to keep the asbestos, a known carcinogen, from becoming airborne where it could be inhaled. After trial, the owner of the demolition and salvage company was found guilty of conspiracy to violate the CAA and two counts of violation of the CAA. He was sentenced to 18 months imprisionment. The owner of the property was found guilty of conspiracy to violate the CAA, six counts of violation of the CAA, making

263. United States v. Bragg, 207 F.3d 394 (7th Cir. 2000).
264. Bragg, 207 F.3d at 397-98.
265. Asbestos is designated by the CAA as a hazardous air pollutant. Exposure to asbestos can cause life-threatening diseases, including asbestosis, cancer, and mesothelioma.
266. U.S. DOJ, Three Men Sentenced to Prison for Participating in a Conspiracy to Use Homeless Men for Illegal Asbestos Removal, http://www.justice.gov/opa/pr/1999/January/032enr.htm (last visited May 29, 2013).
267. 908 F. Supp. 835 (D. Colo. 1995), *reh'g denied*, 925 F. Supp. 1484 (D. Colo. 1996), *interlocutory app. denied*, 106 F.3d 345 (10th Cir. 1997).
268. The case results are summarized at http://www.justice.gov/enrd/3515.htm (last visited Mar. 5, 2014). This summary refers to the case as United States v. Company A and Two Individuals.
269. No. 3:11-CR-241-MOC (W.D.N.C. 2013). This case and two other similar cases for falsification of automobile emissions tests are summarized at U.S. EPA, Summary of Criminal Prosecutions, *available at* http://cfpub.epa.gov/compliance/criminal_prosecution/index.cfm?action=3&prosecution_summary_id=2381 (last visited Mar. 6, 2014).
270. 738 F.3d 719 (6th Cir. 2013), *reh'g denied en banc*, 2014 U.S. App. LEXIS 1966 (2014).

false statements in violation of 18 U.S.C. §1001, and obstruction of justice. He was sentenced to 44 months imprisonment.

In *United States v. Columbus Steel Castings Company, Inc.* (CSC),[271] CSC, an Ohio corporation, owns and operates a steel foundry in Columbus, Ohio. At this foundry, CSC manufactures steel castings for various industries, including the railroad industry. As part of these operations airborne pollutants are generated. Some of the individual processes at the foundry that generate air pollution are required to have emission control devices. CSC had a Title V permit. Following a review of the records from the facility, as well as interviews of CSC employees, it was determined that there have been numerous violations of the Title V permit at the facility. In particular, between 2004 and 2007, there were numerous control device malfunctions and deviations from a number of different permitted processes at the facility. These malfunctions and deviations were neither reported in the monthly nor annual reports. In addition, emissions were not properly vented into a baghouse from the green sand core making and air turntable processes. Also, daily visual emission checks were not conducted at the facility. Lastly, stack tests were not conducted within six months after the expiration of the permits for air arc turntables and the storage silos processes. CSC employees were aware of these permit requirements and were also aware of the violations. CSC pled guilty to six violations of the CAA and was sentenced in November 2011 to 12 months of probation and ordered to pay a $660,000 federal fine, ordered to pay $165,000 as community service to two different Columbus charitable organizations that serve residents who live near the plant. CSC was also ordered to install interlock devices designed to shut down emissions sources when the associated air pollution control equipment is not in operation and a bag leak detection system for the air control equipment for the furnace.

In *United States v. Certified Environmental Services, Inc.*,[272] an environmental laboratory that, among other services, conducted air sampling and performed analysis related to asbestos abatement projects, and three of its supervisory employees, and a supervisor from a former asbestos abatement company, conspired over the course of nearly a decade to falsify lab results used to prove that asbestos removal was done properly. In numerous instances asbestos removal companies represented that homes, schools, and other buildings were free of asbestos contamination when asbestos debris remained behind. CES and three employee defendants were found guilty of conspiring to violate the CAA of committing mail fraud and of defrauding the United States. CES and two employees were also convicted of making false statements. The supervisor of the asbestos abatement company pleaded guilty to conspiracy to defraud the United States, to violating the CAA, to violating the TSCA, and to mail fraud. In October 2011, CES was sentenced to 60 months of probation, ordered to pay a $20,000 federal fine and $117,102 in restitution. One CES supervisor to 3 days incarceration, to 36 months of probation and ordered to pay $5,855 in restitution; another to 3 weeks incarceration, to 60 months of probation and was order to pay restitution in the amount of $23,420; and the third to 3 days incarceration, to 36 months of probation and was ordered to pay $5,855 in restitution. The supervisor of the asbestos abatement company was sentenced to 3 days incarceration, to 36 months of probation and ordered to pay $3,704 in restitution.[273]

In United States v. Hailey,[274] defendant was convicted by a federal jury of eight counts of wire fraud, thirty-two counts of money laundering, and two counts of violating the CAA. The convictions stem from Defendant's scheme to sell $9 million in renewable fuel credits which he fraudulently claimed were produced by his company. Though the company was registered with the EPA as a bio-diesel fuel producer, it did not actually produce the fuel. Over a 21-month period, defendant sold over 35 million "renewable identification numbers" to brokers and oil companies, receiving at least $9 million in profits while producing no actual renewable fuel. Hailey was sentenced to over 12 years imprisonment. The judge enhanced the

---

271. No. 2:11-CR-180(1) (N.D. Ohio 2012). For a summary of this case, *see* U.S. EPA, Summary of Criminal Prosecutions, *available at* http://cfpub.epa.gov/compliance/criminal_prosecution/index.cfm?action=3&prosecution_summary_id=2235 (last visited Mar. 5, 2014). *See also* U.S. Atty's Office, S. D. Ohio, Press Release, *Columbus Steel Castings Pleads Guilty to Violating Clean Air Act* (Jul. 28, 2011), *available at* http://www.justice.gov/usao/ohs/news/07-28-11.html. (last visited Mar. 5, 2014).
272. No. 5-09-CR-319 (N.D.N.Y. 2012).
273. In *U.S. v. Certified Envtl Serv., Inc.*, 800 F.Supp.2d 391 (N.D.N.Y. 2011), the court analyzed the restitution amounts to be awarded to the various defendants under 18 U.S.C. 3664(h), and held that each defendant would be jointly and severally liable to the extent of the restitution order as against that individual defendant. For a summary of the case, *see* EPA, Summary of Criminal Prosecutions, *available at* http://cfpub.epa.gov/enforcement/criminal_prosecution/index.cfm?action=3&prosecution_summary_id=2226 (last visited Mar. 5, 2014).
274. No. 1:11-cr-540 (D. Md. 2012).

sentence upon finding that he had obstructed justice by concealing, selling and spending assets that were protected by court order. Hailey was also ordered to pay restitution of approximately $ 42.2 million to over 20 companies and to forfeit $9.1 million in proceeds from the fraud, including cars, jewelry, his home and bank accounts, which had already been seized by the government.[275]

In United States v. Tyler Pipe Co.,[276] Tyler Pipe pled guilty to two felony counts for violations of the new source review/prevention of significant deterioration provisions of the CAA This was the first criminal prosecution ever undertaken for violation of these provisions. The company paid a $4.5 million criminal fine and agreed to undertake an estimated $11 million in upgrades to its facility to reduce future pollution. The prosecution arose from the facility's construction and operation of a scrap metal furnace used to produce molten iron, a process that generated significant emissions of particulate matter, carbon monoxide, and lead. When the company constructed a new furnace, it failed to apply to the Texas Commission on Environmental Quality for permission to construct and operate the new furnace using enhanced control technology, and instead continued to use the same control technology as for the previous furnace.[277]

In 2008, in *United States v. Hershey Creamery Co.,* the company was charged with failure to develop and maintain a Risk Management Plan (RMP) at two of its facilities.[278] Under the CAA, stationary sources where more than a threshold quantity of regulated substances is present must prepare and implement an RMP to detect and prevent or minimize accidental releases, and to provide prompt emergency response to protect human health and the environment.[279] The implementing regulations require, among other things, that an RMP include procedures for identifying the chemicals that pose safety and environmental risks, notifying and training workers, responding to an accidental release and coordinating with local emergency agencies, assessing risks to neighboring communities, and maintaining and updating the plan as necessary.[280] Hershey pled guilty to a violation of the CAA for failing to have the required RMP based on the presence of anhydrous ammonia, a regulated substance, having falsely certified to the EPA at least twice that it did. The company was sentenced to pay a fine of $100,000 and placed on probation for a year.[281]

Similarly, in *United States v. BP Products N. America, Inc.*,[282] defendants BP Products North America, Inc. (BP) pled guilty to felony violations of the CAA arising from an explosion at a Texas City refinery plant that killed 15 and injured at least 170 workers. The risk management plan regulations under the CAA required BP to implement written procedures to maintain the integrity of process equipment and to inform contractors of the risks involved when it performed a restart of a raffinate splitter. BP admitted to know-

---

275. *See* U.S. EPA, News Release, *Rodney Hailey Sentenced to More Than 12 Years in Prison for Selling $9 Million in Fraudulent Renewable Fuel Credits / Owner of "Clean Green Fuel" falsely claimed his company produced 23 million gallons of renewable fuel* (Feb. 22, 2013), *available at* http://yosemite.epa.gov/opa/admpress.nsf/d0cf6618525a9efb85257359003fb69d/499ba7061892802085257b1a006f9522!OpenDocument (last visited Mar. 5, 2014). As a result of this case, EPA has stated that it is increasing enforcement related to this program and that criminal enforcement has "gone from 15 miles per hour to 75." Ann E. Marimow & Juliet Eilperin, *Renewable-fuels fraud cases expose weakness in EPA program,* Wash. Post, Apr. 14, 2012, *available at* http://www.washingtonpost.com/local/crime/renewable-fuels-fraud-cases-expose-weakness-in-epa-program/2012/04/14/gIQAtGKbHT_story.html (last visited Mar. 6, 2014).

276. Crim. No. 6:05-CR-29 (E.D.Tex., Mar. 2005).

277. In addition to the Tyler Pipe facility, two other prosecutions related to the McWane-related group of cases also involved CAA violations. In *United States v. Atlantic States Cast Iron Pipe Co.,* No. 3:03-CR-00852 (D.N.J. 2006), the company and one plant manager were found guilty of multiple violations, including violating the CAA by burning tires and paint waste in violation of their permit. In *United States v. McWane,* Inc., No. CR 05-00811 (D. Utah 2005), the company and the former general manager of the Pacific States Cast Iron Pipe Co., a McWane company, pled guilty to violation related to the CAA. The company pled guilty to making false statements by submitting falsified emissions reports to the State of Utah and was fined $3 million. The general manager pled guilty to a violation of the CAA by rendering inaccurate a required testing method and was sentenced to 12 months and 1 day in prison and to pay a $20,000 fine. For a summary of all of these cases, see U.S. DOJ, United States v. McWane Corporation (New Jersey, Texas, Utah, Alabama), *available at* http://www.justice.gov/enrd/3409.htm (last visited Mar. 7, 2014).

278. Indictment, United States v. Hershey Creamery Co., No. 08-353 (M.D. Pa. Sept. 2, 2008).

279. 42 U.S.C. § 7412(r)(7).

280. 40 C.F.R. Part 68, Subpart G.

281. U.S. EPA, News Release, *Hershey Creamery Company Pleads Guilty and Pays $100 Fine for Clean Air Act Violation-First Prosecution in the Country for Failure to Implement CAA Risk Management Program* (Nov. 3, 2008), *available at* http://yosemite.epa.gov/opa/admpress.nsf/dc57b08b5acd42bc852573c90044a9c4/a620d5f71121362585257 4f60066ab94!OpenDocument. (last visited Mar. 6, 2014). Although not specifically identified as such, this case was likely the outgrowth of the "Worker Endangerment Initiative," a multi-agency initiative begun in 2005 involving the DOJ Environmental Crimes Section, EPA and OSHA to target and prosecute worker safety-related violations. Hershey had previously been fined by OSHA in 2004 and 2006 for violations of its safety measures. *See* Samuel Howard, *Ice Cream Co. Cops To Criminal Clean Air Violations,* Law360 (Nov. 3, 2008), *available at* http://www.law360.com/articles/75386/ice-cream-co-cops-to-criminal-clean-air-violations (last visited Mar. 6, 2014). The CAA RMP requirements are modeled in large part on OSHA's process safety management (PSM) requirements, 29 C.F.R. §1910.119.

282. 610 F. Supp. 2d 655 (S.D. Tex. 2009).

ingly violating these regulations. The government agreed to accept a plea agreement which stipulated a $50 million fine, three years of probation, and compliance with both an OSHA settlement agreement and an order imposed by the Texas Commission on Environmental Quality. The victims of the explosion objected to the court's acceptance of the plea agreement because they wanted to participate in court hearings, and they believed the sentence was too lenient.

The court held that the plea agreement would be accepted and the fine was not too low. BP pled to the highest offense that could be charged based on the evidence. The court reasoned that a criminal fine is not intended as victim compensation, and BP would spend far more on settling multiple civil cases. Furthermore, the fine was, at that time, the largest criminal fine imposed against a single corporation under the CAA, and the largest criminal fine imposed for a fatal industrial accident.

In *United States v. W.R. Grace*,[283] the company and seven of its executives were indicted for conspiracy to violate the CAA and to defraud the United States, wire fraud, and obstruction of justice regarding the alleged release of asbestos-contaminated vermiculite ore from the mine in response to ongoing serious health problems in the nearby town of Libby, Montana. Defendants were charged with conspiring to knowingly to release asbestos into the ambient air, thereby knowingly placing persons in imminent danger of death or serious bodily injury in violation of the CAA and conspiring to defraud the United States, a dual-object conspiracy. In addition, the indictment charged defendants with three counts of knowing endangerment under the CAA, and with obstruction of justice. In May 2009, a jury in the U.S. District Court for the District of Montana acquitted W.R. Grace and three former executives. The government case was difficult to prove in part because the indictment was filed in 1999, but the mine had closed in 1990. DOJ invested substantial resources in this multi-week trial, but its position was also undermined by its failure to disclose its relationship with a key witness, which resulted in the trial judge denouncing the prosecution in open court for an "inexcusable dereliction of duty."[284]

In March 2005, *The Tyler Pipe Co.*, one of the largest U.S. manufacturers of iron pipes and castings, pled guilty to two felony counts for violations of the new source review/prevention of significant deterioration provisions of the CAA.[285] This was the first criminal prosecution ever undertaken for violation of these provisions. The company paid a $4.5 million criminal fine and agreed to undertake an estimated $11 million in upgrades to its facility to reduce future pollution. The prosecution arose from the facility's construction and operation of a scrap metal furnace used to produce molten iron, a process that generated significant emissions of particulate matter, carbon monoxide, and lead. When the company constructed a new furnace, it failed to apply to the Texas Commission on Environmental Quality for permission to construct and operate the new furnace using enhanced control technology, and instead continued to use the same control technology as for the previous furnace.

In *United States v. Louisiana Pacific Corp.*,[286] the company and individual defendant owners of a plywood mill were indicted for, inter alia, "conspiracy to violate the CAA, tampering with a monitoring device and method, and making false statements. The tampering and several of the false statement charges involved a continuous opacity monitoring system required under a permit issued to LPC in 1988 by the Colorado Department of Health, but replaced in 1992 by a new permit that instead required a camera monitoring system."[287]

---

283. 504 F.3d 745 (9th Cir. 2007), cert. denied, 554 U.S. 918 (2008).

284. Kirk Johnson, *Chemical Company Acquitted in Asbestos Case,* N.Y. Times (May 8, 2009), *available at* http://www.nytimes.com/2009/05/09/us/09grace.html?_r=0 (last visited Mar. 7, 2014). Although seven individuals had been charged in the original indictment, prior to trial, one of the defendants had died, two had been earlier dismissed from the case at the request of the government, and one individual defendant had been granted a separate trial, so the acquittal was for the company and the three remaining individual defendants.

285. U.S. EPA, *Criminal Enforcement, McWane Convictions Summary,* http://www.epa.gov/compliance/resources/cases/civil/mm/mcwane.html (last visited May 29, 2013).

286. 908 F. Supp. 835, 26 ELR 20726 (D. Colo. 1995), *reh'g denied,* 925 F. Supp. 1484, 27 ELR 20405 (D. Colo. 1996), *interlocutory appeal denied,* 106 F.3d 345, 27 ELR 20715 (10th Cir. 1997).

287. ECS, Environmental Crimes Bulletin (Summer 1997), *available at* http://www.regionalassociations.org/common/files/newsletters/ECS_Sum97.pdf.

284. *Id.* at 728-29. [deleted reference in text, but did not delete footnote or renumber after this]

IV. Resource Conservation and Recovery Act

RCRA[288] manages hazardous wastes from their point of generation to disposal, also known as "cradle to grave" regulation. Unlike the CAA and the CWA, which establish limitations on what and how much of a pollutant may lawfully be discharged, RCRA focuses on the manner in which waste materials are managed. Its ultimate goal is to ensure that the storage, transportation, treatment, and disposal of hazardous waste occur in a manner that poses minimal risk to human health and the environment. The key provisions of RCRA relate to both the disposal of solid waste and the treatment and disposal of hazardous waste, which is subject to far more stringent regulation than ordinary solid waste.

For purposes of criminal prosecution, the most important part of the statute is that section which classifies certain waste materials as hazardous and establishes a system for regulating those who generate and manage these wastes. RCRA imposes criminal liability on parties who knowingly violate this hazardous waste regulatory scheme.

A. *Hazardous Waste*

As a threshold matter, RCRA applies only to materials that are "solid wastes" as defined by the statute.[289] Only a subset of solid wastes meets the definition of "hazardous waste" (but all hazardous wastes are solid wastes). The definition of "solid waste" hinges on the concept of "discarding" a substance and are regulated under Subtitle D.[290] Numerous exemptions exist from the definition of solid waste. For example, products intended for re-use or recycling are not considered discarded and may be exempt from the regulations of RCRA, provided certain conditions are met.

Solid wastes that also satisfy the statutory definition of "hazardous" under RCRA are subject to the much more onerous requirements of Subtitle C.[291] A solid waste is considered "hazardous" if it falls into one of two categories: "listed wastes" or "characteristic wastes."[292] "Listed wastes" are those materials the EPA specifically has determined routinely contain hazardous constituents or exhibit hazardous qualities.[293] "Characteristic wastes", are materials that demonstrate certain characteristics: ignitability, corrosivity, reactivity, or toxicity. The burden falls on the waste's generator to identify whether a particular waste product demonstrates one or more of these characteristics.

Listed wastes and characteristic wastes are regulated quite differently under RCRA. Certain characteristic hazardous wastes can be considered non-hazardous solid waste when they are mixed with another substance so that the mixture no longer demonstrates any hazardous characteristic. On the other hand, when a listed hazardous waste is mixed with another solid waste, the resulting mixture remains a hazardous waste regardless of its properties.[294] Furthermore, any wastes derived from the treatment of listed hazardous wastes are also classified as hazardous wastes.[295]

---

288. Pub. L. No. 94-580, 90 Stat. 2795 (1976), RCRA amended in its entirety and completely revised the Solid Waste Disposal Act, Title II, Pub. L. No. 89-272 (1965), and sometimes the provisions of RCRA are still referred to as the Solid Waste Disposal Act or SWDA. RCRA is currently codified at 42 U.S.C. §§6901 – 6992k.
289. 42 U.S.C. §6903(27) (2006). Several large categories of waste are exempt from RCRA, including sewage that passes through public water treatment plants, wastewater discharges regulated by a Clean Water Act permit, mining wastes, coal byproducts, nuclear wastes, and municipal garbage.
290. EPA regulations define a solid waste as "any discarded material" that is not excluded by variance granted under other cited sections of the regulations. 40 C.F.R. 261.2(a)(1). The regulations define "discarded material" as "any material" that is abandoned, recycled, inherently waste-like," or a specifically identified military munition. 40 C.F.R.§ 261.2(a)(2)(i). *See* American Mining Cong. v. EPA, 824 F.2d 1177, 1192-93, (D.C. Cir. 1987). Subtitle D of RCRA is codified at 42 U.S.C. §§6941-6949a.
291. Subtitle C of RCRA is codified at 42 U.S.C. §§6921 – 6939f.
292. 40 C.F.R. §261.3
293. A list of these substances is contained in the *Code of Federal Regulations* at 40 C.F.R. §261.30-261.35.
294. 40 C.F.R. §261.3(a)(2).
295. *Id.* at §261.3(c).

B. *Entities Regulated by RCRA*

Because RCRA creates a system that manages waste from generation to disposal, its regulations apply to all parties dealing with the waste including: (1) generators; (2) transporters; and (3) those that treat, store, or dispose of the waste.

The Subtitle C regulations broadly define the term "generator" to include any person, by site, who (1) first creates or produces a hazardous waste (e.g., from an industrial process) or (2) first brings a hazardous waste into the RCRA Subtitle C system (e.g., imports a hazardous waste into the United States).[296] Pursuant to EPA's regulations, generators must determine if their waste is a listed or characteristic hazardous waste.[297] Nevertheless, the degree of regulation to which a generator is subject depends largely on the amount of hazardous waste the generator produces in a particular calendar month.[298]

RCRA provides for three classes of generators: (1) large quantity generators (LQGs); (2) small quantity generators (SQGs); and (3) conditionally exempt small quantity generators (CESQGs). LQGs that store hazardous waste for no more than ninety days, and SQGs that store hazardous waste for no more than 180 days, are subject to limited regulatory requirements.[299] Generally, LQGs and SQGs must ensure proper storage and labeling and provide appropriate recordkeeping for waste generation and test results. Further, when waste is transported, LQGs and SQGs must create a "manifest" that will accompany the waste through each stage of transportation. CESQGs are not subject to these requirements; however, they must still identify their hazardous waste, comply with storage limit requirements, and ensure proper waste treatment or disposal at an on-or off-site location.[300]

A hazardous waste transporter under Subtitle C is any person engaged in the *off-site* transportation of hazardous waste within the United States, if that transportation requires a manifest.[301] Off-site transportation of hazardous waste includes shipments from a hazardous waste generator's property to another facility for treatment, storage, or disposal; but does not include transportation of hazardous waste within a facility's property or boundary[302] or between geographically contiguous properties, even if such properties are separated by a public road.[303] Transporters are required to obtain an EPA identification number, carry the manifest, and comply with EPA and U.S. Department of Transportation requirements for transportation of hazardous wastes and hazardous materials, respectively.[304]

The RCRA requirements for treatment, storage, and disposal facilities (TSDFs)[305] are more burdensome than those for generators and transporters. Most importantly, a TSDF must obtain a permit from the EPA or an authorized state agency in order to operate legally.[306] A TSDF permit lays out the standards and requirements applicable to the specific activities conducted at that facility, including both general facility standards and standards applicable to each type of unit at the facility. General facility standards cover good management practices, including keeping track of the amount and type of wastes entering the facility, training employees to manage hazardous waste safely, and preparing to avoid and respond to hazardous waste emergencies.[307] In addition, hazardous wastes may be treated, stored, or disposed of in several different types of units. In order to ensure that hazardous wastes are managed properly and in a safe manner, RCRA imposes specific design, construction, operation, maintenance, closure, and financial assurance requirements depending on the type of hazardous waste management unit and facility.[308] These technical standards go beyond the general requirements to ensure that all elements of the TSDF are constructed and operated to prevent releases of hazardous waste into the environment.

---

296. *Id.* at §262.10.
297. *Id.* at §262.11.
298. *Id.* at §262.10.
299. *Id.* at §262.
300. *Id.* at §261.5.
301. 40 C.F.R. §263.10
302. *Id.* at §263.10(b).
303. 40 C.F.R. §262.20(f).
304. *Id.* at §262.20, §263.10.
305. *See id.* 264, 265.
306. 42 U.S.C. §6925.
307. 40 C.F.R. Part 264.
308. *Id.*

C. *Criminal Liability Under RCRA*

RCRA imposes criminal liability for knowing violations of the transport, permit, and reporting/record-keeping regulations. Specifically, Section 3008(d) makes it a crime for any person to:

(1) *knowingly* transport or cause to be transported any hazardous waste to a facility which does not have a permit;

(2) *knowingly* treat, store, or dispose of any hazardous waste without a permit or in knowing violation of any material condition or requirement of such permit or interim status regulations or standards;

(3) *knowingly* omit material information or make any false material statement or representation in any application, label, manifest, record, report, permit, or other document filed, maintained, or used for purposes of regulatory compliance;

(4) *knowingly* generate, store, treat, transport, dispose of, export, or otherwise handle any hazardous waste while *knowingly* destroying, altering, concealing, or failing to file any record, application, manifest, report, or other document required to be maintained or filed for purposes of regulatory compliance;

(5) *knowingly* transport without a manifest, or cause to be transported without a manifest, any hazardous waste;

(6) *knowingly* export a listed or identified hazardous waste without the receiving country's consent or in violation of an international agreement between the United States and the receiving country; or

(7) *knowingly* store, treat, transport, or cause to be transported, dispose of, or otherwise handle any used oil not identified or listed as a hazardous waste *knowing* violation of a material condition of a permit or any other applicable regulations or standards.[309]

Any person convicted of a crime under Section 3008(d) is subject to a fine of up to $50,000 per day and five years' imprisonment. A second RCRA conviction for a violation committed after a first RCRA conviction doubles these penalties.[310] As discussed below, RCRA also contains a knowing endangerment provision, which upon conviction carries a possible penalty of up to $250,000 or 15 years imprisonment for an individual or a $1 million fine for corporations.[311]

In *United States v. MacDonald & Watson Waste Oil Co.*, a court found that the statutory phrase "which does not have a permit" naturally conveys the meaning "which does not have a permit for that substance."[312] Therefore, although a TSDF may have a permit, for some chemical(s), the a defendant can be convicted under Section 3008(d)(1) (knowingly transporting hazardous wastes to an unpermitted TSDF) so long as the permit does not provide for the storage, treatment, or disposal of the specific hazardous waste in question.

A recent criminal case involving the illegal export of hazardous waste could have far-reaching effects and prompt increased federal regulation of electronic waste. In *United States v. Executive Recycling, Inc.*,[313] an electronic waste recycling company and two of its executives were convicted of illegally exporting e-waste, include cathode ray tubes containing lead, overseas. The company had failed to file a Notice of Export and obtain permission of both EPA and the receiving countries prior to exporting the electronic waste. Proper disposal of electronic waste has become an increasingly important issue, and this case, the first of its kind, may signal a change in the regulatory landscape of electronic waste.[314]

---

309. RCRA §3008(d); 42 U.S.C. §6928(d) (emphasis added).
310. *Id.*
311. *Id.* at §6928(e).
312. United States v. MacDonald & Watson Waste Oil Co., 933 F.2d 35, 46 (1st Cir. 1991).
313. 946 F.Supp.2d 1130 (D. Colo. 2013).
314. *See* Peggy Otum, *E-Waste Case Could Bring Changes to E-Waste Recycling Laws,* Law 360 (Jan. 30, 2013), *available at* http://www.law360.com/articles/410501/e-waste-case-could-bring-changes-to-e-waste-recycling-laws (last visited Mar. 10, 2014).

D. *Knowledge Requirement*

A recurring issue in RCRA criminal enforcement proceedings is the level of knowledge a defendant must have in order to trigger criminal liability. The term "knowingly" is critically important to Sections 3008(d)(1) and 3008(d)(2), which contain several elements to which the term "knowingly" could apply. For example, must a defendant knowingly transport, treat, store, or dispose of the waste? Must he know the waste was "hazardous" or that it was a "waste" as defined by RCRA? Must he know the facility did not have a permit? Courts also have considered whether "knowingly" contemplates familiarity with or awareness of the RCRA regulations.

The Third Circuit was the first to address the knowledge requirement under RCRA. In *United States v. Johnson & Towers*,[315] the court found that under Section 3008(d)(2)(A), which criminalizes storage, treatment, or disposal of hazardous waste without a permit, the government must prove knowledge by the defendant of *all elements* of the crime, including knowledge of RCRA's requirements. However, since *Johnson & Towers*, other circuits have consistently held that knowledge of the RCRA regulations is *not required* for a conviction.[316] In these circuits, a defendant need not know that the material was a "waste" or that it was classified as "hazardous" under RCRA. Rather, the prosecution must show only that the defendant was aware of his actions *and* knew that the waste material had the potential to harm persons or the environment. The courts' rationales rely upon the public welfare doctrine, which holds that the probability of regulation is so great for dangerous products that anyone who is aware that he is in possession of them or dealing with them must be presumed to be aware of the regulation.[317]

A greater degree of division exists among the courts of appeals on the issue of whether a showing of knowledge of a facility's permit status is necessary for a conviction. The Third and Eleventh Circuits have determined that the government must show the defendant knew the facility in question lacked the necessary permit.[318] The Ninth and Second Circuits, on the other hand, have held that such knowledge is not necessary.[319] The Ninth Circuit's detailed statutory analysis in *United States v. Hoflin*[320] noted that Sections 3008(d)(2)(B) and 3008(d)(2)(C) reiterate the knowledge requirement, while Section 3008(d)(2)(A) does not.[321] Several courts have expressed support for the Ninth Circuit's reasoning in *Hoflin* and disagreement with the Third Circuit's decision in *Johnson & Towers*, although these courts have not all addressed the issue of a defendant's knowledge of permit status.[322]

The Ninth Circuit later distinguished *Hoflin* from cases of criminal liability under Section 3008(d)(1) (knowingly transporting hazardous waste to an unpermitted facility). In *United States v. Speach*,[323] the court held that a transporter's criminal liability under section 3008(d)(1) *does require* knowledge of a facility's permit status. The court reached this conclusion despite the fact that Section 3008(d)(1), like the subsection at issue in *Hoflin*, does not restate the knowledge requirement. An important distinction between subsections (d)(1) and (d)(2)(A), as noted by the court, is the role of the defendant in RCRA's regulatory scheme. Charges under Subsection (d)(2)(A) are brought against the TSDF's owner or operator, who is in the best position to know of and control the TSDF's permit status. Charges under Subsection (d)(1), on the other hand, are raised against transporters or generators. The Ninth Circuit feared

315. United States v. Johnson & Towers, Inc., 741 F.2d 662, 14 (3d Cir. 1984), *cert. denied,* 469 U.S. 1208 (1985).
316. *See, e.g.,* United States v. Kelley Tech. Coatings, Inc., 157 F.3d 432, 436 (6th Cir. 1998), *reh'g denied,* 1998 U.S. App. LEXIS 29653 (6th Cir. Oct. 19, 1998); United States v. Wagner, 29 F.3d 264, 266 (7th Cir. 1994); United States v. Laughlin, 10 F.3d 961, 965-66 (2d Cir. 1993); United States v. Self, 2 F.3d 1071, 1089-91 (10th Cir. 1993); United States v. Dean, 969 F.2d 187, 191 (6th Cir. 1992); United States v. Goldsmith, 978 F.2d 643, 645 (11th Cir. 1992); United States v. Baytank (Houston), Inc., 934 F.2d 599, 613 (5th Cir. 1991); United States v. Dee, 912 F.2d 741, 745 (4th Cir. 1990), *cert. denied,* 499 U.S. 919; United States v. Hoflin, 880 F.2d 1033, 1037-39 (9th Cir. 1989), *cert. denied,* 493 U.S. 1083.
317. For a discussion of the public welfare doctrine, *see supra* Chap. 4, Part F.
318. United States v. Hayes Int'l Corp., 786 F.2d 1499, 1503-04 (11th Cir. 1986); *Johnson & Towers,* 741 F.2d at 669.
319. *Laughlin,* 10 F.3d at 965-66; *Hoflin,* 880 F.2d at 1037-39.
320. 880 F.2d at 1038.
321. Section 3008(d)(2) provides that any person who knowingly treats, stores, or disposes of any hazardous waste (A) without a permit; or (B*) in knowing violation* of any material condition or requirement of such permit; or (C) *in knowing violation* of any material condition or requirement of any applicable interim status regulation or standards. 42 U.S.C. §6928(d)(2) (emphasis added).
322. *Wagner,* 29 F.3d at 266; *Dean,* 969 F.2d at 191; *Baytank,* 934 F.2d at 613.
323. 968 F.2d 795 (9th Cir. 1992).

innocent conduct could be criminalized if a facility owner or operator misrepresented its permit status to the generator or transporter.[324]

E. Knowing Endangerment

RCRA was the first environmental criminal statute to incorporate a "knowing endangerment" provision. Under Section 3008(e), any person who handles hazardous waste or used oil in violation of the seven criminal provisions found in Section 3008(d) and "knows" at the time the offense is committed "that he thereby places another person in imminent danger of death or serious bodily injury" is subject to additional fines and up to 15 years' imprisonment.[325]

Section 3008(f) establishes various definitions, qualifications, and presumptions related to the elements of proof needed for a knowing endangerment conviction. A person "knows" of an existing circumstance "if he is aware or believes that the circumstance exists" and "is aware or believes that his conduct is substantially certain to cause danger of death or serious bodily injury."[326] That section also provides that knowledge may be imputed to an organization, but not to an individual.[327] To prove actual knowledge, circumstantial evidence may be used, including evidence that an individual took "affirmative steps to shield oneself from relevant information."[328]

Successful prosecutions against individuals have relied heavily on a subjective inquiry and turn on facts that plainly suggest an influence of knowing endangerment. For example, in *United States v. Tumin*,[329] an individual was convicted of abandoning barrels of what he knew to be highly volatile toxic wastes in a residential neighborhood. In *United States v. Hansen*,[330] managers of an unpermitted facility allowed mercury exposure to continue even after they were informed that employees had "extremely high" levels of mercury in their bodies and that the mercury-contaminated waste should be stored in a different manner.

In the context of corporate liability, in *United States v. Protex Ind.*,[331] the Tenth Circuit held in that a corporation may be found liable for knowing endangerment where the corporation *should have known* of the danger of exposure. This case stands in contrast to the actual knowledge requirement espoused by other courts. Here, the court determined, it was enough that the corporation was aware of a *risk* of great harm even if it had not contemplated the specific injuries that resulted.

F. Persons Liable Under RCRA

RCRA makes it a criminal offense for "any person" to commit the violations found in Section 3008(d). These violations generally involve acts performed without a permit or proper records or acts performed in violation of a permit. Usually, these are all responsibilities of the owner or operator of a facility that generates, treats, stores, or disposes of hazardous waste. This raises an important question: can individual employees be held criminally liable?

The Third Circuit addressed this issue in *Johnson & Towers* and determined that criminal liability for treating, storing, or disposing of hazardous waste without a permit could extend to employees who were not personally responsible for obtaining the permit but were in charge of the facility's waste management. The court found it appropriate to give "any person" an expansive definition because RCRA is a "public welfare statute" intended to protect those who are not in a position to protect themselves.[332] Other courts have consistently followed this approach.[333] The outcome may be different for an employee who does not manage the facility's waste.

---

324. *Id.* at 796.
325. 42 U.S.C. §6928(e).
326. *Id.* §6928(f).
327. *Id.*
328. *Id.*
329. No. CR 87-488 (E.D.N.Y. 1988).
330. 262 F.3d 1217 (11th Cir. 2001), *cert. denied,* 535 U.S. 1111 (2002).
331. *See* United States v. Protex Ind., 874 F.2d 740, 19 ELR 21061 (10th Cir. 1989).
332. *Johnson & Towers,* 741 F.2d at 667-68.
333. *See, e.g., Dean,* 969 F.2d at 192-93 (holding that an employee with day-to-day supervision of a facility's production process and employee, and the responsibility to instruct other employees on hazardous waste handling and disposal, is liable under RCRA even though he was not

Despite the expansive definition given to "any person," courts have limited *individual* criminal liability to those with actual knowledge. An individual cannot be held the required knowledge on the basis of *respondeat superior* or the responsible corporate officer doctrine.[334] Instead, the defendant is liable only if he knew that he was taking a prohibited action.

In *United States v. Wasserson*,[335] the Third Circuit considered whether someone who merely generates, but does not carry out the disposal of, hazardous waste can be convicted under subsection (d)(2)(A). Although merely a generator and not a TSDF, the defendant was convicted of knowingly disposing of hazardous waste without a permit. The trial court granted the defendant's motion for judgment of acquittal, holding that one who generates hazardous waste cannot be convicted under subsection (d)(2)(A) without performing the act of disposal. The court of appeals reversed, stating that any of the RCRA offenses can give rise to aiding and abetting liability. The court also rejected the defendant's argument that convicting him of both the transportation offense and the disposal offense would result in duplicate criminal liability for the same conduct. The court explained that each provision constitutes a separate offense because Congress defined transporting, storing, treating, and disposing as separate acts.[336]

Notably, the *Wasserman* decision comes from the Third Circuit, which requires knowledge of a facility's permit status in order to obtain a conviction. The court found that the defendant was "willfully blind" to the waste's ultimate destination and, therefore, had the requisite knowledge that the disposal facility lacked the proper permit.[337] It remains to be seen how other circuits that do not require knowledge of permit status will handle the question of aiding and abetting liability in future cases. This issue raises the same concern addressed by the Ninth Circuit in *Speeach*—that innocent conduct may be criminalized if a TSDF misrepresents its permit status.

G. *Passive Migration*

In *Slott v. Texas*,[338] a Texas appellate court addressed whether, in imposing criminal liability, passive migration of a hazardous waste qualifies as an act of "disposal" under the Texas Water Code, which contains a definition of "disposal" almost identical to that found in RCRA. The defendant argued that because the state had failed to bring action against him within the one year from his initial disposal, the statute of limitations had passed. The state, on the other hand, argued that after the initial disposal, the hazardous waste continued to leak into the soil and that therefore, the defendant continued to dispose of the waste by permitting it to migrate passively into the soil. The state relied on several federal civil cases holding that passive migration of previously dumped waste constitutes an ongoing violation under RCRA.[339] The court found these cases inapplicable to a criminal action, reasoning that "a statute of limitations in the criminal context is to protect the accused from having to defend against stale criminal charges and to prevent punishment for acts committed in the remote past."[340] It explained that under the state's proposed rule, "a potential polluter could be subject to criminal prosecution years after his act of disposal ended."[341] The court concluded that for purposes of criminal prosecution, the term "disposal" does not include the pas-

---

in charge of permitting the facility).

334. *MacDonald & Watson Waste Oil Co.*, 933 F.2d at 54 ("the district court erred by instructing the jury that proof that a defendant was a responsible corporate officer, as described, would suffice to conclusively establish the element of knowledge"); United States v. White, 766 F. Supp. 873, 894-95, 22 ELR 20050 (E.D. Wash. 1991).
335. 418 F.3d 225 (3d Cir. 2005).
336. *Id.* at 233-34.
337. *Id.* at 237-39.
338. 148 S.W.3d 624 (Tex. App. 2004).
339. *See* United States v. Power Eng'g Co., 10 F. Supp. 2d 1145, 1151 (D. Colo. 1998) (the leaking of hazardous waste into the groundwater constitutes continuing disposal of hazardous waste); City of Toledo v. Beazer Materials & Servs., Inc., 833 F. Supp. 646, 656 (N.D. Ohio 1993) (the prior disposal of waste is an ongoing violation); Gache v. Town of Harrison, N.Y., 813 F. Supp. 1037, 1042 (S.D.N.Y. 1993) (same); Acme Printing Ink Co. v. Menard, Inc., 812 F. Supp. 1498, 1512 (E.D. Wis. 1992) (leaking of hazardous substances may constitute a continuous or intermittent violation); United States v. Conservation Chem. Co., 619 F. Supp. 162, 200 (D. Mo. 1985) (disposal occurs when wastes migrate from their initial location); United States v. Price, 523 F. Supp. 1055, 1071 (D.N.J. 1981) (Section 7003 authorizes relief restraining further leaking of waste from a landfill).
340. 148 S.W.3d at 629
341. *Id.*

sive disposal of hazardous wastes. Instead, "some form of affirmative human conduct must accompany a disposal for it to rise to the level of criminal culpability."[342]

H. Federal Enforcement of State Programs

EPA may authorize states to operate their own hazardous waste programs "in lieu of" RCRA so long as the state program is "equivalent to" or "consistent with" the federal baseline program.[343] There are two significant aspects about this arrangement. First, EPA may authorize a state program to cover only part of RCRA's regulatory scheme, without barring federal regulation under other parts of RCRA. Second, pursuant to the criminal provisions of RCRA, it is a federal offense to violate federal regulations promulgated by EPA "or by a State in the case of an authorized State program."[344] Consequently, RCRA allows for federal enforcement, including federal criminal enforcement, of federally authorized state plans.[345]

EPA has promulgated regulations which govern the approval of state hazardous waste programs. These regulations provide that states can adopt and enforce requirements that are "more stringent" or "more extensive" than the federal baseline.[346] Nevertheless, for plans with a "greater scope of coverage," any "additional coverage" is not part of the federally approved program.[347] Thus, the additional coverage is *not* federally enforceable.

In *United States v. Southern Union Co.*,[348] defendant appealed the district court's denial of acquittal and argued that Rhode Island's regulation of CESQGs (conditional exemption for small quantity generators) could not be enforced by the EPA in a federal criminal prosecution under RCRA when the state program is broader than the federal program. Defendant interpreted the EPA regulations as providing that any state rule that is not "required" by federal law "necessarily imposes 'a greater scope of coverage.'"[349] The court declined to adopt this interpretation, concluding that defendant's reading "vitiates the clear distinction between 'more stringent' and 'greater in scope,' collapsing the two terms into one."[350] The court also reasoned that the EPA's interpretation should be deferred to as it was reasonable and not arbitrary and capricious under the Administrative Procedure Act.[351] Defendant also argued that even if the EPA's reading was accepted, state regulation of CESQGs is "additional coverage" under the EPA regulations and not a "more stringent" requirement because CESQG regulation expands coverage to new entities.[352] The court disagreed with this interpretation of the regulations and stated that they already provided for federal regulation of CESQGs. The court concluded that it does not "expand the universe of regulated entities to subject already-regulated entities to fuller regulation" by the state.[353]

V. The Comprehensive Environmental Response, Compensation, and Liability Act

A. Introduction

In 1980, Congress enacted the Comprehensive Emergency Response, Compensation and Liability Act (CERCLA)[354] to create a comprehensive mechanism for handling the problems associated with abandoned and inactive hazardous waste disposal sites. Unlike RCRA, which addresses *current or planned* waste dis-

342. *Id.*
343. 42 U.S.C. §6926.
344. *Id.* §6928(d).
345. United States v. Elias, 269 F.3d 1003, 1012 (9th Cir. 2001), *cert. denied,* 546 U.S. 857 (2005); McDonald & Watson Waste Oil Co., 933 F.2d at 44-45.
346. 40 C.F.R. §271(i).
347. *Id.* §271.1(i)(2).
348. 630 F.3d 17 (1st Cir. 2010), *rev'd on other grounds,*132 S. Ct. 2344 (2012).
349. 630 F.3d at 29.
350. *Id.*
351. *Id.* at 29-30.
352. *Id.* at 30.
353. *Id.*
354. Pub. L. No. 96-510, Title I, 94 Stat. 2767 (1980) (codified as amended at 42 U.S.C. §§9601-9675).

posal, CERCLA responds primarily to *prior* waste disposal practices and imposes liability to ensure remediation of contaminated sites.

At its most basic level, CERCLA requires any person with knowledge of a release of a hazardous substance into the environment to notify EPA and gives the government power to compel parties to clean up those releases. Under CERCLA, both the government and private parties have the authority to recover the costs of cleanup from potentially responsible parties. Although the primary focus of CERCLA is remedial, it does provide for criminal sanctions in certain instances relating to the failure to report or the provision of false information.

B. *Criminal Liability*

CERCLA creates criminal liability for:

> (1) any person in charge of a vessel from which a hazardous substance is released into the navigable waters or adjoining shorelines, the contiguous zone or the EEZ, or in charge of a facility from which a hazardous substance is released, for failing to immediately notify (as soon as they have knowledge of such a release) the appropriate federal agency;[355] 2) any person in charge who submits in a required notification any information which that person knows to be false or misleading;[356] (3) any person who knowingly gives or causes to be given any false information as part of a claim for response costs under the Superfund;[357](4) any person who owns or operates, or at the time of the disposal owned or operated, or who accepted hazardous substances for transport and selected, a non-permitted facility at which hazardous substances are or have been stored, treated, or disposed of and who knowingly fails to notify the EPA of the existence of such facility;[358](5) any person who knowingly destroys, mutilates, erase, disposes of, conceals, or otherwise renders unavailable or unreadable, or who falsifies, any record required to be kept by the EPA regarding a facility where hazardous substances are contained or deposited;[359] and (6) any person not an officer or employee of the United States who knowingly and willfully divulges or discloses information entitled to protection that is obtained as part of an investigation conducted under CERCLA.[360]

Most criminal cases under CERCLA are for failure to notify the appropriate agency of a release of a reportable quantity of a hazardous substance. To establish criminal liability, the government must prove: (1) that the substance released was a "hazardous substance"; (2) that the release was in an amount greater than or equal to the reportable quantity; (3) that it was released from a facility into the environment; (4) that the defendant had knowledge of the release; (5) that the defendant was a "person in charge" of the facility; and (6) that the defendant failed to give immediate notice after learning of the release. Case law is relatively sparse in this area; however, because the civil and criminal provisions of CERCLA are similar, what is meant by elemental terms under CERCLA criminal provisions logically should mirror judicial interpretations of these terms in the civil cases.[361]

1. Person in Charge

CERCLA is defined by Section 9603(b), which requires "any person in charge" of a facility to notify the appropriate agency of a release. Although CERCLA does not separately define the term for "person in charge," it does define "person" as "an individual, firm, corporation, association, partnership, consortium, joint venture, commercial entity, United States Government, state, municipality, commission, political

355. 42 U.S.C. §9603(b). The Emergency Planning and Community Right-to-Know Act (EPCRA), 42 U.S.C. §§11001 - 11050, was passed as part of the Superfund Amendment and Reauthorization Act of 1986, which amended CERCLA. EPCRA contains criminal sanctions for any person who knowingly and willfully fails to report a release of a reportable quantity of certain identified chemicals. *Id.* § 11045(b)(4).
356. *Id.*
357. *Id.* §9612(b).
358. *Id.* §9603(c).
359. *Id.* §9603(d)(2).
360. *Id.* §9604(e)(7). Under EPCRA, any person who knowingly and willfully divulges or discloses any information entitled under the Act to protection as a trade secret is subject to misdemeanor criminal sanctions. 42 U.S.C. §11045(d)(2).
361. *See, e.g., United States v. Hansen,* 262 F.3d 1217, 1254 (11th Cir. 2001) (defining "operator" as described in United States v. Bestfoods, 524 U.S. 51, 66-67 (1998), a civil case involving liability for remedial costs under §9607).

subdivision of a state, or any interstate body."[362] Using this broad definition, prosecutors have brought charges against corporations, owners, operators, corporate officers, and supervisory personnel for failure to notify.

Corporate officers also may be "persons in charge" in appropriate circumstances. Generally, a corporate officer will not be held criminally liable solely based on his position in the corporate hierarchy. Further, unlike the CWA and the CAA, responsible corporate officers are not specifically included as being subject to criminal sanctions. Because there are explicit knowledge requirements for criminal liability in CERCLA, courts may be more reluctant to use the responsible corporate officer doctrine to impose criminal sanctions.[363]

Finally, supervisory personnel, even those of relatively low rank, may be deemed "persons in charge" if they are in a position to detect, prevent, and abate the release of the hazardous substance. In United States v. Carr, the court equated "in charge" with responsibility for an operation that results in a release and held the maintenance foreman who directed workers to dispose of old paint cans liable under CERCLA for failing to report a release of waste paint into a man-made pit.[364] There is no "one person in charge" of a particular facility; multiple people can share this responsibility. To be exposed to potential criminal liability, it is only necessary that a person have or share supervisory control of the facility where the release occurred.[365]

2. Owner or Operator

Because owners and operators are subject to civil liability under CERCLA for cleanup of hazardous releases, courts in criminal cases may look to civil treatment of the definition of "owner or operator" when determining criminal liability.[366] In *United States v. Bestfoods*, the Supreme Court found that an "operator" is one who manages, directs, or conducts a facility's operations "specifically related to pollution, that is, operations having to do with the leakage or disposal of hazardous waste, or decisions about compliance with environmental regulations."[367] The court in *United States v. Hansen* applied the *Bestfoods* definition when upholding the conviction of a defendant for failure to report.[368] Similarly, in *United States v. Greer*, an owner and operator of a waste recycling and transport business who was actively involved in the daily operation of the business was found guilty for failure to notify.[369]

Based on holdings in civil CERCLA cases, it is possible that a corporate parent could be criminally liable for the actions of its subsidiary. In *Bestfoods*, the Supreme Court first acknowledged that a parent could be liable directly as an "operator" if it managed, directed or controlled the subsidiary's operations relating to pollution, such as waste management or compliance with environmental regulation.[370] It further held that a parent could also be liable under traditional corporate law principles; specifically, the corporate veil may be pierced when the "corporate form would otherwise be misused to accomplish certain wrongful purposes."[371]

3. Facility

CERCLA defines a "facility" as "any building, structure, installation, equipment, pipe or pipeline (including any pipe into a sewer or publicly owned treatment works), well, pit, pond, lagoon, impoundment, ditch, landfill, storage container, motor vehicle, rolling stock, or aircraft" or "any site or area where a hazardous substance has been deposited, stored, disposed of, or placed, or otherwise come to be located; but does

362. 42 U.S.C. §9601(21).
363. *See* discussion of the responsible corporate officer doctrine *supra* at Chap. 4, Sec. J.
364. 880 F.2d 1550, 1554 (2d Cir. 1989).
365. *Id.*
366. *See Hansen*, 262 F.3d at 1254 (citing *Bestfoods*, 524 U.S.at 66-67 (1998)).
367. 524 U.S. at 66-67.
368. *Hansen*, 262 F.3d at 1254.
369. 850 F.2d 1447 (11th Cir. 1998).
370. 524 U.S. at 65-66.
371. *Id.* at 62. By definition, the term "owner or operator" does not include "a person, who, without participating in the management of a vessel or facility, holds indicia of ownership primarily to protect his security interest in the vessel or facility." 42 U.S.C. §9601(20)(A).

not include any consumer product in a consumer use or any vessel."[372] The term applies to both physical structures and to areas of property. For example, in *Carr,* the pit into which paint cans were thrown was considered the "facility," not the army base where the pit was located.[373]

In the civil context, the meaning of "facility" has been litigated extensively and, in general has been interpreted quite broadly. For example, in *United States v. Bliss,* the court found that the definition encompasses "both the container from which a hazardous substance has been released and the site where those substances have been placed."[374] Other courts agree with this interpretation, holding that a facility is any area or place where hazardous substances have come to be located.[375]

4. Hazardous Substance

CERCLA defines "hazardous substance" very broadly to include not only specific substances listed in CERCLA itself but also those found in other environmental statutes. The term "hazardous substance" includes:

(A) any substance designated pursuant to Section 311(b)(2)(A) of the Federal Water Pollution Control Act, 33 U.S.C. §1321 (b)(2)(A);

(B) any element, compound, mixture, solution, or substance designated pursuant to Section 9602 of CERCLA;

(C) any hazardous waste having the characteristics identified under or listed pursuant to Section 3001 of the Solid Waste Disposal Act, 42 U.S.C. §6921 (but not including any waste the regulation of which under the Solid Waste Disposal Act, 42 U.S.C. §6901, has been suspended by Act of Congress);

(D) any toxic pollutant listed under Section 307(a) of the Federal Water Pollution Control Act, 33 U.S.C. §1317 (a);

(E) any hazardous air pollutant listed under Section 112 of the Clean Air Act, 42 U.S.C. §7412; and

(F) any imminently hazardous chemical substance or mixture with respect to which the Administrator has taken action pursuant to Section 7 of the Toxic Substances Control Act, 15 U.S.C. §2606. The term does not include petroleum, including crude oil or any fraction thereof which is not otherwise specifically listed or designated as a hazardous substance under subparagraphs (A) through (F), and the term does not include natural gas, natural gas liquids, liquefied natural gas, or synthetic gas usable for fuel (or mixtures of natural gas and such synthetic gas).[376]

The EPA has issued regulations which delineate the substances names in the statutes referred to in Section 9601(14).[377] The regulations further clarify that, although unlisted, any solid waste under RCRA which exhibits the characteristics identified in RCRA regulations is a hazardous waste under CERCLA (these are referred to as "unlisted hazardous substances" in the regulations).[378] Although the definition encompasses a vast number of substances, it excludes petroleum and natural gas products.[379] In *A&W*

372. 42 U.S.C. §9601(9).
373. 880 F.2d at 1551.
374. 667 F. Supp. 1298, 1305 (E.D. Miss. 1987), *amended by* 1991 U.S. Dist. LEXIS 66 (E.D. Mo. Jan. 3, 1991).
375. *See* United States v. Vertac Chem. Corp., 364 F. Supp. 2d 941, 958-60 (E.D. Ark. 2005); United States v. Conservation Chem. Co., 619 F. Supp. 162, 185 (W.D. Mo. 1985); *see also* United States v. JG-24, Inc., 478 F.3d 28, 30 (1st Cir. 2007) (conviction based on release of chemicals from deteriorating metal drums).
376. 42 U.S.C. §9601(14). As is apparent from the definition, the term "hazardous substances" as used in CERCLA is much broader than, and inclusive of, hazardous substances as that term is defined in the CWA. Because discharges of hazardous substances are comprehensively addressed by CERCLA, federal enforcement efforts related to notification of discharges under Section 311, 33 U.S.C. §1321, of the CWA tend to focus on discharges of oil vice hazardous substances.
377. 40 C.F.R. §302.1.
378. *Id.* §302.4(b).
379. 42 U.S.C. §9601(14).

Smelter & Refiners, Inc. v. Clinton, the Ninth Circuit stated that "CERCLA seems to give the [EPA] carte blanche to hold liable anyone who disposes of just about anything."[380]

Many states have statues similar to CERCLA, and these statutes may list some substances as hazardous that CERCLA does not. Therefore, it is important for counsel to review the relevant state provisions before determining a substance is not hazardous and, therefore, not subject to reporting requirements.

5. Released in Reportable Quantity Into Environment

A "release" is "any spilling, leaking, pumping, pouring, emitting, emptying, discharging, injecting, escaping, leaching, dumping, or disposing into the environment (including the abandonment or discarding of barrels, containers, and other closed receptacles containing any hazardous substance or pollutant or contaminant)."[381] Although broadly defined, a release must be reported only when the amount released exceeds a certain amount, the "reportable quantity," and that release is "into the environment." In addition, certain releases are excluded from the reporting requirement, including releases which expose only people indoors in the workplace, emissions from automobiles, releases from naturally occurring radionuclides resulting from mining and excavation activities, and releases resulting from the normal application of fertilizer.[382] In the late 1980s, EPA issued a final rule which interpreted "release" as "the placement of a substance into a facility that is exposed to the environment."[383] In *Fertilizer Inst. v. EPA,* the D.C. Circuit struck down that interpretation and held that an actual release, rather than a threatened release, into the environment must occur to trigger the reporting requirements.[384] Therefore, placing a substance in an unenclosed container does not, by itself, constitute a release.

a. Reportable Quantity

The default reportable quantity for a hazardous substance is one pound, unless superseded by regulations promulgated by EPA.[385] The agency has issued regulations that list the reportable quantity for every regulated substance under CERCLA.[386] Unlisted hazardous substances have the reportable quantity of 100 pounds, unless they exhibit toxicity as defined in EPA's regulations.[387] For wastes that exhibit toxicity, the reportable quantity is the amount listed in the regulations for the contaminant on which the characteristic of toxicity is based.[388] The regulations further clarify that the reportable quantity applies to the waste itself, not merely to the toxic contaminant.[389] The person in charge must immediately report as soon as that person has knowledge of any release of a hazardous substance equal to or exceeding a reportable quantity determined in any 24-hour period.[390]

CERCLA regulations also clarify what substance is relevant when measuring the reportable quantity of a release of mixtures or solutions. If the quantity of all the hazardous constituents of the mixture is known, notification is required where the reportable quantity of any hazardous constituent is released.[391] If the quantity of the hazardous constituent in the mixture is unknown, notification is required where the total amount of the mixture or solution released equals or exceeds the reportable quantity for the hazardous constituent with the lowest reportable quantity.[392] For example, where there has been a release of a substance contaminated with chemical X, and the amount of chemical in the mixture cannot be determined, the

380. A&W Smelter and Refiners, Inc. v. Clinton, 146 F.3d 1107, 1110 (9th Cir. 1998).
381. *Id.* §9601(22).
382. *Id.*
383. 54 Fed. Reg. 22524 (May 24, 1989)
384. 935 F.2d 1303 (D.C. Cir. 1991).
385. 40 C.F.R. §302.5.
386. *Id.* §302.4.
387. *Id.* §302.5(b).
388. *Id.*
389. *Id.*
390. *Id.* §302.6.
391. *Id.* §302.6(b).
392. *Id.*

person in charge is required to report a release if the total amount of substance released exceeds the reportable quantity listed for chemical X.

Notably, in a relatively recent civil action, a court found that chicken production farms that released ammonia from chicken droppings were not exempt from the reporting requirements of CERCLA, despite the fact that there was no generally accepted methodology or model for estimating the amount of ammonia those facilities emit.[393]

b. Environment

Under CERCLA, a person in charge must report only releases "into the environment." "Environment" is defined broadly and includes navigable waters, contiguous zone and EEZ of the United States, and " . . . any other surface water, ground water, drinking water supply, land surface or subsurface strata, or ambient air within the United States or under the jurisdiction of the United States.[394] Releases that occur and are confined indoors are not considered reportable releases.

6. Passive Migration

One problematic and controversial question that has arisen under CERCLA is whether the discovery of historical soil or groundwater contamination constitutes a "release" of hazardous substances. In other words, can an owner be held liable totally under CERCLA due to passive migration of the contaminant through the soil or groundwater even though he was not responsible for the original release? Although the issue has not been addressed in the release-reporting context, courts have considered passive migration in connection with cleanup liability.

In addressing the passive migration issue, courts have distinguished in the civil context between a "release" and a "disposal."[395] Most of these cases consider the imposition of liability on an interim owner, or one who bought the property after the initial disposal but before the contamination was found. In these cases, the meaning of "disposal" is key because CERCLA imposes civil liability on those who owned the property at the time of disposal. If passive migration is considered a disposal under CERCLA, the interim owner would become an original owner subject to liability. Most courts have held that interim owners are not liable for passive migration because "disposal" requires an affirmative act.[396] However, several of these cases indicated that the definition of "release" is broader than disposal and may include passive migration.

One court considered whether current owners of contaminated land can be liable for passive migration of contaminants from a neighboring property. Unlike prior owners, disposal is not a factor in determining the liability of current owners. Rather, liability attaches to the current owner of a facility from which there is a release or a threatened release. Looking to the interim owner cases for guidance, the court held that a "release" encompasses the passive migration of a contaminant.[397]

These cases do not address how the issue should be handled in the release-reporting context. However, because reporting of newly discovered historical contamination only furthers the reporting requirement's purpose to protect the public and the environment by alerting the government to hazardous contamination, and given the courts' broad interpretation of a "release" on the civil liability side, it would be prudent for the owner to report historical contamination as soon as it is discovered. Moreover, the government may

393. Sierra Club, Inc. v. Tyson Foods, Inc., 299 F. Supp. 2d 693, 706 (W.D. Ky. 2003).

394. 42 U.S.C. §9601(8).

395. *See generally* Khara Coleman, Disposing of Leaks and Spills: Passive Disposal of Hazardous Wastes Under CERCLA, 80 Wash. U. L.Q. 945 (2002).

396. *See* Carson Harbor Vill., Ltd. v. Unocal Corp., 270 F.3d 863, 878-79 (9th Cir. 2001), *cert. denied*, 535 U.S. 971 (2002); *see also* Bob's Beverage, Inc. v. Acme, Inc., 264 F.3d 692, 697-98 (6th Cir. 2001) (explaining "disposal" did not occur because contamination was caused by passive migration of hazardous materials present in environment before defendant took any action); ABB Indus. Sys., Inc. v. Prime Tech., Inc., 120 F.3d 351, 358 (2d Cir. 1997), *motion denied*, 32 F. Supp. 2d 38 (D. Conn. 1998); United States v. CDMG Realty Co., 96 F.3d 706 (3d Cir. 1996). Although other cases have held interim owners liable for passive migration, they have done so only in cases where passive leaching occurred from existing equipment. For example, in *Nurad, Inc. v. William E. Hooper & Sons Co.*, 966 F.2d 837 (4th Cir. 1992), *cert. denied*, 506 U.S. 940 (1992), the court found an interim owner liable for passive migration of hazardous substances from an underground storage tank because he had a duty to maintain or inspect the tank for ongoing leaks. *See also* Crofton Ventures Ltd. P'ship v. G&H P'ship, 258 F.3d 292, 297 (4th Cir. 2001).

397. Castaic Lake Water Agency v. Whittaker Corp., 272 F. Supp. 2d 1053, 1076-77 (C.D. Cal. 2003).

take the position that failure to report is negligence or even an affirmative act. If criminal charges were brought based on a release through passive migration, one defense may be that there was no reportable quantity released within the 24-hour time frame.

7. Failure to Notify Immediately

The person in charge of the facility or vessel must report the release of hazardous substance to the National Response Center immediately after obtaining the knowledge that a release of a hazardous substance in a reportable quantity has occurred.[398] The National Response Center operates 24 hours a day, 7 days a week, 365 days a year. A release is most likely also subject to state or local reporting requirements under EPCRA, discussed below.

There are no court cases interpreting what is meant by the term "immediately." Based on EPA administrative enforcement action, whether a report was done immediately is a case-by-case determination.[399] Legislative history regarding this requirement indicates that delays in notification "should not exceed 15 minutes after the person in charge has knowledge of the release, and 'immediate notification' requires shorter delays whenever practicable."[400] Thus, in In re Genicom Corp., the EPA Environmental Appeals Board determined a report two hours after the person in charge had acquired knowledge of the release of a hazardous substance in a reportable quantity was not "immediate."[401] Similarly, in In re United States Leather, Inc., an EPA Administrative Law Judge determined that notification four hours after a spill was not immediate.[402]

7. Knowledge of Release

"Knowledge," under CERCLA, means knowledge that one is doing the statutorily prescribed act, not knowledge that the statute or potential health hazards exist.[403] Therefore, to prove knowledge, the government must show only that the defendant knew or should have known of the release. The government may meet this burden by providing evidence from which the jury can infer knowledge of the release. For example, in *Greer*, there was no evidence that the owner and operator directly told the plant manager to dump the hazardous waste at issue.[404] Rather, he had instructed the plant manager to "handle" the waste. Testimony from other employees showed that the defendant had a practice of dumping wastes illegally when there was a shortage of storage space. The court found this evidence sufficient to support the conviction. Similarly, in *United States v. Catucci*, the defendant had been informed that lawful disposal of two PCB-laden transformers would cost between $8,000 and $10,000 and had arranged for the transformers to be disposed of by volunteers willing to remove the transformers for their scrap value.[405] The court held that such evidence was sufficient to infer the defendant knew the transformers would be disposed of illegally.[406]

8. Submitting False or Misleading Information

Any person who knowingly submits false or misleading information as part of a notification of release or claim for reimbursement is also subject to criminal liability under CERCLA. The statute authorizes sanctions for submitting false or misleading notifications regarding the release of a hazardous substance[407] and

398. The toll-free number of the National Response Center is (800) 424-8802; in Washington, D.C., the number is (202) 267-2675. Reports may also be made online at http://www.nrc.uscg.mil/.
399. *See* In re Nova Chemicals, Inc., Docket No. CERCLA-01-2005-0051 (EPA ALJ, Aug. 2, 2006).
400. Senate Comm. on Environment and Public Works, Superfund Amendments and Reauthorization Act of 1986, S. Rep. No. 99-11, 99th Cong. (1985) at 9.
401. 4 E.A.D. 426 (EAB 1992).
402. Docket No. EPCRA-7-99-0048 (EPA ALJ, February 23, 2000).
403. United States v. Buckley, 934 F.2d 84, 88 (6th Cir. 1991); *see also* United States v. Laughlin, 10 F.3d 961, 966 (2d Cir. 1993) *cert. denied sub nom.*, Goldman v. United States, 511 U.S. 1071 (1994).
404. 850 F.2d 1447 (11th Cir. 1988).
405. 55 F.3d 15 (1st Cir. 1995).
406. *Id.* at 17-18.
407. 42 U.S.C. §9603(b).

for giving or causing to be given any false information as part of a claim for reimbursement of costs associated with cleanup.[408]

10. Failure to Notify of Hazardous Facility

Owners, operators, and transporters must notify the EPA of any facility that treats or has treated, stored, or disposed of hazardous substances, unless that facility is permitted under the RCRA. Failure to do so subjects that person to a maximum fine of $10,000 and/or up to one year in prison. The reporting requirements include: "the location, title, or condition of a facility; and the identity, characteristics, quantity, origin, or condition (including containerization and previous treatment) of any hazardous substances contained or deposited in a facility."[409]

11. Falsification or Destruction of Records

Persons required to provide notification of unpermitted facilities also are required to keep records pertaining to those facilities.[410] Such records should identify the substances and amount of substances stored at the site and should be maintained for fifty years. CERCLA provides for criminal sanctions against persons who knowingly "destroy, mutilate, erase, dispose of, conceal, or otherwise render unavailable or unreadable or falsify" such records.[411]

12. Disclosure of Confidential Information

Under CERCLA, EPA may require additional information relevant to reported releases. Such information is made available to the public unless the information is shown to be confidential. CERCLA and EPCRA make it unlawful for any person to disclose such confidential information.[412]

C. Title III of the Emergency Planning and Community Right-To-Know Act

Title III of the Emergency Planning and Community Right-To-Know Act was enacted as part of the Superfund Amendment and Reauthorization Act of 1986. Like CERCLA, it requires emergency notification of leaks, spills, and other releases of hazardous substances into the environment.[413] Although similar to the notification requirements under CERCLA, there are a few key differences.

First, Title III applies only to owners or operators of facilities that produce, use, or store hazardous substances, rather than to "any person in charge." Second, EPCRA requires notification for not only substances subject to CERCLA reporting but also for materials designated as extremely hazardous substances (EHS).[414] Third, notification must be made to the relevant local emergency planning committee and the state emergency response commission, not to the National Response Center.[415] Finally, a criminal conviction for failure to report under EPCRA requires specific intent, or knowing and willful failure to provide notice, not general knowledge.[416]

Any notice provided pursuant to EPCRA should contain the following information:

- The chemical name or identity of any substance involved in the release;
- Whether the substance is an EHS;

---

408. *Id.* §9612(b)(1).
409. *Id.* §9603(c).
410. *Id.* §9603(d)(1).
411. *Id.* §9603(d)(2).
412. *Id.* §9604(e).
413. *Id.* §11045.
414. *See id.* §11004.
415. *Id.* If the release occurs during transportation, the notice requirements can be satisfied by dialing 911 and providing the relevant information. *Id.* §11004(b).
416. *Id.* §11045(b)(4).

- An estimate of the quantity of substance released;
- The time and duration of the release;
- The environmental medium or media into which the release occurred;
- Any known or anticipated acute or chronic health risks associated with the emergency, as well as advice on medical attention if necessary;
- The proper precautions that should be taken as a result of the release; and
- The name and telephone number of the person to be contacted for further information.[417]

The facility also must supplement the original notice with a written notification as soon as practicable after the release. This follow-up should present and update the original information submitted as well as providing:

- Action taken to respond to and contain the release;
- Any known or anticipated acute or chronic health risks associated with the release; and
- Advice regarding medical attention for exposed individuals.[418]

VI. Toxic Substances Control Act

A. *Introduction*

The Toxic Substance Control Act (TSCA) of 1976[419] was enacted to protect the public and the environment from exposure to numerous chemical substances and mixtures and to fill what were perceived as "gaps" in the regulatory authority provided by other environmental laws. It gives EPA authority to impose reporting, record-keeping, and testing requirements and restrictions on both old and new chemical substances, essentially providing EPA the ability to control the manufacture and use of chemical substances from creation to disposal.[420] The regulations prohibit the manufacture of PCBs and establish complex requirements for the storage, transport, and disposal of existing chemicals. Despite its broad regulatory scope, however, TSCA provides only misdemeanor criminal sanctions for knowing or willful violations of its provisions.

TSCA authorizes EPA to screen existing and new chemicals used in manufacturing and commerce to identify potentially dangerous products or uses that should be subject to federal control. These controls may apply to the production, importation, use, and disposal of chemical substances. The law defines "chemical substance" as "any organic or inorganic substance of a particular molecular identity."[421] Specific chemicals regulated by TSCA include PCBs, asbestos, radon, and lead-based paint. The term "chemical substances" does not include materials regulated under FIFRA (pesticides), the Atomic Energy Act, and the Federal Food, Drug, and Cosmetic Act.[422]

B. *Chemical Testing*

TSCA authorizes EPA to require manufacturers and/or processors to test and report on chemical substances or mixtures whose "manufacture, processing, distribution in commerce, use or disposal" may present an "unreasonable risk of injury to health or the environment," but for which existing data are inadequate to

---

417. *Id.* §11004(b).
418. *Id.* §11004(c).
419. 15 U.S.C. §2601-2697.
420. For example, EPA has adopted extensive regulations governing polychlorinated biphenals (PCBs). The regulations prohibit the manufacture of PCBs and establish complex requirements for the storage, transport, and disposal of existing chemicals. 40 C.F.R. pt. 761.
421. 15 U.S.C. §2602.
422. *Id.*

allow the agency to reasonably determine or predict such effects.[423] The testing rules, found in 40 C.F.R. Part 799, include approximately thirty individual test rule requirements.[424]

C. *Pre-Manufacture Notification and Significant New Use Rules*

TSCA establishes requirements governing pre-manufacture notification and significant new use restrictions. The "pre-manufacture notification" provision directs manufacturers of chemical substances to notify EPA at least ninety days prior to the intended manufacture or import of a "new chemical substance," i.e., a chemical substance that is not on the existing TSCA inventory of chemical substances. TSCA also provides for the compilation of an inventory intended to include all chemical substances currently manufactured in or imported to the United States.[425]

Any chemical substance that is not on the TSCA inventory is considered "new" and thus is subject to the pre-manufacture notification requirements.[426] Subject to certain regulatory exemptions, a new chemical substance cannot be manufactured, processed, imported or sold unless a pre-manufacture notification is submitted to EPA at least 90 days prior to such action.[427]

EPA has 90 days to review a pre-manufacture notification.[428] During this review period, EPA identifies conditions that should be placed on the use of a new chemical substance before it is placed into commerce. There are three possible outcomes to a pre-manufacture notification review:

The agency can take no action. In this case, no restrictions are placed on use of the chemical substance. Almost 90% of reviews end in no action.[429]

EPA can issue a "Section 5(e) Order" to prohibit or limit use of the chemical substance. These orders are issued when EPA determines that there is insufficient information to evaluate the human health and environmental effects of the substance and either (1) the substance may present an unreasonable risk of injury to human health or the environment, or (2) the substance will be produced in substantial quantities and may be anticipated to enter the environment in substantial quantities or that there may be significant or substantial human exposure.[430]

TSCA also gives EPA the authority to (1) identify a "significant new use" of chemical substances that could result in exposures to, or releases of, that chemical which may result in an unreasonable risk to health or the environment, and (2) issue a SNUR for that chemical. A determination by the EPA that a use is "significant" and "new: must be made through agency rulemaking procedures, which include public notice and comment.[431] Manufacturers, importers, and processors of chemical substances to provide notice to EPA of any use of a chemical substance that EPA has determined is a "significant new use."[432] This notification process provides EPA the opportunity to review and, if necessary, place restrictions on the new use. Also, because in practice, any "Section 5(e) Order" is a consent order between EPA and the chemical manufacturer and are binding on only those parties, EPA generally promulgates a SNUR that mimics the consent order to bind other manufacturers, processors, and importers of that chemical to the same terms and conditions.[433]

If EPA determines that the new chemical will present an unreasonable risk of injury to health or the environment, it is required to publish a rule that may prohibit the manufacturing, processing or distri-

423. *Id.* §2603(a).
424. 40 C.F.R. pt. 799.
425. *Id.* §2607(b).
426. *Id.* §2602(9).
427. *Id.* §2604(a)(1); 40 C.F.R. §720.3(v).
428. 15 U.S.C. §2604(g). *See also* U.S. EPA, New Chemicals: Basic Information, http://www.epa.gov/oppt/newchems/pubs/basicinfo.htm (last visited Mar. 12, 2014).
429. U.S. EPA, *New Chemicals: Possible Outcomes of a PMN Review,* http://www.epa.gov/oppt/newchems/pubs/possible.htm (last visited Mar. 12, 2014).
430. *See id. See also* 15 U.S.C. §2604(e).
431. 15 U.S.C. §2604(a)(2).
432. *Id.* §2604(a)(1)(B).
433. EPA may also issue a SNUR in the absence of a Section 5(e) Order if the agency finds that potential new uses differ from those identified in the pre-manufacture notification and could result in increased exposures to, or release of, the substance, and may thereby result in an unreasonable risk to health or the environment. *See* U.S. EPA, *New Chemicals: New Chemical Consent Orders and Significant New Use Rules (SNURs),* http://www.epa.gov/oppt/newchems/pubs/cnosnurs.htm (last visited Mar. 12, 2014).

bution in commerce of the substance; limit the amount of the substance or mixture that may be manufactured, processed or distributed; or take such other actions established by TSCA. Before such a rule is promulgated, EPA may (1) issue an immediately effective proposed rule that places appropriate restrictions on the substance, or (2) issue a proposed order or apply to the U.S. District Court for an injunction to prohibit the substance completely.[434]

D. Substantive Control Rules

EPA also has the broad authority to regulate chemical substances to protect against an "unreasonable risk of injury to health or the environment." If EPA finds that there is a reasonable basis to conclude that manufacture, processing, distribution in commerce, use or disposal of a chemical substance or mixture will present an unreasonable risk of injury to health or environment, it may issue a rule controlling such risks "using the least burdensome requirements."[435] When issuing such a rule, EPA must consider and publish a statement with respect to:

(1) The effects of the chemical substance on health and the magnitude of the exposure of human beings to such substance;

(2) The effect of the chemical substance of the environment and the magnitude of the exposure of the environment to such substance;

(3) The benefits of the chemical substance for various uses and the availability of substitutes for such uses; and

(4) The reasonable ascertainable economic consequences of the rule, after consideration of the effect on the national economy, small business, technological innovation, the environment, and public health.[436]

Rules issued can address all aspects of a chemical's manufacture or import, processing, distribution in commerce, use and disposal. Currently, there are only a few substances subject to such rules: metal-working fluids, PCBs, fully halogenated chlorofluoroalkanes, dioxin, hexavalent chromium, and asbestos.

E. Imminent Hazard Authority

EPA has the authority to take emergency action through the U.S. District Courts to control an "imminently hazardous chemical substance or mixture." A chemical is "imminently hazardous" if it presents an imminent and unreasonable risk of serious or widespread injury to health or the environment.[437] The federal district court may grant any relief "as may be necessary to protect health or the environment from [an] unreasonable risk associated with the chemical substance, mixture, or article" involved in such action. Authorized remedies include seizure of any imminently hazardous chemical substance, mixture, or article.[438]

F. Reporting and Recordkeeping Requirements

"Preliminary assessment information rules" that apply to manufacturers or importers of specifically listed chemical substances. These rules require manufacturers or importers to submit a one-time report containing basic information about the chemical substance.[439] This report must address the quantities of chemical substance manufactured or imported, used as a reactant or in industrial and consumer products, or lost to

434. 15 U.S.C. §2604(f).
435. *Id.* §2605(a).
436. *Id.* §2605(c).
437. *Id.* §2606(f).
438. *Id.* §2606(b).
439. *Id.* §2607. *See* 40 C.F.R. Part 712.

the environment. It also must include information on worker exposure to such substance. EPA periodically updates the list of chemical substances subject to these rules.[440]

The "chemical data reporting rule" (formerly known as the inventory update rule). This rule requires any facility that manufactures or imports more than 25,000 pounds of a chemical substance on the TSCA Inventory to submit data every four years on its production, volume, plant site, and site-limited status of that substance.[441] Facilities that manufacture or import more than 100,000 pounds of a chemical substance must report additional downstream use and exposure information.

Any person who manufactures or distributes into commerce a chemical substance for a commercial purpose must immediately submit to EPA any "information which reasonably supports the conclusion that such substance or mixture presents a substantial risk of injury to health or the environment."[442] This requirement encompasses human health and environmental effects, including widespread and previously unsuspected environmental contamination which has the potential for widespread exposure to human or non-human organisms. Persons who have "actual knowledge" that EPA "has been adequately informed of such information" are exempt from the notification.[443]

Manufacturers, importers, and processors of chemical substances must keep records of "significant adverse reactions" to health or the environment where such reactions are alleged to have been caused by the chemical substance including allegations from any source, including customers, employees, or claims in lawsuits.[444] However, regulated entities are not required to keep comparable records for allegations involving "known human effects."[445] Allegations made may trigger an obligation under the substantial risk reporting provisions.

G. *Export and Import Notifications*

Persons must notify EPA prior to exporting any chemical substances that are subject to specific TSCA requirements.[446] The import of any chemical substance or mixture, or any article containing a chemical substance or mixture, into the United States is prohibited if it fails to comply with a rule in effect under TSCA or if it is offered for entry in violation of orders issued by the agency or a U.S. District Court under sections 2604, 2605, or 2606.[447]

H. *Regulation of PCBs*

Under TSCA, EPA is required specifically to regulate the manufacture, distribution, use, and disposal of PCBs.[448] EPA's implementing regulations prohibit the manufacture, distribution, and use of PCBs except where used in a completely enclosed manner.[449] The regulations also impose recordkeeping, marking, storage, treatment, and disposal requirements.

EPA's PCB rules generally apply to concentrations of 50 parts per million or greater. In *United States v. Ward*,[450] the defendants were convicted of unlawful disposal of oil laced with PCBs. In affirming the conviction, the court of appeals found that evidence consisting of chemical analyses of soil samples indicating a wide range of levels of PCB contamination was sufficient to support a jury finding that the oil sprayed onto the soil had contained the requisite parts per million of PCBs.

---

440. *Id.* §2607(a)(2).
441. 15 U.S.C. §2607(a); 40 C.F.R. Part 704.
442. 15 U.S.C. §2607(a).
443. *Id.* §2607(e).
444. *Id.* §2607(c).
445. 40 C.F.R. §717.12(b).
446. 15 U.S.C. §2611.
447. *Id.* §2612.
448. *Id.* §2605(e).
449. 40 C.F.R. pt. 761.
450. 676 F.2d 94 (4th Cir. 1982), *cert. denied*, 459 U.S. 835 (1982).

I. Special Titles

TSCA also contains several special titles that regulate certain specific substances, including asbestos, lead, and radon.[451] Subchapter II establishes the Asbestos Hazard Emergency Response Act, and Subchapter III creates a program for indoor radon abatement.

J. Criminal Liability Under TSCA

TSCA makes it a misdemeanor for a person to knowingly or willfully violate any of TSCA's provisions or EPA's implementing regulations.[452] A person convicted under this provision is subject to a fine of not more than $25,000 for each day of violation and/or imprisonment of not more than one year.[453]

K. Statutory Prohibitions

Under TSCA, it is unlawful for any person to:

(1) fail or refuse to comply with (a) any rule promulgated or order issued by EPA under Section 2603; (b) any requirement prescribed by Section 2604 or 2605; (c) any rule promulgated or order issued by EPA under section 2604 or 2605; or (d) any requirement of the Asbestos Hazard Emergency Response Act or any rule or order promulgated by EPA under that Act;

(2) use for commercial purposes a chemical substance or mixture which such person knew or had reason to know was manufactured, processed, or distributed in commerce in violation of Section 2604 or 2605; a rule or order issued by EPA under Section 2604 or 2605; or an order issued by the U.S. District Court in action brought under Section 2604 or 2606;

(3) fail or refuse to (a) establish or maintain records; (b) submit reports, notices, or other information, or (c) permit access to or copying of records, as required by TSCA or an EPA implementing rule; or

(4) fail or refuse to permit entry or inspection as required by Section 2610.[454]

L. Elements of Criminal Liability

Criminal liability for violations of TSCA attaches only where those violations are "knowing" or "willful."[455] The prosecution may satisfy the "knowledge" element by showing that the defendant knew it was doing the statutorily prescribed act, and need not show that the defendant knew that the statute or its requirements exist. The government may meet its burden by providing evidence from which the jury can infer knowledge of the release. For example, in *United States v. Catucci*,[456] the defendant had been informed that it would cost between $8,000 and $10,000 for the lawful disposal of two PCB-laden transformers. Despite this knowledge, he arranged for the transformers to be disposed of by volunteers willing to remove the transformers for their scrap value. The court held that such evidence was sufficient for the jury to infer that the defendant knew the transformers would be disposed of illegally.

In *United States v. Pacific Hide & Fur Depot, Inc.*,[457] the corporate owner of a scrap metal yard and its manager were indicted for the illegal disposal of capacitors that contained PCBs. During the trial, the defendants argued that they did not know the capacitor contained PCBs. The government attempted to prove that they had avoided this knowledge deliberately, constituting willful blindness to the nature of the

451. *See* 15 U.S.C. §§2641-2656 (asbestos); §§2661-2671 (radon); §§2681-2692 (lead).
452. *Id.* §2615(b).
453. *Id.*
454. *Id.* §2614. Under §2610, EPA has the authority to enter and inspect premises and to subpoena documents. This authority has been interpreted by the courts to apply broadly. *See* EPA v. Alyeska Pipeline Serv. Co., 836 F.2d 443 (9th Cir. 1988) (a subpoena does not need to relate to a specific violation; rather, it need only be relevant to a lawful purpose under TSCA).
455. 15 U.S.C. §2615(b).
456. 55 F.3d 15, 17-18 (1st Cir. 1995).
457. 768 F.2d 1096 (9th Cir. 1985).

material they were discarding. The jury found the defendants guilty, but the court of appeals reversed on the ground that the evidence was insufficient to support the government's "deliberate avoidance" theory. Thus, the court held that the jury instruction regarding this theory was improper, as it might have implied the defendants had the requisite degree of knowledge.[458]

M. *TSCA Criminal Enforcement*

TSCA does not displace the requirements of other environmental statutes. It therefore is possible that actions constituting a violation of TSCA's provisions also will violate the provisions of other environmental laws, such as CERCLA or RCRA. Because of this overlap, the government may choose to prosecute under several different statutes in the same action. Most criminal actions prosecuted under TSCA have involved violations of the PCB and asbestos provisions.[459] Criminal indictments for violations of TSCA are not common and are usually brought as part of larger criminal actions charging violations of other environmental statutes.

VII. Federal Insecticide, Fungicide, and Rodenticide Act

The Federal Insecticide, Fungicide and Rodenticide Act (FIFRA)[460] establishes the federal program that regulates commerce in and use of pesticides. As originally enacted, the law was aimed primarily at protecting consumers from ineffective products and deceptive labeling. Through a series of amendments over the last fifty years, FIFRA now mandates that EPA regulate the use and sale of pesticides to protect human health and preserve the environment.

The FIFRA regulatory program is complex and contains a long list of prohibited acts potentially subject to criminal sanctions. The primary requirement under FIFRA is that all pesticides be registered by EPA before they are produced and sold. This registration process enables EPA to determine the manufacturing and the terms of use and conditions. FIRFA regulations also establish packaging and labeling requirements for pesticides, experimental use permit provisions, record-keeping obligations and inspection authority, guidance for safe handling and disposal of pesticides, and import/export requirements, and provide for protection of trade secrets.

FIFRA distinguishes among various types of parties associated with pesticide production, distribution, and use, and the statute provides different criminal penalty levels for different parties. As the most practical point of control and enforcement, the most burdensome requirements fall upon pesticide manufactures and producers. Commercial applicators are subject to a higher standard of care than private applicators. With one exception, violations of FIFRA are punishable only as misdemeanors. Accordingly, criminal prosecutions for violation of FIFRA most commonly are brought alongside statues or Title 18 charges.

A. *Definition of "Pesticide"*

Under Section 2(u) of FIFRA, a "pesticide" is "any substance or mixture of substances intended for preventing, destroying, repelling, or mitigating any pest" and "any substance or mixture of substance intended for use as a plant regulator, defoliant, or desiccant . . .."[461] A "pest" is further defined as:

- Any insect, rodent, nematode, fungus, weed, or

---

458. A "deliberate avoidance instruction" is properly given only when a defendant claims lack of guilty knowledge and the proof at trial supports an inference of deliberate ignorance. *See id.* at 1098.

459. *See, e.g.,* United States v. HSKM, Inc., Crim. No. 08-20365 (E.D. Mich. 2008) (Co. pled guilty to violation of TSCA for abandoning a PCB-containing transformer at a closed facility after company went out of business and was sentenced to pay $1.7 million in restitution and serve one year of probation.).

460. 7 U.S.C. §136.

461. *Id.* §136(u).

- Any other form of terrestrial or aquatic plant or animal life or virus, bacteria, or other micro-organism (except viruses, bacteria, or other micro-organisms on or living in man or other living animals) which the [EPA] Administrator declares to be a pest under section 25(c)(1) [of FIFRA].[462]

Thus, FIFRA defines "pesticide" in terms of the intended use of a product rather than the chemical characteristics of the substance. EPA has adopted regulations that define pesticide as "any substance (or mixture of substances) intended for a pesticidal purpose."[463] The regulations list three factors that must be considered when determining whether a substance is "intended for a pesticidal purpose."

- Whether the person who distributes or sells the substance claims that it has a pesticidal purpose or use or contains an active ingredient that can be used to manufacture a pesticide;
- Whether the substance contains an active ingredient and has no commercially valuable use other than for a pesticidal purpose or use or for the manufacture of a pesticide; and
- Whether the person who distributes or sells the substance has actual or constructive knowledge that the substance will be used or is intended for use for a pesticidal purpose.[464]

These factors primarily take the distributor's intent into account, rather than the user's. EPA applies an objective standard when determining intent, i.e., can the producer expect a reasonable consumer to use the product against pests?[465]

EPA and the Food and Drug Administration (FDA) have entered into a Memorandum of Agreement and Memorandum of Understanding to delineate the primary jurisdiction of each agency.[466] In general, EPA exercises authority over disinfectants and sanitizers that do not claim disease controlling properties. FDA, on the other hand, has primary authority over products that control or relieve the effects of parasites, insect bites, diaper rash, athlete's foot, and certain animal diseases. Certain products, such as microbiocides used in paper and other packaging that comes into contact with food and products intended to sanitize food contact surfaces, may require the approval of both agencies.[467]

B. *Registration Requirement*

A core component of FIFRA is the requirement that all pesticides must be registered with EPA.[468] Through the registration process, EPA is able to determine appropriate conditions for the manufacture, distribution, and use of the pesticide. Once these conditions are established, it is unlawful for any reason to use the pesticide in a manner that is not in accordance with those conditions.[469] After a pesticide is registered, the registrant is required to notify EPA of any new facts concerning adverse environmental effects.[470] EPA also must also review periodically pesticide registrations.

A registrant is required to submit to EPA information describing the pesticide, all active ingredients, testing information that demonstrates the pesticide's efficacy and performance, a description of its effects, a proposed label, and other information required under EPA regulations.[471] FIFRA provides that EPA *shall* register a pesticide if it determines that the product works as claimed, the materials submitted in conjunction with its registration application comply with FIFRA requirements, and the expected use of the pes-

---

462. *Id.* §136(t).
463. 40 C.F.R. §152.12.
464. *Id.* §152.12.
465. *See* Pesticide Registration Procedures, Pesticide Data Requirements, 53 Fed. Reg. 15952, 15954 (May 4, 1988); 40 C.F.R. §152.15(c).
466. Memorandum of Understanding Between the Environmental Protection Agency and the Food and Drug Administration, Drug/Pesticide Products for Use on or in Animals, 48 Fed. Reg. 22799 (May 20, 1983); Enforcement of the Federal Insecticide, Fungicide and Rodenticide Act, Registration, Reregistration and Classification Procedures, 44 Fed. Reg. 63749 (Nov. 5, 1979) (EPA final regulation to clarify its policy regarding the registration of pesticide products); Agreement Between Department of Health, Education and Welfare and Environmental Protection Agency, Notice Regarding Matter of Mutual Responsibility, Amendment, 38 Fed. Reg. 24233 (Sept. 6, 1973); Agreement Between Department of Health, Education and Welfare and Environmental Protection Agency, Notice Regarding Matters of Mutual Responsibility, 36 Fed. Reg. 24234 (Dec. 22, 1971) (Memorandum of Agreement).
467. *See* 21 C.F.R. §178.1010; 21 C.F.R. pt. 176; 21 U.S.C. §360(k); 21 C.F.R. §173.320.
468. 7 U.S.C. §136a.
469. *Id.* §136j(a)(1).
470. *Id.* §136d(a)(2).
471. 40 C.F.R. pt. 152.

ticide will not cause unreasonable environmental harm.[472] The statute gives EPA the authority to protect public health and the environment by refusing or placing restrictions on registration of the product. In evaluating what harm is deemed unreasonable, FIFRA applies a balancing test that incorporates the risks and benefits to public health, as well as the risks of the pesticide versus the risks of the pests controlled by the pesticide.[473]

A pesticide registration is very specific and is not valid for all uses of a particular product. Each registration specifies which crops and/or sites, insects, or other pests to which it may be applied, and each use must be supported by research data. Conditional registration may be given in certain circumstances while EPA obtains the data needed to perform a full analysis of the product.

Facilities that produce or manufacture pesticides also must be registered with EPA.[474] Registered establishments must file annual reports that describe the types and amounts of the pesticides manufactured or produced. These registrations are valid for five years and are subject to renewal at the request of the registrant.

C. *Trade Secrets and Data Compensation*

FIFRA provides protection for trade secrets and commercial and financial information obtained by EPA through the required registration submissions.[475] When submitting this information to EPA, the applicant must indicate clearly the information for which a confidentiality claim is being made. EPA may determine that the information is not entitled to confidential treatment but may not publically release the information before notifying the registrant. The applicant then has 30 days to file an action in federal court seeking protection of the information.

D. *Experimental Use Permits*

FIFRA recognizes that in order to register a pesticide, an applicant first may need to test an unregistered substance to acquire the data needed for a registration application. In general, if the applicant performs testing within certain narrow limitations, no registration is required. However, for more extensive testing, FIFRA provides for the issuance of an Experimental Use Permit, which is generally valid for one year. EPA may place conditions on this permit in any manner determined necessary to protect public health and the environment.[476]

E. *EPA Inspections and Recordkeeping Requirements*

All producers of pesticides must maintain records:

- EPA registration number and batch identification information;
- Brand names and quantities of products and devices produced;
- All ingredients used in producing pesticides;
- Pesticide shipment and transfer information;
- Pesticides in inventory;
- Advertisement information;
- Guarantees that the producer has given the pesticide was lawfully registered at the time of sale;
- Exported pesticides;

472. 7 U.S.C. §136a(c)(5).
473. *Id.* §136(bb).
474. *Id.* §136a(c)(5)(C).
475. *Id.* §136h.
476. *Id.* §136(c); 40 C.F.R. pt. 172.

- Disposal of pesticides;
- Records of any relevant tests conducted on humans; and
- Pesticide research data and summaries.[477]

Significant recordkeeping requirements also are imposed on distributors, dealers, and sellers. The producer or other relevant party must allow EPA employees or their representatives to inspect and copy these records upon request.[478] When requesting access to records, the EPA employee or representative must present appropriate credentials and a written statement setting forth the reason for the inspection.

F. *Safe-Handling Disposal Restrictions*

FIFRA requires any person who distributes or sells any canceled or suspended pesticide (including producers, exporters, registrants, application for registration, and commercial applicators) to notify EPA and the appropriate state and/or local officials if he or she possesses such a pesticide.[479] This notice must include the quantity possessed and the location where it is stored. EPA may allow existing stocks of a cancelled pesticide to be sold and used.[480] EPA also may restrict the continued use of the cancelled pesticide by:

- Use of cancellation or suspension orders[481];
- Issuance of a "stop salc, use, or removal" order to a person who owns, controls, or has custody of the pesticide[482];
- Issuance of requirements and procedures for persons who store or transport the pesticide[483]; or
- Recalling the pesticide if it is determined to be necessary to protect human health or the environment.[484]

G. *Import and Export Requirements*

Pesticides prepared or packaged according the specifications of a foreign purchaser and intended solely for export to a foreign country generally are exempt from the majority of FIFRA's requirements. For example, registration is not required if the foreign purchaser signs a statement verifying that it is aware that the pesticide is not registered for use and cannot be sold into the United States. However, most labeling requirements remain in force, and the producer remains responsible for registering its establishment with EPA. Certain record-keeping requirements also remain in effect.[485] EPA has issued guidance on pesticide exports that discusses labeling requirements and purchaser acknowledgement statements.[486]

Under FIFRA, the Secretary of the Treasury, working together with the EPA Administrator, is responsible for monitoring imports of pesticides to the United States.[487] The Customs and Border Protection (CBP) allows imports of pesticides only if they are registered under FIFRA. Unregistered pesticide devices may be imported without FIFRA registration, but they may not have any misleading labels or graphics.[488]

477. 7 U.S.C. §136f(a); 40 C.F.R. §169.2.
478. 7 U.S.C. §136f(b).
479. *Id.* §136d(g)(1).
480. *Id.* §136(d)(a)(1).
481. *Id.*
482. *Id.* §136k(a).
483. *Id.* §136q(a)(2).
484. *Id.* §136q(b)(1).
485. *Id.* §136o(a).
486. Statement of Enforcement Policies and Interpretations, 40 C.F.R. pt. 168.
487. 7 U.S.C. §136o(c).
488. 19 C.F.R. §12.111.

H. *FIFRA Criminal Sanctions*

1. Unlawful Acts

7 U.S.C. §136j(a)(1) of FIFRA makes it unlawful for any person to distribute or sell:

- an unregistered, cancelled, or suspended pesticide;
- a registered pesticide using claims that substantially differ from the claims made in the registration statement;
- a pesticide with a different composition than described in the registration statement;
- a pesticide that has not been colored or discolored pursuant to the requirements of FIFRA;
- an adulterated or misbranded pesticide; or
- a misbranded device.

In addition, Section 136j(a)(2) makes it unlawful for any person to:

- detach, alter, deface, or destroy the label;
- refuse to prepare, maintain or submit any required records or reports, or to allow entry, inspection, copying of records, or sampling authorized under FIFRA;
- give a false guaranty or undertaking;
- reveal or use to one's own advantage any confidential information submitted under the requirements of FIFRA;
- misadvertise a restricted use pesticide;
- distribute, sell, make available for use, or use any registered pesticide for a purpose not in accordance with its restrictions;
- use any registered pesticide in a manner inconsistent with its labeling;
- use any pesticide which is under an experimental use permit contrary to the provisions of such permit;
- violate any "stop sale" order;
- violate any suspension order;
- violate any cancellation order;
- produce a pesticide in violation of the registration requirements;
- knowingly falsify any part of a registration application, application for experimental use permit, or any information, records, or reports required to be filed under FIFRA;
- fail to file any required report;
- add any substance to or take any substance from any pesticide "in a manner that may defeat the purpose" of FIFRA;
- use any pesticide in tests on human beings without fully informing and obtaining consent from the human beings;
- falsify any information relating to the testing of any pesticide submitted to the EPA Administrator;
- submitting false data in support of a registration; or
- violate any regulation issued concerning sale, distribution, and use of unregistered pesticides or regulation concerning storage, disposal, transportation, and recall or pesticides.

The actions enumerated in Section 136j are not a comprehensive listing of all unlawful actions under FIFRA. Rather, a violation of any provision found in FIFRA could subject the offender to criminal prosecution. Therefore, it is important for counsel to be familiar with all substantive provisions of FIFRA and the associated regulations. In addition, EPA has issued enforcement guidance that provides useful information about the appropriate enforcement response and civil penalty amounts for FIFRA violations.

2. Criminal Penalties

7 U.S.C. §136*l*(b) establishes criminal penalties for knowing violations of FIFRA's provisions. "Knowing" means acting with the general intent to take an action that is unlawful, rather than the specific intent to violate a provision of FIFRA.[489] The prosecutor need only prove that the defendant knew it was producing, using, or applying a pesticide in particular manner, not that the defendant knew it was breaking the law.

The severity of the applicable criminal penalty depends on the type of party that violated the law. Registrants, applicants for registration, and producers who knowingly violate any section of FIFRA are subject to a fine of not more than $50,000 or imprisonment for not more than one year, or both.[490] Any commercial applicator of a restricted use pesticide, or any person other than a registrant, applicant, or producer who distributes or sells pesticides or devices, who knowingly violates any provision of FIFRA is subject to a fine of no more than $25,000 or imprisonment for not more than one year, or both.[491] A private applicator, on the other hand, is guilty only of a misdemeanor offense and is subject to fines up to $1,000 and imprisonment for not more than 30 days, or both.[492]

In addition to "knowing" violations of the provisions of FIFRA, any person who, with the intent to defraud, uses or reveals information about formulas of products acquired pursuant to the registration requirements is guilty of a felony and is subject to fines up to $10,000 and up to three years, imprisonment.[493]

Section 136*l*(b)(4) establishes that, if an employee, officer, or agent violates FIFRA, the employer or principal also is liable. In *United States v. Corbin Farm Service*,[494] the court considered whether a farmer could be held criminally liable for the actions of a person applying pesticides on his farm. The court found that the defendant farmer was the intended beneficiary of the application and that the applicator was acting for the farmer. The defendant therefore was held criminally liable.

On the other hand, courts have rejected a strict standard of vicarious liability for corporate officers. To obtain a conviction, the prosecution must show that a corporate officer had actual knowledge of the acts found to be illegal. For example, in *United States v. White*,[495] the government argued that a corporate officer in charge of environmental safety should be held criminally liable for the illegal disposal of pesticides by certain company employees. The government contended that the corporate officer was liable as the party responsible for the handling of hazardous wastes at the company. The court found the officer not liable, however, stating that employment in an oversight position does not, by itself, impose criminal liability on the incumbent.

I. Federal and State Enforcement Issues

FIFRA authorizes states to regulated pesticides both under FIFRA itself and under counterpart state pesticide laws. It is critical for counsel to be familiar with both FIFRA and a state's individual pesticide laws because states may lawfully place more restrictive requirements on pesticides than EPA. Pesticides must be registered both by EPA and the state before distribution.

EPA may delegate primary enforcement authority for illegal uses of pesticide to the states and largely has done so. Delegation is mandatory where EPA determines that the state has adequate pesticide laws

489. *See* United States v. Corbin Farm Serv., 444 F. Supp. 510 (E.D. Cal.), *aff'd*, 578 F.2d 259 (9th Cir. 1978).
490. 7 U.S.C. §136*l*(b)(1)(A).
491. *Id.* §136*l*(b)(1)(B).
492. *Id.* §136*l*(b)(2).
493. *Id.* §136*l*(b)(3).
494. 444 F. Supp. 510 (E.D. Cal.), *aff'd*, 578 F.2d 259 (9th Cir. 1978).
495. 766 F. Supp. 873 (E.D. Wash. 1991).

and procedures for enforcing that law.[496] Delegation may also be achieved through a cooperative agreement between EPA and a state.[497] These cooperative agreements reflect EPA's priorities for inspection and enforcement, and the state agrees to undertake a set number of inspections of various types of persons covered by FIFRA each year. Inspections also may be triggered in response to tips at the federal, state, or local level.

Unlike other environmental statutes, EPA does not have the authority to over file a federal civil enforcement action for unlawful uses. Rather, EPA may only initiate an enforcement action when a state fails to take appropriate enforcement action on its own within thirty days following receipt of a complaint or other information alleging or indicating an illegal use in violation of FIFRA.[498] However, this primary enforcement delegation to states may not prevent the U.S. Department of Justice from bringing a criminal proceeding based on the same facts. In *United States v. Orkin Exterminating Co.*,[499] the defendant argued that enforcement authority under FIFRA belonged exclusively to the states and that the U.S. Attorney General could not bring a criminal prosecution. The court rejected this argument and found that DOJ has inherent enforcement authority, particularly in the area of criminal prosecutions.

EPA has primary enforcement authority over non-use violations, i.e., violations concerning the sale or distribution of pesticides. These violations may include, for example, the failure to report a pesticide's unreasonable effects of the environment, distribution of an unregistered pesticide, and fraudulent labeling, advertising, or registration of a pesticide. Non-use violations may be investigated and prosecuted by the federal government without waiting for the state to exercise its enforcement authority.[500]

J. Federal Enforcement Policy

In December 2009, EPA issued the FIFRA Enforcement Response Policy, which in forms the public of the criteria EPA likely will use in determining the appropriate enforcement response and penalty amount for FIFRA violations.[501] Although this policy applies only to the civil regulatory programs, and DOJ is not bound by EPA's enforcement policies when exercising its prosecutorial authority, the policy may provide useful information regarding the focus in FIFRA enforcement. In particular, the Enforcement Response Policy provides a chart delineating how EPA views the relative severity the severity of various offenses.[502]

VIII. Migratory Bird Treaty Act

The Migratory Bird Treaty Act (MBTA) was originally enacted in 1918 to implement a treaty between the United States and Great Britain (acting on behalf of Canada) and subsequently amended to implement similar treaties and conventions between the United States and Japan (1972), Mexico (1936) and Russia (1976) for the protection of migratory birds.[503] In general, the MBTA proscribes the hunting, capture, possession, and sale of more than eight hundred species of birds.[504] The Secretary of the Interior is responsible for its enforcement.

Under the MBTA, is it unlawful to:

- at any time, by any means or in any manner, pursue, hunt, take, capture, kill, attempt to take, capture, or kill, possess, offer for sale, sell, offer to barter, barter, offer to purchase, purchase, deliver for shipment, ship, export, import, cause to be shipped, exported, or imported, deliver for transportation, transport or cause to be transported, carry or cause to be carried, or receive for shipment, transportation, carriage, or export, any migratory bird, any part, nest, or egg of any such bird, or any

---

496. 7 U.S.C. §136w-1.
497. *Id.*
498. *Id.* §136w-2.
499. 688 F. Supp. 223 (W.D. Va. 1988).
500. *See* U.S. EPA, Office Of Enforcement & Compliance Assurance, Fifra Enforcement Response Policy (Dec. 2009) *available at* http://www2.epa.gov/sites/production/files/documents/fifra-erp1209.pdf (last visited Mar. 13, 2104).
501. *Id.*
502. *See id.*, app. A.
503. Migratory Bird Treaty Act of 1918, ch. 128, 40 Stat. 755 (currently codified as amended at 16 U.S.C. §§703-712).
504. The list of migratory bird species protected by the MBTA appears in 50 C.F.R. §10.13.

product, whether or not manufactured, which consists, or is composed in whole or part, of any such bird or any part, nest, or egg thereof[505];

- ship, transport, or carry from one state, territory or district to another, or through a foreign country, any bird, part, nest or egg that was captured, killed, taken, shipped, transported or carried contrary to the laws from where it was obtained[506];
- take any migratory game bird by the aid of baiting, or on or over any baited area, if the person knows or reasonably should know that the area is a baited area[507]; or
- place or direct the placement of bait on or adjacent to an area for the purpose of causing, inducing, or allowing any person to take or attempt to take any migratory game bird by the aid of baiting on or over the baited area.[508]

Unlike the Endangered Species Act, the MBTA does not provide for an incidental take permit or its equivalent. However, the statute does authorize the Secretary of the Interior to issue take permits,[509] and specific regulations have been issued for various activities, such as the hunting of certain migratory birds.[510]

Criminal liability under section 703 of the MBTA does not require proof that the defendant had specific intent or guilty knowledge.[511] This greatly diminished standard makes MBTA charges attractive to environmental prosecutors in negotiations seeking to resolve criminal investigations with a guilty plea. However, in some cases, courts have found that the mental element of MBTA offense does contain a limiting principle—deaths must be a reasonably foreseeable consequence of the action taken.[512]

A person, association, partnership, or corporation that violates the law or its implementing regulations is guilty of a misdemeanor and subject to a fine of up to $15,000 per violation and six months imprisonment.[513] However, anyone who *knowingly* takes a migratory bird with the intent to sell or offer to sell such bird or *knowingly* sells or offers to sell a migratory bird is guilty of a felony and subject to up to $2,000 per violation and two years' imprisonment.[514]

The MBTA uses very broad language in its prohibition ("it shall be unlawful at *any time*, by *any means* or in *any manner*, to pursue, hunt, take, capture, kill . . . any migratory bird").[515] It has been interpreted to mean that conduct not expressly cited can be included as prohibited conduct.[516] For example, in *United States v. Corbin Farm Service*, the court held that the MBTA prohibits the poisoning of birds, even though "poison" is not specifically listed in the statute.[517] There is a division among the courts, however, as to whether the MBTA prohibits any conduct that may proximately cause a bird death or whether it covers only conduct directed against wildlife.

In *Seattle Audubon Society v. Evans*, the Ninth Circuit found that the MBTA describes only conduct *directed* at birds, such as hunting and poaching, and not acts or omissions having merely the incidental or unintended effect of causing bird deaths.[518] The court held that habitat modification that leads indirectly to bird deaths does not amount to a "taking" of migratory birds within the meaning of the MBTA.[519] In

505. 16 U.S.C. §703 (2006).
506. *Id.* §705.
507. *Id.* §704(b)(1).
508. *Id.* §704(b)(2).
509. *Id.* §704.
510. 50 C.F.R. §20.
511. *See* United States v. Corrow, 119 F.3d 796, 805 (8th Cir. 1997), *cert. denied*, 522 U.S. 1133 (1998); United States v. Pitrone, 115 F.3d 1, 5 (1st Cir. 1997); United States v. Hogan, 89 F.3d 403, 404 (7th Cir. 1996); United States v. Boynton, 63 F.3d 337, 343-44 (4th Cir. 1995); United States v. Engler, 806 F.2d 425, 431 (3d Cir. 1986), *cert. denied*, 481 U.S. 1019 (1987); United States v. FMC Corp., 572 F.2d 902, 907-08 (2d Cir. 1978).
512. *See* United States v. Apollo Energies, Inc., 611 F.3d 679, 689-90 (10th Cir. 2010); United States v. Moon Lake Elec. Ass'n., 45 F. Supp. 2d 1070, 1085 (D. Colo. 1999).
513. 16 U.S.C. §707. Anyone who violates §704(b)(2) shall be fined pursuant to Title 18 of the United States Code and/or imprisoned for not more than one year. *Id.* Section 707 also includes a criminal forfeiture provision that allows seizure of property, such as guns, traps, vehicles and so on, that were used in the commission of an offense.
514. *Id.*
515. 16 U.S.C. §703 (emphasis added).
516. *See* United States v. Corbin Farm Serv., 444 F. Supp. 510, 531-32 (E.D. Cal. 1978), *aff'd*, 578 F.2d 259 (9th Cir. 1978).
517. *Id.*
518. 952 F.2d 297, 302-03 (9th Cir. 1991).
519. *Id.*

Newton County Wildlife Association v. U.S. Forest Service, the Eighth Circuit agreed with *Seattle Audubon Society* and held that timber harvesting that indirectly resulted in the death of migratory birds was not within the scope of activity covered by the MBTA.[520] Several other courts also have found that bird deaths incidental to habitat modification are not covered by the MBTA.[521]

Several courts also have found that bird deaths resulting from various lawful commercial activities fall outside the scope of the MBTA. For example, in *United States v. Brigham Oil and Gas*, the government brought criminal charges under the MBTA against three companies after dead migratory birds were found in their oil reserve pits.[522] The court found that the use of reserve pits in commercial oil development is a legal, commercially useful activity that stands outside the reach of the MBTA.[523]

Reserve pits are not directed at birds or their habitat . . .. The reserve pits have little effect on bird habitat, except to attract occasional birds which mistake the pits for a pond or lake . . . the reserve pits were not created to effect the habitat of migratory birds.[524]

Similarly, in *United States v. Ray Westall Operating, Inc.*, the government prosecuted a company after discovering fifty dead birds in an evaporation pit at its oil production site.[525] The evaporation pit was covered by netting to prevent exposure to birds and was surrounded by a barbed-wire fence.[526] Prior to the bird deaths, however, a switch had malfunctioned, and the water in the pit rose to a level at which the oil pooled above the netting.[527] The court found that "Congress intended to prohibit only conduct directed towards birds and did not intend to criminalize negligent acts or omissions that are not directed at birds, but which incidentally and proximately cause bird deaths."[528] Finally, in *United State v. Chevron USA, Inc.*, a court rejected a plea agreement with respect to the death of thirty-five brown pelicans entrapped in an uncovered offshore oil well caisson on the ground that the activity did not constitute a crime under the MBTA.[529]

Other courts, however, have sustained criminal liability for bird deaths that are indirect result of commercial activities. For example, in *United States v. FMC Corporation*, a company was convicted under the MBTA for the death of birds caused by the release of a toxic chemical into a nearby pond.[530] The company routinely discharged wastewater into the pond; under normal operations, the toxic chemical should not have been present in the wastewater.[531] The court found that the company had manufactured the pesticide, which was known to be highly toxic, and had failed to act to prevent the chemical from reaching the pond.[532]

Similarly, in *United States v. Moon Lake Electrical Association*, an electrical utility that failed to install bird guards for power lines was found criminally liable for the unintended electrocution of migratory birds.[533] The court specifically rejected the defense argument that the MBTA applies only to activities intended to harm birds, such as hunting and trapping.[534] In reaching this conclusion, the court noted an "important and inherent limiting feature" of the MBTA: that liability attaches where the injury "might be reasonably anticipated or foreseen as a natural consequence of the wrongful act."[535] The court in *United States v. Apollo Energies, Inc.* agreed with *Moon Lake*'s "reasonably foreseeable" analysis and upheld a defen-

---

520. 113 F.3d 110, 115 (8th Cir. 1997), *aff'd*, 141 F.3d 803 (8th Cir. Ark.), *cert. denied*, 522 U.S. 1108 (1998).
521. *See* Curry v. U.S. Forest Serv., 988 F. Supp. 541, 549 (W.D. Pa. 1997) (loss of migratory birds as a result of timber sales does not constitute a taking or killing under MBTA); Mahler v. U.S. Forest Serv., 927 F. Supp. 1559, 1574 (S.D. Ind.), *motion denied*, 927 F. Supp. 1559 (S.D. Ind. 1996) (habitat destruction and logging during nesting season do not produce takings of migratory birds); Citizens Interested in Bull Run, Inc., v. Edrington, 781 F. Supp. 1502, 1510 (D. Or. 1991) (proposed timber sale does not violate MBTA despite claim that sale would diminish habitat of northern spotted owl).
522. 840 F. Supp. 2d 1202, 1203 (D.N.D. 2012).
523. *Id.* at 1210-11.
524. *Id.* at 1211.
525. No. CR 05-1516-MV, 2009 U.S. Dist. LEXIS 130674, at *5 (D.N.M. Feb. 25, 2009).
526. *Id.* at *4.
527. *Id.* at **4-5.
528. *Id.* at *19.
529. Crim. No. 09-CR-0132, 2009 U.S. Dist. LEXIS 102682, at *8-*9 (W.D. La. Oct. 30, 2009).
530. 572 F.2d 902, 904-05 (1978).
531. *Id.* at 904.
532. *Id.* at 907.
533. 45 F. Supp. 2d 1070, 1071 (D. Colo. 1999).
534. *Id.* at 1079.
535. *Id.* at 1085.

dant's conviction for bird deaths resulting from unprotected oil field equipment.[536] The court noted that defendant had received notice of the dangers the equipment posed to birds more than a year before the bird deaths in question and had not taken the suggested "bird-proofing."[537]

In *United States v. Khanh Vu*,[538] defendants, Khanh Vu and Seaside Aquaculture, Inc., were indicted for violating the MBTA after killing 90 brown pelicans without a permit. The Government sought to force Seaside Aquaculture to post a $360,000 bond, roughly half of the restitution the Government's experts considered appropriate for the MBTA violation. Defendants filed a motion to reduce the bond. Defendants first argued that restitution was unavailable under the MBTA because 18 U.S.C. §3663 does not explicitly list a violation of the MBTA as a violation eligible for restitution, and the MBTA does not list restitution as a penalty. *See* 16 U.S.C. §707(a). The court rejected this argument, noting that under *United States v. Love*, 431 F.3d 477 (5th Cir. 2001), there are two possible sources for authority for restitution: 18 U.S.C. §3556 and 18 U.S.C. §3583 the provision for imposing conditions on supervised release and authorizing such conditions as allowed under 18 U.S.C. §3563, the conditions for probation, which allows for restitution. to victims of crimes.[539] The court also held that the government can be a "victim" for the purposes of restitution and was in fact a victim in the case at hand because the government would need to "expend funds to rectify the environmental harm" caused by Defendants.[540] The court concluded that restitution was likely to be available if Defendants were convicted but reduced the bond to $50,000.

In *United States v. Duke Energy Renewables, Inc.*, in what appears to be the first plea agreement involving bird strikes at a wind farm, Duke Energy pled guilty to two class "B" misdemeanors under the MBTA for the take of approximately 163 migratory birds at a wind farm owned by Duke Energy. Among other facts, the government alleged that Duke Energy had constructed a portion of the wind farm despite concerns raised by the U.S. Fish and Wildlife Service regarding potential impacts to migratory bird species. Per the terms of the plea agreement, Duke Energy agreed to be placed on probation for a period of 60 months, to implement a migratory bird compliance program (MBCP), to develop an eagle conservation plan (ECP), and to pay fines, restitution, and community service in the amount of $600,000.[541]

IX. The Lacey Act

A. *Overview*

For over a century, the Lacey Act of 1900[542] has been a powerful tool for prosecutors in dealing with fish and wildlife crimes. The Act makes it unlawful for any person to import, export, transport, sell, receive, acquire, or purchase any fish or wildlife or plant taken, possessed, transported, or sold in violation of any law, treaty, or regulation of the United States or in violation of any Indian tribal law, whether in interstate or foreign commerce.[543] By structuring the Act in this fashion, Congress underscored other federal, state, and foreign wildlife laws by making it a separate offense to take, possess, transport, or sell wildlife that has been taken in violation of those laws. Violation of the Act can result in civil penalties of up to $10,000 per violation or a maximum criminal sanction of $20,000 in fines and/or up to five years, imprisonment.[544] All plants or animals taken in violation of the Act are subject to forfeiture. Vessels, vehicles, aircraft, and other equipment used in importing, exporting, transporting, selling, receiving, acquiring, or purchasing of the illegal fish, wildlife, or plants also are subject to forfeiture in cases in which a felony conviction is obtained.[545]

536. 611 F.3d 679, 690 (10th Cir. 2010).
537. *Id.* at 691. *See also* United States v. Citgo Petroleum Corp., 893 F.Supp.2d 841, 848 (S.D. Tex. 2012) (upholding defendant's conviction under the MBTA when migratory birds were trapped in layers of oil in defendant's tanks, which were required to be covered under the CAA and were not, and defendant knew such birds were liable to be trapped and had been for years, and did nothing to stop it.)
538. Case No. V-11-31, 2011 U.S. Dist. LEXIS 59471 (S.D. Tex. June 1, 2011).
539. *Id.* at *4 -*6 (citing United States v. Love, 431 F.3d 477 (5th Cir. 2001).
540. *Id.* at *9-*11.
541. United States v. Duke Energy Renewables, Inc. plea agreement *available at* http://www.eenews.net/assets/2013/11/25/document_gw_01.pdf
542. 16 U.S.C. §§3371-3378.
543. *Id.* §3372.
544. *Id.* §§3373, 3374.
545. *Id.* at §§3371 - 3378.

The Lacey Act is administered by the Departments of the Interior, Commerce, and Agriculture through their respective agencies. These include the U.S. Fish and Wildlife Service, The National Marine Fisheries Service (NMFS), and the Animal and Plant Health Inspection Service.

As originally enacted, the Lacey Act had three main prongs: (1) preservation of game and wild birds by making it a federal crime to poach in one state and sell the game in another; (2) addressing potential problems with the introduction of non-native avian species into native ecosystems (and the resulting decline in native bird species); and, (3) buttressing state laws that already protected game and birds.[546] The Act has been amended several times since its inception, including significant amendments in 1969, 1981, 1988 and 2008, to expand its scope in response to developments in the taking of wildlife.

The 1969 amendments to the Act expanded the category of protected species to include amphibians, reptiles, mollusks, and crustaceans; the maximum criminal penalty was increased to $10,000 and up to one year's imprisonment; the mental state required for a criminal violation was heightened to "knowingly and willfully"; and civil penalties were expanded to apply to negligent violations, i.e., subjecting to liability those who "in the exercise of due care should have known" they were violating the law.[547]

Prompted by indications of a "massive illegal trade in fish and wildlife" perpetrated by "well organized large volume" criminal operations that were generating substantial profits and causing "grim environmental consequences," Congress again amended the Act in 1981.[548] Attempting to keep pace with the fast-growing global trade in illegal wildlife, Congress removed prior heightened "willfully" standard of proof from the statute. Enforcement had been hampered because the courts had interpreted the word "willful" as requiring proof that a defendant knew not only of the protected nature of the wildlife, but also that his conduct violated the Act itself.[549]

The new law prescribed a criminal penalty (similar to the civil penalty added in 1969) for those who "knowingly" committed an act prohibited by the law and knew or should have known through the exercise of due care of the protected nature of the wildlife in question.[550] The amendment also restored coverage of migratory birds (Congress had removed coverage in 1969 over concerns that the provision duplicated protections afforded by the Migratory Bird Treaty Act),[551] and added coverage of indigenous plants.[552] "A bifurcated felony/misdemeanor criminal scheme was also created, dividing the classification of offenses based on factors such as import/export activity, the mental state of the violator, commercial conduct, and the market value of the wildlife involved in the violation."[553] The maximum felony penalty was set at $20,000 and/or five years' imprisonment.[554] The maximum penalty for misdemeanor violations was set at $10,000 and/or one year's imprisonment.[555] The Act's enforcement provisions also were expanded to permit federal wildlife agents to carry firearms, execute arrest and search warrants, and make warrantless arrests for suspected felony violations.[556]

The 1988 amendments created a separate and distinct violation for the falsification of documents related to intended shipments of fish, wildlife, or plants. This change eliminated the previous requirement that the wildlife actually must be imported, exported, or transported before a violation could be found.[557] The felony provision also was amended to require that the violation be "knowing" and that it involve either the import or export of the species, or the sale or purchase of wildlife, fish, or plants with a market value greater than $350.[558]

---

546. Lacey Act, Ch. 553, 31 Stat. 187 (1900) (codified as amended at 16 U.S.C. §§3371-3378).
547. S. Rep. No. 526 at 15, 1969 U.S.C.C.A.N. at 1427; S. Rep. No. 526 at 12-14, 1969 U.S.C.C.A.N. at 1425-27.
548. Lacey Act Amendments of 1981, Pub. L. No. 97-79, 95 Stat. 1073. *See also* S. Rep. No. 123, 97th Cong. (1981), *reprinted in* 1981 U.S.C.C.A.N. 1748.
549. S. Rep. No. 123 at 2, 11, *reprinted in* 1981 U.S.C.C.A.N. at 1749, 1758; H.R. Rep. No. 276 at 32 (letter of Donald Paul Hodel, Undersecretary of the Interior).
550. 16 U.S.C. §§3372, 3373(d) (1981).
551. H.R. Rep. No. 276 at 32 (letter of Donald Paul Hodel, Undersecretary of the Interior); S. Rep. No. 123 at 4, *reprinted in* 1981 U.S.C.C.A.N. at 1748, 1751.
552. S. Rep. No. 123 at 4, *reprinted in* 1981 U.S.C.C.A.N. at 1748, 1751.
553. Robert S. Anderson, *The Lacey Act: America's Premier Weapon in the Fight Against Unlawful Wildlife Trafficking*, 16 Pub. Land L. Rev. 27 (1995).
554. 16 U.S.C. §3373(d) (1981) (amended 1988).
555. *Id.*
556. *Id.* §3375(b) (1981) (amended 1988).
557. Pub. L. No. 100-653, §101, 102 Stat. 3825; 16 U.S.C. §3372(d) (1988).
558. 16 U.S.C. §3373(d)(3) (1988).

The Food, Conservation, and Energy Act of 2008 further amended the Lacey Act to protect a broader range of plants and plant products.[559] Prior to these amendments, the statute defined "plant" in a manner that excluded the majority of known species. The amendments also expanded the scope of prohibitions related to plants, bringing them more in line with the protections afforded to fish and wildlife species.[560] In addition, the amendments made it unlawful to import certain plants and plant products without an import declaration,[561] and added enforcement provisions for the submittal of any false import record.[562]

The import declaration for plants must include the scientific name of the plant, a description of its value and quantity, and the name of the country from which the plant was taken. If a plant species or country of origin cannot be determined, the plant declaration must include a list of possible plant species found in the product or a list of possible countries from which the plant originated.[563] By holding importers responsible for knowing the type of plant product they are importing and where it was harvested, the law makes the supply chain more transparent and thereby seeks to deter trade in illegal plant products.

B. *Criminal Application of the Lacey Act*

The most commonly invoked enforcement provisions of the Lacey Act are those defining trafficking offenses.[564] When read together with the "attempt" provision,[565] the statutory scheme establishes a hierarchy of questions for analyzing any potential trafficking violation:

(1) Is the wildlife, fish, or plant at issue covered by the Lacey Act?

(2) If so, can the government prove that the wildlife, fish, or plant was taken, possessed, transported, or sold in violation of a wildlife-related state, federal, tribal, or foreign law or regulation?

(3) If so, can the government prove that the defendant imported, exported, transported, received, acquired, or purchased the illegal wildlife, fish, or plant, or attempted to do so?

(4) If the underlying law was a state or foreign law, did the accused import, export, transport, receive, acquire, or purchase the wildlife, fish, or plant in interstate or foreign commerce?

(5) If so, are the additional elements necessary for proof of a misdemeanor or felony violation present, such as commercial conduct, market value, and knowledge of the protected nature of the wildlife or plant?[566]

C. *Recent Examples of Criminal Enforcement Under the Lacey Act*

In *United States v. Wright,* Alan Wright pleaded guilty in federal court to violating the Lacey Act by trafficking in and making false records for illegally harvested white-tailed deer.[567] Wright committed these offenses while employed as a wildlife officer for the Ohio Department of Natural Resources. Using his authority as a state official, Wright sold a resident Ohio hunting license to a non-resident hunter, who used that illegal license to kill three white-tailed deer. Wright "checked in" those deer by providing a false Ohio residence address for the non-resident hunter, to make it appear that the deer were killed by an Ohio resident. After the deer were checked in, the non-resident hunter transported them in interstate commerce from Ohio to South Carolina. Wright also seized white-tailed deer antlers from a hunter who had killed a

559. Pub. L. No. 110-246, §8204, 122 Stat. 1664, 2052 (2008). The term "plant" is now defined broadly to mean "[a]ny wild member of the plant kingdom, including roots, seeds, parts, or products thereof, and including trees from either natural or planted forest stands." 16 U.S.C. §3371(f) (2010).
560. *Id.* §3372(a) (2010).
561. *Id.* §3372(f) (2010).
562. *Id.* §3372(d) (2010).
563. I*d.* §§3372(a)(1), (a)(2).
564. *Id.* §3372(a)(4).
565. *See* 74 Fed. Reg. 45415 (Sept. 2, 2009), *available at* http://www.aphis.usda.gov/plant_haelth/lacey_act/.
566. Robert S. Anderson, *The Lacey Act: America's Premier Weapon in the Fight Against Unlawful Wildlife Trafficking,* 16 Pub. Land L. Rev. 27 (1995).
567. No. 1:11-cr-00103-MRB (S.D. Ohio guilty plea entered Feb. 24, 2012) For a summary of the facts, see U.S. DOJ, Press Release, *Former Ohio Wildlife Officer Convicted of Trafficking in White-Tailed Deer* (Feb. 24, 2012), *available at* http://www.justice.gov/opa/pr/2012/February/12-enrd-250.html.

deer illegally, and then knowingly supplied them to another individual who transported them from Ohio to Michigan. However, Wright filed an official state form that falsely reported that he had personally destroyed the antlers. Wright faced a maximum penalty of one year in, prison and a $100,000 fine per count; however, he was sentenced to home detention, five years of probation, and a $1000 fine.[568]

In *United States v. Alvarez*, the defendant pleaded guilty in federal court to violating the Lacey Act and the Migratory Bird Treaty Act (MBTA) by illegally selling and possessing the feathers of anhingas and other migratory birds protected under the MBTA.[569] Alvarez communicated via email with an individual in Louisiana and eventually exchanged two anhinga tails he possessed for a crested caracara tail, a Harris's hawk tail, and $400. Alvarez later sent 14 sets of anhinga tail feathers to the same individual and asked him to photograph and offer the tails for sale over the Internet. Alvarez later received payment from that person after the anhinga tail feathers were sold. The Lacey Act charge carried a maximum penalty of five years in prison and a fine of $250,000; however, Alvarez was sentenced to three years, probation and a $31,000 fine.[570]

In *United States v. Dupont,*[571] Gregory Dupont pleaded guilty in federal court in Louisiana to one felony count of illegally guiding out-of-state sport hunters to unauthorized areas to hunt American alligators in violation of the Lacey Act, the Endangered Species Act, and Louisiana law.[572] Dupont was a licensed alligator hunter; however, he guided his clients to an area which was unapproved (i.e., an area for which he did not have the required Convention on International Trade of Endangered Species (CITES) tags. During this illegal hunt, one of his clients killed an American alligator. Dupont falsely tagged the alligator with a tag for another location in which taking was permissible. Dupont was sentenced to six months in prison, four months in a half-way house, a $3000 fine, and two years, of probation.[573]

In *United States v. Kinder Caviar, Inc.*,[574] two owners of caviar companies and their companies pleaded guilty to violation of the Lacey Act for trafficking in and falsely labeling illegally harvested paddlefish, which are listed on Appendix II of CITES. Appendix II species, or their parts, which are harvested in the United States may be exported only if they are accompanied by a valid export permit issued by the U.S. Fish & Wildlife Service. In the plea agreement, one defendant admitted to making false statements on behalf of Kinder Caviar in a CITES Export Registration Form for paddlefish eggs. Both defendants admitted to transporting the paddlefish from Ohio to Kentucky with the intent to sell them when, in the exercise of due care, they should have known that the fish were harvested in violation of Ohio law. As part of the plea agreement, the boat and truck that were used in furtherance of the Lacey Act crimes were forfeited.[575]

In *United States v. Bruce,*[576] defendants Billy Bruce, Pamela Salyers, and William Salyers were convicted for conspiracy to violate the Lacey Act. The Salyers purchased undersized freshwater washboard mussels from Bruce, processed them, and then sold them in violation of state law regulating the size of mussel that may be harvested. Defendant Pamela Salyers appealed her conviction on the ground that the Government had presented insufficient evidence to prove she knew of or voluntarily joined the conspiracy. The court found the testimony of an undercover agent who had sold illegal mussels to Pamela Salyers while she worked in her husband's business and of two employees who had assisted her in keeping small mussels off of receipts to be sufficient evidence to prove knowledge.

568. Jeffrey L. Frischkorn, *Outdoors: Former wildlife officer's sentencing: No jail time but "no" to hunting/fishing for next five years,* The News-Herald (Jul. 20, 2012), *available at* http://www.news-herald.com/general-news/20120720/outdoors-former-wildlife-officers-sentencing-no-jail-time-but-no-to-huntingfishing-for-next-five-years (last visited Mar. 13, 2014).

569. Case 1:12-cr-00027-CG (S.D. Ala. 2012). For a summary of the facts, see U.S. DOJ, Press Release *Alabama Man Pleads Guilty to Selling Anhinga Feathers* (Feb. 15, 2012), *available at* http://www.justice.gov/opa/pr/2012/February/12-enrd-220.html (last visited Mar. 13, 2014).

570. Judgment in Criminal Case, Dkt. No. 21, U.S. v. Alvarez, Case 1:12-cr-00027-CG (S.D. Ala. May 31, 2012)

571. No. 10-140-BAJ (M.D. La. Jan. 12, 2012).

572. U.S. DOJ, Press Release, *Louisiana Hunting Outfitter Pleads Guilty to Illegally Killing Protected Alligator* (Feb. 10, 2012), *available at* http://www.justice.gov/opa/pr/2012/February/12-enrd-197.html (last visited Mar. 13, 2014).

573. U.S. DOJ, Press Release, *Louisiana Hunting Outfitter Sentenced to Prison for First Felony Conviction for Illegally Hunting Protected Alligators* (Jun. 22, 2012), *available at* http://www.justice.gov/opa/pr/2012/June/12-enrd-793.html (last visited Mar. 13, 2014).No. 1:11-cr-00035-MRB (S.D. Ohio guilty plea entered Jan.17, 2012).

574. Press Release, DOJ, *Kentuckians Convicted of Lacey Act Crimes for Illegally Harvesting and Making False Records for Ohio River Paddlefish* (Jan. 17, 2012), *available at* http://www.justice.gov/opa/pr/2012/January/12-enrd-059.html (last visited Mar. 13, 2014).

575. Fed. Appx. 357 (6th Cir. 2011) (unpublished).

576. Id. at 367-68.999 F.2d 1023, 1027 (6th Cir. 1993).

At sentencing, Defendant Pamela Salyers was sentenced to 12 months and one day and ordered to pay restitution of $50,000, jointly and severally with William Salyers and another defendant, and Defendant William Salyers was sentenced to 20 months and ordered to pay restitution of $50,000, jointly and severally with Pamela Salyers and another defendant. In appealing her sentence, Pamela Salyers argued that the sentence was unreasonable because she eventually cooperated with the investigation and because the district court failed to properly consider the factors in 18 U.S.C. §3553(a). The court dismissed these arguments, finding that she had not submitted any evidence of her cooperation and that the district court judge had applied the §3553(a) factors to give her a sentence "well below" the applicable range.

Defendant William Salyers appealed his sentence on the ground that he should not have been ordered to pay restitution when there was no identifiable victim. He argued that state agencies do not qualify as victims under the Mandatory Victims Restitution Act ("MVRA"). The court disagreed and stated that the government can be a victim for restitution purposes. As the mussels were taken from the waters of several states, the states had "a property interest . . . and [were] entitled to compensation for their loss."[577]

In *United States v. GEM Manufacturing LLC,*[578] GEM was convicted and sentenced in federal court in the Virgin Islands, for knowingly trading in falsely-labeled, protected black coral that was shipped into the United States in violation of the Endangered Species Act and the Lacey Act. The company was sentenced to pay a criminal fine of $1.8 million and an additional $500,000 in community service payments for projects to study and protect black coral. GEM also was ordered to forfeit dozens of jewelry items, ten artistic sculptures, and over 13,655 pounds of raw black coral, the total value of which exceeded $2.17 million. The aggregate financial penalty of $4.47 million makes this the largest for the illegal trade in coral, the largest non-seafood wildlife trafficking financial penalty, and the fourth largest penalty for any case involving the illegal trade in wildlife.[579]

In *United States v. Delaney,*[580] Defendant was convicted of a felony violation of the Lacey Act for the false labeling of fish, as well as a misdemeanor count of false labeling under the Food, Drug, and Cosmetic Act (FDCA). Defendant labeled $8,000 worth of frozen Pollock fillets as cod loins, which sell for approximately one dollar per pound more than Pollock. Defendant also mislabeled approximately $203,000 worth of frozen fish fillets from China as products of Canada, Holland, Namibia and the United States.

Following the conviction, Defendant moved for a judgment of acquittal, arguing that the meaning of "fish or wildlife" within the Lacey Act "does not include animals that spent their entire lives in captivity and which never lived in the wild." The court, however, rejected that argument, stating that the Lacey Act's definition of "wild" would include fish such as the ones that Defendant mislabeled, and therefore denied his motion for judgment of acquittal.[581]

In *United States v. Bengis,*[582] the Government appealed the district court's order denying restitution to South Africa after Defendants were convicted of smuggling South African rock lobsters in violation of the Lacey Act. The Second Circuit held that under the Mandatory Victims Restitution Act (MVRA), the removal of the lobsters was "an offense against property" because South Africa had a property right in the lobsters. As South African law granted the government the right to seize and sell illegally harvested lobsters and keep the proceeds, the court reasoned that Defendants' smuggling operation prevented the South African government from profiting as it ordinarily would have and that this "entitlement to the revenue from the lobsters that were taken illegally does constitute 'property.'"[583] Additionally, the court held that South Africa was a "victim" under the MVRA because its property interest in the lobsters meant it was "directly harmed" by Defendants' criminal actions.[584] In considering the appropriate amount of restitution, the

577. No. 2:11-cr-00019 (D. V.I. sentence entered Oct. 26, 2011).
578. U.S. DOJ, Press Release, *U.S. Virgin Islands Company Sentenced for Illegal Trade of Protected Coral* (Oct. 26, 2011), *available at* http://www.justice.gov/opa/pr/2011/October/11-enrd-1410.html (last visited Mar. 14, 2014).
579. *See id.*
580. 795 F. Supp. 2d 125 (D. Mass. 2011).
581. *Id.* at 127-28.
582. 631 F.3d 33 (2d Cir. 2011), *cert. denied,* 131 S. Ct. 2911 (2011).
583. *Id.* at 38-40.
584. *Id.* at 40-41.

court remanded to the district court and instructed it to multiply the number of illegally obtained lobsters by the market price for lobsters at the time to determine the amount lost by South Africa.[585]

In *United States v. Foiles*,[586] Defendant filed a motion to dismiss his indictment under the Lacey Act, arguing that he should have been charged under the Migratory Bird Treaty Act (MBTA). Defendant was charged with conspiracy to violate the Lacey Act after leading a series of hunts in which he helped hunters take more duck and geese than the set bag limits. Defendant argued that the MBTA was "the more specific statute," but the court agreed with the magistrate judge's reasoning that "when two criminal statutes apply to the same conduct, the Government has the discretion to elect the statute under which to proceed."[587]

X. The Endangered Species Act

A. *Overview*

The Endangered Species Act (ESA) of 1973 is one of the core modern environmental laws passed in the 1970s.[588] The ESA is administered jointly by the Secretaries of Commerce and the Interior. Lead responsibility for the ESA within the Department of the Interior is held by the U.S. Fish and Wildlife Service (FWS), and within the Department of Commerce by the National Oceanic and Atmospheric Administration (NOAA) (which includes the National Marine Fisheries Service; NOAA handles matters involving marine species, while the FWS has responsibility for freshwater fish and all other species. Species that occur in both habitats, such as sea turtles and Atlantic sturgeon, are jointly managed.) Numerous states also have their own programs that protect rare and endangered species. Federal law usually controls in the case of a conflict, unless the state law is more stringent. The predecessor of the ESA was the Endangered Species Preservation Act of 1966,[589] which directed the Secretary of the Interior to "carry out a program in the United States of conserving, protecting, restoring and propagating selected species of native fish and wildlife that are threatened with extinction."[590] The contents of the program were largely unspecified, however, and the law proved ineffective. The statute also authorized the Secretary to use the Land and Water Conservation Fund to purchase land for the program and directed him to publish a list of endangered domestic fish and wildlife. The Department of Interior limited the definition of the crucial term "fish and wildlife" to vertebrates, thereby narrowing the scope of the program. The Act also failed to impose any prohibitions or restrictions on the hunting or trade of such species, or the destruction of their habitats. In March 1967, the first list of 78 endangered species was issued under the Act. It included 14 mammal, 36 bird, 6 reptile and amphibian, and 22 fish species.[591]

The Endangered Species Conservation Act,[592] passed in December 1969, significantly amended and expanded the Endangered Species Preservation Act to provide additional protection to species in danger of "worldwide extinction." It prohibited the importation and subsequent sale in the United States of species listed as endangered, except for a limited set of purposes.[593] The law also expanded the Lacey Act's ban on interstate commerce in protected species to include reptiles, amphibians, mollusks, and crustaceans, in light of rampant poaching of alligators and crocodiles. Eight species of great whales also were included on the protected list. The law further called upon the Secretary to "seek the convening of an international ministerial meeting" to conclude "a binding international convention on the conservation of endangered

585. *Id.* at 41. On remand, the court awarded restitution of approximately $62,000. The defendants argued that this should be offset by the amounts of 40 million rand that had already been forfeited to the South African government and the $7.4 million that had been forfeited to the United States government. The court disagreed, holding that the forfeited assets cannot be used to offset any fine or restitution to which a defendant is sentenced. United States v. Bengis, No. 03 Cr. 308 (LAK) (AJP, 2012 U.S. Dist. LEXIS 115500 (S.D.N.Y Aug. 16, 2012).
586. No. 10-CR-30100, 2011 U.S. Dist. LEXIS 48738 (C.D. Ill. May 6, 2011).
587. *Id.* at *2-*3. *See* United States v. Foiles, No. 10-CR-30100, 2011 WL 1750120 (C.D. Ill. Mar. 29, 2011) (Magistrate Judge Report and Recommendation).
588. 16 U.S.C. §1531.
589. Pub. L. No. 89-669, §§1-3, 80 Stat. 926 (1966).
590. *Id.* §2(a).
591. *78 Species Listed Near Extinction; Udall Issues Inventory With Appeal to Save Them,* N.Y. Times, Mar. 11, 1967, *available at* http://select.nytimes.com/gst/abstract.html?res=F30D16F63F5D107B93C0A81788D85F438685F9 (last visited Mar. 13, 2014).
592. Pub. L. No. 91-135, 83 Stat. 275 (1969).
593. *Id.* §2.

species."[594] This meeting was held in Washington, D.C. in 1973, and produced a global treaty to regulate international trade in endangered plants and animals known as the Convention on International Trade of Endangered Species of Wild Fauna and Flora (CITES).

The ESA was enacted in 1973, after Congress found and declared that "various species of fish, wildlife, and plants in the United States have been rendered extinct as a consequence of economic growth and development untempered by adequate concern and conservation."[595] To address these concerns, Congress enacted a comprehensive law whose purposes are "to provide a means whereby the ecosystems upon which endangered species and threatened species depend may be conserved, to provide a program for the conservation of such endangered species and threatened species, and to take such steps as may be appropriate to achieve the purposes of the treaties and conventions" pursuant to which the United States had pledged to conserve endangered species.[596]

In order to receive protection under the ESA, a species must first be "listed" through a rulemaking conducted by the agency with jurisdiction over that species. Listing decisions are made based upon five criteria set forth in the ESA.[597] Once a species is listed, its critical habitat must be designated in a separate rulemaking to be completed within one year. The annual rate of listing increased steadily from the Ford Administration (47 listings, 15 per year) through the Carter (126 listings, 32 per year), Reagan (255 listings, 32 per year), George H.W. Bush (231 listings, 58 per year), and Clinton (521 listings, 65 per year) Administrations before declining to its lowest rate under George W. Bush (64 listings, 8 per year), and then rebounding somewhat under Obama (average rate of between 25 and 30 annually).[598] "The Obama administration also recently negotiated a historic settlement agreement that will determine whether 757 imperiled species will be protected under the ESA, including 259 candidates,"[599] which was subsequently approved by a federal court.[600]

B. *Criminal Application of the ESA*

Once a species is listed as "endangered" under the ESA, it is a crime for any person to "take" a protected species, subject to certain important exceptions, including protection from bodily harm.[601] To "take" means "to harass, harm, pursue, hunt, shoot, wound, kill, trap, capture, or collect, or attempt to engage in any such conduct."[602] In 1995, implementing regulations that define "harm" to include habitat modification were upheld by the Supreme Court in *Babbitt v. Sweet Home Chapter of Communities for Greater Oregon*.[603]

Knowingly taking or trafficking in endangered species, or violating a permit or certificate issued under the Act, is a criminal violation punishable by a fine of not more than $50,000 or imprisonment for not more than one year per count. The maximum penalty for a corporation for a violation of the Act is a $200,000 fine per count.[604]

C. *Recent Examples of Criminal Enforcement Under the ESA*

Although the ECS typically does not choose to publicize prosecutions brought under the ESA, in recent years there has been an increase in the number of investigations and criminal charges, particularly of indi-

594. *Id.* §5(b).
595. 16 U.S.C. §1531(a)(1).
596. *Id.* §1531(b).
597. *Id.* §1533(a)(1).
598. Dale D. Goble et al., The Endangered Species Act at 30: Vol. 1: Renewing the Conservation Promise 50-67 (Washington, D.C.: Island Press.); J. Harkinson, *Obama: Not So Wild About Wildlife*, Mother Jones, Jan. 6, 2011, *available at* http://www.motherjones.com/environment/2011/01/obama-endangered-species-act (last visited Mar. 14, 2014).
599. Center for Biological Diversity, *A Future for All* (October 2011), *available at* http://www.biologicaldiversity.org/campaigns/esa/pdfs/A-Future-for-All.pdf (last visited Mar. 14, 2014).
600. Story available at http://naturescrusaders.wordpress.com/2011/09/10/2-thumbs-up-award-757-imperiled-species-protected (last visited May 29, 2013).
601. For instance, federal actions that cause "incidental" takes can be excused by an incidental take statement included in a biological opinion issued under §7(a)(2) of the ESA. 16 U.S.C. §1532(a)(2). Additional exceptions include those for pre-act specimens, economic hardship, subsistence and handicraft use by certain Alaskan residents, and scientific or propagation purposes. 16 U.S.C. §§1539(a)(1), (b), (e), (f), (h).
602. *Id.* §1532(19).
603. 515 U.S. 687 (1995).
604. 16 U.S.C. §1540(b)(1).

viduals. It is unlawful to purchase or sell an endangered species in interstate commerce without a permit. In limited circumstances, permits are issued when applicants demonstrate that the sale or transfer of the endangered species will further scientific research, or enhance the propagation and survival of the species.

In *United States v. Xu,*[605] an antique dealer pleaded guilty to smuggling and to violating the ESA in connection with the illegal export of African elephant ivory, in the form of ivory carvings in his carry-on luggage. A Transportation Security Administration officer alerted inspectors with the U.S. Fish & Wildlife Service that the defendant, a Chinese national, was carrying suspected wildlife items in his carry-on luggage based on x-ray screening. The defendant was charged with a felony count for illegal smuggling and a misdemeanor violation of the ESA for knowingly engaging in trade of ivory specimens, contrary to the provisions of CITES.[606] The defendant was sentenced to time already served and four years on probation.[607]

In *United States v. Hawk Field Services LLC,*[608] the company pleaded guilty in federal court to three counts of violating the ESA. The company pleaded guilty in federal court to three counts of violating the ESA. According to the plea agreement, the company admitted that it did not adequately control erosion during construction of natural gas pipelines. This lack of erosion control allowed silt to run downhill to streams, causing sediment to build up at the stream crossing and downstream. This erosion and sedimentation occurred in waters containing the endangered speckled pocketbook mussel, and caused a take of at least one mussel by harassment.[609] The company agreed to pay a $350,000 fine and to donate $150,000 to the National Fish and Wildlife Foundation.[610]

In United States v. Pugh,[611] two individuals and Cole Brothers Circus Inc., pleaded guilty in U.S. District Court in Beaumont, Texas to ESA violations related to the purchase and sale of two Asian elephants which are listed as an "endangered" species.[612] None of the parties possessed a permit that would have authorized such a sale of the elephants. The corporate defendant was sentenced to four years, probation and a $150,000 fine.

Due to the associated custom forms, declarations, permits, and labeling, many cases involving listed species are prosecuted under, or in combination with, more traditional white collar crimes, such as conspiracy and the making of false statements. For example, in *United States v. Jeffery Diaz*, the defendant pled guilty to two felony smuggling counts and two felony false statement counts, stemming from his smuggling of 12 Austrian Eagle Owl eggs into the United States and then lying about this conduct on customs forms and elsewhere.[613] Austrian Eagle Owls are listed as endangered species and are included on the CITES Appendix II list. The defendant was sentenced to 21 months in prison, a $5,000 fine, and three years of supervised release.[614]

In *United States v. Bao Huynh*, the defendant was sentenced to two years, probation after pleading guilty to an ESA violation for attempting to smuggle Asian Arowana, commonly known as "Lucky" fish, into the United States. The defendant attempted to bring a shipment of tropical fish into the United States from Vietnam, but an inspection revealed that five Arowanas were hidden in unmarked bags among other tropical fish.[615]

---

605. No. 1:11-cr-00777-JBW (E.D.N.Y guilty plea entered Dec. 6, 2011).
606. U.S., DOJ, Press Release *Ivory Smuggler Pleads Guilty in New York* (Dec. 6, 2011), *available at* http://www.justice.gov/opa/pr/2011/December/11-enrd-1576.html (last visited Mar. 14, 2014).
607. U.S. DOJ, Env. Crimes Sec., Monthly Bull. (Apr. 2012) at 17, *available at* http://www.justice.gov/enrd/2012/monthly-bulletin-april2012_508.pdf (last visited Mar. 14, 2014).
608. No. 4:11-cr-00060-HDY (E.D. Ark. sentence entered Sept.14, 2011).
609. U.S., DOJ, Press Release, *Natural Gas Company Pleads Guilty in Arkansas in Connection With Fayetteville Shale Pipeline Construction Activities* (Apr. 8, 2011), *available at* http://www.justice.gov/opa/pr/2011/April/11-enrd-437.html (last visited Mar. 14, 2014).
610. U.S. Atty's Off., E.D. Ark., Press Release, *Natural Gas Company Sentenced in Connection with Fayetteville Shale Pipeline Construction Activities* (Sept. 14, 2011), *available at* http://www.justice.gov/usao/are/news/2011/September/petrohawk%20enviro%20sent%20091311.html (last visited Mar. 14, 2014).
611. No. 9:11-cr-00011-MAC (E.D. Tex. *sentence entered* Mar. 17, 2011)
612. U.S. DOJ, Press Release *Circus President and Former Employee Plead Guilty to Violating Endangered Species Act for Unlawful Purchase and Sale of Asian Elephants* (Feb. 23, 2011), *available at* http://www.justice.gov/opa/pr/2011/February/11-enrd-233.html (last visited Mar. 14, 2014).
613. No. 06-CR-0050 (N.D. Cal. *sentence entered* Jun. 25, 2007).
614. U.S. DOJ, Environmental Crimes Monthly Bulletin (Jul. 2007) at 9-10, *available at* http://www.justice.gov/enrd/2007/LPS-191092-v1-ECS_Bulletin_2007_07_Block.PDF (last visited Mar. 14, 2014).
615. No. 06-CR-00247 (C.D. Cal. *sentence entered* Nov. 13, 2006). *See* U.S. DOJ, Environmental Crimes Monthly Bulletin at 11, available athttp://www.justice.gov/enrd/2006/December_2006.pdf (last visited Mar. 14, 2014).

In *United States v. Ivan and Gloria Chu*, two Taiwanese nationals pleaded guilty to nine counts charging, conspiracy, false statements, and violations of both the ESA and the Lacey Act stemming from their involvement in illegal shipments of internationally-protected black coral into the United States. Each of the species of black coral was listed in Appendix II of CITES, and thus was subject to strict trade regulations, including the requirement of a permit in order to export the material. The defendants had falsely labeled coral shipments to conceal the material from U.S. Customs officials. Under the plea agreement, defendant Ivan Chu agreed to a term of 30 months' imprisonment and a $12,500 fine, while his wife agreed to serve 20 months in prison and pay a $12,500 fine.[616]

XI. The Convention on International Trade of Endangered Species of Wild Fauna and Flora

A. *Overview*

The Convention on International Trade of Endangered Species of Wild Fauna and Flora (CITES) is an international treaty, which entered into force in 1975, and regulates international trade in endangered plants and animals, whether alive or dead, in whole or in parts.[617] CITES seeks to control the international movement of endangered plants and animals so that the pressures of international trade do not contribute to the endangerment of the listed species. Covered plants and animals may not be imported or exported without a permit. Before granting an import or export permit, the issuing state must determine that the trade will not be detrimental to the species. "Determining when trade is detrimental is a difficult projection into the future by science. This is a particular challenge in developing countries where wildlife science for many species is nonexistent. If detrimental trade is allowed, knowingly or unknowingly, then the goal of the treaty is frustrated."[618]

Species listed on Appendix I of the treaty are in danger of extinction, and CITES imposes a ban on the commercial trade of those species. Appendix I species require two permits before they may be moved in international trade: an exporting permit and an importing permit.[619] As a result, both the exporting and importing states must agree that the trade will not have a detrimental effect on the species. Species listed on Appendix II are those that might have population level concerns; however, commercial trade is allowed. Appendix II species require that a CITES export permit be issued by state of export (i.e., one finding of non-detrimental effect).[620] The placement of a species in Appendix I or II is a group decision that requires a two-thirds vote of the Parties.[621]

CITES itself does not provide protection for a species or its habitat within the country of origin; it only controls international movement of the species. There is no international police system to enforce the obli-

---

616. No. 10-CR-0003 (D.V.I. guilty plea entered Mar. 11, 2010). *See* U.S. DOJ, Env. Crimes Section Monthly Bulletin (Apr. 2010) at 6-7), *available at* http://www.justice.gov/enrd/2010/April_2010.pdf (last visited Mar. 14, 2014).
617. 27 UST 1087 (signed March 3, 1973, amended June 22, 1979), *available at* http://www.cites.org/eng/disc/E-Text.pdf (last visited Mar. 14, 2014).
618. David Favre, Overview of Convention on International Trade in Endangered Species (2002), *available at* http://www.animallaw.info/articles/ovcites.htmhttp://www.animallaw.info/articles/ovcites.htm (last visited Mar. 14, 2014).
619. For the import permit required under Appendix I:
    (a) the Scientific Authority of the State of import has advised that the import will be for purposes which are not detrimental to the survival of the species involved;
    (b) the Scientific Authority of the State of import must be satisfied that the proposed recipient of a living specimen is suitably equipped to house and care for it; and
    (c) the Management Authority of the State of import must also be satisfied that the specimen is not to be used for primarily commercial purposes.
    CITES, art. 3(3).
620. The criteria for the exporting permit are the same for Appendix I and Appendix II species. Before issuing such a permit, the Authorities of the state of export must find:
    (a) the Scientific Authority of the State of export has advised that such export will not be detrimental to the survival of that species;
    (b) the Management Authority of the State of export is satisfied that the specimen was not obtained in contravention of the laws of that State for the protection of fauna and flora; and
    (c) the Management Authority of the State of export is satisfied that any living specimen will be so prepared and shipped as to minimize the risk of injury, damage to health, or cruel treatment.
    Id. art. 4(2).
621. *Id.* art. 15(1)(b).

gations of the treaty. A party cannot file a complaint or grievance in an international court against another party for violation of the provisions or obligations of CITES. Rather, CITES presumes that enforcement will be done at the national level, and imposes a specific obligation that a Party must adopt domestic legislation which will carry out its requirements.[622] Section 8(a) of the ESA contains the implementing provisions of CITES for the United States.[623]

A violation of CITES occurs when a person fails to obtain the required import and/or export permit for a listed species or falsifies the permit. Knowing violations of the CITES requirements are typically prosecuted under the Lacey Act or the ESA, or more traditional white collar criminal statutes such as conspiracy or false statements.

B. *Recent Examples of Criminal Enforcement of CITES*

In *United States v. Manghis*,[624] the defendant, a nationally recognized artist skilled in etching, imported sperm whale teeth and elephant ivory for his artworks. He was convicted of conspiracy to smuggle and of knowingly importing ivory and sperm whale teeth into the United States and of making false statements to federal investigators. He appealed these convictions and moved for a new trial, raising several arguments. Defendant contended that the Government had failed to show his intent to smuggle since he did not know about CITES or of any required documentation for his imports. The court held that "to convict Mr. Manghis of violating counts two through eight, the Court had to find that Mr. Manghis *knew that his conduct was illegal in some respect,* but the Court did not need to find that he knew of the particular statute or regulation at issue."[625]

Defendant also argued there was insufficient evidence to convict him of conspiracy or of knowing violations of importation laws because he was only a buyer and not an importer. The court rejected this argument, finding that the defendant was responsible for bringing the teeth and ivory into the U.S. because he had personally ordered the supplies on eBay and directly negotiated further purchases with a Ukrainian seller.[626] Defendant argued that he believed his acts were legal because he was importing antique items over 100 years old and had been told this was legal at an art conference. He also argued that he relied on a middle man in the transaction to comply with all documentation. The court found these arguments unconvincing, based on the defendant's emails to various sellers and other publicly available information Defendant had admitted to reading stating that imports such as his must be declared.[627]

Additionally, Defendant argued that his conviction should be voided because he should have been allowed to raise a lesser-included offense defense under the Lacey Act and because he was charged under a general smuggling statute, 18 U.S.C. §545, rather than the more specific Lacey Act. He contended that the Lacey Act creates a misdemeanor violation with a negligence mens rea standard for violations of CITES and is thus a lesser-included offense of the smuggling statute, which requires knowledge. The court held that the lesser-included offense theory was not available because the misdemeanor provision of the Lacey Act is a lesser offense for the felony provision of the Lacey Act and not for 18 U.S.C. §545. The court went on to hold that Defendant was properly charged under the smuggling statute, and not the Lacey Act, because the Lacey Act was intended to "coexist and complement" existing anti-smuggling laws, leaving the government free to choose to bring smuggling charges.[628]

In *United States v. Breitag*,[629] the defendant was convicted in the U.S. District Court for South Dakota for smuggling the hide of a leopard into the United States in violation of CITES. The leopard was killed illegally in South Africa and then smuggled into Zimbabwe, where a false CITES permit was obtained for shipment to the United States. A jury convicted the defendant of violating the Lacey Act, the federal

---

622. *Id.* art. 8(1).
623. *Id.* art. 8(a).
624. No. 08-cr-10090-NG, 2011 U.S. Dist. LEXIS (D. Mass. May 26, 2011).
625. *Id.* at *14.
626. *Id.* at *54-*57.
627. *Id.* at *37-*51.
628. *Id.* at *70-*78.
629. No. 1:09-CR-10035 (D.S.D. sentence entered Feb. 1, 2010).

wildlife statute that makes CITES enforceable. He was required to pay a $20,000 fine and serve six months of home confinement.[630]

In *United States v. Soliz,*[631] a U.S. border patrol agent pled guilty in U.S. District Court in the Southern District of Texas, to a violation of the Lacey Act for attempting to receive fifteen Tanzanian leopard tortoises that had been transported into the United States in violation of CITES.[632] A U.S. Customs inspector intercepted the package containing the tortoises, which was falsely labeled as containing 50 live scorpions, and a U.S. Fish and Wildlife inspector determined that the package contained 14 live leopard tortoises and one dead leopard tortoise. No export permit accompanied the tortoises. The defendant was sentenced to three years of supervised release, community service, and a $1,500 fine.[633]

In *United States v. Andrew Nguyen,*[634] the defendant pleaded guilty to two smuggling violations and one count of a false declaration in connection with the illegal smuggling of cycads protected under CITES. Nguyen originally was charged with conspiring to import cycads, eight counts of smuggling and importing cycads by means of false declarations and statements, and one count of violating the ESA. The defendant agreed to purchase approximately 50 protected plants from a co-conspirator for approximately $26,000. The plants were shipped to Nguyen from Zimbabwe by a second co-conspirator. The permit accompanying the shipment did not authorize the shipment of any of the species in the actual shipment.

XII. Safe Drinking Water Act

The Safe Drinking Water Act (SDWA)[635] is the main federal law that regulates the quality of drinking water in the United States. Congress passed the law in 1974 to protect the public health by ensuring the quality of the nation's public drinking water supply. The law has been amended several times and now requires many actions to protect drinking water and its sources, which include rivers, lakes, reservoirs, springs, and ground water wells. The law is administered through programs that establish standards and treatment requirements for public water supplies, control underground injection of wastes, finance infrastructure projects, and protect sources of drinking water. SDWA applies to every public water system in the United States.[636] It does not regulate private wells which serve fewer than 25 individuals.[637]

Under SDWA, EPA sets standards for drinking water quality and oversees the states, localities, and water suppliers who implement those standards. Most states have been granted "primacy" and have the authority to implement SDWA within their jurisdiction. To assume primacy, states must adopt regulations at least as stringent as national requirements, develop adequate procedures for enforcement, adopt authority for administrative penalties, maintain records, and develop a plan for providing safe drinking water under emergency circumstances.[638] The agency with primary oversight makes sure that water systems test for contaminants, reviews plans for water system improvements, conducts on-site inspections and sanitary surveys, provides training and technical assistance, and takes action against water systems no meeting standards.

---

630. U.S. DOJ Press Release, *South Dakota Man Sentenced for Smuggling Big Game Leopard Hide Into the United States* (Feb. 2, 2010), *available at* http://www.justice.gov/opa/pr/2010/February/10-enrd-116.html.
631. No. 2:09-CR-00282 (S.D. Tex. guilty plea entered Apr. 14, 2009).
632. U.S. DOJ Press Release, *Border Patrol Agent Pleads Guilty for Attempting to Receive Protected Leopard Tortoises* (Apr. 14, 2009), *available at* http://www.justice.gov/opa/pr/2009/April/09-enrd-345.html.
633. U.S. DOJ Press Release, *Former Border Patrol Agent Sentenced for Attempting to Receive Protected Leopard Tortoises* (Aug. 5, 2009), *available at* http://www.justice.gov/opa/pr/2009/August/09-enrd-769.html.
634. No. 2:05-CR-1208 (C.D. Cal. guilty plea entered Nov. 2, 2006), *See* U.S. DOJ, Environmental Crimes Monthly Bulletin (Dec. 2006) at 12-13, *available at* http://www.justice.gov/enrd/2006/December_2006.pdf (last visited Mar. 14, 2014).
635. 42 U.S.C. §§300f-300j-26.
636. *Id.* §300g.
637. The term "public water system" is defined as "a system for the provision to the public of water for human consumption through pipes or other constructed conveyances, if such system has at least fifteen service connections or regulatory serves at least twenty-five individuals." *Id.* §300f(4)(A).
638. *Id.* §300g-2.

A. *Safe Drinking Water Act Enforcement*

SDWA requires public water systems to monitor their water supplies to ensure compliance with drinking water standards. Public water systems must also report their monitoring results to the states. States also conduct their own monitoring to determine system compliance with drinking water regulations. The EPA monitors public water system compliance by reviewing the violation data submitted by the states.

When EPA finds that a public water system in a state with primary enforcement authority does not comply with regulations, EPA must notify the state and the noncompliant system and provide assistance to bring the system into compliance. If the state fails to commence enforcement action within 30 days after this notification, EPA can issue an administrative order or commence a civil action. In a non-primacy state, the EPA must notify an elected local official with jurisdiction over the noncompliant water system before bringing an enforcement action against the system.[639]

Both states and EPA maintain formal enforcement programs to ensure that violations of the SDWA are addressed without delay. When taking enforcement action, the states and EPA generally follow some type of enforcement policy. EPA, for example, has a Drinking Water Enforcement Response Policy, which focuses enforcement attention on the drinking water systems with the most serious or repeated violations.[640] Although the policy applies only to civil and administrative enforcement actions, it may provide insight into the enforcement priorities of EPA.

B. *Safe Drinking Water Act Criminal Provisions*

Certain provisions of SWDA authorize the imposition of significant criminal sanctions. The first prohibits tampering, attempting to tamper, or threatening to tamper with a public drinking water system.[641] Persons convicted of tampering with a public water supply with the intent to harm are subject to 20 years imprisonment and fines in accordance with 18 U.S.C. §3571. Persons convicted of attempting or threatening to tamper with a public water supply with the intent to harm are subject to 10 years imprisonment and fines in accordance with 18 U.S.C. §3571.[642]

The second provision prohibits willful violations of any requirements of an underground injection control (UIC) program.[643] The SDWA authorizes the establishment of state underground injection control programs.[644] The purpose is to protect underground sources of drinking water. EPA has issued regulations containing minimum requirements for state UIC programs to prevent underground injection that endangers drinking water sources.[645] States are also required to prohibit any underground injection that has not been authorized by state permit. Some states have been granted primary authority for enforcing UIC programs. Persons convicted of willful violations of a UIC program are subject to three years imprisonment and fines in accordance with 18 U.S.C. §3571.[646]

Types of UIC program violations that have resulted in criminal sanctions include tampering with underground injection wells to hide a failure to meet testing requirements and the unpermitted construction and operation of injection wells.[647] For example, in *United States v. King*, the manager of a produce farm and cattle feedlot ordered farm workers to inject excess surface fluids, without a permit, into four deep irrigation wells on the property. He was convicted of an unpermitted injection in violation of SDWA. Although the defendant argued that the injection of fluids did not have an adverse impact on the underground source of water, the court held that the government does not need to show adverse impact. Rather, the govern-

639. *Id.* §300g-3.
640. U.S. EPA, Office of Enforcement and Compliance Assurance, *Drinking Water Enforcement Response Policy,*) *available at* http://www2.epa.gov/sites/production/files/documents/drinking_water_erp_2009.pdf (last visited Mar. 14, 2014)..
641. 42 U.S.C. §300i-1; 40 C.F.R. §§141-143.
642. The fine assessed under 18 U.S.C. §3571 is dependent on the class of violation.
643. 42 U.S.C. §300h-2(b); 40 C.F.R. §§144-149.
644. 42 U.S.C. §300(h).
645. 40 C.F.R. pts 144-48.
646. 42 U.S.C. §300h-2(b)(2).
647. *See* United States v. King, 660 F.3d 1071 (9th Cir. 2011), *cert. denied,* 132 S. Ct. 2740 (2012); United States v. Overholt, 307 F.3d 1231 (10th Cir. 2002); United States v. Weatherbee Supply, 22 ELR 10080 (W.D. Ky. 1991); United States v. Jay Woods Oil, Inc., 18 Env't Rep. 502 (E.D. Mich. 1987).

ment must only prove that the defendant willfully failed to comply with a requirement of an applicable underground injection program.[648]

Finally, SDWA also prohibits the interstate sale or manufacture of drinking water coolers that are not lead-free.[649] Persons convicted of knowing violations of this prohibition are subject to five years imprisonment and fines in accordance with 18 U.S.C. §3571.[650]

Although SDWA does not provide criminal sanctions for false reporting, many criminal actions are brought under Title 18 for submitting false information associated with SDWA requirements. For example, in *United States v. Tetreault*, the superintendent of a public waste system was sentenced to one year supervised release and fined $15,000 for falsely reporting that residual chlorine levels met or exceeded the minimum requirement at two of his facilities.[651] Similarly, a water treatment plant supervisor and water quality technician was convicted of making false statements in violation 18 U.S.C. §1001(a)(2) on monthly monitoring reports required under SDWA.[652]

XIII. Fracking—New Issues, Old Statutes

Hydraulic fracturing (fracking), though used colloquially to describe shale oil and gas extraction, actually only applies to one aspect of the extraction process. The entire process involves the well pad set-up, drilling, fracking, production, and closure. If the well is located in a previously undeveloped area, roads and other infrastructure must be constructed in order to accommodate heavy equipment and to transport the drill rig. Depending on the depth to the shale play, wells are drilled approximately 6,000 to 10,000 feet deep. After drilling is completed, the well is stimulated through fracking. A well can be fracked multiple times. Fracking involves pumping large amounts of "fracking fluid" into the well. The fluid is typically 95 to 99.5% water. The remaining proportion of the fluid is comprised of a proppant, usually sand, along with a chemical cocktail designed to reduce friction, that is used to keep the induced fracture opened, inhibit bacterial growth, alter the pH, and prevent scaling and corrosion. Depending on the conditions of the well, fracking can require several million gallons of water, and about 30 to 70% of that water may flow back to the surface.

After fracking, the well moves to the production phase. A well can produce for up to a decade. During production, liquid referred to as "produced water" will flow from the shale oil or gas reserve to the ground surface. Produced water is a briny solution that contains the frack fluid chemicals, hydrocarbons, and potentially naturally occurring radioactive materials contained in the shale formation. The produced water is typically stored in large, open pits or tanks. Produced water presents a challenge to drilling operators because the potentially toxic fluid cannot be released into the environment. After production of the well ceases, the well must be closed and the well pad area restored.[653]

Oil and gas production is typically regulated by states. Nevertheless, eight federal laws potentially regulate aspects of fracking. Those laws are the SDWA, CWA, CAA, RCRA, CERCLA, EPCRA, TSCA, and FIFRA.

The SDWA regulates underground injection of waste materials through a permit program. The Energy Policy Act of 2005 exempted fracking from the SDWA underground injection program, except where diesel fuel was a part of the waste materials.[654] Recently, EPA published permitting guidance for protecting underground sources of drinking water (USDWs) from potential endangerment posed by underground

648. United States v. King, 660 F.3d 1071 (9th Cir. 2011), *cert. denied*, 132 S. Ct. 2740 (2012).
649. 42 U.S.C. §300j-23(b).
650. *Id.* §300j-23(c).
651. United States v. Tetreault, No. 1:12-cr-10146-DPW (D. Mass. Oct. 4, 2012).
652. United States v. Young, No. 6:12-cr-00157-AA (D. Or. July 24, 2012).
653. For an extensive discussion of the fracking process and the risks associated with it, see George E. King, *Hydraulic Fracturing 101: What Every Representative, Environmentalist, Regulator, Reporter, Investor, University Researcher, Neighbor and Engineer Should Know About Estimating Frac Risk and Improving Frac Performance in Unconventional Gas and Oil Wells* (presented at Society of Petroleum Engineers Hydraulic Fracturing Technology Conference, Feb. 6-8, 2012), *available at* http://www.kgs.ku.edu/PRS/Fracturing/Frac_Paper_SPE_152596.pdf (last visited Feb. 25, 2014).
654. Pub. L. No. 109-58, §322, 119 Stat. 594, 694 (2005).

injection where diesel fuels are used.[655] EPA retains, however, the authority under the SDWA to conclude there is an imminent and substantial endangerment to human health.[656]

Fracking also can be regulated under RCRA Subtitles C and D. In 1980, RCRA was amended to temporarily exclude "drilling fluids, produced waters, and other wastes associated with the exploration, development, or production of crude oil, natural gas, or geothermal energy" (E&P wastes) from regulation as hazardous wastes under Subtitle C, directing EPA to conduct a study of E&P wastes and, if it determined regulation was warranted, to submit proposed regulations to Congress, which would take effect only if authorized by Congress.[657] In its report to Congress, EPA found that existing state and federal regulations were generally adequate to regulate E&P wastes, and that regulating E&P wastes under Subtitle C would have a substantial impact on the U.S. economy and would be unnecessary and impracticable.[658] In its regulatory determination, EPA determined that the management of E&P wastes under Subtitle C was not warranted, but instead it would pursue a three-pronged approach to address these wastes: (1) improve existing regulatory programs under RCRA Subtitle D and augment the SDWA and CWA requirements; (2) work with the states to improve their waste management programs; and (3) work with Congress on any additional legislation that might be needed.[659] Since the determination was made in 1988, however, EPA has chosen not to develop regulations under RCRA Subtitle D and no further legislation addressing the issue has been enacted.[660] While well sites wastes originating within the well or generated by field operations such as water separation, demulsifying, degassing, and storage are exempt, RCRA Subtitle C regulations generally apply to other wastes that may be generated at oil and gas wells, such as discarded unused products, solvents used to clean surface machinery, and others, if they are actually hazardous. In 2002, EPA published a guide that identifies, among other things, exempt and nonexempt wastes under RCRA.[661]

If a release of a CERCLA hazardous substance were to occur as a result of fracking operations, the person in charge and others could face liability under CERCLA, but there are two important exclusions that may limit such liability. The first is the exclusion for petroleum and natural gas found in the definition of hazardous substance under CERCLA.[662] Thus, CERCLA would not apply to leaking petroleum products or gas at a fracking site, but would still apply to other discharged or released substances that do meet the definition of a CERCLA hazardous substance. The second CERCLA exclusion is for federally permitted releases.[663] CERCLA defines a federally permitted release to include any underground injection of fluids authorized under the SDWA, any discharges of wastewater authorized under the CWA, and other discharges or emissions authorized under other delineated statutes. This includes any underground injection of fluids or other materials authorized under any applicable state law for the production or enhanced recovery of oil or natural gas and any reinjection of production fluids or materials.[664]

There are currently no federal laws requiring companies to submit detailed information regarding the chemical composition of fracking fluids.[665] The oil and gas industry is exempt from the provision of EPCRA under which EPA requires industrial and federal facilities with more than ten employees to

655. U.S. EPA, Office of Water, *Permitting Guidance for Oil and Gas Hydraulic Fracturing Activities Using Diesel Fuel: Underground Injection Control Program Guidance #84* (Feb. 2014), *available at* http://water.epa.gov/type/groundwater/uic/class2/hydraulicfracturing/upload/epa816r14001.pdf (last visited Mar. 14, 2014).
656. *See* U.S. Gov't Accountability Office (GAO), Rpt. to Congressional Requesters, *Unconventional Oil and Gas Development: Key Environmental and Public Health Requirements,* at 22 (GAO-12-874, Sept. 2012).
657. Solid Waste Disposal Act Amendments of 1980, Pub. L. No. 96-482, §7, 94 Stat. 2334, 2336-37 (codified at 42 U.S.C. §6921(b)(2)).
658. U.S. EPA, Report to Congress: Management of Wastes from the Exploration, Development, and Production of Crude Oil, Natural Gas, and Geothermal Energy (Dec. 1987), *available at* http://nepis.epa.gov/Adobe/PDF/20012D4P.PDF (last visited Mar. 14, 2014).
659. 53 Fed. Reg. 25, 446, 25, 450 (Jul. 6, 1988).
660. In September 2010, the Natural Resources Defense Council submitted a petition to EPA requesting regulation of waste associated with the exploration, development, or production of oil, natural gas, and geothermal energy, asserting that EPA can and should revisit the determination not to regulate these wastes because, among other things, the underlying assumptions—concerning the availability of alternative disposal practices, the adequacy of state regulations, and economic harm to the oil and gas industry are no longer valid. Nat. Resources Defense Council, Petition to The Honorable Lisa Jackson, Administrator, U.S. EPA (Sept. 8, 2010), *available at* http://docs.nrdc.org/energy/files/ene_10091301a.pdf (last visited Mar. 14, 2014). To date, no action on the petition has been taken by EPA.
661. U.S. EPA, Exemption of Oil and Gas Exploration and Production Wastes from Federal Hazardous Waste Regulations (Oct. 2002), *available at* http://www.epa.gov/osw/nonhaz/industrial/special/oil/oil-gas.pdf (last visited Mar. 14, 2014).
662. 42 U.S.C. §9601(14).
663. *Id.* §9607(j).
664. *Id.* §9601(10).
665. Brandon J. Murrill, *Hydraulic Fracturing: Chemical Disclosure Requirements,* Rep. No. R42461 (CONG. RES. SERV., Jun. 19, 2012), *available at* http://www.fas.org/sgp/crs/misc/R42461.pdf (last visited Mar. 14, 2014).

report the toxic chemicals they release, store, and transfer.[666] The release notification provisions of EPCRA do apply to oil and gas well sites. These provisions require companies that produce, use, or store certain chemicals to notify state and local emergency planning authorities of certain releases that would affect the community.[667]

Similarly, there are currently no requirements under TSCA for oil and gas companies to report on the chemicals they use for fracking. Recently, more than 100 environmental advocacy organizations petitioned EPA to promulgate rules under TSCA for chemicals used in oil and gas exploration or production.[668] In response, EPA indicated that it would initiate a rulemaking to gather available data on the chemicals used in fracking, but has to date not yet issued a proposed rule to do so. Whatever requirements may be forthcoming, EPA indicated that it would discuss any reporting requirements with the states, industry, and public interest groups to "minimize reporting burdens and costs, take advantage of existing information, and avoid duplication of efforts."[669]

FIFRA requires that EPA register new pesticides; pesticide registration is a very specific process that is not valid for all uses of a particular chemical. Instead, each registration describes the chemical and its intended use (such as sites on which it may be applied), and each use must be supported by research data. Some pesticides registered under FIFRA are used in hydraulic fracturing, and EPA has approved registrations of some pesticides for this purpose.[670]

The two primary statutes that are used to regulate fracking operations are the CAA and the CWA. Under the CAA, in 2012, EPA issued regulations covering, among other things, emissions of volatile organic compounds (VOCs) from gas fracking operations.[671] The regulations require new fracking operations and refracking operations be conducted under a process known as "green completions" or "reduced emissions completions" for gas wells; under this process, natural gas that would be otherwise vented to the atmosphere during the completion process is cleaned and captured for reuse.[672] The requirements are phased in – until January 1, 2015, VOC emissions can be reduced at new fracking sites by either using a "completion combustion device" (flaring), or by using the green completion process. After January 15, 2015, all wells must employ the green completion process.[673]

Fracking is a very water-intensive process. After a well is fractured, the majority of the fluid is returned to the surface. This is called "flowback," and it typically contains chemical residues as well as other components, including potentially significant amounts of radioactive materials as well as salts and metals. Additionally, the wells generally continue to produce water from the formation throughout their production lives. Often the flowback is reused and injected into other wells for disposal.[674] However, if the flowback cannot be reused, it cannot be discharged into the waters of the United States unless it is done in accor-

666. 40 C.F.R. §§ 372.22.,372.23. However, under EPCRA, owners and operators of storage facilities holding in excess of 10,000 pounds of any hazardous chemical must submit chemical inventory information ("Tier II reports") to the state emergency response commission ("SERC"), local emergency planning committee ("LEPC"), and the local fire department in the area where the facilities are located. 42 U.S.C. §11022(0)(1); 40 C.F.R. §317.10.

667. Three types of releases must be reported: (1) release of extremely hazardous substances for which notification is also required under CERCLA §103(c), (2) release of extremely hazardous substances for which notification is not required under CERCLA §103(c), but above reporting thresholds and subject to additional conditions, and (3) release of other hazardous substances for which notification is also required under CERCLA §103(c), subject to CERCLA reporting thresholds or 1 pound default threshold. 42 U.S.C. §11004(a).

668. Earthjustice et al., Petition to Lisa P. Jackson, U.S. EPA, Administrator (Aug. 4, 2011), http://www.epa.gov/oppt/chemtest/pubs/Section_21_Petition_on_Oil_Gas_Drilling_and_Fracking_Chemicals8.4.2011.pdf.

669. U.S. EPA, Ltr. From Asst. Administrator Stephen A Owens to Deborah Goldberg, Earthjustice (Nov. 23, 2011), http://www.epa.gov/oppt/chemtest/pubs/EPA-Letter-to-Earthjustice-on-TSCA-Petition.pdf. *See also* 78 Fed. Reg. 41768 (Jul. 11, 2013) (explaining reasons for EPA response to petition).

670. *See* EPA Eyes Novel Use Of FIFRA To Address Fracking, Prompting New Concern, InsideEPA.COM (Oct. 26, 2012), http://insideepa.com/Superfund-Report/Superfund-Report-10/29/2012/epa-eyes-novel-use-of-fifra-to-address-fracking-prompting-new-concern/menu-id-1094.html.

671. 77 Fed. Reg. 49,900 (Aug. 16, 2012). Hydraulically fractured oil wells are exempt from these requirements. In addition certain types of wells, such as exploratory, delineation and low-pressure wells, do not have to employ the green completions process. *Id.* at 49,499.

672. For a more detailed explanation of this process, *see* Richard K. Lattanzio, Air Quality Issues in Natural Gas Systems, Rep. No. R42833 (Cong. Research Serv., Mar. 4, 2013), *available at* http://www.civil.northwestern.edu/docs/Tight-Shale-Gas-2013/Air-Quality-Issues-Natural-Gas-Ratner-2013.pdf (last visited Mar. 14, 2014).

673. 77 Fed. Reg. at 49,499.

674. Adam Vann, Brandon J. Murrill & Mary Tiemann, *Hydraulic Fracturing Selected Legal Issues,* Rep. No. R43152 (Cong. Research Serv., Nov. 15, 2013) at 7.

dance with the provisions of the CWA.[675] This typically means that a NPDES permit must be obtained.[676] The CWA is the most frequently used statute to pursue fracking-related criminal enforcement actions.

In 2009, an oil and gas exploration company, Nami Resources Company, LLC, plead guilty to charges of violating the ESA and the CWA.[677] The company paid a fine of $50,000. The charges stemmed from a fracking operation in Kentucky. Investigators concluded that the fracking fluids at four gas wells adjacent to a stream were not disposed of properly. The fluids, including hydrochloric acid, were discharged into the stream. The discharge wiped out aquatic flora and fauna in a substantial portion of the stream, including two federally threatened blackside dace. The small minnows were found dead just downstream of the well. This case was the first enforcement action concerning the blackside dace and represents the largest ESA-based fine assessed in Kentucky. The CWA charge was based on the unpermitted discharge of drilling and fracking fluids from a point source in violation of 33 U.S.C. §§1311(a) and 1319(c)(1)(A).[678]

In 2011, Integrated Production Services, LLC, pled guilty to negligently violating the CWA in connection with fracking operations.[679] In 2007, a tank situated next to a drilling pad leaked 400 to 700 gallons of hydrochloric acid into an area surrounded by a berm. The area inside the berm was flooded due to recent heavy rainfall. Instead of conducting a proper cleanup of the hazardous acid, the site supervisor breached the berm with a pickup truck and the acid-laden water flowed into a nearby creek. The company agreed to pay a $140,000 criminal fine and a $22,000 community service payment to conduct ecological studies and remediation of the contaminated stream. The company received a two-year probation where it is responsible for implementing a $38,000 environmental compliance program to train its employees in proper hazardous waste handling and spill response. The crew supervisor pled guilty to a misdemeanor violation of the CWA and was sentenced to two years of probation and a fine of $2,500.

In 2012, Chesapeake Appalachia, LLC (Chesapeake), a subsidiary of Chesapeake Energy Corporation, faced criminal and civil actions for fracking-related violations of the CWA.[680] Chesapeake operates numerous fracking operations in West Virginia. In 2008, Chesapeake hired and directed contractors to create access to a fracking well by spreading 60 tons of gravel and rock into a stream bed. The fill impacted sensitive wetlands and completely obliterated a natural waterfall. On three other occasions, Chesapeake directed and supervised the contractor to discharge gravel from dump trucks into the stream. Neither Chesapeake nor the contractors obtained a CWA permit prior to the discharges of gravel and filling of the stream.

After an investigation, Chesapeake pled guilty to three counts of illegally discharging gravel in violation of the CWA. Chesapeake admitted that the discharge and spreading of the 60 tons of rock into the stream bed was for the purposes of creating a roadway so that its contractors could access a well extracting natural gas from the Marcellus Shale. Chesapeake agreed to pay $200,000 for each CWA violation and a two-year probation. EPA's special agent for criminal enforcement in West Virginia noted that this was the highest criminal penalty associated with fracking.

XIV. Transportation Statutes

Chemicals and pollutants that are regulated under the environmental laws are often also regulated for safety purposes, particularly in their transportation, as they pose threats to public health and the environment. As a result, criminal sanctions associated with laws that govern the transportation of hazardous chemicals and pollutants also will be available to Government prosecutors in the event of environmental incidents.

---

675. 33 U.S.C. §1311(a).

676. *Id.* §1342(a).

677. United States v. Nami Resources Co., No. 6:09-cr-00054-JBT-1 (E.D. Ky. Oct. 15, 2009).

678. U.S. Fish & Wildlife Serv., Office of Law Enforcement, *Case at a Glance: U.S. v. Nami Resources Company, LLC,* https://www.fws.gov/home/feature/2009/pdf/NamiInvestigation.pdf.

679. U.S. DOJ, Press Release, *Texas Natural Gas and Oil Drilling Contractor Pleads Guilty to Negligent Violation of Clean Water Act in Oklahoma* (Oct. 11, 2011), *available at* http://www.justice.gov/opa/pr/2011/October/11-enrd-1342.html (last visited May 29, 2013).

680. U.S. Atty's Office, N.D. W Va., Press Release, *Chesapeake Appalachia Sentenced for Clean Water Act Violations* (Dec. 3, 2012), *available at* http://www.justice.gov/usao/wvn/news/2012/december/chesapeake.html (last visited May 29, 2013).

A. *Hazardous Materials Transportation Act*

Shipments of hazardous materials in less than bulk quantities are regulated under the Hazardous Materials Transportation Act (HMTA).[681] Hazardous materials (HazMat) are those substances or materials that have been determined to pose an unacceptable risk to health, safety and property when transported in commerce, and includes hazardous substances, hazardous wastes, marine pollutants, pesticides, and toxic or radioactive materials, among other types of materials that have been determined to be hazardous by the Secretary of Transportation. Shipments of HazMat regulated under the HMTA are those shipped in packagings, including containers such as gas cylinders, cargo tank motor vehicles and tank cars, as well as chemicals and pollutants in other smaller packagings, including chemicals for household use.

A person that knowingly[682] alters, removes, destroys or tampers with a marking, label, placard, or description on a document required under the HMTA or HazMat regulations, or with a package, package component, motor vehicle, rail freight car, aircraft or vessel used to transport hazardous materials, is liable for felony sanctions. Additionally, a person that willfully[683] or recklessly[684] violates the HMTA or a regulation, order, special permit or approval issued under the HMTA is also liable for felony sanctions.[685] Imprisonment is increased for any violation involving the release of a HazMat that results in death or bodily injury.[686]

The Pipeline and Hazardous Materials Safety Administration (PHMSA) in the Department of Transportation (DOT) is responsible for coordinating a national safety program for the transportation of HazMat, including implementing and enforcing the HMTA regulations (HazMat regulations).[687] Additionally, the modal agencies within the DOT, including the Federal Aviation Administration (FAA), the Federal Motor Carrier Safety Administration and the Federal Railroad Administration, as well as the Office of the Inspector General, are involved in the enforcement of the HazMat regulations. For shipments by sea, the U.S. Coast Guard is the modal agency primarily responsible for enforcement of the HazMat transportation regulations. Finally, the various State enforcement agencies work with the Federal agencies to enforce the hazmat regulations.

The regulations implemented under the HMTA include, among other things, requirements for manifesting, labeling, marking and packaging of materials, as well as for training of employees that handle HazMat. The regulations apply to persons that transport HazMat in commerce (carriers), cause HazMat to be transported in commerce (shippers), and manufacture or maintain packagings for HazMat, among other persons.[688]

B. *Pipeline Safety Act*

The transportation of hazardous liquids and gas in bulk by pipeline is also regulated by the PHMSA under the Pipeline Safety Act (PSA).[689] The PSA provides felony criminal sanctions for knowingly and willfully

681. 49 U.S.C. §§5101 et seq.

682. A person acts knowingly when (a) the person has actual knowledge of the facts giving rise to the violation, or (b) a reasonable person acting in the circumstances and exercising reasonable care would have that knowledge. Knowledge of the existence of a statutory provision or a regulation or requirement is not an element of the offense. 49 U.S.C. §5124(b).

683. A person acts willfully when the person has knowledge of the facts giving rise to the violation and the person has knowledge the conduct was unlawful. *Id.* at §5124(c).

684. A person acts recklessly when the person displays a deliberate indifference or conscious disregard to the consequences of their conduct. *Id.* at §5124(d).

685. *Id.* at §5124(a). As an example, in 2006, the president and registered agent of a Florida import/export company was ordered to forfeit two Piper aircrafts valued at a combined $150,000 and was sentenced to two years in prison for illegally transporting radioactive HazMat and for making false representations to Government agents. The defendant contracted with an oil refining company in the Bahamas to transport radioactive Iridium-192 to and from the Bahamas. The company was not licensed or certified to handle or transport radioactive HazMat. The defendant never submitted the HazMat manifests required by law, nor did he disclose the HazMat to Customs officials when it was shipped from the Bahamas to Florida while hidden in a wing compartment of the aircraft. *See* Press Release, DOT IG, Owner of Florida Import/Export Company Sentenced to Forfeit Two Private Aircraft for Illegally Transporting Radioactive Hazardous Materials (HazMat) (Aug. 4, 2006), *available at* http://www.oig.dot.gov/library-item/3482. For a discussion of the issue of forfeiture of the aircraft in conjunction with this case, see *United States v. DeGregory*, 480 F. Supp. 2d 1302 (S.D. Fla. 2006).

686. *Id.*

687. 49 C.F.R. pts. 100-185.

688. *Id.* §171.1.

689. 49 U.S.C. §60101.

violating specific requirements of the Act or regulations or orders issued under the Act.[690] Persons who knowingly and willfully damage or destroy an interstate gas pipeline facility, an interstate hazardous liquid pipeline facility, or an intrastate gas pipeline or hazardous liquid pipeline facility affecting interstate or foreign commerce are subject to increased imprisonment and fines, and if such damage or destruction results in a death, may be imprisoned for any term of years or life.[691] Felony criminal sanctions are also provided for persons that knowingly and willfully engage in excavation activities without using an available one-call information system to establish the location of underground facilities, or does not pay attention to appropriate location information or markings for pipeline facilities, and as a result, damages the pipeline so as to result in death, serious bodily harm, or more than $50,000 property damage, or damages a pipeline and does not report the damage to the pipeline operator or proper authorities, or causes the release of more than 50 barrels of liquid from a hazardous liquid pipeline facility.[692]

The largest criminal fine ever assessed under the PSA was in a case that also underscores the relationship between the laws governing the safe transportation of hazardous liquids and the possible environmental consequences when those laws are violated. In June 1999, a pipeline used to transport gasoline ruptured and caused a massive explosion in Bellingham, Washington. In addition, approximately 236,000 gallons of gasoline were discharged into nearby creeks, where the gasoline ignited and caused three deaths. Two pipeline companies and three individuals involved in the operation of the pipeline entered into plea agreements with the Government.[693]

Olympic Pipe Line Company pleaded guilty and Equilon Pipe Line Company pleaded *nolo contendre* to violating the PSA, specifically a regulation issued under the Act setting minimum standards relating to training of their operating personnel. They also pleaded guilty and *nolo contendre* respectively to a negligent discharge into the navigable waters of the United States in violation of the CWA. Olympic also pleaded guilty to the unlawful discharge of refuse into a navigable water of the United States without a permit in violation of the Refuse Act. Under the plea agreements, Olympic paid a criminal fine of $6 million, and Equilon paid a criminal fine of $15 million. Both were also placed on probation for five years.

In addition to the corporate pleas, a Manager and a Supervisor of Product Movement for Olympic each pleaded guilty to knowingly and willfully violating a regulation under the PSA that set minimum training standards for Olympic's operating personnel. The Manager was sentenced to 6 months in prison and 200 hours of community service. The Supervisor was sentenced to 30 days in prison, 30 days of home detention with electronic monitoring, and 150 hours of community service. An Olympic control operator pleaded guilty to negligently causing the discharge of gasoline into a navigable water of the United States in violation of the CWA. He was sentenced to one year of probation and 100 hours of community service.

XV. Common Title 18 Offenses in Environmental Crimes Cases

Prosecutors often include traditional criminal law charges in indictments for environmental criminal cases. They do so for several reasons: additional counts in an indictment increase the pressure on the accused to enter into a plea agreement; traditional criminal law charges are often easier for the jury to understand than an environmental statutory offense, and thus more likely to result in a conviction; and additional counts proven at trial can increase the severity of the sentence.

The most common "add-on" white collar allegations charged in environmental prosecutions include: (1) making false or misleading statements to federal officials; (2) obstruction of justice or destruction of evidence; and (3) conspiracy. As a result, it is important for environmental defense counsel to have a working understanding of these types of charges and to understand how they typically are invoked by prosecutors in environmental criminal cases.

---

690. *Id.* §60123(a).
691. *Id.* §60123(b).
692. *Id.* §60123(d).
693. For a summary of the guilty pleas and the sentencing in the case, *see* U.S. Atty's Office, W.D. Wash., Press Release, *Two Pipeline Companies and Three Employees Enter Pleas in Criminal Case Arising From the June 1999 Gasoline Pipeline Rupture in Bellingham, Washington* (Dec. 11, 2002), *available at* http://www.pipelinesafetytrust.com/docs/usdoj_doc2.pdf; Ericka Pizzillo, *Former Pipeline Officials Going to Prison for Blast*, Bellingham Herald (June 19, 2003), *available at* http://www.hermit.cc/Pipeline/PRESS/2003/BH190603.htm.

A. *False or Misleading Statements*

18 U.S.C. §1001 makes it a crime, "within the jurisdiction of the executive, legislative, or judicial branch of the Government of the United States," to: (1) conceal a material fact from a federal official; (2) make a false statement or representation to a federal official; or (3) make or use a false writing or document. Due to the mandatory permitting and reporting requirements of most environmental statutes and the familiarity of government investigators with the hallmarks of false statements, Section 1001 charges are common in environmental prosecutions.

1. Essential Elements of False and Misleading Statement Offenses

A conviction for concealment of a material fact under Section 1001(a)(1) requires the government to prove:

(1) the defendant concealed a material fact by trick, scheme or artifice;

(2) the defendant did so knowingly and willfully;

(3) the defendant had a duty to disclose the fact; and

(4) the concealment was in relation to a matter within the jurisdiction of the executive, legislative, or judicial branch of the United States Government.[694]

To support a conviction for a false statement or representation under Section 1001(a)(2), the prosecution must establish:

(1) the defendant made a statement;

(2) the statement was false or fraudulent;

(3) the statement was material;

(4) the statement was made knowingly and willfully; and

(5) the statement was in relation to a matter within the jurisdiction of a department or agency of the United States.[695]

To obtain a conviction for making or using a false writing or document under Section 1001(a)(3), the government must prove:

(1) the defendant made or used a false document or writing;

(2) the statement was false or fraudulent;

(3) the statement was material;

(4) the statement was made knowingly and willfully; and

(5) the statement was in relation to a matter within the jurisdiction of a department or agency of the United States.[696]

---

694. United States v. Kingston, 971 F.2d 481, 489 (10th Cir. 1992), *cert. denied,* 474 U.S. 825 (1985); United States v. Swaim, 757 F.2d 1530, 1533 (5th Cir. 1985); *see also* United States v. Blackley, 167 F.3d 543, 550-51 (D.C. Cir. 1999), *cert. denied,* 528 U.S. 868 (1999).

695. *See* United States v. Moore, 612 F.3d 698, 700-01 (D.C. Cir. 2010), *cert. denied,* 556 U.S. 1235 (2009); United States v. Dedman, 527 F.3d 577, 598 (6th Cir. 2008); United States v. Rice, 449 F.3d 887, 892 (8th Cir. 2006), *cert. denied,* 549 U.S. 1040 (2006); United States v. Sarihifard, 155 F.3d 301, 306 (4th Cir. 1998).

696. *See* United States v. White, 492 F.3d 380, 396 (6th Cir. 2007) (citing United States v. Raithatha, 385 F.3d 1013, 1022; United States v. Hatch, 434 F.3d 1, 4 (1st Cir. 2006)).

2. Key Concepts for False or Misleading Statement Offenses

a. Knowingly and Willfully

A prosecutor must prove that a defendant's false or misleading statement was made knowingly and willfully. "Knowingly" requires proof only that the defendant acted with knowledge of the falsity.[697] However, the law is unsettled with respect to whether the term "willfully" requires proof that the defendant acted with the specific intent to deceive the federal government or that the defendant had actual knowledge that the false statement would be in violation of the law.[698] Prior to the mid-1990s, courts were nearly uniform in holding that the mens rea element of a Section 1001 offense required proof only that that the defendant consciously and deliberately made a statement that he knew was false; it did not, however, require proof that the defendant had a specific intent to violation Section 1001 or knew that this conduct would be unlawful.[699] The United States Attorney's Manual and many jurisdictions continue to adhere to this construction of the mens rea element of Section 1001.[700] In a series of decisions, the Supreme Court outlined situations in which "willful" violations of certain highly technical regulatory statutes may require proof that the defendant knew that the conduct was unlawful.[701] These decisions have led some courts to hold that a defendant must have "knowledge of the general unlawfulness" of the false statement to satisfy the "willful" element of a Section 1001 charge.[702]

b. Materiality

A statement is material if it is capable of influencing or affecting a governmental function.[703] It must be emphasized that a statement need only be *capable* of influencing the decision making process to fall within the scope of the statute. Whether the false statement *actually* influenced or affected the decision making process is irrelevant.[704]

c. Jurisdiction

The Supreme Court has explained that "the term 'jurisdiction' [of a federal entity] should not be given a narrow or technical meaning for purposes of §1001."[705] The jurisdictional element is established if the statement concerns a situation in which the government "has the power to exercise authority."[706] Further, if a federal agency has statutory authority for accessing information, jurisdiction under Section 1001 may be established, even if the agency does not actually access the information at issue.[707] For example, false entries in a business's internal records may fall within the jurisdiction of Section 1001 if a federal agency

697. *See* United States v. Geisen, 612 F.3d 471, 487 (6th Cir. 2010), *cert. denied*, 131 S. Ct. 1813 (2011); United States v. Lange, 528 F.2d 1280, 1287-89 (5th Cir. 1976).
698. *See* United States v. Moore, 612 F.3d 698, 702-04 (D.C. Cir. 2010) (Kavanaugh, J., concurring); United States v. Brandt, 546 F.3d 912, 916 (7th Cir. 2008); United States v. Whab, 355 F.3d 155, 162 (2d Cir. 2004), *cert. denied*, 541 U.S. 1004 (2004).
699. United States v. Yermian, 468 U.S. 63, 73 (1984); United States v. Laughlin, 26 F.3d 1523, 1527 (10th Cir. 1994), *cert. denied*, 513 U.S. 965 (1994); United States v. Hildebrandt, 961 F.2d 116, 118 (8th Cir. 1992), *cert. denied*, 506 U.S. 878 (1992); United States v. Carrier, 654 F.2d 559, 561 (9th Cir. 1981); United States v. Lange, 528 F.2d 1280, 1288 (5th Cir. 1976).
700. *See, e.g.*, United States v. Newell, 658 F.3d 1, 15 (1st Cir. 2011), *cert. denied*, 132 S. Ct. 430 (2011); United States v. Lupton, 620 F.3d 790, 806 (7th Cir. 2010), *cert. denied*, 131 S. Ct. 1544 (2011); U.S. Attorney's Manual, Criminal Resource Manual at 910.
701. *See* Cheek v. United States, 498 U.S. 192, 201 (1991); Ratzlaf v. United States, 510 U.S. 135, 137 (1994); Bryan v. United States, 524 U.S. 184, 193-96 (1998).
702. *See, e.g.*, United States v. Starnes, 583 F.3d 196, 211 (3d Cir. 2009).
703. United States v. Gaudin, 515 U.S. 506, 509 (1995) (quoting Kungys v. United States, 485 U.S. 759, 770 (1988)), *cert. denied*, 513 U.S. 1087 (1995); *see also* United States v. Moore, 612 F.3d 668, 701 (D.C. Cir. 2010).
704. United States v. Boffil-Rivera, 607 F.3d 736, 741-42 (11th Cir. 2010); United States v. Logan, 250 F.3d 350, 361 (6th Cir. 2001), *cert. denied*, 534 U.S. 895 (2001); United States v. Sarihifard, 155 F.3d 301, 307 (4th Cir. 1998); United States v. Vaughn, 797 F.2d 1485, 1490 (9th Cir. 1986).
705. Bryson v. United States, 396 U.S. 64, 70 (1969).
706. United States v. Rodgers, 466 U.S. 475, 479 (1984), *cert. denied*, 131 S. Ct. 999 (2011); *see also* United States v. Jackson, 608 F.3d 193, 196-97 (4th Cir. 2010); United States v. Atalig, 502 F.3d 1063, 1068 (9th Cir. 2007); United States v. White, 270 F.3d 356, 363 (6th Cir. 2001).
707. United States v. Cota, 2008 U.S. Dist. LEXIS 65911 **8-9 (N.D. Cal. July 21, 2008); United States v. Hooper, 596 F.2d 219, 223 (7th Cir. 1979); *see also* United States v. Gibson, 881 F.2d 318, 322 (6th Cir. 1989).

has the authority to demand and review those records to assure compliance with a federal program.[708] At its broadest, the jurisdictional reach of Section 1001 extends to any conduct which "which might result in the frustration of authorized government functions," even if the statement is not made to a federal official.[709] A defendant need not be aware of the federal involvement to violate Section 1001.[710]

d. Duty to Disclose

To obtain a conviction for concealment of a material fact, unlike that for false representation, the prosecutor must prove that the defendant had a legal duty to disclose the fact concealed. The government also must establish that the law required disclosure of the information at the time the defendant allegedly concealed it.[711] The "duty to disclose" element of Section 1001(a)(1) can be established by demonstrating that a federal statute, regulation, agency form, or regulator's questions required such disclosure.[712]

3. Common Uses of False or Misleading Statement Offenses in Environmental Criminal Cases

a. Lying to Government Officials

Section 1001 prosecutions often arise from instances in which persons lie to inspectors or investigators or submit false information in response to official requests. Such prosecutions are common in situations where persons who are eventually charged with environmental crimes attempt to conceal the existence of the violations by lying or preventing agencies from discovering incriminating material during the early stages of an investigation.

For example, in *United States v King*,[713] an Idaho Department of Agriculture inspector asked the defendant where an exposed valve and buried pipe led. The defendant responded that the valve led to the farm's irrigation system, when it in fact led directly to an underground well. The defendant was charged under Section 1001 for lying about the endpoint of the valve, as well as for unlawfully injecting wastewater into underground wells in violation of the Safe Drinking Water Act. Notwithstanding that the defendant's false statement was made to a state inspector, the court held that statement concerned a violation of federal law and therefore was within the jurisdiction of the United States.

b. Vessel Pollution Cases

In pursuing its "Vessel Pollution Initiative," the DOJ ECS routinely invokes Section 1001 to prosecute foreign flagged vessels involved in alleged instances of marine pollution that would otherwise be outside United States jurisdiction.

In *United States v. Royal Caribbean Cruises Ltd.*,[714] the Coast Guard observed a cruise ship discharging oil off the coast of the Bahamas. When the vessel docked in Miami, the agency conducted an inspection, during which it discovered that the vessel's ORB failed to document the discharge. The Southern District of Florida denied Royal Caribbean's motion to dismiss a criminal charge under Section 1001, holding that the United States had jurisdiction to prosecute a false statement charge if the statement occurred in a domestic port, even if it lacked jurisdiction to prosecute the underlying environmental discharge.

In the intervening years since *Royal Caribbean*, similar prosecutions have been filed against numerous other shipping companies and individuals, including: Evergreen International, S.A. ($25 million penalty);

---

708. *See, e.g.*, United States v. Rutgard, 116 F.3d 1270, 1287 (9th Cir. 1997).
709. United States v. Green, 745 F.2d 1205, 1210 (9th Cir. 1985); United States v. Starnes, 583 F.3d 196, 208 (3d Cir. 2009).
710. United States v. Yermian, 468 U.S. 63, 73-74 (1984).
711. United States v. Mubayyid, 658 F.3d 35, 70 (1st Cir. 2011), *cert. denied*, 132 S. Ct. 2378 (2012); United States v. Curran, 20 F.3d 560, 566 (3d Cir. 1994).
712. United States v. Mubayyid, 658 F.3d 35, 70 (1st Cir. 2011); United States v. Stewart, 433 F.3d 273, 318-19 (2d Cir. 2006); United States v. Kingston, 971 F.2d 481, 489 (10th Cir. 1992).
713. 660 F.3d 1071 (9th Cir. 2011), *cert. denied*, 132 S. Ct. 2740 (2012).
714. 11 F. Supp. 2d 1358 (S.D. Fla. 1998).

The National Navigation Company ($7.25 million penalty); MSC Ship Management ($10.5 million penalty); Clipper Marine Services ($4.75 million penalty); Wallenius Ship Management, Pte., Ltd. ($6.5 million penalty); Rick Stickle (33 month sentence of imprisonment for Chairman of Sabine Transportation); Overseas Shipholding Group ($37 million penalty); Irika Shipping S.A. ($4 million penalty); OMI ($4.2 million fine).[715]

According to the DOJ, "criminal penalties imposed in vessel pollution cases over the past ten years have totaled over $200,000,000, and responsible shipboard officers and shore-side officials have been sentenced to more than 17 years of incarceration." It should come as no surprise that DOJ ECS attorneys continue to devote much attention towards enforcing the Vessel Pollution Initiative.

c. Submission of Reports and Permit Applications

Most environmental regulatory statutes, including the CAA, CWA, CERCLA, and RCRA, include mandatory permitting and reporting requirements. As a result, the government routinely includes false statement charges in those cases in addition to charges involve substantive violations of the underlying statute.

For example, in *United States v. Panyard*,[716] the defendant submitted a signed CWA discharge permit application to the authorized state regulatory authority. The application stated that defendant's company was in compliance with pretreatment discharge standards even though it was discharging untreated wastewater into municipal sewers. In addition to facing CWA charges for the unpermitted discharges, the defendant was charged and convicted under Section 1001 for signing the false report, as well as for directing employees to falsify discharge logs and lie to EPA investigators.

B. *Obstruction of Justice/Destruction of Evidence*

Several federal criminal statutes, generally referred to as the obstruction of justice statutes, criminalize a broad range of improper conduct aimed at avoiding prosecution. The omnibus obstruction of justice provision, 18 U.S.C. §1503, broadly provides, "Whoever . . . corruptly or by threats or force, or by any threatening letter or communication, influences, obstructs, or impedes, or endeavors to influence, obstruct, or impede, the due administration of justice, shall be [guilty of an offense]." Section 1503 serves as a catchall for conduct that is intended to influence, obstruct, or impede a pending judicial or grand jury proceeding.[717] Federal prosecutors have applied it to prosecute a wide range of conduct, including destroying documents, suborning perjury, and lying to a grand jury.[718]

Various forms of obstructive conduct also may fall within the bounds of a handful of more specific statutes. Among the more commonly encountered obstruction provisions is 18 U.S.C. §1505, which prohibits the obstruction of proceedings before federal departments, agencies, and committees, but is comparable to Section 1503 in other material respects. Similarly, 18 U.S.C. §1512(a) criminalizes attempts to use threats or violence to prevent witnesses from speaking with law enforcement authorities, and 18 U.S.C. §1512(c) makes it an offense to destroy documents or other evidence. Destroying or making false entries in records also commonly results in charges under 18 U.S.C. §1519.

Typically, obstruction occurs after the initiation of a federal investigation. However, a recent decision by the Court of Appeals for the Sixth Circuit, *United States v. Kernell*,[719] has clarified that the language of 18 U.S.C. §1519 covers certain actions taken prior to the initiation of any federal inquiry as well.[720] In *Kernell*, the defendant had illegally accessed the email account of then-Alaska governor and vice-presidential

715. U.S. DOJ, Vessel Pollution Enforcement, http://www.justice.gov/enrd/3395.htm (last visited May 29, 2013).
716. 403 F. App'x 17 (6th Cir. 2010).
717. United States v. Aguilar, 515 U.S. 593, 598 (1995).
718. *See* U.S. Attorney's Manual, Criminal Resource Manual 1724 (hereinafter Criminal Resource Manual) (listing examples).
719. 667 F.3d 746, 750-51 (6th Cir. Tenn. 2012), *cert. denied*, 133 S. Ct. 259 (2012).
720. 18 U.S.C. §1519 states:

> Whoever knowingly alters, destroys, mutilates, conceals, covers up, falsifies, or makes a false entry in any record, document, or tangible object with the intent to impede, obstruct, or influence the investigation or proper administration of any matter within the jurisdiction of any department or agency of the United States or any case filed under title 11, *or in relation to or contemplation of any such matter or case*, shall be fined under this title, imprisoned not more than 20 years, or both. (Emphasis added.)

candidate, Sarah Palin. The defendant posted online about his activities, including that he had deleted certain information from his computer out of fear of being investigated.[721] There was no question that the federal investigation into the defendant's activities began after the information had been deleted from his computer. After being convicted under Section 1519, the defendant appealed on the grounds that the statute was unconstitutionally vague and that there was insufficient evidence to convict him of a violation.

The Sixth Circuit upheld the district court's decision, confirming that obstruction of justice in advance of the initiation of a federal proceeding is permissible in certain circumstances. The appellate court's reasoning was similar to that in *United States v. Russell,* where a district court held that Section 1519 was not unconstitutionally vague because "the common understanding of 'in relation to' and 'in contemplation of,'" allows a "person of ordinary intelligence. . . reasonable opportunity to understand that destroying a tangible object with the intent to obstruct a federal investigation, or doing so with reference to, or with the purpose of effecting a federal investigation, *or in anticipation of, or envisioning,* such an investigation, is prohibited, but that doing so coincidentally is not."[722]

Although coincidental destruction of documents does not give rise to the level of intent required under 18 U.S.C. §1519, it remains to be seen what level of circumstantial evidence will suffice in convincing a jury that the destruction of information was "other than" coincidental. Although the 'in contemplation of' or 'in relation to' language of 18 U.S.C. §1519 does not yet appear to have been applied in an environmental criminal case, it is likely only a matter of time before it is.

1. Essential Elements of Obstruction of Justice

To obtain a conviction under Section 1503, the prosecution must prove:

- There was a pending judicial or grand jury proceeding constituting the administration of justice;
- The defendant knew or had notice of the proceeding; and
- The defendant acted corruptly to influence, obstruct, or impede the proceeding.[723]

2. Key Concepts for Obstruction of Justice

a. Corrupt Motive

Generally, the government must show that the defendant knowingly and intentionally undertook an action for which interference with an official proceeding was a reasonably foreseeable result.[724] Although the government is not required to prove that the defendant had the specific purpose of obstructing justice, it must establish that the conduct was prompted, at least in part, by an improper motive.[725]

b. Endeavored

The government needs to show only that the defendant "endeavored" to obstruct justice, not that the effort actually succeeded. To satisfy the "endeavored" element, the government needs to show something less than for an "attempted" obstruction. For example, a court held that a defendant's instruction to one of his employees to tell a juror that he was a friend and a "nice guy" constituted an endeavor to improperly influence that juror.[726]

721. *Id.* at 749.
722. United States v. Russell, 639 F. Supp. 2d 266, 240 (D. Conn. 2007) (emphasis added).
723. *See* United States v. Quattrone, 441 F.3d 153, 170 (2d Cir. 2006); United States v. Fassnacht, 332 F.3d 440, 447-48 (7th Cir. 2003); United States v. Thomas, 916 F.2d 647, 651 (11th Cir. 1990).
724. *See, e.g.,* United States v. Phillips, 583 F.3d 1261, 1264-65 (10th Cir. 2009), *cert. denied,* 558 U.S. 1100 (2009); United States v. Reich, 479 F.3d 179, 185-86 (2d Cir. 2007), *cert. denied,* 552 U.S. 819 (2007); United States v. Matthews, 505 F.3d 698, 706 (7th Cir. 2007).
725. *See* United States v. Barfield, 999 F.2d 1520, 1524 (11th Cir. 1993), *cert. denied,* 522 U.S. 875 (1997) (citing United States v. Thomas, 916 F.2d 647, 651 (11th Cir. 1990) (internal citations omitted)).
726. United States v. Tedesco, 635 F.2d 902, 907 (1st Cir. 1980), *cert. denied,* 452 U.S. 962 (1981).

c. Proceeding

Under Section 1503, the alleged obstruction must have occurred in the course of a pending civil or criminal proceeding, and the defendant must have been aware of the pending proceeding.[727] A grand jury proceeding constitutes a proceeding under Section 1503 and is considered pending once "a subpoena [has been] issued in furtherance of an actual grand jury investigation, i.e., to secure a presently contemplated presentation of evidence before a regularly sitting grand jury."[728] It is important to note, however, that under some obstruction statutes, such as 18 U.S.C. §1512 (tampering with a witness to or victim of unlawful conduct), an official proceeding need not be pending; it need only be foreseeable.[729] In addition, under Section 1505 (obstruction of certain federal agency activities), the term "proceeding" has been interpreted broadly to include investigative and adjudicative functions of an agency.[730]

Importantly, routine EPA and OSHA inspections for which no search warrant is required may constitute "pending proceedings" for purposes of an obstruction charge.[731] For example, in *United States v. Stickle*,[732] the court held that a Coast Guard boarding constituted a "pending proceeding," based on the agency's "discretionary or adjudicative power" and the "power to enhance [its] investigations through the issuance of subpoenas or warrants."[733]

3. Common Uses of Obstruction Offenses in Environmental Criminal Cases

Obstruction charges routinely accompany criminal environmental charges. For example, in *United States v. Technic Services Inc.*,[734] a joint inspection by EPA and OSHA found numerous problems with the defendant's asbestos remediation work at a closed-down pulp mill, including potential air monitoring violations and disposal of asbestos-containing wastewater through a drain that emptied into a nearby bay. The defendant provided EPA with a statement signed by thirteen employees claiming that no wastewater was being unlawfully discharged. After further investigation, the corporate defendant was charged with seven counts of obstruction of justice under 18 U.S.C. §1505, in addition to a CAA violation for improper asbestos air monitoring and a CWA violation for the wastewater discharges. One of the obstruction charges was based on tampering with the personal air monitoring devises worn by workers. The other six obstruction charges arose from the defendant's efforts to obtain signatures from employees falsely claiming that no unlawful wastewater discharges had occurred. The defendant was convicted of the substantive CAA and CWA violations and all seven of the obstruction charges, although one of the obstruction charges was overturned on appeal on evidentiary grounds.

The ECS routinely uses obstruction of justice charges in prosecuting vessel pollution cases. For instance, on July 8, 2010, Irika Shipping S.A., pleaded guilty to felony obstruction of justice charges related to concealing deliberate vessel pollution from a Greek flagged cargo ship, the M/V Iorana. In pleading guilty, the company admitted in a joint factual statement that it obstructed justice in various ways, including: senior ship officers made false statements to the Coast Guard; crew members were told to lie to the Coast Guard; and evidence of illegal dumping was destroyed. The stipulated $4 million penalty included a $3 million criminal fine and $1 million in organizational community service payments that funded various marine environmental projects.[735]

---

727. United States v. Aguilar, 515 U.S. 593, 599 (1995); United States v. Williams, 874 F.2d 968, 977 (5th Cir. 1989).
728. *See* United States v. Walasek, 527 F.2d 676, 678-79 (3d Cir. 1975).
729. *See* Arthur Andersen LLP v. United States, 544 U.S. 696, 707-08 (2005); United States v. Kaplan, 490 F.3d 110, 125-26 (2d Cir. 2007).
730. *See* United States v. Browning, Inc., 572 F.2d 720, 723-24 (10th Cir. 1978) (quoting United States v. Fruchtman, 421 F.2d 1019 (6th Cir. 1970)), *cert. denied*, 439 U.S. 822 (1978).
731. *See, e.g.*, United States v. W.R. Grace, Inc., Indictment, *available at* http://fl1.findlaw.com/news.findlaw.com/hdocs/docs/asbestos/uswrgrace20705ind.pdf (last visited May 30, 2013); United States v. Atlantic Cast Iron Pipe Company, Indictment, *available at* http://www.justice.gov/opa/pr/2006/April/06_enrd_250.html (last visited May 30, 2013).
732. 355 F. Supp. 2d 1317 (S.D. Fla. 2004), *aff'd*, 454 F.3d 1265 (11th Cir. 2006).
733. *Id.* at 1329.
734. 314 F.3d 1031 (9th Cir. 2002).
735. *See* Press Release, DOJ, Ship Management Corp. to Pay $4 Million Penalty for Concealing Deliberate Pollution (July 9, 2010), *available at* http://www.justice.gov/opa/pr/2010/July/10-enrd-788.html.

C. *Conspiracy*

Because environmental crimes almost always involve multiple individuals, conspiracy charges are frequently included in the charges against the accused. A corporation also may be convicted of conspiracy, including a conspiracy based solely on actions with its own employees.[736]

1. Essential Elements of Conspiracy

To obtain a conviction under the general federal conspiracy statute, 18 U.S.C. §371, an environmental prosecutor must prove:

(1) an agreement between two or more persons;

(2) to accomplish an illegal objective; and

(3) an overt act committed by one or more of the coconspirators in furtherance of the conspiracy.[737]

2. Key Concepts for Conspiracy

a. Agreement

The key element of a conspiracy is an agreement by two or more persons to commit an unlawful act with a common purpose.[738] While the co-conspirators need not agree on the details of their criminal enterprise, they must be aware of the overall nature and objective of the joint scheme.[739] Because there rarely is direct evidence of a conspiratorial agreement between parties, a defendant's actions may provide circumstantial evidence of the agreement.[740]

c. Illegal Objective

The goal of the conspiracy must be either to defraud or hinder a lawful federal government objective or to violate a federal law. To obtain a conviction on a charge of conspiracy to violate a federal statute, the government must prove at least the degree of criminal intent necessary for a conviction of the substantive offense itself.[741]

c. Overt Act

The overt act requirement ensures that the alleged conspiracy has gone further than mere scheming. Any overt act by any conspirator, lawful or not, which furthers the conspiracy satisfies this requirement.[742] A conspirator is held liable under the statute for the acts of his co-conspirators during the period of his participation in the conspiracy, whether he knew of these actions or not.

---

736. *See* United States v. Peters, 732 F.2d 1004, 1008 (1st Cir. 1984); United States v. S & Vee Cartage Co., Inc., 704 F.2d 914, 920 (6th Cir. 1983), *cert. denied*, 464 U.S. 935 (1983); United States v. Hartley, 678 F.2d 961 (11th Cir. 1982), *cert. denied*, 459 U.S. 1170 (1983); United States v. Consol. Coal Co., 424 F. Supp. 577 (S.D. Ohio 1976); *see also* McAndrew v. Lockheed Martin Corp., 206 F.3d 1031, 1038-39 (11th Cir. 2000).

737. Braverman v. United States, 317 U.S. 49 (1942); United States v. Thompson, 518 F.3d 832, 853 (10th Cir. 2008); United States v. Ndiaye, 434 F.3d 1270, 1294 (11th Cir. 2006); United States v. Gosselin World Wide Moving, NV, 411 F.3d 502, 516 (4th Cir. 2005), *cert. denied*, 547 U.S. 1002 (2006); United States v. Hasson, 333 F.3d 1264, 1270 (11th Cir. 2003), *cert. denied*, 543 U.S. 1173 (2005).

738. *See* United States v. Chandler, 376 F.3d 1303, 1315 (11th Cir. 2004); United States v. Borelli, 336 F.2d 376, 384 (2d Cir. 1964).

739. *See* Blumenthal v. United States, 332 U.S. 539, 557 (1947); United States v. Chandler, 376 F.3d 1303, 1315 (11th Cir. 2004); United States v. Downing, 297 F.3d 52, 57 (2d Cir. 2002).

740. *See* United States v. Thompson, 518 F.3d 832, 853 (10th Cir. 2008).

741. *See* United States v. Feola, 420 U.S. 671, 686 (1975); United States v. Bedford, 536 F.3d 1148, 1155 (10th Cir. 2008), *cert. denied*, 555 U.S. 1191 (2009); United States v. Soy, 454 F.3d 766, 768 (7th Cir. 2006), *cert. denied*, 549 U.S. 1065 (2006).

742. United States v. Pursley, 474 F.3d 757, 768 (10th Cir. 2007), *cert. denied*, 552 U.S. 829 (2007); Omari v. Gonzales, 419 F.3d 303, 309 n.12 (5th Cir. 2005); United States v. Medina, 761 F.2d 12, 15 (1st Cir. 1985).

3. Common Uses of Conspiracy Offenses in Environmental Criminal Cases

The prosecution in *United States v. Overholt*,[743] illustrates how environmental prosecutors employ conspiracy charges. An environmental services company and a trucking company developed a joint scheme to unlawfully dispose of untreated wastewater. Instead of transporting the wastewater to the environmental services company's treatment facility, the parties agreed that the trucking company would deliver the untreated wastewater directly to a disposal well. The presidents of both companies were charged and convicted of a five-object conspiracy for conspiring unlawfully to dispose of wastewater in violation of the Solid Waste Disposal Act and transport hazardous waste without a manifest in violation of the RCRA.

United States v. Fountain,[744] is another example of the common use of conspiracy charges in environmental criminal cases. Two defendants operated a fishing business that was harvesting oysters in violation of state law. Based largely on circumstantial evidence regarding their positions and management roles in the company, both defendants were charged and convicted of conspiring to violate the Lacey Act, as well as substantive Lacey Act violations. Further, under application of the *Pinkerton* doctrine,[745] one of the defendants was found criminally liable for the Lacey Act false record offense committed by the other defendant in furtherance of the conspiracy.

743. 307 F.3d 1231 (10th Cir. 2002).
744. 277 F.3d 714 (5th Cir. 2001).
745. *See* Pinkerton v. United States, 328 U.S. 640 (1946), *rehearing denied*, 328 U.S. 818 (1946).

Environmental Crimes Deskbook

Appendix I Memorandum From Earl E. Devaney, Director, Office of Criminal Enforcement, to All EPA Employees Working in or in Support of the Criminal Enforcement Program, The Exercise of Investigative Discretion (Jan. 12, 1994)

UNITED STATES ENVIRONMENTAL PROTECTION AGENCY
WASHINGTON, D.C. 20460

January 12, 1994

OFFICE OF ENFORCEMENT

MEMORANDUM

SUBJECT: The Exercise of Investigative Discretion

FROM: Earl E. Devaney, Director
Office of Criminal Enforcement

TO: All EPA Employees Working in or in Support of the Criminal Enforcement Program

I. Introduction

As EPA's criminal enforcement program enters its second decade and embarks on a period of unprecedented growth, this guidance establishes the principles that will guide the exercise of investigative discretion by EPA Special Agents. This guidance combines articulations of Congressional intent underlying the environmental criminal provisions with the Office of Criminal Enforcement's (OCE) experience operating under EPA's existing criminal case-screening criteria.[1]

In an effort to maximize our limited criminal resources, this guidance sets out the specific factors that distinguish cases meriting criminal investigation from those more appropriately pursued under administrative or civil judicial authorities.[2]

Indeed, the Office of Criminal Enforcement has an obligation to the American public, to our colleagues throughout EPA, the regulated community, Congress, and the media to instill confidence that EPA's criminal program has the proper mechanisms in place to ensure the discriminate use of the powerful law enforcement authority entrusted to us.

II. Legislative Intent Regarding Case Selection

The criminal provisions of the environmental laws are the most powerful enforcement tools available to EPA. Congressional intent underlying the environmental criminal provisions is unequivocal: criminal enforcement authority should target the most significant and egregious violators.

The Pollution Prosecution Act of 1990 recognized the importance of a strong national environmental criminal enforcement program and mandates additional resources necessary for the criminal program to fulfill its statutory mission. The sponsors of the Act recognized that EPA had long been in the posture of reacting to serious violations only after harm was done, primarily due to limited resources. Senator Joseph I. Lieberman (Conn.), one of the co-sponsors of the Act, explained that as a result of limited resources, "[hellip] few cases are the product of reasoned or targeted focus on suspected wrongdoing." He also expressed his hope that with the Act's provision of additional Special Agents, "[hellip] EPA would be able to bring cases that would have greater deterrent value than those currently being brought."

Further illustrative of Congressional intent that the most serious of violations should be addressed by criminal enforcement authority is the legislative history concerning the enhanced criminal provisions of RCRA:

> [The criminal provisions were] intended to prevent abuses of the permit system by those who obtain and then knowingly disregard them. It [RCRA sec. 3008(d)] is not aimed at punishing minor or technical variations from permit regulations or conditions if the facility operator is acting responsibly. The Department of Justice has exercised its prosecutorial discretion responsibly under similar provisions in other statutes and the con-

1. This guidance incorporates by reference the policy document entitled *Regional Enforcement Management: Enhanced Regional Case Screening* (December 3, 1990).
2. This memorandum is intended only as internal guidance to EPA. It is not intended to, does not, and may not be relied upon to, create a right or benefit, substantive or procedural, enforceable at law by a party to litigation with the United States, nor does this guidance in any way limit the lawful enforcement prerogatives, including administrative or civil enforcement actions, of the Department of Justice and the Environmental Protection Agency.

ferees assume that, in light of the upgrading of the penalties from misdemeanor to felony, similar care will be used in deciding when a particular permit violation may warrant criminal prosecution under this Act. H.R. Conf. Rep. No. 1444, 96th Cong., 2d Sess. 37, reprinted in 1980 U.S. Code Cong. & Admin. News 5036.

While EPA has doubled its Special Agent corps since passage of the Pollution Prosecution Act, and has achieved a presence in nearly all federal judicial districts, it is unlikely that OCE will ever be large enough in size to fully defeat the ever-expanding universe of environmental crime. Rather, OCE must maximize its presence and impact through discerning case-selection, and then proceed with investigations that advance EPA's overall goal of regulatory compliance and punishing criminal wrongdoing.

III. Case Selection Process[3]

The case selection process is designed to identify misconduct worthy of criminal investigation. The case selection process is not an effort to establish legal sufficiency for prosecution. Rather, the process by which potential cases are analyzed under the case selection criteria will serve as an affirmative indication that OCE has purposefully directed its investigative resources toward deserving cases.

This is not to suggest that all cases meeting the case selection criteria will proceed to prosecution. Indeed, the exercise of investigative discretion must be clearly distinguished from the exercise of prosecutorial discretion. The employment of OCE's investigative discretion to dedicate its investigative authority is, however, a critical precursor to the prosecutorial discretion later exercised by the Department of Justice.[4]

At the conclusion of the case selection process, OCE should be able to articulate the basis of its decision to pursue a criminal investigation, based on the case selection criteria. Conversely, cases that do not ultimately meet the criteria to proceed criminally, should be systematically referred back to the Agency's civil enforcement office for appropriate administrative or civil judicial action, or to a state or local prosecutor.

IV. Case Selection Criteria

The criminal case selection process will be guided by two general measures—significant environmental harm and culpable conduct.

A. Significant Environmental Harm

The measure of significant environmental harm should be broadly construed to include the presence of actual harm, as well as the threat of significant harm, to the environment or human health. The following factors serve as indicators that a potential case will meet the measure of significant environmental harm.

Factor 1. *Actual* harm will be demonstrated by an illegal discharge, release or emission that has an identifiable and significant harmful impact on human health or the environment. This measure will generally be self-evident at the time of case selection.[5]

Factor 2. The *threat* of significant harm to the environment or human health may be demonstrated by an actual or threatened discharge, release or emission. This factor may not be as readily evident, and must be assessed in light of all the facts available at the time of case selection.

Factor 3. Failure to report an actual discharge, release or emission within the context of Factors 1 or 2 will serve as an additional factor favoring criminal investigation. While the failure to report, alone, may be a criminal violation, our investigative resources should generally be targeted toward those cases in which the failure to report is coupled with actual or threatened environmental harm.

Factor 4. When certain illegal conduct appears to represent a trend or common attitude within the regulated community, criminal investigation may provide a significant deterrent effect incommensurate with its singular environmental impact. While the single violation being considered may have a relatively insignificant impact on human health or the environment, such violations, if multiplied by the numbers in a cross-section of the regulated community, would result in significant environmental harm.

---

3. The case *selection* process must not be confused with the Regional Case Screening Process. The relationship between the Regional Case Screening Process and case selection are discussed further at "VI.", below.

4. Exercise of this prosecutorial discretion in all criminal cases is governed by the principles set forth in the Department of Justice's *Principles of Federal Prosecution.*

5. When this factor involves a fact situation in which the risk of harm is so great, so immediate and/or irremediable, OCE will always cooperate and coordinate with EPA's civil enforcement authorities to seek appropriate injunctive or remedial action.

B. *Culpable Conduct*

The measure of culpable conduct is not *necessarily* an assessment of criminal intent, particularly since criminal intent will not always be readily evident at the time of case selection. Culpable conduct, however, may be indicated at the time of case selection by several factors.

Factor 1. History of repeated violations.

While a history of repeated violations is not a prerequisite to a criminal investigation, a potential target's compliance record should always be carefully examined. When repeated enforcement activities or actions, whether by EPA, or other federal, state and local enforcement authorities, have failed to bring a violator into compliance, criminal investigation may be warranted. Clearly, a history of repeated violations will enhance the government's capacity to prove that a violator was aware of environmental regulatory requirements, had actual notice of violations and then acted in deliberate disregard of those requirements.

Factor 2. Deliberate misconduct resulting in violation.

Although the environmental statutes do not require proof of specific intent, evidence, either direct or circumstantial, that a violation was deliberate will be a major factor indicating that criminal investigation is warranted.

Factor 3. Concealment of misconduct or falsification of required records.

In the arena of self-reporting, EPA must be able to rely on data received from the regulated community. If submitted data are false, EPA is prevented from effectively carrying out its mandate. Accordingly, conduct indicating the falsification of data will always serve as the basis for serious consideration to proceed with a criminal investigation.

Factor 4. Tampering with monitoring or control equipment.

The overt act of tampering with monitoring or control equipment leads to the certain production of false data that appears to be otherwise accurate. The consequent submission of false data threatens the basic integrity of EPA's data and, in turn, the scientific validity of EPA's regulatory decisions. Such an assault on the regulatory infrastructure calls for the enforcement leverage of criminal investigation.

Factor 5. Business operation of pollution-related activities without a permit, license, manifest or other required documentation.

Many of the laws and regulations within EPA's jurisdiction focus on inherently dangerous and strictly regulated business operations. EPA's criminal enforcement resources should clearly pursue those violators who choose to ignore environmental regulatory requirements altogether and operate completely outside of EPA's regulatory scheme.

V. Additional Considerations When Investigating Corporations

While the factors under measures IV. A and B, above, apply equally to both individual and corporate targets, several additional considerations should be taken into account when the potential target is a corporation.

In a criminal environmental investigation, OCE should always investigate individual employees and their corporate[6] employers who may be culpable. A corporation is, by law, responsible for the criminal act of its officers and employees who act within the scope of their employment and in furtherance of the purposes of the corporation. Whether the corporate officer or employee personally commits the act, or directs, aids, or counsels other employees to do so is inconsequential to the issue of corporate culpability.

Corporate culpability may also be indicated when a company performs an environmental compliance or management audit, and then knowingly fails to promptly remedy the noncompliance and correct any harm done.[7] On the other hand, EPA policy strongly encourages self-monitoring, self-disclosure, and self-correction.[8] When self-auditing has been conducted (followed up by prompt remediation of the noncompliance and any resulting harm) and full,

6. The term "corporate" or "corporation", as used in this guidance, describes any business entity, whether legally incorporated or not.
7. In cases of self-auditing and/or voluntary disclosure, the exercise of prosecutorial discretion is addressed in the Department of Justice policy document entitled "Factors in Decisions on Criminal Prosecutions for Environmental Violations in the Context of Significant Voluntary Compliance or Disclosure Efforts by the Violator" (July 1, 1991).
8. See EPA's policy on environmental audits, published at 51 Fed. Reg. 25004 (July 9, 1986)

complete disclosure has occurred, the company's constructive activities should be considered as mitigating factors in EPA's exercise of investigative discretion. Therefore, a violation that is voluntarily revealed and fully and promptly remedied as part of a corporation's systematic and comprehensive self-evaluation program generally will not be a candidate for the expenditure of scarce criminal investigative resources.

VI. Other Case Selection Considerations

EPA has a full range of enforcement tools available—administrative, civil-judicial, and criminal. There is universal consensus that less flagrant violations with lesser environmental consequences should be addressed through administrative or civil monetary penalties and remedial orders, while the most serious environmental violations ought to be investigated criminally. The challenge in practice is to correctly distinguish the latter cases from the former.

The case-selection factors' described in this guidance should provide the foundation for the communication process that necessarily follows in the Regional Case Screening Process. This guidance envisions application of the case-selection factors first, to be followed by the recurring scrutiny of cases during the Regional Case Screening process.

The fundamental purpose of Regional Case Screening is to consider criminal enforcement in the greater context of all available EPA enforcement and environmental response options, to do so early (at the time of each case opening) before extensive resources have been expended, and to identify, prioritize, and target the most egregious cases. Regional Case Screening is designed to be an ongoing process in which enforcement cases are periodically reviewed to assess not only the evidentiary developments, but should also evaluate the clarity of the legal and regulatory authorities upon which a given case is being developed.[9]

In order to achieve the objectives of case screening, all cases originating within the OCE must be presented fully and fairly to the appropriate Regional program managers. Thorough analysis of a case using the case-selection factors will prepare OCE for a well-reasoned presentation in the Regional Case Screening process. Faithful adherence to the OCE case-selection process and active participation in the Regional Case Screening Process will serve to eliminate potential disparities between Agency program goals and priorities and OCE's undertaking of criminal investigations.

Full and effective implementation of these processes will achieve two important results: it will ensure that OCE's investigative resources are being directed properly and expended efficiently, and it will foreclose assertions that EPA's criminal program is imposing its powerful sanctions indiscriminately.

VII. Conclusion

The manner in which we govern ourselves in the use of EPA's most powerful enforcement tool is critical to the effective and reliable performance of our responsibilities, and will shape the reputation of this program for years to come. We must conduct ourselves in keeping with these principles which ensure the prudent and proper execution of the powerful law enforcement authorities entrusted to us.

9. The legal structure upon which a criminal case is built—e.g., statutory, regulatory, case law, preamble language and interpretative letters—must also be analyzed in terms of Agency enforcement practice under these authorities. Thorough discussion of this issue is beyond the scope of this document, but generally, when the clarity of the underlying legal authority is in dispute, the more appropriate vehicle for resolution lies, most often, in a civil or administrative setting.

Environmental Crimes Deskbook

Appendix 2 U.S. DOJ, Factors in Decisions on Criminal Prosecutions for Environmental Violations in the Context of Significant Voluntary Compliance or Disclosure Efforts by the Violator (July 1, 1991)

U.S. Department of Justice

Washington, D.C. 20530

July 1, 1991

Factors in Decisions on Criminal Prosecutions for Environmental Violations in the Context of Significant Voluntary Compliance or Disclosure Efforts by the Violator

I. Introduction

It is the policy of the Department of Justice to encourage self-auditing, self-policing and voluntary disclosure of environmental violations by the regulated community by indicating that these activities are viewed as mitigating factors in the Department's exercise of criminal environmental enforcement discretion. This document is intended to describe the factors that the Department of Justice considers in deciding whether to bring a criminal prosecution for a violation of an environmental statute, so that such prosecutions do not create a disincentive to or undermine the goal of encouraging critical self-auditing, self-policing, and voluntary disclosure. It is designed to give federal prosecutors direction concerning the exercise of prosecutorial discretion in environmental criminal cases and to ensure that such discretion is exercised consistently nationwide. It is also intended to give the regulated community a sense of how the federal government exercises its criminal prosecutorial discretion with respect to such factors as the defendant's voluntary disclosure of violations, cooperation with the government in investigating the violations, use of environmental audits and other procedures to ensure compliance with all applicable environmental laws and regulations, and use of measures to remedy expeditiously and completely any violations and the harms caused thereby.

This guidance and the examples contained herein provide a framework for the determination of whether a particular case presents the type of circumstances in which lenience would be appropriate.

II. Factors to Be Considered

Where the law and evidence would otherwise be sufficient for prosecution, the attorney for the Department should consider the actors contained herein, to the extent they are applicable, along with any other relevant factors, in determining whether and how to prosecute. It must be emphasized that these are examples of the types of factors which could be relevant. They do not constitute a definitive recipe or checklist of requirements. They merely illustrate some of the types of information which is relevant to our exercise of prosecutorial discretion.

It is unlikely that any one factor will be dispositive in any given case. All relevant factors are considered and given the weight deemed appropriate in the particular case. See *Federal Principles of Prosecution* (U.S. Dept. of Justice, 1980), Comment to Part A.2; Part B.3.

A. *Voluntary Disclosure*

The attorney for the Department should consider whether the person[1] made a voluntary, timely and complete disclosure of the matter under investigation. Consideration should be given to whether the person came forward promptly after discovering the noncompliance, and to the quantity and quality of information provided. Particular consideration should be given to whether the disclosure substantially aided the government's investigatory process, and whether it occurred before a law enforcement cr regulatory authority (federal, state or local authority) had already obtained knowledge regarding noncompliance. A disclosure is not considered to be "voluntary" if that disclosure is already specifically required by law, regulation, or permit.[2]

---

1. As used in this document, the terms "person" and "violator" are intended to refer to business and nonprofit entities as well as individuals.
2. For example, any person in charge of a vessel or of an on shore facility or an offshore facility is required to notify the appropriate agency of the United States Government of any discharge of oil or a hazardous substance into or upon *inter alia* the navigable waters of the United States. Section 311(b) (5) of the Clean Water Act, 33 U.S.C. 1321(b)(5), as amended by the Oil Pollution Act of 1990, Pub. L. No. 101-380, §4301(a), 104 Stat. 485, 533 (1990).

B. *Cooperation*

The attorney for the Department should consider the degree and timeliness of cooperation by the person. Full and prompt cooperation is essential, whether in the context of a voluntary disclosure or after the government has independently learned of a violation. Consideration should be given to the violator's willingness to make all relevant information (including the complete results of any internal or external investigation and the names of all potential witnesses) available to government investigators and prosecutors. Consideration should also be given to the extent and quality of the violator's assistance to the government's investigation.

C. *Preventive Measures and Compliance Programs*

The attorney for the Department should consider the existence and scope of any regularized, intensive, and comprehensive environmental compliance program; such a program may include an environmental compliance or management audit. Particular consideration should be given to whether the compliance or audit program includes sufficient measures to identify and prevent future noncompliance, and whether the program was adopted in good faith in a timely manner.

Compliance programs may vary but the following questions should be asked in evaluating any program: Was there a strong institutional policy to comply with all environmental requirements? Had safeguards beyond those required by existing law been developed and implemented to prevent noncompliance from occurring? Were there regular procedures, including internal or external compliance and management audits, to evaluate, detect, prevent and remedy circumstances like those that led to the noncompliance? Were there procedures and safeguards to ensure the integrity of any audit conducted? Did the audit evaluate all sources of pollution (*i.e.*, all media), including the possibility of cross-media transfers of pollutants? Were the auditor's recommendations implemented in a timely fashion? Were adequate resources committed to the auditing program and to implementing its recommendations? Was environmental compliance a standard by which employee and corporate departmental performance was judged?

D. *Additional Factors Which May Relevant*

1. Pervasiveness of Noncompliance

Pervasive noncompliance may indicate systemic or repeated participation in or condonation of criminal behavior. It may also indicate the lack of a meaningful compliance program. In evaluating this factor, the attorney for the Department should consider, among other things, the number and level of employees participating in the unlawful activities and the obviousness, seriousness, duration, history, and frequency of noncompliance.

2. Internal Disciplinary Action

Effective internal disciplinary action is crucial to any compliance program. The attorney for the Department should consider whether there was an effective system of discipline for employees who violated company environmental compliance policies. Did the disciplinary system establish an awareness in other employees that unlawful conduct would not be condoned?

3. Subsequent Compliance Efforts

The attorney for the Department should consider the extent of any efforts to remedy any ongoing noncompliance. The promptness and completeness of any action taken to remove the source or the noncompliance and to lessen the environmental harm resulting from the noncompliance should be considered. Considerable weight should be given to prompt, good-faith efforts to reach environmental compliance agreements with federal cr state authorities, or both. Full compliance with such agreements should be a factor in any decision whether to prosecute.

III. Application of These Factors to Hypothetical Examples[3]

These examples are intended to assist federal prosecutors in their exercise of discretion in evaluating environmental cases. The situations facing prosecutors, of course, present a wide variety of fact patterns. Therefore, in a given case, some of the criteria may be satisfied while others may not. Moreover, satisfaction of various criteria may be a mat-

3. While this policy applies to both individuals and organizational violators, these examples focus particularly upon situations involving organizations.

ter of degree. Consequently, the effect of a given mix of factors also is a matter of degree. In the ideal situation, if a company fully meets all of the criteria, the result may be a decision not to prosecute that company criminally. Even if satisfaction of the criteria is not complete, still the company may benefit in terms of degree of enforcement response by the government. The following hypothetical examples are intended to illustrate the operation of these guidelines.

Example 1:

This is the ideal case in terms of criteria satisfaction and consequent prosecution leniency.

1. Company A regularly conducts a comprehensive audit of its compliance with environmental requirements.
2. The audit uncovers information about employees' disposing of hazardous wastes by dumping them in an unpermitted location.
3. An internal company investigation confirms the audit information. (Depending upon the nature of the audit, this follow-up investigation may be unnecessary.)
4. Prior to the violations the company had a sound compliance program, which included clear policies, employee training, and a hotline for suspected violations.
5. As soon as the company confirms the violations, it discloses all pertinent information to the appropriate government agency; it undertakes compliance planning with that agency; and it carries out satisfactory remediation measures.
6. The company also undertakes to correct any false information previously submitted to the government in relation to the violations.
7. Internally the company disciplines the employees actually involved in the violations, including any supervisor who was lax in preventing or detecting the activity. Also, the company reviews its compliance program to determine how the violations slipped by and corrects the weaknesses found by that review.
8. The company discloses to the government the names of the employees actually responsible for the violations, and it cooperates with the government by providing documentation necessary to the investigation of those persons.

Under these circumstances Company A would stand a good chance of being favorably considered for prosecutorial leniency, to the extent of not being criminally prosecuted at all. The degree of any leniency, however, may turn upon other relevant factors not specifically dealt with in these guidelines.[4]

Example 2:

At the opposite end of the scale is Company Z, which meets few of the criteria. The likelihood of prosecutorial leniency, therefore, is remote. Company Z's circumstances may include any of the following:

1. Because an employee has threatened to report a violation to federal authorities, the company is afraid that investigators may begin looking at it. An audit is undertaken, but it focuses only upon the particular violation, ignoring the possibility that the violation may be indicative of widespread activities in the organization.
2. After completing the audit, Company Z reports the violations discovered to the government.
3. The company had a compliance program, but it was effectively no more than a collection of paper. No effort is made to disseminate its content, impress upon employees its significance, train employees in its application, or oversee its implementation.
4. Even after "discovery" of the violation the company makes no effort to strengthen its compliance procedures.
5. The company makes no effort to come to terms with regulators regarding its violations. It resists any remedial work and refuses to pay any monetary sanctions.

4. For example, if the company had a long history of noncompliance, the compliance audit was done only under pressure from regulators, and a timely audit would have ended the violations much sooner, those circumstances would be considered.

6. Because of the non-compliance, information submitted to regulators over the years has been materially inaccurate, painting a substantially false picture of the company's true compliance situation. The company fails to take any steps to correct that inaccuracy.

7. The company does not cooperate with prosecutors in identifying those employees (including managers) who actually were involved in the violation, and it resists disclosure of any documents relating either to the violations or to the responsible employees.

In these circumstances leniency is unlikely. The only positive action is the so-called audit, but that was so narrowly focused as to be of questionable value, and it was undertaken only to head off a possible criminal investigation. Otherwise, the company demonstrated no good faith either in terms of compliance efforts or in assisting the government's full understanding of the violation and [see original].

Nonetheless, these factors do not assume the prosecution of Company Z. As with Company A, above, circumstances may be present which affect the balance s [see original] prosecutors. For example, the effect of the violation of substance, duration, or amount) may be such that pro would not consider it to be an appropriate criminal case Administrative or civil proceedings may be considered a appropriate response.

Other Examples:

Between these extremes there is a range of possibilities. The presence, absence, or degree of any criterion may aid prosecution's exercise of discretion. Below are some [see original] such effects:

1. In a situation otherwise similar to that of Company A above, Company B performs an audit that is very like in scope and probably reflects no more than an effort prosecution. Despite that background, Company B is cooperative in terms of both bringing itself into [see original] and providing information regarding the crime and perpetrators. The result could be any of a number outcomes, including prosecution of a lesser charge decision to prosecute the individuals rather than the company.

2. Again the situation is similar to Company A's, but Company C refuses to reveal any information regarding the individual violators. The likelihood of the government's prosecuting the company are substantially increased.

3. In another situation similar to Company A's, Company D chooses to "sit on" the audit and take corrective action without telling the government. The government learns of the situation months or years after the fact.

   A complicating fact here is that environmental regulatory programs are self policing: they include a substantial number of reporting requirements. If reports which in fact presented false information are allowed to stand uncorrected, the reliability of this system is undermined. They also may lead to adverse and unfair impacts upon other members of the regulated community. For example, Company D failed to report discharges of X contaminant into a municipal sewer system, discharges that were terminated as a result of an audit. The sewer authority, though, knowing only that there have been excessive loadings of X, but not knowing that Company D was a source, tightens limitations upon all known sources of X. Thus, all of those sources incur additional treatment expenses, but Company D is unaffected. Had Company D revealed its audit results, the other companies would not have suffered unnecessary expenses.

   In some situations, moreover, failure to report is a crime. *See, e.g.*, 33 U.S.C. §1321(b)(5) and 42 U.S.C. §9603(b). To illustrate the effect of this factor, consider Company E, which conducts a thorough audit and finds that hazardous wastes have been disposed of by dumping them on the ground. The company cleans up the area and tightens up its compliance program, but does not reveal the situation to requlators. Assuming that a reportable quantity of a hazardous substance was released, the company was under a legal obligation under 42 U.S.C. §9603(b) to report that release as soon as it had knowledge of it, thereby allowing regulators the opportunity to assure proper clean up. Company E's knowing failure to report the release upon learning of it is itself a felony.

   In the cases of both Company D and Company E; consideration would be given by prosecutors for remedial efforts; hence prosecution of fewer or lesser charges might result. However, because Company D's silence adversely affected others who are entitled to fair regulatory treatment and because Company E deprived those legally responsible for evaluating cleanup needs of the ability to carry out their functions, the likelihood of their totally escaping criminal prosecution is significantly reduced.

4. Company F's situation is similar to that of Company B. However, with regard to the various violations shown by the audit, it concentrates upon correcting only the easier, less expensive, less significant among them. Its lackadaisical approach to correction does not make it a strong candidate for leniency.

5. Company G is similar to Company D in that it performs an audit and finds violations, but does not bring them to the government's attention. Those violations do not involve failures to comply with reporting requirements. The company undertakes a program of gradually correcting its violations. When the government learns of the situation, Company G still has not remedied its most significant violations, but claims that it certainly planned to get to them. Company G could receive some consideration for its efforts, but its failure to disclose and the slowness of its remedial work probably mean that it cannot expect a substantial degree of leniency.

6. Comprehensive audits are considered positive efforts toward good faith compliance. However, such audits are not indispensable to enforcement leniency. Company H's situation is essentially identical to that of Company A, except for the fact that it does not undertake a comprehensive audit. It does not have a formal audit program, but, as a part of its efforts to ensure compliance, does realize that it is committing an environmental violation. It thereafter takes steps otherwise identical to those of Company A in terms of compliance efforts and cooperation. Company H is also a likely candidate for leniency, including possibly no criminal prosecution.

In sum, mitigating efforts made by the regulated community will be recognized and evaluated. The greater the showing of good faith, the more likely it will be met with leniency. Conversely, the less good faith shown, the less likely that prosecutorial discretion will tend toward leniency.

IV. Nature of This Guidance

This guidance explains the current general practice of the Department in making criminal prosecutive and other decisions after giving consideration to the criteria described above, as well as any other criteria that are relevant to the exercise of criminal prosecutorial discretion in a particular case. This discussion is an expression of, and in no way departs from, the long tradition of exercising prosecutorial discretion. The decision to prosecute "generally rests entirely in [the prosecutor's] discretion." *Bordenkircher v. Hayes*, 434 U.S. 357, 364 (1978).[5] This discretion is especially firmly held by the criminal prosecutor.[6] The criteria set forth above are intended only as internal guidance to Department of Justice attorneys. They are not intended to, do not, and may not be relied upon to create a right or benefit, substantive or procedural, enforceable at law by a party to litigation with the United States, nor do they in any way limit the lawful litigative prerogatives, including civil enforcement actions, of the Department of Justice or the Environmental Protection Agency. They are provided to guide the effective use of limited enforcement resources, and do not derive from, find their basis in, nor constitute any legal requirement, whether constitutional, statutory, or otherwise, to forego or modify any enforcement action or the use of any evidentiary material. See *Principles of Federal Prosecution* (U.S. Dept. of Justice, 1980) p. 4; *United States Attorneys' Manual* (U.S. Dept. of Justice, 1986) 1-1.000.

5. Although some statutes have occasionally been held to require civil enforcement actions, *see, e.g.*, *Dunlop v. Bachowski*, 421 U.S. 560 (1975), those are unusual cases, and the general rule is that both civil and criminal enforcement is at the enforcement agency's discretion where not prescribed by law. *Heckler v. Chaney*, 470 U.S. 821, 830-35 (1985); *Cutler v. Hayes*, 818 F.2d 879, 893 (D.C. Cir. 1987) (decisions not to enforce are not reviewable unless the statute provides an "inflexible mandate").

6. *Newman v. United States*, 382 F.2d 479, 480 (D.C. Cir. 1967).

Environmental Crimes Deskbook

Appendix 3 EPA Audit Policy (Website)

EPA's Audit Policy

The EPA Audit Policy (PDF), (11 pp, 262K, About pdf) formally titled "Incentives for Self-Policing: Discovery, Disclosure, Correction and Prevention of Violations," safeguards human health and the environment by providing several major incentives for regulated entities to voluntarily come into compliance with federal environmental laws and regulations.

To take advantage of these incentives, regulated entities must voluntarily discover, promptly disclose to EPA, expeditiously correct, and prevent recurrence of future environmental violations. Disclosures are often preceded by consultation between EPA and the regulated entity, so that they can discuss mutually acceptable disclosure details, compliance, and audit schedules can be discussed.

Summary of Incentives: Significant penalty reductions. Civil penalties under the environmental laws generally have two components, an amount assessed based upon the severity or "gravity" of the violation, and the amount of economic benefit a violator received from failing to comply with the law.

- **No gravity-based penalties if all nine of the Policy's conditions are met**. EPA retains its discretion to collect any economic benefit that may have been realized as a result of noncompliance.
- **Reduction of gravity-based penalties by 75%** where the disclosing entity meets all of the Policy's conditions except detection of the violation through a systematic discovery process.

No recommendation for criminal prosecution for entities that disclose criminal violations if all of the applicable conditions under the Policy are met. "Systematic discovery" is not a requirement for eligibility for this incentive, although the entity must be acting in good faith and adopt a systematic approach to preventing recurring violations. Refer to the Audit Policy for a complete discussion of issues relating to disclosure of criminal violations.

No routine requests for audit reports would be made. EPA reaffirms its Environmental Auditing Policy Statement, in effect since 1986, to refrain from routine requests for audit reports. That is, EPA has not and will not routinely request copies of audit reports to trigger enforcement investigations.

How Do I Make a Voluntary Disclosure Under EPA's Audit Policy?

An entity has 21 days from the time it discovers a violation has, or may have, occurred to disclose the violation in writing to EPA. Discovery is when any officer, director, employee or agent of the facility has an objectively reasonable basis for believing that a violation has, or may have occurred. Entities should make the disclosure to the EPA Regional Office where the affected facility is located. Voluntary self-disclosures for violations should be sent to the appropriate Audit Policy Contact. Violations of the Emergency Planning and Community Right -to-Know Act can be submitted electronically to EPA. In the event of violations affecting more than one Region, entities should contact EPA Headquarters.

The disclosure should at a minimum identify the means of discovery, type of violation, and facility location. EPA encourages companies to review our Sample Disclosure Follow-Up Letter and the Self-Disclosure Questionnaire in Attachment A of that letter to get a sense of the type of information needed about the violation(s) being disclosed in order to process the submission.

Before self-disclosing, you may wish to consult one or more of U.S. EPA's policies and guidance which deal with self-disclosures and incentives for compliance.

Conditions for Penalty Mitigation

Entities that satisfy the following conditions are eligible for Audit Policy benefits. Even if your entity fails to meet the first condition - systematic discovery - you can still be eligible for 75% penalty mitigation, and a recommendation for no criminal prosecution of the violations against your entity.

- **Systematic discovery** of the violation through an environmental audit or the implementation of a compliance management system.
- **Voluntary discovery** of the violation was not detected as a result of a legally required monitoring, sampling or auditing procedure.
- **Prompt disclosure** in writing to EPA within 21 days of discovery or such shorter time as may be required by law. Discovery occurs when any officer, director, employee or agent of the facility has an objectively reasonable basis for believing that a violation has or may have occurred.
- **Independent discovery and disclosure** before EPA or another regulator would likely have identified the violation through its own investigation or based on information provided by a third-party.
- **Correction and remediation** within 60 calendar days, in most cases, from the date of discovery.
- **Prevent recurrence** of the violation.
- **Repeat violations are ineligible**, that is, the specific (or closely related) violations have occurred at the same facility within the past 3 years or those that have occurred as part of a pattern at multiple facilities owned or operated by the same entity within the past 5 years; if the facility has been newly acquired, the existence of a violation prior to acquisition does not trigger the repeat violations exclusion.
- **Certain types of violations are ineligible** such as those that result in serious actual harm, those that may have presented an imminent and substantial endangerment, and those that violate the specific terms of an administrative or judicial order or consent agreement.
- **Cooperation** by the disclosing entity is required.

Please refer to the Audit Policy (PDF), (11 pp, 262K About pdf)"Incentives for Self-Policing: Discovery, Disclosure, Correction and Prevention of Violations", 65 FR 19,618 (04/11/00) for a more detailed discussion of eligibility and the application of the Audit Policy. Additional information about the Audit Policy and its use is available from the following:

- Questions and Answers concerning U.S. EPA's Audit Policy (also called Self-Disclosure Policy).
  - Audit Policy Interpretive Guidance (January 1997) (PDF) (40 pp, 1MB, About pdf) This guidance was developed to answer frequently asked questions regarding the implementation of the original Audit Policy issued in 1995 (60 FR 66,706 (December 22, 1995)).
  - Audit Policy: Frequently Asked Questions 2007 (PDF) (13 pp, 235K, About PDF) This document describes the differences between the original Audit Policy and the 2000 Policy and is intended to supplement the 1997 Interpretive Guidance.

- EPA's Audit Policy: Tailored Incentives for New Owners
  On August 1, 2008, EPA published in the Federal Register its "Interim Approach to Applying the Audit Policy to New Owners (16 pp, 120K, About PDF) ("Interim Approach)." The Interim Approach describes tailored Audit Policy incentives for new owners that want to make a "clean start" at their recently acquired facilities by addressing environmental noncompliance that began prior to acquisition.

- eDisclosure -- EPA's Electronic Audit Policy Self-Disclosure System
  EPA is piloting a web-based system to allow companies to electronically self-disclose violations under EPA's Audit Policy. eDisclosure makes it easier and faster to self-report environmental violations. It also speeds up EPA's processing of self-disclosures by ensuring that each disclosure contains complete information. Facilities nationwide can use eDisclosure to disclose violations of the Emergency Planning and Community Right-to-Know Act, and facilities located in EPA Region 6 states -- Arkansas, Louisiana, New Mexico, Oklahoma and Texas -- can also use eDisclosure to disclose violations of other environmental laws. Once EPA has gained experience with electronic self-disclosures, EPA will refine the system, as necessary, and decide whether to expand, on a nationwide basis, the eDisclosure system to allow regulated entities to electronically self-disclose violations of other federally enforceable environmental requirements for possible incentives under the Audit Policy. For more on Electronic Self-Disclosure.

- Corporate Audit Agreements
  A Corporate Audit Agreement allows an entity (such as corporation, university or other organization with many facilities or facility locations within its authority) to plan a corporate-wide or facility-wide audit with an advanced understanding between the entity and EPA regarding schedules for conducting the audit and disclosing violations beyond the current 21-day disclosure requirement for single-facility disclosures. In return for the advanced agreement of an audit and disclosure schedule, the facility would receive the benefits of EPA's Audit Policy as applicable.

- Audit Protocols
  Audit protocols assist the regulated community in developing programs at individual facilities to evaluate their compliance with environmental requirements under federal law. The protocols are intended solely as guidance in this effort. The regulated community's legal obligations are determined by the terms of applicable environmental facility-specific permits, underlying statutes and applicable state and local law.

- Audit Policy Self-Disclosure & Regional Contacts
  Once a violation has been discovered, a company has 21 days from the time of that discovery to disclose in writing the violation to EPA. The initial disclosure should identify the means of discovery, type of violation, and facility location.

- "Audit Policy Update" Newsletter
  The Audit Policy Update Newsletters, published between 1996-2001 by EPA's Office of Regulatory Enforcement, Office of Enforcement and Compliance Assurance provides information on the changes to the Audit Policy and other information relating to its use.

- *"Enforcement Alert"* Newsletter
  This informational newsletter published by EPA's Office of Civil Enforcement, Office of Enforcement and Compliance Assurance. It is intended to inform and educate the public and the regulated community about important environmental enforcement issues, recent trends, and significant enforcement actions. It calls attention to such matters as the need for voluntary corporate audits.

Sample Documents for Use in Self-Disclosing Environmental Violations under EPA's Audit Policy

- Sample Status Report (PDF) (5 pp, 40K, About pdf)
  Some companies have used this report to provide information to EPA during the course of conducting an audit. The initial report, and subsequent periodic progress reports, have helped identify issues early in the auditing process and assisted in the overall progress of the audit.

- Sample Disclosure Follow-up Letter (PDF) (5 pp, 22K, About pdf)
  This is an example of what the Agency sends a company after receiving a self disclosure pursuant to EPA's Audit Policy. The letter provides companies with clear guidance on the kind of information needed by EPA to better understand the potential violations and determine whether a company's disclosure meets the conditions of the Audit Policy.

Audit Policy User's Survey (November 13, 1998)

Under a contract EPA conducted a voluntary and confidential survey of companies that have disclosed environmental violations under the EPA Audit Policy. The intent of the survey was to aide EPA to better serve the regulated community and to help EPA evaluate and improve the Audit Policy.

- Audit Policy Survey Invitation and Form (PDF) (9 pp, 179K, About pdf)
- Audit Policy Survey Results (PDF) (29pp, 364K, About pdf)

Environmental Crimes Deskbook

Appendix 4 U.S. Attys. Manual-Prosecution of Organizations

9-28.000 PRINCIPLES OF FEDERAL PROSECUTION OF BUSINESS ORGANIZATIONS [FN1]

9-28.100	Duties of Federal Prosecutors and Duties of Corporate Leaders
9-28.200	General Considerations of Corporate Liability
9-28.300	Factors to Be Considered
9-28.400	Special Policy Concerns
9-28.500	Pervasiveness of Wrongdoing Within the Corporation
9-28.600	The Corporation's Past History
9-28.700	The Value of Cooperation
9-28.710	Attorney-Client and Work Product Protections
9-28.720	Cooperation: Disclosing the Relevant Facts
9-28.730	Obstructing the Investigation
9-28.740	Offering Cooperation: No Entitlement to Immunity
9-28.750	Qualifying for Immunity, Amnesty, or Reduced Sanctions Through Voluntary Disclosures
9-28.760	Oversight Concerning Demands for Waivers of Attorney-Client Privilege or Work Product By Corporations Contrary to This Policy
9-28.800	Corporate Compliance Programs
9-28.900	Restitution and Remediation
9-28.1000	Collateral Consequences
9-28.1100	Other Civil or Regulatory Alternatives
9-28.1200	Selecting Charges
9-28.1300	Plea Agreements with Corporations

9-28.100 Duties of Federal Prosecutors and Duties of Corporate Leaders

The prosecution of corporate crime is a high priority for the Department of Justice. By investigating allegations of wrongdoing and by bringing charges where appropriate for criminal misconduct, the Department promotes critical public interests. These interests include, to take just a few examples: (1) protecting the integrity of our free economic and capital markets; (2) protecting consumers, investors, and business entities that compete only through lawful means; and (3) protecting the American people from misconduct that would violate criminal laws safeguarding the environment.

In this regard, federal prosecutors and corporate leaders typically share common goals. For example, directors and officers owe a fiduciary duty to a corporation's shareholders, the corporation's true owners, and they owe duties of honest dealing to the investing public in connection with the corporation's regulatory filings and public statements. The faithful execution of these duties by corporate leadership serves the same values in promoting public trust and confidence that our criminal cases are designed to serve.

A prosecutor's duty to enforce the law requires the investigation and prosecution of criminal wrongdoing if it is discovered. In carrying out this mission with the diligence and resolve necessary to vindicate the important public interests discussed above, prosecutors should be mindful of the common cause we share with responsible corporate leaders. Prosecutors should also be mindful that confidence in the Department is affected both by the results we achieve and by the real and perceived ways in which we achieve them. Thus, the manner in which we do our job as prosecutors—including the professionalism we demonstrate, our willingness to secure the facts in a manner that encourages corporate compliance and self- regulation, and also our appreciation that corporate prosecutions can potentially harm blameless investors, employees, and others—affects public perception of our mission. Federal prosecutors recognize that they must maintain public confidence in the way in which they exercise their charging discretion. This endeavor requires the thoughtful analysis of all facts and circumstances presented in a given case. As always, professionalism and civility play an important part in the Department's discharge of its responsibilities in all areas, including the area of corporate investigations and prosecutions.

[new August 2008]

9-28.200 General Considerations of Corporate Liability

A. General Principle: Corporations should not be treated leniently because of their artificial nature nor should they be subject to harsher treatment. Vigorous enforcement of the criminal laws against corporate wrongdoers, where appropriate, results in great benefits for law enforcement and the public, particularly in the area of white collar crime. Indicting corporations for wrongdoing enables the government to be a force for positive change of corporate culture, and a force to prevent, discover, and punish serious crimes.

B. Comment: In all cases involving corporate wrongdoing, prosecutors should consider the factors discussed further below. In doing so, prosecutors should be aware of the public benefits that can flow from indicting a corporation in appropriate cases. For instance, corporations are likely to take immediate remedial steps when one is indicted for criminal misconduct that is pervasive throughout a particular industry, and thus an indictment can provide a unique opportunity for deterrence on a broad scale. In addition, a corporate indictment may result in specific deterrence by changing the culture of the indicted corporation and the behavior of its employees. Finally, certain crimes that carry with them a substantial risk of great public harm—*e.g.*, environmental crimes or sweeping financial frauds—may be committed by a business entity, and there may therefore be a substantial federal interest in indicting a corporation under such circumstances.

In certain instances, it may be appropriate, upon consideration of the factors set forth herein, to resolve a corporate criminal case by means other than indictment. Non-prosecution and deferred prosecution agreements, for example, occupy an important middle ground between declining prosecution and obtaining the conviction of a corporation. These agreements are discussed further in USAM 9-28.1000. Likewise, civil and regulatory alternatives may be appropriate in certain cases, as discussed in USAM 9-28.1100.

Where a decision is made to charge a corporation, it does not necessarily follow that individual directors, officers, employees, or shareholders should not also be charged. Prosecution of a corporation is not a substitute for the prosecution of criminally culpable individuals within or without the corporation. Because a corporation can act only through individuals, imposition of individual criminal liability may provide the strongest deterrent against future corporate wrongdoing. Only rarely should provable individual culpability not be pursued, particularly if it relates to high-level corporate officers, even in the face of an offer of a corporate guilty plea or some other disposition of the charges against the corporation.

Corporations are "legal persons," capable of suing and being sued, and capable of committing crimes. Under the doctrine of *respondeat superior*, a corporation may be held criminally liable for the illegal acts of its directors, officers, employees, and agents. To hold a corporation liable for these actions, the government must establish that the corporate agent's actions (i) were within the scope of his duties and (ii) were intended, at least in part, to benefit the corporation. In all cases involving wrongdoing by corporate agents, prosecutors should not limit their focus solely to individuals or the corporation, but should consider both as potential targets.

Agents may act for mixed reasons—both for self-aggrandizement (both direct and indirect) and for the benefit of the corporation, and a corporation may be held liable as long as one motivation of its agent is to benefit the corporation. *See United States v. Potter*, 463 F.3d 9, 25 (1st Cir. 2006) (stating that the test to determine whether an agent is acting within the scope of employment is "whether the agent is performing acts of the kind which he is authorized to perform, and those acts are motivated, at least in part, by an intent to benefit the corporation."). In *United States v. Automated Medical Laboratories, Inc.*, 770 F.2d 399 (4th Cir. 1985), for example, the Fourth Circuit affirmed a corporation's conviction for the actions of a subsidiary's employee despite the corporation's claim that the employee was acting for his own benefit, namely his "ambitious nature and his desire to ascend the corporate ladder." *Id.* at 407. The court stated, "Partucci was clearly acting in part to benefit AML since his advancement within the corporation depended on AML's well-being and its lack of difficulties with the FDA." *Id.*; *see also United States v. Cincotta*, 689 F.2d 238, 241-42 (1st Cir. 1982) (upholding a corporation's conviction, notwithstanding the substantial personal benefit reaped by its miscreant agents, because the fraudulent scheme required money to pass through the corporation's treasury and the fraudulently obtained goods were resold to the corporation's customers in the corporation's name).

Moreover, the corporation need not even necessarily profit from its agent's actions for it to be held liable. In *Automated Medical Laboratories*, the Fourth Circuit stated:

> [B]enefit is not a "touchstone of criminal corporate liability; benefit at best is an evidential, not an operative, fact." Thus, whether the agent's actions ultimately redounded to the benefit of the corporation is less significant than whether the agent acted with the intent to benefit the corporation. The basic purpose of requiring that an agent have acted with the intent to benefit the corporation, however, is to insulate the corporation from criminal liability for actions of its agents which may be *inimical* to the interests of the corporation or which may have been undertaken solely to advance the interests of that agent or of a party other than the corporation.

770 F.2d at 407 (internal citation omitted) (quoting *Old Monastery Co. v. United States*, 147 F.2d 905, 908 (4th Cir. 1945)).

[new August 2008]

9-28.300 Factors to Be Considered

A. General Principle: Generally, prosecutors apply the same factors in determining whether to charge a corporation as they do with respect to individuals. *See* USAM 9-27.220 *et seq*. Thus, the prosecutor must weigh all of the factors normally considered in the sound exercise of prosecutorial judgment: the sufficiency of the evidence; the likelihood of success at trial; the probable deterrent, rehabilitative, and other consequences of conviction; and the adequacy of noncriminal approaches. *See id.* However, due to the nature of the corporate "person," some additional factors are present. In conducting an investigation, determining whether to bring charges, and negotiating plea or other agreements, prosecutors should consider the following factors in reaching a decision as to the proper treatment of a corporate target:

1. the nature and seriousness of the offense, including the risk of harm to the public, and applicable policies and priorities, if any, governing the prosecution of corporations for particular categories of crime (see USAM 9-

28.400);

2. the pervasiveness of wrongdoing within the corporation, including the complicity in, or the condoning of, the wrongdoing by corporate management (see USAM 9-28.500);

3. the corporation's history of similar misconduct, including prior criminal, civil, and regulatory enforcement actions against it (see USAM 9-28.600);

4. the corporation's timely and voluntary disclosure of wrongdoing and its willingness to cooperate in the investigation of its agents (see USAM 9-28.700);

5. the existence and effectiveness of the corporation's pre-existing compliance program (see USAM 9-28.800);

6. the corporation's remedial actions, including any efforts to implement an effective corporate compliance program or to improve an existing one, to replace responsible management, to discipline or terminate wrongdoers, to pay restitution, and to cooperate with the relevant government agencies (see USAM 9-28.900);

7. collateral consequences, including whether there is disproportionate harm to shareholders, pension holders, employees, and others not proven personally culpable, as well as impact on the public arising from the prosecution (see USAM 9-28.1000);

8. the adequacy of the prosecution of individuals responsible for the corporation's malfeasance; and

9. the adequacy of remedies such as civil or regulatory enforcement actions (see USAM 9-28.1100).

B. Comment: The factors listed in this section are intended to be illustrative of those that should be evaluated and are not an exhaustive list of potentially relevant considerations. Some of these factors may not apply to specific cases, and in some cases one factor may override all others. For example, the nature and seriousness of the offense may be such as to warrant prosecution regardless of the other factors. In most cases, however, no single factor will be dispositive. In addition, national law enforcement policies in various enforcement areas may require that more or less weight be given to certain of these factors than to others. Of course, prosecutors must exercise their thoughtful and pragmatic judgment in applying and balancing these factors, so as to achieve a fair and just outcome and promote respect for the law.

In making a decision to charge a corporation, the prosecutor generally has substantial latitude in determining when, whom, how, and even whether to prosecute for violations of federal criminal law. In exercising that discretion, prosecutors should consider the following statements of principles that summarize the considerations they should weigh and the practices they should follow in discharging their prosecutorial responsibilities. In doing so, prosecutors should ensure that the general purposes of the criminal law—assurance of warranted punishment, deterrence of further criminal conduct, protection of the public from dangerous and fraudulent conduct, rehabilitation of offenders, and restitution for victims and affected communities—are adequately met, taking into account the special nature of the corporate "person."

[new August 2008]

9-28.400 Special Policy Concerns

A. General Principle: The nature and seriousness of the crime, including the risk of harm to the public from the criminal misconduct, are obviously primary factors in determining whether to charge a corporation. In addition, corporate conduct, particularly that of national and multi-national corporations, necessarily intersects with federal economic, tax, and criminal law enforcement policies. In applying these Principles, prosecutors must consider the practices and policies of the appropriate Division of the Department, and must comply with those policies to the extent required by the facts presented.

B. Comment: In determining whether to charge a corporation, prosecutors should take into account federal law enforcement priorities as discussed above. See USAM 9-27.230. In addition, however, prosecutors must be aware of the specific policy goals and incentive programs established by the respective Divisions and regulatory agencies. Thus, whereas natural persons may be given incremental degrees of credit (ranging from immunity to lesser charges to sentencing considerations) for turning themselves in, making statements against their penal interest, and cooperating in the government's investigation of their own and others' wrongdoing, the same approach may not be appropriate in all circumstances with respect to corporations. As an example, it is entirely proper in many investigations for a prosecutor to consider the corporation's pre-indictment conduct, *e.g.*, voluntary disclosure, cooperation, remediation or restitution, in determining whether to seek an indictment. However, this would not necessarily be appropriate in an antitrust investigation, in which antitrust violations, by definition, go to the heart of the corporation's business. With this in mind, the Antitrust Division has established a firm policy, understood in the business community, that credit should not be given at the charging stage for a compliance program and that amnesty is available only to the first corporation to make full disclosure to the government. As another example, the Tax Division has a strong preference for prosecuting responsible individuals, rather than entities, for corporate tax offenses. Thus, in determining whether or not to charge a corporation, prosecutors must consult with the Criminal, Antitrust, Tax, Environmental and Natural Resources, and National Security Divisions, as appropriate.

[new August 2008]

9-28.500 Pervasiveness of Wrongdoing Within the Corporation

is therefore held responsible for the acts of such persons fairly attributable to it. Charging a corporation for even minor misconduct may be appropriate where the wrongdoing was pervasive and was undertaken by a large number of employees, or by all the employees in a particular role within the corporation, or was condoned by upper management. On the other hand, it may not be appropriate to impose liability upon a corporation, particularly one with a robust compliance program in place, under a strict *respondeat superior* theory for the single isolated act of a rogue employee. There is, of course, a wide spectrum between these two extremes, and a prosecutor should exercise sound discretion in evaluating the pervasiveness of wrongdoing within a corporation.

B. Comment: Of these factors, the most important is the role and conduct of management. Although acts of even low-level employees may result in criminal liability, a corporation is directed by its management and management is responsible for a corporate culture in which criminal conduct is either discouraged or tacitly encouraged. As stated in commentary to the Sentencing Guidelines:

> Pervasiveness [is] case specific and [will] depend on the number, and degree of responsibility, of individuals [with] substantial authority ... who participated in, condoned, or were willfully ignorant of the offense. Fewer individuals need to be involved for a finding of pervasiveness if those individuals exercised a relatively high degree of authority. Pervasiveness can occur either within an organization as a whole or within a unit of an organization.

USSG § 8C2.5, cmt. (n. 4).

[new August 2008]

9-28.600 The Corporation's Past History

A. General Principle: Prosecutors may consider a corporation's history of similar conduct, including prior criminal, civil, and regulatory enforcement actions against it, in determining whether to bring criminal charges and how best to resolve cases.

B. Comment: A corporation, like a natural person, is expected to learn from its mistakes. A history of similar misconduct may be probative of a corporate culture that encouraged, or at least condoned, such misdeeds, regardless of any compliance programs. Criminal prosecution of a corporation may be particularly appropriate where the corporation previously had been subject to non-criminal guidance, warnings, or sanctions, or previous criminal charges, and it either had not taken adequate action to prevent future unlawful conduct or had continued to engage in the misconduct in spite of the warnings or enforcement actions taken against it. The corporate structure itself (*e.g.*, the creation or existence of subsidiaries or operating divisions) is not dispositive in this analysis, and enforcement actions taken against the corporation or any of its divisions, subsidiaries, and affiliates may be considered, if germane. *See* USSG § 8C2.5(c), cmt. (n. 6).

[new August 2008]

9-28.700 The Value of Cooperation

A. General Principle: In determining whether to charge a corporation and how to resolve corporate criminal cases, the corporation's timely and voluntary disclosure of wrongdoing and its cooperation with the government's investigation may be relevant factors. In gauging the extent of the corporation's cooperation, the prosecutor may consider, among other things, whether the corporation made a voluntary and timely disclosure, and the corporation's willingness to provide relevant information and evidence and identify relevant actors within and outside the corporation, including senior executives.

Cooperation is a potential mitigating factor, by which a corporation—just like any other subject of a criminal investigation—can gain credit in a case that otherwise is appropriate for indictment and prosecution. Of course, the decision not to cooperate by a corporation (or individual) is not itself evidence of misconduct, at least where the lack of cooperation does not involve criminal misconduct or demonstrate consciousness of guilt (*e.g.*, suborning perjury or false statements, or refusing to comply with lawful discovery requests). Thus, failure to cooperate, in and of itself, does not support or require the filing of charges with respect to a corporation any more than with respect to an individual.

B. Comment: In investigating wrongdoing by or within a corporation, a prosecutor is likely to encounter several obstacles resulting from the nature of the corporation itself. It will often be difficult to determine which individual took which action on behalf of the corporation. Lines of authority and responsibility may be shared among operating divisions or departments, and records and personnel may be spread throughout the United States or even among several countries. Where the criminal conduct continued over an extended period of time, the culpable or knowledgeable personnel may have been promoted, transferred, or fired, or they may have quit or retired. Accordingly, a corporation's cooperation may be critical in identifying potentially relevant actors and locating relevant evidence, among other things, and in doing so expeditiously.

This dynamic—*i.e.*, the difficulty of determining what happened, where the evidence is, and which individuals took or promoted putatively illegal corporate actions—can have negative consequences for both the government and the corporation that is the subject or target of a government investigation. More specifically, because of corporate attribution principles concerning actions of corporate officers and employees (*see, e.g., supra* section II), uncertainty about exactly who authorized or directed apparent corporate misconduct can inure to the detriment of a corporation. For example, it may not matter under the law which of several possible executives or leaders in a chain of command approved of or authorized criminal conduct; however, that information if known might bear on the propriety of a particular disposition short of indictment of the corporation. It may not be in the interest of a corporation or the government for a charging decision to be made in the absence of such information, which might occur if, for example, a statute of limitations were relevant and authorization by any one of the officials were enough to justify a charge under the law. Moreover, and at a minimum, a protracted government investigation of such an issue could, as a collateral consequence, disrupt the corporation's business operations or even depress its stock price.

For these reasons and more, cooperation can be a favorable course for both the government and the corporation. Cooperation benefits the government—and ultimately shareholders, employees, and other often blameless victims—by allowing prosecutors and federal agents, for example, to avoid protracted delays, which compromise their ability to quickly uncover and address the full extent of widespread corporate crimes. With cooperation by the corporation, the government may be able to reduce tangible losses, limit damage to reputation, and preserve assets for restitution. At the same time, cooperation may benefit the corporation by enabling the government to focus its investigative resources in a manner that will not unduly disrupt the corporation's legitimate business operations. In addition, and critically, cooperation may benefit the corporation by presenting it with the opportunity to earn credit for its efforts.

[new August 2008]

9-28.710 Attorney-Client and Work Product Protections

The attorney-client privilege and the attorney work product protection serve an extremely important function in the American legal system. The attorney-client privilege is one of the oldest and most sacrosanct privileges under the law. *See Upjohn v. United States*, 449 U.S. 383, 389 (1981). As the Supreme Court has stated, "[i]ts purpose is to encourage full and frank communication between attorneys and their clients and thereby promote broader public interests in the observance of law and administration of justice." *Id.* The value of promoting a corporation's ability to seek frank and comprehensive legal advice is particularly important in the contemporary global business environment, where corporations often face complex and dynamic legal and regulatory obligations imposed by the federal government and also by states and foreign governments. The work product doctrine serves similarly important goals.

For these reasons, waiving the attorney-client and work product protections has never been a prerequisite under the Department's prosecution guidelines for a corporation to be viewed as cooperative. Nonetheless, a wide range of commentators and members of the American legal community and criminal justice system have asserted that the Department's policies have been used, either wittingly or unwittingly, to coerce business entities into waiving attorney-client privilege and work-product protection. Everyone agrees that a corporation may freely waive its own privileges if it chooses to do so; indeed, such waivers occur routinely when corporations are victimized by their employees or others, conduct an internal investigation, and then disclose the details of the investigation to law enforcement officials in an effort to seek prosecution of the offenders. However, the contention, from a broad array of voices, is that the Department's position on attorney-client privilege and work product protection waivers has promoted an environment in which those protections are being unfairly eroded to the detriment of all.

The Department understands that the attorney-client privilege and attorney work product protection are essential and long- recognized components of the American legal system. What the government seeks and needs to advance its legitimate (indeed, essential) law enforcement mission is not waiver of those protections, but rather the facts known to the corporation about the putative criminal misconduct under review. In addition, while a corporation remains free to convey non-factual or "core" attorney-client communications or work product—if and only if the corporation voluntarily chooses to do so—prosecutors should not ask for such waivers and are directed not to do so. The critical factor is whether the corporation has provided the facts about the events, as explained further herein.

[new August 2008]

9-28.720 Cooperation: Disclosing the Relevant Facts

Eligibility for cooperation credit is not predicated upon the waiver of attorney-client privilege or work product protection. Instead, the sort of cooperation that is most valuable to resolving allegations of misconduct by a corporation and its officers, directors, employees, or agents is disclosure of the relevant *facts* concerning such misconduct. In this regard, the analysis parallels that for a non-corporate defendant, where cooperation typically requires disclosure of relevant factual knowledge and not of discussions between an individual and his attorneys.

Thus, when the government investigates potential corporate wrongdoing, it seeks the relevant facts. For example, how and when did the alleged misconduct occur? Who promoted or approved it? Who was responsible for committing it? In this respect, the investigation of a corporation differs little from the investigation of an individual. In both cases, the government needs to know the facts to achieve a just and fair outcome. The party under investigation may choose to cooperate by disclosing the facts, and the government may give credit for the party's disclosures. If a corporation wishes to receive credit for such cooperation, which then can be considered with all other cooperative efforts and circumstances in evaluating how fairly to proceed, then the corporation, like any person, must disclose the relevant facts of which it has knowledge.[FN2]

(a) Disclosing the Relevant Facts—Facts Gathered Through Internal Investigation

Individuals and corporations often obtain knowledge of facts in different ways. An individual knows the facts of his or others' misconduct through his own experience and perceptions. A corporation is an artificial construct that cannot, by definition, have personal knowledge of the facts. Some of those facts may be reflected in documentary or electronic media like emails, transaction or accounting documents, and other records. Often, the corporation gathers facts through an internal investigation. Exactly how and by whom the facts are gathered is for the corporation to decide. Many corporations choose to collect information about potential misconduct through lawyers, a process that may confer attorney-client privilege or attorney work product protection on at least some of the information collected. Other corporations may choose a method of fact- gathering that does not have that effect—for example, having employee or other witness statements collected after interviews by non-attorney personnel. Whichever process the corporation selects, the government's key measure of cooperation must remain the same as it does for an individual: has the party timely disclosed the relevant facts about the putative misconduct? That is the operative question in assigning cooperation credit for the disclosure of information—*not* whether the corporation discloses attorney-client or work product materials. Accordingly, a corporation should receive the same credit for disclosing facts contained in materials that are not protected by the attorney- client privilege or attorney work product as it would for disclosing identical facts contained in materials that are so protected.[FN3] On this point the Report of the House Judiciary Committee, submitted in connection with the attorney-client privilege bill passed by the House of Representatives (H.R. 3013), comports with the approach required here:

> [A]n ... attorney of the United States may base cooperation credit on the facts that are disclosed, but is prohibited from basing cooperation credit upon whether or not the materials are protected by attorney-client privilege or attorney work product. As a result, an entity that voluntarily discloses should receive the same amount of cooperation credit for disclosing facts that happen to be contained in materials not protected by attorney-client privilege or attorney work product as it would receive for disclosing identical facts that are contained in materials protected by attorney-client privilege or attorney work product. There should be no differentials in an assessment of cooperation (i.e., neither a credit nor a penalty) based upon whether or not the materials disclosed are protected by attorney-client privilege or attorney work product.
>
> H.R. Rep. No. 110-445 at 4 (2007).

In short, so long as the corporation timely discloses relevant facts about the putative misconduct, the corporation may receive due credit for such cooperation, regardless of whether it chooses to waive privilege or work product protection in the process.[FN4] Likewise, a corporation that does not disclose the relevant facts about the alleged misconduct—for whatever reason—typically should not be entitled to receive credit for cooperation.

Two final and related points bear noting about the disclosure of facts, although they should be obvious. First, the government cannot compel, and the corporation has no obligation to make, such disclosures (although the government can obviously compel the disclosure of certain records and witness testimony through subpoenas). Second, a corporation's failure to provide relevant information does not mean the corporation will be indicted. It simply means that the corporation will not be entitled to mitigating credit for that cooperation. Whether the corporation faces charges will turn, as it does in any case, on the sufficiency of the evidence, the likelihood of success at trial, and all of the other factors identified in Section III above. If there is insufficient evidence to warrant indictment, after appropriate investigation has been completed, or if the other factors weigh against indictment, then the corporation should not be indicted, irrespective of whether it has earned cooperation credit. The converse is also true: The government may charge even the most cooperative corporation pursuant to these Principles if, in weighing and balancing the factors described herein, the prosecutor determines that a charge is required in the interests of justice. Put differently, even the most sincere and thorough effort to cooperate cannot necessarily absolve a corporation that has, for example, engaged in an egregious, orchestrated, and widespread fraud. Cooperation is a relevant potential mitigating factor, but it alone is not dispositive.

(b) Legal Advice and Attorney Work Product

Separate from (and usually preceding) the fact-gathering process in an internal investigation, a corporation, through its officers, employees, directors, or others, may have consulted with corporate counsel regarding or in a manner that concerns the legal implications of the putative misconduct at issue. Communications of this sort, which are both independent of the fact-gathering component of an internal investigation and made for the purpose of seeking or dispensing legal advice, lie at the core of the attorney-client privilege. Such communications can naturally have a salutary effect on corporate behavior—facilitating, for example, a corporation's effort to comply with complex and evolving legal and regulatory regimes.[FN5] Except as noted in subparagraphs (b)(i) and (b)(ii) below, a corporation need not disclose and prosecutors may not request the disclosure of such communications as a condition for the corporation's eligibility to receive cooperation credit.

Likewise, non-factual or core attorney work product—for example, an attorney's mental impressions or legal theories—lies at the core of the attorney work product doctrine. A corporation need not disclose, and prosecutors may not request, the disclosure of such attorney work product as a condition for the corporation's eligibility to receive cooperation credit.

(i) Advice of Counsel Defense in the Instant Context

Occasionally a corporation or one of its employees may assert an advice-of-counsel defense, based upon communications with in- house or outside counsel that took place prior to or contemporaneously with the underlying conduct at issue. In such situations, the defendant must tender a legitimate factual basis to support the assertion of the advice-of-counsel defense. *See, e.g.*, *Pitt v. Dist. of Columbia*, 491 F.3d 494, 504-05 (D.C. Cir. 2007); *United States v. Wenger*, 427 F.3d 840, 853-54 (10th Cir. 2005); *United States v. Cheek*, 3 F.3d 1057, 1061-62 (7th Cir. 1993). The

Department cannot fairly be asked to discharge its responsibility to the public to investigate alleged corporate crime, or to temper what would otherwise be the appropriate course of prosecutive action, by simply accepting on faith an otherwise unproven assertion that an attorney—perhaps even an unnamed attorney—approved potentially unlawful practices. Accordingly, where an advice-of-counsel defense has been asserted, prosecutors may ask for the disclosure of the communications allegedly supporting it.

(ii) Communications in Furtherance of a Crime or Fraud

Communications between a corporation (through its officers, employees, directors, or agents) and corporate counsel that are made in furtherance of a crime or fraud are, under settled precedent, outside the scope and protection of the attorney- client privilege. *See United States v. Zolin*, 491 U.S. 554, 563 (1989); *United States v. BDO Seidman, LLP*, 492 F.3d 806, 818 (7th Cir. 2007). As a result, the Department may properly request such communications if they in fact exist.

[new August 2008]

9-28.730 Obstructing the Investigation

Another factor to be weighed by the prosecutor is whether the corporation has engaged in conduct intended to impede the investigation. Examples of such conduct could include: inappropriate directions to employees or their counsel, such as directions not to be truthful or to conceal relevant facts; making representations or submissions that contain misleading assertions or material omissions; and incomplete or delayed production of records.

In evaluating cooperation, however, prosecutors should not take into account whether a corporation is advancing or reimbursing attorneys' fees or providing counsel to employees, officers, or directors under investigation or indictment. Likewise, prosecutors may not request that a corporation refrain from taking such action. This prohibition is not meant to prevent a prosecutor from asking questions about an attorney's representation of a corporation or its employees, officers, or directors, where otherwise appropriate under the law.[FN6] Neither is it intended to limit the otherwise applicable reach of criminal obstruction of justice statutes such as 18 U.S.C. § 1503. If the payment of attorney fees were used in a manner that would otherwise constitute criminal obstruction of justice—for example, if fees were advanced on the condition that an employee adhere to a version of the facts that the corporation and the employee knew to be false—these Principles would not (and could not) render inapplicable such criminal prohibitions.

Similarly, the mere participation by a corporation in a joint defense agreement does not render the corporation ineligible to receive cooperation credit, and prosecutors may not request that a corporation refrain from entering into such agreements. Of course, the corporation may wish to avoid putting itself in the position of being disabled, by virtue of a particular joint defense or similar agreement, from providing some relevant facts to the government and thereby limiting its ability to seek such cooperation credit. Such might be the case if the corporation gathers facts from employees who have entered into a joint defense agreement with the corporation, and who may later seek to prevent the corporation from disclosing the facts it has acquired. Corporations may wish to address this situation by crafting or participating in joint defense agreements, to the extent they choose to enter them, that provide such flexibility as they deem appropriate.

Finally, it may on occasion be appropriate for the government to consider whether the corporation has shared with others sensitive information about the investigation that the government provided to the corporation. In appropriate situations, as it does with individuals, the government may properly request that, if a corporation wishes to receive credit for cooperation, the information provided by the government to the corporation not be transmitted to others—for example, where the disclosure of such information could lead to flight by individual subjects, destruction of evidence, or dissipation or concealment of assets.

[new August 2008]

9-28.740 Offering Cooperation: No Entitlement to Immunity

A corporation's offer of cooperation or cooperation itself does not automatically entitle it to immunity from prosecution or a favorable resolution of its case. A corporation should not be able to escape liability merely by offering up its directors, officers, employees, or agents. Thus, a corporation's willingness to cooperate is not determinative; that factor, while relevant, needs to be considered in conjunction with all other factors.

[new August 2008]

9-28.750 Qualifying for Immunity, Amnesty, or Reduced Sanctions Through Voluntary Disclosures

In conjunction with regulatory agencies and other executive branch departments, the Department encourages corporations, as part of their compliance programs, to conduct internal investigations and to disclose the relevant facts to the appropriate authorities. Some agencies, such as the Securities and Exchange Commission and the Environmental Protection Agency, as well as the Department's Environmental and Natural Resources Division, have formal voluntary disclosure programs in which self-reporting, coupled with remediation and additional criteria, may qualify the corporation for amnesty or reduced sanctions. Even in the absence of a formal program, prosecutors may consider a corporation's timely and voluntary disclosure in evaluating the adequacy of the corporation's compliance program and its management's commitment to the compliance program. However, prosecution and economic policies specific to the industry or statute may require prosecution notwithstanding a corporation's willingness to cooperate. For example, the Antitrust Division has a policy of offering amnesty only to the first corporation to agree to cooperate. Moreover, amnesty, immunity, or reduced sanctions may not be appropriate where the corporation's business is permeated with fraud or other crimes.

[new August 2008]

9-28.760 Oversight Concerning Demands for Waivers of Attorney-Client Privilege or Work Product Protection By Corporations Contrary to This Policy

The Department underscores its commitment to attorney practices that are consistent with Department policies like those set forth herein concerning cooperation credit and due respect for the attorney-client privilege and work product protection. Counsel for corporations who believe that prosecutors are violating such guidance are encouraged to raise their concerns with supervisors, including the appropriate United States Attorney or Assistant Attorney General. Like any other allegation of attorney misconduct, such allegations are subject to potential investigation through established mechanisms.

[new August 2008]

9-28.800 Corporate Compliance Programs

A. **General Principle:** Compliance programs are established by corporate management to prevent and detect misconduct and to ensure that corporate activities are conducted in accordance with applicable criminal and civil laws, regulations, and rules. The Department encourages such corporate self-policing, including voluntary disclosures to the government of any problems that a corporation discovers on its own. However, the existence of a compliance program is not sufficient, in and of itself, to justify not charging a corporation for criminal misconduct undertaken by its officers, directors, employees, or agents. In addition, the nature of some crimes, *e.g.*, antitrust violations, may be such that national law enforcement policies mandate prosecutions of corporations notwithstanding the existence of a compliance program.

B. **Comment:** The existence of a corporate compliance program, even one that specifically prohibited the very conduct in question, does not absolve the corporation from criminal liability under the doctrine of *respondeat superior. See United States v. Basic Constr. Co.*, 711 F.2d 570, 573 (4th Cir. 1983) ("[A] corporation may be held criminally responsible for antitrust violations committed by its employees if they were acting within the scope of their authority, or apparent authority, and for the benefit of the corporation, even if ... such acts were against corporate policy or express instructions."). As explained in *United States v. Potter*, 463 F.3d 9 (1st Cir. 2006), a corporation cannot "avoid liability by adopting abstract rules" that forbid its agents from engaging in illegal acts, because "[e]ven a specific directive to an agent or employee or honest efforts to police such rules do not automatically free the company for the wrongful acts of agents." *Id.* at 25-26. *See also United States v. Hilton Hotels Corp.*, 467 F.2d 1000, 1007 (9th Cir. 1972) (noting that a corporation "could not gain exculpation by issuing general instructions without undertaking to enforce those instructions by means commensurate with the obvious risks"); *United States v. Beusch*, 596 F.2d 871, 878 (9th Cir. 1979) ("[A] corporation may be liable for acts of its employees done contrary to express instructions and policies, but ...the existence of such instructions and policies may be considered in determining whether the employee in fact acted to benefit the corporation.").

While the Department recognizes that no compliance program can ever prevent all criminal activity by a corporation's employees, the critical factors in evaluating any program are whether the program is adequately designed for maximum effectiveness in preventing and detecting wrongdoing by employees and whether corporate management is enforcing the program or is tacitly encouraging or pressuring employees to engage in misconduct to achieve business objectives. The Department has no formulaic requirements regarding corporate compliance programs. The fundamental questions any prosecutor should ask are: Is the corporation's compliance program well designed? Is the program being applied earnestly and in good faith? Does the corporation's compliance program work? In answering these questions, the prosecutor should consider the comprehensiveness of the compliance program; the extent and pervasiveness of the criminal misconduct; the number and level of the corporate employees involved; the seriousness, duration, and frequency of the misconduct; and any remedial actions taken by the corporation, including, for example, disciplinary action against past violators uncovered by the prior compliance program, and revisions to corporate compliance programs in light of lessons learned.[FN7] Prosecutors should also consider the promptness of any disclosure of wrongdoing to the government. In evaluating compliance programs, prosecutors may consider whether the corporation has established corporate governance mechanisms that can effectively detect and prevent misconduct. For example, do the corporation's directors exercise independent review over proposed corporate actions rather than unquestioningly ratifying officers' recommendations; are internal audit functions conducted at a level sufficient to ensure their independence and accuracy; and have the directors established an information and reporting system in the organization reasonably designed to provide management and directors with timely and accurate information sufficient to allow them to reach an informed decision regarding the organization's compliance with the law. *See, e.g., In re Caremark Int'l Inc. Derivative Litig.*, 698 A.2d 959, 968-70 (Del. Ch. 1996).

Prosecutors should therefore attempt to determine whether a corporation's compliance program is merely a "paper program" or whether it was designed, implemented, reviewed, and revised, as appropriate, in an effective manner. In addition, prosecutors should determine whether the corporation has provided for a staff sufficient to audit, document, analyze, and utilize the results of the corporation's compliance efforts. Prosecutors also should determine whether the corporation's employees are adequately informed about the compliance program and are convinced of the corporation's commitment to it. This will enable the prosecutor to make an informed decision as to whether the corporation has adopted and implemented a truly effective compliance program that, when consistent with other federal law enforcement policies, may result in a decision to charge only the corporation's employees and agents or to mitigate charges or sanctions against the corporation.

Compliance programs should be designed to detect the particular types of misconduct most likely to occur in a particular corporation's line of business. Many corporations operate in complex regulatory environments outside the normal experience of criminal prosecutors. Accordingly, prosecutors should consult with relevant federal and state agencies with the expertise to evaluate the adequacy of a program's design and implementation. For instance, state and federal banking, insurance, and medical boards, the Department of Defense, the Department of Health and Human Services, the Environmental Protection Agency, and the Securities and Exchange Commission have considerable experience with compliance programs and can be helpful to a prosecutor in evaluating such programs. In addition, the Fraud Section of the Criminal Division, the Commercial Litigation Branch of the Civil Division, and the Environmental Crimes Section of the Environment and Natural Resources Division can assist United States Attorneys' Offices in finding the appropriate agency office(s) for such consultation.

[new August 2008]

9-28.900 Restitution and Remediation

A. General Principle: Although neither a corporation nor an individual target may avoid prosecution merely by paying a sum of money, a prosecutor may consider the corporation's willingness to make restitution and steps already taken to do so. A prosecutor may also consider other remedial actions, such as improving an existing compliance program or disciplining wrongdoers, in determining whether to charge the corporation and how to resolve corporate criminal cases.

B. Comment: In determining whether or not to prosecute a corporation, the government may consider whether the corporation has taken meaningful remedial measures. A corporation's response to misconduct says much about its willingness to ensure that such misconduct does not recur. Thus, corporations that fully recognize the seriousness of their misconduct and accept responsibility for it should be taking steps to implement the personnel, operational, and organizational changes necessary to establish an awareness among employees that criminal conduct will not be tolerated.

Among the factors prosecutors should consider and weigh are whether the corporation appropriately disciplined wrongdoers, once those employees are identified by the corporation as culpable for the misconduct. Employee discipline is a difficult task for many corporations because of the human element involved and sometimes because of the seniority of the employees concerned. Although corporations need to be fair to their employees, they must also be committed, at all levels of the corporation, to the highest standards of legal and ethical behavior. Effective internal discipline can be a powerful deterrent against improper behavior by a corporation's employees. Prosecutors should be satisfied that the corporation's focus is on the integrity and credibility of its remedial and disciplinary measures rather than on the protection of the wrongdoers.

In addition to employee discipline, two other factors used in evaluating a corporation's remedial efforts are restitution and reform. As with natural persons, the decision whether or not to prosecute should not depend upon the target's ability to pay restitution. A corporation's efforts to pay restitution even in advance of any court order is, however, evidence of its acceptance of responsibility and, consistent with the practices and policies of the appropriate Division of the Department entrusted with enforcing specific criminal laws, may be considered in determining whether to bring criminal charges. Similarly, although the inadequacy of a corporate compliance program is a factor to consider when deciding whether to charge a corporation, that corporation's quick recognition of the flaws in the program and its efforts to improve the program are also factors to consider as to appropriate disposition of a case.

[new August 2008]

9-28.1000 Collateral Consequences

A. **General Principle:** Prosecutors may consider the collateral consequences of a corporate criminal conviction or indictment in determining whether to charge the corporation with a criminal offense and how to resolve corporate criminal cases.

B. **Comment:** One of the factors in determining whether to charge a natural person or a corporation is whether the likely punishment is appropriate given the nature and seriousness of the crime. In the corporate context, prosecutors may take into account the possibly substantial consequences to a corporation's employees, investors, pensioners, and customers, many of whom may, depending on the size and nature of the corporation and their role in its operations, have played no role in the criminal conduct, have been unaware of it, or have been unable to prevent it. Prosecutors should also be aware of non-penal sanctions that may accompany a criminal charge, such as potential suspension or debarment from eligibility for government contracts or federally funded programs such as health care programs. Determining whether or not such non-penal sanctions are appropriate or required in a particular case is the responsibility of the relevant agency, and is a decision that will be made based on the applicable statutes, regulations, and policies.

Virtually every conviction of a corporation, like virtually every conviction of an individual, will have an impact on innocent third parties, and the mere existence of such an effect is not sufficient to preclude prosecution of the corporation. Therefore, in evaluating the relevance of collateral consequences, various factors already discussed, such as the pervasiveness of the criminal conduct and the adequacy of the corporation's compliance programs, should be considered in determining the weight to be given to this factor. For instance, the balance may tip in favor of prosecuting corporations in situations where the scope of the misconduct in a case is widespread and sustained within a corporate division (or spread throughout pockets of the corporate organization). In such cases, the possible unfairness of visiting punishment for the corporation's crimes upon shareholders may be of much less concern where those shareholders have substantially profited, even unknowingly, from widespread or pervasive criminal activity. Similarly, where the top layers of the corporation's management or the shareholders of a closely-held corporation were engaged in or aware of the wrongdoing, and the conduct at issue was accepted as a way of doing business for an extended period, debarment may be deemed not collateral, but a direct and entirely appropriate consequence of the corporation's wrongdoing.

On the other hand, where the collateral consequences of a corporate conviction for innocent third parties would be significant, it may be appropriate to consider a non-prosecution or deferred prosecution agreement with conditions designed, among other things, to promote compliance with applicable law and to prevent recidivism. Such agreements are a third option, besides a criminal indictment, on the one hand, and a declination, on the other. Declining prosecution may allow a corporate criminal to escape without consequences. Obtaining a conviction may produce a result that seriously harms innocent third parties who played no role in the criminal conduct. Under appropriate circumstances, a deferred prosecution or non-prosecution agreement can help restore the integrity of a company's operations and preserve the financial viability of a corporation that has engaged in criminal conduct, while preserving the government's ability to prosecute a recalcitrant corporation that materially breaches the agreement. Such agreements achieve other important objectives as well, like prompt restitution for victims.[FN8] Ultimately, the appropriateness of a criminal charge against a corporation, or some lesser alternative, must be evaluated in a pragmatic and reasoned way that produces a fair outcome, taking into consideration, among other things, the Department's need to promote and ensure respect for the law.

[new August 2008]

9-28.1100 Other Civil or Regulatory Alternatives

A. **General Principle:** Non-criminal alternatives to prosecution often exist and prosecutors may consider whether such sanctions would adequately deter, punish, and rehabilitate a corporation that has engaged in wrongful conduct. In evaluating the adequacy of non-criminal alternatives to prosecution—*e.g.*, civil or regulatory enforcement actions—the prosecutor may consider all relevant factors, including:

1. the sanctions available under the alternative means of disposition;
2. the likelihood that an effective sanction will be imposed; and
3. the effect of non-criminal disposition on federal law enforcement interests.

B. **Comment:** The primary goals of criminal law are deterrence, punishment, and rehabilitation. Non-criminal sanctions may not be an appropriate response to a serious violation, a pattern of wrongdoing, or prior non-criminal sanctions without proper remediation. In other cases, however, these goals may be satisfied through civil or regulatory actions. In determining whether a federal criminal resolution is appropriate, the prosecutor should consider the same factors (modified appropriately for the regulatory context) considered when determining whether to leave prosecution of a natural person to another jurisdiction or to seek non-criminal alternatives to prosecution. These factors include: the strength of the regulatory authority's interest; the regulatory authority's ability and willingness to take effective enforcement action; the probable sanction if the regulatory authority's enforcement action is upheld; and the effect of a non-criminal disposition on federal law enforcement interests. See USAM 9-27.240, 9-27.250.

[new August 2008]

9-28.1200 Selecting Charges

A. **General Principle:** Once a prosecutor has decided to charge a corporation, the prosecutor at least presumptively should charge, or should recommend that the grand jury charge, the most serious offense that is consistent with the nature of the defendant's misconduct and that is likely to result in a sustainable conviction.

B. **Comment:** Once the decision to charge is made, the same rules as govern charging natural persons apply. These rules require "a faithful and honest application of the Sentencing Guidelines" and an "individualized assessment of the extent to which particular charges fit the specific circumstances of the case, are consistent with the purposes of the Federal criminal code, and maximize the impact of Federal resources on crime." See USAM 9-27.300. In making this determination, "it is appropriate that the attorney for the government consider, *inter alia*, such factors as the [advisory] sentencing guideline range yielded by the charge, whether the penalty yielded by such sentencing range ...is proportional to the seriousness of the defendant's conduct, and whether the charge achieves such purposes of the criminal law as punishment, protection of the public, specific and general deterrence, and rehabilitation." *Id.*

[new August 2008]

9-28.1300 Plea Agreements with Corporations

A. **General Principle:** In negotiating plea agreements with corporations, as with individuals, prosecutors should generally seek a plea to the most serious, readily provable offense charged. In addition, the terms of the plea agreement should contain appropriate provisions to ensure punishment, deterrence, rehabilitation, and compliance with the plea agreement in the corporate context. Although special circumstances may mandate a different conclusion, prosecutors generally should not agree to accept a corporate guilty plea in exchange for non-prosecution or dismissal of charges against individual officers and employees.

B. **Comment:** Prosecutors may enter into plea agreements with corporations for the same reasons and under the same constraints as apply to plea agreements with natural persons. See USAM 9-27.400-530. This means, *inter alia*, that the corporation should generally be required to plead guilty to the most serious, readily provable offense charged. In addition, any negotiated departures or recommended variances from the advisory Sentencing Guidelines must be justifiable under the Guidelines or 18 U.S.C. § 3553 and must be disclosed to the sentencing court. A corporation should be made to realize that pleading guilty to criminal charges constitutes an admission of guilt and not merely a resolution of an inconvenient distraction from its business. As with natural persons, pleas should be structured so that the corporation may not later "proclaim lack of culpability or even complete innocence." See USAM 9-27.420 (b)(4), 9-27.440, 9-27.500. Thus, for instance, there should be placed upon the record a sufficient factual basis for the plea to prevent later corporate assertions of innocence.

A corporate plea agreement should also contain provisions that recognize the nature of the corporate "person" and that ensure that the principles of punishment, deterrence, and rehabilitation are met. In the corporate context, punishment and deterrence are generally accomplished by substantial fines, mandatory restitution, and institution of appropriate compliance measures, including, if necessary, continued judicial oversight or the use of special masters or corporate monitors. *See* USSG §§ 8B1.1, 8C2.1, *et seq*. In addition, where the corporation is a government contractor, permanent or temporary debarment may be appropriate. Where the corporation was engaged in fraud against the government (*e.g.*, contracting fraud), a prosecutor may not negotiate away an agency's right to debar or delist the corporate defendant.

In negotiating a plea agreement, prosecutors should also consider the deterrent value of prosecutions of individuals within the corporation. Therefore, one factor that a prosecutor may consider in determining whether to enter into a plea agreement is whether the corporation is seeking immunity for its employees and officers or whether the corporation is willing to cooperate in the investigation of culpable individuals as outlined herein. Prosecutors should rarely negotiate away individual criminal liability in a corporate plea.

Rehabilitation, of course, requires that the corporation undertake to be law-abiding in the future. It is, therefore, appropriate to require the corporation, as a condition of probation, to implement a compliance program or to reform an existing one. As discussed above, prosecutors may consult with the appropriate state and federal agencies and components of the Justice Department to ensure that a proposed compliance program is adequate and meets industry standards and best practices. See USAM 9-28.800.

In plea agreements in which the corporation agrees to cooperate, the prosecutor should ensure that the cooperation is entirely truthful. To do so, the prosecutor may request that the corporation make appropriate disclosures of relevant factual information and documents, make employees and agents available for debriefing, file appropriate certified financial statements, agree to governmental or third-party audits, and take whatever other steps are necessary to ensure that the full scope of the corporate wrongdoing is disclosed and that the responsible personnel are identified and, if appropriate, prosecuted. See generally USAM 9-28.700. In taking such steps, Department prosecutors should recognize that attorney-client communications are often essential to a corporation's efforts to comply with complex regulatory and legal regimes, and that, as discussed at length above, cooperation is not measured by the waiver of attorney-client privilege and work product protection, but rather is measured by the disclosure of facts and other considerations identified herein such as making witnesses available for interviews and assisting in the interpretation of complex documents or business records.

These Principles provide only internal Department of Justice guidance. They are not intended to, do not, and may not be relied upon to create any rights, substantive or procedural, enforceable at law by any party in any matter civil or criminal. Nor are any limitations hereby placed on otherwise lawful litigative prerogatives of the Department of Justice.

[new August 2008]

FN 1. While these guidelines refer to corporations, they apply to the consideration of the prosecution of all types of business organizations, including partnerships, sole proprietorships, government entities, and unincorporated associations.

FN 2. There are other dimensions of cooperation beyond the mere disclosure of facts, of course. These can include, for example, providing non-privileged documents and other evidence, making witnesses available for interviews, and assisting in the interpretation of complex business records. This section of the Principles focuses solely on the disclosure of facts and the privilege issues that may be implicated thereby.

FN 3. By way of example, corporate personnel are typically interviewed during an internal investigation. If the interviews are conducted by counsel for the corporation, certain notes and memoranda generated from the interviews may be subject, at least in part, to the protections of attorney-client privilege and/or attorney work product. To receive cooperation credit for providing factual information, the corporation need not produce, and prosecutors may not request, protected notes or memoranda generated by the lawyers' interviews. To earn such credit, however, the corporation does need to produce, and prosecutors may request, relevant factual information—including relevant factual information acquired through those interviews, unless the identical information has otherwise been provided—as well as relevant non-privileged evidence such as accounting and business records and emails between non-attorney employees or agents.

FN 4. In assessing the timeliness of a corporation's disclosures, prosecutors should apply a standard of reasonableness in light of the totality of circumstances.

FN 5. These privileged communications are not necessarily limited to those that occur contemporaneously with the underlying misconduct. They would include, for instance, legal advice provided by corporate counsel in an internal investigation report. Again, the key measure of cooperation is the disclosure of factual information known to the corporation, not the disclosure of legal advice or theories rendered in connection with the conduct at issue (subject to the two exceptions noted in USAM 9-28.720(b)(i-ii)).

FN 6. Routine questions regarding the representation status of a corporation and its employees, including how and by whom attorneys' fees are paid, sometimes arise in the course of an investigation under certain circumstances—to take one example, to assess conflict-of-interest issues. Such questions can be appropriate and this guidance is not intended to prohibit such limited inquiries.

FN 7. For a detailed review of these and other factors concerning corporate compliance programs, see USSG § 8B2.1.

FN 8. Prosecutors should note that in the case of national or multi-national corporations, multi-district or global agreements may be necessary. Such agreements may only be entered into with the approval of each affected district or the appropriate Department official. See USAM 9-27.641.

Environmental Crimes Deskbook

Appendix 5 U.S. EPA, Incentives for Self-Policing: Discovery, Disclosure, Correction, and Prevention of Violations, 65 Fed. Reg. 19618 (Apr. 11, 2000)

Federal Register

Tuesday,
April 11, 2000

Part VII

Environmental Protection Agency

Incentives for Self-Policing: Discovery, Disclosure, Correction and Prevention of Violations; Notice

19618 **Federal Register** / Vol. 65, No. 70 / Tuesday, April 11, 2000 / Notices

ENVIRONMENTAL PROTECTION AGENCY

[FRL–6576–3]

Incentives for Self-Policing: Discovery, Disclosure, Correction and Prevention of Violations

AGENCY: Environmental Protection Agency (EPA, or Agency).

ACTION: Final Policy Statement.

SUMMARY: EPA today issues its revised final policy on "Incentives for Self-Policing: Discovery, Disclosure, Correction and Prevention of Violations," commonly referred to as the "Audit Policy." The purpose of this Policy is to enhance protection of human health and the environment by encouraging regulated entities to voluntarily discover, promptly disclose and expeditiously correct violations of Federal environmental requirements. Incentives that EPA makes available for those who meet the terms of the Audit Policy include the elimination or substantial reduction of the gravity component of civil penalties and a determination not to recommend criminal prosecution of the disclosing entity. The Policy also restates EPA's long-standing practice of not requesting copies of regulated entities' voluntary audit reports to trigger Federal enforcement investigations. Today's revised Audit Policy replaces the 1995 Audit Policy (60 FR 66706), which was issued on December 22, 1995, and took effect on January 22, 1996. Today's revisions maintain the basic structure and terms of the 1995 Audit Policy while clarifying some of its language, broadening its availability, and conforming the provisions of the Policy to actual Agency practice. The revisions being released today lengthen the prompt disclosure period to 21 days, clarify that the independent discovery condition does not automatically preclude penalty mitigation for multi-facility entities, and clarify how the prompt disclosure and repeat violation conditions apply to newly acquired companies. The revised Policy was developed in close consultation with the U.S. Department of Justice (DOJ), States, public interest groups and the regulated community. The revisions also reflect EPA's experience implementing the Policy over the past five years.

DATES: This revised Policy is effective May 11, 2000.

FOR FURTHER INFORMATION CONTACT: Catherine Malinin Dunn (202) 564–2629 or Leslie Jones (202) 564–5123.

Documentation relating to the development of this Policy is contained in the environmental auditing public docket (#C–94–01). An index to the docket may be obtained by contacting the Enforcement and Compliance Docket and Information Center (ECDIC) by telephone at (202) 564–2614 or (202) 564–2119, by fax at (202) 501–1011, or by email at docket.oeca@epa.gov. ECDIC office hours are 8:00 am to 4:00 pm Monday through Friday except for Federal holidays. An index to the docket is available on the Internet at www.epa.gov/oeca/polguid/enfdock.html. Additional guidance regarding interpretation and application of the Policy is also available on the Internet at www.epa.gov/oeca/ore/apolguid.html.

SUPPLEMENTARY INFORMATION: This Notice is organized as follows:

I. Explanation of Policy
A. Introduction
B. Background and History
C. Purpose
D. Incentives for Self-Policing
1. Eliminating Gravity-Based Penalties
2. 75% Reduction of Gravity-Based Penalties
3. No Recommendations for Criminal Prosecution
4. No Routine Requests for Audit Reports
E. Conditions
1. Systematic Discovery of the Violation Through an Environmental Audit or a Compliance Management System
2. Voluntary Discovery
3. Prompt Disclosure
4. Discovery and Disclosure Independent of Government or Third-Party Plaintiff
5. Correction and Remediation
6. Prevent Recurrence
7. No Repeat Violations
8. Other Violations Excluded
9. Cooperation
F. Opposition to Audit Privilege and Immunity
G. Effect on States
H. Scope of Policy
I. Implementation of Policy
1. Civil Violations
2. Criminal Violations
3. Release of Information to the Public
II. Statement of Policy—Incentives for Self-Policing: Discovery, Disclosure, Correction and Prevention
A. Purpose
B. Definitions
C. Incentives for Self-Policing
1. No Gravity-Based Penalties
2. Reduction of Gravity-Based Penalties by 75%
3. No Recommendation for Criminal Prosecution
4. No Routine Request for Environmental Audit Reports
D. Conditions
1. Systematic Discovery
2. Voluntary Discovery
3. Prompt Disclosure
4. Discovery and Disclosure Independent of Government or Third-Party Plaintiff
5. Correction and Remediation
6. Prevent Recurrence
7. No Repeat Violations
8. Other Violations Excluded
9. Cooperation
E. Economic Benefit
F. Effect on State Law, Regulation or Policy
G. Applicability
H. Public Accountability
I. Effective Date

I. Explanation of Policy

A. Introduction

On December 22, 1995, EPA issued its final policy on "Incentives for Self-Policing: Discovery, Disclosure, Correction and Prevention of Violations" (60 FR 66706) (Audit Policy, or Policy). The purpose of the Policy is to enhance protection of human health and the environment by encouraging regulated entities to voluntarily discover, disclose, correct and prevent violations of Federal environmental law. Benefits available to entities that make disclosures under the terms of the Policy include reductions in the amount of civil penalties and a determination not to recommend criminal prosecution of disclosing entities.

Today, EPA issues revisions to the 1995 Audit Policy. The revised Policy reflects EPA's continuing commitment to encouraging voluntary self-policing while preserving fair and effective enforcement. It lengthens the prompt disclosure period to 21 days, clarifies that the independent discovery condition does not automatically preclude Audit Policy credit in the multi-facility context, and clarifies how the prompt disclosure and repeat violations conditions apply in the acquisitions context. The revised final Policy takes effect May 11, 2000.

B. Background and History

The Audit Policy provides incentives for regulated entities to detect, promptly disclose, and expeditiously correct violations of Federal environmental requirements. The Policy contains nine conditions, and entities that meet all of them are eligible for 100% mitigation of any gravity-based penalties that otherwise could be assessed. ("Gravity-based" refers to that portion of the penalty over and above the portion that represents the entity's economic gain from noncompliance, known as the "economic benefit.") Regulated entities that do not meet the first condition—systematic discovery of violations—but meet the other eight conditions are eligible for 75% mitigation of any gravity-based civil penalties. On the criminal side, EPA will generally elect not to recommend criminal prosecution by DOJ or any other prosecuting authority for a disclosing entity that meets at least conditions two through nine—regardless of whether it meets the systematic discovery requirement—as long as its self-policing, discovery and disclosure were conducted in good faith and the entity adopts a systematic approach to preventing recurrence of the violation.

The Policy includes important safeguards to deter violations and protect public health and the environment. For example, the Policy requires entities to act to prevent recurrence of violations and to remedy any environmental harm that may have occurred. Repeat violations, those that result in actual harm to the environment, and those that may present an imminent and substantial endangerment are not eligible for relief under this Policy. Companies will not be allowed to gain an economic advantage over their competitors by delaying their investment in compliance. And entities remain criminally liable for violations that result from conscious disregard of or willful blindness to their obligations under the law, and individuals remain liable for their criminal misconduct.

When EPA issued the 1995 Audit Policy, the Agency committed to evaluate the Policy after three years. The Agency initiated this evaluation in the Spring of 1998 and published its preliminary results in the **Federal Register** on May 17, 1999 (64 FR 26745). The evaluation consisted of the following components:

- An internal survey of EPA staff who process disclosures and handle enforcement cases under the 1995 Audit Policy;
- A survey of regulated entities that used the 1995 Policy to disclose violations;
- A series of meetings and conference calls with representatives from industry, environmental organizations, and States;
- Focused stakeholder discussions on the Audit Policy at two public conferences co-sponsored by EPA's Office of Enforcement and Compliance Assurance (OECA) and the Vice President's National Partnership for Reinventing Government, entitled "Protecting Public Health and the Environment through Innovative Approaches to Compliance";
- A **Federal Register** notice on March 2, 1999, soliciting comments on how EPA can further protect and improve public health and the environment through new compliance and enforcement approaches (64 FR 10144); and
- An analysis of data on Audit Policy usage to date and discussions amongst EPA officials who handle Audit Policy disclosures.

The same May 17, 1999, **Federal Register** notice that published the evaluation's preliminary results also proposed revisions to the 1995 Policy and requested public comment. During the 60-day public comment period, the Agency received 29 comment letters, copies of which are available through the Enforcement and Compliance Docket and Information Center. (See contact information at the beginning of this notice.) Analysis of these comment letters together with additional data on Audit Policy usage has constituted the final stage of the Audit Policy evaluation. EPA has prepared a detailed response to the comments received; a copy of that document will also be available through the Docket and Information Center as well on the Internet at www.epa.gov/oeca/ore/apolguid.html.

Overall, the Audit Policy evaluation revealed very positive results. The Policy has encouraged voluntary self-policing while preserving fair and effective enforcement. Thus, the revisions issued today do not signal any intention to shift course regarding the Agency's position on self-policing and voluntary disclosures but instead represent an attempt to fine-tune a Policy that is already working well.

Use of the Audit Policy has been widespread. As of October 1, 1999, approximately 670 organizations had disclosed actual or potential violations at more than 2700 facilities. The number of disclosures has increased each of the four years the Policy has been in effect.

Results of the Audit Policy User's Survey revealed very high satisfaction rates among users, with 88% of respondents stating that they would use the Policy again and 84% stating that they would recommend the Policy to clients and/or their counterparts. No respondents stated an unwillingness to use the Policy again or to recommend its use to others.

The Audit Policy and related documents, including Agency interpretive guidance and general interest newsletters, are available on the Internet at www.epa.gov/oeca/ore/apolguid. Additional guidance for implementing the Policy in the context of criminal violations can be found at www.epa.gov/oeca/oceft/audpol2.html.

In addition to the Audit Policy, the Agency's revised Small Business Compliance Policy ("Small Business Policy") is also available for small entities that employ 100 or fewer individuals. The Small Business Policy provides penalty mitigation, subject to certain conditions, for small businesses that make a good faith effort to comply with environmental requirements by discovering, disclosing and correcting violations. EPA has revised the Small Business Policy at the same time it revised the Audit Policy. The revised Small Business Policy will be available on the Internet at www.epa.gov/oeca/smbusi.html.

C. Purpose

The revised Policy being announced today is designed to encourage greater compliance with Federal laws and regulations that protect human health and the environment. It promotes a higher standard of self-policing by waiving gravity-based penalties for violations that are promptly disclosed and corrected, and which were discovered systematically—that is, through voluntary audits or compliance management systems. To provide an incentive for entities to disclose and correct violations regardless of how they were detected, the Policy reduces gravity-based penalties by 75% for violations that are voluntarily discovered and promptly disclosed and corrected, even if not discovered systematically.

EPA's enforcement program provides a strong incentive for compliance by imposing stiff sanctions for noncompliance. Enforcement has contributed to the dramatic expansion of environmental auditing as measured in numerous recent surveys. For example, in a 1995 survey by Price Waterhouse LLP, more than 90% of corporate respondents who conduct audits identified one of the reasons for doing so as the desire to find and correct violations before government inspectors discover them. (A copy of the survey is contained in the Docket as document VIII–A–76.)

At the same time, because government resources are limited, universal compliance cannot be achieved without active efforts by the regulated community to police themselves. More than half of the respondents to the same 1995 Price Waterhouse survey said that they would expand environmental auditing in exchange for reduced penalties for violations discovered and corrected. While many companies already audit or have compliance management programs in place, EPA believes that the incentives offered in this Policy will improve the frequency and quality of these self-policing efforts.

D. Incentives for Self-Policing

Section C of the Audit Policy identifies the major incentives that EPA provides to encourage self-policing, self-disclosure, and prompt self-correction. For entities that meet the conditions of the Policy, the available incentives include waiving or reducing gravity-based civil penalties, declining to recommend criminal prosecution for regulated entities that self-police, and refraining from routine requests for audits. (As noted in Section C of the Policy, EPA has refrained from making routine requests for audit reports since issuance of its 1986 policy on environmental auditing.)

1. Eliminating Gravity-Based Penalties

In general, civil penalties that EPA assesses are comprised of two elements: the economic benefit component and the gravity-based component. The economic benefit component reflects the economic gain derived from a violator's illegal competitive advantage. Gravity-based penalties are that portion of the penalty over and above the economic benefit. They reflect the egregiousness of the violator's behavior and constitute the punitive portion of the penalty. For further discussion of these issues, see "Calculation of the Economic Benefit of Noncompliance in EPA's Civil Penalty Enforcement Cases," 64 FR 32948 (June 18, 1999) and "A Framework for Statute-Specific Approaches to Penalty Assessments," #GM–22 (1984), U.S. EPA General Enforcement Policy Compendium.

Under the Audit Policy, EPA will not seek gravity-based penalties for disclosing entities that meet all nine Policy conditions, including systematic discovery. ("Systematic discovery" means the detection of a potential violation through an environmental audit or a compliance management system that reflects the entity's due diligence in preventing, detecting and correcting violations.) EPA has elected to waive gravity-based penalties for violations discovered systematically, recognizing that environmental auditing and compliance management systems play a critical role in protecting human health and the environment by identifying, correcting and ultimately preventing violations.

However, EPA reserves the right to collect any economic benefit that may have been realized as a result of noncompliance, even where the entity meets all other Policy conditions. Where the Agency determines that the economic benefit is insignificant, the Agency also may waive this component of the penalty.

EPA's decision to retain its discretion to recover economic benefit is based on two reasons. First, facing the risk that the Agency will recoup economic benefit provides an incentive for regulated entities to comply on time. Taxpayers whose payments are late expect to pay interest or a penalty; the same principle should apply to corporations and other regulated entities that have delayed their investment in compliance. Second, collecting economic benefit is fair because it protects law-abiding companies from being undercut by their noncomplying competitors, thereby preserving a level playing field.

2. 75% Reduction of Gravity-based Penalties

Gravity-based penalties will be reduced by 75% where the disclosing entity does not detect the violation through systematic discovery but otherwise meets all other Policy conditions. The Policy appropriately limits the complete waiver of gravity-based civil penalties to companies that conduct environmental auditing or have in place a compliance management system. However, to encourage disclosure and correction of violations even in the absence of systematic discovery, EPA will reduce gravity-based penalties by 75% for entities that meet conditions D(2) through D(9) of the Policy. EPA expects that a disclosure under this provision will encourage the entity to work with the Agency to resolve environmental problems and begin to develop an effective auditing program or compliance management system.

3. No Recommendations for Criminal Prosecution

In accordance with EPA's Investigative Discretion Memo dated January 12, 1994, EPA generally does not focus its criminal enforcement resources on entities that voluntarily discover, promptly disclose and expeditiously correct violations, unless there is potentially culpable behavior that merits criminal investigation. When a disclosure that meets the terms and conditions of this Policy results in a criminal investigation, EPA will generally not recommend criminal prosecution for the disclosing entity, although the Agency may recommend prosecution for culpable individuals and other entities. The 1994 Investigative Discretion Memo is available on the Internet at http://www.epa.gov/oeca/ore/ aed/comp/acomp/a11.html.

The "no recommendation for criminal prosecution" incentive is available for entities that meet conditions D(2) through D(9) of the Policy. Condition D(1) "systematic discovery" is not required to be eligible for this incentive, although the entity must be acting in good faith and must adopt a systematic approach to preventing recurring violations. Important limitations to the incentive apply. It will not be available, for example, where corporate officials are consciously involved in or willfully blind to violations, or conceal or condone noncompliance. Since the regulated entity must satisfy conditions D(2) through D(9) of the Policy, violations that cause serious harm or which may pose imminent and substantial endangerment to human health or the environment are not eligible. Finally, EPA reserves the right to recommend prosecution for the criminal conduct of any culpable individual or subsidiary organization.

While EPA may decide not to recommend criminal prosecution for disclosing entities, ultimate prosecutorial discretion resides with the U.S. Department of Justice, which will be guided by its own policy on voluntary disclosures ("Factors in Decisions on Criminal Prosecutions for Environmental Violations in the Context of Significant Voluntary Compliance or Disclosure Efforts by the Violator," July 1, 1991) and by its 1999 Guidance on Federal Prosecutions of Corporations. In addition, where a disclosing entity has met the conditions for avoiding a recommendation for criminal prosecution under this Policy, it will also be eligible for either 75% or 100% mitigation of gravity-based civil penalties, depending on whether the systematic discovery condition was met.

4. No Routine Requests for Audit Reports

EPA reaffirms its Policy, in effect since 1986, to refrain from routine requests for audit reports. That is, EPA has not and will not routinely request copies of audit reports to trigger enforcement investigations. Implementation of the 1995 Policy has produced no evidence that the Agency has deviated, or should deviate, from this Policy. In general, an audit that results in expeditious correction will reduce liability, not expand it. However, if the Agency has independent evidence of a violation, it may seek the information it needs to establish the extent and nature of the violation and the degree of culpability.

For discussion of the circumstances in which EPA might request an audit report to determine Policy eligibility, see the explanatory text on cooperation, section I.E.9.

E. Conditions

Section D describes the nine conditions that a regulated entity must meet in order for the Agency to decline to seek (or to reduce) gravity-based penalties under the Policy. As explained in section I.D.1 above, regulated entities that meet all nine conditions will not face gravity-based civil penalties. If the regulated entity meets all of the conditions except for D(1)—systematic discovery—EPA will reduce gravity-based penalties by 75%. In general, EPA will not recommend criminal prosecution for disclosing entities that meet at least conditions D(2) through D(9).

1. Systematic Discovery of the Violation Through an Environmental Audit or a Compliance Management System

Under Section D(1), the violation must have been discovered through either (a) an environmental audit, or (b) a compliance management system that reflects due diligence in preventing, detecting and correcting violations. Both "environmental audit" and "compliance management system" are defined in Section B of the Policy.

The revised Policy uses the term "compliance management system" instead of "due diligence," which was used in the 1995 Policy. This change in nomenclature is intended solely to conform the Policy language to terminology more commonly in use by industry and by regulators to refer to a systematic management plan or systematic efforts to achieve and maintain compliance. No substantive difference is intended by substituting the term "compliance management system" for "due diligence," as the Policy clearly indicates that the compliance management system must reflect the regulated entity's due diligence in preventing, detecting and correcting violations.

Compliance management programs that train and motivate employees to prevent, detect and correct violations on a daily basis are a valuable complement to periodic auditing. Where the violation is discovered through a compliance management system and not through an audit, the disclosing entity should be prepared to document how its program reflects the due diligence criteria defined in Section B of the Policy statement. These criteria, which are adapted from existing codes of practice—such as Chapter Eight of the U.S. Sentencing Guidelines for organizational defendants, effective since 1991—are flexible enough to accommodate different types and sizes of businesses and other regulated entities. The Agency recognizes that a variety of compliance management programs are feasible, and it will determine whether basic due diligence criteria have been met in deciding whether to grant Audit Policy credit.

As a condition of penalty mitigation, EPA may require that a description of the regulated entity's compliance management system be made publicly available. The Agency believes that the availability of such information will allow the public to judge the adequacy of compliance management systems, lead to enhanced compliance, and foster greater public trust in the integrity of compliance management systems.

2. Voluntary Discovery

Under Section D(2), the violation must have been identified voluntarily, and not through a monitoring, sampling, or auditing procedure that is required by statute, regulation, permit, judicial or administrative order, or consent agreement. The Policy provides three specific examples of discovery that would not be voluntary, and therefore would not be eligible for penalty mitigation: emissions violations detected through a required continuous emissions monitor, violations of NPDES discharge limits found through prescribed monitoring, and violations discovered through a compliance audit required to be performed by the terms of a consent order or settlement agreement. The exclusion does not apply to violations that are discovered pursuant to audits that are conducted as part of a comprehensive environmental management system (EMS) required under a settlement agreement. In general, EPA supports the implementation of EMSs that promote compliance, prevent pollution and improve overall environmental performance. Precluding the availability of the Audit Policy for discoveries made through a comprehensive EMS that has been implemented pursuant to a settlement agreement might discourage entities from agreeing to implement such a system.

In some instances, certain Clean Air Act violations discovered, disclosed and corrected by a company prior to issuance of a Title V permit are eligible for penalty mitigation under the Policy. For further guidance in this area, see "Reduced Penalties for Disclosures of Certain Clean Air Act Violations," Memorandum from Eric Schaeffer, Director of the EPA Office of Regulatory Enforcement, dated September 30, 1999. This document is available on the Internet at www.epa.gov/oeca/ore/apolguid.html.

The voluntary requirement applies to discovery only, not reporting. That is, any violation that is voluntarily discovered is generally eligible for Audit Policy credit, regardless of whether reporting of the violation was required after it was found.

3. Prompt Disclosure

Section D(3) requires that the entity disclose the violation in writing to EPA within 21 calendar days after discovery. If the 21st day after discovery falls on a weekend or Federal holiday, the disclosure period will be extended to the first business day following the 21st day after discovery. If a statute or regulation requires the entity to report the violation in fewer than 21 days, disclosure must be made within the time limit established by law. (For example, unpermitted releases of hazardous substances must be reported immediately under 42 U.S.C. 9603.) Disclosures under this Policy should be made to the appropriate EPA Regional office or, where multiple Regions are involved, to EPA Headquarters. The Agency will work closely with States as needed to ensure fair and efficient implementation of the Policy. For additional guidance on making disclosures, contact the Audit Policy National Coordinator at EPA Headquarters at 202–564–5123.

The 21-day disclosure period begins when the entity discovers that a violation has, or may have, occurred. The trigger for discovery is when any officer, director, employee or agent of the facility has an objectively reasonable basis for believing that a violation has, or may have, occurred. The "objectively reasonable basis" standard is measured against what a prudent person, having the same information as was available to the individual in question, would have believed. It is not measured against what the individual in question thought was reasonable at the time the situation was encountered. If an entity has some doubt as to the existence of a violation, the recommended course is for the entity to proceed with the disclosure and allow the regulatory authorities to make a definitive determination. Contract personnel who provide on-site services at the facility may be treated as employees or agents for purposes of the Policy.

If the 21-day period has not yet expired and an entity suspects that it will be unable to meet the deadline, the entity should contact the appropriate EPA office in advance to develop disclosure terms acceptable to EPA. For situations in which the 21-day period already has expired, the Agency may accept a late disclosure in the exceptional case, such as where there are complex circumstances, including where EPA determines the violation could not be identified and disclosed within 21 calendar days after discovery.

EPA also may extend the disclosure period when multiple facilities or acquisitions are involved.

In the multi-facility context, EPA will ordinarily extend the 21-day period to allow reasonable time for completion and review of multi-facility audits where: (a) EPA and the entity agree on the timing and scope of the audits prior to their commencement; and (b) the facilities to be audited are identified in advance. In the acquisitions context, EPA will consider extending the prompt disclosure period on a case-by-case basis. The 21-day disclosure period will begin on the date of discovery by the acquiring entity, but in no case will the period begin earlier than the date of acquisition.

In summary, Section D(3) recognizes that it is critical for EPA to receive timely reporting of violations in order to have clear notice of the violations and the opportunity to respond if necessary. Prompt disclosure is also evidence of the regulated entity's good faith in wanting to achieve or return to compliance as soon as possible. The integrity of Federal environmental law depends upon timely and accurate reporting. The public relies on timely and accurate reports from the regulated community, not only to measure compliance but to evaluate health or environmental risk and gauge progress in reducing pollutant loadings. EPA expects the Policy to encourage the kind of vigorous self-policing that will serve these objectives and does not intend that it justify delayed reporting. When violations of reporting requirements are voluntarily discovered, they must be promptly reported. When a failure to report results in imminent and substantial endangerment or serious harm to the environment, Audit Policy credit is precluded under condition D(8).

4. Discovery and Disclosure Independent of Government or Third Party Plaintiff

Under Section D(4), the entity must discover the violation independently. That is, the violation must be discovered and identified before EPA or another government agency likely would have identified the problem either through its own investigative work or from information received through a third party. This condition requires regulated entities to take the initiative to find violations on their own and disclose them promptly instead of waiting for an indication of a pending enforcement action or third-party complaint.

Section D(4)(a) lists the circumstances under which discovery and disclosure will not be considered independent. For example, a disclosure will not be independent where EPA is already investigating the facility in question. However, under subsection (a), where the entity does not know that EPA has commenced a civil investigation and proceeds in good faith to make a disclosure under the Audit Policy, EPA may, in its discretion, provide penalty mitigation under the Audit Policy. The subsection (a) exception applies only to civil investigations; it does not apply in the criminal context. Other examples of situations in which a discovery is not considered independent are where a citizens' group has provided notice of its intent to sue, where a third party has already filed a complaint, where a whistleblower has reported the potential violation to government authorities, or where discovery of the violation by the government was imminent. Condition D(4)(c)—the filing of a complaint by a third party—covers formal judicial and administrative complaints as well as informal complaints, such as a letter from a citizens' group alerting EPA to a potential environmental violation.

Regulated entities that own or operate multiple facilities are subject to section D(4)(b) in addition to D(4)(a). EPA encourages multi-facility auditing and does not intend for the "independent discovery" condition to preclude availability of the Audit Policy when multiple facilities are involved. Thus, if a regulated entity owns or operates multiple facilities, the fact that one of its facilities is the subject of an investigation, inspection, information request or third-party complaint does not automatically preclude the Agency from granting Audit Policy credit for disclosures of violations self-discovered at the other facilities, assuming all other Audit Policy conditions are met. However, just as in the single-facility context, where a facility is already the subject of a government inspection, investigation or information request (including a broad information request that covers multiple facilities), it will generally not be eligible for Audit Policy credit. The Audit Policy is designed to encourage regulated entities to disclose violations before any of their facilities are under investigation, not after EPA discovers violations at one facility. Nevertheless, the Agency retains its full discretion under the Audit Policy to grant penalty waivers or reductions for good-faith disclosures made in the multi-facility context. EPA has worked closely with a number of entities that have received Audit Policy credit for multi-facility disclosures, and entities contemplating multi-facility auditing are encouraged to contact the Agency with any questions concerning Audit Policy availability.

5. Correction and Remediation

Under Section D(5), the entity must remedy any harm caused by the violation and expeditiously certify in writing to appropriate Federal, State, and local authorities that it has corrected the violation. Correction and remediation in this context include responding to spills and carrying out any removal or remedial actions required by law. The certification requirement enables EPA to ensure that the regulated entity will be publicly accountable for its commitments through binding written agreements, orders or consent decrees where necessary.

Under the Policy, the entity must correct the violation within 60 calendar days from the date of discovery, or as expeditiously as possible. EPA recognizes that some violations can and should be corrected immediately, while others may take longer than 60 days to correct. For example, more time may be required if capital expenditures are involved or if technological issues are a factor. If more than 60 days will be required, the disclosing entity must so notify the Agency in writing prior to the conclusion of the 60-day period. In all cases, the regulated entity will be expected to do its utmost to achieve or return to compliance as expeditiously as possible.

If correction of the violation depends upon issuance of a permit that has been applied for but not issued by Federal or State authorities, the Agency will, where appropriate, make reasonable efforts to secure timely review of the permit.

6. Prevent Recurrence

Under Section D(6), the regulated entity must agree to take steps to prevent a recurrence of the violation after it has been disclosed. Preventive steps may include, but are not limited to, improvements to the entity's environmental auditing efforts or compliance management system.

7. No Repeat Violations

Condition D(7) bars repeat offenders from receiving Audit Policy credit. Under the repeat violations exclusion, the same or a closely-related violation must not have occurred at the same facility within the past 3 years. The 3-year period begins to run when the government or a third party has given the violator notice of a specific violation, without regard to when the original violation cited in the notice actually occurred. Examples of notice include a complaint, consent order, notice of violation, receipt of an inspection report, citizen suit, or receipt of penalty mitigation through a compliance assistance or incentive project.

When the facility is part of a multi-facility organization, Audit Policy relief is not available if the same or a closely-related violation occurred as part of a pattern of violations at one or more of these facilities within the past 5 years. If a facility has been newly acquired, the existence of a violation prior to acquisition does not trigger the repeat violations exclusion.

The term "violation" includes any violation subject to a Federal, State or local civil judicial or administrative order, consent agreement, conviction or plea agreement. Recognizing that minor violations sometimes are settled without a formal action in court, the term also covers any act or omission for which the regulated entity has received a penalty reduction in the past. This condition covers situations in which the regulated entity has had clear notice of its noncompliance and an opportunity to correct the problem.

The repeat violation exclusion benefits both the public and law-abiding entities by ensuring that penalties are not waived for those entities that have previously been notified of violations and fail to prevent repeat violations. The 3-year and 5-year "bright lines" in the exclusion are designed to provide regulated entities with clear notice about when the Policy will be available.

8. Other Violations Excluded

Section D(8) provides that Policy benefits are not available for certain types of violations. Subsection D(8)(a) excludes violations that result in serious actual harm to the environment or which may have presented an imminent and substantial endangerment to public health or the environment. When events of such a consequential nature occur, violators are ineligible for penalty relief and other incentives under the Audit Policy. However, this condition does not bar an entity from qualifying for Audit Policy relief solely because the violation involves release of a pollutant to the environment, as such releases do not necessarily result in serious actual harm or an imminent and substantial endangerment. To date, EPA has not invoked the serious actual harm or the imminent and substantial endangerment clauses to deny Audit Policy credit for any disclosure.

Subsection D(8)(b) excludes violations of the specific terms of any order, consent agreement, or plea agreement. Once a consent agreement has been negotiated, there is little incentive to comply if there are no sanctions for violating its specific requirements. The exclusion in this section also applies to violations of the terms of any response, removal or remedial action covered by a written agreement.

9. Cooperation

Under Section D(9), the regulated entity must cooperate as required by EPA and provide the Agency with the information it needs to determine Policy applicability. The entity must not hide, destroy or tamper with possible evidence following discovery of potential environmental violations. In order for the Agency to apply the Policy fairly, it must have sufficient information to determine whether its conditions are satisfied in each individual case. In general, EPA requests audit reports to determine the applicability of this Policy only where the information contained in the audit report is not readily available elsewhere and where EPA decides that the information is necessary to determine whether the terms and conditions of the Policy have been met. In the rare instance where an EPA Regional office seeks to obtain an audit report because it is otherwise unable to determine whether Policy conditions have been met, the Regional office will notify the Office of Regulatory Enforcement at EPA headquarters.

Entities that disclose potential criminal violations may expect a more thorough review by the Agency. In criminal cases, entities will be expected to provide, at a minimum, the following: access to all requested documents; access to all employees of the disclosing entity; assistance in investigating the violation, any noncompliance problems related to the disclosure, and any environmental consequences related to the violations; access to all information relevant to the violations disclosed, including that portion of the environmental audit report or documentation from the compliance management system that revealed the violation; and access to the individuals who conducted the audit or review.

F. Opposition to Audit Privilege and Immunity

The Agency believes that the Audit Policy provides effective incentives for self-policing without impairing law enforcement, putting the environment at risk or hiding environmental compliance information from the public. Although EPA encourages environmental auditing, it must do so without compromising the integrity and enforceability of environmental laws. It is important to distinguish between EPA's Audit Policy and the audit privilege and immunity laws that exist in some States. The Agency remains firmly opposed to statutory and regulatory audit privileges and immunity. Privilege laws shield evidence of wrongdoing and prevent States from investigating even the most serious environmental violations. Immunity laws prevent States from obtaining penalties that are appropriate to the seriousness of the violation, as they are required to do under Federal law. Audit privilege and immunity laws are unnecessary, undermine law enforcement, impair protection of human health and the environment, and interfere with the public's right to know of potential and existing environmental hazards.

Statutory audit privilege and immunity run counter to encouraging the kind of openness that builds trust between regulators, the regulated community and the public. For example, privileged information on compliance contained in an audit report may include information on the cause of violations, the extent of environmental harm, and what is necessary to correct the violations and prevent their recurrence. Privileged information is unavailable to law enforcers and to members of the public who have suffered harm as a result of environmental violations. The Agency opposes statutory immunity because it diminishes law enforcement's ability to discourage wrongful behavior and interferes with a regulator's ability to punish individuals who disregard the law and place others in danger. The Agency believes that its Audit Policy provides adequate incentives for self-policing but without secrecy and without abdicating its discretion to act in cases of serious environmental violations.

Privilege, by definition, invites secrecy, instead of the openness needed to build public trust in industry's ability to self-police. American law reflects the high value that the public places on fair access to the facts. The Supreme Court, for example, has said of privileges that, "[w]hatever their origins, these exceptions to the demand for every man's evidence are not lightly created nor expansively construed, for they are in derogation of the search for truth." *United States* v. *Nixon*, 418 U.S. 683, 710 (1974). Federal courts have unanimously refused to recognize a privilege for environmental audits in the context of government investigations. See, *e.g., United States* v. *Dexter Corp.*, 132 F.R.D. 8, 10 (D.Conn. 1990)

19624 Federal Register / Vol. 65, No. 70 / Tuesday, April 11, 2000 / Notices

(application of a privilege "would effectively impede [EPA's] ability to enforce the Clean Water Act, and would be contrary to stated public policy.") Cf. In re Grand Jury Proceedings, 861 F. Supp. 386 (D. Md. 1994) (company must comply with a subpoena under Food, Drug and Cosmetics Act for self-evaluative documents).

G. Effect on States

The revised final Policy reflects EPA's desire to provide fair and effective incentives for self-policing that have practical value to States. To that end, the Agency has consulted closely with State officials in developing this Policy. As a result, EPA believes its revised final Policy is grounded in commonsense principles that should prove useful in the development and implementation of State programs and policies.

EPA recognizes that States are partners in implementing the enforcement and compliance assurance program. When consistent with EPA's policies on protecting confidential and sensitive information, the Agency will share with State agencies information on disclosures of violations of Federally-authorized, approved or delegated programs. In addition, for States that have adopted their own audit policies in Federally-authorized, approved or delegated programs, EPA will generally defer to State penalty mitigation for self-disclosures as long as the State policy meets minimum requirements for Federal delegation. Whenever a State provides a penalty waiver or mitigation for a violation of a requirement contained in a Federally-authorized, approved or delegated program to an entity that discloses those violations in conformity with a State audit policy, the State should notify the EPA Region in which it is located. This notification will ensure that Federal and State enforcement responses are coordinated properly.

For further information about minimum delegation requirements and the effect of State audit privilege and immunity laws on enforcement authority, see "Statement of Principles: Effect of State Audit/Immunity Privilege Laws on Enforcement Authority for Federal Programs," Memorandum from Steven A. Herman et al, dated February 14, 1997, to be posted on the Internet under www.epa.gov/oeca/oppa.

As always, States are encouraged to experiment with different approaches to assuring compliance as long as such approaches do not jeopardize public health or the environment, or make it profitable not to comply with Federal environmental requirements. The Agency remains opposed to State legislation that does not include these basic protections, and reserves its right to bring independent action against regulated entities for violations of Federal law that threaten human health or the environment, reflect criminal conduct or repeated noncompliance, or allow one company to profit at the expense of its law-abiding competitors.

H. Scope of Policy

EPA has developed this Policy to guide settlement actions. It is the Agency's practice to make public all compliance agreements reached under this Policy in order to provide the regulated community with fair notice of decisions and to provide affected communities and the public with information regarding Agency action. Some in the regulated community have suggested that the Agency should convert the Policy into a regulation because they feel doing so would ensure greater consistency and predictability. Following its three-year evaluation of the Policy, however, the Agency believes that there is ample evidence that the Policy has worked well and that there is no need for a formal rulemaking. Furthermore, as the Agency seeks to respond to lessons learned from its increasing experience handling self-disclosures, a policy is much easier to amend than a regulation. Nothing in today's release of the revised final Policy is intended to change the status of the Policy as guidance.

I. Implementation of Policy

1. Civil Violations

Pursuant to the Audit Policy, disclosures of civil environmental violations should be made to the EPA Region in which the entity or facility is located or, where the violations to be disclosed involve more than one EPA Region, to EPA Headquarters. The Regional or Headquarters offices decide whether application of the Audit Policy in a specific case is appropriate. Obviously, once a matter has been referred for civil judicial prosecution, DOJ becomes involved as well. Where there is evidence of a potential criminal violation, the civil offices coordinate with criminal enforcement offices at EPA and DOJ.

To resolve issues of national significance and ensure that the Policy is applied fairly and consistently across EPA Regions and at Headquarters, the Agency in 1995 created the Audit Policy Quick Response Team (QRT). The QRT is comprised of representatives from the Regions, Headquarters, and DOJ. It meets on a regular basis to address issues of interpretation and to coordinate self-disclosure initiatives. In addition, in 1999 EPA established a National Coordinator position to handle Audit Policy issues and implementation. The National Coordinator chairs the QRT and, along with the Regional Audit Policy coordinators, serves as a point of contact on Audit Policy issues in the civil context.

2. Criminal Violations

Criminal disclosures are handled by the Voluntary Disclosure Board (VDB), which was established by EPA in 1997. The VDB ensures consistent application of the Audit Policy in the criminal context by centralizing Policy interpretation and application within the Agency.

Disclosures of potential criminal violations may be made directly to the VDB, to an EPA regional criminal investigation division or to DOJ. In all cases, the VDB coordinates with the investigative team and the appropriate prosecuting authority. During the course of the investigation, the VDB routinely monitors the progress of the investigation as necessary to ensure that sufficient facts have been established to determine whether to recommend that relief under the Policy be granted.

At the conclusion of the criminal investigation, the Board makes a recommendation to the Director of EPA's Office of Criminal Enforcement, Forensics, and Training, who serves as the Deciding Official. Upon receiving the Board's recommendation, the Deciding Official makes his or her final recommendation to the appropriate United States Attorney's Office and/or DOJ. The recommendation of the Deciding Official, however, is only that—a recommendation. The United States Attorney's Office and/or DOJ retain full authority to exercise prosecutorial discretion.

3. Release of Information to the Public

Upon formal settlement, EPA places copies of settlements in the Audit Policy Docket. EPA also makes other documents related to self-disclosures publicly available, unless the disclosing entity claims them as Confidential Business Information (and that claim is validated by U.S. EPA), unless another exemption under the Freedom of Information Act is asserted and/or applies, or the Privacy Act or any other law would preclude such release. Presumptively releasable documents include compliance agreements reached under the Policy (see Section H) and descriptions of compliance management systems submitted under Section D(1).

Any material claimed to be Confidential Business Information will be treated in accordance with EPA regulations at 40 CFR Part 2. In determining what documents to release, EPA is guided by the Memorandum from Assistant Administrator Steven A. Herman entitled "Confidentiality of Information Received Under Agency's Self-Disclosure Policy," available on the Internet at www.epa.gov/oeca/sahmemo.html.

II. Statement of Policy—Incentives for Self-Policing: Discovery, Disclosure, Correction and Prevention of Violations

A. Purpose

This Policy is designed to enhance protection of human health and the environment by encouraging regulated entities to voluntarily discover, disclose, correct and prevent violations of Federal environmental requirements.

B. Definitions

For purposes of this Policy, the following definitions apply:

"Environmental Audit" is a systematic, documented, periodic and objective review by regulated entities of facility operations and practices related to meeting environmental requirements.

"Compliance Management System" encompasses the regulated entity's documented systematic efforts, appropriate to the size and nature of its business, to prevent, detect and correct violations through all of the following:

(a) Compliance policies, standards and procedures that identify how employees and agents are to meet the requirements of laws, regulations, permits, enforceable agreements and other sources of authority for environmental requirements;

(b) Assignment of overall responsibility for overseeing compliance with policies, standards, and procedures, and assignment of specific responsibility for assuring compliance at each facility or operation;

(c) Mechanisms for systematically assuring that compliance policies, standards and procedures are being carried out, including monitoring and auditing systems reasonably designed to detect and correct violations, periodic evaluation of the overall performance of the compliance management system, and a means for employees or agents to report violations of environmental requirements without fear of retaliation;

(d) Efforts to communicate effectively the regulated entity's standards and procedures to all employees and other agents;

(e) Appropriate incentives to managers and employees to perform in accordance with the compliance policies, standards and procedures, including consistent enforcement through appropriate disciplinary mechanisms; and

(f) Procedures for the prompt and appropriate correction of any violations, and any necessary modifications to the regulated entity's compliance management system to prevent future violations.

"Environmental audit report" means the documented analysis, conclusions, and recommendations resulting from an environmental audit, but does not include data obtained in, or testimonial evidence concerning, the environmental audit.

"Gravity-based penalties" are that portion of a penalty over and above the economic benefit, *i.e.*, the punitive portion of the penalty, rather than that portion representing a defendant's economic gain from noncompliance.

"Regulated entity" means any entity, including a Federal, State or municipal agency or facility, regulated under Federal environmental laws.

C. Incentives for Self-Policing

1. No Gravity-Based Penalties

If a regulated entity establishes that it satisfies all of the conditions of Section D of this Policy, EPA will not seek gravity-based penalties for violations of Federal environmental requirements discovered and disclosed by the entity.

2. Reduction of Gravity-Based Penalties by 75%

If a regulated entity establishes that it satisfies all of the conditions of Section D of this Policy except for D(1)—systematic discovery—EPA will reduce by 75% gravity-based penalties for violations of Federal environmental requirements discovered and disclosed by the entity.

3. No Recommendation for Criminal Prosecution

(a) If a regulated entity establishes that it satisfies at least conditions D(2) through D(9) of this Policy, EPA will not recommend to the U.S. Department of Justice or other prosecuting authority that criminal charges be brought against the disclosing entity, as long as EPA determines that the violation is not part of a pattern or practice that demonstrates or involves:

(i) A prevalent management philosophy or practice that conceals or condones environmental violations; or

(ii) High-level corporate officials' or managers' conscious involvement in, or willful blindness to, violations of Federal environmental law;

(b) Whether or not EPA recommends the regulated entity for criminal prosecution under this section, the Agency may recommend for prosecution the criminal acts of individual managers or employees under existing policies guiding the exercise of enforcement discretion.

4. No Routine Request for Environmental Audit Reports

EPA will neither request nor use an environmental audit report to initiate a civil or criminal investigation of an entity. For example, EPA will not request an environmental audit report in routine inspections. If the Agency has independent reason to believe that a violation has occurred, however, EPA may seek any information relevant to identifying violations or determining liability or extent of harm.

D. Conditions

1. Systematic Discovery

The violation was discovered through:

(a) An environmental audit; or

(b) A compliance management system reflecting the regulated entity's due diligence in preventing, detecting, and correcting violations. The regulated entity must provide accurate and complete documentation to the Agency as to how its compliance management system meets the criteria for due diligence outlined in Section B and how the regulated entity discovered the violation through its compliance management system. EPA may require the regulated entity to make publicly available a description of its compliance management system.

2. Voluntary Discovery

The violation was discovered voluntarily and not through a legally mandated monitoring or sampling requirement prescribed by statute, regulation, permit, judicial or administrative order, or consent agreement. For example, the Policy does not apply to:

(a) Emissions violations detected through a continuous emissions monitor (or alternative monitor established in a permit) where any such monitoring is required;

(b) Violations of National Pollutant Discharge Elimination System (NPDES) discharge limits detected through required sampling or monitoring; or

(c) Violations discovered through a compliance audit required to be performed by the terms of a consent order or settlement agreement, unless the audit is a component of agreement terms to implement a comprehensive environmental management system.

3. Prompt Disclosure

The regulated entity fully discloses the specific violation in writing to EPA within 21 days (or within such shorter time as may be required by law) after the entity discovered that the violation has, or may have, occurred. The time at which the entity discovers that a violation has, or may have, occurred begins when any officer, director, employee or agent of the facility has an objectively reasonable basis for believing that a violation has, or may have, occurred.

4. Discovery and Disclosure Independent of Government or Third-Party Plaintiff

(a) The regulated entity discovers and discloses the potential violation to EPA prior to:

(i) The commencement of a Federal, State or local agency inspection or investigation, or the issuance by such agency of an information request to the regulated entity (where EPA determines that the facility did not know that it was under civil investigation, and EPA determines that the entity is otherwise acting in good faith, the Agency may exercise its discretion to reduce or waive civil penalties in accordance with this Policy);

(ii) Notice of a citizen suit;

(iii) The filing of a complaint by a third party;

(iv) The reporting of the violation to EPA (or other government agency) by a "whistleblower" employee, rather than by one authorized to speak on behalf of the regulated entity; or

(v) imminent discovery of the violation by a regulatory agency.

(b) For entities that own or operate multiple facilities, the fact that one facility is already the subject of an investigation, inspection, information request or third-party complaint does not preclude the Agency from exercising its discretion to make the Audit Policy available for violations self-discovered at other facilities owned or operated by the same regulated entity.

5. Correction and Remediation

The regulated entity corrects the violation within 60 calendar days from the date of discovery, certifies in writing that the violation has been corrected, and takes appropriate measures as determined by EPA to remedy any environmental or human harm due to the violation. EPA retains the authority to order an entity to correct a violation within a specific time period shorter than 60 days whenever correction in such shorter period of time is feasible and necessary to protect public health and the environment adequately. If more than 60 days will be needed to correct the violation, the regulated entity must so notify EPA in writing before the 60-day period has passed. Where appropriate, to satisfy conditions D(5) and D(6), EPA may require a regulated entity to enter into a publicly available written agreement, administrative consent order or judicial consent decree as a condition of obtaining relief under the Audit Policy, particularly where compliance or remedial measures are complex or a lengthy schedule for attaining and maintaining compliance or remediating harm is required.

6. Prevent Recurrence

The regulated entity agrees in writing to take steps to prevent a recurrence of the violation. Such steps may include improvements to its environmental auditing or compliance management system.

7. No Repeat Violations

The specific violation (or a closely related violation) has not occurred previously within the past three years at the same facility, and has not occurred within the past five years as part of a pattern at multiple facilities owned or operated by the same entity. For the purposes of this section, a violation is:

(a) Any violation of Federal, State or local environmental law identified in a judicial or administrative order, consent agreement or order, complaint, or notice of violation, conviction or plea agreement; or

(b) Any act or omission for which the regulated entity has previously received penalty mitigation from EPA or a State or local agency.

8. Other Violations Excluded

The violation is not one which (a) resulted in serious actual harm, or may have presented an imminent and substantial endangerment, to human health or the environment, or (b) violates the specific terms of any judicial or administrative order, or consent agreement.

9. Cooperation

The regulated entity cooperates as requested by EPA and provides such information as is necessary and requested by EPA to determine applicability of this Policy.

E. Economic Benefit

EPA retains its full discretion to recover any economic benefit gained as a result of noncompliance to preserve a "level playing field" in which violators do not gain a competitive advantage over regulated entities that do comply. EPA may forgive the entire penalty for violations that meet conditions D(1) through D(9) and, in the Agency's opinion, do not merit any penalty due to the insignificant amount of any economic benefit.

F. Effect on State Law, Regulation or Policy

EPA will work closely with States to encourage their adoption and implementation of policies that reflect the incentives and conditions outlined in this Policy. EPA remains firmly opposed to statutory environmental audit privileges that shield evidence of environmental violations and undermine the public's right to know, as well as to blanket immunities, particularly immunities for violations that reflect criminal conduct, present serious threats or actual harm to health and the environment, allow noncomplying companies to gain an economic advantage over their competitors, or reflect a repeated failure to comply with Federal law. EPA will work with States to address any provisions of State audit privilege or immunity laws that are inconsistent with this Policy and that may prevent a timely and appropriate response to significant environmental violations. The Agency reserves its right to take necessary actions to protect public health or the environment by enforcing against any violations of Federal law.

G. Applicability

(1) This Policy applies to settlement of claims for civil penalties for any violations under all of the Federal environmental statutes that EPA administers, and supersedes any inconsistent provisions in media-specific penalty or enforcement policies and EPA's 1995 Policy on "Incentives for Self-Policing: Discovery, Disclosure, Correction and Prevention of Violations."

(2) To the extent that existing EPA enforcement policies are not inconsistent, they will continue to apply in conjunction with this Policy. However, a regulated entity that has received penalty mitigation for satisfying specific conditions under this Policy may not receive additional penalty mitigation for satisfying the same or similar conditions under other policies for the same violation, nor will this Policy apply to any violation that has received penalty mitigation under other policies. Where an entity has failed to meet any of conditions D(2) through D(9) and is therefore not eligible for penalty relief under this Policy, it may still be eligible for penalty

relief under other EPA media-specific enforcement policies in recognition of good faith efforts, even where, for example, the violation may have presented an imminent and substantial endangerment or resulted in serious actual harm.

(3) This Policy sets forth factors for consideration that will guide the Agency in the exercise of its enforcement discretion. It states the Agency's views as to the proper allocation of its enforcement resources. The Policy is not final agency action and is intended as guidance. This Policy is not intended, nor can it be relied upon, to create any rights enforceable by any party in litigation with the United States. As with the 1995 Audit Policy, EPA may decide to follow guidance provided in this document or to act at variance with it based on its analysis of the specific facts presented. This Policy may be revised without public notice to reflect changes in EPA's approach to providing incentives for self-policing by regulated entities, or to clarify and update text.

(4) This Policy should be used whenever applicable in settlement negotiations for both administrative and civil judicial enforcement actions. It is not intended for use in pleading, at hearing or at trial. The Policy may be applied at EPA's discretion to the settlement of administrative and judicial enforcement actions instituted prior to, but not yet resolved, as of the effective date of this Policy.

(5) For purposes of this Policy, violations discovered pursuant to an environmental audit or compliance management system may be considered voluntary even if required under an Agency "partnership" program in which the entity participates, such as regulatory flexibility pilot projects like Project XL. EPA will consider application of the Audit Policy to such partnership program projects on a project-by-project basis.

(6) EPA has issued interpretive guidance addressing several applicability issues pertaining to the Audit Policy. Entities considering whether to take advantage of the Audit Policy should review that guidance to see if it addresses any relevant questions. The guidance can be found on the Internet at www.epa.gov/oeca/ore/apolguid.html.

H. Public Accountability

EPA will make publicly available the terms and conditions of any compliance agreement reached under this Policy, including the nature of the violation, the remedy, and the schedule for returning to compliance.

I. Effective Date

This revised Policy is effective May 11, 2000.

Dated: March 30, 2000.

Steven A. Herman,

Assistant Administrator for Enforcement and Compliance Assurance.

[FR Doc. 00–8954 Filed 4–10–00; 8:45 am]

BILLING CODE 6560–50–P

Environmental Crimes Deskbook

Appendix 6 U.S. EPA, Small Business Compliance Policy, 65 Fed. Reg. 19630 (Apr. 11, 2000)

Federal Register

Tuesday,
April 11, 2000

Part VIII

Environmental Protection Agency

Small Business Compliance Policy; Notice

19630 Federal Register / Vol. 65, No. 70 / Tuesday, April 11, 2000 / Notices

ENVIRONMENTAL PROTECTION AGENCY

[FRL–6576–4]

Small Business Compliance Policy

AGENCY: Environmental Protection Agency (EPA).

ACTION: Final Policy Statement.

SUMMARY: The Environmental Protection Agency (EPA) today issues its revised final *Small Business Compliance Policy* to expand the options allowed under the Policy for discovering violations and to establish a time period for disclosure. This Policy was originally titled the *Policy on Compliance Incentives for Small Businesses.* This Policy is intended to promote environmental compliance among small businesses by providing incentives for voluntary discovery, prompt disclosure, and prompt correction of violations. The Policy accomplishes this in two ways: by setting forth guidelines for the Agency to apply in reducing or waiving penalties for small businesses that come forward to disclose and make good faith efforts to correct violations, and by deferring to State, local and Tribal governments that offer these incentives. Major revisions released today include lengthening the prompt disclosure period from 10 to 21 calendar days and broadening the applicability of the Policy to violations uncovered by small businesses through any means of voluntary discovery.

DATES: This policy is effective May 11, 2000.

ADDRESSES: Additional documentation relating to the development of this policy is contained in the Office of Enforcement and Compliance Assurance (OECA) public docket (EC–P–1999–009). An index to the docket may be obtained by contacting the Enforcement and Compliance Docket and Information Center by telephone at (202) 564–2614 or (202) 564–2119, by fax at (202) 564–1011, or by email at docket.oeca@epa.gov. Office hours are 8:00 a.m. to 4:00 p.m., Monday through Friday, except legal holidays. An additional contact is Ginger Gotliffe (202) 564–7072; fax (202) 564–009; e-mail: gotliffe.ginger@epa.gov.

SUPPLEMENTARY INFORMATION:

Introduction

Five years ago, EPA reorganized its compliance programs. This reorganization was undertaken by Administrator Browner with a goal of making EPA's enforcement and compliance programs more effective in protecting public health, safety and the environment. The reorganization also improved and enhanced EPA's ability to reach out to small businesses with information to help them comply with environmental requirements. Five years after the reorganization, EPA conducted outreach efforts to obtain feedback on compliance and enforcement activities, on ways to further improve public health, safety and the environment through compliance efforts, and on actions the Agency has taken over the past five years. From these and other outreach efforts and from meetings and conference calls with interested stakeholder groups, OECA received feedback that improvements were needed to both its Audit Policy and to its Small Business Policy. In response to that feedback, OECA reviewed ways to improve these Policies.

Background and History

EPA issued two incentives policies in 1995 and 1996. The "Incentives for Self-Policing: Discovery, Disclosure, Correction and Prevention of Violations," informally known as the "Audit Policy," was issued in December 1995. See 60 FR 66706 (Dec. 22, 1995). The purpose of the Audit Policy, which is available to entities of any size, is to enhance protection of human health, safety and the environment by encouraging regulated businesses to voluntarily discover, promptly disclose, expeditiously correct and prevent violations of federal environmental law. Benefits available to businesses that qualify for the Audit Policy include reductions in the amount of civil penalties and no recommendation for prosecution of potential criminal violations. The Audit Policy has been recently modified, and the Final revised Audit Policy is being published today in the **Federal Register**.

To address the special needs of small businesses EPA issued the "Policy on Compliance Incentives for Small Businesses," which is commonly called the "Small Business Policy," in June 1996. See 61 FR 27984 June 3, 1996. The Small Business Policy implements section 223 of the Small Business Regulatory Enforcement Fairness Act (SBREFA) of 1996. The term "small business" will be used throughout this Policy, however this term will also cover entities such as small governments and small organizations as defined in SBREFA. Under the existing Small Business Policy, EPA will waive or reduce civil penalties whenever a small business makes a good faith effort to comply with environmental requirements by discovering violations as part of a government sponsored compliance assistance program or a voluntary environmental audit, promptly disclosing those violations, and correcting them in a timely manner. If the small business meets all the criteria in the policy, including violation history, correction timeframe, and lack of harm, EPA will waive 100% of the gravity component of the civil penalty. Moreover, EPA will defer to State, local and Tribal actions that are consistent with the criteria set forth in this Policy. The Small Business Policy provides penalty reduction as an incentive for small businesses, who are less likely than large businesses to have sophisticated environmental expertise, to ask for compliance assistance. This policy was also simpler for small businesses to use.

There are several notable differences between the existing Audit Policy and Small Business Policy. First, the policies allow penalty reduction for violations discovered in different ways. The Audit Policy addresses violations discovered through systematic methods such as audits as well as through non-systematic methods. The Small Business Policy applies only to violations discovered through audits and during government sponsored on-site compliance assistance activities. Second, the penalty reduction granted by the policies varies. The Audit Policy provides 100% reduction of the gravity component of the penalty (explained below) for systematic discoveries (i.e., part of a regular audit program) and 75% for non-systematic discoveries. The Small Business Policy grants provides up to 100% reduction of the gravity component of the penalty for violations discovered either through regular audits or during government sponsored on-site compliance assistance activities. Finally, the period within which violations must be corrected is different. Under the Audit Policy, businesses must correct a violation within up to 60 days of its discovery of the violation to qualify for penalty reduction. Under the Small Business Policy, a business must generally correct a violation within 180 days of its discovery to qualify for penalty reduction, and within 360 days if the correction involves pollution prevention modifications.

In addition to these notable differences, the Audit Policy addresses several issues not covered by the Small Business Policy; criminal conduct and multi-facility disclosures. The Small Business Policy is inapplicable for criminal violations. Violations that may involve criminal conduct can be addressed under the Audit Policy. In the unlikely situation where a disclosure involves a multi-facility business, the Agency will identify the relevant provisions of the Audit and Small Business Policies.

Changes to Policy

EPA is today making several major changes to the Small Business Compliance Policy. All of these changes will make it easier for small businesses to take advantage of the Small Business Compliance Policy. These changes result from EPA's evaluation of comments received on our proposed modification of the Small Business Compliance Policy, which was published on July 29, 1999. See 64 FR 41116.

The following sections discuss the two major changes that we have made to the Small Business Compliance Policy: expansion of options for discovery of violations and lengthening the disclosure period.

1. Expanded Options for Discovery of Violations

Comments submitted to EPA suggested that this Policy should be expanded to include violations that are discovered by a variety of compliance assistance activities, including participation in compliance programs or the use of tools that have been developed or sponsored by EPA, the States, and local, private and non-profit assistance providers. Based on its evaluation of those comments, EPA has decided in the revised Small Business Compliance Policy to allow small businesses to obtain penalty relief if violations are discovered by any voluntary means in addition to discovery as the result of government sponsored on-site compliance assistance activities or environmental audits. For example, voluntary discovery could result from compliance management systems (CMSs), pollution prevention assessments, participation in mentoring programs, training classes, use of on-line compliance assistance centers, and use of checklists. These programs and activities need not be associated with environmental regulatory agencies, but may be associated with any public, private, or non-profit organization. The Agency wants to encourage participation in those programs or activities that could increase compliance, improve efficiency, and reduce pollution.

There are a variety of activities and sources of information that a small business can use to learn more about environmental regulatory requirements. EPA and the States provide various forms of compliance assistance. Some State assistance programs are run as confidential services to the small business community. If a small business wishes to obtain a corrections period under this policy after receiving compliance assistance from a confidential program, the business must promptly disclose the violations to the EPA or the State or Tribal government agency which is applying a similar policy and comply with the other provisions of this Policy.

2. Clarify and Lengthen the Disclosure Period

This revised Small Business Compliance Policy extends the time period within which the small business must fully disclose a violation from 10 to 21 calendar days. The original Policy required "prompt disclosure" for compliance assistance discovery and 10 day disclosure for discoveries made through an environmental audit. Lengthening the disclosure period to 21 calendar days regardless of how the violation was discovered will give small businesses more opportunity to make use of the Small Business Compliance Policy while allowing EPA to get timely reporting of violations. Such timely reporting provides the Agency with clear notice of violations that have or may have occurred and the opportunity to respond if necessary, as well as an accurate picture of a given businesses's compliance record. Lengthening the disclosure period to 21 calendar days is also consistent with a similar change that EPA made to the Audit Policy.

EPA received comment that there might be situations where small businesses would not able to disclose within the 21 calendar day period. Therefore the revised Small Business Compliance Policy addresses this issue. Where the 21 calendar day disclosure period has not expired and a small business knows that it will be unable to disclose within that time period, the small business is advised to contact the appropriate EPA Office before the period expires to request additional time. For situations in which the 21 calendar day disclosure period has already expired, the Agency may accept a late disclosure in the exceptional case, such as where there are complex circumstances. In such instances, the small business will need to demonstrate that an exceptional case exists.

With the broadening of the options for the discovery of violations, there was some concern by one commenter in a follow-up conversation about the event that triggers the beginning of the 21 calendar day disclosure period. The 21 calendar day disclosure period begins when the small business discovers that a violation has, or may have, occurred. Discovery occurs when any officer, director, employee or agent of the facility becomes aware of any facts that reasonably lead him or her to believe that a violation has or may have occurred at the facility.

Other Issues Addressed by Public Comment

There were also issues that the public commented on, either through outreach activities or in response to the Agency's proposed modifications. These covered reduction of penalties, implementation of the policy, and the combination of the Audit Policy and the Small Business Compliance Policy.

1. Penalty Reduction

EPA did not change the Small Business Compliance Policy provisions on reducing or eliminating the gravity component of civil penalties that it would otherwise seek. Civil penalties are made up of two components: a gravity component and an economic benefit component. The gravity component typically reflects the nature of the violations, the duration of the violations, the environmental, safety or public health impacts of the violations, good faith efforts by the business to promptly remedy the violation, and the business's overall record of compliance with environmental requirements. Under this Policy, the Agency will grant 100% reduction of the gravity component of the penalty for violations provided all the other criteria in the policy are met. The Agency believes the incentive of 100% reduction of the gravity component should encourage small businesses to disclose violations promptly and correct them within the specified time period.

The economic benefit component typically reflects any monetary advantage a small business has derived from the violations. For example, if a small business significantly reduced its expenses by not purchasing and installing an emission control device to meet regulatory requirements, then that small business has gained an economic benefit or advantage over its competitors who have complied with the environmental requirements. We received a comment that the possibility of being subject to the economic benefit component of a civil penalty would keep small businesses from using the policy. However, other commenters stated that the economic benefit component should be retained to protect law abiding small businesses from being placed at a competitive disadvantage to those which do not comply.

EPA retains discretion to consider and collect economic benefit where a significant benefit was gained, although based on its experience, the Agency does not anticipate the need to exercise this discretion often. To date, the vast majority of the disclosures under the Audit Policy and all of the disclosures under the Small Business Compliance Policy have not necessitated recovery of economic benefit.

2. Implementation of the Policy

EPA has modified the Small Business Compliance Policy in format and language to provide the information in a more understandable manner. This in part helps to respond to comments about how we have implemented the Policy. In addition, when they become available, EPA will provide a fact sheet, contact list, and other information about the Policy at the EPA web site (*http:// www.epa.gov/oeca/smbusi.html*) to increase the usefulness of the Policy. We will also ensure that other internet sites such as EPA's Small Business Ombudsman web site and the Compliance Assistance Center's web sites (9 Centers available at http:// www.epa.gov/oeca/centers) link to this information about the Policy. EPA staff and other compliance assistance activities and initiatives will also provide information about the Small Business Compliance Policy.

Enhanced implementation of the Policy also involves improved procedures and coordination within EPA. EPA Headquarters and Regional staff working on the Audit Policy as well as this Small Business Compliance Policy are coordinating on issues and procedures to ensure national consistency in its application and to improve the timeliness of the Agency's review of each disclosure. In most circumstances, EPA will respond to a small business within 60 days of disclosure of a violation.

3. Combining Both Compliance Incentives Policies

As part of the Agency's evaluations of the Audit and Small Business Policies and given the similarities between the two Policies, EPA asked for comments on the advisability of combining them. In particular, the Agency was interested in whether small businesses would be more likely to audit (or seek compliance assistance) and self-disclose violations if the two policies were merged. EPA received a range of comments supportive of combining the two policies if doing so would simplify the process for small businesses. After a careful review, EPA decided that it is preferable for small businesses to have a separate policy tailored specifically for them. The Small Business Compliance Policy: (1) Is shorter and simpler, (2) contains additional benefits for small businesses such as a longer correction period and 100% penalty reduction of the gravity component for all covered violations, and (3) can be more easily distributed with compliance assistance materials developed just for small businesses.

We expect these changes to enable more small businesses to use the policy and thereby promote environmental compliance.

Small Business Compliance Policy

A. Introduction and Purpose

The Small Business Compliance Policy is intended to promote environmental compliance among small businesses by providing incentives for them to make use of compliance assistance programs, environmental audits, or compliance management systems (CMS), or to participate in any activities that may increase small businesses' understanding of the environmental requirements with which they must comply. The Policy accomplishes this in two ways: by waiving or reducing civil penalties to which a small business might otherwise be subject, and by deferring to States and local governments or tribal authorities that offer these incentives consistent with the criteria established in this Policy.

EPA will waive or reduce the gravity component of civil penalties whenever a small business makes a good faith effort to comply with environmental requirements by:

(1) Voluntarily discovering a violation,

(2) Promptly disclosing the violation within the required time period, and

(3) Expeditiously correcting the violation within the proper timeframe.

To obtain the benefits of the Policy, the facility must also meet criteria on violation history, lack of harm, and criminal conduct.

B. Background

This Policy implements section 223 of the Small Business Regulatory Enforcement Fairness Act (SBREFA) of 1996.

C. Applicability

This Policy applies to facilities owned by small businesses as defined here. A small business is a person, corporation, partnership, or other entity that employs 100 or fewer individuals (across all facilities and operations owned by the small business).[1] Entities, as defined under SBREFA, also include small governments and small organizations. Facilities that are operated by municipalities or other local governments may be covered under the Small Communities Policy (see *http:// www.epa.gov/oeca/scpolcy.html*). Facilities that are disclosing violations involving multiple facilities should refer to the sections on multiple facilities in the Policy on Incentives for Self-Policing: Discovery, Disclosure, Correction and Prevention of Violations (the Audit Policy) of April 11, 2000.

This Policy supersedes the previous version of the policy which was called the Policy on Compliance Incentives for Small Businesses and became effective on June 10,1996. To the extent that this Policy may differ from the terms of applicable enforcement response policies (including penalty policies) under media-specific programs, this document supersedes those policies.

D. How Small Businesses Can Qualify for Penalty Reduction

EPA will eliminate or reduce the gravity component of civil penalties against small businesses based on the following criteria:

1. Discovery is Voluntary

The small business discovers a violation on its own before an EPA or State inspection. For example, a small business may discover violations after receiving compliance assistance, conducting an environmental audit or participating in mentoring programs. Other activities that may be useful in discovering violations include establishing CMS, using compliance checklists, reading materials on complying with environmental requirements, using compliance assistance center web sites, and attending training classes.

The violation must be identified voluntarily, and not through a monitoring or sampling requirement prescribed by statute, regulation, permit, judicial or administrative order, or consent agreement. For example, emissions violations discovered through a continuous emissions monitor (or alternative monitor established in a permit), violations of National Pollutant Discharge Elimination System (NPDES) discharge limits discovered through required sampling or monitoring, and violations discovered through a compliance audit required to be performed by terms of a consent order or settlement order are not eligible for penalty reduction under the policy.

[1] The number of employees should be considered as full-time equivalents on an annual basis, including contract employees. Full-time equivalents means 2,000 hours per year of employment. For example, see 40 CFR 372.3.

2. Disclosure Period is Met

i. The small business must voluntarily disclose a specific violation fully and in writing to EPA or the State within 21 calendar days after the small business has discovered that the violation has occurred, or may have occurred. Prompt disclosure is evidence of the small business's good faith in wanting to achieve or return to compliance as soon as possible. For purposes of this Policy, the time at which a small business discovers that a violation has or may have occurred begins when any officer, director, employee, or agent of the facility becomes aware of any facts that reasonably lead him or her to believe that a violation may exist. If a small business has some doubt as to the existence of a violation, EPA recommends that the business make a prompt disclosure and allow the regulatory authorities to make a definitive determination. This will ensure that the small business meets the disclosure period requirement.

ii. The disclosure of the violation must occur before the violation was otherwise discovered by, or reported to EPA, the appropriate state or local regulatory agency. See section F.1 of the Policy below. Good faith also requires that a small business cooperate with EPA and in a timely manner provide such information requested by EPA to determine applicability of this Policy.

iii. If a small business wishes to obtain a corrections period after receiving compliance assistance from a confidential assistance program, the business may still take advantage of the policy by disclosing the violation to the appropriate regulatory agency.

3. Violation is Corrected

The business corrects the violation within the corrections period set forth below. Small businesses are expected to remedy the violations within the shortest practicable period of time. Correcting the violation includes remediating any environmental harm associated with the violation, as well as putting into place procedures to prevent the violation from happening again.

i. For any violation that cannot be corrected within 90 calendar days of its discovery, the small business must submit a written schedule, or the agency may, at its sole discretion, elect to issue a compliance order with a schedule, as appropriate. The small business must correct any violations within 180 calendar days after the date that they were discovered.

ii. If the small business intends to correct the violation by putting into place pollution prevention measures, the business may take an additional period of up to 180 calendar days, *i.e.,* up to a period of 360 calendar days from the date the violation is discovered.

4. When the Policy Does Not Apply

The Policy *does not* apply if:

a. The facility has the following noncompliance history:

i. It has previously *received* a warning letter, notice of violation, or field citation, or been subject to a citizen suit or any other enforcement action by a government agency for a violation of the same requirement within the past three years.

ii. It has been granted penalty reduction under this Policy (or a similar State or Tribal policy) for a violation of the same or a similar requirement within the past three years.

iii. It has been subject to two or more enforcement actions for violations of environmental requirements in the past five years, even if this is the first violation of this particular requirement.

b. The violation was discovered through an information request, inspections, field citations, reported to a federal, state or local agency by a member of the public or a "whistleblower" employee, identified in notices of citizen suits, previously reported to an agency, or through an investigation unless the facility can demonstrate that it did not know that the agency had initiated the investigation and has disclosed in good faith.

c. The violation has caused actual serious harm to public health, safety, or the environment;

d. The violation is one that may present an imminent and substantial endangerment to public health, safety or the environment; or

e. The violation involves criminal conduct.

E. Penalty Reduction Guidelines That EPA Will Follow

EPA will exercise its enforcement discretion to eliminate or reduce civil penalties as follows.

1. EPA will waive the gravity component of the civil penalty if a small business satisfies all of the criteria in section D. If, however a small business has obtained a significant economic benefit from the violation(s), EPA will still waive 100% of the gravity component of the penalty, but may seek the full amount of the significant economic benefit associated with the violations.[2] EPA anticipates that such a significant economic benefit will occur infrequently. However, EPA retains its discretion to ensure that small businesses that comply with public health protections are not put at a serious competitive disadvantage by those who have not complied.

2. If a small business does not fit within the guideline E.1.immediately above, this Policy does not provide any special penalty reduction. However, if a small business has otherwise made a good faith effort to comply, EPA has discretion, pursuant to its applicable enforcement response or penalty policies, to waive or reduce civil penalties.[3]

3. Further, the Agency's enforcement response and penalty policies may allow for penalty reduction where the small business is able to document an inability to pay all or a portion of the penalty. Penalty reduction in this situation allows the small business to stay in business and to finance compliance. See *Guidance on Determining a Violator's Ability to Pay a Civil Penalty* of December 1986 (see http://www.epa.gov/oeca/ore/aed/comp/acomp/a1.html). Penalties also may be reduced pursuant to the *Final EPA Supplemental Environmental Projects Policy* of May 1998 (63 FR 24796, June 5, 1998, available at http://www.epa.gov/oeca/sep/sepfinal.html) and *Incentives for Self-Policing: Discovery, Disclosure, Correction and Prevention of Violations Policy of April 11, 2000.*

4. This Policy sets forth how the Agency expects to exercise its enforcement discretion in deciding on an appropriate enforcement response and determining an appropriate civil penalty for violations by small businesses. It states the Agency's views as to the proper allocation of enforcement resources. This Policy is not final agency action and is intended as guidance. It does not create any rights, duties, obligations, or defenses, implied or otherwise, in any third parties.

F. Enforcement for Violations Not Promptly Corrected

To ensure that this Policy enhances and does not compromise public health and the environment, a business remains subject to all applicable enforcement response policies (which may include discretion whether or not to take formal enforcement action) for all violations that were not remedied within the corrections period. The

[2] The "gravity component" of the penalty includes everything except the economic benefit amount.

[3] For example, in some media specific penalty policies, the penalty calculation may be reduced to account for good faith efforts to comply.

penalty in such action may include the time period before and during the correction period.

G. Applicability to States and Tribes

Small businesses may take advantage of small business policies that many States have developed. EPA recognizes that states and tribes are partners in enforcement and compliance assurance and may have adopted their own penalty mitigation policies in Federally-authorized, approved or delegated programs. Therefore, EPA will generally defer to State and Tribal penalty mitigation for self disclosures as long as the State policy meets minimum requirements for Federal delegation and is generally consistent with the criteria set forth in this Policy. Whenever a State agency or Tribe provides a penalty waiver or mitigation or a correction period to a small business pursuant to this Policy or a similar policy, that State or Tribe should notify the appropriate EPA Region to ensure coordination and to request that EPA defer to that action. Similarly, EPA will notify the appropriate State agency or Tribe whenever EPA applies this policy to ensure coordination and request the States defer to EPA's action. Regional contacts, along with other materials about the Policy, will be posted at the EPA web page (*http://www.epa.gov/oeca/smbusi.html*) as they become available.

H. Effective Date

This revised Policy is effective May 11, 2000.

Dated: April 5, 2000.

Sylvia K. Lowrance,

Acting Assistant Administrator for Enforcement and Compliance Assurance.

[FR Doc. 00–8955 Filed 4–10–00; 8:45 am]

BILLING CODE 6560–50–P

Environmental Crimes Deskbook

Appendix 7 ENRD Parallel Proceedings Policy

ENVIRONMENT AND NATURAL RESOURCES DIVISION DIRECTIVE 2008-02

PARALLEL PROCEEDINGS POLICY[1]

I. INTRODUCTION

This Directive sets forth the policy of the Environment and Natural Resources Division (ENRD) for coordinated enforcement of the criminal and civil provisions of statutes under its purview.[2] The Environmental Crimes Section (ECS), Environmental Enforcement Section (EES), Environmental Defense Section (EDS), and Wildlife and Marine Resources Section (WMRS) routinely work with statutes that authorize both civil and criminal enforcement. To optimize effective enforcement of these statutes, the Division may sometimes pursue both civil and criminal enforcement actions against the same or related defendants for the same or related conduct.

Nevertheless, legal requirements prohibit or control some kinds of cooperation between prosecutors and civil attorneys working on overlapping cases. This Directive sets forth restrictions to ensure compliance with those requirements and to avoid unnecessary litigation. In some cases, these restrictions exceed what the law requires. All of the restrictions set forth in this Directive must be followed unless the Assistant Attorney General (AAG) or his or her designee directs otherwise in a particular case.

This Policy is primarily directed at those sections involved in the enforcement of laws designed to address pollution problems and wildlife protection: ECS, EDS, EES and WMRS. Other sections may be covered by this Policy in individual circumstances. Section IV does not apply when the Division is defending a civil lawsuit and pursuing a criminal investigation or prosecution involving the same or related matters. In such cases, the AAG may issue instructions appropriate for the circumstances.

In cases where the parallel proceeding is being handled by a U.S. Attorney's Office, another Division, or another agency, ENRD attorneys should exchange parallel proceedings policies with their counterparts. If the policies differ in any substantial way, ENRD attorneys should consult with their supervisor regarding the appropriate course of action. It may be appropriate to prepare a memorandum setting forth the policies and practices that will apply to a

---

[1] This action is taken pursuant to the authority set forth at 28 C.F.R. § 0.65.

[2] Pursuant to the Attorney General's memorandum of July 28, 1997, United States Attorneys' Offices and Department Litigating Divisions are directed to establish a system for coordinating criminal, civil, and administrative law enforcement. This memorandum provides guidelines for Environment and Natural Resources Division attorneys and is written to be consistent with the Attorney General's memorandum.

particular case or cases. Unless otherwise directed, ENRD attorneys should follow the direction contained in this Policy.

This Policy supersedes Directive 99-21, Integrated Enforcement Policy, dated April 20, 1999.

II. DEFINITIONS

For the purposes of this document, parallel proceedings means overlapping criminal and civil or administrative enforcement activities with respect to the same or related parties and that deal with the same or a related course of conduct. The overlapping activities may be undertaken simultaneously or sequentially. These activities include enforcement actions brought to obtain criminal sanctions, civil penalties, injunctive relief, compliance orders, or cost recovery, as well as pre-filing activities directed at enforcement, including investigative efforts.

III. GENERAL PRINCIPLES GOVERNING PARALLEL PROCEEDINGS

Division attorneys shall follow the principles set forth below in exercising their enforcement discretion. Some of the following limitations may not be required by law and are established as a matter of policy to avoid unnecessary litigation issues. Within the boundaries of these requirements, Division civil and criminal attorneys should coordinate investigations and cases as necessary to protect human health, the environment, and other interests of the United States, and to obtain just results.

1. ECS, EDS, EES, and WMRS shall evaluate their cases to determine whether civil or criminal enforcement, or both, is appropriate. The type of enforcement assigned the case by the originating agency should be given careful consideration, and section managers should consult with the agency in making this determination.

2. When it appears that a parallel proceeding may be appropriate, civil and criminal attorneys should exchange information and evidence received from agencies as early as possible in the process, conduct joint investigations where appropriate, and consult together on an ongoing basis, subject to legal and ethical constraints, including those discussed in this Policy.

3. Attorneys may only conduct civil and administrative discovery when justified by genuine civil or administrative case purposes. The administrative and civil discovery process may not be used as a pretext to obtain information for a criminal investigation.

4. Notwithstanding the above limitations, any information obtained as the result of legitimate civil and administrative discovery may be freely shared with criminal

enforcement attorneys.

5. Civil attorneys shall neither confirm nor deny the existence of a criminal investigation to any person outside the Department. Civil attorneys should report any such inquiries to their supervisor, and coordinate with ECS regarding whether any additional steps are necessary.

6. Federal Rule of Criminal Procedure 6(e) ("Rule 6(e)"), governing the disclosure of information related to grand jury proceedings, must be complied with at all times.

7. After a grand jury has been convened in an investigation, ECS attorneys shall not share with civil attorneys information obtained from the criminal investigation unless the information is part of the pre-grand jury record and the fact that it is part of the pre-grand jury record is documented, or there has been court authorization to do so. However, when appropriate, and in accordance with the procedures set forth in Part IV.E. below, ECS supervisors may authorize disclosure of information collected after a grand jury has been convened if it is documented that disclosure of the information will not reveal a matter occurring before the grand jury.

8. Civil and criminal attorneys should consult with each other on legal issues to ensure that the Division takes consistent positions on the interpretation of regulations and statutes.

9. Although the availability of civil relief may be considered in making criminal charging decisions, see United States Attorneys Manual § 9-27.250, criminal prosecution shall not be used as a threat to obtain civil settlement. Conversely, civil enforcement shall not be used as a threat to resolve a criminal matter. See Directive 99-20, Global Settlement Policy.

10. Civil and/or criminal sanctions may be appropriate in any given case. However, once a decision has been made that criminal sanctions are appropriate, Division attorneys shall not permit a defendant to trade civil relief in exchange for a reduction in criminal penalties.

11. At the Section level, decisions about the initiation, conduct, and conclusion of cases shall be made solely by criminal attorneys and their supervisors with respect to criminal cases, and by civil attorneys and their supervisors with respect to civil cases. Unless directed to the contrary by the AAG, criminal plea agreements and civil settlements shall be negotiated separately, and must separately satisfy the appropriate criminal and civil criteria.

IV. PROCEDURES

In conjunction with the general principles outlined above, the following guidelines and procedures should be followed:

A. Cross-Referrals

Civil attorneys should consider the possibility that their civil case may include criminal conduct, and should remain alert for information indicating criminality. For example, a civil case yielding evidence of falsification of data, concealment of evidence, or repeated violations despite prior enforcement efforts should alert the trial attorney to potential criminal liability. If a referral package received from an agency includes evidence of potential criminal violations, or if such evidence emerges at any time during the course of a civil proceeding, the attorney handling the matter should consult with section management and the matter should be brought to the attention of ECS.

Similarly, ECS attorneys must be alert to situations in which civil enforcement may be appropriate; for example, when it appears that an injunction to halt ongoing unlawful activity or remedial action is necessary, or when an investigation reveals a violation of law, but there is insufficient evidence of criminal mental state. ECS shall adopt procedures to ensure that, when appropriate, matters that ECS declines for criminal prosecution are referred to EES, EDS or WMRS. ECS attorneys shall not include in the materials sent to civil attorneys grand jury material subject to Rule 6(e), unless a court order has been obtained.

ECS, EDS, EES, and WMRS Section Chiefs shall establish procedures for submitting the facts of appropriate cases to other sections for review, as well as for tracking and reporting the progress and outcome of other sections' review.

B. Consultations

As appropriate, criminal and civil attorneys should consult about cases (including sharing information), subject to requirements set forth in Section IV.E., including Rule 6(e). Further, Division attorneys should coordinate positions regarding legal issues to ensure that the Division takes consistent positions on the interpretation of regulations and statutes. They also should notify their counterparts in other sections of milestones in a case of interest, such as seeking an indictment, filing a complaint, seeking injunctive relief, setting discovery deadlines, setting trial dates, and beginning or ending settlement negotiations. Information about ENRD's litigation plans is confidential information and must not be shared outside the Department.

C. Joint Investigations

When a case may be appropriate for both criminal and civil enforcement, the Division encourages joint investigations prior to initiating the grand jury process. Civil and criminal attorneys jointly investigating a matter may together undertake fact-finding activities such as interviewing witnesses and gathering documents. The circumstances of each case will dictate the extent to which the investigation should be undertaken jointly. Once the grand jury process has begun, joint investigative activity shall not be initiated or continued without the approval of the AAG.

In any joint investigation, civil and criminal attorneys each must have a good faith basis for every information-gathering action taken, independent of the investigatory needs of their counterpart. The administrative and civil discovery process may not be used as a pretext to obtain information for a criminal investigation. However, any information obtained as the result of legitimate civil and administrative discovery may be freely shared with criminal enforcement attorneys. Civil attorneys should ensure that criminal attorneys are aware of any protective orders or other restrictions on the use of the information. Information obtained in a criminal investigation may be shared with civil attorneys, subject to the requirements that: (a) the information was obtained for a criminal enforcement purpose, and (b) the disclosure of such information does not violate Rule 6(e) or the policies described in Parts III or IV of this document. Civil attorneys also shall observe any confidentiality requirements, such as those protecting informant identity and the criminal investigatory process. Civil and criminal attorneys should also coordinate their selection of expert witnesses, as further discussed in Section IV.E. below.

When a joint investigation has been undertaken prior to the commencement of the grand jury process, civil and criminal attorneys should create a record of what information has been gathered through means other than the grand jury process. When there is a parallel proceeding, ECS attorneys are encouraged to consider whether there are alternatives to the use of a grand jury subpoena for obtaining needed information.

It may be appropriate for civil and criminal attorneys to prepare a joint memorandum to their respective Section Chiefs outlining a plan for a joint investigation. Under any circumstances, civil and criminal attorneys should ensure that supervisors are kept informed of the progress of a joint investigation, including any parallel proceedings issues that have arisen.

D. Charging and Litigation Decisions

Decisions about civil cases shall be made only by civil attorneys and their supervisors. Decisions about criminal cases shall be made only by criminal attorneys and their supervisors. The AAG has responsibility for related civil and criminal cases handled by the Division. The DAAGs may, as directed by the AAG, supervise related civil and criminal cases or coordinate among themselves in the supervision of such cases.

Criminal attorneys should carefully consider the timing of bringing a case before a grand jury, and generally should not do so until the benefits of this action outweigh the disadvantages to both the criminal and civil proceedings. Attorneys should consider developing as much evidence as possible before the grand jury is used.

When proceeding with both criminal and civil enforcement, the Division generally will delay the civil case until criminal proceedings are resolved.[3] However, the Division will assess the circumstances of each matter, and may decide to proceed in some other fashion. Factors that may weigh in favor of not delaying the civil proceeding include:

(1) the civil violations present a threat to public health or the environment such that injunctive relief should not be delayed;

(2) the defendant's assets are in danger of dissipation;

(3) there is an imminent statute of limitations or bankruptcy deadline for the civil claim;

(4) there is only a marginal relationship between the civil and criminal violations; and

(5) civil proceedings are in an advanced stage when the potential criminal liability is brought to light.

When a civil complaint is to be filed before resolution of a criminal matter, the civil and criminal attorneys and their supervisors should consult and consider various case management tools that may serve to minimize the likelihood that defendants may attempt to use the civil discovery process to undermine the criminal investigation.

E. Parallel Proceedings and Compliance with Grand Jury Rules

Subject to certain exceptions, Rule 6(e) prohibits government attorneys from disclosing "a matter occurring before the grand jury."[4] Rule 6(e) must be complied with at all times.

---

[3] Criminal proceedings typically precede civil actions because of Speedy Trial Act considerations, the more substantial deterrent and punitive effect of criminal sanctions, and because results in criminal cases can be used as collateral estoppel in favor of the government in subsequent civil cases on the same issues.

[4] For example, there is an exception to this rule for forfeiture actions under 18 U.S.C. § 3322(a). In a civil forfeiture case, a prosecutor can disclose grand jury information to a Department civil forfeiture attorney for use in a complaint, restraining order, or other pleading filed, as well as at trial, without a disclosure order. However, without first obtaining a judicial order, neither a prosecutor nor a Department civil forfeiture attorney may disclose grand jury information to a seizing agency's attorneys for use in an administrative forfeiture proceeding or to government contract employees who may be assisting in the preparation of the civil forfeiture

Except as otherwise provided in this Policy, after a grand jury has begun to conduct an investigation, ECS attorneys should not share with civil attorneys information obtained from the criminal investigation unless the information is part of the pre-grand jury record and the fact that it is part of the pre-grand jury record is documented, or there has been court authorization to do so. This requirement exceeds the legal requirements imposed by Rule 6(e) and is established by the Division as a matter of policy and to avoid unnecessary litigation.

If an attorney believes that an exception to this general requirement is warranted with respect to a particular piece of non-grand jury information,[5] the attorney should consult with the appropriate ECS supervisor, who may authorize the disclosure of the information. Any authorization of the disclosure of such information must be documented in writing, and should include an analysis specific to the circuit where the case is pending of why the disclosure of the information does not fall within the prohibitions of Rule 6(e). If the disclosure is to be made by a person other than a DOJ attorney, the authorization by the DOJ attorney to that person to disclose the information must be in writing, and shall include a description of the information to be shared, the source of that information, and who may receive it. Attorneys may also consult with ECS management about seeking a court order under Rule 6(e) allowing the disclosure of grand jury information.

After commencement of a grand jury proceeding, civil attorneys may continue to obtain information through the civil discovery process, so long as they have a good faith basis for seeking the information for the civil case. ECS attorneys shall not direct civil discovery strategy. Subject to that requirement, once information is obtained by a civil attorney it may be freely provided to criminal enforcement attorneys.

To the extent possible, civil and criminal attorneys should coordinate their selection of expert witnesses. Division attorneys should consider whether a particular expert witness would be better used for the civil or criminal case, balancing such factors as the likely pace of each proceeding, the respective needs of each case, and the availability of alternative experts. When

---

case.

Where this or other exceptions to Rule 6(e) clearly apply, Division attorneys are not subject to the information sharing restrictions set forth in this subsection, but should instead look to the law governing each particular case. In such instances, Division attorneys should coordinate closely with section management to ensure compliance with all applicable legal requirements.

[5] For example, an exception to this general rule may be warranted when a particular piece of information was not obtained through the grand jury process or presented to the grand jury, and these facts are documented; or when grand jury subpoenas have been served, but a prosecutor receives information apart from the grand jury process while responses to the grand jury subpoenas are pending.

civil attorneys have used expert witnesses in developing the civil case, these experts may be made available to the criminal attorneys. Criminal attorneys shall not provide to these experts information obtained after commencement of the grand jury process, except as otherwise provided above. However, if the civil case has concluded, including all possible appeals, this policy does not restrict ECS attorneys from providing information subject to Rule 6(e) to a former civil case expert who may be useful to the criminal prosecution. Criminal case expert witnesses sometimes may be made available for use in civil cases, to be determined on a case-by-case basis and subject to the limitations of this policy and Rule 6(e).

V. CASE RESOLUTION

The negotiated resolution of civil and criminal proceedings is governed by the Division's policy on global settlements. See Directive 99-20, Global Settlement Policy. In general, criminal plea agreements and civil settlements shall be negotiated separately, must separately satisfy the appropriate criminal and civil criteria, and must be embodied in separate documents. Those documents should make clear that the criminal plea does not resolve the civil case, and the civil settlement does not resolve the criminal case. Criminal prosecution shall not be used as a threat to obtain civil settlement. Conversely, the Division shall not use civil enforcement as a threat to resolve a criminal matter. Division attorneys shall not permit a defendant to trade civil relief in exchange for a reduction in criminal penalties.

Attorneys should be aware that, under Hudson v. United States, 522 U.S. 93 (1997), neither the imposition of a civil penalty nor a criminal disposition will bar subsequent proceedings under the other option against the same entity for the same violations. However, it is possible that a civil penalty or sanction could be so punitive as to be deemed a criminal penalty and, in such circumstances, successive civil and criminal proceedings might be barred as a violation of the Double Jeopardy Clause. Thus, attorneys should be aware of anticipated fines or penalties in a parallel proceeding to avoid any unintended consequences leading to the barring of other relief.

VI. TRAINING

The Division will continue to provide training to its attorneys about criminal and civil cases, the benefits of integrated enforcement, important issues that arise in the two types of cases, and implementation of this Policy. For example, ECS will help train civil attorneys to identify potential criminal liability in civil cases, to recognize Fourth and Fifth Amendment concerns that may arise when there is a parallel criminal proceeding, and to understand the criminal process. Civil attorneys will help educate ECS attorneys about civil process, civil remedies and the elements of a civil case so they will be able to determine when an ECS matter should be submitted to a civil section and when a case slated to remain on ECS's docket should be reviewed by civil attorneys due to issues such as injunctive relief or limitations.

VII. EFFECT OF THIS POLICY

This policy provides only internal guidelines for the Environment and Natural Resources Division of the Justice Department. The policy does not create any rights, substantive or procedural, that are enforceable at law by any party. No limitations are hereby placed on otherwise lawful prerogatives of the Justice Department.

Date: 12 December 2008

Ronald J. Tenpas
Assistant Attorney General
Environment & Natural Resources Division

Environmental Crimes Deskbook

Appendix 8 EPA Criminal Enforcement and Compliance Results

VENABLE LLP

Cases – 2011 Statistics:

FY2011 Enforcement & Compliance Annual Results
Criminal Enforcement

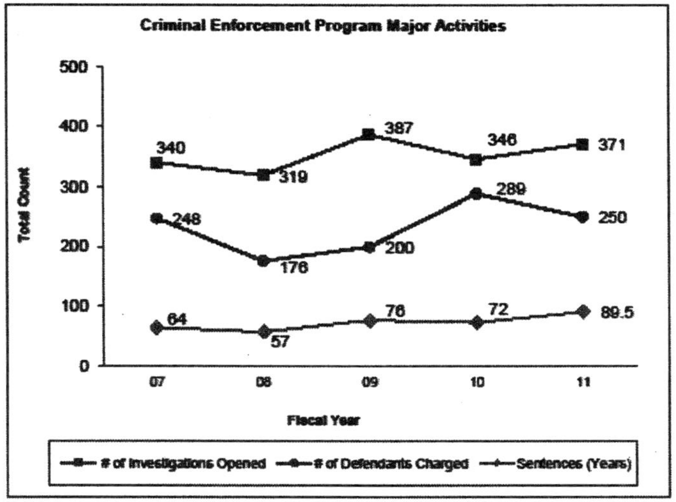

- In FY 2011, 371 **environmental crime investigations were opened. The** second highest number of new cases since FY 2007.
- The increase reflects the 2008-2010 strategy to increase the number of special agents back up to the minimum of 200, as mandated by the 1990 Pollution Prosecution Act.
- Criminal charges were brought against **249 defendants in FY 2011,** the second highest number since FY 2007. Of the 249 defendants , 197 were individuals and 52 were companies. Charging individuals, where warranted, enhances deterrence because only individuals face potential incarceration.
- In FY 2011, **individual defendants were sentenced to a total of 89.5 years of incarceration.***

Note: The 248 defendants charged in FY 2007 is different than the number which appeared on FY 2007 report (226). FY 2007 number failed to include the defendants in several additional cases that were also charged during FY 2007.

* The total level of incarceration in FY 2011 was reduced by 43 years as a consequence of prior Supreme Court decisions which made the U.S. federal sentencing guidelines discretionary rather than mandatory.

FY2011 Data Source: Criminal Case Reporting System; Source for previous years: annual Criminal Case Reporting System data.

VENABLE LLP

Cases – 2011 Statistics:

FY2011 Enforcement & Compliance Annual Results

Criminal Enforcement

Value of Fines & Restitution and Court Ordered Environmental Projects

(Inflation/Deflation Adjusted to FY 11 Dollars)

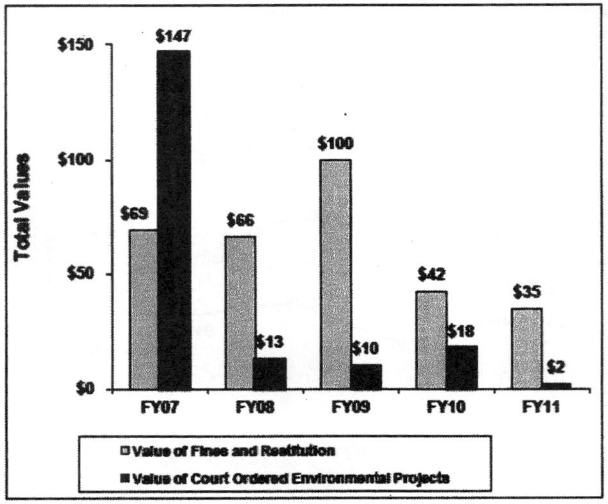

- Both court-ordered environmental projects and criminal fines fluctuate based primarily on the presence or absence of a small number of cases with large organizational fines.
- Criminal defendants were assessed a total of $35 million in fines and restitution in FY 2011. The largest single fine was $11.8 million. By comparison, in FY 2009, one company was assessed a single fine of $50 million (the largest ever assessed under the Clean Air Act)
- In FY 2011, U.S. District Court judges assessed $2 million in court ordered environmental projects., e.g. environmentally beneficial projects that a judge orders criminal defendants to pay for or undertake themselves.
- In FY 07, one case contained projects valued at an estimated $119 million (before being adjusted for inflation). In FY 2010, one case had projects valued at an estimated $12 million.

Note: All prior FY dollar figures in this report are adjusted to reflect the current value in FY 2011 dollars based on the monthly rate of inflation/deflation as determined by the U.S. Department of Labor Consumer Price Index for All Urban Consumers.

FY2011 Data Source: Criminal Case Reporting System; Source for previous years: Annual Criminal Case Reporting System data.

12/8/2011 U.S. Environmental Protection Agency 14

6

Environmental Crimes Deskbook

Appendix 9 U.S. Coast Guard Maritime Law Enforcement Manual, App. V, Environmental Crimes: Voluntary Disclosure Policy

Appendix V
Environmental Crimes: Voluntary Disclosure Policy

Introduction

This appendix provides information on the Coast Guard's environmental crimes voluntary disclosure policy.

In this Appendix

This appendix contains the following information:

Topic	See Page
Introduction	V-3
Definitions	V-3
Compliance Management System	V-3
Self-Policing	V-4
Conditions to Qualify for Participation	V-4
Other Issues	V-8

Appendix V – Environmental Crimes: Voluntary Disclosure Policy

Voluntary Disclosure Policy

Introduction

This Policy is designed to enhance the protection of human health and the marine environment by encouraging regulated entities to voluntarily discover, disclose, correct, and prevent violations of Federal environmental requirements.

Definitions

V.1. Environmental audit report

The documented analysis, conclusions, and recommendations resulting from an environmental audit, but does not include data obtained in, or testimonial evidence concerning, the environmental audit.

V.2. Regulated entity

Any entity regulated under Federal environmental laws.

Compliance Management System

Introduction

The Disclosure Policy uses the term "compliance management system" instead of "due diligence". The term "compliance management system" is intended solely to conform the Policy language to terminology more commonly in use by industry and by regulators to refer to a systematic management plan or systematic efforts to achieve and maintain compliance. No substantive difference is intended by substituting the term "compliance management system" for "due diligence," as the Policy clearly indicates that the compliance management system must reflect the regulated entity's due diligence in preventing, detecting and correcting violations.

Compliance management programs that train and motivate employees to prevent, detect and correct violations on a daily basis are a valuable complement to periodic auditing. Where the violation is discovered through a compliance management system and not through an inspection, the disclosing entity should be prepared to document how its program reflects the due diligence criteria defined in V.3. of this Manual. These criteria, which are adapted from existing codes of practice—such as Chapter Eight of the U.S. Sentencing Guidelines for organizational defendants, effective since 1991—are flexible enough to accommodate different types and sizes of businesses and other regulated entities. The Coast Guard recognizes that a variety of compliance management programs are feasible, and it will determine whether basic due diligence criteria have been met in deciding whether to grant credit under the Disclosure Policy.

V.3. Regulated Entity's Documented Systematic Efforts

Encompasses the regulated entity's efforts, to prevent, detect and correct violations through all of the following:

- Compliance policies, standards and procedures that identify how vessel employees and agents are to meet the requirements of laws, regulations, enforceable agreements and other sources of authority for environmental requirements;
- Assignment of overall responsibility for overseeing compliance with policies, standards, and procedures, and assignment of specific responsibility for assuring compliance aboard each vessel;
- Mechanisms for systematically assuring that compliance policies, standards and procedures are being carried out, including monitoring and auditing systems reasonably designed to detect and correct violations, periodic evaluation of the overall performance

of the compliance management system, and a means for employees or agents to report violations of environmental requirements without fear of retaliation;

- Efforts to communicate effectively the regulated entity's standards and procedures to all employees and other agents;
- Appropriate incentives to managers and employees to perform in accordance with the compliance policies, standards and procedures, including consistent enforcement through appropriate disciplinary mechanisms; and
- Procedures for the prompt and appropriate correction of any violations, and any necessary modifications to the regulated entity's compliance management system to prevent future violations.

Self-Policing

V.4 Incentives for self-policing

If a regulated entity establishes that it satisfies conditions in V.5. of the Disclosure Policy, the Coast Guard will not recommend to the U.S. Department of Justice or other prosecuting authority that criminal charges be brought against the disclosing entity, as long as the Coast Guard determines that the violation is not part of a pattern or practice that demonstrates or involves:

- A prevalent management philosophy or practice that conceals or condones environmental violations; or
- High-level corporate officials' or managers' conscious involvement in, or willful blindness to, violations of Federal environmental law.

Whether or not the Coast Guard recommends the regulated entity for criminal prosecution under this section, the Coast Guard may recommend for prosecution the criminal acts of individual managers or employees under existing policies guiding the exercise of enforcement discretion.

Conditions to Qualify for Participation

Introduction

This section provides information regarding conditions that a regulated entity must meet in order to qualify for participation in the Coast Guard's voluntary disclosure policy.

Pursuant to the Coast Guard's Voluntary Disclosure Policy, any violation must have been discovered through either an environmental audit, or a compliance management system that reflects due diligence in preventing, detecting and correcting violations. Both "environmental audit" and "compliance management system" are defined in sections V.1. and V.3. of this Manual.

V.5. Conditions

The conditions discussed in sections V.5.a. through V.5.h. must be met for a regulated entity to qualify for participation in the Coast Guard's Voluntary Disclosure Policy.

Appendix V – Environmental Crimes: Voluntary Disclosure Policy

V.5.a. Voluntary Discovery

The violation was discovered voluntarily and not through a legally mandated monitoring or sampling requirement prescribed by statute, regulation, judicial or administrative order, or consent agreement. This does not include violations discovered through a compliance audit required to be performed by the terms of a consent order or settlement agreement, unless the audit is a component of agreement terms to implement a comprehensive environmental management system.

The voluntary requirement applies to discovery only, not reporting. That is, any violation that is voluntarily discovered is generally eligible for Disclosure Policy credit, regardless of whether reporting of the violation was required after it was found.

V.5.b. Prompt Disclosure

Requires that the regulated entity disclose the violation in writing to the Coast Guard within 21 calendar days of discovery. This disclosure is not required to be a complete investigation of the violation by the regulated entity, but must clearly identify the known particulars of the specific incident. If the 21st day after discovery falls on a weekend or Federal holiday, the disclosure period will be extended to the first business day following the 21st day after discovery. If a statute or regulation requires the entity to report the violation in fewer than 21 days, disclosure must be made within the time limit established by law. (For example, unpermitted discharges of oil or hazardous substances must be reported immediately under 33 USC 1321(b)(5).) Disclosures under this policy should be made to the nearest Coast Guard unit, the National Response Center, and, where applicable, to individuals predesignated in response plans or, where multiple Regions are involved, to Coast Guard Headquarters. For additional guidance on making disclosures, contact Commandant (CG-941).

The 21-day disclosure period begins when the regulated entity discovers that a violation has, or may have, occurred. The trigger for discovery is when any officer, director, employee or agent of the regulated entity has an objectively reasonable basis for believing that a violation has, or may have, occurred. The "objectively reasonable basis" standard is measured against what a prudent person, having the same information as was available to the individual in question, would have believed. It is not measured against what the individual in question thought was reasonable at the time the situation was encountered. If a regulated entity has some doubt as to the existence of a violation, the recommended course is for the entity to proceed with the disclosure and allow the regulatory authorities to make a definitive determination.

If the 21-day period has not yet expired and an entity suspects that it will be unable to meet the deadline, the entity should contact the appropriate Coast Guard office, in advance, to develop disclosure terms acceptable to the Coast Guard. For situations in which the 21-day period has already expired, the Coast Guard may accept a late disclosure in the exceptional case, such as where there are complex circumstances, including where the Coast Guard determines the violation could not be identified and disclosed within 21 calendar days after discovery.

The Coast Guard may also extend the disclosure period when multiple vessels are involved. In the multi-vessel context, the Coast Guard will ordinarily extend the 21-day period to allow regulated entities reasonable time for completion and review of multi-vessel audits where: (a) the Coast Guard and the regulated entity agree on the timing and scope of the audits prior to their commencement; and (b) the vessels to be audited are identified in advance. In the acquisitions context, the Coast Guard will consider extending the prompt disclosure period on a case-by-case basis. The 21-day disclosure period will begin on the date of discovery by the acquiring entity, but in no case will the period begin earlier than the date of acquisition.

It is critical for the Coast Guard to receive timely reporting of violations in order to have clear notice of the violations and the opportunity to respond if necessary. Prompt disclosure is also evidence of the regulated entity's good faith in wanting to achieve or return to compliance as soon as possible. The integrity of Federal environmental law depends upon timely and accurate reporting. The public relies on timely and accurate reports from the regulated community, not only to measure compliance but also to evaluate health or environmental risks and to gauge progress in reducing pollutant loadings. The Coast Guard expects the Disclosure Policy to encourage the kind of vigorous self-policing that will serve these objectives and does not intend that it justify delayed reporting. When violations of reporting requirements are voluntarily discovered, they must be promptly reported. When a failure to report results in imminent and substantial endangerment or serious harm to the environment, Disclosure Policy credit is precluded under condition V.5.g.

V.5.c. Discovery and Disclosure Independent of Government or Third-Party Plaintiff

The regulated entity must discover the violation independently. That is, the violation must be discovered and identified before the Coast Guard or another government agency likely would have identified the problem either through its own investigative work or from information received through a third party. This condition requires regulated entities to take the initiative to find violations on their own and disclose them promptly instead of waiting for an indication of a pending enforcement action or third-party complaint.

Specifically, the regulated entity discovers and discloses the potential violation to the Coast Guard prior to:

- The commencement of a Federal, State or local agency inspection or investigation;
- Notice by a third party;
- The reporting of the violation to the Coast Guard or other government agency by a "whistleblower" employee, rather than by one authorized to speak on behalf of the regulated entity; or,
- Imminent discovery of the violation by a regulatory agency.

Regulated entities that own or operate multiple vessels are subject to section V.5.b. in addition to V.5.a. The Coast Guard encourages multi-vessel auditing and does not intend for the "independent discovery" condition to preclude availability of the voluntary disclosure policy when multiple vessels are involved. Thus, if a regulated entity owns or operates multiple vessels, the fact that one of its vessels is the subject of an investigation, inspection, information request or third-party complaint, does not automatically preclude the Coast Guard from granting Disclosure Policy credit for disclosures of violations self-discovered at the other vessels, assuming all other policy conditions are met. However, just as in the single-vessel context, where a vessel is already the subject of a government inspection, investigation or information request (including a broad information request that covers multiple vessels), it will generally not be eligible for Disclosure Policy credit. The Disclosure Policy is designed to encourage regulated entities to disclose violations before any of their vessels are under investigation, not after the Coast Guard discovers violations aboard the regulated entity's vessel. Nevertheless, the Coast Guard retains its full discretion under the Disclosure Policy to waive a recommendation of criminal prosecution for good-faith disclosures made in the multi-vessel context.

V.5.d. Correction and Remediation

The regulated entity must correct the violation within 60 calendar days from the date of discovery, or as expeditiously as possible. The Coast Guard retains the authority to order an entity to correct a violation within a specific time period shorter than 60 days whenever correction in such shorter period of time is feasible and necessary to protect public health and the environment adequately. If more than 60 days will be needed to correct the violation, the regulated entity must so notify the Coast Guard, in writing, before the 60-day period has passed. Where appropriate, to satisfy conditions of this section and V.5.e, the Coast Guard may require a regulated entity to enter into a publicly available written agreement, administrative consent order, or judicial consent decree as a condition of obtaining relief under the Voluntary Disclosure Policy particularly where compliance or remedial measures are complex or a lengthy schedule for attaining and maintaining compliance or re-mediating harm is required. In all cases, the regulated entity will be expected to do its utmost to achieve or return to compliance as expeditiously as possible.

V.5.e. Prevent Recurrence

The regulated entity must agree to take steps to prevent a recurrence of the violation after it has been disclosed. Preventive steps may include, but are not limited to, improvements to the entity's environmental auditing efforts or compliance management system.

V.5.f. No Pattern of Violations

Bars repeat offenders from receiving Disclosure Policy credit. The specific violation (or a related violation) has not occurred previously within the past three years involving the same vessel, and has not occurred within the past five years as part of a pattern involving multiple vessels owned or operated by the same entity. If a vessel has been newly acquired, the existence of a violation prior to acquisition does not trigger the repeat violations exclusion.

Commandant (CG-3PCA) will makc thc final determination of whether or not a previous violation is "related" for the purpose of applying this section. For the purposes of this section, a violation is:

- A violation of Federal, State or local environmental law identified in a judicial or administrative order, consent agreement or order, complaint, or notice of violation, conviction or plea agreement; or
- Any act or omission for which the regulated entity has previously received leniency from the Coast Guard or a State or local agency.

The repeat violation exclusion benefits both the public and law-abiding entities by ensuring that the recommendation of criminal prosecution is not waived for those regulated entities that have previously been notified of violations and fail to prevent repeat violations. The three-year and five-year "bright lines" in the exclusion are designed to provide regulated entities with clear notice about when the Disclosure Policy will be available.

The three-year period begins to run when the government, a third party, or the regulated entity has notice of a specific violation, without regard to when the original violation cited in the notice actually occurred. Examples of notice include a complaint, consent order, notice of violation, receipt of an inspection report, citizen suit, or previous treatment under the voluntary disclosure policy.

V.5.g. Other Violations Excluded

- Violation resulted in serious actual harm, or may have presented an imminent and substantial endangerment, to human health or the environment. However, this condition does not bar a regulated entity from qualifying for Disclosure Policy relief solely because the violation involves release of a pollutant to the environment, to the extent such releases do not necessarily result in serious actual harm or an imminent and substantial endangerment.

- Violates specific terms of any judicial or administrative order, consent agreement, or plea agreement. Once a consent agreement has been negotiated, there is little incentive to comply if there are no sanctions for violating its specific requirements. The exclusion in this section also applies to violations of the terms of any response, removal or remedial action covered by a written agreement.

V.5.h. Cooperation

The regulated entity must cooperate with the Coast Guard and provide it with the information needed to determine Disclosure Policy applicability. The regulated entity must not hide, destroy, or tamper with possible evidence following discovery of potential environmental violations. In order for the Coast Guard to apply the Disclosure Policy fairly, it must have sufficient information to determine whether its conditions are satisfied in each individual case.

Responsible parties that disclose potential criminal violations may expect a thorough review by the Coast Guard. In criminal cases, entities will be expected to provide, at a minimum, the following: access to all requested documents; access to all employees of the disclosing entity; assistance in investigating the violation, any noncompliance problems related to the disclosure, and any environmental consequences related to the violations; access to all information relevant to the violations disclosed, including that portion of the environmental audit report or documentation from the compliance management system that revealed the violation; and access to the individuals who conducted the audit or review.

Other Issues

V.6. Privilege or immunity

The Coast Guard remains firmly opposed to statutory environmental audit privileges that shield evidence of environmental violations and undermine the public's right to know, as well as to blanket immunities, particularly immunities for violations that reflect criminal conduct, present serious threats or actual harm to health and the environment, allow non-complying companies to gain an economic advantage over their competitors, or reflect a repeated failure to comply with Federal law. The Coast Guard reserves its right to take necessary actions to protect public health or the environment by enforcing against any violations of Federal law.

V.7. Applicability

This Disclosure Policy applies to criminal violations under all of the Federal environmental statutes that the Coast Guard administers. This Policy sets forth factors for consideration that will guide the Coast Guard in the exercise of its enforcement discretion. The Policy is not final agency action and is intended only as guidance. This Policy is not intended, nor can it be relied upon, to create any rights enforceable by any party in litigation with the United States. The Coast Guard may decide to follow guidance provided in this Manual or to act at variance with it based on its analysis of the specific facts presented. This Policy may be revised without public notice to reflect changes in the Coast Guard's approach to providing incentives for self-policing by regulated entities, or to clarify and update text. For purposes of this Policy, violations discovered pursuant to an environmental audit or compliance management system may be considered voluntary.

V.8. Public accountability

The Coast Guard will make publicly available the terms and conditions of any compliance agreement reached under this Policy, including the nature of the violation, the remedy, and the schedule for returning to compliance.

Appendix V – Environmental Crimes: Voluntary Disclosure Policy

Environmental Crimes Deskbook

Appendix 10 Clipper Trojan Indictment

2006R00751/BAH

UNITED STATES DISTRICT COURT
DISTRICT OF NEW JERSEY

UNITED STATES OF AMERICA	:	Hon. ______________
v.	:	Crim. No. ______________
CLIPPER WONSILD TANKERS HOLDING A/S, CLIPPER MARINE SERVICES A/S, and TROJAN SHIPPING CO., LTD.	:	18 U.S.C. § 371 33 U.S.C. § 1908(a) 18 U.S.C. § 1001 18 U.S.C. § 1505 18 U.S.C. § 1519 18 U.S.C. § 2

I N D I C T M E N T

The Grand Jury in and for the District of New Jersey, sitting in Newark, charges:

COUNT ONE
(Conspiracy - 18 U.S.C. § 371)

1. At all times relevant to this Indictment, unless otherwise indicated:

The Defendants

a. Defendant CLIPPER WONSILD TANKERS HOLDING A/S (hereinafter "CLIPPER WONSILD TANKERS") was a Danish corporation headquartered in Copenhagen, Denmark, that commercially operated a fleet of approximately 55 ocean-going transport vessels. As a commercial operator, CLIPPER WONSILD TANKERS was responsible for the chartering and trading of vessels on the open market.

b. Defendant CLIPPER MARINE SERVICES A/S (hereinafter "CLIPPER MARINE SERVICES," formerly known as CRESCENT MARINE

SERVICES A/S) was a Danish corporation with offices in Denmark and the United Kingdom that managed the technical aspects of all chemical and product tankers (approximately 28 vessels) in the fleet that defendant CLIPPER WONSILD TANKERS commercially operated. As a technical manager, CLIPPER MARINE SERVICES was responsible for overseeing the day-to-day operations of the vessels, ensuring compliance with safety and environmental regulations, and ensuring that vessels were crewed by qualified personnel.

c. Defendant TROJAN SHIPPING CO., LTD. (hereinafter, "TROJAN SHIPPING"), was a Bahamian corporation with offices in the Bahamas, and was the registered owner of the M/T CLIPPER TROJAN.

d. Defendants CLIPPER WONSILD TANKERS, CLIPPER MARINE SERVICES and TROJAN SHIPPING were part of the Clipper Group A/S, an international shipping consortium that controlled approximately 240 vessels.

The M/T CLIPPER TROJAN

e. The M/T CLIPPER TROJAN was a Bahamas-registered, ocean-going chemical tanker weighing approximately 9,553 gross tons with an International Maritime Organization ("IMO") number of 9140451. The M/T CLIPPER TROJAN was owned by defendant TROJAN SHIPPING, commercially operated by defendant CLIPPER WONSILD TANKERS, and technically managed by defendant CLIPPER MARINE

SERVICES.

f. The M/T CLIPPER TROJAN had a crew of approximately 20 people, who were hired through a crewing agency based in Manila, the Philippines, on contract by defendant CLIPPER MARINE SERVICES.

g. Approximately seven seamen of different ranks worked in the M/T CLIPPER TROJAN's Engine Department, including a Chief Engineer, Second Engineer, Third Engineer, Fourth Engineer, Pipe Fitter, and two Motormen. A Motorman typically assisted the engineers in cleaning and maintaining engineering machinery. The Chief Engineer reported directly to the Master of the vessel, and both reported to shore-based managers of defendant CLIPPER MARINE SERVICES. The Chief Engineer had overall responsibility for the operation of the Engine Department, including the supervision of daily operations, formulation and implementation of engine room procedures, and verification that all systems, including certain pollution prevention equipment, were functioning properly.

h. On or about May 13, 2006, defendant CLIPPER MARINE SERVICES appointed co-conspirator Fernando Magnaye as Chief Engineer of the M/T CLIPPER TROJAN. As Chief Engineer, co-conspirator Fernando Magnaye, along with those who served under him in the Engine Department of the M/T CLIPPER TROJAN, acted as an officer and agent of defendants CLIPPER WONSILD TANKERS, CLIPPER MARINE SERVICES and TROJAN SHIPPING CO. with respect to the engine room operations of the M/T CLIPPER TROJAN, any discharges or transfers of oily wastes from the M/T CLIPPER TROJAN, record-keeping relating to such discharges and transfers, and compliance with laws and regulations relating to such discharges, transfers and record-keeping.

The Act to Prevent Pollution from Ships and the MARPOL Protocol

i. The Act to Prevent Pollution from Ships ("APPS"), 33 U.S.C. §§ 1901 et seq., was enacted by Congress in or around 1980 to implement two related international treaties to which the United States is a signatory: the 1973 International Convention for the Prevention of Pollution from Ships and the Protocol of 1978 Relating to the International Convention for the Prevention of Pollution from Ships. Together, these treaties were known as the "MARPOL Protocol".

j. The MARPOL Protocol was the result of an international consensus that the significant pollution produced by ships in international waters could be prevented effectively only if each participating nation enforced the MARPOL Protocol's rules and regulations. APPS made the MARPOL Protocol applicable to vessels registered in the United States or operating in United States waters.

k. APPS also authorized the United States Coast Guard (the "Coast Guard"), now an agency within the Department of Homeland Security, to promulgate regulations implementing the

MARPOL Protocol. The Coast Guard's implementing regulations served to insure compliance with the MARPOL Protocol and to prevent pollution in United States waters. 33 U.S.C. §§ 1907(c)(1) and (c)(2); 33 C.F.R. §§ 151.01 et seq.

The Prevention of Oil Pollution from Ocean-Going Vessels

l. A principal source of water pollution addressed by the Coast Guard regulations and the MARPOL Protocol was the oil sludge and oil-contaminated water generated by virtually all large ships. The normal operation of an ocean-going ship produces a significant quantity of oil sludge due to the processing of fuel oil and lubricating oil. In addition, the engineering machinery of virtually all ocean-going vessels produces large amounts of oily water that collects in a ship's bilges and which must be discharged for the ship to remain seaworthy.

m. The oil sludge and oil-contaminated bilge water are collected in tanks designed to hold the oily wastes for proper disposal. On board the M/T CLIPPER TROJAN, the oil sludge was collected in a Bilge Sludge Oil Tank and the oil-contaminated bilge water was collected in the Bilge Tank. Crew members in the engine room of ocean-going ships, including the M/T CLIPPER TROJAN, measured or "sounded" the contents of the tanks into which oil sludge and bilge water were collected in order to determine when the oily waste was in need of disposal. Such measurements were recorded in a "sounding log".

n. The MARPOL Protocol and regulations implemented pursuant to APPS provided that only water containing no more than fifteen parts of oil per million may be discharged directly into the sea. 33 C.F.R. §§ 151.10(a)(5) and (b)(3); MARPOL Annex I, Reg. 9(4). Oil-contaminated bilge water could be processed through a pollution-control device known as an Oily Water Separator, which removed oil contamination from bilge water to produce water containing no more than fifteen parts of oil per million, which was pumped overboard through an overboard discharge valve. APPS and the MARPOL Protocol also required that oil sludge, which could not be processed through pollution control equipment, had to be disposed of by either off-loading it to shore or burning it in a ship's incinerator.

The Requirement that Vessels Maintain an Oil Record Book

o. To insure that oily wastes were properly processed and disposed of, the regulations implemented pursuant to APPS and the MARPOL Protocol provided that with regard to vessels of more than 400 gross tons, the person or persons in charge of an operation involving the transfer or disposal of oily wastes was required to fully record every operation, without delay and on a tank to tank basis, in a log known as an Oil Record Book. Any transfer or disposal of oily waste was required to be recorded in the Oil Record Book. 33 C.F.R. §§ 151.25(a), (d), and (h);

MARPOL Annex I, Reg. 20. For example, upon incineration of oil sludge, the responsible officer was required to record the quantity of oil sludge disposed of, the tanks emptied, the total time of the operation, and the date of the operation. The responsible officer also was required to sign or initial his name after every entry in the Oil Record Book.

The Coast Guard's Authority

p. The Coast Guard was authorized to conduct inspections to determine whether vessels in U.S. waters were in compliance with MARPOL, APPS and other applicable federal regulations. In connection with inspections, the Coast Guard was authorized to examine the vessel's Oil Record Book to determine, among other things, whether the vessel had operable pollution prevention equipment, whether it posed a danger to United States ports and waters, and whether the vessel had discharged oily waste in violation of law. 33 C.F.R. §§ 151.23(a)(3) and 151.23(c). In conducting inspections, the Coast Guard relied on a ship's Oil Record Book and statements of the crew to determine whether the vessel's crew was properly handling oily waste. 33 C.F.R. § 151.23(c).

q. With regard to the improper disposal of oily wastes in international waters, the Coast Guard was authorized, upon entry of a vessel into United States waters, to deny the vessel entry into a United States port, 33 U.S.C. §§ 1223,

1228(a), or to detain a vessel for inspection and investigation by the nation in which the ship was registered, 33 U.S.C. § 1223(b)(1).

r. As an ocean-going chemical tanker weighing more than 400 gross tons, the M/T CLIPPER TROJAN was required to maintain an accurate Oil Record Book. On the M/T CLIPPER TROJAN, the Chief Engineer was responsible for recording transfers and disposals of oil in the Oil Record Book and was required to sign or initial next to each such entry.

The Conspiracy

2. From at least as early as on or about January 5, 2006 through on or about June 15, 2006, in Port Newark and the internal waters and ports of the United States, in the District of New Jersey, and elsewhere, defendants

CLIPPER WONSILD TANKERS HOLDING A/S,
CLIPPER MARINE SERVICES A/S, and
TROJAN SHIPPING CO., LTD.,

by and through the acts of their agents and employees, including co-conspirator Fernando Magnaye and others serving under him in the Engine Department of the M/T CLIPPER TROJAN, who were acting within the scope of their agency and employment and with the intent to benefit the defendants, did knowingly and willfully conspire and agree with each other and others to:

A. Defraud the United States: To hamper, hinder, impede, impair and obstruct by craft, trickery, deceit, and dishonest means, the lawful and legitimate functions of the United States Coast Guard in enforcing the MARPOL Protocol, APPS, and the regulations promulgated thereunder; and

B. Violate the laws of the United States as set forth below:

(i) Failure to Maintain an Oil Record Book: To knowingly and willfully violate the MARPOL Protocol, Chapter 33 of Title 33 of the United States Code, and the regulations issued thereunder by failing to maintain an Oil Record Book for the M/T CLIPPER TROJAN in which all discharges, disposals and transfers of oil and oily waste, including all overboard discharges of oil sludge and oil-contaminated bilge water, were fully recorded, contrary to Title 33, United States Code, Section 1908(a) and Title 33, Code of Federal Regulations, Sections 151.25(a) and 151.25(h);

(ii) False Statements and Writings: To knowingly and willfully make materially false, fictitious, and fraudulent statements and representations, and make and use false writings and documents knowing the same to contain materially false, fictitious, and fraudulent statements and entries, in a matter within the jurisdiction of the Executive Branch of the United States, namely the United States Coast Guard and the Department of Homeland Security, contrary to Title 18, United States Code, Section 1001;

(iii) Obstruction of Proceedings: To corruptly influence, obstruct and impede, and endeavor to influence, obstruct, and impede the due and proper administration of the law under which a pending proceeding, namely, an inspection and investigation of the M/T CLIPPER TROJAN, was being had before a department and agency of the United States, namely, the United States Coast Guard and the Department of Homeland Security, contrary to Title 18, United States Code, Section 1505; and

(iv) Concealment of Tangible Objects in Federal Investigation: To knowingly and willfully alter, destroy, mutilate, conceal, and cover up a tangible object with the intent to impede, obstruct and influence the investigation and proper administration of a matter, namely an inspection and investigation of the M/T CLIPPER TROJAN, within the jurisdiction of a department and agency of the United States, namely the United States Coast Guard and the Department of Homeland Security, contrary to Title 18, United States Code, Section 1519.

Objects of the Conspiracy

3. It was an object of the conspiracy to illegally discharge oil sludge and oil-contaminated bilge water directly into the ocean and to conceal and cover up the illegal discharges to avoid detection by governmental authorities.

Manner and Means

4. Among the manner and means used by the defendants and their co-conspirators to effectuate this conspiracy and to further its objectives were the following:

a. It was part of the conspiracy that defendants CLIPPER WONSILD TANKERS, CLIPPER MARINE SERVICES, and TROJAN SHIPPING created and maintained, on paper, separate corporate entities when, in fact, all three defendants operated as a single entity and as agents for one another.

b. It was further part of the conspiracy that, with respect to the MARPOL Protocol, APPS, and the regulations promulgated thereunder, defendants CLIPPER WONSILD TANKERS, CLIPPER MARINE SERVICES, and TROJAN SHIPPING failed to provide sufficient training to crew members of the M/T CLIPPER TROJAN and failed to diligently enforce company policies.

c. It was further part of the conspiracy that defendants CLIPPER WONSILD TANKERS, CLIPPER MARINE SERVICES, and TROJAN SHIPPING caused crew members of the M/T CLIPPER TROJAN to execute affidavits falsely certifying that the crew members had received briefings on the MARPOL Protocol and APPS before the crew members boarded the M/T CLIPPER TROJAN.

d. It was further part of the conspiracy that defendants CLIPPER WONSILD TANKERS, CLIPPER MARINE SERVICES, and TROJAN SHIPPING maintained a special bypass hose on board the M/T CLIPPER TROJAN that was used to pump oil sludge and oil-contaminated bilge water directly overboard.

e. It was further part of the conspiracy that defendants CLIPPER WONSILD TANKERS, CLIPPER MARINE SERVICES, and TROJAN SHIPPING, in order to pump oil sludge and oil-contaminated bilge water directly overboard, removed an elbow assembly that connected the Oily Water Separator to the overboard discharge valve and replaced it with the special bypass hose, which was connected at the other end to either the Bilge Sludge Oil Tank or Bilge Tank.

f. It was further part of the conspiracy that defendants CLIPPER WONSILD TANKERS, CLIPPER MARINE SERVICES, and TROJAN SHIPPING, in order to avoid detection, conducted the improper discharges of oily waste at night and, once the pumping was complete, disassembled the bypass hose connection and replaced the elbow assembly on the overboard discharge valve.

g. It was further part of the conspiracy that on or about the dates and in the amounts listed in the table below, defendants CLIPPER WONSILD TANKERS, CLIPPER MARINE SERVICES, and

TROJAN SHIPPING used the bypass hose to discharge and cause the discharge of oil-contaminated bilge waste directly overboard into the ocean, thus bypassing the Oily Water Separator and other required pollution prevention equipment:

Discharges of Contaminated Bilge	
Date	**Approximate Quantity (cubic meters)**
March 19-20, 2006	11.72
March 31- April 1, 2006	3.33
April 15-16, 2006	4.945
April 22-23, 2006	2.75
May 2-3, 2006	4.145
May 15-16, 2006	1.97
May 18-20, 2006	5.65
June 4-5, 2006	3.615

h. It was further part of the conspiracy that on or about the dates and in the amounts listed in the table below, defendants CLIPPER WONSILD TANKERS, CLIPPER MARINE SERVICES, and TROJAN SHIPPING used the bypass hose to discharge and cause the discharge from the M/T CLIPPER TROJAN of oil sludge directly overboard into the ocean rather than incinerating or off-loading the oil sludge as required under the MARPOL Protocol:

Date	**Approximate Quantity (cubic meters)**
May 23-24, 2006	1.59
May 31-June 1, 2006	2.29

i. It was further part of the conspiracy that defendants CLIPPER WONSILD TANKERS, CLIPPER MARINE SERVICES, and TROJAN SHIPPING, in order to conceal the overboard discharges of oily waste, failed to record the overboard discharges of oil sludge and oil-contaminated bilge water in the Oil Record Book for the M/T CLIPPER TROJAN, and made affirmatively false entries in the Oil Record Book stating that the oil sludge had been incinerated and that the oil-contaminated bilge water had been processed in the Oily Water Separator.

j. It was further part of the conspiracy that on or about June 15, 2006, defendants CLIPPER WONSILD TANKERS, CLIPPER MARINE SERVICES, and TROJAN SHIPPING knowingly maintained and caused to be maintained, and had available for inspection, a materially false Oil Record Book for the M/T CLIPPER TROJAN during its port call in Port Newark, New Jersey, and presented such false Oil Record Book to the Coast Guard during the Coast Guard's inspection of the M/T CLIPPER TROJAN on or about June 15, 2006 knowing that it contained material omissions and materially false, fictitious and fraudulent entries.

k. It was further part of the conspiracy that defendants CLIPPER WONSILD TANKERS, CLIPPER MARINE SERVICES, and TROJAN SHIPPING affirmatively attempted to conceal the overboard discharges of oily waste by, among other things, painting the overboard discharge valve prior to entering U.S. waters and secreting the bypass hose and pump that were used for the discharges in a workshop.

l. It was further part of the conspiracy that defendants CLIPPER WONSILD TANKERS, CLIPPER MARINE SERVICES, and TROJAN SHIPPING attempted to impede, obstruct, and influence the Coast Guard's investigation into improper discharges of oily waste and false record-keeping practices by knowingly making false statements to the Coast Guard which included the claims that the M/T CLIPPER TROJAN's Oil Record Book was accurate; that no illegal or improper overboard discharges of oily waste had occurred aboard the M/T CLIPPER TROJAN; that the hose and pump used to discharge oily waste overboard had been used instead to transfer fuel from a forward tank to an aft tank; and that the M/T CLIPPER TROJAN had offloaded oil sludge during a port call in Albany, New York on or about June 11-14, 2006.

m. It was further part of the conspiracy that defendants CLIPPER WONSILD TANKERS, CLIPPER MARINE SERVICES, and TROJAN SHIPPING attempted to impede, obstruct, and influence the Coast Guard's investigation by directing various crew members to make false statements to the Coast Guard.

n. It was further part of the conspiracy that defendants CLIPPER WONSILD TANKERS, CLIPPER MARINE SERVICES, and TROJAN SHIPPING attempted to impede, obstruct, and influence the Coast Guard's investigation by fabricating and deploying a device that would ensure that the Coast Guard took a false reading of the contents of the Bilge Sludge Oil Tank, and then throwing the device overboard after the Coast Guard's inspection on or about June 15, 2006.

Overt Acts

5. In furtherance of the conspiracy and to effect the objects thereof, defendants CLIPPER WONSILD TANKERS, CLIPPER MARINE SERVICES, and TROJAN SHIPPING, by and through the acts of their agents and employees, who were acting within the scope of their agency and employment and with the intent to benefit the defendants, committed and caused to be committed within Port Newark, in the District of New Jersey, and elsewhere, the following overt acts among others:

a. Overt Act 1: From on or about January 5, 2006 to on or about January 31, 2006, defendants CLIPPER WONSILD TANKERS CLIPPER MARINE SERVICES, and TROJAN SHIPPING caused crew members of the M/T CLIPPER TROJAN to execute affidavits falsely certifying that the crew members had received briefings on the MARPOL Protocol and APPS.

b. Overt Acts 2-11: On or about the dates listed in the table below, defendants CLIPPER WONSILD TANKERS, CLIPPER MARINE SERVICES, and TROJAN SHIPPING, by and through the Chief Engineer of the M/T CLIPPER TROJAN, omitted illegal and improper discharges of oil sludge and oil-contaminated bilge water from entries made in the Oil Record Book of the M/T CLIPPER TROJAN:

Overt Acts 2-11 (Omissions of Overboard Discharges)	
Overt Act	**Date**
2	March 19-20, 2006
3	March 31-April 1, 2006
4	April 15-16, 2006
5	April 22-23, 2006
6	May 2-3, 2006
7	May 15-16, 2006
8	May 18-20, 2006
9	May 23-24, 2006
10	May 31-June 1, 2006
11	June 4-5, 2006

c. Overt Acts 12-18: On or about the dates listed in the table below, among others, defendants CLIPPER WONSILD TANKERS, CLIPPER MARINE SERVICES, and TROJAN SHIPPING, by and through the Chief Engineer of the M/T CLIPPER TROJAN, created entries in the Oil Record Book of the M/T CLIPPER TROJAN falsely stating that oil sludge had been incinerated or that oil-contaminated bilge water had been processed through the Oily Water Separator:

Overt Acts 12-18 (Affirmatively False Entries in ORB)	
Overt Act	**Date**
12	May 18, 2006
13	May 23, 2006
14	May 24, 2006
15	June 4, 2006
16	June 5, 2006
17	June 6, 2006
18	June 7, 2006

d. Overt Act 19: On or about June 15, 2006, defendants CLIPPER WONSILD TANKERS, CLIPPER MARINE SERVICES, and TROJAN SHIPPING, by and through the Chief Engineer of the M/T CLIPPER TROJAN, presented and caused to be presented for inspection to the Coast Guard a false Oil Record Book for the M/T CLIPPER TROJAN.

e. Overt Act 20: On or before June 15, 2006, defendants CLIPPER WONSILD TANKERS, CLIPPER MARINE SERVICES, and

TROJAN SHIPPING, by and through the Chief Engineer and Pipe Fitter of the M/T CLIPPER TROJAN, painted the overboard discharge valve of the M/T CLIPPER TROJAN and maintained the newly painted overboard discharge valve during the Coast Guard's inspection on or about June 15, 2006.

f. Overt Acts 21-24: On or about June 15, 2006, defendants CLIPPER WONSILD TANKERS, CLIPPER MARINE SERVICES, and TROJAN SHIPPING, by and through the Chief Engineer of the M/T CLIPPER TROJAN, knowingly made the following false statements to Coast Guard inspectors:

Overt Acts 21-24 (False Statements)	
Overt Act	**False Statement**
21	that the M/T CLIPPER TROJAN's Oil Record Book was accurate
22	that no illegal or improper discharges of oily waste had occurred aboard the M/T CLIPPER TROJAN
23	that the pipes and pump used to discharge oily waste overboard had been used instead to transfer fuel from a forward tank to an aft tank
24	that the M/T CLIPPER TROJAN had offloaded oily waste during a port call in Albany, New York on June 11-14, 2006

g. Overt Act 25: On or about June 15, 2006, defendants CLIPPER WONSILD TANKERS, CLIPPER MARINE SERVICES, and TROJAN SHIPPING, by and through the Chief Engineer of the M/T CLIPPER TROJAN, directed the Fourth Engineer, Pipe Fitter, and two Motormen to deny to the Coast Guard that any discharges of oily waste had occurred aboard the M/T CLIPPER TROJAN.

h. Overt Act 26: On or about June 15, 2006, defendants CLIPPER WONSILD TANKERS, CLIPPER MARINE SERVICES, and TROJAN SHIPPING, by and through the Chief Engineer of the M/T CLIPPER TROJAN, directed the Second Engineer to claim responsibility for the transfer of oil sludge and oil-contaminated bilge waste.

i. Overt Act 27: On or about June 15, 2006, defendants CLIPPER WONSILD TANKERS, CLIPPER MARINE SERVICES, and TROJAN SHIPPING, by and through the Chief Engineer, Pipe Fitter and Fourth Engineer of the M/T CLIPPER TROJAN, fabricated and deployed a pipe that would render a false reading of the contents of the Bilge Sludge Oil Tank during the Coast Guard's anticipated sounding of that tank, and kept the pipe in place during the Coast Guard's inspection on or about June 15, 2006.

j. Overt Act 28: On or about June 15, 2006, defendants CLIPPER WONSILD TANKERS, CLIPPER MARINE SERVICES, and TROJAN SHIPPING, by and through the Fourth Engineer of the M/T CLIPPER TROJAN, disposed of the pipe that had been fabricated to render a false reading of the contents of the Bilge Sludge Oil Tank during the Coast Guard's anticipated sounding of that tank.

In violation of Title 18, United States Code, Section 371.

COUNT TWO
(Act to Prevent Pollution from Ships - 33 U.S.C. § 1908(a), 18 U.S.C. § 2)

1. Paragraphs 1 and 3 through 5 of Count One of this Indictment are re-alleged and incorporated herein.

2. On or about June 15, 2006, in Port Newark and the internal waters and ports of the United States, in the District of New Jersey, and elsewhere, defendants

CLIPPER WONSILD TANKERS HOLDING A/S,
CLIPPER MARINE SERVICES A/S, and
TROJAN SHIPPING CO., LTD.,

by and through the acts of their agents and employees, including the Chief Engineer of the M/T CLIPPER TROJAN, who were acting within the scope of their agency and employment and with the intent to benefit the defendants, did knowingly and willfully violate the MARPOL Protocol, Chapter 33 of Title 33 of the United States Code, and the regulations issued thereunder, including Title 33, Code of Federal Regulations, Section 151.25, by failing to maintain an Oil Record Book for the M/T CLIPPER TROJAN in which all discharges, disposals and transfers of oil and oily waste, including all overboard discharges of oil sludge and oil-contaminated bilge water, were fully recorded.

In violation of Title 33, United States Code, Section 1908(a) and Title 18, United States Code, Section 2.

COUNT THREE
(False Writings - 18 U.S.C. §§ 1001(a)(3) and 2)

1. Paragraphs 1 and 3 through 5 of Count One of this Indictment are re-alleged and incorporated herein.

2. On or about June 15, 2006, in Port Newark and the internal waters and ports of the United States, in the District of New Jersey, defendants

CLIPPER WONSILD TANKERS HOLDING A/S,
CLIPPER MARINE SERVICES A/S, and
TROJAN SHIPPING CO., LTD.,

by and through the acts of their agents and employees, including the Chief Engineer of the M/T CLIPPER TROJAN, who were acting within the scope of their agency and employment and with the intent to benefit the defendants, did knowingly and willfully make and use materially false writings and documents, namely the Oil Record Book for the M/T CLIPPER TROJAN, in a matter within the jurisdiction of the Executive Branch of the United States, namely the United States Coast Guard and Department of Homeland Security, knowing that such writings and documents contained materially false, fictitious, and fraudulent statements and entries.

In violation of Title 18, United States Code, Sections 1001(a)(3) and 2.

COUNTS FOUR THROUGH TEN
(Obstruction of Justice - 18 U.S.C. §§ 1505 and 2)

1. Paragraphs 1 and 3 through 5 of Count One of this Indictment are re-alleged and incorporated herein.

2. On or about June 15, 2006, in Port Newark and the internal waters and ports of the United States, in the District of New Jersey and elsewhere, defendants

CLIPPER WONSILD TANKERS HOLDING A/S,
CLIPPER MARINE SERVICES A/S, and
TROJAN SHIPPING CO., LTD.,

by and through the acts of their agents and employees, including the crew members of the M/T CLIPPER TROJAN identified in the table below, who were acting within the scope of their agency and employment and with the intent to benefit the defendants, did corruptly influence, obstruct, and impede, and endeavor to influence, obstruct and impede, the due and proper administration of the law under which a pending proceeding, namely, an inspection and investigation of the M/T CLIPPER TROJAN pursuant to 33 U.S.C. §§ 1907(c)(1) and (c)(2) and 33 C.F.R. §§ 151.01 et seq., was being had before a department and agency of the United States, namely, the United States Coast Guard and the Department of Homeland Security, by committing the acts identified and described in the table below.

[redacted]		
Count	**Crew Member(s)**	**Obstructive Act**
4	Chief Engineer, Pipe Fitter	painting the overboard discharge valve before the M/T CLIPPER TROJAN entered United States waters in order to conceal its use for the discharge of oily waste, and maintaining the newly painted overboard discharge valve during the Coast Guard's inspection on or about June 15, 2006
5	Chief Engineer	knowingly making the false statement to Coast Guard inspectors that the M/T CLIPPER TROJAN's Oil Record Book was accurate and that no illegal or improper discharges of oily waste had occurred aboard the M/T CLIPPER TROJAN
6	Chief Engineer	knowingly making the false statement to Coast Guard inspectors that the M/T CLIPPER TROJAN had offloaded oily waste during a port call in Albany, New York on or about June 11-14, 2006
7	Chief Engineer	knowingly making the false statement to Coast Guard inspectors that the pipes and pump used to discharge oily waste overboard had been used instead to transfer fuel from a forward tank to an aft tank
8	Chief Engineer	directing the Fourth Engineer, Pipe Fitter, and two Motormen to deny to the Coast Guard that any discharges of oily waste had occurred aboard the M/T CLIPPER TROJAN
9	Chief Engineer	directing the Second Engineer to claim responsibility for the transfer and disposal of oil sludge and oil-contaminated bilge waste when, in fact, such transfers had been directed by the Chief Engineer
10	Chief Engineer, Fourth Engineer, Pipe Fitter	fabricating and deploying a pipe that would render a false reading of the contents of the Bilge Sludge Oil Tank during the Coast Guard's anticipated sounding of that tank

In violation of Title 18, United States Code, Sections 1505 and 2.

COUNT ELEVEN
(Concealment of Tangible Object - 18 U.S.C. §§ 1519 and 2)

1. Paragraphs 1 and 3 through 5 of Count One of this Indictment are re-alleged and incorporated herein.

2. On or about June 15, 2006, in Port Newark and the internal waters and ports of the United States, in the District of New Jersey, and elsewhere, defendants

CLIPPER WONSILD TANKERS HOLDING A/S,
CLIPPER MARINE SERVICES A/S, and
TROJAN SHIPPING CO., LTD.,

by and through the acts of their agents and employees, including the Fourth Engineer of the M/T CLIPPER TROJAN, who were acting within the scope of their employment and with the intent to benefit the defendants, did knowingly and willfully alter, destroy, mutilate, conceal, and cover up a tangible object with the intent to impede, obstruct and influence the investigation and proper administration of a matter, namely an inspection and investigation of the M/T CLIPPER TROJAN pursuant to 33 U.S.C. §§ 1907(c)(1) and (c)(2) and 33 C.F.R. §§ 151.01 et seq., within the jurisdiction of a department and agency of the United States, namely the United States Coast Guard and the Department of Homeland Security, by discarding the pipe that had been fabricated to render a false reading of the contents of the Bilge

Sludge Oil Tank during the Coast Guard's anticipated sounding of that tank.

In violation of Title 18, United States Code, Sections 1519 and 2.

A TRUE BILL

FOREPERSON

CHRISTOPHER J. CHRISTIE
United States Attorney

CASE NUMBER: ____________

United States District Court
District of New Jersey

UNITED STATES OF AMERICA

v.

CLIPPER WONSILD TANKERS HOLDING A/S, CLIPPER MARINE SERVICES A/S, and TROJAN SHIPPING CO., LTD.

INDICTMENT FOR

18 U.S.C. §§ 371, 1001, 1505, 1519 & 2
33 U.S.C. § 1908

A True Bill,

____

Foreperson

CHRISTOPHER J. CHRISTIE
U.S. ATTORNEY
NEWARK, NEW JERSEY

BRADLEY A. HARSCH
ASSISTANT U.S. ATTORNEY
(973) 645-2700

USA-48AD 8
(Ed. 1/97)

Environmental Crimes Deskbook

Appendix 11 Mylonakis Jury Instructions

UNITED STATES DISTRICT COURT
SOUTHERN DISTRICT OF TEXAS
HOUSTON DIVISION

UNITED STATES OF AMERICA,	§	
	§	
VS.	§	CRIMINAL ACTION NO. H-09-492
	§	
IOANNIS MYLONAKIS, *et al*,	§	
	§	
Defendants.	§	

INSTRUCTIONS TO THE JURY

The following instructions were presented to the jury on the 27 day of April, 2010.

Signed this 27th day of April, 2010.

KENNETH M. HOYT
UNITED STATES DISTRICT COURT

INTRODUCTION TO FINAL INSTRUCTIONS

Members of the Jury:

In any jury trial there are, in effect, two judges. I am one of the judges; the other is the jury. It is my duty to preside over the trial. I decide what evidence is proper for your consideration. It is also my duty to explain the rules of law that you must follow in arriving at your verdict.

First, I will give you some general instructions that apply in every case, for example, instructions about the burden of proof and how to judge the credibility of witnesses. Then I will give you some specific rules of law about this particular case, and finally I will explain to you the procedures you should follow in your deliberations.

DUTY TO FOLLOW INSTRUCTIONS

You, as jurors, are the judges of the facts. But in determining what actually happened, it is your sworn duty to follow all of the rules of law as I explain them to you.

You have no right to disregard or give special attention to any one instruction. You are not allowed to question the wisdom or correctness of any rule I may state to you. You must not substitute or follow your own opinion as to what the law is or ought to be. It is your duty to apply the law as I explain it to you, regardless of the consequences.

It is also your duty to base your verdict solely upon the evidence, without prejudice or sympathy. That was the promise you made and the oath you took before being accepted by the parties as jurors, and they have the right to expect nothing less.

PRESUMPTION OF INNOCENCE, BURDEN OF PROOF, REASONABLE DOUBT

The indictment or formal charge against the defendant is not evidence of guilt. Indeed, the defendant is presumed by the law to be innocent. The law does not require a defendant to prove his innocence or produce any evidence at all. The government has the burden of proving the defendant guilty beyond a reasonable doubt, and if it fails to do so, you must acquit the defendant.

While the government's burden of proof is a strict or heavy burden, it is not necessary that the defendant's guilt be proved beyond all possible doubt. It is only required that the government's proof exclude any "reasonable doubt" concerning the defendant's guilt.

A "reasonable doubt" is a doubt based upon reason and common sense after careful and impartial consideration of all the evidence in the case. Proof beyond a reasonable doubt, therefore, is proof of such a convincing character that you would be willing to rely and act upon it without hesitation in the most important of your own affairs.

EVIDENCE - EXCLUDING WHAT IS NOT EVIDENCE

As I told you earlier, it is your duty to determine the facts. In doing so, you must consider only the evidence presented during the trial. Evidence includes the sworn testimony of the witnesses and the exhibits. Remember that any statements, objections, or arguments made by the lawyers are not evidence. The function of the lawyers is to point out those things that are most significant or most helpful to their side of the case, and in so doing to call your attention to certain facts or inferences that might otherwise escape your notice. In the final analysis, however, it is your own recollection and interpretation of the evidence that controls in the case. What the lawyers say is not binding upon you.

During the trial I sustained objections to certain questions and exhibits. You must disregard those questions and exhibits entirely. Do not speculate as to what the witness would have said if permitted to answer the question or as to the contents of an exhibit. Also, certain testimony or other evidence has been ordered stricken from the record and you have been instructed to disregard this evidence. Do not consider any testimony or other evidence which has been stricken in reaching your decision. Your verdict must be based solely on the legally admissible evidence and testimony.

Also, do not assume from anything I may have done or said during the trial that I have any opinion concerning any of the issues in this case. Except for the instructions to you on the law, you should disregard anything I may have said during the trial in arriving at your own findings as to the facts.

EVIDENCE - INFERENCES - DIRECT AND CIRCUMSTANTIAL

While you should consider only the evidence, you are permitted to draw such reasonable inferences from the testimony and exhibits as you feel are justified in light of common experience. In other words, you may make deductions and reach conclusions that reason and common sense lead you to draw from the facts which have been established by the evidence.

In considering the evidence you may make deductions and reach conclusions which reason and common sense lead you to make; and you should not be concerned about whether the evidence is direct or circumstantial. "Direct evidence" is the testimony of one who asserts actual knowledge of a fact, such as an eye witness. "Circumstantial evidence" is proof of a chain of events and circumstances indicating that something is or is not a fact. The law makes no distinction between the weight you may give to either direct or circumstantial evidence.

SUMMARIES AND CHARTS NOT RECEIVED IN EVIDENCE

Certain charts have been shown to you solely to help explain the facts disclosed by the books, records, and other documents which are in evidence in the case. These charts and summaries are not evidence or proof of any facts. You should determine the facts from the evidence.

CREDIBILITY OF WITNESSES

It is your job to decide whether the government has proved the guilt of the defendant beyond a reasonable doubt. In doing so, you must consider all of the evidence. This does not mean, however, that you must accept all of the evidence as true or accurate.

You are the sole judges of the credibility or "believability" of each witness and the weight to be given the witness's testimony. An important part of your job will be making judgments about the testimony of the witnesses including the defendant who testified in this case. You should decide whether you believe all or any part of what each person had to say, and how important that testimony was. In making that decision I suggest that you ask yourself a few questions: Did the person impress you as honest? Did the witness have any particular reason not to tell the truth? Did the witness have a personal interest in the outcome of the case? Did the witness have any relationship with either the government or the defense? Did the witness seem to have a good memory? Did the witness clearly see or hear the things about which he or she testified? Did the witness have the opportunity and ability to understand the questions clearly and answer them directly? Did the witness's testimony differ from the testimony of other witnesses? These are a few of the considerations that will help you determine the accuracy of what each witness said.

The testimony of a defendant should be weighed and his credibility evaluated in the same way as that of any other witness.

Your job is to think about the testimony of each witness you have heard and decide how much you believe of what each witness had to say. In making up your mind and reaching a verdict, do not make any decisions simply because there were more witnesses on one side than on the other. Do not reach a conclusion on a particular point just because there were more witnesses testifying for one side on that point.

ACCOMPLICE – INFORMER - IMMUNITY

During the trial, the government also called as witnesses certain alleged accomplices. The testimony of an alleged accomplice, and the testimony of one who provides evidence against a defendant as an informer for pay or for immunity from punishment or for personal advantage or vindication, must always be examined and weighed by the jury with greater care and caution than the testimony of ordinary witnesses. You, the jury, must decide whether the witness's testimony has been affected by any of those circumstances, or by the witness's interest in the outcome of the case, or by prejudice against the defendant, or by the benefits that the witness has received either financially or as a result of being immunized from prosecution. You should keep in mind that such testimony is always to be received with caution and weighed with great care.

You should never convict any defendant upon the unsupported testimony of such a witness unless you believe that testimony beyond a reasonable doubt.

IMPEACHMENT BY PRIOR INCONSISTENCIES

The testimony of a witness may be discredited by showing that the witness testified falsely concerning a material matter, or by evidence that at some other time the witness said or did something, or failed to say or do something, which is inconsistent with the testimony the witness gave at this trial.

Earlier statements of a witness were not admitted in evidence to prove that the contents of those statements are true. You may consider the earlier statements only to determine whether you think they are consistent or inconsistent with the trial testimony of the witness and therefore whether they affect the credibility of that witness.

If you believe that a witness has been discredited in this manner, it is your exclusive right to give the testimony of that witness whatever weight you think it deserves.

ON OR ABOUT

You will note that the indictment charges that the offenses were committed on or about January 15, 2009, February 18, 2009, and between on or about November 29, 2008 and January 21, 2009. The government does not have to prove that the crimes were committed on that exact date, so long as the government proves beyond a reasonable doubt that the defendant committed the crimes charged in the indictment on a date reasonably near the date stated in the indictment for each count.

CAUTION - CONSIDER ONLY CRIMES CHARGED

You are here to decide whether the government has proved beyond a reasonable doubt that the defendant is guilty of the crimes charged. The defendant is not on trial for any act, conduct, or offense not alleged in the indictment. Neither are you concerned with the guilt of any other person or persons not on trial as a defendant in this case.

CAUTION – PUNISHMENT

If a defendant is found guilty, it will be my duty to decide what the punishment will be. You should not be concerned with punishment in any way. It should not enter your consideration or discussion of the case.

AIDING AND ABETTING (AGENCY)
18 U.S.C. § 2

The guilt of a defendant in a criminal case may be established without proof that the defendant personally did every act constituting the offense alleged. The law recognizes that, ordinarily, anything a person can do for himself may also be accomplished by him through the direction of another person as his or her agent, or by acting in concert with, or under the direction of, another person or persons in a joint effort or enterprise.

If another person is acting under the direction of the defendant or if the defendant joins another person and performs acts with the intent to commit a crime, then the law holds the defendant responsible for the acts and conduct of such other persons just as though the defendant had committed the acts or engaged in such conduct.

Before any defendant may be held criminally responsible for the acts of others it is necessary that the accused deliberately associate himself in some way with the crime and participate in it with the intent to bring about the crime.

Of course, mere presence at the scene of a crime and knowledge that a crime is being committed are not sufficient to establish that a defendant either directed or aided and abetted the crime unless you find beyond a reasonable doubt that the defendant was a participant and not merely a knowing spectator.

In other words, you may not find any defendant guilty unless you find beyond a reasonable doubt that every element of the offense as defined in these instructions was committed by some person or persons, and that the defendant voluntarily participated in its commission with the intent to violate the law.

For you to find the defendant guilty of this crime, you must be convinced that the government has proved each of the following beyond a reasonable doubt:

First: That the offense of violating the Act to Prevent Pollution from Ships (Counts One and Two) or making a False Statement (Count Six and Seven) or Obstruction (Count Eleven) was committed by some person;

Second: That the defendant associated with the criminal venture;

Third: That the defendant purposefully participated in the criminal venture; and

Fourth: That the defendant sought by action to make that venture successful.

"To associate with the criminal venture" means that the defendant shared the criminal intent of the principal. This element cannot be established if the defendant had no knowledge of the principal's criminal venture.

"To participate in the criminal venture" means that the defendant engaged in some affirmative conduct designed to aid the venture or assisted the principal of the crime.

"KNOWINGLY" – TO ACT

The word "knowingly," as that term is used from time to time in these instructions, means that the act was done voluntarily and intentionally, not because of mistake or accident.

UNANIMITY OF THEORY

Your verdict, whether it is guilty or not guilty, must be unanimous. The following instructions apply to the unanimity requirement in each count.

(Read Counts of Indictment)

The government does not have to prove all manner and means for you to return a guilty verdict on these charges. Proof beyond a reasonable doubt on one is enough. But in order to return a guilty verdict, all twelve of you must agree that the same one has been proved.

ACT TO PREVENT POLLUTION FROM SHIPS
33 U.S.C. 1908(a)

Counts One and Two of the Indictment charges Defendant Ioannis Mylonakis with violating 33 U.S.C. § 1908(a), the Act to Prevent Pollution from Ships, by failing to maintain an accurate Oil Record Book as to various discharges of oily waste from the M/T Georgios M on or about January 15, 2009 and February 18, 2009 as required under the MARPOL Protocol.

In order for a defendant to be found guilty on this count, the government must prove each of the following elements beyond a reasonable doubt:

First, the *M/T Georgios M* is a foreign flag ocean going vessel in excess of 150 tons and is therefore required to maintain an Oil Record Book onboard the ship;

Second, the defendant was the master or other person in charge of the *Georgios M* and was responsible for the maintenance of the Oil Record Book;

Third, a disposal of oil residue as described in 33 C.F.R. § 151.25 took place onboard the ship;

Fourth, the defendant knowingly entered an inaccurate description of the disposal or omitted a required Oil Record Book entry;

Fifth, the Oil Record Book of the ship was materially false because an inaccurate description of the disposal was entered or omitted a required Oil Record Book entry;

Sixth, the defendant knew that the Oil Record Book of the ship was materially false because an inaccurate description of the disposal was entered or omitted from the Oil Record Book; and

Seventh, the defendant knew that the Oil Record Book maintained and used on the ship was materially false because it contained an inaccurate description of the disposal or omitted from the Oil Record Book.

You are instructed that 33 C.F.R. § 151.25 is a regulation implementing the MARPOL Protocol, which requires that any disposal of oil residue from a ship into the ocean must be accurately entered into the Oil Record Book.

An act is done knowingly if the defendant is aware of the act and does not act or fail to act through ignorance, mistake or accident. The government is not required to prove that the defendant knew that his acts or omissions were unlawful. You may consider evidence of the defendant's words, acts, or omissions, along with all the other evidence, in deciding whether the defendant acted knowingly.

FALSE STATEMENTS TO FEDERAL AGENCIES AND AGENTS

Title 18, United States Code, Section 1001, makes it a crime for anyone to knowingly and willfully make a false or fraudulent statement in any matter within the jurisdiction of the executive, legislative, or judicial branch of the Government of the United States.

For you to find the defendant guilty of this crime, you must be convinced that the government has proved each of the following beyond a reasonable doubt:

First: That the defendant made a false statement to the United States Coast Guard and the Department of Homeland Security regarding a matter within their jurisdiction;

Second: That the defendant made the statement intentionally, knowing that it was false;

Third: That the statement was material; and

Fourth: That the defendant made the false statement with the specific intent of misleading the United States Coast Guard and the Department of Homeland Security.

A statement is material if it has a natural tendency to influence, or is capable of influencing, a decision of the United States Coast Guard and the Department of Homeland Security.

An act is done knowingly if the defendant is aware of the act and does not act or fail to act through ignorance, mistake or accident. The government is not required to prove that the defendant knew that his acts or omissions were unlawful. You may consider evidence of the defendant's words, acts, or omissions, along with all the other evidence, in deciding whether the defendant acted knowingly.

The word "willfully," as that term has been used from time to time in these instructions, means that the act was committed voluntarily and purposely, with the specific intent to do something the law forbids; that is to say, with bad purpose either to disobey or disregard the law.

It is not necessary to show that the United States Coast Guard and the Department of Homeland Security were in fact misled.

OBSTRUCTION
18 U.S.C. § 1519

Count Eleven of the Indictment charges Defendant Ioannis Mylonakis with failure to record discharges of bilge and oily sludge and falsely recording discharges and disposal of bilge and oily sludge wastes as being processed through proper pollution prevention equipment in violation of 18 U.S.C. § 1519. These acts were allegedly committed between November 29, 2008 and January 21, 2009.

In order for a defendant to be found guilty on this count, the government must prove each of the following elements beyond a reasonable doubt:

First, the defendant knowingly altered, concealed, covered up, falsified and made a false entry in a record or document that was material; and

Second, the defendant did so with the specific intent to impede, obstruct and influence the investigation or proper administration of any department or agency or the United States.

A statement is material if it has a natural tendency to influence, or is capable of influencing, a decision of the United States Coast Guard and the Department of Homeland Security.

An act is done knowingly if the defendant is aware of the act and does not act or fail to act through ignorance, mistake or accident. The government is not required to prove that the defendant knew that his acts or omissions were unlawful. You may consider evidence of the defendant's words, acts, or omissions, along with all the other evidence, in deciding whether the defendant acted knowingly.

DUTY TO DELIBERATE – VERDICT FORM

To reach a verdict, whether it is guilty or not guilty, all of you must agree. Your verdict must be unanimous on each count of the indictment. Your deliberations will be secret. You will never have to explain your verdict to anyone.

It is your duty to consult with one another and to deliberate in an effort to reach agreement if you can do so. Each of you must decide the case for yourself, but only after an impartial consideration of the evidence with your fellow jurors. During your deliberations, do not hesitate to reexamine your own opinions and change your mind if convinced that you were wrong. But do not give up your honest beliefs as to the weight or effect of the evidence solely because of the opinion of your fellow jurors, or for the mere purpose of returning a verdict.

Remember at all times, you are judges--judges of the facts. Your duty is to decide whether the government has proved the defendant guilty beyond a reasonable doubt.

When you go to the jury room, the first thing that you should do is select one of your number as your foreperson, who will help to guide your deliberations and will speak for you here in the courtroom.

A form of verdict has been prepared for your convenience.

The foreperson will write the unanimous answer of the jury in the space provided for each count of the Indictment, either guilty or not guilty. At the conclusion of your deliberations, the foreperson should date and sign the verdict.

If you need to communicate with me during your deliberations, the foreperson should write the message and give it to the marshal. I will either reply in writing or bring you back into the court to answer your message.

Bear in mind that you are never to reveal to any person, not even to the court, how the jury stands, numerically or otherwise, on any count of the indictment, until after you have reached a unanimous verdict.

COUNTS ONE AND TWO
(Act to Prevent Pollution from Ships - 33 U.S.C. 1908(a))

10. The Grand Jury re-alleges and incorporates by reference herein paragraphs 1 through 9 of this Indictment and further charges:

11. On or about the dates in the table below in the corresponding ports, each constituting a separate count under this Indictment, and within the navigable waters of the United States in the Southern District of Texas, the defendant,

IOANNIS MYLONAKIS,

did knowingly fail to maintain an Oil Record Book for the *M/T Georgios M* in which all disposals of oil residue, overboard discharges, and disposals of oily bilge waste water were required to be fully recorded. Specifically, the defendant maintained an Oil Record Book that: (1) falsely and affirmatively claimed that discharges of oily bilge waste water had been made through the use of an Oil Water Separator and that sludges had been incinerated; (2) failed to disclose overboard discharges of oily sludge and oily bilge waste water made through bypass equipment and without the use of a properly functioning Oil Water Separator and oil monitoring equipment; (3) failed to record all tank to tank transfers, including transfers from the bilge tank into the drain oil tank; and (4) created the overall false and misleading impression that the vessel was being operated properly and was fully maintaining an accurate Oil Record Book:

COUNT	ON OR ABOUT	IN THE PORT OF
1	January 15, 2009	Corpus Christi, Texas
2	February 18, 2009	Texas City, Texas

All in violation of Title 33, United States Code, Section 1908(a), Title 18, United States Code, Section 2, and Title 33, Code of Federal Regulations, Section 151.25.

COUNTS SIX AND SEVEN
(False Statements - 18 U.S.C. § 1001(a)(2))

14. The Grand Jury re-alleges and incorporates by reference herein paragraphs 1 through 9 of this Indictment and further charges:

15. From on or about the dates in the table below in the corresponding ports, each constituting a separate count under this Indictment, and within the navigable waters of the United States in the Southern District of Texas, the defendant,

IOANNIS MYLONAKIS,

in a matter within the jurisdiction of the United States Coast Guard and the Department of Homeland Security, did knowingly and willfully use and cause to be used a materially false writing to wit: the Oil Record Book for the *M/T Georgios M*, knowing the same to contain a materially false, fictitious, and fraudulent statement, entry and representation, in that the Oil Record Book for the *M/T Georgios M* failed to state and omitted the fact that: (1) the vessel's Oil Water Separator had been by-passed; (2) oily bilge waste water had been discharged directly into the ocean without first being processed through the ship's Oil Water Separator;(3) sludge wastes

has been discharged directly overboard; and (4) that there were transfers of oily bilge waste water from the bilge tank to the drain oil tank, when in truth and in fact, as the defendant then and there well knew, some volume of the oil-contaminated bilge wastes and sludges not recorded in the Oil Record Book had been discharged overboard , and oily bilge waste water not recorded in the Oil Record Book had been transferred into the drain oil tank and sludge tank:

COUNT	ON OR ABOUT	IN THE PORT OF
6	January 15, 2009	Corpus Christi, Texas
7	February 18, 2009	Texas City, Texas

All in violation of Title 18, United State Code, Sections 1001(a)(2) and 2.

COUNT ELEVEN
(Obstruction - 18 U.S.C. § 1519)

18. The Grand Jury re-alleges and incorporates by reference herein paragraphs 1 through 9 and paragraphs 11 and 15 of this Indictment and further charges:

19. Between on or about November 29, 2008, and January 21, 2009, the defendant,

IOANNIS MYLONAKIS,

with the intent to impede, obstruct and influence the investigation or proper administration of a matter within the jurisdiction of the United States Coast Guard and the Department of Homeland Security and in relation to and in contemplation of an investigation and matter within the Southern District of Texas and elsewhere, did knowingly alter, conceal, cover up, falsify and made a false entry in a record or document to wit: the defendant:

A. failed to record discharges of bilge and oily sludge wastes made without using proper pollution prevention equipment;

B. falsely recorded discharges and disposal of bilge and oily sludge wastes as being processed through proper pollution prevention equipment when in fact the bilge and oily sludge wastes were discharged directly overboard into the ocean;

All in violation of Title 18, United States Code, Sections 1519 and 2.

Environmental Crimes Deskbook

Appendix 12 *United States v. W.R. Grace et al.* Superseding Indictment (Mont. 2005)

SUE ELLEN WOOLDRIDGE
Assistant Attorney General, ENRD
DAVID M. UHLMANN
Chief, Environmental Crimes Section
KEVIN M. CASSIDY
Trial Attorney
Environmental Crimes Section

WILLIAM W. MERCER
United States Attorney
KRIS A. MCLEAN
Assistant U.S. Attorney
U.S. Attorney's Office
P.O. Box 8329
Missoula, MT 59807
105 E. Pine, 2nd Floor
Missoula, MT 59802
Phone: (406) 542-8851
FAX: (406) 542-1476

ATTORNEY FOR PLAINTIFF
UNITED STATES OF AMERICA

FILED
BILLINGS DIV.
2005 JUN 26 AM 10 13
PATRICK E. DUFFY, CLERK
BY
DEPUTY CLERK

IN THE UNITED STATES DISTRICT COURT

FOR THE DISTRICT OF MONTANA

MISSOULA DIVISION

UNITED STATES OF AMERICA, Plaintiff, vs. W.R. GRACE, ALAN R. STRINGER, HENRY A. ESCHENBACH, JACK W. WOLTER, WILLIAM J. McCAIG, ROBERT J. BETTACCHI, O. MARIO FAVORITO, ROBERT C. WALSH Defendants.	CR 05 - 07 -M-DWM **SUPERSEDING INDICTMENT** CONSPIRACY (Count I) Title 18 U.S.C. §371 (Penalty: Five years imprisonment, $250,000 fine, and three years supervised release; $1,000,000 fine per violation for organization) CLEAN AIR ACT VIOLATIONS (Counts II, III, IV) Title 42 U.S.C. § 7413(c)(5)(A) Title 18 U.S.C § 2 (Penalty: Fifteen years imprisonment, $250,000 fine, and three years supervised release; $1,000,000 fine per violation for organization)

	OBSTRUCTION OF JUSTICE **(Counts V, VI, VII, VIII)** **18 U.S.C. §§ 1505, 2** **(Penalty: Five years imprisonment, $250,000 fine, and three years supervised release)**

THE GRAND JURY CHARGES:

INTRODUCTION

A. BACKGROUND

At all times material to this Indictment:

1. In the late 1800s, gold miners discovered a significant body of vermiculite ore in an area located in the mountains approximately seven miles northeast of the town of Libby, Montana (the "Libby Mine").

2. Vermiculite is a mineral that expands, or pops, at high temperatures in an "expansion" or "exfoliation" process.

3. Expanded vermiculite that originated at the Libby Mine had many uses, including as an attic insulation (marketed as "Zonolite Attic Insulation"), as an ingredient in fireproofing products (marketed as "Monokote"), as an ingredient in masonry fill, and as an additive in potting soils and fertilizers.

4. The vermiculite deposits at the Libby Mine were contaminated with amphibole asbestos. The amphibole asbestos found at the Libby Mine is composed of a family of closely related minerals including tremolite, winchite, richterite, actinolite and others. This amphibole asbestos has been commonly called "tremolite" and, for the purposes of this Indictment, it will be referred to as "tremolite," "tremolite asbestos" and "amphibole asbestos."

5. On or about 1939, the Zonolite Company (originally known as Universal Zonolite Insulation Company) was formed to mine and process vermiculite from the ore deposit at the Libby Mine.

6. Pursuant to the Agreement and Plan of Reorganization dated January 17, 1963, between W.R. Grace & Co., a Connecticut corporation, and the Zonolite Company ("Zonolite Agreement"), W.R. Grace & Co. acquired "substantially all of the properties and assets of Zonolite" under the terms and conditions contained in that agreement.

7. The employees of the Zonolite Company remained at the mine and processing facilities as employees of W.R. Grace & Co.

8. W.R. Grace & Co. operated the Libby Mine until on or about 1992.

9. W.R. Grace & Co. acquired the rights to the name "Zonolite" as part of the transaction with the Zonolite Company and continued to manufacture and sell Zonolite's product line, including vermiculite concentrate, expanded vermiculite, and Zonolite Attic Insulation.

10. In 1988, W.R. Grace & Co., the same Connecticut corporation that entered into the Zonolite Agreement, changed its name to W.R. Grace & Co. - Conn. as part of a corporate reorganization, and became a subsidiary of a newly-created New York corporation named W.R. Grace & Co. In 1998, W.R. Grace & Co., a Delaware corporation, was incorporated. W.R. Grace & Co. - Conn., became a wholly owned subsidiary of the Delaware corporation.

11. For the purposes of this Indictment, "W.R. GRACE" refers to W.R. Grace & Co., a Connecticut corporation, both before and after it changed its name to W.R. Grace & Co.-Conn. in 1988.

12. As part of its operations, defendant W.R. GRACE mined and milled vermiculite ore at the Libby Mine. The milled vermiculite ore was known as "vermiculite concentrate."

13. As part of its operations, defendant W.R. GRACE disposed of mining waste and mill tailings (a waste product of the milling process) at the Libby Mine.

14. From on or about 1963 until on or about 1991, defendant W.R. GRACE operated a Screening Plant, a processing plant at which vermiculite concentrate was separated into different sized grades through a mechanical screening process (the "Screening Plant").

15. Prior to the mid-1970s, the Screening Plant was located at the Libby Mine.

16. After the mid-1970s, the Screening Plant was located down Rainy Creek Road from the Libby Mine, at the intersection of Highway 37 and Rainy Creek Road on the bank of the Kootenai River, about four miles from Libby, Montana.

17. Prior to the construction of the new Screening Plant at the intersection of Highway 37 and Rainy Creek Road, defendant W.R. GRACE used this property as a holding point for vermiculite concentrate trucked from the Screening Plant at the Libby Mine.

18. A facility known as the "Export Plant" was located across the railroad tracks from downtown Libby, Montana near where Highway 37 crosses the Kootenai River.

19. From on or about 1963 to at least on or about 1992, defendant W.R. GRACE trucked small amounts (relative to the volume shipped to customers from the rail loading station near the Screening Plant) of vermiculite concentrate to the Export Plant from the Screening Plant, where it was stockpiled and then placed in bags for distribution to locations in other states.

20. Defendant W.R. GRACE shipped the vermiculite concentrate (in hopper railroad cars or, in lesser amounts, in bags) to defendant W.R. GRACE owned and licensed expansion facilities and to customers throughout the United States.

21. In the operation of the Screening Plant, there were occasionally spills, processing errors, or lack of demand for certain size grades of vermiculite concentrate.

22. At various times between 1963 and 1992, defendant W.R. GRACE placed the vermiculite concentrate that had spilled, vermiculite concentrate that was affected by processing errors, or vermiculite concentrate of a grade for which there was no immediate demand in various locations on the grounds of the Screening Plant.

23. At various times between 1963 and 1990, defendant W.R. GRACE allowed employees and residents of Libby, Montana to take vermiculite concentrate for their personal use.

24. At some unknown time in the 1970s, an employee of defendant W.R. GRACE informed the Libby Public School District that vermiculite materials from the Libby Mine could be used as a surface for the Libby High School running track.

25. At some unknown time, employees of defendant W.R. GRACE transported vermiculite materials to the Libby High School and the Libby Junior High School

where they were laid and served as a surface for the running tracks at both schools for approximately seven years.

26. On or about 1981, employees of defendant W.R. GRACE transported vermiculite materials to Plummer Elementary School in Libby, Montana where they were laid and served as the foundation for an outdoor ice skating rink.

27. In 1990, defendant W.R. GRACE ceased vermiculite mining at the Libby Mine. Defendant W.R. GRACE continued vermiculite processing operations at the Libby Mine and the Screening Plant until approximately 1992.

28. In the mid-1990s, defendant W.R. GRACE sold several of the properties associated with its former vermiculite operations in and near Libby, Montana.

29. On or about December 17, 1993, defendant W.R. GRACE sold the Screening Plant to Lincoln County residents Mel and Lerah Parker.

30. From approximately 1993 to on or about June, 2000, Mel and Lerah Parker used the Screening Plant for commercial operations (a commercial nursery and mushroom farm) and their personal residence.

31. From on or about 1977 to on or about 1994, the defendant W.R. GRACE leased a portion of the Export Plant to various people and entities to use for organized youth baseball games and practices.

32. From on or about 1987 to sometime before on or about May 12, 1994, defendant W.R. Grace leased a portion of the Export Plant to Jim Regh, Melvin Burnett, and others for use as their place of business.

33. In separate transactions on or about May 12, 1994 and on or about February 23, 1995, defendant W.R. GRACE transferred portions of the former Export Plant property to the City of Libby.

34. From on or about 1995 to on or about 1997, the City of Libby leased a portion of the Export Plant to various people and entities to use for organized youth baseball games and practices.

35. From on or about May 12, 1994 to on or about 2000, the City of Libby leased a portion of the Export Plant to Melvin Burnett, who used the location for a retail lumber yard and related operations.

36. On or about 1994, defendant W.R. GRACE sold to an entity known as Kootenai Development Corporation ("KDC") approximately 3,600 acres of mountainous land that comprises the Libby Mine, 1,200 acres of which had been actively mined, and an approximately 20-acre parcel now known as the "Flyway," which is located between Highway 37 and the Kootenai River, adjacent to and south of the former Screening Plant.

37. On or about November 23, 1999, Environmental Protection Agency ("EPA") representatives arrived in Libby, Montana to investigate reports of a potential hazardous waste emergency relating to asbestos contaminated vermiculite.

38. As a result of its investigation, EPA concluded that the conditions at the site presented an imminent and substantial threat to human health and the environment. The site was ultimately declared a Superfund Site pursuant to federal law. As of December 31, 2001, EPA had incurred 55,100,000.00 dollars in cleanup costs.

39. At various dates alleged in this Indictment, defendant ALAN R. STRINGER held different positions with defendant W.R. GRACE, including: from on or about September 8, 1981 to on or about 1988, he was the Libby Mine Supervisor; from on or about 1988 to on or about 1994, he was the General Manager of Operations at the Libby Mine; and from on or about 1999 to the present, he served as defendant W.R. GRACE's representative relating to EPA's Superfund Cleanup.

40. At various dates alleged in this Indictment, defendant HENRY "HARRY" A. ESCHENBACH held different positions with defendant W.R. GRACE, including: from on or about 1971 to on or about 1977, he was an Industrial Hygienist in the Industrial Chemicals Group ("ICG"); and from on or about 1977 to on or about December 31, 1996, he was the Director of Health, Safety, and Toxicology for ICG.

41. At various dates alleged in this Indictment, defendant JACK W. WOLTER held different positions with defendant W.R. GRACE, including: from on or about September 15, 1975 to on or about 1988, he was Vice-President of Mining and Engineering for the Construction Products Division ("CPD"); and from on or about 1988 to on or about 1994, he was Vice-President and General Manager of CPD.

42. At various dates alleged in this Indictment, defendant WILLIAM J. McCAIG held different positions with defendant W.R. GRACE, including: from on or about January, 1971, he was a Maintenance Engineer at the Libby Mine; from on or about 1976 to on or about 1979, he was Maintenance Superintendent at the Libby Mine; from on or about 1979 to on or about 1988, he was General Manager

of Operations at the Libby Mine; and from on or about 1988 to on or about August 31, 1995, he was Manufacturing Manager of Specialty Vermiculite of CPD Business Unit in Enoree, South Carolina.

43. At various dates alleged in this Indictment, defendant ROBERT J. BETTACCHI held different positions with defendant W.R. GRACE, including: from on or about 1979 to on or about 1986, he was General Manager of CPD; from on or about 1986 to on or about 1989, he was Vice-President of CPD; and from on or about 1989 to the present, he was President of CPD and Senior Vice-President of defendant W.R. GRACE.

44. At various dates alleged in this Indictment, defendant O. MARIO FAVORITO held different positions with defendant W.R. GRACE, including: from on or about 1970 to on or about 1993, he was corporate legal counsel for ICG; and from an unknown time but no earlier than on or about 1993 to the present, he was Assistant Secretary of defendant W.R. GRACE and Chief Group Counsel.

45. At various dates alleged in this Indictment, defendant ROBERT C. WALSH held different positions with defendant W.R. GRACE, including: from on or about 1982 to on or about 1989, he was President of CPD; from on or about 1989 to an unknown time he was Executive Vice President of Grace Specialty Chemicals Co.; and from an unknown time to on or about 1994, he was Senior Vice-President of defendant W.R. GRACE.

46. From 1976 to 1990 the Directors, Officers, and Shareholders of W.R. GRACE enjoyed at least $140 million in after tax profits arising largely from products made with vermiculite contaminated with tremolite asbestos from the Libby Mine.

B. ASBESTOS RELATED DISEASES

47. Modern science has not established a safe level for asbestos exposure for which there is no increased risk of disease.

48. Airborne exposure to tremolite asbestos by breathing into human lungs causes scarring of the lung tissues and can cause the disease known as "asbestosis."

49. Asbestosis is a progressive disease that destroys the human lung's ability to absorb oxygen, and in severe cases, results in severe disability or death.

50. The rate of asbestosis mortality of the Libby population is 40 to 80 times higher than expected when compared to rates for Montana and the United States.

51. Airborne exposure to tremolite asbestos causes lung cancer in humans.

52. The rate of lung cancer mortality of the Libby population is approximately 30 percent higher than expected when compared to rates for Montana and the United States.

53. Airborne exposure to tremolite asbestos can cause an aggressive and fatal form of cancer in humans known as "mesothelioma." This form of cancer is extremely rare, resulting in no more than 9 cases per 1 million individuals in the United States general population, and is uniquely associated with exposure to asbestos. This form of cancer is not related to cigarette smoking.

54. Over twenty cases of mesothelioma have been identified to date among persons who lived or worked in Libby. This is a significant finding for this small population of approximately 8,000 people.

55. Airborne exposure to tremolite asbestos can cause the disease of pleural fibrosis, which is scarring of the pleural tissues surrounding the lungs. Pleural fibrosis can

result in impaired functioning of the lungs, and in more severe cases, disability and death. The development and progression of pleural fibrosis is not related to cigarette smoking.

56. Pleural fibrosis is associated with a greater risk of developing mesothelioma and lung cancer.

57. To date, approximately 1,200 residents of the Libby, Montana area have been identified as having asbestos related pleural abnormalities as a result of being exposed to tremolite asbestos produced by W.R. GRACE at the Libby Mine. Of this group, 70 percent are not former employees at the Libby Mine. Individuals have been identified with asbestos related disease whose only exposure to asbestos has been through asbestos containing vermiculite from the Libby Mine located throughout the community.

58. Asbestos related diseases have a latency period ranging from 3 to 40 years or more. That is, a person exposed to asbestos by breathing will not manifest symptoms of disease until 3 to 40 or more years after exposure.

59. Airborne exposure to tremolite asbestos can cause bloody pleural effusions. A bloody pleural effusion is a pathological collection of bloody fluid between the pleural lining and the lung. They are considered to be a possible manifestation of early stages of mesothelioma.

C. STATUTORY BACKGROUND

I. CLEAN AIR ACT

60. The Clean Air Act ("CAA"), 42 U.S.C. § 7401 *et seq.*, is the United States' comprehensive air pollution control statute. The purpose of the CAA is "to protect

and enhance the quality of the nation's air resources." 42 U.S.C. § 7401(b)(1); *see also* 42 U.S.C. § 7470.

61. Under the CAA, any person who knowingly releases into the ambient air any hazardous air pollutant or any extremely hazardous substance, and who knows at the time that he thereby places another person in imminent danger of death or serious bodily injury is subject to criminal penalties. 42 U.S.C. § 7413(c)(5)(A).

62. Asbestos is a hazardous air pollutant. 42 U.S.C. § 7412(b)(1).

63. A "person" includes a corporation, individual and "any responsible corporate officer." 42 U.S.C. § 7602(e); 42 U.S.C. § 7413(c)(6).

64. Congress defined "serious bodily injury" as "bodily injury which involves a substantial risk of death, . . . extreme physical pain, . . . or protracted loss or impairment of the function of a bodily member, organ, or mental faculty." 42 U.S.C. § 7413(c)(5)(F).

II. TOXIC SUBSTANCES CONTROL ACT

65. The Toxic Substances Control Act, 15 U.S.C. § 2601 et. seq. ("TSCA"), regulates chemical substances and mixtures whose manufacture, processing, distribution in commerce, use, or disposal may present an unreasonable risk of injury to health or the environment.

66. Section 8(e) of TSCA, 15 U.S.C. § 2607(e) requires that any person who manufactures, processes, or distributes in commerce a chemical substance or mixture and who obtains information that reasonably supports the conclusion that such substance or mixture presents a substantial risk of injury to health or the environment shall immediately inform the Administrator of EPA of such

information, unless the person has actual knowledge that the Administrator has been adequately informed of such information.

67. At times relevant to this Indictment, EPA interpreted the requirement under TSCA 8(e) that a person "immediately inform" the Administrator to be met if the person submitted the information to EPA within 15 working days after the date the person obtained such information.

III. COMPREHENSIVE ENVIRONMENTAL RESPONSE, COMPENSATION AND LIABILITY ACT (SUPERFUND)

68. The Comprehensive Environmental Response, Compensation and Liability Act, 42 U.S.C. § 9601 et seq. ("CERCLA" or "Superfund"), authorizes designated EPA personnel to conduct response actions to address releases or threatened releases of hazardous substances into the environment. 42 U.S.C. § 9604(a)(1). Asbestos is defined as a "hazardous substance" under CERCLA and EPA's implementing regulations. 42 U.S.C. § 9601(14); 40 C.F.R. 302.4.

69. Under Section 104(e)(2) of CERCLA, 42 U.S.C. § 9604(e)(2), designated EPA personnel "may require any person who has or may have information relevant to any of the following to furnish, upon reasonable notice, information and documents relating to such matter:

(A) The identification, nature, and quantity of materials which have been or are generated, treated, stored, or disposed of at a vessel or facility or transported to a vessel or facility.

(B) The nature or extent of a release or threatened release of a hazardous substance or pollutant or contaminant at or from a vessel or facility.

(C) Information relating to the ability of a person to pay for or perform a cleanup.

COUNT I
(Conspiracy)

70. Paragraphs 1 through 69 are incorporated here as if set forth in full.

71. That beginning on or about 1976, and continuing until on or about 2002, at Libby, and other locations within and without the District of Montana, the defendants, W.R. GRACE, ALAN R. STRINGER, HENRY A. ESCHENBACH, JACK W. WOLTER, WILLIAM J. McCAIG, ROBERT J. BETTACCHI, O. MARIO FAVORITO, and ROBERT C. WALSH, and others known and unknown to the grand jury did knowingly combine, conspire and agree among themselves and others:

OBJECTS OF THE CONSPIRACY

a. To knowingly release and cause to be released into the ambient air a hazardous air pollutant, namely asbestos, and at the time knowingly placed persons, including: families of employees of W.R. GRACE Libby vermiculite mining and processing operations; residents of Libby, Montana and surrounding communities in Lincoln County; and others in imminent danger of death or serious bodily injury in violation of 42 U.S.C. § 7413(c)(5)(A).

b. To defraud the United States and others by impairing, impeding, and frustrating the governmental functions of the United States, including the United States Environmental Protection Agency (EPA) and the Department of Health and Human Services, specifically, the National Institute for Occupational Safety and Health ("NIOSH");

being federal agencies responsible for administering federal laws and regulations designed to protect public health and safety and the environment in violation of 18 U.S.C.§ 371.

72. It was a purpose of the conspiracy to conceal and misrepresent the hazardous nature of the tremolite asbestos contaminated vermiculite, thereby enriching defendants and others.

73. It was a purpose of the conspiracy to increase profits and avoid liability by misleading the government and preventing the government from using its authorities to protect against risks to human health and the environment associated with the manufacture, processing, distribution, commerce, use, handling, disposal, and release of tremolite asbestos contaminated vermiculite.

MANNER AND MEANS OF THE CONSPIRACY

The following manner and means, among others, were used by the defendants to effectuate and perpetuate the conspiracy set forth above:

74. It was part of the conspiracy that the defendants obtained knowledge of the hazardous nature of the tremolite asbestos contaminated vermiculite through various means, including, but not limited to: scientific testing and analysis, including animal studies; epidemiological studies of employees; employee medical screening and examinations; employee medical record reviews; collection and evaluation of a deceased employee's lung tissue; review of employee death certificates; conducting employee morbidity and mortality studies; employee autopsy reviews; review of medical and scientific literature; reviewing

reports from insurance carriers; and reviewing employee worker's compensation claims.

75. It was part of the conspiracy that the defendants obtained knowledge of the propensity of tremolite asbestos contaminated vermiculite, when disturbed, to release fibers into the ambient air (also known as "friability") through various means, including, but not limited to: product testing, including attic simulation and vermiculite materials handling tests ("drop tests"); and air and bulk sampling at the Libby Mine and other defendant W.R. GRACE facilities in and around Libby, Montana, at defendant W.R. GRACE owned and licensed expansion plants, at the facilities of customers using vermiculite materials, and at the Libby High School track.

76. It was part of the conspiracy that the defendants concealed the full extent of their knowledge of the hazardous nature and friability of the tremolite asbestos contaminated vermiculite from employees of defendant W.R. GRACE Libby vermiculite mining and processing operations; families of employees of defendant W.R. GRACE Libby vermiculite mining and processing operations; industrial customers of defendant W.R. GRACE Libby vermiculite products; employees of industrial customers of defendant W.R. GRACE Libby vermiculite products; residents of Libby, Montana and surrounding communities in Lincoln County, Montana; and government authorities.

77. It was part of the conspiracy that the defendants obstructed, impeded, and frustrated the governmental authorities by withholding information regarding the hazardous nature and friability of the tremolite asbestos contaminated vermiculite

and asserting that the Libby Mine operations and Libby vermiculite posed no risk to public health and safety and the environment.

78. It was part of the conspiracy that the defendants marketed and sold tremolite asbestos contaminated vermiculite and products containing tremolite asbestos contaminated vermiculite.

79. It was part of the conspiracy that the defendants sold and leased tremolite asbestos contaminated real property and withheld information about the contamination from the purchasers of the property.

80. It was part of the conspiracy that defendants provided and distributed tremolite asbestos contaminated vermiculite material to the community, resulting in releases of asbestos into the ambient air in and around Libby, Montana and surrounding communities in Lincoln County, Montana.

81. It was part of the conspiracy that defendants caused W.R. GRACE employees and their personal effects and clothing to be contaminated with tremolite asbestos and allowed them to leave the Libby mine with these contaminated clothes, resulting in releases of tremolite asbestos into the ambient air in and around Libby, Montana and surrounding communities in Lincoln County, Montana.

82. It was part of the conspiracy that the defendants falsely described, concealed from, and failed to reveal to the government the hazardous nature and friability of the tremolite asbestos in the Libby vermiculite and the health hazards associated with exposure to tremolite asbestos.

83. It was part of the conspiracy that the defendants obstructed, impaired, impeded, and misled EPA during the course of EPA's emergency response to the asbestos contamination in and around Libby, Montana.

OVERT ACTS

In furtherance of the conspiracy and to effect its objectives, defendants, together with each other and with other persons known and unknown to the grand jury committed numerous overt acts in the District of Montana and elsewhere including, but not limited to, the following:

Eschenbach Study

84. Sometime prior to August 23, 1976, defendant ESCHENBACH gathered information regarding the lung health of defendant W.R. GRACE employees at the Libby Mine. This information was reported by an employee of defendant W.R. GRACE to defendant WOLTER in a memo dated August 23, 1976:

> Statistics provided by Harry Eschenbach indicated of eighteen (18) age sixty-five (65) normal retirements, three (3) had normal chests, one (1) had no records and fourteen (14) had positive lung disease, i.e. either significant scar tissue on the lung or significant fibrosis; there have been five (5) long term disability claims, three (3) of these were employees with six (6) years of service and two (2) with between fifteen (15) and twenty-five (25) years of service. Sixty-three (63) percent of all Libby employees with over ten (10) years of service test positive.

Commission of the Fairleigh Dickinson Animal Toxicology Study (Hamster Study)

85. On or about March 15, 1976, defendants W.R. GRACE and co-conspirators contracted with Dr. William Smith of Fairleigh Dickinson University to conduct animal toxicological studies on Libby Mine tremolite asbestos and vermiculite for

70,000.00 dollars (the "Hamster Study"). The contract between defendant W.R. GRACE and Dr. Smith prohibited Dr. Smith from publishing the results of the study in scientific literature without the permission of defendant W.R. GRACE.

86. From on or about January 1977 through approximately October 1977, Dr. Smith and an employee of defendant W.R. GRACE provided regular status reports to defendants W.R. GRACE, FAVORITO, ESCHENBACH, and WOLTER on the findings of the Hamster Study showing progressive evidence of asbestos related lung disease, including a significant incidence of mesothelioma.

87. On or about May 25, 1978, Dr. Smith provided defendant W.R. GRACE a preliminary draft Final Report of the Hamster Study. The draft report concluded that 10 hamsters had died of mesothelioma, and that the findings of tumors were evidence that tremolite asbestos fibers in the sizes tested were carcinogenic (caused cancer).

88. A consultant hired by defendant W.R. GRACE revised Dr. Smith's preliminary draft Final Report including the removal of the statement that the findings of tumors in response to tremolite asbestos fibers were evidence that tremolite asbestos fibers in the sizes tested were carcinogenic (caused cancer). Defendant W.R. GRACE did not grant Dr. Smith permission to publish the results of the study in scientific literature.

The Enbionics Review

89. On or about March 29, 1977, an employee of defendant W.R. GRACE wrote a memo directing another employee of defendant W.R. GRACE to coordinate a meeting to discuss a professional epidemiological study of defendant W.R.

20

Environmental Crimes Deskbook

Appendix 13 Gibson Guitar NPA

U.S. Department of Justice

United States Attorney
Middle District of Tennessee

Suite A-961
110 9th Avenue South
Nashville, Tennessee 37203-3870

Telephone (615) 736-5151
Fax (615) 736-5323

July 27, 2012

Donald A. Carr, Esq.
William M. Sullivan Jr., Esq.
Pillsbury Winthrop Shaw Pittman, LLP
2300 N Street, NW
Washington, DC 20037

Re: Gibson Guitar Corporation

Dear Mr. Carr and Mr. Sullivan:

On the understandings specified below, the United States Attorney's office for the Middle District of Tennessee (hereinafter referred to as "this Office") and the United States Department of Justice, Environmental Crimes Section (hereinafter referred to as "ECS"), (hereinafter collectively referred to as "the Government"), and Gibson Guitar Corp. (hereinafter referred to as "Gibson"), by its undersigned attorneys, pursuant to the authority granted by Gibson's Board of Directors, hereby enter into this Criminal Enforcement Agreement ("the Agreement").

This Agreement is part of a resolution of criminal matters relating to allegations that Gibson ordered, purchased, or imported ebony and/or other wood originating in Madagascar, and ebony and rosewood originating in India, to the United States in violation of the Lacey Act, Title 16, United States Code, Section 3371, *et seq.* and other applicable civil and criminal laws, including, but not limited to Conspiracy, Title 18, United States Code, Section 371. A related agreement resolves the related civil forfeiture matters as further described below.

By this Agreement the Government agrees that it will not prosecute any criminal action, against Gibson (except for criminal tax violations, as to which the Government cannot and does not make any agreement) related to violations of the Lacey Act or any other law resulting from Gibson's order, purchase, or importation of ebony and/or other wood from Madagascar and ebony and rosewood from India, from the beginning of this matter through the date of execution of this Agreement, including without limitation, from June 2008 through September 2009, as described, in part, in Appendix A (Statement of Facts) hereto, which is incorporated by reference herein. The Government enters into this Agreement based, in part, on the following factors: (a) Gibson's voluntary disclosure of the facts described in Appendix A; (b) Gibson's cooperation with the Government and the investigation conducted by the Fish and Wildlife Service; (c) remedial efforts already undertaken, and to be undertaken, by Gibson, as described in Appendix B (Lacey Act Compliance Plan) hereto, which is incorporated by reference herein; (d) unique considerations relative to Malagasy/U.S. diplomatic relations; and (e) the evidence discovered during the course of the investigation.

It is understood that Gibson accepts and acknowledges responsibility for the conduct set forth in Appendix A. The parties agree that their public statements regarding this Agreement will not contradict the statement of facts in Appendix A.

No information given by or on behalf of Gibson as of the date of this Agreement or at the request of the Government (or any other information directly or indirectly derived there from) will be used against Gibson in any prosecution by the Government or other action against Gibson related to these matters. In the event of any material breach of this Agreement by Gibson, the preceding sentence shall become ineffective. This Agreement does not provide any protection against prosecution for any crimes except as set forth herein, and applies only to Gibson, and not to any other entities or individuals except as set forth in this Agreement. Gibson expressly understands that the protections provided to Gibson under this Agreement shall not apply to any acquirer or successor entities unless and until such acquirer or successor formally adopts and executes this Agreement.

This Agreement shall have a term of eighteen months from the date of this Agreement, except as specifically provided herein. It is understood that for the eighteen month term of this Agreement, Gibson shall: (a) commit no criminal violations; (b) truthfully and completely disclose, upon request, non-privileged information with respect to the activities of Gibson, its current and former directors, officers, and employees, and others, concerning the import or purchase of ebony or other woods for use in manufacturing guitars; and (c) bring to the Government's attention all criminal conduct by, or criminal investigations of, Gibson or any of its senior managerial employees, that comes to the attention of Gibson or its senior management, as well as any administrative proceeding or civil action brought by any governmental authority that alleges fraud or criminal violations by or against Gibson.

During the term of this Agreement, Gibson shall: (a) cooperate fully with the Government and any law enforcement agency designated by the Government regarding Lacey Act investigations (b) assist the Government in any Lacey Act investigation or prosecution arising out of the conduct described in this Agreement by providing logistical and technical support for any meeting, interview, grand jury proceeding, or any trial or other court proceeding concerning the Lacey Act; (c) use its best efforts promptly to secure the attendance and truthful statements or testimony of any officer, agent, or employee at any meeting or interview or before the grand jury or at any trial or other court proceeding; and (d) respond to requests for all non-privileged information, documents, records, or tangible evidence or any designated law enforcement agency inquiries concerning a Lacey Act investigation or prosecution.

It is understood that Gibson agrees to pay a monetary penalty of $300,000 to the United States. Gibson must pay this sum within ten days of executing this Agreement. Pursuant to the Lacey Act, 16 U.S.C. § 3375(d), the payment of the penalty imposed shall be directed to the Lacey Act Reward Account. Gibson acknowledges that no tax deduction may be sought in connection with this payment.

It is further understood that Gibson agrees to make a community service payment of $50,000 to the National Fish and Wildlife Foundation ("NFWF") to be used by NFWF or another organization selected by NFWF for the purpose of funding a project or projects related to research and/or activities to promote the conservation, identification, and/or propagation of protected tree species used in the musical instruments industry as well as the forests in which those species occur. Gibson acknowledges that no tax deduction may be sought in connection with this payment and that it shall not advertise this community service payment except as being a condition for resolving this matter.

It is further understood that Gibson will continue to strengthen its compliance, bookkeeping, and internal controls standards and procedures, as set forth in Appendix B. Gibson further agrees to report to the Government regarding its compliance with this Agreement at the mid-point of the term of the Agreement (9 months after its execution) and 60 days prior to the expiration of the 18-month term of the Agreement.

The Government and Gibson acknowledge and agree that certain questions and inconsistencies now exist regarding the tariff classification of ebony and rosewood fingerboard blanks pursuant to the Indian government's Foreign Trade Policy. Accordingly, the Government will not undertake enforcement actions related to Gibson's future orders, purchases, or imports of ebony and rosewood fingerboard blanks from India, unless and until the Government of India provides specific clarification that ebony and rosewood fingerboard blanks are expressly prohibited by laws related to Indian Foreign Trade Policy. The Government agrees to provide Gibson notice of any such clarification from the Government of India in the future and a reasonable period of time (60 days or as otherwise agreed) to address the potential change in the understanding of the law as it relates to shipments received by or en route to Gibson.

This Agreement shall have force and effect only upon the occurrence of both: (a) execution of this Agreement by the Government and Gibson; and (b) execution of a Civil Settlement Agreement in three civil forfeiture actions before the United States District Court for the Middle District of Tennessee: (a) United States v. Ebony Wood in Various Forms, Civ. No. 3:10-cv-00747, (b) United States v. 25 Bundles of Indian Ebony Wood, Civ. No. 3:11-cv-00913, and (c) United States v. Indian Ebony and Rosewood, Civ. No. 3:12-mc-00014 (in which a complaint has not yet been filed), whereby Gibson will withdraw any and all claims interposed in U.S. v. Ebony Wood in Various Forms, Civ. No. 3:10-cv-00747, pertaining to wood from Madagascar, and will withdraw any and all claims and file corresponding petitions for remission and mitigation, as provided by law, in the remaining two actions referenced in (b) and (c) above, pertaining to wood from India, which the Government does not oppose.

It is also understood that, if the Government determines that Gibson has committed crimes under the Lacey Act subsequent to the date of signing of this Agreement, determines that Gibson has given false, incomplete, or misleading testimony or information at any time, or should Gibson otherwise violate any material provision of this Agreement, Gibson shall thereafter be subject to prosecution for any federal violation of which the Government has knowledge. Any such prosecution that is not time-barred by the applicable statute of limitations on the date of the signing of this Agreement may be commenced against Gibson, notwithstanding the expiration of the statute of limitations between the signing of this Agreement and expiration of the term of this agreement plus one year. Thus, by signing this Agreement, Gibson agrees that the statute of limitations with respect to any prosecution that is not time-barred on the date that this Agreement is signed shall be tolled for the term of this Agreement plus one year.

It is further understood that, if the Government determines that Gibson has committed any crime after signing this Agreement, or that Gibson has given false, incomplete, or misleading testimony or information, or has otherwise violated any provision of this Agreement, the Government may proceed with further investigation and enforcement. In such further enforcement, Gibson shall not seek to suppress: a) any statements made by Gibson (through any of its current or former officers, directors, or employees) to the Government or other designated law enforcement agents in furtherance of the negotiation of the Agreement or between the date of the Agreement and the violation of the Agreement (including Appendix A hereto and any future testimony given by Gibson or its employees, agents, and officers, before any tribunal), under Rule 410 of the Federal Rules of Evidence or any other statutes, rules, or Constitutional provisions specifically pertaining to statements made to the Government during the course of plea discussions; and b) any information or evidence derived from leads based on any statements made by Gibson (through any of its current or former officers, directors, or employees) to the Government or other designated law enforcement agents in furtherance of the negotiation of the Agreement or between the date of the Agreement and the violation of the Agreement (including Appendix A hereto and any future testimony given by Gibson or its employees, agents, and officers, before any tribunal), under Rule 410 of the Federal Rules of Evidence or any other statutes, rules, or Constitutional provisions specifically pertaining to statements made to the Government during the course of plea discussions.

It is further understood that this Agreement does not bind any federal, state, local, or foreign prosecuting authority other than the Government as defined in this Agreement. The Government will, however, bring the cooperation of Gibson to the attention of other prosecuting and investigative offices, if requested by Gibson.

It is further understood that Gibson and the Government may disclose this Agreement and the attached appendices to the public.

With respect to this matter, from the date of execution of this agreement forward, this Agreement supersedes all prior, if any, understandings, promises, and / or conditions between the Government and Gibson. No additional promises, agreements, or conditions have been entered into than those set forth in this Agreement and none will be entered into unless in writing and signed by all parties.

Sincerely,

JERRY E. MARTIN
United States Attorney

JOHN K. WEBB
Deputy Chief, Criminal Division

IGNACIA S. MORENO
Assistant Attorney General
Environment and Natural Resources Div.

LANA N. PETTUS
Trial Attorney

JAMES B. NELSON
Trial Attorney

Acknowledged and Agreed by:

Donald A. Carr, Esq.
Attorney for Gibson Guitar Corp.

Date

William M. Sullivan, Jr., Esq.
Attorney for Gibson Guitar Corp.

Date

Bruce Mitchell
Executive Vice President, General Counsel, and
Corporate Secretary
Gibson Guitar Corp.

Date

JERRY E. MARTIN
United States Attorney

JOHN K. WEBB
Deputy Chief, Criminal Division

IGNACIA S. MORENO
Assistant Attorney General
Environment and Natural Resources Div.

LANA N. PETTUS
Trial Attorney

JAMES B. NELSON
Trial Attorney

Acknowledged and Agreed by:

Donald A. Carr, Esq.
Attorney for Gibson Guitar Corp.

Date

William M. Sullivan, Jr., Esq.
Attorney for Gibson Guitar Corp.

Date

Bruce Mitchell
Executive Vice President, General Counsel, and
Corporate Secretary
Gibson Guitar Corp.

Date

JERRY E. MARTIN
United States Attorney

JOHN K. WEBB
Deputy Chief, Criminal Division

IGNACIA S. MORENO
Assistant Attorney General
Environment and Natural Resources Div.

LANA N. PETTUS
Trial Attorney

JAMES B. NELSON
Trial Attorney

Acknowledged and Agreed by:

Donald A. Carr, Esq.
Attorney for Gibson Guitar Corp.

7-26-12
Date

William M. Sullivan, Jr., Esq.
Attorney for Gibson Guitar Corp.

7/26/12
Date

Bruce Mitchell
Executive Vice President, General Counsel, and
Corporate Secretary
Gibson Guitar Corp.

7/26/012
Date

APPENDIX A

STATEMENT OF FACTS

The parties agree that the facts to be resolved by this agreement are as follows:

1. Defendant Gibson Guitar Corp. ("Gibson") is a privately-held corporation incorporated in Delaware and headquartered and doing business in Nashville, Tennessee. It has a number of different divisions and subsidiaries that manufacture a variety of musical instruments, most notably guitars. Gibson's U.S. guitar manufacturing plants are located in Nashville (Gibson Electric/Gibson USA and part of Gibson Custom); Memphis, Tennessee (Gibson Custom); and Bozeman, Montana (Gibson Acoustic). Gibson also owns the guitar brand, Epiphone, which manufactures guitars in factories outside of the United States, including in China. The majority owners of Gibson are Henry Juskiewicz and David Berryman.

2. The manufacture of guitars includes the manufacture and use of parts called "fretboards," also referred to as "fingerboards." The fretboard of a guitar is the piece attached to the neck of the guitar, immediately under the strings. Technically, on a musical instrument that has frets, a fretboard may be distinguished from a fingerboard by the installation of frets that run perpendicular to the length of the fingerboard. Ebony is one type of wood used by Gibson to make fretboards for its guitars. "Fingerboard blanks" are sawn boards of wood manufactured into fretboards, by drying, cutting, and shaping them, among other steps. (See Figures 1 – 4). Gibson and others frequently refer to what this Agreement describes as "fingerboard blanks," simply as fingerboards. Gibson typically purchases wood in the form of fingerboard blanks cut to particular specifications (length, width, and thickness) from a variety of suppliers.

Figure 1 - Fretboard and two fingerboard blanks

Figure 2 - Fretboard and two fingerboard blank, edgewise

Figure 3 - Examples of progression of the manufacturing process from fingerboard blank to fretboard.

Figure 4 - Fretboards attached to guitar necks..

3. Madagascar Ebony (*Diospryos spp.*) is the term used to describe members of the genus *Disopryos* found naturally on the island of Madagascar. Madagascar Ebony is a slow-growing tree species and supplies are considered threatened in its native environment due to over-exploitation. Both legal and illegal logging of Madagascar Ebony and other tree species have significantly reduced Madagascar's forest cover. Madagascar's forests are home to many rare endemic species of plants and animals.

4. Gibson ordered ebony fingerboard blanks to use in the manufacture of guitars from T.N. GMBH, a company based in Hamburg, Germany. Based upon documentation now in Gibson's possession, T.N. purchased some of its ebony fingerboard blanks from R.T., a forestry operator in Madagascar. Gibson maintains that specific information concerning that sourcing was not provided to Gibson by T.N. when Gibson placed its orders. Gibson assumed, without asking, that T.N. had undertaken to provide it with lawfully harvested and exported materials and, after the execution of the search warrant in this case, T.N. represented to Gibson that it had supplied legally obtained and exported materials.

Malagasy Law and the Status of Ebony

5. The parties acknowledge that the following memoranda and orders were part of the applicable body of law in Madagascar relating to the harvest and export of ebony:

   a. Departmental Memorandum 001/06/MINENVEF/Mi, issued on February 15, 2006, by the Ministry of the Environment, Water, and Forests mandated that any stockpiles of ebony not declared to the Madagascar government prior to February 15, 2006, were illegal.

   b. Madagascar Interministerial Order 16.030/2006 was issued in September 2006 by three Malagasy Ministries: the Ministry of the Environment, Water, and Forests; the Ministry of Economy, Finance, and Budget; and the Ministry of Industrialization, Trade and Private Sector Development. Articles 1 and 5 of Interministerial Order 16.030/2006. Order 16.030/2006 banned all harvest of ebony and prohibited the export of ebony except in the form of "finished wood" or "finished products." According to the Department's translation of Interministerial Order 16.030/2006, the order further defined "finished" wood as "any wood that has been shaped and processed to its final use and is no longer capable of being modified." Interministerial Order 16.030/2006, Article 6, musical instrument parts, including "guitar fingerboards," were listed as one example of "finished products;" however, "fingerboard blanks" are not specifically listed.

c. In late 2008, the Republic of Madagascar compiled inventory records of existing stocks of previously harvested Madagascar ebony and rosewood. After compiling the inventory and determining whether any wood in the stockpiles was legal, "exceptional authority" was granted to specific forest operators to export specific quantities of ebony logs and rosewood pieces and logs. Interministerial Order 003/2009. R.T., who supplied Madagascar ebony to T.N., was listed in the order as being granted exceptional authority to export pieces of rosewood from his stockpiles. R.T. was not listed as having been granted exceptional authority to export ebony logs.

June 2008 Madagascar Trip

6. At the invitation of Greenpeace and other non-profit environmental groups, on June 9, 2008, a Gibson wood product specialist ("Gibson representative") flew to Madagascar for a "fact finding" trip with a group called the "MusicWood Coalition," spearheaded by Greenpeace. The trip was designed to assess the potential for supporting sustainable forestry in Madagascar. Part of the justification for the Gibson representative's participation in the trip was that the ebony species preferred for some of Gibson's instruments is found in Madagascar.

7. In connection with the trip, the Gibson representative received a translation of Madagascar Interministerial Order 16.030/2006, banning the harvest of ebony and the export of any ebony products that were not in finished form. The translation of the Order received by the Gibson representative stated that "fingerboards" are considered "finished" under Madagascar Law. Participants in the MusicWood Coalition trip to Madagascar, including the Gibson representative, were informed by trip organizers that, under the organizers' interpretation of the 2006 Interministerial Order, the harvest of ebony was illegal and that instrument part "blanks" would be considered "unfinished" and, therefore, considered illegal to export.

8. Following the trip, one of the trip organizers, produced a trip report that contained the following statements, among others:

   a. "There are many legal issues pending on wood harvesting and export particularly with ebony and rosewood. It is currently illegal to harvest or export ebony."

   b. "Currently, all wood products have to be in a final finished form before they can be exported. This issue would have to be addressed as instrument makers require wood blanks and pieces that can be further processed to desired dimensions. A possible export contract document that specified dimensions was suggested by the chief law enforcement officer that was traveling with us as a way to comply with finished form regulations. This would have to [be] negotiated at the government level."

c. "It is currently illegal to harvest any species from natural forests until permitting has been resolved."

d. "Proving legality is a major problem and tracking woods from origin is even harder."

e. "There are at least two companies that have controlled the wood export for ebonies and rosewoods both of which sell to [T.N.].... We visited [R.T.]'s ([T.N.] supplier) wood yard and he is obviously a main player in the market....His wood is under temporary seizure and cannot be moved."

The trip report, containing the above statements, was also attached to an email sent to the Gibson representative and Gibson's President. The Gibson representative forwarded an email, with the trip report attached, to a Gibson wood purchaser and others.

Gibson Ebony Purchases After June 2008

9. Based on documentation received by Gibson, T .N. continued to receive shipments of wood from R.T., including ebony fingerboard blanks, exported from Madagascar in 2007, after Interministerial Order 16.030/2006 became effective.

10. According to import documentation as described in the table below, Gibson continued to order Madagascar ebony fingerboard blanks after June 20, 2008. According to import documentation, shipments of Madagascar Ebony fingerboard blanks destined for Gibson entered the United States on the following dates, at the following ports, in the following amounts, for the following invoiced amounts:

Arrival Date	**10/2/2008**	**12/22/2008**	**4/2/2009**	**9/28/2009**
Port of Entry	Charleston, SC	Newark, NJ	Charleston, SC	New York, NY
Quantity (pcs.)	5147	2014	9066	7133
Invoice Amount	$52,036.17	$32,505.96	$100,985.16	$76,317.59

11. Gibson's President received from the Gibson representative, as early as April 2007, information that Gibson had purchased Madagascar ebony from T.N. The trip report emailed to Gibson's President and the Gibson representative indicated that R.T. was a supplier for T.N.'s Madagascar wood. The Gibson representative reported to his superiors on February 25, 2009, that in light of political instability and violence in Madagascar, R.T. would be able to supply T.N. with ebony "for the grey market," referring to wood that was not documented to be the product of sustainable forestry practices.

12. Gibson placed and confirmed orders for, and accepted delivery of, at least some of the shipments of Madagascar ebony fingerboard blanks listed in paragraph 10 and scheduled delivery of shipments of Madagascar ebony fingerboard blanks listed in paragraph 10 after June 20, 2008. Gibson also made payments to T.N. and its agent, a Connecticut-based import company, toward the purchase of the Madagascar ebony fingerboard blanks after June 20, 2008.

13. For the shipment of Madagascar ebony fingerboard blanks that entered the United States on September 28, 2009, the Madagascar customs documents reflect the ebony was described as classified under series 4418.9010 of the Harmonized Tariff Code ("HTC") when it left Madagascar. The 4418 series applies to "Builders' joinery and carpentry of wood, including cellular wood panels and assembled flooring panels; shingles, and shakes." HTC 4418.90 applies to a subcategory of "other" within the larger category of wood used by builders. Subcategories under 4418.90 include "drilled or notched lumber studs," "wood flooring," arches, roof trusses, and "prefabricated partitions and panels for buildings."

14. The U.S. Customs documents reflect that when the September 28, 2009, shipment entered the United States, T.N., acting though a U.S.-based agent, declared the ebony for U.S. Customs purposes under a different tariff classification, HTC series 4407 (wood sawn or chipped lengthwise, sliced or peeled, whether or not planed, sanded, or end-jointed), from that used when then shipment left Madagascar. No evidence exists to demonstrate that Gibson prepared or participated in the preparation of the tariff classifications at issue.

15. Between June 20, 2008, and November 17, 2009, Gibson did not ask for or obtain paperwork or official assurances from officials in Madagascar that the wood it was purchasing from Madagascar through its German supplier was legally harvested and exported from Madagascar, notwithstanding the information received by Gibson during the June 2008 trip to Madagascar. Before November 2009, Gibson further did not ask for additional paperwork or other confirmation from its supplier that the wood it was purchasing from Madagascar was legally harvested and exported, although

T.N. supplied information to Gibson purporting to represent the wood's legality after the execution of the search warrant. Instead, Gibson relied on the fact that T.N. was an established, FSC chain of custody certified supplier. Before ordering or accepting delivery of the fingerboards, Gibson should have taken a more active role and exercised additional diligence with respect to documentation of legal forestry practices in the areas of Madagascar from which those shipments from its wood supplier may have originated. Information received by the Gibson representative during the June 2008 trip to Madagascar was not further investigated or acted upon, prior to the continuing placement of orders with the supplier, T.N. Information sent to company management by the Gibson representative and others following the June 2008 trip to Madagascar also was not further investigated or acted upon, prior to the continuing placement of orders with the supplier, T.N. Instead, Gibson continued to purchase Madagascar ebony after June 20, 2008.

16. The investigation into the harvest and export of valuable tone woods served important environmental and law enforcement objectives, and accordingly, Gibson ceased acquisitions from Madagascar following the execution of the search warrants. Gibson now recognizes that its duties under the Lacey Act with respect to the acquisition of musical instrument parts from foreign sources include reasonable corroboration of the circumstances of their harvest and export, so as to guard against the acquisition of wood of illegal origin.

APPENDIX B

Lacey Act Compliance Program

1 Compliance Objectives

As an industry leader, Gibson is committed to helping to conserve, protect and restore threatened forest habitats and safeguarding the future of natural resources critical to making musical instruments. A large part of this commitment is the support and use of legally harvested and exported sustainable wood sources. Compliance with relevant laws including the Lacey Act (16 U.S.C. §§ 3371 *et seq.*), amendments, or regulatory interpretations of the Lacey Act, is a critical component of a transparent, legal, and sustainable supply chain. The objective of this compliance program is to support legal wood sourcing through the implementation of a structured Lacey Act compliance program, which will expand upon the sustainability goals of Gibson's existing Responsible Wood Purchasing Policy. This document sets forth Gibson's policies, procedures and processes with regard to Lacey Act compliance ("Lacey Act Compliance Program").

2 Legal Background

The Lacey Act is the oldest wildlife protection statute in the United States. Initially enacted to protect animal species, the Lacey Act was amended, effective May 22, 2008, to include plant species. A major rationale for the inclusion of plant species in the Lacey Act was to prevent trade in illegally harvested lumber and wood products made from illegally harvested lumber.

2.1 General Prohibitions Under the Lacey Act

The Lacey Act makes it unlawful to:

- Trade in any plant that is taken, possessed, transported, or sold in violation of the laws of the United States, a State, Indian Tribe, or any foreign law that protects plants;
- Falsify or submit falsified documents, accounts or records of any plant covered by the Lacey Act;
- Import plants and plant products (with some exemptions) without an import declaration.

As it concerns Gibson, the definition of plant contained in the Lacey Act includes wood used for the purposes of manufacturing guitars or guitar parts. The full text of the Lacey Act can be found at attachment A. In addition, a useful reference guide can be found at http://www.aphis.usda.gov/plant_health/lacey_act/index.shtml.

2.2 Lacey Act Penalties

Violations of the Lacey Act carry serious penalties for companies and individuals. In addition to civil fines and forfeiture of goods, criminal penalties may also attach to individuals or companies found to have knowingly and, in some cases with lack of due care, violated the Lacey Act.

A misdemeanor violation of the Lacey Act, punishable by 1 year in prison and a fine of $100,000 ($200,000 for companies), may be found if, in the exercise of due care, the individual or the company should have known the wood it purchased was illegally taken, possessed, transported or sold. Felony culpability, punishable by 5 years in prison and a $250,000 ($500,000 for companies), may lie for knowing violations of the Lacey Act.

2.3 Due Care Standard

To exercise due care, one must use the degree of care which a reasonably prudent person would exercise under the same or similar circumstances. The exercise of due care will minimize the risk of purchasing plant products that were harvested or traded illegally. A Lacey Act violation may also occur if an individual or company fails to exercise due care in evaluating its supply chain.

The obligation to exercise due care accordingly requires that certain reasonable steps be undertaken to ensure that the Lacey Act is not being violated and wood is not being purchased in violation of the relevant laws in the place of origin. As such, Gibson seeks to enhance its current due care standards when purchasing wood products. As a part of this effort all purchasing staff at each division are trained annually (see Section 3.5) to follow this legal compliance plan and shall adhere to the following steps prior to purchasing any wood product:

- Step 1: Communicate with suppliers about Gibson's policies to determine any challenges the supplier may have in implementing the policies and work with the supplier to solve the issue.
- Step 2: Ask Questions to find as much information as possible regarding the supplier and where wood based products are originating, using "Gibson's Legal Compliance Procurement Checklist" (example questions from which are attached hereto at attachment A) to determine whether the product meets Gibson's minimum requirements for known/legal wood products.
- Step 3: Do not rely solely on the checklist to identify risky sources, but conduct independent research and exercise care before making a purchase. This may include internet research, consultation with U.S. or foreign-based experts or authorities, arranging an on site supplier/forest visit, if possible, or speaking with local authorities and/or experts on documentation required for legal export and the validity of such documentation received from the supplier. (see Sections 3.2 and 3.3)
- Step 4: Request sample documentation prior to wood purchase to reasonably ensure that all forms provide sufficient information to comply with the Lacey Act requirements and to assist in verifying the validity of the documentation as described in Step 3.
- Step 5: Make a determination based on a review of all of the information collected.
- Step 6: Maintain records documenting all efforts to ensure legality.
- Step 7: In the event uncertainty exists regarding satisfaction of the above criteria or the ultimate determination of legal compliance, Gibson's policy is that Gibson should not pursue the purchase.

3 Gibson Policies and Procedures

Gibson is committed to exercising due care in determining whether prospective wood sources are legal prior to purchase. Gibson's due care standard is outlined in Section 2.3 and supplemented by Gibson's policies and procedures. Gibson will not knowingly purchase wood that has been illegally harvested or exported from its country of origin. If Gibson discovers that an importer/supplier has engaged in illegal activities, it will cease business dealings with the violating entity and, where appropriate, notify the relevant enforcement agency.

3.1 Procurement of Wood

Gibson's objective is to procure wood products sourced from forests where legal harvest and chain of custody can be verified and from recycled sources. Gibson encourages all of its suppliers to work with a third-party certification group, such as the Forest Stewardship Council (FSC), to validate the legality and sustainability of their harvesting practices. Gibson requires that wood suppliers who claim their product is "certified" maintain valid FSC or equivalent certification and that the certification number (CoC # in the case of FSC) be listed on each invoice. These third-party certified claims will be verified on an annual basis by Gibson during its Supply Chain Audit (see section 3.4). Gibson also requires that all shipments of wood that it receives, whether from the original wood supplier or an importer, include copies of all relevant import forms and declarations (including required Lacey Act Plant declarations) and export documentation, including from the country of origin and/or harvest. All Gibson importers and suppliers will also be required to furnish to Gibson copies of any applicable export or business licenses that they maintain to be updated on at least an annual basis.

3.2 Verification of Foreign Law and Foreign Certifications/Licenses

When working with a new supplier or new country of origin, or during the annual Supply Chain Audit for existing suppliers and sources, Gibson will make a reasonable inquiry into the foreign laws governing the protection and export of wood from the country of origin where Gibson wood purchases originate. Gibson will make such inquiry directly of applicable foreign government agencies or, if appropriate, of practitioners of law in such countries. Gibson will also work with third-party certifiers, non-profit organizations or NGOs dedicated to sustainable sourcing practices to supplement its inquiry into foreign law.

3.3 Using Watch Lists and Other Resources to Determine Risk

When working with a new supplier or new country of origin, or during the annual Supply Chain Audit for existing suppliers and sources, Gibson will research available information on illegal logging practices to perform a risk assessment at the species level, considering source location, using the following key resources to determine or clarify risk:

- CITES (Convention on International Trade in Endangered Species) listed tree species;
- IUCN (International Union for the Conservation of Nature) Red List of Threatened Plants;

- National endangered or threatened species lists (typically listed in government legislation, natural heritage databases, etc.) – available through government agencies or conservation-oriented NGOs; and,
- UNEP-WCMC (World Conservation Monitoring Centre) tree species database (http://www.unep-wcmc.org/trees/trade/ara_ang.htm).

Gibson will refer to the sources above to identify countries and regions that are substantially impacted by illegal logging. In addition to consulting the above sources, Gibson will use reasonable efforts to research any available industry or governmental guidance related to the appropriate measures for verifying the legality of wood originating from countries designated as high risk by any reliable third-party certifier, governmental agency or NGO. At annual training sessions (see Section 3.5) the results of Gibson's risk assessment will be relayed to Gibson employees involved in purchasing. In addition, any purchases from countries or regions designated as high risk will require a heightened level of diligence.

For instance, in addition to complying with all other Gibson policies and procedures, wood can only be purchased from a country source identified as high risk if (a) the product is certified against a chain of custody or traceability standard, (b) the supplier certificate is valid and the scope includes the product supplied, (c) the product has been traced by Gibson along an unbroken and verified chain of custody from the purchaser back to the source entirely by obtaining supplier certification codes on documentation for that product down to forest level, and (d) the harvest and export of the species is not restricted or prohibited in the source country.

3.4 Supply Chain Audit

On an annual basis Gibson will conduct an audit of its wood purchasing practices that evaluates all documents, certifications, licenses, and other records associated with its wood purchases to ensure compliance with Gibson's Lacey Act Compliance Program. During this audit, Gibson will evaluate the adherence to existing laws governing the protection and export of wood from all countries where Gibson wood purchases originate. At this time, Gibson will also make inquiries of foreign government agencies, third-party certifiers, non-profit organizations, or NGOs as to changes in foreign forestry or export laws. To the extent practical, the Supply Chain Audit will include audits of each division's application of the Compliance Program. The Supply Chain Audit will identify any material weaknesses in Gibson's Lacey Act Compliance Program and establish appropriate corrective action, to include amending the compliance program as necessary to reflect changes in the laws.

3.5 Training

On an annual basis, following the Supply Chain Audit, Gibson will conduct Lacey Act compliance training seminars with employees and managers responsible for wood purchases to reinforce the importance of complying with Gibson's Lacey Act Compliance Program and to provide updates on applicable law, high risk countries, and identified weaknesses in compliance. A training record will be created for each training session. As necessary, Gibson will also conduct training sessions for wood suppliers to educate them on Gibson legality requirements and to provide them with links to existing resources.

3.6 Retention of Records

All records associated with Gibson's Lacey Act Compliance Program will be retained for at leas 5 years.

3.7 Disciplinary Action for Non-Compliance

Any Gibson employee that is found to have violated any of the procedures contained in Gibson's Lacey Act Compliance Program will be subject to discipline and possible termination. Gibson will maintain records related to any such disciplinary action in the personnel files of any impacted employee.

4 Conclusion

Gibson is committed to a successful implementation of its Lacey Act Compliance Program and the broader goals of sustainable and lawful sourcing that the program seeks to promote. Gibson will endeavor to share its methods and results of its compliance efforts with others in the musical instrument manufacturing industry in an effort to be a leader in this area.

ATTACHMENT A – SAMPLE CHECKLIST QUESTIONS

1. Does supplier have long standing relationships with the supplier/s (exporter) of this product? How long?
2. Do the supplier/s of this supplier buy this product from 'spot markets'?
3. Does supplier regularly question their suppliers regarding the origin of this product?
4. Did supplier provide you with all required documentation?
    a. e.g., for non high risk countries, a written and signed document from supplier identifying companies included in the full supply chain of the product back to the harvesting entity/ies, including name and location of the harvesting entity/ies and Forest Management Unit.
    b. A list of supplying companies harvesting wood from source forests and copies of the associated harvesting permits for supplied product and/or other form of authorization from the forest owner, including, for example:
        i. species, district of origin information and any other related harvesting or purchasing agreements.
    c. Evidence of compliance with timber transportation documents: Copies of transport or sales permits with specification of species and volumes as applicable.
5. Have you reviewed the documents and verified that they meet Gibson requirements?
6. Is there any reason for supplier to believe that paperwork from their suppliers may not be authentic for this product?
7. Is there a ban on exports from this region/country?
8. Have you checked on approved species/products with State/Province for that supplier?, etc.)
9. Have you retained copies of required documentation?
10. Is this supplier sourcing from a high risk country?

11. If yes, verify that additional required procedures were followed, e.g.,

a. **product is certified against a Chain of Custody or Traceability Standard,**

b. **the supplier certificate is valid and the scope includes the product supplied,**

c. **the product has been traced by Gibson along an unbroken and verified chain of custody from the purchaser back to the source entirely by obtaining supplier certification codes on documentation for that product down to forest level, and**

d. **the harvest and export of the species is not restricted or prohibited in the source country.**

Sample checklist items.doc

Environmental Crimes Deskbook

Appendix 14 Search Warrant

CONFIDENTIAL

SUPERIOR COURT OF NEW JERSEY
LAW DIVISION - CRIMINAL
COUNTY OF WARREN

CORRECTED

STATE OF NEW JERSEY)
) ss.
COUNTY OF WARREN)

SEARCH WARRANT

TO: STATE INVESTIGATOR MICHAEL KANE, ANY OFFICER OF THE NEW JERSEY DIVISION OF CRIMINAL JUSTICE, OR ANY LAW ENFORCEMENT OFFICER HAVING JURISDICTION.

1. This matter being opened to the Court by State Investigator Michael Kane on application for the issuance of a search warrant for the premises of Atlantic States Cast Iron Pipe (Atlantic States), a division of McWane, Inc., located at 183 Sitgreaves Street, Phillipsburg, New Jersey, and the Court having reviewed the affidavit under oath of State Investigator Michael Kane and being satisfied therefrom that probable cause exists to believe that evidence of violations of the following laws of the State of New Jersey is located therein: the crime of unlawfully causing a hazardous discharge required to be reported pursuant to the Spill Compensation and Control Act, contrary to N.J.S.A. 2C:17-2a(2); and the crime of discharging a pollutant without a permit, contrary to N.J.S.A. 58:10A-6a and N.J.S.A. 58:10A-10f(1)(a). The Court hereby grants the State the right to search the premises of Atlantic States Cast Iron Pipe in the following manner:

2. The premises to be searched are more particularly described as follows.

The multiple addresses for the facility, as listed in the Office of the Phillipsburg Tax Assessor's records are 183 Sitgreaves Street, 181 Sitgreaves Street, 1 Jefferson Street, and 1 Limekiln Road, Phillipsburg, New Jersey. The property occupies Block

2001, Lot 1, Block 1904, Lot 21, Block 2008, Lots 1, 2, 3 and 4, Block 2503, Lot 9, and Block 2506, Lot 21. The total area is 25.339 acres.

This is an industrial manufacturing facility which extends for approximately five city blocks. The facility is used for the production of ductile pipe. The property is bordered on the north by Stockton Street, on the west by Sitgreaves Street, on the south by Center Street, and on the east by Conrail heavy freight line railroad tracks. On the northwest corner of the property, the corner of Stockton and Sitgreaves Streets, is a large white sign with bluish-gray lettering which reads, "Atlantic States Pipe. A Division of McWane, Inc." Extending from the northern border of the property to the south, the first building is a dark gray corrugated steel building which is a city block in length. There is a silver steel rectangular structure on the top of this building and additional gabled portions on the southern and eastern sides of the building. This gabled portion is silver in color. Rising above the large gray steel building is the most distinctive feature of the complex. This feature consists of two green smoke stacks. The western most stack is approximately double the circumference as the eastern stack. Both stacks have a helical feature which extends from the outer circumference of each stack and runs vertically around each stack extending where they are visible from the street, from the base to the top of the stacks.

Proceeding south along Sitgreaves Street, the next building is a two story red brick structure with a sign, to the left side of the door, hanging from a bracket which reads "Atlantic States Pipe. A Division of McWane, Inc." There is a one story brick building attached to the two story structure extending to the south. Immediately south of the one story red brick structure is a dark gray corrugated steel building with no windows on the side facing out towards Sitgreaves.

Running south, the next building is a three story red brick building. Continuing south is the entrance gate to the property. The gate is across from McKeen Street. On the gate is a large white sign reading, "Atlantic States Pipe, A Division of McWane, Inc." Continuing south from the gate is a medium gray guard shack. A red and white striped wooden gate, with red lights affixed to the edge, controls access to the property. The gate is vertically rotating which opens to the south. A two story brick building is next to the guard shack, which opens onto a large open yard where pipe is stored. A very large warehouse type of building is to the south of the yard. The size of this building is comparable to a large airplane hangar. The structure appears to be about forty feet high where it ultimately tapers into a point where the roof line extends upward for another fifteen feet. Across from the facility, four city streets intersect Sitgreaves Street from the west. The four intersecting streets from the north are Jefferson Street, McKeen Street, Smith Avenue and Abbott Street.

3. You are commanded to search, with the assistance of necessary personnel, the premises of Atlantic States, as previously described in paragraph 2 above for any physical evidence and documents relating to violations of <u>N.J.S.A.</u> 2C:17-2a(2), and <u>N.J.S.A.</u> 58:10A-6a and <u>N.J.S.A.</u> 58:10A-10f(1)(a). The search is to include any offices, furnaces, outbuildings, trailers, drums, pits, sludge piles and smoke stacks. The search is to encompass any and all desks, filing cabinets, storage cabinets, bookcases, shelves, closets, locker rooms, bathrooms upon which any and all of the above-described items are stored, and anyplace where documents and physical evidence related to the enumerated crimes in this paragraph are or may be located.

You are hereby commanded to:

(1) search for and seize records, documentation, lists, notes, telephone numbers and correspondence which reflect the names of companies and/or individuals involved in the treatment, transportation and disposal of hazardous waste or solid waste material generated by Atlantic States;

(2) search for and seize any documents which would indicate either the origination, the generation and/or disposal of hazardous waste or toxic pollutants from Atlantic States;

(3) search for and seize all records on site for evidence of cleaning of the furnaces, personnel scheduling records, company procedures for disposal/cleanup of spills on the property, all notifications concerning spills and other environmentally sensitive incidents;

(4) search the facility and seize samples from all waste pits;

(5) inspect the system from which the discharges originated;

(6) search the facility and seize samples of all oils or cleaning substances that could have been utilized for the cleaning of the foundry furnaces;

(7) search for and seize any documents which reflect any transportation and/or disposal of hazardous waste or toxic pollutants from Atlantic States;

(8) search for and seize any documents relating to the collection and handling of any hazardous substances, hazardous wastes or toxic pollutants from Atlantic States;

(9) Obtain samples of any possible pollutants or hazardous wastes or substances or toxic pollutants from any drums, containers, cans, vats or vessels located at Atlantic States;

(10) obtain samples of any soil which appears to be contaminated by pollutants or hazardous waste;

(11) conduct a floroscene dye test of the storm drains located on the site for the purpose of determining the course the oily discharge followed when released from the facility;

(12) conduct a dye test to determine the concentration and type of materials being discharged.

4. You are further commanded to seize all physical evidence (as fully described in the preceding paragraph) relating to the violations of law as set forth at the beginning of this warrant.

5. You are further commanded in the event you seize any of the above-described evidence to give a receipt for the property so seized to the person from whom it was taken, or in the absence of such person, to leave a copy of this warrant, together with such receipt, upon the premises from which the property was taken.

6. You are also authorized to take photographs and use videotape cameras during the execution of the warrant and to be accompanied by all necessary personnel during the execution of the warrant.

7. You are further commanded to execute this warrant within ten (10) days from the issuance hereof, between the hours of 6:00 a.m. to 6:00 p.m., and are authorized to continue the execution of this warrant and to re-enter the premises at any time and on as many occasions as are reasonably necessary to complete the gathering of evidence for a period not to exceed ten (10) days after the issuance of this warrant. During this time period, the State will not be required to maintain a continuous presence, unless

you so deem it necessary to preserve evidence.

8. You are authorized to use any personnel necessary to execute this warrant.

9. You are commanded after completing the execution of this warrant to make a prompt return to the Court.

10. Given and issued under my hand at 8:50 o'clock, a. m., this 23rd* day of February, 2000, at Belvidere, N.J.

JUDGE OF THE SUPERIOR COURT

* This search warrant was signed on Feb 23, 2000, but inadvertently not dated. This correction adds the date when the search warrant was signed.

2-24-00

J.S.C.

JOHN F. KINGFIELD

-6-

Environmental Crimes Deskbook

Appendix 15 McWane (N.D. Ala.) Court Jury Instructions (4.5.05)

FILED
2005 Apr-07 PM 02:09
U.S. DISTRICT COURT
N.D. OF ALABAMA

IN THE UNITED STATES DISTRICT COURT FOR THE NORTHERN DISTRICT OF ALABAMA SOUTHERN DIVISION

UNITED STATES OF AMERICA

v. **CR 04-PT-199-S**

MCWANE, INC., JAMES DELK, MICHAEL DEVINE, CHARLES "BARRY" ROBISON, and DONALD BILLS

Defendants.

ORDER

The attached are draft proposed jury instructions. The parties will bring to the conference on April 11 written objections, proposed additions and proposed changes.

DONE and **ORDERED** this the 7th day of April, 2005.

Robert B. Propst

ROBERT B. PROPST
SENIOR UNITED STATES DISTRICT JUDGE

COURT'S INSTRUCTIONS

Members of the Jury:

It is now my duty to instruct you on the rules of law that you must follow and apply in deciding this case. When I have finished you will go to the jury room and begin your discussions–what we call your deliberations.

It will be your duty to decide whether the Government has proved beyond a reasonable doubt the specific facts necessary to find a Defendant guilty of a crime charged in the indictment.

You must make your decision only on the basis of the testimony and other evidence presented here during the trial; and you must not be influenced in any way by either sympathy or prejudice for or against the Defendant or the Government.

You must follow the law as I explain it to you whether you agree with that law or not; and you must follow all of my instructions as a whole. You may not single out, or disregard, any of the Court's instructions on the law.

The indictment or formal charge against any Defendant is not evidence of guilt. Indeed, every Defendant is presumed by the law to be innocent. The law does not require a Defendant to prove innocence or to produce any evidence at all. The government has the burden of proving a Defendant guilty beyond a reasonable doubt, and if it fails to do so you must find that Defendant not guilty.

Thus, while the Government's burden of proof is a strict or heavy burden, it is not necessary that a Defendant's guilt be proved beyond all possible doubt. It is only required that the Government's proof exclude any "reasonable doubt" concerning the Defendant's guilt.

A "reasonable doubt" is a real doubt, based upon reason and common sense after careful and impartial consideration of all the evidence in the case.

Proof beyond a reasonable doubt, therefore, is proof of such a convincing character that you would be willing to rely and act upon it without hesitation in the most important of your own affairs. If you are convinced that a Defendant has been proved guilty beyond a reasonable doubt, say so. If you are not convinced, say so.

As I said earlier, you must consider only the evidence that I have admitted in the case. The term "evidence" includes the testimony of the witnesses and the exhibits admitted in the record. Remember that anything the lawyers say is not evidence in the case. It is your own recollection and interpretation of the evidence that controls. What the lawyers say is not binding upon you. Also, you should not assume from anything I may have said that I have any opinion concerning any of the issues in this case. Except for my instructions to you on the law, you should disregard anything I may have said during the trial in arriving at your own decision concerning the facts.

In considering the evidence you may make deductions and reach conclusions which reason and common sense lead you to make; and you should not be unduly concerned about whether the evidence is direct or circumstantial. "Direct evidence" is the testimony of one who asserts actual knowledge of a fact, such as an eye witness. "Circumstantial evidence" is proof of a chain of facts and circumstances tending to prove, or disprove, any fact in dispute. The law makes no distinction between the weight you may give to either direct or circumstantial evidence.

Now, in saying that you must *consider* all of th evidence, I do not mean that you must *accept* all of the evidence as true or accurate. You should decide whether you believe what each witness had to say, and how important that testimony was. In making those decisions you may believe or disbelieve any witness, in whole or in part. Also, the number of witnesses testifying concerning any particular dispute is not controlling.

In deciding whether you believe or do not believe any witness I suggest that you ask yourself a few questions: Did the witness impress you as one who was telling the truth? Did the witness have any particular reason not to tell the truth? Did the witness have a personal interest in the outcome of the case? Did the witness seem to have a good memory? Did the witness have the opportunity and ability to observe accurately the things he or she testified about? Did the witness appear to understand the questions clearly and answer them directly? Did the witness's testimony differ from other testimony or other evidence?

You should also ask yourself whether there was evidence tending to prove that a witness testified falsely concerning some important fact; or, whether there was evidence that at some other time a witness said or did something, or failed to say or do something, which was different from the testimony the witness gave before you during the trial.

You should keep in mind, of course, that a simple mistake by a witness does not necessarily mean that the witness was not telling the truth as he or she remembers it, because people naturally tend to forget some things or remember other things inaccurately. So, if a witness has made a misstatement, you need to consider whether it was simply an innocent lapse of memory or an intentional falsehood; and the significance of that may depend on whether it has to do with an important fact or with only an unimportant detail.

When knowledge of a technical subject matter might be helpful to the jury, a person having special training or experience in that technical field is permitted to state an opinion concerning those technical matters.

Merely because such a witness has expressed an opinion, however, does not mean that you must accept that opinion. The same as with any other witness, it is up to you to decide whether to rely upon it.

The charges against the defendants in this case are before you in the form of counts which allege the violations of various federal offenses against one or more defendants. The charges against each defendant in each count are to be considered separately by you as to each defendant as if that defendant were on trial before you separately.

The guilt of a Defendant in a criminal case may be proved without evidence that the Defendant personally did every act involved in the commission of the crime charged. The law recognizes that, ordinarily, anything a person can do for one's self may also be accomplished through direction of another person as an agent, or by acting together with, or under the direction of, another person or persons in a joint effort.

So, if the acts or conduct of an agent, employee or other associate of a Defendant are willfully directed or authorized by that Defendant, or if a Defendant aids and abets another person by willfully joining together with that person in the commission of a crime, then the law holds that Defendant responsible for the conduct of that other person just as though the Defendant had personally engaged in such conduct.

However, before any Defendant can be held criminally responsible for the conduct of others it is necessary that the Defendant willfully associate in some way with the crime, and willfully participate in it. Mere presence at the scene of a crime and even knowledge that a crime is being committed are not sufficient to establish that a Defendant either directed or aided and abetted the crime. You must find beyond a reasonable doubt that the Defendant was a willful participant and not merely a knowing spectator.

I will instruct you as to the essential elements which the Government must prove beyond a reasonable doubt as to each count and each defendant.

COUNTS 2-22

Counts 2 through 22 of the indictment each charge violations of the same federal statutes. Counts 2 through 11 charge violations of these statutes against only the Defendants McWane, Inc., James Delk and Michael Devine. Counts 12 through 22 charge violations of these same federal statutes against only the Defendants McWane, Inc, and James Delk.

Various federal statutes in Title 33 of the United States Code known as the Clean Water Act prohibit discharges of pollutants into the "waters of the United States" except in accordance with a permit. These permits known as National Pollutant Discharge Elimination System ("NPDES') permits impose limits on the types and amount of pollutants that can be discharged from a facility into the waters of the United States. Title 33, Section 1319(c)(2)(A) provides that it is unlawful for any person to knowingly violate a permit condition or limitation of a NPDES permit issued by the federal Environmental Protection Agency ("EPA") or by an authorized state agency, which condition or limitation implements one or more specified provisions of said Clean Water Act.

Sections 1319(c)(2)(A) and 1311(a) of Title 33 of the United States Code provide, in part, that any person who knowingly discharges a pollutant without a Clean Water Act permit or in violation of a Clean Water Act permit commits a crime.

Counts 2-11 of the Indictment allege that in or about the months of May 1999 through February 2000, Defendants McWane, Inc., James Delk, and Michael Devine, knowingly discharged or caused the discharge of process wastewater from stormwater outfall DSN002 into Avondale Creek in violation of Defendant McWane, Inc's. NPDES permit because that permit only allowed for the discharge of "stormwater runoff from industrial activity."

Counts 12-22 of the Indictment allege that in or about the months of March 2000 through January 2001, Defendants McWane, Inc. and James Delk knowingly discharged or caused the discharge of process wastewater from stormwater outfall DSN002 into Avondale Creek in violation of Defendant McWane, Inc.'s NPDES permit because that permit only allowed for the discharge of "stormwater runoff from industrial activity."

To find any Defendant guilty of Counts 2-22, you must unanimously agree that each and every one of the following events has been proven by the Government beyond a reasonable doubt:

First, that on or about the dates alleged in the Indictment, the Defendant knowingly, and not accidentally, discharged or caused a discharge;

Second, that the Defendant knew (he)(it) was discharging a pollutant or causing a pollutant to be discharged;

Third, that the Defendant knew that the content of the discharge was process wastewater and was not, in fact, stormwater;

Fourth, that the Defendant knew that the water was discharged from the point source DSN002 into Avondale Creek;

Fifth, that the Defendant knew that Avondale Creek was a water of the United States; and

Sixth, that the Defendant discharged or caused the discharge knowing that such discharge violated McWane, Inc.'s NODES permit. In other words, if storm water was discharged, or if a Defendant thought he or it was discharging storm water when he or it was actually discharging process wastewater, then you must find that Defendant not guilty.

In each of Counts 2 through 22, the Government has alleged that illegal discharges occurred during a particular calendar month. In order to convict a Defendant of any such count, you must all unanimously agree, in connection with the elements described previously, that

____

Only if you are convinced that the Government has met its burden of proof beyond any reasonable doubt as to each and every one of these elements may you return a guilty verdict as to any specific count. If you have a reasonable doubt about any of these elements, then you must find the Defendant not guilty of the charge.

With regard to Counts 2 through 22, in order to convict a Defendant you must find, beyond a reasonable doubt, that the Defendant discharged "process wastewater" as it is defined by McWane, Inc.'s NODES Permit into Avoidable Creek. If you do not find that a Defendant discharged process wastewater, as it is defined, into Avoidable Creek, but discharged a different type of water—such as storm water runoff from industrial activity—into Avoidable Creek, you must find the Defendant not guilty of any such count in Counts 2 through 22.

COUNT 23

Count 23 of the indictment alleges that on or about May 26, 1999, Defendants McWane, Inc., James Deck, and Michael Devine, knowingly discharged or caused the discharge of process wastewater from the Creek Clarified Outfall DSN001 into Avoidable Creek in violation of Defendant McWane, Inc.'s NODES permit limit for oil and grease. To find a Defendant guilty of Count 23, you must unanimously agree beyond a reasonable doubt to each of the following:

First, that on or about May 26, 1999, the Defendant knowingly, and not accidentally, discharge or caused a discharge;

Second, that the Defendant knew at the time of discharge that (he)(it) was discharging a pollutant;

Third, that the Defendant knew that the content of the discharge, when properly analyzed, would return a result of more than 15 milligrams per liter of oil and grease;

Fourth, the contents of the discharge, when properly analyzed, in fact returned a result of more than 15 milligrams per liter of oil and grease;

Fifth, that the Defendant knew that the water was discharged from the Creek Clarified Outfall DSN001 into Avoidable Creek;

Sixth, that the Defendant knew that Avoidable Creek was a water of the United States;

Seventh, that the Defendant discharged or caused the discharge knowing that such discharge violated McWane, Inc.'s NODES permit.

The word "knowingly" as it is used in Counts 2-23 of the indictment means that the act was done voluntarily and intentionally and not by mistake or accident. To prove a knowing violation of the Clean Water Act as charged in Counts 2-23, the Government must meet its burden of proof beyond a reasonable doubt that the Defendant was aware of the act, and that the Defendant's actions or failure to act were not the result of mistake, ignorance, accident, negligence, or carelessness. In order for you to find any Defendant guilty of a violation of Counts 2-23, you must find, beyond a reasonable doubt, that the Defendant acted knowingly with regard to each element of the offense that I described above. It is not enough for the Government to prove only that a discharge exceeded a permit limit. The Government must meet its burden of proof beyond a reasonable doubt that the Defendant acted knowingly. You should consider the Defendants' behavior in light of all of the circumstances and the instructions that I give you in determining whether the Government has established beyond a reasonable doubt that each Defendant has acted knowingly. Negligence alone on the part of a Defendant is not enough to establish knowing conduct.

The term "negligence" means failure to use reasonable care. In other words, the Government must prove more than that a Defendant failed to act as a reasonably prudent person would under the same circumstances. To find a Defendant guilty of Counts 2 through 23, the Government has the burden to prove, beyond a reasonable doubt, that Defendant acted knowingly. If the Government proves only that the Defendant acted negligently, you must find that Defendant not guilty.

The government is not required to prove that the discharge of pollutants caused any damage or harm in order to establish the criminal offense charged under Counts 2-23.

As to Counts 2-23, the term "pollutant" includes solid waste, chemical wastes, heat, rock, sand, and industrial waste discharged into water. As to Counts 2-23, a "water of the United States" includes any stream which may eventually flow into a navigable stream or river. The Government does not have to prove that the stream into which a discharge is made is itself navigable in fact. What it must prove is that the stream into which the discharge is made may eventually flow directly or indirectly into a navigable stream or river. The stream into which the discharge is made may be natural or manmade and may flow continuously or only intermittently, as long as it may eventually flow directly or indirectly into a navigable stream or river whose use affects interstate commerce.

With regard to the Clean Water Act counts in the indictment, that is counts 2-23, a person may be found guilty as a "responsible corporate officer" if the government proves beyond a reasonable doubt:

1. that he had knowledge of the facts that gave rise to the violation;
2. that he had the authority and capacity to prevent the violation; and
3. that he failed to prevent the violation.

COUNT 24

Count 24 of the Indictment charges Defendants McWane, Inc. and Robinson with knowingly and willfully making a false statement to the EPA in violation of 18 U.S.C. § 1001. This statute states that whoever, in any matter within the jurisdiction of the executive branch of the Government of the United States, knowingly and willfully makes any materially false, fictitious, or fraudulent statement or representation commits the offense of making a false statement.

Count 24 alleges that the Defendants McWane, Inc. and Robinson knowingly and willfully certified falsely that the documents submitted or transmitted to the EPA by McWane, Inc. were "true, accurate and complete." Specifically, Count 24 alleges that on September 15, 2000, Defendants McWane, Inc. and Robinson submitted a certification to the EPA accompanying a set of documents requested by the EPA. The documents were prepared by other McWane, Inc. employees from 1995 to 2000, and many involved inspections conducted at the McWane, Inc. plant. The certification in question states:

> I certify under penalty of law that this document and all attachments were prepared under my direction or supervision in accordance with a system designed to ensure that qualified personnel properly gather and evaluate the information submitted. Based on my inquiry of the person or persons who manage the system, or those persons directly responsible for gathering the information, I certify that the information submitted is, to the best of my knowledge and belief, true, accurate, and complete. I am aware that there are significant penalties for submitting false information, including the possibility of fine and imprisonment for knowing violations.

The Government alleges that some of the inspection forms submitted to the EPA with the certification were false and, that Defendant Robinson signed the certification knowing such forms were false.

In order to meet its burden of proof that a Defendant is guilty of making a false statement to the United States, the Government must establish beyond a reasonable doubt that:

(1) on or about the date specified, a Defendant made the statement as detailed in the indictment;

(2) the statement or representation was false, fictitious or fraudulent

(3) the Defendant made the false, fictitious or fraudulent statement intentionally, knowing that the statement was false at the time it was made;

(4) the statement was material;

(5) the statement was within the jurisdiction of an agency of the United States; and

(6) the Defendant made the false statement with the intent to deceive the EPA.

<u>First Element – Statement or Representation</u>

The first element that the Government must prove beyond a reasonable doubt is that the individual Defendant made a statement or representation. Thus, the Government must prove either that the individual Defendant physically made or otherwise personally prepared the specific statement alleged to be false, or that he caused to be made the specific statement alleged to be false.

<u>Second Element – False, Fictitious or Fraudulent Statement</u>

The second element that the Government must prove beyond a reasonable doubt is that the statement or representation was false, fictitious, or fraudulent. A statement or representation is "false" or "fictitious" if it was untrue when made, and the person making it or causing it to be made knew at the time that it was untrue. A statement or representation is "fraudulent" if it was untrue when made, and it was made or caused to be made with the specific intent to deceive the EPA.

As I have said, the statement that you must consider in this Count is the certification signed by Mr. Robinson, not the inspection forms submitted with the certification. Even if you find that some of the inspection forms were false, you may only find the Defendants guilty of Count 24 if Mr. Robinson signed the certification knowing the inspections were false. Again, the allegations in the Indictment are based on the falsity of the certification, not the inspection forms.

In addition, if a statement was literally true at the time that it was made, it is not a false statement under the law. If you find that the statement alleged in Count 24, the certification, was literally true on or about the dates the statement was made, you must find the Defendant not guilty on that count.

Third Element – Knowing and Willful Conduct

The third element that the Government must prove beyond a reasonable doubt is that the Defendant acted knowingly and willfully. An act is done knowingly if it is done purposely and voluntarily, as opposed to mistakenly or accidentally. A person acts "knowingly," as that term is used in these instructions, if that person acts consciously and with awareness and comprehension and not because of ignorance, mistake or misunderstanding or other similar reasons. To find Defendants Robinson or McWane, Inc. guilty of Count 24, the Government must prove beyond a reasonable doubt that the Defendants had personal knowledge that the specific statement alleged was false.

A person who makes, submits, or uses a statement or writing which that person believes to be truthful does not "knowingly" make, submit, or use a false, fictitious, or fraudulent statement. Under Count 24, if you find the Government did not prove beyond a reasonable doubt that Defendant

Robinson had personal knowledge that the specific inspection forms submitted to the EPA were false, you must find him not guilty. As I have previously instructed you, Count 24 alleges that the certification is a false statement, not the inspection forms. To find Mr. Robinson guilty, the Government must prove beyond a reasonable doubt that he had personal knowledge that one or more inspection forms submitted to the EPA with the certification were false. If the Government has not presented proof beyond a reasonable doubt that Defendant Robinson had personal knowledge that the inspection forms were false when he signed the certification, you must find him not guilty. An act is done willfully if it is done with an intention to do something the law forbids, with a bad purpose to disobey the law. A person acts "willfully," as that term is used in these instructions, when that person acts deliberately, voluntarily, and intentionally. Under Count 24, if you find that Defendant Robinson did not act willfully, that is deliberately, voluntarily and intentionally in signing the certification accompanying the inspection forms submitted to the EPA, you must find him not guilty of Count 24. If you so find, then, because Defendant McWane, Inc. can act only through its employees or agents, you must also find Defendant McWane, Inc. not guilty of this Count.

Fourth Element – Materiality

The Government must also prove beyond a reasonable doubt that the statement or representation was material. A statement is material if it could have influenced the EPA, in its normal decisions or activities. Proof of actual reliance on the statements by the EPA is not required. The test is whether the false statement had the capacity to impair or pervert the functioning of a governmental agency. In other words, a misrepresentation is material if it related to an important fact, as distinguished from some unimportant or trivial detail.

If you determine that the certification was false, then you may consider whether it was material, that is, whether it could have influenced the EPA's decision or activities. If you determine that the certification was not material, you must find the Defendants not guilty.

Fifth Element – Matter Within the Jurisdiction of the United States Government

As I have told you, the fifth element with respect to Count 24 is that the statement was made with regard to a matter within the jurisdiction of an agency or department of the Government of the United States. I charge you that the EPA is a department of the United States Government.

To be within the jurisdiction of a department or agency of the United States Government means that the statement must concern an authorized function of that department or agency.

Sixth Element – Intent to Deceive

As I have told you, the sixth element that the Government must prove beyond a reasonable doubt is that the Defendant made the statement for the purpose of misleading the EPA. In this case, if you find that the Government has not proven beyond a reasonable doubt that Defendant Robinson acted with the purpose of misleading the EPA when he signed the certification accompanying the inspection forms, you must find him not guilty. If you find that Defendant Robinson did not act with the purpose of misleading the EPA, because Defendant McWane, Inc. can act only through its employees or agents, you must also find Defendant McWane, Inc. not guilty.

As I have said, the statement at issue in Count 24 is the certification submitted to the EPA on September 15, 2000. To find Defendants McWane, Inc. and Robinson guilty of making a knowing and willful false statement, all jurors must agree that the same inspection form submitted to the EPA with the certification, is, in fact, false, fictitious, or fraudulent. Moreover, all jurors must find that Defendant Robinson had personal knowledge of the falsity of the same inspection form submitted with the certification, and that Defendant acted willfully and with the intent to deceive as to the falsity of the same inspection form. If you do not unanimously agree that the same inspection form was false, fictitious, or fraudulent, and that the Defendants knowingly and willfully made the certification accompanying the false statement with the intent to deceive, you must find the Defendants not guilty.

The "good faith" of the Defendants, if you so find, is a complete defense to the allegations in Count 24 of the Indictment.

A person who makes a statement or representation, or causes another person to make a statement or representation, on a belief, opinion, or interpretation honestly held is not punishable under the provisions of 18 U.S.C. § 1001 merely because the belief, opinion, or interpretation eventually turns out to be inaccurate, incorrect, or wrong. An honest mistake in judgment or an honest error in management does not rise to the level of criminal conduct.

The law is written to subject to criminal punishment only those people who intentionally make a statement or representation that they know to be false at the time it was made. A statement made with "good faith" belief in its accuracy does not amount to a false statement and is not a crime. This is so even if the statement is, in fact, erroneous.

While the term "good faith" has no precise definition, it encompasses, among other things, a belief or opinion honestly held and an absence of malice or ill will.

In determining whether or not the Government has proven beyond a reasonable doubt that the Defendants acted with the specific intent to make a statement that they knew to be false at the time it was made, the jury must consider all the evidence in the case bearing on the Defendants' state of mind.

The burden of proving good faith does not rest with the Defendants because the Defendants do not have any obligation to prove anything in this case. It is the Government's burden to prove to you, beyond a reasonable doubt, that Defendants acted with the specific intent to make a statement or representation that they knew to be false at the time the statement was made.

If the evidence in the case leaves you with a reasonable doubt as to whether the Defendants acted with the specific intent to make a statement or representation that they knew to be false at the time the statement was made, you must find the Defendants not guilty of Count 24.

As you have heard, the Government has alleged that Defendant Robinson made a false statement by signing the certification that accompanied the inspection forms submitted to the EPA. If you find that Defendant Robinson acted in good faith in signing the certification, you must find him not guilty because the Government has not established that Defendant Robinson acted with specific intent. In that event, as I have previously instructed you, because Defendant McWane, Inc. can act only through its employees and agents, you must also find Defendant McWane, Inc. not guilty of Count 24.

COUNT 25

Only Defendant McWane, Inc. is charged in Count 25 with obstruction of justice in violation of Section 1505 of Title 18 of the United States Code, and with aiding and abetting in violation of Section 2 of Title 18 of the United State Code. It is alleged that during an EPA compliance sampling inspection on April 25 to 27, 2000, McWane, Inc. provided the false and misleading information that "there is sufficient recycling of wastewater that the facility normally would not have a discharge." Title 18, United States Code, Section 1505, makes it a crime for anyone corruptly, by threats or force, or by any threatening letter or communication, to endeavor to influence, obstruct or impede the due administration of justice under which any pending proceeding is being had before any agency of the United States. Count 25 alleges that Defendant McWane, Inc. corruptly endeavored to influence, obstruct or impede the due administration of justice in connection with a pending proceeding before the EPA.

The defendant can be found guilty of that offense only if all of the following facts are proved beyond a reasonable doubt:

First: That there was a proceeding pending before the United States EPA as described in the Indictment.

Second: That the defendant knew of the pending proceeding and influenced, obstructed, impeded, or endeavored to influence, obstruct, and impede the due administration of justice in that proceeding;

Third: That the defendant's act was done "corruptly," that is, that the defendant acted knowingly and dishonestly, with the specific intent to influence, obstruct, or impede the due administration of justice; and

Fourth: That the obstructive act must have a relationship in time, causation, or logic with the proceeding allegedly obstructed.

While it must be proven beyond a reasonable doubt that the Defendant corruptly endeavored to influence, obstruct or impede the due administration of justice as alleged, and that the natural and probable effect of the Defendant's acts would be to influence, obstruct or impede the due administration of justice, it is not necessary for the Government to prove that the EPA proceeding was in fact influenced or obstructed or impeded in any way.

The defendant can only be found guilty of the offense charged in Count 25 if you conclude that a "pending proceeding" existed at the time the allegedly obstructive acts occurred. You may determine that there was a pending proceeding before the EPA, as alleged by the Government, only if you unanimously determine, beyond a reasonable doubt, that the compliance sampling inspection conducted by the EPA on or about April 25 through April 27, 2000, was an investigation based upon specific prior information that called for an investigation. A routine agency inspection not based upon prior specific information does not constitute a pending proceeding. Thus, if you determine that the compliance sampling inspection conducted by the EPA on or about April 25 through 27, 2000, was nothing more than a routine agency inspection, the Government has not met its burden of proof, and you should find that Defendant McWane, Inc. is not guilty of Count 25.

In order to find a defendant guilty of obstruction, you must find beyond a reasonable doubt that the Defendant falsely and misleadingly provided information that "there is sufficient recycling of wastewater that the facility normally would not have a discharge," and in doing so, intentionally endeavored corruptly to influence, obstruct or impede a pending proceeding. Again, "corruptly" means to act knowingly and dishonestly, with the specific intent to influence, obstruct, or impede the due administration of justice.

COUNT 1

The last count that I will instruct you with reference to is Count 1. Count 1 does not allege the violations of any federal offenses as such. What it does is to allege a conspiracy or unlawful agreement by two or more of the defendants to violate one or more of the offenses charged in (1) Counts 2 through 23 of the indictment, that is to knowingly discharge or cause the discharge of a pollutant from a point source into the waters of the United States in violation of a NODES permit; (2) Count 24 of the indictment, that is to knowingly and willfully make materially false, fictitious and fraudulent statements and representations in matters within the jurisdiction of the EPA; and (3) Count 25, that is to corruptly influence, obstruct, or impede or endeavor to influence obstruct or impede, the due and proper administration of law under which a pending proceeding is being had before the EPA.

In addition to alleging that the objects of the alleged conspiracy were to commit the offenses alleged in Counts 2 through 23, 24 and 25, Count 1 also alleges that there was an unlawful agreement or conspiracy to defraud the United States.

Thus, the Indictment alleges two different types of conspiracy in Count 1: conspiracy to violate Federal law and conspiracy to defraud the United States. I will instruct you as to both types of conspiracies. In order to find the Defendants guilty of a conspiracy, you must unanimously agree on which type of conspiracy the Government has presented evidence beyond a reasonable doubt. In other words, if five of you conclude that Defendants were only guilty of conspiracy to violate a specific Federal law and seven of you find Defendants only guilty of conspiracy to defraud the United States, you must find Defendants not guilty.

The Indictment alleges that the Defendants conspired (1) to knowingly violate the Clean Water Act, (2) to defraud the United States by obstructing the EPA in enforcing federal environmental laws and regulations, (3) to knowingly and willfully make a false statement to the

EPA in a matter within its jurisdiction, and (4) to corruptly obstruct a pending proceeding before the EPA.

The relevant Federal statute on this subject is 18 U.S.C. § 371. It provides: "If two or more persons conspire . . . to commit any offense against the United States . . . and one or more of such persons do any act to effect the object of the conspiracy, each [is guilty of an offense against the United States]."

The same act also provides: "If two or more persons conspire to defraud the United States, or any agency thereof in any manner or for any purpose, and one or more of such persons do any act to effect the object of the conspiracy, each [is guilty of a crime].".

A "conspiracy" is an agreement between two or more persons to join together to accomplish some unlawful purpose. It is a kind of "partnership in crime" in which each member becomes the agent of every other member. For you to find a Defendant guilty of this crime, you must be convinced that the Government has met its burden of proof beyond a reasonable doubt as to each of following as to that Defendant or Defendants:

<u>First</u>: That a Defendant and at least one other person made an agreement: (1) to knowingly violate the Clean Water Act, (2) to defraud the United States by obstructing the EPA in enforcing federal environmental laws and regulation, (3) to knowingly and willfully make a false statement to the EPA in a matter within its jurisdiction, or (4) to corruptly obstruct a pending proceeding before the EPA;

<u>Second</u>: That the Defendant knowingly and willfully became a member of the conspiracy;

Third: That one of the members of the conspiracy knowingly committed at least one of the overt acts in the Indictment; and

Fourth: That the overt acts which you find to have been committed were committed to further some objective of the conspiracy.

The first element that the Government must prove beyond a reasonable doubt to establish the offense of conspiracy is that two or more persons entered into the unlawful agreement alleged in the Indictment

In order for the Government to satisfy this element, the Government must prove beyond a reasonable doubt that there was a mutual understanding, either spoken or unspoken, between two or more people to cooperate with each other to accomplish an unlawful act.

Involvement in an event, even with knowledge that a crime is being committed is not sufficient to establish an unlawful agreement. Nor does the fact that certain persons may have associated with each other, worked together, participated in meetings together, or communicated with each other in person or by document necessarily establish proof of the existence of a conspiracy. Moreover, a person who has no knowledge of a conspiracy, but who happens to act in a way which advances some purpose of a conspiracy, does not thereby become a conspirator. Negligent conduct on the part of a Defendant alone does not make him a conspirator. In other words, to establish the existence of a conspiracy, the Government must prove beyond a reasonable doubt an agreement to achieve a common unlawful purpose. To find a Defendant guilty of the conspiracy alleged in Count One, you must find beyond a reasonable doubt that the Defendant agreed to knowingly violate the

Clean Water Act, to defraud the United States by obstructing the EPA in enforcing federal environmental laws and regulations, to knowingly and willfully make a false statement to the EPA in a matter within its jurisdiction, or to corruptly obstruct a pending proceeding before the EPA. Thus, if you find that a Defendant did not agree on one or more of those things, you must find the Defendant not guilty of Count One.

The second element that the Government must prove beyond a reasonable doubt to establish the offense of conspiracy is that the Defendant knowingly, willfully and voluntarily became a member of the conspiracy.

If you are satisfied that the conspiracy alleged in the Indictment existed, you must next ask yourselves who the members of that conspiracy were. In deciding whether the Defendant whom you are considering was, in fact, a member of the conspiracy, you should consider whether the defendant knowingly and willfully joined the conspiracy. Did he participate in it with knowledge of its unlawful purpose and with the specific intention of furthering its objective?

I want to caution you, however, that association with, working with, meeting with, or communicating with one or more members of the conspiracy, whether that conspirator is a defendant in this case or not, does not in and of itself make the Defendant a member.

I also want to caution you that knowledge or acquiescence, without participation, in the unlawful plan is not sufficient. Moreover, the fact that the acts of a Defendant, without knowledge, happen to further the purposes or objectives of the conspiracy does not make the defendant a member. Either negligence or careless conduct is not enough. More is required under the law.

What is necessary is that the Defendant must have participated with knowledge of at least some of the purposes or objectives of the conspiracy and with the intention of aiding in the accomplishment of those unlawful ends, namely (1) to knowingly violate the Clean Water Act, (2) to defraud the United States by obstructing the EPA in enforcing federal environmental laws and regulations, (3) to knowingly and willfully making a false statement to the EPA in a matter within its jurisdiction, or (4) to corruptly obstruct a pending proceeding before the EPA.

In sum, the Defendant, with an understanding of the unlawful character of the conspiracy, must have intentionally engaged, advised or assisted in it for the purpose of furthering the illegal undertaking, in order to become a conspirator.

The third element that the Government must prove beyond a reasonable doubt to establish the offense of conspiracy is that at least one of the overt acts alleged in the Indictment was knowingly and willfully committed by at least one of the conspirators, at or about the time and place alleged.

In order for the Government to satisfy this element, it is not required that all of the overt acts alleged in the Indictment be proven; it is sufficient if the Government proves beyond a reasonable doubt one such act; but in that event, in order to return a verdict of guilty, you must unanimously agree upon which act was done.

Not everything an alleged conspirator does constitutes an overt act. Conspirators often do things that are not a part of any agreement with others. You should understand that the law recognizes that this is particularly true of acts intended to cover-up an offense, since such acts are common to offenses that are not conspiracies. Thus, an act done by a conspirator, on his own, in an attempt to cover-up a conspiracy is not an act in furtherance of the conspiracy unless there was a common agreement among the conspirators that such acts would be committed for the purpose of achieving the objects of the conspiracy.

You must also find that the overt act occurred while the conspiracy was still in existence.

The fourth, and final, element that the Government must prove beyond a reasonable doubt is that the overt act was committed for the purpose of carrying out the unlawful agreement.

In order for the Government to satisfy this element, it must prove, beyond a reasonable doubt, that at least one overt act was knowingly and willfully done, by at least one conspirator, in furtherance of some unlawful object or purpose of the conspiracy, as alleged in the Indictment. Once again, you must all agree upon which act was done and the unlawful object or purpose of the conspiracy.

As I have stated, with regard to the alleged conspiracy, the indictment charges that the Defendants knowingly and willfully combined, conspired, confederated and agreed with each other and others known and unknown to the Grand Jury, to commit the following offenses against the United States and the laws thereof:

a. To knowingly discharge and cause the discharge of a pollutant from a point source into the waters of the United States, in violation of a permit;

b. To defraud the United States, that is, to hamper, hinder, impede, impair, and obstruct by craft, trickery, deceit, and dishonest means, the lawful and legitimate functions of the EPA in enforcing federal environmental laws and regulations;

c. To knowingly and willfully make materially false, fictitious, and fraudulent statements and representations in matters within the jurisdiction of the EPA, an agency of the executive branch of the Government of the United States; and

d. To corruptly influence, obstruct, and impede, and endeavor to influence, obstruct, and impede, the due and proper administration of law under which a pending proceeding is being had before the EPA, an agency of the United States.

It is charged, in other words, that Defendants conspired to commit four separate, substantive crimes or offenses.

In such a case it is not necessary for the Government to prove that the Defendants under consideration willfully conspired to commit all of those substantive offenses. It would be sufficient if the Government proves, beyond a reasonable doubt, that the Defendants willfully conspired with someone to commit at least one of those offenses; but in that event, in order to return a verdict of guilty, you must unanimously agree upon which of the offenses the Defendants conspired to commit.

In other words, in reaching your conclusion, you must determine whether the Government has met its burden of proof and proven, beyond a reasonable doubt, some or all of the objects of the conspiracy. You must be unanimous as to which, if any, objects the conspiracy was undertaken to accomplish.

Whether there existed a single unlawful agreement, or many such agreements, or indeed, no agreement at all, is a question of fact for you, the jury, to determine in accordance with the instructions I have given you. Here, the Government has the burden of proving, beyond a reasonable doubt, the existence of only one overall conspiracy. If you find there was no conspiracy at all, or if you find there were several separate and independent conspiracies with various groups of members that did not include a Defendant, then you must find that Defendant not guilty.

When two or more people join together to further one common unlawful design or purpose, a single conspiracy exists. By way of contrast, multiple conspiracies exist when there are separate unlawful agreements to achieve distinct purposes.

Proof of several separate and independent conspiracies is not proof of the single, overall conspiracy alleged in the Indictment, unless one of the conspiracies proved happens to be the single conspiracy described in the Indictment.

If you find that the conspiracy alleged in the Indictment did not exist, you cannot find any defendant guilty of the single conspiracy alleged in the Indictment. This is so even if you find that some conspiracy other than the one alleged in the Indictment existed, even though the purpose of both conspiracies may have been the same and even though there may have been some overlap in membership.

Similarly, if you find that a particular Defendant was a member of another conspiracy, and not the one alleged in the Indictment, then you must find that Defendant not guilty of the conspiracy count.

Therefore, what you must do is determine whether the conspiracy alleged in the Indictment existed. If it did, you then must determine the nature of the conspiracy and who were its members.

If you find that a central core of conspirators recruited separate groups of co-conspirators to carry out the various functions of the illegal enterprise and that none of those recruits had knowledge of or connection with any other and dealt independently with the core conspirators, then you must find that there is not a single conspiracy, but rather multiple separate conspiracies. In that case, you must find Defendants not guilty of Count One.

The law requires the Government to bring criminal allegations within certain time limits. The limits are what we call "statutes of limitations." These statutes of limitations in this case required the Government to file the Indictment within five years of the alleged offenses. The Indictment was returned on May 25, 2004, which means that there cannot be a conviction for an alleged offense which occurred before May 25, 1999.

The Government has the burden of proving that at least one overt act occurred after May 25, 1999. As I have told you, an "overt act" is an act by a conspirator intended to help achieve the objects of the alleged conspiracy. In order to find Defendants guilty of conspiracy, you must find, beyond a reasonable doubt, that at least one of the overt acts proven to be in furtherance of the alleged conspiracy was committed within five years of the date of Indictment. The jury must unanimously agree on that overt act. If you find that a conspiracy existed, and that it included some or all of the Defendants, <u>but</u> that it ended on or before May 25, 1999, then you must find the

Defendants not guilty of criminal conspiracy.

With regard to an organizational defendant such as a corporation, its knowledge is the state of mind and the sum of the knowledge of all of its employees and agents. That is, the corporation's knowledge is the totality of what all of the employees and agents knew within the scope of their employment. You may use the sum of what the separate employees and agents knew when determining the corporation's knowledge. As with individuals, knowledge is usually established by surrounding facts and circumstances as of the times the acts in question occurred, and the reasonable inferences to be drawn from them.

As you know, defendant McWane, Inc. is a corporation and not an individual. A corporation, of course, may act only through natural persons who are known as its agents. In general, any agent or representative of a corporation possessing adequate authority may bind the corporation by that person's acts, declarations and omissions. In order to find McWane, Inc. guilty, you must find that there is proof beyond a reasonable doubt of all of the essential elements of the offense, through the acts or omissions of employees or agents of the corporation who must have been acting within the scope of their authority.

An act or omission is within the scope of employment if it is sufficiently related to the duties that the individual was employed to perform, if it was done substantially within the time and space limits of the job, and was motivated, at least in part, by a purpose to serve or benefit the corporation. An act or omission is not within the scope of the employee's authority if it is different in kind from that authorized, far beyond the authorized time or space limits, or too little actuated by a purpose to serve the master. The scope of authority of these agents is a question of fact for you to decide just as other fact questions in the case.

In the context of a conspiracy allegation, the conspiracy can be between McWane, Inc. and one or more of its employees.

A separate crime or offense is charged against one or more of the Defendants in each count of the indictment. Each charge, and the evidence pertaining to it, should be considered separately. Also, the case of each Defendant should be considered separately and individually. The fact that you may find any one or more of the Defendants guilty or not guilty of any of the offenses charged should not affect your verdict as to any other offense or any other Defendant.

I caution you, members of the Jury, that you are here to determine from the evidence in this case whether each Defendant is guilty or not guilty. Each defendant is on trial only for the specific offense alleged in the indictment.

When the Government alleges that a defendant committed a particular offense or offenses, the defendant may be convicted of that specific offense or offenses and not an offense for which he was not charged. Even if you believe that the Government has met its burden of proof, beyond a reasonable doubt, that a Defendant has committed an offense, you cannot find that Defendant guilty of that offense if you determine that it was not an offense in the Indictment.

Also, the question of punishment should never be considered by the jury in any way in deciding the case. If a Defendant is convicted the matter of punishment is for the Judge alone to determine later.

Any verdict you reach in the jury room, whether guilty or not guilty, must be unanimous. In other words, to return a verdict you must all agree. Your deliberations will be secret; you will never have to explain your verdict to anyone.

It is your duty as jurors to discuss the case with one another in an effort to reach agreement if you can do so. Each of you must decide the case for yourself, but only after full consideration of the evidence with the other members of the jury. While you are discussing the case do not hesitate to reexamine your own opinion and change your mind if you become convinced that you were wrong. But do not give up your honest beliefs solely because the others think differently or merely to get the case over with.

Remember, that in a very real way you are judges–judges of the facts. Your only interest is to seek the truth from the evidence in the case.

When you go to the jury room you should first select one of your members to act as your foreperson. The foreperson will preside over your deliberations and will speak for you here in court.

A form of verdict has been prepared for your convenience.

You will take the verdict form to the jury room and when you have reached unanimous agreement you will have your foreperson fill in the verdict form date and sign it, and then return to the courtroom.

If you should desire to communicate with me at any time, please write down your message or question and pass the note to the marshal (courtroom deputy) who will bring it to my attention.

I will then respond as promptly as possible, either in writing or by having you returned to the courtroom so that I can address you orally. I caution you, however, with regard to any message or question you might send, that you should not tell me your numerical division at the time.

Environmental Crimes Deskbook

Appendix 16 Sample Employee Rights Form (Contracts)

Advisory Memo to Employees of XXXXXXX Regarding Contacts by Government Investigators

[DATE]

This memo is being circulated for the purpose of advising employees of XXXXXXX that they may be contacted by government investigators who want to interview them. These interviews will most likely be related to the current investigation of XXXXXXX. Such contacts with these investigators might occur on the job or during off-hours, at home, or away from company premises.

This memo is also intended to provide employees with general guidance about their rights, duties, and obligations with respect to possible contact by investigators. Employees should be aware of the following:

1. Government investigators have a legal right to contact employees and to <u>request</u> an interview. However, they do not have any legal authority by which they can <u>force</u> employees to speak with them or to submit to an interview. It is improper for investigators to resort to threats or intimidation in order to obtain an interview.

2. Employees have the right to speak with investigators as well as the right to refuse to speak to them. They also have the right to have an attorney present during any interview, to confer with an attorney before an interview, and to end an interview at any time.

3. XXXXXXX has hired ______________________ of XXXXXX in XXXXXX to represent it with regard to this investigation. In order to ensure that employees understand their rights, duties, and obligations, XXXXXXX can also arrange, at its expense, for legal representation of employees who may be approached by government investigators. A lawyer can be made available to consult with employees who have further questions about their rights and obligations <u>regardless</u> of whether they have been approached by a government investigator.

4. Although you are encouraged to make use of the legal services at the company's expense, you do have a right to forego such representation. You may choose to deal with the government investigators directly. You may also choose to secure some other lawyers at your own expense.

5. Statements made to a government investigator may constitute legal admissions that can later be used as evidence against the company, the employee, or both in an administrative, civil, or criminal proceeding.

6. Employees who choose to submit to an interview should tell the truth and should state as fact only those matters that they know to be fact. It is unwise to guess or speculate.

7. Neither speaking to government investigators nor declining to speak to them at this time will prevent or foreclose compulsory grand jury testimony in the future. Legal counsel is available to consult with present and former employees regarding their rights and obligations if served with a grand jury subpoena.

8. If the government has approached you with questions about your job or the company, or if you become aware that the government has approached another employee (whether current or former), consultant, or contractor of the company regarding similar concerns, please call __________________.

Should you have any questions regarding this memorandum, please contact ______________.

Environmental Crimes Deskbook

Appendix 17 Sample Document Hold Notice

Sample Litigation Hold Notice

To: [ALL RELEVANT XXXXXX EMPLOYEES]

From: XXXXXXX, Company Counsel

Re: Notice to Preserve and Retain Certain Records

Date: July X, 20XX

Please be advised that XXXXXX recently received a grand jury subpoena issued by the U.S. District Court for the XXXXX District of XXXXX requesting the production of certain categories of documents related to ____________________.

In light of the subpoena, XXXXX has a duty to preserve and maintain certain documents, records and electronically stored information ("ESI"), as more fully described below. Until further written notice from me, XXXXX and its employees must take all reasonable steps to preserve all documents, records and ESI that is or may reasonably be considered relevant to the following categories:

1.
2.
3.
4.

All XXXXX personnel *must preserve and not discard, destroy, modify or delete any documents and electronically stored information in your possession, custody, or control, in whatever form they now exist, that relate to the categories listed above*.

Electronically stored information includes, but is not limited to, all initial, interim, draft, and final versions of the following: e-mail, voice mail, and other electronic communications (*e.g.*, logged IM); databases (e.g., Access, SQL, Exchange, etc.); digitized images; database spreadsheets (e.g., Excel, etc.); word processing documents; PowerPoint® slides and presentations; computerized calendars and personal information manager (PIM) or personal digital assistant (PDA) information; internet usage, telephone, and network access logs; billing, accounting, or ledger entries; web sites and web pages; and all similar data that is stored on, utilized on, or transmitted via a computer or computer network, including the Internet. ESI also includes metadata, which is information about a particular record or data set which describes how, when and by whom it was collected, created, accessed, modified and how it is formatted. All hardware and storage media containing such electronically stored information must be preserved, regardless of whether duplicates of the information exist on other hardware, systems, or platforms.

Going forward, please apply the same instructions in this Memorandum to any documents created in the future that relate to any of the categories listed above.

Please be certain to err on the side of preservation, and to promptly raise any questions or concerns you may have about this Memorandum or your preservation obligations by contacting Company counsel in this matter, XXXXXX (phone number) or XXXXXXXX (phone number). Thank you for your cooperation.

Environmental Crimes Deskbook

Appendix 18 Miranda Reading to Companies (*Upjohn* Warning)

Sample *Upjohn* Warning

I am a lawyer from Corporation A. I represent only Corporation A, and I do not represent you. I am conducting this interview to gather facts in order to provide legal advice for Corporation A. This interview is part of an investigation to determine the facts and circumstances of X in order to advise Corporation A how best to proceed.

Your communications with me are protected by the attorney-client privilege But the attorney-client privilege belongs solely to Corporation A, not you. That means that Corporation A alone may elect to waive the attorney-client privilege and reveal our discussion to third parties. Corporation A alone may decide to waive the privilege and disclose this discussion to such third parties as federal or state agencies, at its sole discretion, and without notifying you.

In order for an interview such as this to remain privileged, it must be kept confidential. To help keep this interview confidential, the Company asks you *not* to disclose the substance of it to any third party, including other employees or anyone outside of the company. You may of course discuss this interview with your own lawyer.

Do you have any questions?

Are you willing to proceed?

Environmental Crimes Deskbook

Appendix 19 Developing an Effective Environmental and Monitoring Compliance Program

Environmental Compliance Programs

Companies can mitigate the risks presented by a government criminal investigation by developing and implementing a comprehensive environmental compliance program because:

- an effective compliance program will prevent many incidents that could lead to government investigation, and thus avoid not only criminal liability, but potential civil or administrative sanctions as well;
- violations discovered through an effective compliance program will give the company the opportunity to disclose violations or incidents voluntarily, potentially allowing the company to take advantage of government voluntary disclosure provisions that could result in a recommendation against criminal prosecution and/or reductions in civil penalty assessments;
- the existence of an effective compliance program will be an important bargaining tool in trying to convince the government that an environmental violation is most appropriately handled as a civil or administrative matter rather than a criminal case;
- if the case is handled civilly or administratively, the compliance program will help in reducing civil penalties and in avoiding administrative sanctions, such as suspension and debarment from obtaining government contracts or subsidies;
- an effective corporate compliance program can be the basis of a good defense at trial, particularly if a company is charged with negligence or intentional misconduct; and
- even if an environmental violation is criminally prosecuted, a comprehensive, effective corporate compliance program could head off a highly intrusive, court-mandated compliance program that is often imposed as a condition of probation for corporations in the event of a conviction, or as a condition of a plea agreement.

A. The Importance of Having an Effective Compliance Program

In 1999, the Deputy Attorney General of the United States, Eric Holder, issued a Memorandum entitled, "Bringing Criminal Charges Against Corporations."[1] This memorandum promulgated guidance to prosecutors, "Federal Prosecution of Corporations," regarding the factors that should generally be considered when making charging decisions against a corporation. There have been subsequent iterations of this guidance,[2] but with each reiteration, the existence and effectiveness of a corporate compliance program that addresses the subject of the suspected violation has consistently been on of the factors that is required to be considered by the prosecutor. The guidance notes that while no compliance program can ever prevent all criminal activity, the "critical factors in evaluating any program are whether the program is adequately designed for maximum effectiveness in preventing and detecting wrongdoing by employees and whether corporate management is enforcing the program or is tacitly encouraging or pressuring employees to engage in misconduct to achieve business objectives."[3]

The guidance also establishes other factors to be considered. In some instances, the ability to meet these factors will also, by necessity, rely heavily on the existence of a comprehensive and effective compliance program. For instance, one factor to be considered is the pervasiveness of wrongdoing within the corporation, with the most important aspect being the role of management in establishing a corporate culture that either discourages or tacitly encourages criminal conduct.[4] Obviously, the promulgation and implementation of a comprehensive and effective corporate compliance program is a strong management statement that it is doing everything it can to discourage criminal or other aberrant conduct, and to discover and appropriately deal with instances of noncompliance.

---

1. U.S. DOJ, Memorandum from Eric Holder, Deputy Attorney General, to Heads of Department Components and All U.S. Attorneys, *Subject: Bringing Criminal Charges Against Corporations* (June 16, 1999), *available at* http://www.justice.gov/criminal/fraud/documents/reports/1999/charging-corps.PDF.
2. The second iteration was the so-called "Thompson Memo," Memorandum from Larry D. Thompson, Deputy Attorney General, to Heads of Department Components and United States Attorneys, *Subject: Principals of Federal Prosecution of Business Organizations* (Jan. 20, 2003), *available at* http://www.americanbar.org/content/dam/aba/migrated/poladv/priorities/privilegewaiver/2003jan20_privwaiv_dojthomp.authcheckdam.pdf. The current guidance, the so-called "McNulty Memo," was promulgated on August 28, 2008, and has been incorporated into the U.S. Attorney's Manual. Dept. of Justice, U.S. Attorneys' Manual, Title 9, ch. 9-28.000, *Principles of Federal Prosecution of Business Organizations, available at* http://www.justice.gov/usao/eousa/foia_reading_room/usam/title9/28mcrm.htm (last visited Mar. 27, 2014) [hereinafter *USAM Principles*].
3. *USAM Prinicples, supra* note 2, at §9-28.800 B.
4. *Id.* §9-28.500 B.

Likewise, another factor the memorandum requires to be considered is the past compliance history of the corporation. In this regard, the memorandum states that a corporation is expected to learn from its mistakes.[5] This, of course, is the purpose of compliance programs—to discover nonconformities or violations, to learn from these problems, and to implement changes in corporate policies and procedures to address these problems and prevent their reoccurrence.

B. Mitigation Under the Federal Sentencing Guidelines for Organizations

Even if a corporation has an effective compliance program, it may still be prosecuted for environmental violations.[6] However, if the company is prosecuted, and is convicted or pleads guilty, the existence of an effective compliance program will be an important factor in determining an appropriate sentence.

U.S. government policies generally seek to reward corporate compliance and diligence. The United States Sentencing Guidelines for Organizations[7] give companies an opportunity to directly reduce the financial penalties for criminal violations of Federal laws if they have in place "an effective program to prevent and detect violations of law."[8] The Guidelines establish elements for what an effective compliance program should include.[9]

Although the financial penalty provisions of the Sentencing Guidelines for Organizations do not apply to corporate environmental crimes,[10] there will be situations in which the direct mitigation of financial penalties for a corporate compliance program under the organizational Sentencing Guidelines will be applicable. In addition to charging violations of an environmental statute, prosecutors frequently charge companies with common law criminal violations, such as false statements or conspiracy. In such cases, the Sentencing Guidelines for Organizations do apply, and the existence of an effective compliance program as a mitigating factor could reduce the fines awarded for these offenses substantially.[11]

The probation, restitution and remediation (clean up) provisions of the Guidelines also apply to environmental violations, including the provisions applicable to corporate probation. These require that the court order a term of probation (typically five years) if, at the time of sentencing, an organization having 50 or more employees does not have an effective program to prevent and detect violations of law.[12] Further, if probation is ordered, the Guidelines recommend that the court impose as a condition of probation that such a compliance program be developed and submitted to the court for approval along with a schedule for implementation. The court will further require that periodic progress reports be submitted to the court or the probation officer.[13] In many cases, the compliance program will be overseen by appropriate federal agencies, such as the EPA or the U.S. Coast Guard.

C. General Benefits of an Effective Environmental Compliance Program

Over and above the enforcement implications, comprehensive corporate environmental compliance programs help companies identify small compliance problems before they become large ones. Among other things, environmental compliance programs help companies to:

- reaffirm to all levels of management and employees the value of improved compliance and pollution prevention efforts, and prevent employee misconduct;
- verify the environmental compliance of the company's facilities and operations, and ensure accurate certification of environmental compliance in reports required under permits and regulations;
- ensure accuracy in SEC disclosures;[14]

---

5. *Id.* §9-28.600 B.
6. The *USAM Principles* guidance notes that "[t]he existence of a corporate compliance program, even one that specifically prohibited the very conduct in question, does not absolve the corporation from criminal liability under the doctrine of *respondeat superior*." *Id.* §9-28.800 B (citing United States v. Basic Constr. Co., 711 F.2d 570, 573 (4th Cir. 1983)).
7. United States Sentencing Comm'n, Guidelines Manual (Nov. 2013) [hereinafter Sentencing Guidelines], *available at* http://www.ussc.gov/Guidelines/2013_Guidelines/index.cfm (last visited Feb. 10, 2014).
8. *See id.* §8C2.5(f).
9. *See infra* text accompanying note 16.
10. Sentencing Guidelines, *supra* note 7, §8C2.1, Commentary.
11. The Guidelines, while still relevant, are no longer mandatory in light of the Supreme Court's decision in *United States v. Booker*, 543 U.S. 220 (2005). *See* Ch. 8, *Sentencing*, Section I.F.
12. Sentencing Guidelines, *supra* note 7, §8D1.1(a)(3).
13. *Id.* §8D1.4(c).
14. The SEC requires reporting of certain environmentally related matters that materially affect the finances of the corporation. Specifically, SEC regulations require that:

    > Appropriate disclosure also shall be made as to the material effects that compliance with Federal, State and local provisions which have been enacted or adopted regulating the discharge of materials into the environment, or otherwise relating to the protection of

- prioritize compliance concerns and provide a method for allocating capital to address environmental problems;
- generate company protocols that help facilities to better manage themselves and that allow headquarters to better monitor the performance of the company's operations;
- provide a forum for employees to report any information concerning violations or potential problems for management attention;
- anticipate and respond to emergency situations;
- enhance the company's reputation in the business community and as a good business partner for blue chip companies who have compliance programs in place for not only themselves, but agents and subcontractors with whom they do business; and
- enhance the company's goodwill and reputation as a good corporate citizen with the government, the media and the general public.[15]

D. Developing an Effective Environmental Compliance Program

For two reasons, the most important criteria to consider when developing an environmental compliance program are those applicable to corporate compliance programs under the U.S. Sentencing Guidelines for Organizations. First, these are the criteria that Department of Justice prosecutors are familiar with and will likely use in assessing the effectiveness of any corporate compliance program. Second, these criteria will also be consulted by the court in determining whether the compliance program is effective for purposes of determining appropriate fines, probation, restitution and remediation.

In brief, in order to have an effective compliance program, a company must exercise due diligence to prevent and detect criminal conduct and otherwise promote an organizational structure that encourages ethical conduct and a commitment to compliance with the law. The Guidelines require that, under such a program:

- the company's governing authority (*e.g.*, board of directors) must be knowledgeable about the content and operation of the compliance program and exercise reasonable oversight with respect to the implementation and effectiveness of the program;
- specific high-level personnel in the company must be assigned overall responsibility for the program;
- specific individuals in the company must be delegated day-to-day operational responsibility for the program, and these individuals must report periodically to high-level personnel and to the governing authority on the effectiveness of the program;
- individuals delegated responsibility for the compliance program must be given adequate resources, appropriate authority and direct access to the governing authority or an appropriate subgroup of the governing authority;
- the company must use due care not to delegate discretion to individuals in the company whom the company knew, or should have known through the exercise of due diligence, have engaged in illegal activities or other conduct inconsistent with the compliance program;
- the company must have a schedule and system to ensure employees are effectively trained on the company's standards and procedures for environmental compliance, and that information is disseminated to employees on their roles and responsibilities;
- the company must have monitoring and auditing systems in place to detect violations by company employees and agents and have in place a reporting system, such as a hotline, through which employees and agents can report environmental violations without fear of retribution;

> the environment, may have upon the capital expenditures, earnings and competitive position of the registrant and its subsidiaries. The registrant shall disclose any material estimated capital expenditures for environmental control facilities for the remainder of its current fiscal year and its succeeding fiscal year and for such further periods as the registrant may deem materials.

17 C.F.R. §229.101(c)(1)(xii).

15. The good will generated by establishing a comprehensive environmental management system with government agencies can result in significant reduction in regulatory compliance inspections and more efficient permitting. For instance, under Wisconsin's "Green Tier" program, Wis. Stat. §§299.80-.85, participants that either agree to implement an effective EMS or have an effective EMS in place and sign contracts with the Wisconsin Department of Natural Resources have benefits that include reduced red tape through designation of a single contact person with the agency, quicker turnaround on permits and the fewest number of inspections allowable. For information regarding this program, see http://dnr.wi.gov/topic/greentier/.

- the company must consistently enforce the standards and policies in place through both appropriate incentives to perform in accordance with the compliance program, and through appropriate disciplinary actions for employees who engage in criminal conduct or who fail to take reasonable steps to prevent or detect an offense; and
- after a violation has been detected, the company must take all reasonable steps to respond to the violation and prevent further similar violations, including modifying its compliance program if necessary to address shortfalls discovered in the program.[16]

16. SENTENCING GUIDELINES, *supra* note 7, §8B2.1(b).

Notes

Notes

Notes

Notes

Notes

Notes